Frommer's®

POSTCARDS

ISRAEL

At the Dome of the Rock, a gloriously beautiful Islamic shrine, one can spend hours soaking up the rich atmosphere and breathtaking views. See chapter 4. © Richard Passmore/Tony Stone Images.

In the Negev desert, hear the spine-tingling quiet of rock and sun and time. See chapter 10. © Dave G. Houser Photography.

The Red Sea is an awe-inspiring natural aquarium, rich with tropical marine life and one of the best places on earth for fabulous scuba diving and snorkeling. See chapters 10 and 11. © Kevin Cullimore/Tony Stone Images.

The Dome of the Rock, one of the Islamic world's crowning architectural achievements, covers the rock believed to have been the altar of the First and Second Temples and also the point from which the Prophet Muhammad glimpsed Heaven during the miraculous night journey. See chapter 4. © Sarah Stone/Tony Stone Images.

In the Garden of Gethsemane, beautifully tended gardens of ancient olive trees and bougainvillea lead to the Byzantine-style Church of All Nations, built by people from 16 different countries. See chapter 4. © Glen Allison/Tony Stone Images.

Christianity's holiest place, the Church of the Holy Sepulcher, is divided among the six oldest Christian sects: Roman Catholic, Armenian Orthodox, Greek Orthodox, Egyptian Coptic, Ethiopian, and Syrian Orthodox. See chapter 4. © Robert Holmes Photography.

High above the shores of the Dead Sea sits King Herod's palace fortress at Masada—a site of haunting magnificence and what many believe is one of the most heroic and tragic incidents in Jewish history. See chapter 10. © Harvey Lloyd/The Stock Market.

Luxurious Dead Sea spas and resorts provide a comfortable base for exploring the desert and enjoying the sea. For our top picks on where to soak, stretch, and be pampered, see chapter 10. © David G. Houser Photography.

This evocative monument commemorating Jewish World War II soldiers can be seen at the Yad VaShem Memorial in West Jerusalem. See chapter 4. © Dave G. Houser Photography.

Over the centuries, the Western Wall, a fragment of the wall built by Herod around the Temple Mount, has come to symbolize the indestructible attachment of the Jewish people to the land of Israel. See chapter 4. © Robert Holmes Photography.

Mineral-rich black mud from the Dead Sea is believed to possess therapeutic powers. See chapter 10. © Dave G. Houser Photography.

At Bet Shean you'll see the best-preserved Roman theater in Israel. For more about this fascinating city's archeological treasures, see chapter 9. © Dave G. Houser Photography.

The restored port of Old Jaffa, the most romantic urban spot in Israel, is filled with galleries, shops, seaside cafes and restaurants, and vistas of minarets, Crusader ruins, and bustling, modern Tel Aviv. See chapter 6. © Richard Passmore/Tony Stone Images.

The mysterious 2,000-year-old Nabatean city of Petra, carved from the walls of a desert canyon and the highlight of excursion tours into Jordan from Israel. See chapter 11. © Glen Allison/Tony Stone Images.

Frommer's®

3rd
Edition

Israel

by Robert Ullian

IDG Books Worldwide, Inc.
An International Data Group Company
Foster City, CA • Chicago, IL • Indianapolis, IN • New York, NY

ABOUT THE AUTHOR

Educated at Amherst College and Columbia University, **Robert Ullian** is a writer whose work has appeared in *Esquire, Mademoiselle,* and *The Boston Phoenix.* A recipient of a National Endowment for the Arts grant in fiction, he has taught art and writing at Hampshire College and the University of Massachusetts in Amherst and is also the author of books on Venice and Morocco.

IDG BOOKS WORLDWIDE, INC.

An International Data Group Company
919 E. Hillsdale Blvd.
Suite 400
Foster City, CA 94404

Find us online at **www.frommers.com**

ISBN 0-02-863742-9
ISSN 1086-4024

Editors: Claudia Kirschhoch, Justin Lapatine
Production Editor: Donna Wright
Photo Editor: Richard Fox
Design by Michele Laseau
Staff Cartographers: John Decamillis, Roberta Stockwell, Elizabeth Puhl
Page creation by Kendra Span and Elizabeth Brooks

SPECIAL SALES

For general information on IDG Books Worldwide's books in the U.S., please call our Consumer Customer Service department at 1-800-762-2974. For reseller information, including discounts, bulk sales, customized editions, and premium sales, please call our Reseller Customer Service department at 1-800-434-3422.

Manufactured in the United States of America

5 4 3 2 1

Contents

List of Maps

To Janet Ullian and to Jacob and Katherine Slomin.

ACKNOWLEDGMENTS

Special gratitude goes to my research assistant Sadek Shweiki. Born in Jerusalem and educated at Hampshire College in Amherst, Massachusetts, where he majored in psychology and intercultural communication, Sadek brings a careful understanding of Middle Eastern and American societies to this book.

I would like to thank Zahara Schatz of the Jerusalem Artists House, Michael Goldstein of the Israel Museum, and Motti Belinco, Janet K. Rodgers, Rita and Norman Perlmutter, Ilana Nadir, Shlomo Morgon, Marietta Samuel, David Perlmutter, Raed Saadah, Wendy Geri, Miriam Cohen, Khaled Shweiki, Ellen Oppenheim, Ev and Ray Lipson, Fran and Haim Shapiro, Ali Kleibo, Patti Parson, Jos Ullian, and Abbey Nachtomi, all of whom contributed their ideas, enthusiasm, and efforts to this book. Mr. Raed Saadeh was exceptionally kind to offer special assistance and advice about Jericho.

Finally, I would like to thank my neighbors in Abu Tor, Jerusalem, who made me so welcome while I lived and worked there, and whenever I returned. I hope readers of this book will find such friends in this very special land.

AN INVITATION TO THE READER

In researching this book, I discovered many wonderful places—hotels, restaurants, shops, and more. I'm sure you'll find others. Please tell me about them, so I can share the information with your fellow travelers in upcoming editions. If you were disappointed with a recommendation, I'd love to know that, too. Please write to:

Frommer's Israel, 3rd Edition
Frommer's Travel Guides
1633 Broadway
New York, NY 10019

AN ADDITIONAL NOTE

Please be advised that travel information is subject to change at any time—and this is especially true of prices. We therefore suggest that you write or call ahead for confirmation when making your travel plans. The author, editors, and publisher cannot be held responsible for the experiences of readers while traveling. Your safety is important to us, however, so we encourage you to stay alert and be aware of your surroundings. Keep a close eye on cameras, purses, and wallets, all favorite targets of thieves and pickpockets.

WHAT THE SYMBOLS MEAN

✪ Frommer's Favorites

Our favorite places and experiences—outstanding for quality, value, or both.

The following abbreviations are used for credit cards:

AE	American Express	EURO	Eurocard
CB	Carte Blanche	JCB	Japan Credit Bank
DC	Diners Club	MC	MasterCard
DISC	Discover	V	Visa
ER	EnRoute		

FIND FROMMER'S ONLINE

www.frommers.com offers up-to-the-minute listings on almost 200 cities around the globe—including the latest bargains and candid, personal articles updated daily by Arthur Frommer himself. No other Web site offers such comprehensive and timely coverage of the world of travel.

The Best of Israel, Jordan & Sinai

A journey to Israel is a journey to a place where the past and present call out to travelers in astonishing ways. You will find messages and meaning everywhere you turn in this intense land, and why not? For this land and its history lie at the very center of the consciousness of Western civilization.

Israel is amazingly dramatic and diverse, the more so when you realize the entire country is the size of New Jersey. When you find yourself in the silent, haunting desertscape near the Dead Sea, spotting ibexes on sheer cliffs that are dotted with caves like those in which the Dead Sea Scrolls lay hidden for more than 18 centuries, it can be hard to believe that less than 60 minutes away is the 19th-century east European ghetto world of Jerusalem's orthodox Mea Shearim quarter. A few blocks east of Mea Shearim, you'll find the labyrinthine medieval Arab bazaars of the Old City, with ancient church bells and calls to prayer from the city's minarets punctuating your wanderings. Hop into a sherut (shared taxi) to Tel Aviv on downtown Jerusalem's Jaffa Road, and in less than an hour in a world of white skyscrapers, surfboards, and bikinis on the beach, with the Mediterranean lapping at your feet. Two hours to the north, and you can be exploring ruined Crusader castles in the green forests of the Galilee mountains.

As a visitor and long-term resident, I have had the opportunity to see Israel from a number of different perspectives. Twenty-five years ago, the country was an austere, no-frills society—Israelis lived with few luxuries. Today, the country's economy is booming, the standard of living has skyrocketed, and many surveys rank Israel's per capita income among the top 20 in the world. Israel is becoming a nation with a lively sense of style and a taste for the good life. Luxury and better-quality hotel accommodations and resorts are going up all over the country, and visitors will find an interesting array of fine restaurants and shopping opportunities geared to Israeli society at large rather than to visitors. With the Israeli-Jordanian and Israeli-Egyptian peace treaties, a journey to Israel can also easily include an excursion to the fabulous ancient Nabatean city of Petra in Jordan; a diving or snorkeling odyssey off the Sinai Peninsula; or a jaunt over to Egypt to see the pyramids and explore Khan-el-Khalili, the legendary bazaar of Cairo.

This book will help direct you, as an independent traveler, to some of the best and most authentic experiences Israel has to offer. Israel is an easy country to explore and get close to if you know the ropes. We hope to lead you to experiences that will be both personal and rewarding.

1 The Best Travel Experiences

- **Visiting the Dome of the Rock and the Temple Mount** (Jerusalem): Built by the early Islamic rulers of Jerusalem in A.D. 691 on the site of the Temple of Solomon, the Dome of the Rock is one of the most beautiful structures ever created. It is the crown upon a 4,000-year tradition of Western monotheistic belief. One can spend hours on the Temple Mount soaking up the atmosphere and the dazzling views. You might first visit the Temple Mount on a tour, but come back and experience the power of this extraordinary place on your own. See chapter 4.

- **Journeying Into the Past at Mea Shearim:** Mea Shearim is the Hassidic Jewish quarter of Jerusalem, little more than a century old, but in the dress and customs of its inhabitants, and in its tangle of courtyards and alleyways, it is a miraculously surviving fragment of the world of east European Jewry that disappeared forever into the Holocaust. A visitor to Mea Shearim may feel like a dreamer wandering the past; nothing in the neighborhood can be scrutinized too intensely (residents will not permit you to stare at them or photograph them, nor will they allow anything resembling a tour group to troop their streets). Many visitors will revere the strict discipline and religious devotion evident in Mea Shearim; others will be troubled by its many constraints. But a walk through these streets will give you insight into the powerful traditions that continue to make Israel unique. See chapter 4.

- **An Evening Stroll Through Old Jaffa:** The beautifully restored Casbah of Old Jaffa is probably the most romantic urban spot in the country, filled with galleries, shops, cafes, restaurants, and vistas of minarets and Crusader ruins against the sunset and the sea. See chapter 6.

- **Exploring the Eastern Shore of the Sea of Galilee:** The Sea of Galilee is Israel's greatest natural treasure, and its lyrical shores were the birthplace of Christianity. It is also almost miraculous in its loveliness—a sapphire/turquoise freshwater lake surrounded by the mountains of the Galilee and the Golan. The eastern shore is less developed and gives you a better chance to feel the lake's poetry. There are eucalyptus-shaded beaches where you can have a late afternoon swim and picnic and watch the silver and lavender twilight descend behind the mountains on the western shore of the lake, which sparkles with the lights of farm settlements and kibbutzim. See chapter 9.

- **Freewheeling in the Galilee:** This is the place to rent a car for a few days and explore Israel's most beautiful countryside—forested mountains, rushing streams, waterfalls, and oceans of wildflowers in late winter and early spring. Among the region's treasures are ruined Roman-era synagogues, crusader castles, ancient churches, and the walled Casbah of Akko beside the Mediterranean. There are also the warm, sparkling waters of the Sea of Galilee to swim in from April to early November. See chapter 9.

- **Touching the Desert:** These are not just endless sandy wastes; the deserts of Israel encompass the unworldly and ethereal Dead Sea, the mysterious, abandoned Nabatean cities of Avdat and Shivta, the haunting fortress of Masada, canyon oases, and vast erosion craters that are geological encyclopedias of past eons. These landscapes were the crucible in which monotheism was born. Don't let the desert be just a 45-minute ride to the Dead Sea on a tour bus from Jerusalem. If you can, spend the night at a guest house or hostel near Masada before you make the ascent at dawn. Or join an overnight llama trek in the Ramon Crater. See chapter 10.

Israel

LEBANON

SYRIA

GOLAN HEIGHTS

Metula

Rosh Ha-Niqra
Nahariyya
Kiryát Shmona
Katzrin
Akko
85
Safed
Gamla
Haifa
Nazareth
Tiberias
77
Sea of Galilee

2
Megiddo
90

Caesarea
65
Bet Shean

Netanya
Jenin

Herzlia
WEST BANK
Nablus

Tel-Aviv
Bat Yam
Ramallah
Ramla
Rishon Letzion
4
Jericho
Rehovot
Allenby Bridge
Ashdod
1
Jerusalem
Bethlehem

Ashkelon

Kiryat Gat
Hebron

Gaza
Amman

GAZA STRIP
Ein Gedi
Masada

Beersheva
Arad
Ein Boqeq
Neve Zohar
Dimona
Sodom

Sdeh Boker

10
NEGEV

Mitzpeh Ramon

EGYPT

90

Yotvata

Eilat
Aqaba
Gulf of Aqaba

JORDAN

Jordan River

Dead Sea

Mediterranean Sea

0 ___ 50 Mi
0 ___ 50 Km

Areas occupied by Israel since 1967

3

- **Snorkeling in the Red Sea:** The Red Sea, with its coral reefs, is an awe-inspiring natural aquarium. Rich with tropical marine life, it's one of the best places on earth for scuba diving and snorkeling. At the Coral Beach Nature Reserve just south of Eilat, there's enough to fascinate experts, yet wonders are accessible to all levels of swimmers—dazzling fish abound even in waist-deep water. Experienced divers can scuba dive at the Coral Island, a few miles down the coast from Eilat, or make an excursion into the Egyptian Sinai to the even more extraordinary reefs off Nuweiba, Dahab, and the legendary Ras Muhammad at Sharm-el-Sheik. See chapter 10.

- **Sampling the Music Scene:** Israel has an oversupply of magnificent musicians; even suburbs of Tel Aviv and small cities like Beersheva are home to orchestras that would be the envy of many world capitals. You may find the Israel Philharmonic Orchestra performing at Tel Aviv's Mann Auditorium, or the acclaimed Rishon-Le-Zion Symphony Orchestra (filled with new immigrants from the former Soviet Union) giving a visiting concert at the Haifa Auditorium. But also look out for an outdoor performance of *Carmen* in the Valley of the Sultan's Pool, just at the foot of the walls of Jerusalem; a night of Mozart at the 2,000-year-old Roman amphitheater beside the sea at Caesaria; Yemenite wedding singers or Arabic oudists performing at free municipal concerts inside Jerusalem's Jaffa Gate; Israeli African-American blues and jazz musicians at clubs in Tel Aviv; or festivals like the Chamber Music Days at Kibbutz Kfar Blum, the Red Sea Jazz Festival in Eilat, or the Jacob's Ladder Folk Festival held each summer in the Galilee.

2 The Most Evocative Ancient Sites

People come to Israel to touch the past. The events that occurred here in ancient times and the stories and legends that arose in Israel are firmly planted in the minds of more than a billion people throughout the world.

- **City of David:** Now the Arab village of Silwan (in the Bible, Siloam), this is the oldest part of Jerusalem, located on a ridge that slopes downhill just south of the present Old City. David, Solomon, and the prophets walked here. By late Roman times, warfare had advanced to the point where this area was too low to be easily defended and it was left outside the walls of Jerusalem. The ancient gardens of Siloam inspired the Song of Songs; now an overgrown orchard of fig and pomegranate trees, watered by the same Gihon Spring that was used by the prophets to anoint the kings of Judah, the gardens still stand at the foot of modern-day Silwan. The City of David is best visited on an organized tour or with a guide. See chapter 3.

- **Northwest Shore of the Sea of Galilee:** This enchantingly lovely corner of the lake, in many ways the birthplace of one of the world's great religions, was the landscape of Jesus' ministry. Centering on the ruins of Capernaum (once a fishing town, and the site of St. Peter's house), and Tagba, where the multitudes were fed with the Miracle of the Loaves and the Fishes, the shoreline is dominated by the Mount of Beatitudes. Churches and archaeological excavations mark the locations of New Testament events. See chapter 9.

- **Bar'am Synagogue:** In the northern Galilee, near the Lebanese border, this is the best preserved and perhaps most beautiful of the many ruined synagogues of antiquity. Built in the 4th century A.D., it was once the centerpiece of a small town in the breathtaking wooded mountains of this northern region. See chapter 9.

- **Masada:** On an almost inaccessible mountaintop high above the shores of the Dead Sea, Herod built this legendary palace fortress; in A.D. 73, more than 75 years after his death, it became the last stronghold of the First Revolt against Rome. Here the last Jews to live under their own rule (until the creation of the State of Israel in 1948) committed suicide on the eve of their conquest by Roman armies. The meaning of this mass suicide is fiercely debated by Israelis today. Even without the drama of Masada's last stand, the site is one of haunting, audacious magnificence. See chapter 10.

3 The Most Important Holy Places

The great sacred sites all possess extraordinary power, mystery, and beauty, at least partly conveyed upon them by centuries, if not millennia, of reverence. The ownership and histories of Israel's holy places are often a matter of contention and debate, not only among the three great monotheistic religions, but also among sects within these religions. These listings are in the order in which they appear in the book.

- **The Western Wall** (Jerusalem): Part of a vast retaining wall built by Herod around the Temple Mount, this is the most visible structure remaining from the Second Temple complex. Judaism's great legacy to the world is spiritual, but the massive stones of the Wall, each with its perfectly carved border, are testimony to the physical grandeur of the ancient Jewish world. Over the centuries, this enduring fragment of the Temple complex has come to symbolize the indestructible attachment of the Jewish people to the land of Israel. For more than 1,000 years, under Islamic governments, the Wall was the closest point that Jews were permitted to approach to the place where the ancient Temple of Jerusalem once stood. Because of the sanctity of the Temple Mount itself, very observant Jews do not go farther than the Wall to this day. See chapter 4.
- **Dome of the Rock** (Jerusalem): A gloriously beautiful Islamic shrine, built in A.D. 691, covers the rock believed to have been the altar or foundation stone of the First and Second Temples. According to Jewish tradition, the rock was the altar upon which Abraham prepared to sacrifice Isaac; Islamic tradition holds that it was Abraham's first son, Ishmael, the father of the Arabic people, whom Abraham was called upon to sacrifice, either at this rock, or at Mecca. The rock is also believed to have been the point from which the Prophet Muhammad ascended to glimpse heaven during the miraculous night journey described in the 17th Sura of the Koran.
- **El Aksa Mosque** (Jerusalem): On the southernmost side of the Temple Mount, built in A.D. 720, this is the third most important Muslim place of prayer after Mecca and Medina. See chapter 4.
- **Church of the Holy Sepulcher** (Jerusalem): Christianity's holiest place, this church covers the traditional sites of the crucifixion, entombment, and resurrection of Jesus. Built about A.D. 330, the complex is carefully divided among the Greek Orthodox, Roman Catholic, Armenian Orthodox, Coptic, Syrian, and Ethiopian churches. See chapter 4.
- **Mount of Olives** (Jerusalem): Overlooking the Old City of Jerusalem from the east, the mount offers a sweeping vista of the entire city. Here, Jesus wept at a prophetic vision of Jerusalem lying in ruins; in the Garden of Gethsemane, on the lower slope of the mount, Jesus was arrested; and the ridge of the Mount of Olives is the place from which, according to tradition, Jesus ascended to heaven. An encampment site for Jewish pilgrims in ancient times, the Mount of Olives contains Judaism's most important graveyard. See chapter 4.

- **Church of the Nativity** (Bethlehem): This church marks the site of Jesus' birth-place. It is the oldest surviving church in the Holy Land; the Persians spared it during their invasion in A.D. 614 because, according to legend, they were impressed by a representation of the Magi (fellow Persians) that decorated the building. See chapter 5.
- **Tomb of the Patriarchs** (Hebron, on the West Bank): This is the burial place of Abraham, Isaac, and Jacob, as well as their wives, Sarah, Rebecca, and Leah (Rachel, the second wife of Jacob, is buried in Bethlehem). It's surrounded by massive walls built by King Herod, and venerated by both Jews and Muslims. Rights to this place are a point of bitter contention between the Islamic and Jewish worlds. See chapter 5.
- **Baha'i Gardens** (Akko): At the northern edge of Akko, this site marks the tomb of the founder and prophet of the Baha'i faith, Baha' Allah. As such, it is the holiest place for members of the Baha'i faith. See chapter 7.
- **Baha'i Shrine and Gardens** (Haifa): The shrine was built to memorialize the remains of one of the Baha'i faith's martyrs, Bab Mirza Ali Muhammad, who was executed by Persian authorities in 1850. See chapter 8.
- **Mount Sinai** (Sinai Peninsula, Egypt): Controversy still rages over which of the Sinai's mountains is the true site where the Ten Commandments were given to Moses, but the traditional identification of Mount Sinai is very ancient. An isolated Byzantine monastery at the foot of the mountain adds to the mysterious aura. The view from the top of Mount Sinai at dawn is among the most awe-inspiring sights you will ever see. See chapter 10.

4 The Best Ancient Cities

Israel and neighboring Jordan are filled with ruins of lost, ancient cities from every part of their long histories. In Herodian-Roman times, the population of Judea and the Galilee may have been around three million. Almost 2 millennia of wars, religious rivalries, persecutions, and misgovernment drove the population down to less than half a million by the start of the 19th century. Even knowledge of the location of many ancient sites was forgotten. Now dazzling physical monuments to the past are being recovered at a rapid pace.

- **Zippori** (Sepphoris, near Nazareth): A cosmopolitan Jewish-Hellenistic city, it was the capital of the Galilee in Roman and Talmudic times. Especially interesting because it may have been familiar to Jesus, Zippori's highlights include a colonnaded street; a mosaic synagogue floor depicting the zodiac; and the beautiful mosaic portrait of a woman dubbed "the Mona Lisa of the Galilee," recently discovered in a late Roman-era villa. See chapter 9.
- **Caesaria** (on the coast between Tel Aviv and Haifa): Built by Herod as the great harbor and seaport of his kingdom, this was the splendid administrative capital of Roman Palestine. There are impressive, vast ruins of the Roman city (including two theaters), as well as of the crusader-era city, made all the more romantic by the waves lapping at the ancient stones. Caesaria was an important Byzantine Christian city, but it is not a biblical site. See chapter 7.
- **Megiddo** (Armageddon, about 20 miles southeast of Haifa): This town stood in the path of invading armies from ancient to modern times. It is an encyclopedia of Near Eastern archeology with more than 20 levels of habitation from 4,000 B.C. to A.D. 400 having been discovered here. The water tunnel dug from inside the fortified town to the source of water outside the walls in the 9th century B.C. is a miracle of ancient engineering. See chapter 9.

- **Korazim** (Galilee): A Roman-Byzantine–era Jewish town in the hills just northeast of the Sea of Galilee, this is a beautiful place, with sweeping views of the lake. Portions of ruins still stand. A black basalt synagogue, with beautifully carved detailing, and some surrounding houses, also of local black basalt, give a good idea of what the more than 100 towns once in this area must have been like. Jesus visited Korazim, but developed little following there. See chapter 9.
- **Gamla** (Golan Heights): Once a small Roman-era Jewish city located on a ridge in the Golan Heights, the site has a story chillingly similar to that of Masada, but the number of dead was far greater. In A.D. 67, at the beginning of the First Jewish Rebellion against Rome, Gamla was overrun by Roman soldiers, and as many as 9,000 townspeople flung themselves from the cliff, choosing death over subjugation. This dramatic site is especially beautiful amid late winter wildflowers and waterfalls. A ruined synagogue, one of the few that can be dated to the Second Temple period, is also here. See chapter 9.
- **Bet Shean** (Jordan Valley): This place has been continuously inhabited for the past 6,000 years. A vast, Roman-Byzantine city with colonnaded streets and a theater that could house 5,000 people once stood here, although by the 19th century, Bet Shean was a small village. Remnants of earlier civilizations can be seen on the ancient *tel* (Hebrew for a mound composed of layers of cities) above the Roman ruins. See chapter 9.
- **Petra** (Jordan): The legendary 2,000-year-old Nabatean capital carved from the walls of a desert canyon is now the highlight of excursion tours into Jordan from Israel. The entire Petra experience, including the trek into the canyon, has an air of adventure and mystery—especially if you plan 1 or 2 nights (or more) at Petra and give yourself time to get a feel for the place early in the morning and in the evening, before the hordes of visitors arrive. See chapter 11.

5 The Best Nature & Outdoor Experiences

Israel's diverse landscapes and unusual natural phenomena provide opportunities for interesting outdoor pursuits, many of which you might never have thought of in connection with a trip here.

- **Digging for a Day:** Joining an archaeological dig as a volunteer requires a definite commitment of time, money, and backbreaking labor. However, you can often arrange to dig for a day and get a close-up look at the hard work and thrills involved in bringing so much of Israel's history to light. Contact the Municipal Tourist Information Office in Jerusalem for current options. The digging season is during the dry summer months. See chapter 2.
- **Hiking Down Wadi Kelt:** This hike, manageable for most walkers, takes you down one of the extraordinary canyons leading from the Judean mountains to the Jordan Valley and the Dead Sea. On the route, you pass the ancient and almost inaccessible Monastery of Saint George, built into the walls of the canyon above the stream of Wadi Kelt. This dramatic canyon may soon be under the control of the Palestinian Authority. At present, it should only be visited by an organized group tour. See chapter 5.
- **Hiking to Gamla:** A beautiful trail throughout the year, in late winter this 1- to 2-hour hike in the Golan takes you past wildflowers, streams, and waterfalls. The reward at the end of the trail is the dramatic ruined city of Gamla (see "The Best Ancient Cities," above). The countryside is also dotted with prehistoric dolmens and Stone Age tombs. This walk brings you into contact with nature, archaeology, and a very moving piece of Israeli history. Plan additional time for the return walk, although a shorter trail is also available. See chapter 9.

- **Llama Trekking in the Ramon Crater** (Negev): In the Negev Highlands, near Mitzpe Ramon, this geological encyclopedia can be visited on a speedy, bone-dismantling Jeep tour, or on a rather arduous hike. Or you can experience the mysterious quiet of the desert as you explore the crater accompanied by a guide, with a llama to carry your water and equipment. This novel approach can be arranged for a variety of itineraries as well as longer excursions with overnight camping and Bedouin-style cookouts. The Alpaca Farm and travel agencies in Mitzpe Ramon can set it up for you at reasonable prices. See chapter 10.

- **Diving and Snorkeling the Reefs of Eilat:** The Red Sea coral reefs are among the most interesting and easily accessible in the world; anyone who can swim even moderately well can snorkel and enjoy the underwater scene. If you want to scuba dive, you must bring your certification from abroad or obtain a license in Israel. Eilat is home to a number of diving schools offering short- and longer-term programs, plus classes in underwater photography. Once you've seen the coral reef just off the shores of southern Eilat, you can graduate to a dive cruise of the more extensive reefs of the Coral Island. You can snorkel in the Coral Beach Nature Preserve for less than $20, including rental of gear, or you can join diving cruises that begin at $40 for a dive. See chapter 10.

- **Diving at Dahab** (Sinai Peninsula): Just across the border from Eilat is the Sinai Peninsula's extraordinary reefs and clear, light-filled water. Reefs teeming with exotic marine life extend all the way down the coast; perhaps the most famous is the suicidal Blue Hole, off the town of Dahab (but not recommended by this book). At the southernmost tip of Sinai, just beyond the new resort center at Sharm-el-Sheik is the Egyptian National Park at Ras Muhammad. You'll need a visa for Egypt rather than a Sinai Only visa to reach this diver's paradise. Diving schools in Eilat and good Eilat travel agents and discounters can arrange diving-package excursions to Sinai where hotel prices are bargains compared to Israeli rates. See chapter 10.

6 The Best Beaches

Israel's four seas (the Mediterranean, the Sea of Galilee, the Dead Sea, and the Red Sea) offer an amazing variety of swimming experiences. The beaches of Israel look beautiful, but be careful about going in the water. Unusually strong riptides, whirlpools, and undertows along the Mediterranean coast can claim the strongest swimmer. Never swim in unguarded areas. Along much of the coast, especially north of Tel Aviv, the beaches seem sandy, but a few steps into the surf, and you're standing on a rocky shelf—not a good place to be when waves come crashing down. Pollution is also a serious problem, as it is throughout the Mediterranean. Israel's beach standards are much higher than those of most Mediterranean countries, but on many days, garbage from other countries swirls along the coast. At Nahariya, Akko, and the Poleg Nature Reserve (8km or 4.8 mi. south of Netanya), which have no sewage treatment plants, I would hesitate to put my head in the water. Israelis play compulsive paddle-ball on any stretch of beach they're on, regardless of sleeping sunbathers in the line of fire. Expect beaches to be lively; watch out for sea urchins and stinging coral in the Red Sea, and the burning medusas (jellyfish) that attack the Mediterranean beaches in July.

- **Gordon Beach** (Tel Aviv): Perhaps the most accessible place to sample the Mediterranean, this free municipal beach has showers and a friendly mix of Israelis, new Russian immigrants, and tourists from luxury hotels. There are nearby places to take a break for a snack or meal, the sand is passably clean, and when the tide is clear, the beach is a pleasure. See chapter 6.

- **Mikmoret Beach** (between Netanya and Caesaria): If you have a car, this is a life-guarded, slightly sheltered, out-of-the-way beach with a restaurant, showers, and changing rooms. To the south, the beach goes on straight for miles, good for long walks. In-season entrance is $2.40 per person, deducted from your restaurant bill if you have a full meal. See chapter 7.

- **Aqueduct Beach** (just north of Caesaria): An ancient Roman aqueduct gives this beach its name and travel-poster ambience. There are no showers or amenities or crowds except on summer weekends, when vendors sell drinks and snacks. Not good for swimming if the water is rough, but on calm days, as you float in the Mediterranean and gaze at the romantic ruins, you know it's not the Jersey Shore. Currently the beach is free, with an impromptu parking area. See chapter 7.

- **Ein Gev Holiday Village Beach** (Sea of Galilee): The freshwater Sea of Galilee is warm and cleansing, spiritually as well as physically. You have to be a guest at the Ein Gev Holiday Village to be allowed to use the beach here, but it's the prettiest one on the lake, with a date palm grove and thick lawns stretching down to the water, which is relatively free of foot-stubbing rocks. Just to the south of Ein Gev are several miles of eucalyptus-shaded beaches along the road (in summer there's a $3 parking fee); they're rockier underwater, but very pleasant when not crowded with weekenders. Late afternoon often brings real breakers to the eastern shore of the lake; twilight here is soft and magical. See chapter 9.

- **Ein Gedi Beach** (Dead Sea): Everyone should experience swimming in the Dead Sea, the strangest body of water and the lowest point on the face of the earth. The extremely high salt content makes you feel like a cork; if you float, it's impossible to keep much of yourself underwater. The salt and minerals in the water are believed to be therapeutic, but the water will sting any cuts on your skin, and if you stay in too long, you'll be pickled. At Ein Gedi Beach, there are freshwater showers as well as a restaurant. High daytime temperatures mean that even in winter a dip may be possible. See chapter 10.

- **Coral Beach Nature Reserve** (Eilat): The Nature Reserve has staked out a strip of beach alongside Eilat's best reefs. Here you can snorkel among dazzling fish and coral formations, and even take interesting scuba expeditions. Snorkeling gear is for rent, and there are showers, changing areas, and snack facilities. This beach is not good for recreational swimming—unless you wear a face mask and foot protection, you can easily step on the quills of a sea urchin, or be cut and burned by stinging coral. See chapter 10.

- **Dolphin Reef Beach** (Eilat): A good choice for everyday swimming in the Red Sea, Dolphin Reef is the most picturesque beach in Eilat, with thatched umbrellas, a shady garden cafeteria, and a thatched-roof, sand-floor pub/restaurant for when you want to be out of the sun. It also has a resident dolphin population in the water, separated from the human swimming area by a net fence. You can swim under supervision in the dolphin zone for $30 a half hour; or better yet, stay in the roomy people's zone (with a sandy, nearly sea-urchin-free bottom) and enjoy watching the dolphins leap and frolic. See chapter 10.

- **Nuweiba Hilton Coral Resort Beach** (Sinai Peninsula, Egypt): If you want to really beach out for a few days at a comfortable resort that has a low-rise desert architectural style, and a quiet, distant end-of-the-earth ambience, with the mountains of Arabia facing you across the water, this is the place. There are beaches for swimming and snorkeling, a pool, and you can take wonderful excursions from here to the haunting interior of the Sinai. See chapter 10.

7 The Best Museums

Israel's museums are relatively new, innovative, and interactive. They display the discoveries of the past, of the self, and of nationhood that are happening so intensively every day in Israeli society. The most interesting museums are those that could only be found in Israel.

- **Israel Museum** (Jerusalem): Although it only opened in 1965, in 3 decades the Israel Museum has made its place on the world museum map. Its greatest treasures, beautifully exhibited, include a number of the Dead Sea Scrolls; a dazzling, all-encompassing collection of archaeological finds from Israel; a vast treasury of world Judaica and costumes, including reconstructions of the interiors of synagogues brought to Israel from Italy, Germany, and Cochin, India; and excellent collections of primitive, pre-Colombian, European, and modern art, including the exciting Billy Rose Sculpture Garden. There's also an enticing Children's Wing. See chapter 4.

- **L. A. Mayer Memorial Museum of Islamic Art** (Jerusalem): An undervisited treasure, with an excellent collection of Islamic and Middle Eastern art, and well-chosen special and visiting exhibitions. See chapter 4.

- **Sir Isaac and Lady Edith Wolfson Museum** (Jerusalem): Right in the heart of Jerusalem, this little-known gem consists of a large but intimate private collection of Judaica from all over the world. It is exhibited on the fourth floor of Hechal Shlomo, the Great Synagogue complex on King George Street. See chapter 4.

- **Yad VaShem Memorial** (Jerusalem): This large complex is a memorial to the six million Jews killed by the Nazis during World War II. Part of the museum is a teaching experience, with films, photographs, and documents pertaining to the Holocaust; part is an archive in which information about each individual victim will be gathered and kept. A third part of the complex consists of memorial structures, gardens, and installations such as the Avenue of the Righteous, in memory of those who risked their lives to shelter Jews; the darkened, terrifying interior of the Children's Memorial; and the tragic sculpture of the Valley of Destroyed Communities. No visitor can leave unaffected. See chapter 4.

- **Bet Hatfutzot, The Diaspora Museum** (Tel Aviv): Not a museum in terms of displaying actual genuine artifacts, Bet Hatfutzot is rather a state-of-the-art multimedia exhibit that illustrates the histories of Jewish communities throughout the world. It's fascinating, fun, and the special visiting exhibitions are always worthwhile. See chapter 6.

- **Eretz Israel Museum** (Tel Aviv): This museum covers many aspects of the land of Israel, including its natural history, flora and fauna, archaeology, folklore, and traditional crafts. Highlights include a bazaar filled with craftspeople demonstrating such skills from antiquity as glass blowing, olive pressing, weaving, and pottery making; an extraordinary collection of ancient glass; and excavations of a tell (an ancient mound) located on the grounds of the museum. See chapter 6.

- **Tel Aviv Museum of Art** (Tel Aviv): Notable for strong collections of Israeli and contemporary European (including Russian) art, the museum has just begun to exhibit its newest gift: the Jaglom Collection of Impressionist and Post-Impressionist Art. There is a lively program of public events, performances, and special exhibitions. See chapter 6.

8 The Best Luxury Hotels

The hotel scene in Israel is presently in the process of a truly massive change. International chains have been building new hotels throughout Israel as well as in Sinai and Jordan, and upgrading many older properties.

- **The King David Hotel** (Jerusalem, ☎ 02/620-8888): Built in 1930 during the British Mandate, the King David has outlasted the British Empire and continues to sail on, immaculate, elegant, and up-to-date in every way. The Nubian, fez-adorned lobby attendants of the 1930s are no longer here, but the King David is thick with atmosphere and ambience, and VIPs from Henry Kissinger and Warren Christopher to Barbra Streisand and Bob Dylan seem to pop up here. The gardened swimming pool and views of the walls of the Old City are a real plus. See chapter 3.
- **American Colony Hotel** (Jerusalem, ☎ 02/627-9777): This beautiful, atmospheric, gardened enclave was a 19th-century pasha's villa. As an international meeting place between the worlds of East and West Jerusalem, it attracts journalists, writers, archaeologists, and all sorts of VIPs, and is probably the most savvy, romantic spot in the Middle East. Some of the suites, furnished with antiques and traditional crafts, are as splendid as anything you'll find in the region, yet prices are comparatively reasonable. The hotel's Saturday afternoon luncheon buffet is famous throughout the country. See chapter 3.
- **Tel Aviv Sheraton Hotel & Towers** (Tel Aviv, ☎ 03/521-1111): The most fun of Tel Aviv's five-star hotels—right on the beach, but steps away from the city's restaurant and gallery district—feels like an urban resort. Restaurant services here are probably the best of any hotel in the country, topped off by the Twelve Tribes Restaurant with an elegant, luxurious menu that's both inventive and kosher. Mediterranean views from many of the guest rooms, complete with dazzling sunsets, are a plus, as is the very efficient business center. See chapter 6.
- **Tel Aviv Hilton** (Tel Aviv, ☎ 03/522-4111): With an unequaled staff, business center, guest services, and CYBEX health club the Hilton is the doyenne of Tel Aviv's beachfront hotels. Suites and better-category rooms are beautifully furnished and decorated; the sheltered beach offers a resort atmosphere, but the kosher sushi bar hints at the Hilton's role as a center for business and tourism exchanges between Asia and the Middle East. See chapter 6.
- **Dan Carmel Hotel** (Haifa, ☎ 04/830-6306): With sweeping views from its site at the top of the Carmel Range, as well as a careful staff and a relaxing, gardened pool enclave, this hotel, built in the 1960s, is regarded as Haifa's best. The better guest rooms, newly renovated and with views of the bay, are beautifully decorated and well worth the extra money. Lower-category rooms still have a style that recalls the Eisenhower era. See chapter 8.
- **Herod's Sheraton Resort and Spa** (North Beach, Eilat, ☎ 07/638-0000): Opened in 1999, this blockbuster's public areas are the most sumptuous in Israel. With architectural touches echoing Middle Eastern traditions, and staff costumed in "ancient" garb, the effect may seem a bit Hollywoodesque, but you know you're not staying in just another cookie cutter hotel. The Red Sea is steps away. See chapter 10.
- **Petra Movenpick Hotel** (Petra, Jordan, ☎ 962 03/214-7111): Right at the entrance to Petra National Park (which makes more than one foray into Petra each day possible) the Movenpick is the best blend of contemporary and traditional

Middle Eastern design I've seen in the region. Without being kitschy, public areas are atmospheric and exciting. The rooftop cafe at night is an easy place for travelers to meet and swap experiences under the stars; the dinner buffet is the best around. See chapter 11.

- **Taybet Zeman Hotel and Resort** (Petra, Jordan, ☎ **962 03/215-0111**): The stone houses and lanes of an abandoned Bedouin village in the mountains above Petra have been turned into the rooms and suites of a charming, atmospheric, quality resort. Vistas are awesome; the village market is a shopping arcade; each room is uniquely decorated with Bedouin crafts; local country musicians serenade at night—all a 20-minute drive from the wonders of Petra. See chapter 11.

9 The Best Value Hotels

This selection of hotel choices runs from splurges to economy strategies; each establishment offers something special.

- **Saint Mark's Lutheran Guest House** (Jerusalem, ☎ **02/628-2120**): Beautiful, atmospheric, and immaculate, with gardens above the main Arab bazaar, this is the best possible place to stay in the Old City, and one of the most remarkable little hotels in the country. Depending on the value of the German mark, a double could run from $70 to $75. See chapter 3.
- **Jerusalem Tower Hotel** (Jerusalem, ☎ **02/620-9209**): At this well-run moderate hotel located on the upper floors of a high-rise, you're right in the center of everything—restaurants, cafes, shopping—but high above the street noise, and with luck, you'll have a dazzling view. It's around $130 for a double, but on El Al's Sunsational Package the rate can be under $60. See chapter 3.
- **Jerusalem Inn Hotel** (Jerusalem, ☎ **02/625-2757**): Just a short walk from the Old City, and 1¹/₂ blocks from Zion Square and the bustling Ben Yehuda and Yoel Salomon malls, this small hotel offers tidy, no-frills doubles with a touch of style and excellent beds for $68 to $86, depending on the time of year. The management constantly upgrades the rooms with new equipment and services, yet keeps its rates the most reasonable in town for this quality. See chapter 3.
- **YMCA Three Arches Hotel** (Jerusalem, ☎ **02/625-7111**): This is in no way your average YMCA; instead, it's a respected hotel frequented by savvy travelers. For $145 you get a well-appointed double in a landmark building (designed by the same architect who created New York's Empire State Building), right across the street from the famed King David Hotel. Remember, you'd pay three or four times as much across the street! See chapter 3.
- **Saint Andrew's Hospice** (Jerusalem, ☎ **02/673-2401**): One of the most dramatic and atmospheric sites in West Jerusalem, on a vista-sweeping hilltop overlooking the Old City, this Church of Scotland guest house offers simple rooms in an interesting 1930s-style building, and a hearty, welcoming staff. See chapter 3.
- **Jerusalem Hotel** (East Jerusalem, ☎ **02/628-3282**): A small place run by a well-informed, attentive family, the Jerusalem Hotel offers a pleasant garden restaurant with live music a number of times a week, and a general atmosphere that makes it seem like a very affordable version of the renowned American Colony Hotel. See chapter 3.
- **Church of Scotland Center Guest House** (Tiberias, ☎ **06/672-3769**): With its 19th-century buildings, beautiful terraces, and overgrown gardens looking out on the Sea of Galilee, this well-run guest house seems almost like a villa on the Italian coast, and welcomes visitors of all faiths. Rooms are simple but have recently been redone; doubles go for $80. See chapter 9.

- **Ein Gev Holiday Village** (Sea of Galilee, ☎ **06/665-9800**): The Ein Gev Kibbutz has bungalows, caravans, and basic doubles set in eucalyptus and date palm groves right on the shores of the Sea of Galilee. It's a paradisiacal place to unwind and swim the warm waters of the lake. The kibbutz runs an excellent fish restaurant a mile down the road. Book this in the kibbutz package, and the price becomes very reasonable. See chapter 9.
- **Vered Ha-Galil Guest Farm** (Galilee, ☎ **06/693-5785**): Set in the hills a few miles north of the Sea of Galilee, this intimate, family run place began as a simple horseback riding lodge and over 4 decades has slowly been turned into a small Garden of Eden. It offers a variety of rustic, charming accommodations and well-informed, personal attention; you don't have to come here for riding, but if you do, the programs are probably the best in the country. See chapter 9.
- **Bed-and-Breakfast in a Galilee Arab Village** (☎ **04/990-1555**): This program introduces both foreign visitors and Jewish Israelis to the many Arab Israeli communities of the Galilee countryside. You can make a special request to stay with a family in residence, or you can choose a guest flat where breakfast will be brought in by the owner from his or her own house. Either way, your room will be immaculate, and filled with amenities and personal touches that convey a real sense of hospitality. See chapter 9.
- **Howard Johnson Ruth Rimon Inn** (Safed, ☎ **06/699-4666**): In a country with few really romantic, atmospheric hotels, this upper-moderate–range inn, a collection of beautiful buildings from Ottoman times, is a real winner and an example of what might be done elsewhere in the country. A stay here helps make the often-elusive magic of Safed more tangible. See chapter 9.
- **Isaac H. Taylor Youth Hostel** (Masada, ☎ **07/658-4349**): Right at the base of Masada, overlooking the Dead Sea, this large, modern Israel Youth Hostel Association establishment allows you to overnight in the desert and make the ascent to Masada in the cool dawn hours. Midweek during off-season, you can often arrange a private double with bathroom for around $45. See chapter 10.
- **Isrotel Riviera Apartment Hotel** (Eilat, ☎ **800/552-0141** in the U.S.): A block from the beach, units built around a pool can accommodate two to four people, and are equipped with kitchenettes, TVs, and other useful amenities. Although not a kibbutz guest house, a double here can be booked as part of the Kibbutz Guest House 7-Night Package Plan (see chapter 2), the most affordable way to have nonscruffy accommodations in costly Eilat. See chapter 10.
- **Sanafir Tourist Village** (Sharm-el-Sheik, Sinai, ☎ **20 62/600-197**): With an inventive architectural design that draws on traditional Middle Eastern *khans*, or travelers' inns, Sanifir is a lively place where it's easy to meet fellow travelers, and an affordable alternative to the big package resort villages of Na'ama Bay. It's a few blocks from the beach, but it has charm, comfort, and maintains something of the spirit of exotic adventure that was once part of a trip to Sharm-el-Sheik. See chapter 10.

10 The Best Luxury Dining

Until the 1980s, it was almost considered anti-Zionist to spend money and effort on gourmet cuisine. Israel was a practical, egalitarian society, and good, healthful fresh food was all that was necessary to create a sturdy population. Humans do not live by falafel alone, however, and Israel has developed a group of truly fine, personal restaurants, many rooted in French tradition, but also exploring the traditions of the Mediterranean Rim.

- **Ocean Bistro** (Jerusalem): Although Jerusalem is a mountain city, this is Israel's masterpiece restaurant for fish and seafood. Service is formal but friendly, and the menu takes light, natural preparation to levels of perfection that are sublime. See chapter 3.
- **Darna** (Jerusalem): Craftsmen and interior designers from Morocco were brought to Jerusalem to create this authentic, atmospheric restaurant that celebrates the traditions of Israel's large Moroccan Jewish population. The fine Moroccan cuisine matches the graceful service and ambience. See chapter 3.
- **Le Divellec** (Hilton Hotel, Jerusalem): Excellent by any standard, this quietly elegant restaurant is the best luxury kosher restaurant in the country, with an exquisite menu of foie gras, fish, and meat. See chapter 3.
- **American Colony Hotel** (Jerusalem): The Saturday luncheon buffet in the Arabesque Room is a Jerusalem tradition, with real atmosphere as well as a vast, all-you-can-eat buffet of excellent Middle Eastern and continental choices. Sadly, this treat is only for lunch, and only a once-a-week affair. See chapter 3.
- **Twelve Tribes** (Tel Aviv): Long admired for its inventive menu of nouvelle cuisine, prepared within the rules of kashruth under executive chef Hans Lelie, the restaurant has moved toward a slightly rustic, earthy style that doesn't try to disguise the basic elements of the foods being presented. It's the best hotel restaurant in Tel Aviv. See chapter 6.
- **Mika** (Tel Aviv): This is Israeli Fusion cuisine, served in a New York SoHo-like setting and done with style that is sometimes exquisitely delicate, and sometimes delightfully audacious. Every meal fascinates. Lunch specials are a bargain. See chapter 6.
- **Capot Tmarim** (Tel Aviv): A carefully re-created enclave of 1930s Tel Aviv architecture and decor is the setting for Ofer Gal's menu of brilliant Mediterranean Rim creations presented with careful attention to detail and is at the very top of Tel Aviv's luxury restaurants. See chapter 6.
- **Keren** (Jaffa): Occupying a wooden house brought to Jaffa by ship from America more than 100 years ago, Keren abounds in romantic charm. The elegant, always interesting French menu with touches of Mediterranean Rim is a constant joy. See chapter 6.
- **Yoe'ezer Wine Bar** (Jaffa): Set inside the cavernous arches of a crusader-era building, this is a gourmand's paradise created by noted Israeli journalist and food writer Shaul Evron. Here, at your leisure, you can sample from an Elysian collection of European and Israeli wines, accompanied by wonderful breads and cheeses, or feast on a menu of exquisite, richly prepared dishes. See chapter 6.
- **Ocean** (Herzlia): This brand-new restaurant is the dream of Eyal Shani, creator of Jerusalem's Ocean Bistro. Here the carefully herbed meats, fish, and seafood are prepared in special citrus wood ovens that bring out exquisite flavor. With a style that combines inventiveness and simplicity, this is well worth the taxi from Tel Aviv. See chapter 7.
- **Picciotto** (Zichron Yaacov): Named for its founder and former chef, an ex-fighter pilot who has moved on to the world of computers, this is a delightful Mediterranean Rim restaurant set in a 19th-century cottage; not cheap, but by Israeli standards a very good value. See chapter 7.
- **1873** (Haifa): Named for the year in which the quaint cottage it occupies was built, this French restaurant is the gastronomic jewel of Haifa, and a must for that special afternoon or night out. It's also surprisingly affordable. See chapter 8.

- **Voila** (Haifa): A small, intimate place that specializes in fondues and French/Swiss cuisine, the atmosphere here is semiromantic; the food is rich, rustic, and expertly prepared. See chapter 8.
- **Au Bistro** (Eilat): This French/Belgian gem is presided over by chef Michel Torjiman, who turns out nightly miracles. Au Bistro is reasonably priced, and runs circles around its competition in Eilat's big hotels. See chapter 10.

11 The Best Moderate Dining

Israel is filled with interesting, affordable restaurants ranging from authentic ethnic to natural Mediterranean Rim, and from kosher Indian or kosher Mexican to gracefully inventive French. In order to be accessible to kosher diners, many Israeli restaurants offer vegetarian-only menus that are imaginative and affordable. The following is a selection of unusual choices for atmosphere, good food, and good value, but you'll find many other fabulous restaurants throughout this book.

- **Eucalyptus** (Jerusalem): This is a must for sampling genuine, beautifully prepared, home-style Israeli food. Chef Moshe Basson blends traditional recipes, local herbs and spices, and seasonal vegetables and fruits into some of the best Arabic-style chicken Mahlouba and homemade Middle Eastern dishes in the country. Mr. Basson's explanations of his recipes are an added treat. See chapter 3.
- **Misadonet** (Jerusalem): This Kurdish restaurant has one of the best home-style kitchens in the country. The dish to die for here is Mama Nomi's *giri-giri,* a rich creation of lamb hearts stuffed with rice, meat, raisins, walnuts, and pine nuts, all served in a curried apricot sauce. Kubbeh soups, each distinctively flavored, are also quite special. See chapter 3.
- **Yemenite Step** (Jerusalem): Here you can sample *mellawach* (flaky Yemenite phyllo crepes) filled with spiced meats, chicken, or vegetables. Yemenite garnishes, soups, and vegetables are especially worthwhile—it's popular with both Jerusalemites and visitors. See chapter 3.
- **Pepperoni's** (Jerusalem): With its bountiful first-course buffet, ever-changing main-course selections, atmospheric building, and bargain fixed-price meals, this is always a great choice for an interesting meal in the relaxed, Mediterranean style. See chapter 3.
- **Spaghettim** (Jerusalem): This fabulous restaurant offers a vast array of spaghettis in fantastic sauces loaded with fresh ingredients. The Jerusalem branch, set in an old Ottoman-era mansion with a delightful dining garden, is an especially romantic location, but there's also a branch in Tel Aviv. See chapters 3 and 6.
- **Cacao at the Cinémathèque** (Jerusalem): The view of the Old City walls from the terrace here is breathtaking, the crowd is intelligent and stylish, and the menu is very affordable. Salads, peasant sandwiches, and an excellent but reasonably priced fish menu are offered. In cold weather, the indoor dining room can be smoky, but in good weather, a meal or dessert on the terrace is a must. See chapter 3.
- **Kohinoor** (Jerusalem): This kosher Indian restaurant provides a rare opportunity for kosher visitors to sample well-prepared Indian cuisine. The all-you-can-eat luncheon buffets are very affordable. The nonkosher Tandoori restaurants (Tel Aviv, Eilat, and Herzlia) of the same chain are equally excellent, elegant, and a good value. See chapters 3, 6, 7, and 10.
- **Ali Oli** (Tel Aviv): Without being fancy or pretentious, this place has style, spirit, and heavenly fish and seafood prepared in light, Mediterranean Rim style.

Prices are reasonable—a great place to wine and dine the night away. See chapter 6.

- **Manta Ray** (Tel Aviv): On an empty stretch of beach between Tel Aviv and Jaffa, this beach pavilion is open to the sea, the sound of the waves, and the Mediterranean sunset. It serves stylishly prepared fish and seafood, and is a good choice for breakfast or leisurely lunches and dinners. See chapter 6.
- **Margaret Tayar's** (Jaffa): This is a small, authentic place a short walk from trendy Old Jaffa, with a covered terrace overlooking the sweeping Tel Aviv shoreline, and a master cook who loves to see people enjoying her creations. Jaffa's fishers adore Margaret—she gets first choice of the catch. This is a one-woman tour de force. Always call to confirm hours. One of the very best restaurants in the country at any price. See chapter 6.
- **Abu Christo** (Old Akko): Fresh fish and a covered dining terrace right beside the sea give this restaurant a delightful Greek Island harborside ambience. You can put together a feast here, complete with Middle Eastern appetizers, for $15 to $20. See chapter 7.
- **Decks** (Tiberias): Named for its vast deck jutting into the Sea of Galilee, Decks does superb meats and vegetables grilled over olive, hickory, and citrus fires and gives you vistas, and, at times, the option of a free evening cruise. The breast of mullard, a duck-goose hybrid, is amazing, as is the special shoulder of baby lamb. See chapter 9.
- **Dushara** (Mamshit National Park): An interesting, delicious experiment in re-creating ancient dishes, this restaurant is set amid the Nabatean ruins of Mamshit, in the northern Negev. It's one of the Negev's modern treasures. See chapter 10.
- **Eddie's Hideaway** (Eilat): In a tourist town at the end of the earth, where most restaurants plan for customers they'll never see again, Eddie puts his heart into every meal and keeps coming up with menus that are delicious and inventive. See chapter 10.
- **Abu Ahmed's New Orient Restaurant** (Amman, Jordan): Jordan is famous for its Middle Eastern food, and this moderate restaurant serves some exquisite examples of Arabic cuisine in a pleasant bungalow with a garden terrace. See chapter 11.
- **Kan Zeman** (Yeduda, outside Amman, Jordan): This vast Middle Eastern buffet is accompanied in the evenings by Arabic musicians and dancers—it's touristy, but Jordanians and travellers alike love it—a national institution! See chapter 11.

Planning a Trip to Israel   2

In this chapter, the where, when, and how of your trip are discussed—the advanced planning that gets your trip together and takes it on the road.

1 The Regions in Brief

It doesn't take much time to get from one region of Israel to another, but you'll find the country is enormously varied. A quick review of the country will help you to decide where you want to spend your time.

JERUSALEM   This city is of course, the jewel in the crown. It is many worlds: modern and timeless; Jewish and Arab; religious and nonreligious. The walled, labyrinthine Old City has been named a World Heritage Site; in addition to being a perfectly preserved, living walled town with more than 4,000 years of history, it contains the great holy places of Judaism, Christianity, and Islam—the Temple Mount with the Dome of the Rock and the El Aksa Mosque, the Western Wall, and the Church of the Holy Sepulcher. Highlights of the New City include the remarkable Israel Museum, which houses the Dead Sea Scrolls as well as many other treasures, and Yad Vashem, the haunting Holocaust Memorial and Museum. Most travelers want to spend as much time as possible here, exploring and becoming acquainted with this extraordinary city.

THE DEAD SEA   Easy to visit for a day using Jerusalem as your base, the Dead Sea is also a good place to visit for a few days as the first part of a jaunt into the Negev Desert. The almost impregnable Herodian Fortress of **Masada,** is the most dramatic ancient site in the country, perched on a plateau above the Dead Sea. It was here that the last Jewish resisters against Rome committed suicide rather than surrender. The beautiful canyon oasis of **Ein Gedi** is another attraction here, as is the unique experience of trying to sink in the mineral-heavy Dead Sea. The southern Israeli shore of the Dead Sea is now lined with world-famous spa/hotels, offering therapeutic and beauty packages.

THE NEGEV   The southern 60% of Israel is desert and semidesert; it contains beautiful **nature reserves,** and is great for hiking and nature tours. This part of the country, least visited by tourists, is the most mysterious and spiritual part of Israel. **Eilat,** at the southern tip of the Negev, is a world unto itself—a mirage rising out of the sand with dozens of new high-rise megahotels and fancy restaurants grouped on

Factoid

For a map of these regions of Israel, see chapter 1.

the city's few miles of Red Sea shoreline. Long famous for its coral reef and laid back snorkeling and diving, Eilat's new motto is: "Make yourself a destination and people will come." Indeed the city is booming and now definitely upmarket. The **Sinai Coast,** a bit farther south, offers reefs that are more spectacular, a landscape more dramatic and less developed, and hotels that are considerably less expensive.

TEL AVIV   It seems to many like it must be in a different country from Jerusalem. Full of energy and verve, it has great restaurants, good beaches (with free samba dancing at least one evening a week in summer); and three inventive museums: the Diaspora Museum, the Eretz Israel Museum, and the Tel Aviv Museum of Art. From April to October, Tel Aviv is a good first stop in Israel—you can spend a day or two at the beach recovering from jet lag before plunging into the rest of the country.

THE MEDITERRANEAN COAST   If you want to relax on the beach, get to know this area. The coast is a good base. **Ashkelon,** at the southern end, has a few hotels, good weather, rough water, and is just becoming a tourist destination. **Netanya,** in the midcoast region, is a favorite of older, longer term English and French-speaking travelers. It has lots of hotels in all price ranges, and many apartments and studios for rent. The ruined Roman- and crusader-era city of **Caesaria** is the most dramatic archaeological site along the coast; further north, the Old City of **Akko,** with its bazaars, cafes and minarets beside the Mediterranean, is the most exotic site. **Kibbutz** and moshav holiday villages, from Nasholim, south of Haifa, right up to the northernmost coast, are good spots for a pleasant beach break from touring.

HAIFA   Israel's third major city offers a spirit and face quite different from Jerusalem or Tel Aviv. It is a business and industrial city, but it's so beautifully laid out on a stepped mountain overlooking the harbor, that it's quite memorable. Haifa makes a good urban base for exploring the northwestern part of the country.

THE GALILEE   Israel's northern region is lovely countryside, with forested mountains and olive groves dotted with Arab cities and towns, kibbutzim, and the remains of ancient ruined cities, synagogues and churches. At the heart of the Galilee, is the freshwater **Sea of Galilee,** a lyrically beautiful lake, made all the more special by its association with both New and Old Testament sites. The Galilee offers great hiking and nature trails, but it's also a good place to rent a car for a few days, and freewheel.

THE WEST BANK/PALESTINIAN AUTHORITY AREAS   This is a countryside of classic biblical landscapes that so far have been less developed than those inside Israel. The major cities of the West Bank are lively, but only the old neighborhoods are architecturally beautiful or atmospheric. **Bethlehem,** birthplace of Jesus, is just 5 miles south of Jerusalem and will be a major destination during 2000–2001. Further south, **Hebron,** a city rich in history for both Jews and Muslims, is best visited on organized tours. **Nablus,** site of the biblical Shechem, is the major Palestinian city in the northern part of the region, surrounded by graceful, mountainous countryside. At present, it too, is best visited on organized tours. Jerusalem is a good base for forays into this region.

JORDAN   Israel's neighbor offers dramatic, totally unspoiled landscapes as well as magnificent sites from ancient times, like the legendary rock-hewn city of **Petra,** in the southern part of the country, and the extensive Roman/Byzantine ruins of **Jerash,** in the north. Hotels are a bargain compared to those in Israel, and some, like the charming Taybet Zeman and the Movenpick at Petra, or the new Movenpick Dead Sea Spa Hotel, are designed with exoticism and inventiveness. Far larger than Tel Aviv or Jerusalem, **Amman,** Jordan's capital, is not really a town for tourists, but it's a lively metropolis that will give you a sense of the New Middle East.

2 Visitor Information & Entry Requirements

VISITOR INFORMATION

The Ministry of Tourism maintains information offices overseas, known as the Israel Government Tourist Office (IGTO). Readers in the Unites States and Canada can contact the **IGTO North American Information Center** (☎ **888/77-ISRAEL;** www.goisrael.com; e-mail: info@goisrael.com). **U.S.** offices are: 5 S. Wabash Ave., Chicago, IL 60603 (☎ **312/782-4306**); 6380 Wilshire Blvd., Suite 1718, Los Angeles, CA 90048 (☎ **213/658-7462** or 213/658-7463); 5151 Belt Line Rd., Suite 1289 Dallas, TX 75240 (☎ **800/472-6364**); and 800 Second Ave., New York, NY 10117 (☎ **212/499-5650**).

In **Australia,** contact Australia-Israel Chamber of Commerce, Tourism Dept., 395 New South Head Rd., Double Bay NSW 2028, Sydney (☎ **2-9326-1700;** fax 2-9326-1676; e-mail: aicc@mpx.com.au).

Canadians can head to 180 Bloor St. West, Suite 700, Toronto, ON M5S 2V6 (☎ **800/669-2369;** fax 416/964-2420). In **South Africa,** the office is at Nedbank Gardens, 5th Floor, 33 Bath Ave., Rosebank, 2196 Johannesburg (☎ **11/788-1703**), and in the **United Kingdom,** 18 Great Marlborough St., London W1V 1AF (☎ **071/434-3651**).

Note: Be sure to contact the nearest branch of the Israel Government Tourist Office for updated information on special events in conjunction with the **Year 2000,** planned for the 2,000th anniversary of the birth of Jesus.

ENTRY REQUIREMENTS

Visas are given free to U.S., U.K., and Canadian citizens, without prior application, when they enter Israel and show passports that are valid for at least 9 months beyond the time of arrival. The tourist visa is good for 3 months and can be extended for another 3 consecutive months at any office of the Ministry of the Interior (you may be asked to prove you have adequate funding for your extended stay). For residents of New Zealand, Australia, and Ireland visas are issued free upon entry and are valid for 3 months. To work, study, or settle in Israel, you need the proper permit before arrival.

If you plan to visit Arab countries, ask for your visa stamp to be placed on a piece of paper separate from your passport (if your passport is stamped by the Israelis, that stamp will close most Arab-world doors). Israeli passport control is accustomed to this request and will cooperate.

CUSTOMS

You can bring $150 worth of tax-free gifts into the country. You can also bring in 250 cigarettes, one bottle ($^4/_5$ quart) of liquor, and a reasonable amount of film. When you leave you can convert up to $3,000 back into foreign currency at the airport, so keep your bank receipts.

3 Money

The basic unit of currency is the **new Israel shekel (NIS)**. We estimate that during the time span of this edition, the value of the shekel will be approximately **NIS 4.5 to $1. This means 1 shekel is approximately 22¢.** Over the past 5 years, the general value of the new Israeli shekel has been in a constant, slow fall in relation to the American dollar. During the time span of this edition, you may even find the rate of exchange moving closer to NIS 5 to the dollar, but uncertainties in the Israeli economy could alter this trend. British travelers will find the rate of exchange to be approximately **NIS 6.8 to £1; 1 shekel is about 14 new pence.** We have tried to make an estimate of what prices and exchange rates should be on average during the 2000–2002 period. Readers using this book early in the time span of this edition, may find actual prices a bit lower than those we quote; later, actual prices may be a bit higher.

The shekel is divided into 100 agorot, and the smallest denomination you will encounter is a copper-colored 5-agorot coin. There are 10-agorot copper-colored coins, and larger, copper 50-agorot (half shekel) coins, all useful for bus fare. The 1-shekel coin is a tiny silver buttonlike object that is extremely easy to lose. Hang onto a few 1-shekel coins: pay phones in restaurants and hotels often only take 1-shekel coins instead of the cheaper per-call telephone cards. There is also a 5- and 10-shekel coin, as well as 10-, 20-, 50-, and 100-shekel notes. The new, small 10-shekel coins are not popular; they coexist with 10-shekel notes, a few of which will be around during the time span of this edition.

Warning: Black-market street dealers sometimes try to pass off pre-1985 old shekel notes in denominations of 500 and 1,000. These notes have **no value** and are not in circulation, although their design is exactly like current notes of lower denominations. Be certain that all currency notes you accept are clearly marked "New Sheqels" in English.

The Shekel & the Dollar

At this writing NIS 1 equals approximately 22¢, or NIS 4.5 to $1, and this was the rate of exchange used to calculate the dollar values given in this guide. One shekel is about 14 new pence, or NIS 6.8 to £1. This rate fluctuates from time to time and may not be the same when you travel to Israel. Therefore, the following table should be used only as a guide:

NIS	U.S.$	U.K.£	NIS	U.S.$	U.K.£
1	.22	.14	20	4.40	2.80
2	.44	.28	25	5.50	3.50
3	.66	.42	30	6.60	4.20
4	.88	.56	40	8.80	5.60
5	1.10	.70	50	11.00	7.00
6	1.32	.84	100	22.00	14.00
7	1.54	.98	125	27.50	17.50
8	1.76	1.12	150	33.00	21.00
9	1.98	1.26	200	44.00	28.00
10	2.20	1.40	500	110.00	70.00
15	3.30	2.10	1,000	220.00	140.00

What Things Cost in Israel	U.S. $
Set taxi fare from Ben-Gurion Airport to Jerusalem	
(daytime)	37.00
(nights and Shabbat)	48.00
Sherut (shared limo or van) from Ben-Gurion Airport to any address in Jerusalem (per person)	9.50
Bus fare from Ben-Gurion Airport to Jerusalem	3.35
Bus fare from Ben-Gurion Airport to Tel Aviv	3.35
Local phone call from public phone	.22–.33
Double room at Jerusalem Hilton Hotel (expensive)	310.00–395.00
Double room at Laromme Hotel (expensive)	187.00–276.00
Double room at Jerusalem YMCA, King David Street (upper moderate)	145.00
Double room at Ha-Nagid Hotel (moderate)	110.00–150.00
Double room at Jerusalem Inn Hotel (inexpensive)	68.00–86.00
Meal for one at Ocean Bistro Restaurant (luxury)	40.00–80.00
Meal for one at Stanley's (expensive)	15.00–30.00
Meal for one at Misadonet (moderate)	13.00–20.00
Meal for one at Spaghettim(budget)	8.00–15.00
Shwarma at Moshiko's (superbudget)	3.50
Beer	2.90
Coca-Cola	1.30
Cup of coffee	1.60–2.80
Admission to Israel Museum	7.20
Ticket to attraction in Jerusalem Festival	35.00 and up
Ticket to small folk or classical concert	10.00–33.00
Municipal bus fare	1.30

CREDIT CARDS   The major credit cards—American Express, MasterCard, Visa, Access, and EuroCard—are accepted at most hotels, at many restaurants and shops, and for cash advances at banks. Some banks accept one card, but not others: Try the local branch of Bank Leumi le-Israel and the Israel Discount Bank for Visa; for MasterCard, try a Bank Ha-Poalim or United Mizrachi branch.

ATM CARDS   Automated-teller machines at *some* **Bank Ha-Poalim** and **Mizrachi Bank** branches are now connected to the CIRRUS-NYCE systems. Your foreign ATM card will only work at those few machines in each major city that are equipped with ATMs that carry the CIRRUS, NYCE, or PLUS sign. Your American account will be debited and you will receive shekels from the machine. The exchange rate is usually a bit better than for cash or traveler's checks, as it is figured at the commercial rate. At press time, Israeli banks charge no fee for ATM use. Check with your home bank about service charges for withdrawals from overseas ATMs. If you're going to use this method of exchanging money, it's a good idea to open an account at a bank that doesn't charge for ATM transactions at foreign banks—otherwise service fees can really accumulate.

Note: Don't wait until you're down to your last shekel before going to the ATM. International computers are often down for hours at a time; ATMs are not restocked at Sabbath or on holidays. In small towns and rural areas, there may not be any CIRRUS, NYCE, or PLUS ATMs, so you'll need to use traveler's checks.

TRAVELER'S CHECKS   Traveler's checks in major hard currencies are accepted at all banks and money-changers. Always take your passport when changing traveler's checks. Personal checks are sometimes accepted, but you can never depend on it. Ask the merchant before you assume you can pay with a personal check.

4 When to Go

CLIMATE   The Israeli seasons are somewhat different from those in the United States and western Europe. To start with, the Israeli winter doesn't normally involve snow, except for Mount Hermon on the Golan Heights—although there are occasional flurries every couple of years in Jerusalem and Upper Galilee. Winter in Israel starts with showers in October and continues through periodic heavy rainfalls from November to March. Swimming is out in the Mediterranean during this time, except during occasional heat waves, although you can usually swim in Eilat and the Dead Sea in the winter.

From late March to September, it seldom rains at all. You can count on constant sunshine during the summer months. In late February and the beginning of March, the entire country seems to turn green from the winter rains, and wildflower displays in the Galilee and the Golan regions are truly spectacular. In the months that follow, the heat gathers intensity, reaching its peak in July and August, when the only relatively cool spots are Jerusalem and the high mountains around Safed. The landscape is dry and parched by May, but by September temperatures are falling off a bit.

Generally, Israel's Mediterranean climate is somewhat like that of Southern California: intense summer heat and sunshine, breezy nights, the coastal winds of winter. In addition, Israel also experiences hot and dry desert winds at the beginning and end of the summer, although a *hamsin* can occur anytime from March to November. These south and eastern winds are named after the Arabic word *fifty,* since the wind was traditionally believed to blow for 50 days a year. Thankfully, it doesn't.

In winter (November through March), cold rain systems move in from the north. Because they are prevented from continuing south by the constant tropical weather systems of Africa, these storms can stall over Israel for days until they rain themselves out. If you find a few days of your trip hampered by constant rain, your reward will be the chance to visit pine forests near Jerusalem and in the Galilee as fragrant and misty as those of the Pacific Northwest. You'll see the countryside carpeted with wildflowers and a rare, fragile veil of greenery.

ISRAEL'S CALENDAR(S)   If awards were given for "daily" confusion, or for having the maximum number of holidays a year, Israel would probably win them all.

Israel's Average Temperatures °F

	Jan	Mar	May	July	Sept	Nov
Jerusalem	39–57	52–66	61–80	67–83	66–82	50–66
Tel Aviv	48–66	55–71	60–79	71–87	70–83	55–75
Haifa	50–62	55–70	62–76	71–83	72–83	59–70
Tiberias	54–69	57–79	68–92	77–98	72–96	62–77
Eilat	52–72	67–75	73–97	80–105	80–100	59–82

Israel "officially" operates on two separate systems for determining day, month, and year: the Jewish calendar with its roots in ancient Canaanite and Babylonian tradition, dating from some 5,750-odd years ago, and the Gregorian calendar, used in most countries, including the United States. Recognized, but "unofficial," are even more calendars, such as the Julian (Julius Caesar) calendar, which runs 13 days behind the Gregorian; and the Muslim era, which counts the years from A.D. 622, when the Prophet Muhammad led the *hejira* from Mecca to Medina. Not only do these calendars disagree about dates, but also about whether time is measured by sun, moon, or a combination of the two, and when the year should start and end. (I've never calculated how many New Year celebrations occur each year in Israel, but I do know of at least three Christmases.)

HOLIDAYS   Israeli holidays and events will affect your visit in several important ways. First, hotels and campsites will fill to capacity and rates will rise by as much as 20%. Next, transportation and restaurant service may be curtailed or completely suspended, and places of entertainment may be closed. On the other hand, a holiday is a special occasion, and you won't want to miss the events that may take place.

Israel is also a most confusing place when it comes to the weekly holiday schedule. Jews stop work at midafternoon on Friday; some Muslims at sundown on Thursday (although many shops remain open on Friday); most Christians all day on Sunday. In Tel Aviv, no buses run from late Friday afternoon until Saturday after sundown, although small private minibuses cover the main routes. In Jerusalem, buses run only in the Arab neighborhoods on Saturday; in Haifa, there's partial bus service on Saturday. In nonreligious Eilat, there is no public transport on Shabbat. Some shops open just as others are closing for a holiday.

Lots of religious holidays change dates each year. The entire Muslim religious calendar starts 11 days earlier each year—it's a lunar calendar. This means the Islamic holy month of Ramadan, when Muslims may not eat or drink during daylight hours (and when Western visitors may not visit the mosques on the Temple Mount in Jerusalem), slowly migrates across the year. How to keep your wits amid all these openings and closings? Read the following information carefully.

THE JEWISH SABBATH   The Bible states that the seventh day is one of rest—a time when no work can be done. For Orthodox Jews, this means no fires are lit, no human beings or animals can be made to work, no machines can be operated, no traveling can be done, no money handled, no business transacted. So officially that's the way it is in most of Israel, where the Sabbath, or *Shabbat,* is celebrated on Saturday. By 2 or 3pm on a Friday afternoon, depending on whether it's winter or summer (Shabbat begins at sundown), most shops have closed for the day. Buses and trains stop running at least an hour before Shabbat, and the movie houses are closed at night. There is a growing list of exceptions: in central Tel Aviv, many restaurants, cafes, discos, and theaters close on Friday afternoon for a few hours, but reopen on Friday night; Haifa has always had a quiet alternative Friday nightlife; and in Jerusalem, a number of cinemas and restaurants (nonkosher) remain open; recently the pub area around Jerusalem's Russian Compound has begun to boom, and Friday nights are very busy.

On Saturday, almost all shops throughout the country are closed (except for a few cafes and Arab or Christian establishments in Jerusalem's Old City) and nearly all transportation stops (only Haifa has limited municipal bus service at this time, and only taxis or small sherut companies ply in or between cities). Gas stations are mostly open on Shabbat, since few are located in religious neighborhoods. Most admission-free museums are ordinarily open for part of Shabbat; entrance tickets, when required, must sometimes be bought from private-duty guards outside the museum entrance. A few strictly kosher restaurants follow this same no-money-handling rule, accepting only advanced prepaid orders for Shabbat meals, which will often be cooked in advance and served tepid or cold; 99% of kosher restaurants, however, will be closed. Also, do watch for signs in restaurants or hotel dining rooms asking you not to smoke, so as not to offend Orthodox guests. (Lighting a cigarette or turning on a light switch are considered forms of starting a fire, which is an act of work forbidden on Shabbat.)

Precise hours for the duration of Shabbat, which vary according to the time of sunset, are listed in the Friday *Jerusalem Post.* The restarting of buses and reopening of cinemas and restaurants can be quite late in summer, as Shabbat does not end until you can see three stars in the sky at one glance.

Most Israelis are not Sabbath observant and love to travel on their day off, so if you want to drive on Saturday, you'll find the roads to beaches and parks quite busy. About the only people who'll try to stop you are the ultrareligious Jews, such as those in Jerusalem's Mea Shearim section. There they tend to get rather heated about people who ignore their interpretation of Shabbat restrictions. Many streets in religious areas will be blocked with boulders; most ultraorthodox neighborhoods in Jerusalem and Bnei Brak, near Tel Aviv, have official permission to close their streets to traffic. Don't even think of trying to drive in or up to such areas. You can be stoned, and you will have little or no help from the police.

Israelis work 6 days a week, and as almost everything is shut down on Friday nights, Saturday nights are for staying up late and partying. By nightfall, transportation services resume, and movie houses begin selling tickets for evening shows. By dark, all entertainment places are usually packed full, including the many sidewalk cafes. Restaurants need about an hour after the end of Shabbat to assemble their staffs and prepare things before they open their doors to the public. You won't get the best possible meal at a restaurant on Saturday night—conditions are crowded, staffs are harried, and many items will have been prepared on Thursday or Friday.

Israel Calendar of Events

Here's a general guide to when holidays and festivals occur. Keep in mind that a Jewish holiday that generally falls in March, say, may some years fall on a late date in February. Note also that not all Jewish holidays are subject to Sabbath-like prohibitions and closings. Holidays on which things do close down are indicated by an asterisk (*). **Celebration of each holiday commences at sundown on the evening before the date listed.**

For updated information about holidays, special events, and festivals, check with your nearest IGTO office. In North America, call the **Israel Tourism Information Center** at ☎ **888-77-ISRAEL;** www.goisrael.com; e-mail: info@goisrael.com.

January/February
- **Israeli Arbor Day (Tu b'Shevat):** Thousands of singing and dancing schoolchildren traipse off to plant trees all over the country. January 8, 2001; January 22, 2002.

March
- **Purim (Feast of Lots):** Recalling how Queen Esther saved her people in Persia (5th century B.C.), this is an exciting time when folks, especially children, dress up in fancy or zany (or sometimes irreligious) costumes, have parties, parade in

the streets, give gifts, spray shaving cream at passersby, and generally make merry. In Jerusalem and Safed, which are considered walled cities, Purim is celebrated 1 day later than in the rest of the country. March 21, 2000; March 9, 2001; February 26, 2002.

April

- **Pesach (Passover)*:** No bread, beer, or other foods containing leavening are obtainable for 7 days (8 days outside Israel), and hotel and restaurant meals may cost more because of the culinary complexities. Many restaurants simply shut down for this period of time. During the days just before the holidays, housewives furiously clean their kitchens, and houses in general, to render them spotless and free of any stray bits of leavening. The first night of the holiday is devoted to a seder, a family meal and ritual recalling the exodus of the ancient Israelites from Egypt. (In the Diaspora, the seder is held on both the first and second nights of Passover.) Many hotels and restaurants have special seders for tourists. The first and last days of this holiday are Sabbath-like affairs, which means the country more or less closes down. April 19 to April 25, 2000; April 8 to 14, 2001; March 28 to April 3, 2002.

April/May

- **Holocaust Memorial Day (Yom Ha-Shoah)*:** Marking the time of the year in 1945 when the last of the concentration camps in Europe were liberated, and the Holocaust came to an end. All places of entertainment are closed. As the day begins (like all Jewish days, at nightfall) most restaurants are closed, although public transportation continues and most shops and businesses are open. At 11am on Yom Ha-Shoah, a siren sounds throughout the nation, and a period of silence is observed in memory of the six million who perished. A special memorial ceremony is held at Yad VaShem in Jerusalem. Some places for simple meals and snacks are open during the day. April 20, 2001; April 9, 2002.
- **Memorial Day*:** One week after Yom Ha-Shoah, the nation remembers its war dead. Restaurants and places of public entertainment are closed, but transportation operates and most shops are open. Again, at 11am, a siren sounds, and a period of silence is observed. Throughout the country, memorial services are held. April 27, 2001; April 16, 2002.
- **Independence Day:** The day after Memorial Day, Israel commemorates the day in 1948 when the British Mandate ended, and the State of Israel was proclaimed. It is celebrated with house parties and municipal fireworks at night. April 28, 2001; April 17, 2002.

May/June

- **Lag b'Omer:** Ending 33 days of mourning, this is the chief happy celebration for the Hasidim, who leave Jerusalem and other cities at this time to sing and dance around bonfires at the Meiron tomb of the mystical Rabbi Shimon Bar Yochai, in Galilee. There are also Sephardic pilgrimages to the tombs of great rabbis. Children around the country also sing, dance, and light evening bonfires. May 11, 2001; May 1, 2002.
- **Shavuot (Pentecost)*:** The early summer harvest celebration is a joyous time, a special favorite of agricultural settlements. It is often marked by plays, entertainment, and children dressed in white, wearing floral crowns. Since it also recalls the receipt of the Ten Commandments, as well as the bringing of the "first fruits" to the temple, it is observed as a religious holiday. Dairy foods such as blintzes and cheesecakes are traditionally prepared for the holiday, and at synagogues

throughout the country, as well as at the Western Wall, the Torah is read throughout the night. June 9, 2000; May 28, 2001; May 17, 2002.

- **Abu Gosh Music Festival:** A new festival held in the Arab-Israeli village of Abu Gosh, in the hills west of Jerusalem. Classical and religious music is performed in the village's two churches; there's street performances and arts and crafts. Each year at Shavuot and Sukkot.

- **Israel/Jerusalem Festival of the Performing Arts:** In late spring, music groups and theater and dance companies come from all over the world to perform. For exact dates e-mail info@israel2000.tourism.gov.il.

July/August

- **Tisha b'Av:** The fast day on the ninth day of the month of Av is a time set aside to remember the destruction of the First and Second Temples, which by ominous coincidence were destroyed on the same calendar day in the years 586 B.C. and A.D. 70, respectively. Entertainment facilities are closed. Many restaurants are closed. August 10, 2000; July 29, 2001.

- **Israeli Folkdance Festival,** Karmiel, in the Galilee: Jewish ethnic dancers come from around the world for this festival held in early July.

- **Jerusalem International Film Festival:** Increasingly prestigious, with many offerings from both mainstream and exotic countries. At the Jerusalem Cinémathèque, it takes place the first 2 weeks in July. For more information, contact ☎ 02/672-4131; www.jer-cin.org.il; or e-mail: jer-cin@jer-cin.org.il.

- **Jerusalem Arts and Crafts Festival:** Held in the Sultan's Pool in the valley outside the western walls of the Old City, the contemporary Israeli craft booths are not usually of a high level, but the large International Craft Section is excellent. Performances by Israeli musicians every night. Late July.

- **Hebrew Song Festival:** This event takes place at Arad, in the Negev, in late July. Because of a stampede that resulted in a number of deaths and injuries during the 1995 festival, the future of this event is in doubt.

- **Jacob's Ladder Country, Folk, and Blues Festival,** Gan HaShlosha (Sachne): An important event, it is held in the Galilee each year, on the first weekend in July.

- **Red Sea Jazz Festival,** Eilat: The jazz festival is held in Eilat in July or August.

September/October

- **The Jerusalem International Chamber Music Festival:** Produced by the Jerusalem Symphony Orchestra under the directorship of pianist Elena Bashkirova, this festival offers an array of internationally famous musicians performing classic chamber music.

- **Rosh Hashonah (Jewish New Year)*:** The start of the High Holy Days. Since the Jewish calendar starts in September or October, that's when the new year falls. It is a 2-day religious festival, not an occasion for revels but rather for solemn contemplation and prayer. Almost everything in the Jewish sector of the country is closed. September 30 to October 1, 2000; September 18 to 19, 2001.

- **Yom Kippur (Day of Atonement)*:** Ten days after the Jewish year begins, the High Holy Days culminate in the most solemn of Jewish holidays. Observant Jews spend nearly the whole day in synagogue. Places of worship are crowded, but the large synagogues reserve seats for tourists, and some of the larger hotels organize their own services. Yom Kippur is a fast day, but hotel dining rooms serve guests who wish to eat. Everything comes to a standstill; even television and radio stations suspend broadcasting. October 9, 2000; September 28, 2001.

- **Sukkot (Feast of Tabernacles)*:** Beginning 5 days after Yom Kippur, this 7-day holiday recalls how Moses and the Children of Israel dwelled in "booths" (or "sukkot") as they left Egypt to wander in the desert. Observant families have meals and services in specially built, highly decorated yet simple huts, located outside in gardens or on balconies. Sukkot is also a harvest festival and thus an agricultural and kibbutz favorite. In ancient times, the harvest of Sukkot was the most important of the annual pilgrimage festivals to Jerusalem. On the first and last days of Sukkot, Sabbath-like restrictions are observed. October 14 to 21, 2000; October 2 to 9, 2001.
- **Simhat Torah*:** As Sukkot ends, Jews rejoice that they have the Torah (the Law); street festivities in Jerusalem and Tel Aviv mark this day. On Simhat Torah, cantors read the final verses of the Torah (the first five books of the Bible), and then start again at its beginning. October 21, 2000; October 9, 2001

November

- **Olive Festival:** In recent years, both Jewish and Arab communities in the Galilee have come to mark the November Olive Harvest period with at least a dozen local festivals of traditional foods, music, crafts, and dance. It's partly a genuine grassroots reawakening of ancient traditions, and partly aimed at both Israeli and foreign tourists. Check with the Nazareth and Akko Tourist Information offices for the best listings.

December

- **Hanukkah:** Celebrates the victory of the Maccabees over Syrian-Greeks and the consequent rededication of the Temple in 164 B.C. For 8 days this history-based holiday is marked by the nightly lighting of the Hanukkiah, or eight-branch menorah (as opposed to the traditional seven-branch menorah, which is a more ancient symbol of the Jewish people). December 22 to 29, 2000; December 10 to 17, 2001.
- **Ramadan:** The Islamic holy month migrates through the year. It begins approximately 10 days earlier each year, and the exact first and last days depend on astronomical sightings in Saudi Arabia. December 9, 2000 to January 9, 2001; November 30, or December 1 2001 to January 1, 2002.
- **International Choir Concerts:** These take place in Bethlehem on December 24.
- **Liturgica,** Jerusalem: A week of choral music organized by the Jerusalem Symphony Orchestra in late December.

5 The Active Vacation Planner

BIKING   Check with the **Jerusalem Cyclists Club,** 16 Harazim St. (☎ 02/ 643-8386,** ask for Gershon; or 02/561-9416, ask for Benni). They give advice on bicycle rentals and interesting routes; they often lead bike tours that begin at 7am on Saturdays at the Binyanei Ha-Oma International Convention Center near the Jerusalem Holiday Inn Hotel.

In the Tel Aviv area, the **Israel Cyclists Touring Club** (☎ 03/685-6262) promotes guided tours between March and October. Generally, the tours are 8, 9, or 14 days, and packages include accommodations, meals, a guide, bus transportation when necessary, entrance fees to sights on the itinerary, and insurance. Contact the ICTC for further information. You can also contact **Galgalei Ha'Etz** for racing and touring event information (☎ 03/572-7031). The **Red Sea Sports Center** in Eilat (☎ 07/ 637-9835) rents bikes and is in touch with tours and bike events in Israel's southern region.

CAMPING Beautiful, interesting sites and serviceable facilities mark Israel's camping scene. If you want, you can stay in a hut or trailer (caravan), complete with electricity. Modern showers and conveniences are always nearby, and kiosks supplement or provide all your food needs. Some camping sites even offer mobile homes—fully furnished units with a living room, two bedrooms, kitchen, bathroom, and toilet. These can accommodate up to six people. Bed linens are supplied, as well as kitchen utensils. There's usually good transportation to each location.

You can avoid paying value-added tax (VAT) if you pay for your campsite in foreign currency. Fees skyrocket on weekends, Jewish holidays, and during summer school vacation. There's a minimum 3-day charge on Rosh Hashanah and Shavuot Passover, Sukkot, and other Jewish holidays.

Package deals including airport transfers, auto rentals, and more, are available. Contact the **Israel "Chalets" and Camping Union,** P.O. Box 53, Nahariya 22100 (☎ **04/992-5392**), for rates, literature, and further information.

By the way, you'll be glad to know that containers of propane and butane gas are readily available in Israel, and many of them have American-style fittings, so you can use your stateside stove or lantern in Israel. French "camping gaz" tanks are also available.

HIKING & NATURE WALKS The **Society for Protection of Nature in Israel (SPNI)** offers overnight treks, detailed hiking trips, and active package tours throughout Israel, with accommodations in many price categories. They also offer excellent nature walks through the wadis and deserts near Jerusalem and day tours of the Jerusalem Old and New Cities. For information, brochures, and reservations call ☎ **800/323-0035** or 718/645-3370 in the U.S., www.spni.org.il, e-mail: Tourism@spni.org.il; in the U.K., call ☎ **0171-957-4300.**

MARATHONS The **Tel Aviv Half Marathon** takes place in mid-March. The **Mount Tabor Run** is usually held during the third week in March. On the Sea of Galilee, the 4-kilometer (2$\frac{1}{2}$-mi.) **Sea of Galilee Crossing Swim** from Kibbutz Ha-On to Zemach is held each year in July or August. For information, contact the GTIO office.

6 Learning Vacations & Special Programs

LANGUAGE SCHOOLS In order to absorb enormous numbers of new immigrants over the past 5 decades, Israel has developed intensive Hebrew language programs, centered around an institution called an *ulpan*. If you plan an extended visit to Israel, you should know that a good many kibbutzim operate *ulpanim* that are based on the principle of working for your education, room, and board. In exchange for half a day of Hebrew-language classroom instruction, you work the other half day in a job assigned by the kibbutz—in the fields, kitchen, or wherever you are needed.

The Jewish Agency—in the United States, abroad, and in Israel—makes the arrangements for you to do work/study at a specific kibbutz. In the United States, send requests for information to the **Kibbutz Program Center,** 110 E. 59th St., 4th Floor, New York, NY 10022 (☎ **800/247-7852** or 212/318-6130; fax 212/832-2597; e-mail: kibbutzdsk@aol.com). In Israel, apply to the **Kibbutz Program Center Volunteer Office,** 18 Frishman St., Tel Aviv (☎ **03/527-8874;** fax 03/523-9966). To enter a program, in most cases, you must be between 18 and 32, speak a reasonable amount of English, and you must make a commitment of at least 2 months. You must provide a medical certificate to show you are in good health, and show proof that you have health insurance, a round-trip airline ticket, and at least $250. Classes are mixed, and your classmates may be Argentinean, Polish, Romanian, Moroccan, Iranian, Russian, and Ethiopian new immigrants.

Study at ulpanim in Israel not affiliated with kibbutzim may be accepted for credit or fulfillment of language requirements at a number of American universities.

The three big cities have ulpanim where you pay a fee. There are 3-, 8-, 12-, and 20-week courses, very reasonably priced. If you're interested, apply to the **JCC Ulpan Center,** 16 W. 65th St., New York, NY 10023 (☎ **212/580-0099**).

The well-established **Ulpan Akiva,** P.O. Box 6086, Netanya 42160, Israel (☎ **09/835-2312/3**; fax 09/865-2919; www.ulpan-akiva.org.il; e-mail: ulpanakv@ netvision.net.il), offers intensive, live-in programs in both Hebrew and Arabic for varying periods of time in a pleasant seaside community. Ulpan Akiva supplements its language programs with a full range of tours and social and cultural activities. Courses at Ulpan Akiva are accepted for credit at a number of American universities.

KIBBUTZ VOLUNTEERS   You can volunteer for work in most of Israel's 250 kibbutzim or communal settlements. The work can be difficult, and can range from agricultural labor to kitchen, laundry, or factory work, 6 hours a day, 6 days a week. Most kibbutzim offer room, board, pocket money, lectures, and trips around Israel to their volunteer workers. Many volunteers find the experience rewarding, but a major complaint is that the lifelong kibbutz members remain aloof and isolated from the constantly changing temporary volunteers, and volunteers' high expectations of becoming a true part of kibbutz life are not generally realized. Also, be aware that there are different groups of kibbutzim based on various ideologies. All kibbutzim share a great commitment to developing the land; most are opposed to settlements in the Occupied Territories. The Hashomer Hatzair Kibbutz Movement is the most actively committed to civil rights and liberal social issues throughout the country; the mainstream United Kibbutz Movement (the largest in Israel) is more middle-of-the-road. There is also a religious kibbutz movement. Most kibbutzim accept volunteers of any nationality or religion.

In kibbutzim that have an ulpan program, you can often study Hebrew intensively while you work. See above for information on how to contact the Kibbutz Program Centers in New York and Tel Aviv.

Volunteers For Israel, 330 W. 42nd St., Room 1618, New York, NY 10036 (☎ **212/643-4848**; fax 212/643-4855), is an organization that arranges volunteer support positions such as typing, repair work, and KP duty with noncombat sectors of the Israeli military. We've had letters from readers in all age groups over 20 testifying to interesting experiences in this program. You sleep and eat at military bases, wear fatigues, and after you fulfill your 3-week obligations, you are eligible for a special El Al discount fare. Application to this program requires a nonrefundable $100 application fee.

ARCHAEOLOGICAL DIGS   You can volunteer to work at an archaeological dig if you are 18 or older, prepared to stay for at least 2 weeks, and capable of doing strenuous work in a hot climate. You will have to pay your own fare to and from Israel. Most excavations take place between June and October, but there are off-season digs. Lectures are given at some sites, and some offer academic credit for the work. If you'd like to join a dig, it's best to inquire as far in advance as possible.

The best summary of current digs is found each year in the January/February issue of the magazine ***Biblical Archaeology Review,*** P.O. Box 7026, Red Oak, IA 51591, available at many libraries and newsdealers. *Biblical Archeology Review's* listings include exactly whom to contact for information about joining each specific dig, as well as estimates on expenses for volunteers and a description of each dig's recent finds. The

The Year 2000–2001 Millennial Celebrations

Many special events are planned in 2000–01 in conjunction with the ongoing Millennial Celebrations, which will probably bring unprecedented numbers of tourists to Israel. For an update on events, contact the **IGTO North American Information Center** (☎ **888/77-ISRAEL**), or contact your nearest branch of the IGTO (e-mail: info@goisrael.com). Much additional information about the celebrations and pilgrimage activities **2000–2001,** planned for the 2,000th anniversary of the birth of Jesus should become available during the time span of this edition.

Israel Ministry of Tourism North American InfoCenter (☎ **888/77-ISRAEL**) will also give you general, updated information about finding a suitable dig.

The **Biblical Archaeology Society,** 4710 41st St., NW, Washington, D.C. 20016 (☎ **800/221-4644** or 202-364-2636; www.bib-arch.org; e-mail: bibarch@clark,net), which publishes the *Biblical Archaeology Review,* organizes archaeology-based study tours of Israel and the surrounding region. The **Israel Archaeological Society,** 467 Levering Ave., Los Angeles, CA 90024 (☎ **800/477-2358** or 310/472-9449; e-mail: archaeology@mindspring.com), is another organization concerned with this field— they will send you schedules of their events and free videos.

SPECIAL PROGRAMS

PLANT A TREE   Once in Israel, you can plant a tree with your own hands and feel some connection with the physical development and beauty of the country. It costs $10 a tree, and the Jewish National Fund will tell you how it's done. All tourism information offices will have current information on tree planting in their localities.

JEWISH-ARAB DIALOGUE PROGRAMS   One out of every six Israeli citizens living inside the pre-1967 boundaries of Israel is Arabic. There are a growing number of dialogue and intercultural understanding projects inside Israel for Israeli Arabs and Jews; you will often find Israelis from English-speaking countries, armed with democratic traditions and experience living in multicultural societies, at the forefront of these projects. Visitors to Israel may observe these organizations and participate in lectures and tours that illuminate the problems and possibilities that exist in dialogue and understanding; students and professionals, including educators, psychologists, creative artists, and social workers, can often volunteer to participate in these programs. This can be an offbeat but interesting way to encounter one of the most hopeful sides of Israeli society.

The **Abraham Fund** is a nonprofit organization that works to enhance coexistence between Israel's Jewish and Arab citizens. The fund supports a variety of coexistence programs across Israel ranging from Arab-Jewish dialogue groups and intercultural classrooms and education experiences to projects in music, art, and theater. Individuals or groups interested in visiting projects on-site are welcome, and should contact the Abraham Fund, 477 Madison Ave., 4th Floor, New York, NY 10022, (☎ **800/ 301-3863** or 212/303-9421; e-mail:info@abrahamfund.org). Visiting these projects can add a fascinating and inspiring dimension to your trip.

Neve Shalom/Wahat al Salaam, 99761 Doar Na Shimshon, Israel (☎ **02/ 991-7160;** fax 02/991-7412; e-mail: nswasinn@trendline.co.il), is a unique Israeli-Palestinian cooperative village near Jerusalem that sponsors programs for visiting youth groups, including meetings with Jewish and Palestinian youth; programs for peace-oriented groups, focusing on area peace organizations; and tours for pilgrim groups, focusing on religious sites and the Holy Land's significance to Judaism, Christianity, and Islam. Neve Shalom/Wahat al Salaam (which means "Oasis of Peace") has an international conference and visitor's center, guest house, and restaurant on its premises, and offers half- and full-day lecture programs for $11 to $17 per person. Individuals and groups of less than 15 people will be added to larger groups.

New Israel Fund & Shatil Volunteer Programs, 1625 K St. NW, Suite 500, Washington, DC 20006 (☎ **202/223-3333;** fax 202/659-2789; e-mail: shatil@shatil.nif.org.il), is concerned with human rights and intercultural understanding inside Israel. It sponsors professional exchange, volunteer and intern projects, social change fellowships, and village volunteer-in-residence programs.

CULINARY TOURS The **Israel Programs Foundation,** 1098 S. Milwaukee Ave., Wheeling, IL 60090 (☎ **800/826-4525;** fax 847/541-8092; www.ipf.org; e-mail: ipf@ipf.org), affiliated with the movement for Conservative Judaism, offers a 12-day Culinary Gourmet and Israel Culture tour in the fall for $3,900; you must be over 18. If this does not fit in with your plans, they may be able to direct you to packagers offering tours designed around Israel's varied cuisines.

7 Health & Insurance

HEALTH

You do not need to take any special precautions for traveling to Israel. Vaccinations are not necessary unless you have spent the preceding 14 days in a country where there is an epidemic of a disease such as cholera or smallpox. Take along an adequate supply of any prescription drugs you need as well as a prescription that uses the generic name of the drug you are using.

INSURANCE

There are three kinds of travel insurance: trip cancellation, medical, and lost luggage coverage. **Trip cancellation insurance** is a good idea if you have paid a large portion of your vacation expenses up front. The other two types of insurance, however, don't make sense for most travelers. Rule number one: Check your existing policies before you buy any additional coverage.

Your **existing health insurance** should cover you if you get sick while on vacation (though if you belong to an HMO, you should check to see whether you are fully covered when away from home). If you need hospital treatment, most health insurance plans and HMOs will cover out-of-country hospital visits and procedures, at least to some extent. However, most make you pay the bills up front at the time of care, and you'll get a refund after you've returned and filed all the paperwork. Members of **Blue Cross/Blue Shield** can now use their cards at select hospitals in most major cities worldwide (☎ **800/810-BLUE;** www.bluecares.com/blue/bluecard/wwn for a list of hospitals). For independent travel health-insurance providers, see below. Your **homeowner's insurance** should cover stolen luggage.

The differences between travel assistance and insurance are often blurred, but in general the former offers on-the-spot assistance and 24-hour hot lines (mostly oriented toward medical problems), while the latter reimburses you for travel problems (medical, travel, or otherwise) after you have filed the paperwork. The coverage you should consider will depend on how much protection is already contained in your existing health insurance or other policies. Some credit- and charge-card companies may insure you against travel accidents if you buy plane, train, or bus tickets with their cards. Before purchasing additional insurance, read over your policies and agreements carefully. Call your insurers or credit/charge-card companies if you have any questions.

Some **credit cards** (American Express and certain gold and platinum Visa and MasterCards, for example) offer automatic flight insurance against death or dismemberment in case of an airplane crash.

If you do require additional insurance, try one of the companies listed below. But don't pay for more than you need. Among the reputable issuers of travel insurance are: **Access America,** 6600 W. Broad St., Richmond, VA 23230 (☎ 800/284-8300); **Travel Guard International,** 1145 Clark St., Stevens Point, WI 54481 (☎ 800/826-1300); **Travel Insured International,** Inc., P.O. Box 280568, East Hartford, CT 06128 (☎ 800/243-3174); and **Columbus Travel Insurance,** 279 High St., Croydon CR0 1QH (☎ 020/7375-0011 in London; www.columbusdirect.co.uk).

Companies specializing in accident and medical care include: **MEDEX International,** P.O. Box 5375, Timonium, MD 21094-5375 (☎ 888/MEDEX-00 or 410/453-6300; fax 410/453-6301; www.medexassist.com); **Travel Assistance International** (Worldwide Assistance Services, Inc.), 1133 15th St. NW, Suite 400, Washington, DC 20005 (☎ 800/821-2828 or 202/828-5894; fax 202/828-5896); and for scuba divers, **The Divers Alert Network** (DAN) (☎ 800/446-2671 or 919/684-2948).

8 Tips for Travelers with Special Needs

FOR PEOPLE WITH DISABILITIES

A disability shouldn't stop anyone from traveling. There are more resources out there than ever before. **Yad Sarah Institute,** Yad Sarah House, Jerusalem 91609 (☎ 02/644-4444; fax 02/625-9294; www.yadsarah.org.il; e-mail: info@yadsarah.org.il), Israel's largest voluntary organization, lends without charge canes, crutches, walkers, wheelchairs, high-tech medical rehab equipment, oxygen, and other medical equipment (security deposit required). Yad Sarah offers advice on transportation and other special problems; contact the Public Relations Director, Overseas Department, in advance to book airport pick up and help with special needs. There are more than 70 Yad Sarah branches throughout the country; most services are free.

A handy and detailed guide entitled *Access in Israel: A Guide for the Disabled and Those with Problems Getting Around,* is published by Pauline Hephaistos Survey Projects, 39 Bradley Gardens, West Ealing, London W13 18HE, England. This charitable organization does not charge a set price, and in fact will send you a copy for free. But each copy actually costs them about £4, and they ask that you make a contribution in a similar amount, if you can, to cover costs. The 122-page guide includes useful maps of easily traversed routes, including Jerusalem's Old City, and a handy guide to hotels, kibbutz inns, youth hostels, and their conditions of access. It even covers access and transportation situations at the major airports such as New York's JFK, Chicago's O'Hare, London's Heathrow, and Lod's Ben-Gurion. This guide can often be obtained in the United States through the **Travel Information Service** (☎ 215/456-9603), Moss Rehabilitation Hospital, 1200 W. Tabor Rd., Philadelphia, PA 19141. The cost is $7 plus postage. Telephone for assistance before ordering this guide. The **Moss Rehab Hospital** (☎ 215/456-9600) has been providing friendly and helpful phone advice and referrals to disabled travelers for years through its Travel Information Service (www.mossresourcenet.org).

FOR LONG-TERM VISITORS

The **Association of Americans and Canadians in Israel (AACI)** is mainly North American immigrants to Israel, but you can join the AACI or participate in many of its social activities, lectures, theater performances, and tours even if you're only planning to be in the country for a month or two. The AACI sponsors get-togethers on American holidays, English tutoring for new Ethiopian immigrants, singles events, counseling on retirement in Israel, legal advice, and generally promotes the well-being of the country's English speaking community. AACI offices in Jerusalem, 6 Mane St. (☎ **02/561-7151;** fax 02-566-1186), and in Netanya, 28 Shmuel Ha-Naziv St. (☎ **09/833-0950**), are especially active, but there are branches throughout the country, including Haifa, Tel Aviv, and in the Negev. Check the *In Jerusalem* and the *Tel Aviv City Lights* supplements to the Friday *Jerusalem Post* for their list of activities. The AACI Web site is www.aaci.org.il.

FOR SENIORS

The **Association of Americans and Canadians in Israel (AACI)** sponsors many social activities, tours for seniors, and has support groups (see above).

If you want something more than the average vacation or guided tour, try **Elderhostel,** 75 Federal St., Boston, MA 02110-1941 (☎ **877/426-8056;** www. elderhostel.org), or the University of New Hampshire's **Interhostel** (☎ **800/733-9753**), both variations on the same theme: educational travel for senior citizens. On these escorted tours, the days are packed with seminars, lectures, and field trips, and the sightseeing is all led by academic experts. In Israel, Elderhostel programs include tours and other group activities. Most courses last about 3 weeks and many include airfare, accommodations in student dormitories or modest inns, meals, and tuition. Write or call for a free catalog, which lists upcoming courses and destinations.

Don't be shy about asking for discounts, but always carry some kind of identification, such as a driver's license, that shows your date of birth. Also, mention the fact that you're a senior citizen when you first make your travel reservations. For example, many hotels offer seniors discounts. In most cities, people over the age of 60 qualify for reduced admission to theaters, museums, and other attractions, and discounted fares on public transportation.

FOR SINGLE TRAVELERS

Budget hotels and hostels, such as the Jerusalem Inn Hotel and Jerusalem Inn Guest House in Jerusalem (see chapter 3) or Tel Aviv's Gordon Inn (see chapter 6), offer a welcoming atmosphere of camaraderie.

The **Society for Protection of Nature in Israel (SPNI)** in Jerusalem, 13 Helena Ha-Malka St. (☎ **02/624-4605;** fax 02/625-4953); in Tel Aviv, 19 Ha-Sharon St. (☎ **03/638-8674;** fax 03/638-3940); and in Haifa, 8 Menachem St. (☎ **04/ 866-4135**), offers intelligent and unusual tours, ranging from walks, treks, hikes, and field trips of a few hours to package tours throughout Israel and into Jordan and Egypt. You can obtain a current brochure of SPNI offerings and make reservations from North America by contacting the **American Friends of SPNI,** 1842 Coney Island Ave., Brooklyn, NY 11230 (☎ **800/323-0035** or 718/645-3370; fax 718/645-3440; www.spini.org.il). You can also book SPNI tours through tour operators/wholesalers that specialize in travel to Israel, such as **Excursions Unlimited Tours,** 545 Madison Ave., New York, NY 10022 (☎ **800/726-8687** or 212/ 755-9150). In the United Kingdom, you can make arrangements for SPINI tours at 180 Oxford St., London W1NOEL (☎ **020/7957-4300;** www.spini.org.il).

Several tour organizers cater to solo travelers as well. **Experience Plus** (☎ 800/685-4565; fax 907/484-8489) offers an interesting selection of single-only trips.

Travel Buddies (☎ 800/998-9099 or 604/533-2483) runs single-friendly tours with no singles supplement. **The Single Gourmet Club,** 133 E. 58th St., New York, NY 10022 (☎ 212/980-8788; fax 212/980-3138), is an international social, dining, and travel club for singles, with offices in 21 cities in the United States and Canada, and one in London.

FOR FAMILIES

Israel is a young country with a young population. After a week in the country, you get used to the surprising number of babies, baby carriages, and playgrounds.

The better hotels, and even most of the smaller ones, will know who to call for baby-sitting services, so the front desk is your first resort. Car seats are available from rental firms, but you must reserve one as early as possible. Disposable diapers, called *tafnukim,* are sold at some drugstores, but they are relatively expensive. Baby food is not available in the variety that exists in the United States. Look into **Jerusalem Adventures** (☎ and fax **02/536-3449;** www.tourisrael.co.il), a company specializing in tours and activities for kids and for families with kids.

FOR WOMEN TRAVELERS

For women travelers, Israel is not too different from Europe or the United States. It is important to remember to dress modestly when visiting holy places of Judaism, Islam, and Christianity. East Jerusalem, the Old City of Jerusalem, the West Bank, Jordan, and Egypt are largely Arabic societies, and unless women travelers are guarded in their dress and behavior, there will be insults and unwanted advances. It is important to remember that most women in these countries do not venture far from their houses unless they are in the company of a husband, relatives, or at least one other woman. Women travelers may seem to be breaking the rules of propriety simply by being alone. It is always best to try to have at least one traveling companion nearby. Modest dress and behavior also helps to avoid unwanted attention. In Middle Eastern society, a woman alone, seen drinking in public, walking on the streets with a bare midriff or shorts, is not respectable, and will often not receive even common courtesy.

FOR GAY & LESBIAN TRAVELERS

In Israel, laws prohibiting homosexual relationships between consenting adults were canceled in 1988. Since then, a number of judicial decisions and governmental orders have begun to reinforce more understanding attitudes in Israeli society. Israel remains a socially traditional, family values oriented society with a large religious sector. There is a small but increasingly open gay community in Tel Aviv; less so in Haifa and Eilat. In Jerusalem, the gay community is more discreet and less accessible to outsiders. **The Society for Protection of Personal Rights** (☎ 03/629-3681; e-mail: sspr@netvision.net.il) operates the White Line (☎ 03/629-2797), a gay and lesbian hot line on Tuesdays, Thursdays, and Sundays from 7:30 to 11:30pm. In Arabic societies such as Jordan, Egypt/Sinai, and the Palestine Authority, homosexual activity is against the law, and largely hidden.

There are also two good, biannual English-language gay guidebooks, both focused on gay men but including information for lesbians as well. You can get the *Spartacus International Gay Guide* or *Odysseus* from most gay and lesbian bookstores, or order them from A Different Light Bookstore (☎ 800/343-4002 or 212/989-4850). Both lesbians and gays might want to pick up a copy of *Gay Travel A to Z* ($16). The *Ferrari Guides* (www.q-net.com) is yet another very good series of gay and lesbian guidebooks.

FOR STUDENTS

The discounts offered to students traveling in Israel are among the best in the world. Students are treated royally, via an elaborate program of reductions that lower the tab in youth hostels and hotels, on buses and trains, even in swimming pools, restaurants, and places of entertainment.

Your passport to all these savings is an international student ID card, available through a number of organizations. The best resource for students is the **Council on International Educational Exchange,** or CIEE (www.ciee.org). They can set you up with an ID card (see below), and their travel branch, Council Travel Service (☎ **800/226-8624;** www.counciltravel.com), is the biggest student travel agency operation in the world. It can get you discounts on plane tickets, rail passes, and the like. Ask them for a list of CTS offices in major cities so you can keep the discounts flowing (and aid lines open) as you travel.

From CIEE you can obtain the student traveler's best friend, the $18 **International Student Identity Card** (ISIC). It's the only officially acceptable form of student identification, good for cut rates on rail passes, plane tickets, and other discounts. It also provides you with basic health and life insurance and a 24-hour help line. If you're no longer a student but are still under 26 you can get a GO 25 card from the same people, which will get you the insurance and some of the discounts (but not student admission prices in museums).

In Canada, Travel CUTS, 200 Ronson St., Ste. 320, Toronto, ONT M9W 5Z9 (☎ **800/667-2887** or 416/614-2887; www.travelcuts.com), offers similar services. **Campus Travel,** 52 Grosvenor Gardens, London SW1W 0AG (☎ **020/7730-3402;** www.campustravel.co.uk), opposite Victoria Station, is Britain's leading specialist in student and youth travel.

International Youth Hostel Cards are available in the United States from **American Youth Hostels,** 733 15th St. NW, Room 840, Washington, DC 20005 (☎ **202/ 783-6161;** fax 202/783-6171); in the United Kingdom, from the **Youth Hostel Association,** Trevelyan House, 8 St. Stephen's Hill, St. Albans, Hertfordshire AL1 2DY, England (☎ **01727/855-215**).

If you arrive in Israel equipped with student and hostel cards, then you can go directly to the central train and bus stations in any of the three major cities to receive discounts on their routes throughout the country. Your student card gives you discounts on Mano Seaways ferries between Israel and Greece, as well as discounts on Neot Ha Kikar tours, and entrance fees to museums, parks, and nature reserves. Always keep your school identification card or a letter from your school handy as an extra verification of your student status.

ISRAEL STUDENTS TRAVEL ASSOCIATION (ISSTA)   When you arrive in Israel, make your first stop ISSTA, which does an excellent job of looking after visiting young people. ISSTA offices in Israel are at 128 Ben-Yehuda St., Tel Aviv (☎ **03/ 521-0555**); 31 Ha-Nevi'im St., Jerusalem (☎ **02/625-2799**); and 2 Balfour St., Haifa (☎ **04/866-9139**). Hours are usually 9am to 1pm and 3 to 6pm; offices close on Wednesday and Friday at 1pm, and all day Saturday. With proof of student status, you can buy an International Student Identification Card from ISSTA for NIS 33 ($9.20).

ISSTA's staff is composed of young people, specialists in the field of student and youth travel. Here the student is treated as a first-class client and is offered a wide variety of special services, planned and developed by people who fully understand the student's needs and problems.

ISSTA operates tours within Israel ranging from 4 to 7 days; they're open to individual as well as group bookings. The tour price includes bed-and-breakfast accommodations, entrance fees, a tour bus, and a government-licensed guide.

Members of students' families—husband or wife and children—are now allowed to fly to and from Israel on student charter flights, at the same rates and subject to the same conditions as the student in the family. Remember that penalties for canceling out of a charter can be severe, baggage allowances can be far less than on normal flights, and charter carriers to Israel can be draconian about charges for overweight baggage.

9 Organized Tours & Package Tours

TOURS & PACKAGES

Most major airlines serving Israel offer a variety of package arrangements that include discounts on accommodations throughout the country, as well as organized and escorted tours and itineraries. El Al and Tower Air, specializing in travel to Israel, have the widest variety of choices in all price ranges. El Al, for example, offers tours such as "The Holyland Experience," with emphasis on Christian sites in Israel. For more information on these tours and packages, call **El Al** at ☎ **800/EL-AL-SUN** in the United States. **TWA Getaway Vacations** (☎ **800/438-2929**) offers a wide range of well-designed all-inclusive tour packages for Israel, and also for Jordan and Egypt. You don't have to be a TWA passenger to buy these packages. TWA Getaway Vacations hotel choices and guided programs are excellent, and you can buy additional nights at hotels in the packages at considerable discounts, in case you want to stay on a few extra days. Airlines and private travel agencies in Israel also offer escorted tours of Jordan and Egypt that originate from Israel.

You'll find a wide choice of escorted day trips (usually by bus) inside Israel offered by the **United** and **Egged** agencies. Virtually any hotel desk can book you into United and Egged tours on a day or so notice—no commission. These tours originate from every major city. The Society for Protection of Nature in Israel (see "Hiking & Nature Walks," above) arranges tours and packages with an emphasis on nature and outdoor activities.

TRAVEL FROM ISRAEL TO CAIRO & SINAI

You can often travel from Israel to destinations that are expensive or complicated to reach by direct flight from the United States or Canada.

BY PLANE   If you plan to go by air to Cairo or the Sinai, a tour package can offer lower rates to counter the high cost of flying. El Al has four flights a week between Cairo and Tel Aviv, and similar service is operated by the Egyptian airline, Air Sinai. Cost is $145 one way, $290 round-trip, and the flight takes about 45 minutes. Excursion fare on El Al is only $170 round-trip if you buy your ticket as an add-on when you purchase an El Al round-trip flight from the United States to Israel. Many travel agents (especially in Israel) can come up with air/hotel packages or all inclusive tour packages from Israel to Cairo and elsewhere in Egypt for amazingly low prices.

BY BUS   You can easily get from Tel Aviv to Cairo and back by signing up for one of the daily (except Saturday) bus tours that can be booked by most travel agencies. Buses leave from Jerusalem, pick up more passengers in Tel Aviv (if not already full), and then head for Cairo. The trip takes 10 to 12 hours, depending on border procedures and delays. Sign up for the one-way bus ($17 to $25), the round-trip bus ($30 to $40), or a tour that gives you hotel, or hotel and sightseeing, or the works: a full-blown guided tour of all the Nile's treasures. Students get good discounts.

BY CAR   You cannot drive an Israeli rental car into Egypt, and that includes the Sinai. If you make the trip in your own vehicle you must obtain a permit to take a vehicle into Egypt from the **Consular Section, Ministry for Foreign Affairs,** Hakirya, Romema, 91950 Jerusalem (☎ **02/530-3111**).

PRIVATE GUIDES

Israel is an easy country for English speakers to explore on their own, but if you are considering hiring a private guide for part of your visit, it will be necessary to plan well in advance. The county has a system of licensing guides who have completed an extensive program of preparatory training. Private guides arrange all the logistics of travel during the times they are under hire, and can take you to major sites as well as out-of-the-way places efficiently. For those with little time, this can be a restful way to get a great deal done in depth. The government licensing program has helped to raise the general quality of guides in Israel, but you still may find yourself engaging a guide whose personality or politics don't exactly mesh well with yours. Or, despite English-language requirements, you may encounter a guide who is not especially articulate. Beware of guides who are on their cellular phones taking other bookings and making arrangements as they drive you through pristine deserts in their Land Rovers, which can destroy the atmosphere of a tour. Check ahead of time about a guide's policy on turning off his cell phone. It is a good idea to ask friends who have visited Israel for personal recommendations, and to discuss plans with a prospective private guide by phone, in order to get a feel for his or her approach before making a commitment. Most good professional guides have put together a brochure or video that will give you an indication of their styles and approaches.

Approximate rates for a private guide are $200 per day for a Jerusalem tour by foot and taxi; $300 to $400 a day for a licensed and insured guide with a vehicle within Israel. There can be extra charges for over 9 hours per day and for off-road trips and use of off-road vehicles. If your guide accompanies you overnight, the fee should include the cost of his or her hotel room (in many places, a licensed guide will receive a discount—your guide will know where he can be put up at a discount rate). If you engage an Israeli guide to arrange excursions into Jordan and to accompany you on these trips, the rate could be $660 to $700 per day, including a vehicle and hotel accommodations.

Following are some guides with unusual background qualifications and specialties in nature, archaeological, and active tours. If they are not able to meet your time specifications or interests, they may be able to refer you to other guides who will better match your needs.

American-born **David Perlmutter,** POB 8015 Jerusalem 91080 Israel (☎ mobile phone **054/201-353** or 02/991-8626; fax 02/991-2229; www.israeladventure.com; e-mail: davidper@netvision.net.il), was a guide for the Society for Protection of Nature in Israel and helped design that organization's hikes and tours. He specializes in off-road tours in Israel and Jordan in a comfortable four-wheel-drive vehicle as well as photography, culinary, and cultural tours.

Judy Stacey Goldman, Gan Rehavia Aleph apt. 6, 92461 Jerusalem (☎ **02/ 624-5827;** fax 02-623-3834; e-mail: judebob@netvision.net.il), is the coauthor of *The Underground Guide to Jerusalem* and *The Underground Guide to Tel Aviv,* two lively insider books on the country's two major metropolitan areas as well as a book about Israeli food. Ms. Goldman was born in Canada.

Izat Abu Rabia, Kibbutz Shefayim, Israel (☎ mobile phone **52/262-465;** fax 09/959-5555), is another licensed guide who has worked with the Society for Protection of Nature in Israel. Mr. Abu Rabia is an Israeli Bedouin who speaks English,

Hebrew, and Arabic and is recommended for his energy, knowledge of the country-side (especially the desert), and local cultural and music traditions.

Rabbi Jeffrey Bearman, POB 11022, Jerusalem 91110 (☎ and fax **02/676-5197;** e-mail: rabbjeff@netvision.net.il), is a Reform rabbi (somewhat unusual in Israel) and a licensed guide. **Ido Katz,** 24 Yakinton St., Oranit 44813 (☎ **03/938-2540;** fax 03/902-1541; e-mail: katzzi@ashur.cc.biu.ac.il), an archaeologist, is observant Ortho-dox Jewish. **David Silvera** (☎ and fax **03/516-5265;** www.globus.com; e-mail: dragoman@internet-zahav.net) speaks Italian, English, and French.

Laura Nelson-Levy (☎ **02/543-4602)** is a young former American and a thoughtful specialist in family tours. **Miriam Feinberg Vamoosh** (☎ **02/534-5071)** is an especially articulate guide, who writes about Israel. She has published a book about the spiritual aspects of Israel's landscape. **Ada Ben-Gera,** Moshav Ben Zion 60910 Israel (☎ **09/748-5022),** also with an SPNI background, specializes in Jeep tours of Israel, Sinai, and Jordan.

10 Getting There

BY PLANE

The airline you choose can have a major effect on what your trip to Israel will be like. Some airlines offer a wide variety of gateway cities with direct flights that can make the very long flight to Ben-Gurion considerably easier. You'll find that some flights have New York transfers or European layovers (sometimes an hour or two, sometimes for a full day or overnight); a day in London or an evening in Prague or Bucharest might be a welcome addition for some, but for others it might be just one more tir-ing obstacle. Some European airline flights with long stopovers even include a free overnight hotel, which travelers with unlimited time may find attractive.

Check the time of your flight departure from Israel. Many flights to North America leave at 6 or 7am, which means you must be at the airport by 3 or 4am. For some, this is ideal—you have maximum use of your last day in Israel, and can skip having a hotel room for the final night. For others who prefer to get a good night's sleep, an early afternoon flight that gets you back to North America just in time for bed the same day can make your adjustment to your normal schedule much easier.

Check into youth fares, senior discounts, and family plans. Some airlines offer them; others only at limited times or not at all. If you're eligible, the savings can be substantial. Remember, you must shop around. The rules constantly change, and your travel agent may not take the time to dig up the best buy for you.

Finally, for religious reasons, some airlines cannot fly to or from Israel from Friday afternoon through Saturday night. If time is short, and you need to begin your trip right after work on Friday, this can be an overriding consideration. On the other hand, a flight that leaves Friday at 8pm but has poor connections may not get you to Tel Aviv that much earlier.

El Al (☎ **800/223-6700** or 212/768-9200 in the U.S.; 800/EL-AL-SUN for information about packages; 0345/125725 in the U.K.; 800/361-6174 in Canada), Israel's national carrier, has the largest schedule of nonstop and direct flights between Israel and New York, Chicago, Miami, Baltimore/Washington, D.C., and Los Ange-les. There is also nonstop service from Newark to Tel Aviv.

El Al also provides many special services to help make the trip to Israel as conve-nient and secure as possible. There are also special night-before check-in services for El Al passengers in Boro Park (Brooklyn), as well as from Jerusalem, Haifa, and Tel Aviv. If you'd like to take in the Pyramids on your trip to the Middle East, El Al pas-sengers from North America may purchase an add-on ticket from Tel Aviv to Cairo for $170, a considerable saving over the regular fare.

As the airline of a country in which tourism is a major part of the economy, El Al has developed the best-priced land-package arrangements in the business. See "Package Tours," above, for information about El Al's excellent "Sunsational" packages. An additional consideration, especially for flights outside the United States, is the fact that El Al's security is extremely thorough. El Al does not fly on the Jewish Sabbath, which means there are no flights in the air from Friday afternoon until Saturday night.

Tower Air (☎ 800/34-TOWER) is a small airline that for the past decade has specialized in the New York–Israel route. It offers daily nonstop service (except Friday) between JFK Airport in New York and Tel Aviv. More U.S. passengers fly to Israel on Tower Air than on any other American airline, making Tower the number-one U.S. carrier to Israel. Tower offers a number of useful bargains. I especially like the premier economy class ticket, which gives you a guaranteed empty seat beside you, so that you can stretch out on the long flight; many times the premier economy section is empty enough that you can recline across three adjacent seats. This ticket also includes an excellent upgraded meal and personal service. You are not required to purchase the upgrade on a round-trip basis: You pay only for the part of your trip you choose to upgrade. Tower Air offers long-term tickets, good for 6 months, as well as youth fares (valid for 1 year) and special promotional fares that are excellent bargains. Like El Al, Tower does not have flights to or from Israel on the Jewish Sabbath.

TWA (☎ 800/892-4141) does fly to Israel on the Sabbath. It offers nonstop flights, but with its large network of routes, you can also arrange for stopovers. It also offers the opportunity for frequent-flyer bonuses good for travel in the United States. **Continental Airlines** began direct service between Newark, New Jersey, and Tel Aviv in 1999. Its prices are competitive, and it plans to offer better in-flight service than other carriers flying nonstop between North America and Israel.

Alitalia is the European airline that carries the largest number of passengers between North America and Israel. For the years **2000–2001,** with many travelers planning to visit both Rome and Israel, Alitalia will be planning extra flights and land packages that will be worth looking into. In terms of food, and in-flight service and comforts, Alitalia and other European carriers like Swissair and Lufthansa tend to outshine El Al, Tower, and TWA. No European carrier, however, offers nonstop flights between North America and Israel.

British Airways has often led the field in promotional fares from Britain to Israel. The national carriers of Belgium, Romania, the Czech Republic, Poland, and Hungary sometimes offer fares to Israel at slightly bargain rates. These, and other European airlines, can provide unique stopover possibilities and packages. Note that refunds from some European airlines can be unusually difficult to obtain.

Royal Jordanian Airlines (☎ 800/RJ-TOURS-8) currently has a reciprocal arrangement with El Al, Tower Air, and TWA: Passengers from North America can take those airlines to Ben-Gurion Airport in Israel, tour Israel, travel overland to Jordan, and return home from Amman on Royal Jordanian; or they can do the Jordanian leg of the trip first, and return home via Israel. Royal Jordanian Airlines flies from Chicago via Shannon Airport to Amman; and from New York via Amsterdam to Amman. Numerous European stopovers can be arranged. Royal Jordanian Airlines also flies between Amman and Ben-Gurion, which lets you avoid the time-consuming hassle of the Allenby Bridge Border crossing. A 3- to 30-day round-trip Amman-Ben Gurion fare is $135. Royal Jordanian offers excellent land package arrangements for those traveling to Jordan.

AIRFARES   Airfares are in a constant state of flux. The following El Al fares, therefore, are guidelines that were correct at press time.

The year is divided into low season, high season, and shoulder season, and each type of ticket has different fare periods. Thus, you may find that if you buy a 6- to 90-day excursion ticket, you might only be able to fly at the low winter rate up to April 3; but if you buy a 6- to 60-day APEX supersaver fare (for several hundred dollars less), you can fly at the winter rate only until March 23. You'll have to check with your travel agent for exact dates. Do it early.

Super APEX 6- to 30-Day Fare, New York–Tel Aviv   Special fares on selected flights are priced from approximately $900 in low season to $1,300 in high season. You must stay at least 6 days and complete your travel within 30 days, and your ticket must be bought at least 14 days in advance. Super APEX Fares for London–Tel Aviv–London run from £339 in low season to approximately £409 in high season. Super APEX Fares are also available on routes between Montreal or Toronto and Israel.

APEX 6- to 60-Day Fare, New York–Tel Aviv   Somewhat higher than the Super APEX Fare, ranging in price from about $1,066 in low season to $1,460 in high season, this ticket offers greater flexibility. You can travel for a longer period of time and you are allowed one free stopover en route either to or from Tel Aviv from any gateway city in the United States. If you must cancel within 14 days of your flight, there is a fee, but the ticket is refundable. The London–Tel Aviv APEX Fare ranges from £379 in low season to £449 in high season.

Special Short-Term Promotional Fares   El Al's **Instant Fares** are extraordinary bargains, usually offered without advance notice and for only limited periods of time. You must pay for these tickets within 72 hours of booking, and you must be sure to check on cancellation penalties, but bargains abound. For example, in the summer peak season, El Al recently offered a round-trip London–Tel Aviv fare on its Tuesday night flight of £290 and round-trip fare on other days of the week for £400. El Al and Tower Air, both closely tied to the Israeli tourism industry, often do promotions when the country seems short on tourists. It is always a good idea to call the airlines directly in order to learn exactly what promotional fares may be available, then check with a good travel agent or an agent that specializes in travel to Israel. Promotional fares are sometimes unadvertised and only available through agents.

Fares Between Tel Aviv & Cairo   With many travelers adding excursions to Egypt onto their Israeli vacations, this short 1¹/₂-hour flight route has become increasingly important. Normal coach fare from Tel Aviv to Cairo is $145 each way; $290 round-trip. El Al offers a special round-trip rate of $170 if purchased in conjunction with a round-trip El Al ticket from the United States to Israel. If you plan to stay in Israel for some amount of time, you may be able to find local Israeli travel discounters offering slightly lower fares on local Egyptian and Israeli airlines.

CHARTER FLIGHTS   Chartering a whole plane or a section of one and filling it with budget-minded travelers is still one of the best ways to save money on a flight.

The disadvantages are these: The flight may be canceled due to insufficient demand; it may be delayed on departure, sometimes for several hours; you are committed to fly on specific flights, and it may be impossible to switch to other flights. If you miss the flight, you may lose your money.

BUCKET SHOPS   Travelers from London to Israel can easily locate bargains on one-way and round-trip flights (usually charters) to Israel, advertised in bucket shops throughout the city. Note that on many of these charters, baggage-weight restrictions are mercilessly enforced (handbags and hand luggage are often weighed in with the allowance, and there are steep penalties for excess weight). The bucket shop scene from

New York is less freewheeling, and occurs mostly in the form of discounters buying up blocks of seats on scheduled flights. You can often find round-trip tickets from New York to Tel Aviv for around $650, but there are always restrictions and disadvantages to these fares. Check out both the special regulations and the carrier being used.

Because of security considerations, traveling to Israel as a courier for an overnight air freight firm (an option many budget-conscious travelers like to explore) is unusually difficult.

ARRIVING & DEPARTING

Ben-Gurion International Airport, at Lod on the outskirts of Tel Aviv, serves the whole country. Other, smaller airports exist in Jerusalem, Tel Aviv, Haifa, Rosh Pinna, and Eilat, but most points within Israel are so easily accessible by bus and *sherut* (shared limo or van) that few people spend the relatively large amount to fly.

After landing and passing through immigration and security, you'll be in the Arrivals Hall waiting for your baggage. There are lots of people on hand to help you here, including a fully staffed tourist office, a hotel reservations desk, car-rental desks, and a desk for the helpful Voluntary Tourist Service representatives. From the Arrivals Hall you pass through Customs, then you're outside, in Israel.

AIRPORT TRANSPORTATION   By Bus   Egged operates buses more or less every half hour from the airport to Jerusalem at a price of NIS 20 ($4.40). This is not the optimum way to get to Jerusalem if you have heavy baggage, especially since the price of a sherut, or shared taxi that will take you right to your destination in Jerusalem is just under $10. The bus trip takes about 45 minutes. Schedules are posted by the bus ticket window that is in the low building amid the bus stops. Going by bus, you can be at your hotel in Jerusalem within 2 hours after your plane has landed.

To get to Tel Aviv from the airport, take the **United Tours Airport Shuttle Service** bus no. 222 that departs at least once every hour, usually more frequently, between 4am and midnight (on Saturday, noon to midnight). It leaves the airport, stops at the El Al Air Terminal at the Central Railway Station, then stops near the Bnei Dan Youth Hostel, and then travels all along the waterfront boulevard, Ha-Yarkon Street, stopping at each cluster of hotels. The trip from the airport to your hotel should take a half hour; the fare is NIS 20 ($4.40). There are also buses to Haifa and several other points directly from the airport. Check the schedules next to the bus ticket window.

By Sherut   A sherut is a shared van. The sherut service is to the right as soon as you exit from the terminal. Sherut service from the airport to Jerusalem is highly regulated, with a fixed fare (a drop under $10) for the trip from Ben-Gurion to almost any address point within Jerusalem. The price posted on the sign by the parked sheruts may be out of date—shekel prices rise frequently although the dollar equivalent stays the same. Notice what the other passengers are paying, and then pay exactly the same, not a penny more, for the trip right to your hotel door. There is no charge for normal baggage.

EL AL CHECK-IN SERVICE   Passengers on El Al flights who are leaving from Jerusalem, Tel Aviv, Haifa, or Eilat can use El Al's in-city precheck-in service, for which there is a service charge of around NIS 15 ($3) per person. You must check with El Al for updated information about all El Al precheck in cities throughout Israel.

Some details you should know about early check-in: You can check in only the night before your flight is scheduled to depart; early check-in is not applicable to all flights (you can't check in early for some night flights, for example); you must have your ticket, passport, and payment receipt for the airport departure tax when you check in, just as though you were at the airport. Your bags will be inspected right there in the El Al office, and then sent directly to the aircraft. The next day, you need to arrive at the airport only in time for passport control, security check, and boarding, for which you must figure 1¼ hours. Without early check-in, you're required to be at the airport 2¼ hours before flight time. This is no idle deadline, by the way. You could miss your flight if you ignore this time limit.

BY SHIP

FROM ITALY, GREECE & CYPRUS   Several car ferries make the journey to Haifa from Venice, Piraeus (Athens), Heraklion (Crete), Rhodes, and Limassol (Cyprus). Ships include the **Stability Line**'s *Vergina* and the **Sol Maritime Services'** *Sol Phryne,* which are either Greek- or Cypriot-flag vessels.

The usual route is Piraeus, Rhodes, Limassol, Haifa, with each port being reached on a different day. Standard itinerary calls for departure from Piraeus (Athens) on Thursday, arriving in Haifa on Sunday. The route and departure days are the same for the ships when they leave Haifa; that is, departures are on Sunday. These schedules can change according to the seasons, so use them as a general indication only; get the latest details in Piraeus or Haifa.

While several of these ships have good accommodations and service, others are not so hot. Conditions can change from season to season, so check out the ship in advance, if possible. It's also a good idea to pack some food along, even if you intend to buy your meals on board. Sometimes the dining rooms run out of food before everyone has dined. Don't depend on buying food in the ports of call either, as arrival and departure might be in the middle of the night.

Prices are higher from June to September. Prices may range from $90 for a deck chair to $260 for a berth in a cabin with shower and toilet, including three meals. Cars and motorcycles are charged a separate fee. For bookings and exact prices, go to any major travel agent in Athens, Crete, Limassol, Rhodes, or in Israel. There are connections to Turkey via Rhodes.

11 Getting Around

BY PLANE

If you can afford it, and if traveling overland on hot days just isn't your cup of tea, then by all means use **Arkia,** Israel's inland air service. There are no flights on the Sabbath, but otherwise daily flights connect Tel Aviv with Eilat and Rosh Pina (Safed/Tiberias), Jerusalem with Eilat and Rosh Pina, and Haifa with Eilat. Other flights are scheduled according to demand, as the seasons change. A round-trip flight from Tel Aviv to Eilat, for example, costs $160. You can book flights on Arkia through your home travel agent. Arkia's central toll-free number in Israel is ☎ **1-800/ 444-888.**

Arkia also sponsors very popular air tours, including journeys from Tel Aviv and Jerusalem to Eilat. Or you can design your own tour, gather a group of people, and charter an Arkia aircraft, from nine-seaters to Boeing 737s.

You can book tickets and check flight schedules at any travel agency; information is also available at GTIO throughout the world.

BY TRAIN

Trains are even cheaper than buses, but Israel Railways trains don't run nearly as often, and at press time, only cities along the coast are served—Tel Aviv, Haifa, and Nahariya (with local stops made along the way). Although some of the trains are ancient, they are usually roomy, and the routes run through some of central Israel's most beautiful areas. At press time, service to Jerusalem has been suspended, but check to see if it has been restored when you're in Israel. Unlike the Tel Aviv–Jerusalem highway route, the final portion of the train route runs through the beautiful Judean Hills, a winding, mountain-clinging ride through a magical and rugged landscape. The International Student Identity Card holder obtains a 25% to 50% train discount.

Excepting the Sabbath and religious holidays, trains run daily. Operations close earlier on Friday and before holidays. For train information, call ☎ **03/577-4000.** In Tel Aviv, the Central Train Station (sometimes called North Station) is on Arlosoroff Street near Haifa Road.

BY BUS

Most city and intercity bus routes are operated by two cooperative-shareholder companies, Dan and Egged. Their equipment varies widely. Depending on the whim of fortune, you'll take your intercity bus ride in either spanking-new buses with red upholstery and efficient air-conditioning or in a run-down, torn-upholstered, dirty-windowed, breathlessly hot bus.

Buses run from about 5:30am until late evening. In major cities, most routes operate until midnight. If possible, you should avoid bus travel at rush hours (7 to 8am and 4 to 6pm). On Friday and the eves of Jewish holidays, most buses run only until about 2 or 3 hours before sunset. Except for partial city bus service in East Jerusalem, the West Bank, and Haifa, there is no bus service throughout the country from Friday afternoon until Saturday evening.

Both Dan and Egged have discount fare plans for both city and intercity buses. For instance, in Jerusalem, Tel Aviv, or Haifa, ask for a 25-ride *kartisiya,* one of the multifare cards that are right at the driver's fingertips next to the single-fare tickets. The kartisiya gives you one or two free rides, and frees you from having to fumble for change. If you are a senior citizen or a student, show your identification. The driver will sell you a multifare card at a regular, senior, or student discount. The color of the card is different for each category. Each time you get on a bus, the driver will punch your card. At $1.20, city bus tickets are not all that expensive, but why pay even that when you can pay less? The kartisiya is not supposed to be transferable, but there is rarely a problem if two people together present it as a fare. Just say *pa-mai-yim* and the driver will punch the kartisiya twice.

As for intercity travel, Egged offers 14-, 21-, and 30-day passes good for unlimited travel throughout the country. Ask at any **Egged Tours** office for details. Egged offices are open Sunday through Thursday from 7am to 8pm, on Friday from 7am to 2pm and closed Saturday. Students can apply for discounts here.

BY SHERUT & TAXI

SHERUTS   The Israeli sherut ("service" in Hebrew) is a shared limo or van that goes from city to city or point to point within a city. They supplement city and intercity bus routes and often go where the bus doesn't go. On Saturday in many parts of the country, they are the only transportation available. Sheruts usually make regular stops close to the central bus stations of the cities they service, but by and large, they'll let you off at any bus stop in or out of the city along their routes. These days they're mostly eight-passenger vans. Sheruts won't depart for intercity runs until each eight-passenger vehicle is full (or almost so).

Sherut fares can be a shekel or so higher than the bus; in times of heavy competition, sheruts will match the fares on Egged. Service is often faster and more comfortable. Sheruts from Jerusalem to Tel Aviv leave from Rav Kook Street, just across Jaffa

Road from Zion Square. If you are staying in the center of town, this is much more convenient than taking a bus to Jerusalem's Central Bus Station and waiting on line for the bus to Tel Aviv. There is no charge for a child under 5 traveling on the lap of an adult. Sometimes two children under 5 pay one adult fare. For each additional child under 5, the full fare is required. Smoking is supposed to be forbidden inside sheruts.

Note: When looking for a sherut, always ask before climbing in to see that it truly is a sherut. Otherwise, a gloating driver may whisk you to your destination at taxi rates.

TAXIS   Each municipality sets taxi fares and issues a chart quoting current fares. But in all cases, it's good to agree on an amount before you get in the cab, as many cabbies ignore the meters. That avoids any unpleasantness at the end—and there is often unpleasantness. Having trouble finding a taxi on Shabbat? Go to a big hotel entrance.

BY CAR

CAR RENTALS   Car-rental agencies, both international and local, rent small cars at about $45 to $70 a day, depending on the season, the company, and the size of the car, and whether you've booked ahead from your own country for an advance payment special package. These rates are for such cars as Fiats and Autobianchis. Apply ahead of time for the discount cards that all international car-rental companies currently offer. At the very least, they may get you an automatic upgrade. Remember, if you plan to travel in the summer, or drive to the Negev and Eilat, you'll want a car with air-conditioning.

Avis (☎ **800/638-4016** or 201/750-2050) and **Sixt/Reliable** (☎ **877/4-SHALOM** or 212/541-5029) are two international car-rental companies represented in North America by packagers that specialize in car rentals in Israel. Avis (Dan Rent-A-Car) is staffed by Israeli agents who can advise you about your driving plans, and offers free maps. Both offices are worth checking out.

Driving is one of the best ways to see Israel, but it can be extraordinarily expensive if you don't realize what's involved. The very cheapest cars are often not available, even though their rental prices are widely publicized by agencies. Your best deal will be on a weekly, unlimited-kilometer basis. As the deductible on the agency-provided collision insurance is a staggering $750 to $1,000, you'll want to protect yourself against that much liability for damage to the car. So you must initial the little block that shows you want the collision damage waiver insurance, which will cost $10 to $12 per day. In Israel only a gold MasterCard will exempt you from other mandatory insurance charges. Thus, a balance sheet of what you'll actually end up paying for an economy car rental may look like this:

Basic weekly charge, unlimited kilometers	$290
Collision damage waiver, 7 days at $10 per day	$70
Gasoline, 100 liters at 90¢ per liter	$90
Total	$450

This works out to $66.70 per day for one of the cheapest cars available at the best rates offered by the big companies.

These figures are an average of going rates. You'll save significant sums by shopping around. Be sure to ask in advance what the collision damage waiver will cost, because, as you can see from the figures above, it ends up being a significant sum.

You should not be misled by firms offering extremely low daily rental rates, such as $6 or $8. The daily rental rate is only a small portion of the total rental bill, which also includes the collision damage waiver and the kilometer charge.

Your best bargain may be a package purchased with your flight. El Al's "Sunsational" car package, starting at $17 per day with unlimited mileage (available only for El Al passengers), is generally unbeatable. Reserving and prepaying from the United States through the Israel Tourism Center or a travel discounter can also cut costs.

Some smaller Israeli companies offer no rental charge on Shabbat, although you do have to pay Saturday insurance (if it is a religious company, you may be on your honor not to drive on Shabbat). Others offer free transportation from the airport to your hotel if you want to start the rental later in your trip. Companies offering such services are often more expensive, but you may find these extras worthwhile.

Eldan (☎ **800/938-5000** or 888/243-5326 in the U.S. and Canada, or 212/629-6090 in New York; www.eldan.co.il/), the largest Israeli rental car firm, is always worth looking into. Its fleet of cars is larger and more varied than those of the international agencies. Eldan also offers more offices and service centers throughout the country than any of its competitors, so if you have a breakdown, you have a better chance of getting a replacement quickly. In 2000, Eldan plans to have affiliations with a variety of Israeli hotels; packages and discounts at moderately priced hotels will be available in conjunction with Eldan rental cars. **Tamir** (☎ **800/868-2647**) is another Israeli car-rental agency with a North American reservations office. Tamir's services include delivery and pick-up in major Israeli cities, though not in Eilat.

It's a good idea to reserve a car as far in advance as possible. Except in holiday periods, a day in advance should be enough time to secure some kind of vehicle, but keep in mind that cars with automatic transmission are often in short supply. The earlier you reserve, the more certain you can be of getting the car you want, when you want it.

Almost every major car-rental company has a Jerusalem office on King David Street, between the Hilton and King David hotels; in Tel Aviv, the offices are on Ha-Yarkon Street, between the Dan and the Sheraton hotels. If you don't happen to pass the agency you want, your hotel or any travel agent will be glad to arrange the rental.

Special Considerations When Renting a Car in Israel   Be aware: Visitors are cautioned to deal only with reputable rental companies, only to sign contracts after reading them thoroughly in a language completely understood, and to make sure of proper and full insurance coverage. If you are asked to sign a part of your contract written in Hebrew, make certain it is explained to you and note in writing beside your signature that you do not read Hebrew. Car theft incidence in Israel is very high—you do not want to be held responsible for the cost of an entire car!

Note: No cars rented in Israel are insured for travel in the West Bank and Gaza, although most companies do permit travel on Route 1, the main east-west highway from Jerusalem to the Dead Sea, and Route 90, the main north-south road along the Dead Sea and the Jordan Valley from Jericho to Tiberias. Clarify these regulations each time you rent a car.

Be sure to go with the car-rental worker who makes note of dents and marks when you rent your car. Insist that every mark be noted on your contract, including marks on rubber bumpers—no matter how unimportant they may seem, you'll be charged for them when you return the car.

Age minimums for rentals vary from company to company, but usually you must be 21 years old to rent or drive a rental car in Israel. Seniors over 70 may have a difficult time finding an agency that will rent to them. Check American companies in the United States for their rental policies in Israel. You may pay more for insurance if you're under a certain age.

DRIVING RULES   Although Israel honors American, Canadian, and U.K. driver's licenses, if you plan to drive in other countries you might want to have an International Driver's License, which should be obtained in advance in your hometown.

The local automobile club, **MEMSI** (☎ **03/564-1121;** fax 03/566-0493), has its main office in Tel Aviv at 20 Rehov Ha-Rakevet, Tel Aviv 65117; office hours are 8:30am to 7pm, until 1pm on Friday; closed Saturday. The Jerusalem office of MEMSI is at 31 Ben Yehuda St. (☎ **02/625-9711;** fax 02/625-5994); office hours same as Tel Aviv. MEMSI offers AAA members the following services: information on touring, hotels, car hire, and so on; emergency assistance on the roads, patrolled by radio-controlled yellow vans with MEMSI's name and emblem; and good road maps (for sale) of Israel.

Provided a visitor's foreign car registration is valid and the driver is in possession of a valid driver's license, a car may be brought into Israel for a period of up to 1 year. No customs document or customs duty deposit is required.

This is a tough country for autos. Auxiliary roads are rarely wide and straight, and once you're off the main highways, you're faced with winding, narrow mountain roads, particularly in the Golan Heights and the Negev.

Be aware that among Israeli drivers, brashness on the road is the national sport. Drivers are often aggressive and impatient; tailgating is the norm, not the exception.

Other hazards? Rains bring up loose gravel and dirt and make for unstable, slippery conditions. Flash floods occur in the desert during the rainy season, often gutting low sections of the highway.

PARKING & TOLLS   There are no toll roads or bridges in Israel, so this is not an expense. The number of cars in Israel has quadrupled during the past few years, so Israel now has real, honest-to-goodness traffic jams, and a parking problem in the big cities. In Jerusalem, Tel Aviv, Tiberias, and other main cities, when you park on streets in downtown areas during daylight hours, you must display a parking card in the passenger window. This is a strip of paper with punched tabs for the hours of the day. You tear a tab to designate the month, day, and hour when you parked. Cards can be purchased at newsstands or from lottery ticket vendors. Meter parking is just being introduced in cities like Jerusalem and Tel Aviv. Parking on many residential streets in Jerusalem and Tel Aviv will soon be by residential sticker only.

GASOLINE   Gasoline comes as 91 octane at about 80¢ per liter, and 96 octane at about 90¢ per liter. Rental cars are often "required" to have the higher-octane gas. These gas prices work out to about $2.70 to $3.60 per U.S. gallon.

Gas stations are plentiful enough on main roads, except that on Saturday some of them are closed. And on Saturday and Jewish holidays it's virtually impossible to have a flat tire repaired in the Jewish sections of Israel.

BREAKDOWNS/ASSISTANCE   Your car-rental agency will supply you with numbers to call in case of emergencies. Bigger companies usually have better service.

12 Tips on Accommodations

The eleventh commandment in Israel is: THOU SHALT NOT PAY FULL PRICE FOR YOUR HOTEL ROOM. Travel agents and packagers that specialize in Israel, as well as airlines like El Al, offer land arrangements that can get you into many expensive and moderate hotels, including kibbutz guest houses and hotels, at prices far below the official rack rates we quote in our listings. But you need to plan ahead, at least for part of your itinerary, in order to take advantage of these bargains.

Rates quoted for hotel rooms in this book are in dollars only. As of now, only a few small hotels, hostels, and pensions in Israel will quote you room or bed rates in shekels.

A note on hotel room taxes: If you are not an Israeli citizen and you pay your hotel bill in foreign currency (dollars, marks, francs) in the form of cash, traveler's checks, or credit card, you won't be subject to Israel's additional 17% value-added tax (VAT), a tax that is normally added onto the price of any shekel purchase. Thus, it's a good idea to put hotel restaurant meals and drinks and such on the hotel bill rather than paying for them on the spot with cash shekels. Every time you pay in shekels, you're paying that tax, whether it's shown as a separate charge or hidden in the total price.

In Jordan, a 13% tax is added to all room rates regardless of how you pay, and a standard 10% service tax is also added. If you ask about a room rate in Jordan, you will be told the amount, "plus-plus," meaning plus 13% plus 10%.

Many Israeli and most West Bank hotels add a 15% service charge to your hotel bill. These prices are per room, not per person. The hotel may quote prices differently: "Double room for $15 per person plus 15% service."

When making reservations or buying a hotel package, always check whether the rate quoted includes tax and service.

Virtually every Israeli hotel will provide a large breakfast to guests included in the room rate. In 99% of Israeli hotels, the breakfast will be kosher; most are buffet. Very few East Jerusalem, West Bank, or Sinai or Jordanian hotels serve kosher meals. Many offer buffet breakfasts, but some only offer a continental breakfast.

Children up to the age of 6 are usually allowed a 50% reduction on the extra-person rate if they stay in the same room with their parents. Policies vary for children under 18 at different hotels. Most international hotel chains offer some kind of family plan.

HOTELS & RESERVATIONS

With more and more Israeli hotels affiliated with international chains, you can often get 5-, 7-, or 10-night discount plans if you decide to make your bookings within one hotel chain. There are all kinds of ever-changing bargains floating around. Holiday Inns, which includes Crowne Plaza hotels, usually has a "kids are free" plan. Some chains offer discounts linked to certain airline tickets and frequent-flyer programs. Hilton Hotels offered a 50% discount to guests over 60 years of age. Most of the big hotel chains in Sinai, including Movenpick and Hilton, have deals that average 50% off for much of the year if you book directly through their international reservation centers. At times there are family and student discounts, and if you buy a package at a hotel chain, you may also be able to add in an excellent deal on a car rental as well.

HOTEL CHAINS The major hotel chains in Israel include **Dan Hotels Israel** (☎ **800/223-7773** in the U.S. or 212/752-6120 in New York state, 0800/731-2789 in the U.K.; www.danhotels.com; e-mail: danhtls@danhotels.com); **Isrotel** (☎ **888/ 669-5700** or 888/ISROTEL; 201/556-9669 in the U.S. and Canada; ☎ 0181/ 997-6423, fax 1081/998-6607 in the U.K.; www.isrotel.co.il); **Atlas Hotels** (☎ **800/444-TELL** in the U.S.; 09/90-300-200 in the U.K.; www.hotelbook.com; e-mail: atlashot@netvision.net.il); **Hilton Hotels** (☎ **800/HILTONS**); **Sheraton Hotels** (☎ **800/325-3535** in the U.S. and Canada; 0800/353535 in the U.K.; 800/07-3535 in Australia); **Hyatt Hotels** (☎ **800/233-1234** in the U.S. and Canada; 44/181/335-1220 in the U.K.); **Mercure Hotels** (☎ **800/MERCURE** in the U.S. and Canada; 44/181/741-3100 in the U.K.; 800/64-22-44 in Australia); **Ramada** (☎ **800/468-1902** in the U.S. and Canada; 0800-181-737 in the U.K.);

Holiday Inn (☎ 800/465-4329 in the U.S. and Canada); and **Movenpick Hotels** (☎ 800/ 34-HOTEL or 203/454-0090 in the U.S. and Canada; 31 70/337-3700 in the U.K. and Netherlands).

KIBBUTZ ACCOMMODATIONS   If you plan to travel through the countryside and stay at kibbutz holiday villages, resorts, and guest houses, contact the **Israel Tourism Center,** or **ITC** (☎ 888/669-5700 or 201/556-9669 in the U.S. and Canada; e-mail: israelhotels@worldnet.att.net). This office represents the Kibbutz Hotel Chain, as well as Israel's Isrotel Hotel chain. The ITC will send you current brochures and information about discount packages available through these chains, make and confirm reservations, and arrange prepaid car-rental packages. In many cases, the car-rental arrangements you can make at ITC will be less expensive than those you'll find through other channels. The ITC can expand the Kibbutz Hotel packages to include a range of moderate and luxury nonkibbutz choices in Eilat, Jerusalem, and Mitspe Ramon. The ITC also makes bed-and-breakfast arrangements, and represents a new organization of less-expensive Moshav and Kibbutz Bed-and-Breakfast Country Lodgings throughout the country (see below). The ITC is recommended by the Israel Ministry of Tourism.

You can also make reservations for Kibbutz hotels, and for Kibbutz Country Lodging Bed-and-Breakfast accommodations through the **Kibbutz Hotels Chain** office, 1 Smolanskin St., POB 3139, Tel Aviv 61031 (☎ **03/524-6161;** fax 03-527-8088; www.kibbutz.co.il: e-mail: info@kibbutz.co.il).

RESERVATIONS THROUGH PACKAGERS   All kinds of packagers constantly put together hotel deals that you can buy as an independent traveler, regardless of what airline you fly. If things are slow, a hotel or hotel chain may arrange to let a packager sell a block of its rooms at lower than usual rates. It can truly pay to shop around; also see what kind of deals your own travel agent may be able to come up with.

Travelmania (www.travelmania.com) is one of many new online agencies: pick your destination in Israel, dates, and your price range, and a number of hotels will come up on screen with the bargain rates currently being offered (check against our "Where to Stay" listings to see how good the deals really are). Whenever booking online, always check to see whether rates include tax, service, and booking fees.

If you want to speak to an actual human being while making your plans, and clarify hidden costs, try a packager like **Affordable Israel** (☎ 800/221-0203 or 212/ 541-5009) which continuously updates its prices and accommodation deals. In addition to general discounts on hotel rooms, Affordable Israel also specializes in Spa Vacations and works with a number of hotel chains to come up with special rates for room, meals, and treatments; at press time, it offered excellent deals at the independent Nirvanna Dead Sea Spa.

TOUR OPERATORS   Booking a completely organized, all-inclusive escorted tour through a travel agent is another option. The advantages are that everything is taken care of for you, from airport transfers and your program of daily guided tours to the decisions about where you'll have lunch and dinner. Of course, you pay more for this kind of all-inclusive deal, and you sacrifice your freedom to wander and explore on your own. There are many, many companies selling group tours at many price levels and for travelers with many different interests. If your agent only has one or two tours to show you, by all means look elsewhere.

RESERVATIONS BY MAIL   If you should write for hotel reservations, be certain to print or type both your letter of inquiry and the address on the outer envelope.

Kibbutz Hotel Accommodations

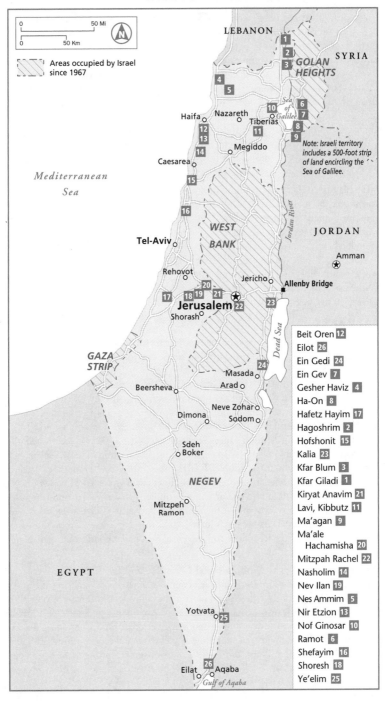

0 ____ 50 MI
0 ____ 50 Km

Areas occupied by Israel since 1967

LEBANON

SYRIA

GOLAN HEIGHTS

Sea of Galilee

Note: Israeli territory includes a 500-foot strip of land encircling the Sea of Galilee.

Haifa
Nazareth
Tiberias
Megiddo
Caesarea

Mediterranean Sea

WEST BANK

Jordan River

JORDAN

Amman

Tel-Aviv

Rehovot

Jericho
Allenby Bridge

Jerusalem
Shorash

GAZA STRIP

Dead Sea

Masada
Arad
Beersheva
Neve Zohar
Dimona
Sodom

Sdeh Boker

NEGEV

Mitzpeh Ramon

EGYPT

Yotvata

Eilat Aqaba
Gulf of Aqaba

Beit Oren 12
Eilot 26
Ein Gedi 24
Ein Gev 7
Gesher Haviz 4
Ha-On 8
Hafetz Hayim 17
Hagoshrim 2
Hofshonit 15
Kalia 23
Kfar Blum 3
Kfar Giladi 1
Kiryat Anavim 21
Lavi, Kibbutz 11
Ma'agan 9
Ma'ale Hachamisha 20
Mitzpah Rachel 22
Nasholim 14
Nev Ilan 19
Nes Ammim 5
Nir Etzion 13
Nof Ginosar 10
Ramot 6
Shefayim 16
Shoresh 18
Ye'elim 25

49

Israeli post office and hotel personnel often have difficulty reading English handwriting. Also, zip codes in Israel are similar to American zip codes; it is advisable to write them in front of the name of the Israeli city or town in order to avoid confusing unwary American postal workers. Zip codes are still not used by everyone in Israel, but the codes are important for smaller towns. I can't stress enough that if you write, you should start the reservations process very early. It can take 2 weeks for a letter to reach Israel by air, and another 2 weeks for the reply, as well as the time for the hotel to go through its paperwork. If you wish a confirmation, enclose International Reply Coupons (on sale at any post office) to pay return postage.

If you choose to make arrangements by telephone, remember that when it's 7am EST in New York, it's 2pm in Israel. Also, many Israeli hotels will have only limited staff during the Shabbat (Friday evening to Saturday evening).

HOTEL SEASONS   Israel's hotels fill up during certain seasons and holidays, and you should be prepared with advanced reservations, secured by a deposit. Generally speaking, hotels are busiest during July and August, and on the major Jewish and Christian holidays such as Passover, Easter, Rosh Hashanah, and Yom Kippur, Hanukkah, and Christmas. For detailed information, and a full list of holiday dates, see the "Israel Calendar of Events," earlier in this chapter.

Off-season is generally November through February (except for Hanukkah/Christmas/New Year's). It is, however, the busiest season in Eilat, which has almost perfect, sunny weather when it's chilly up north.

PACKAGES

AIRLINE PACKAGES   Some of the best bargains in Israeli hotel accommodations are offered by El Al, the national carrier of Israel, but you can only buy them in conjunction with the **"Sunsational Israel"** package that includes 5 nights at Jerusalem's centrally located Jerusalem Tower Hotel or Tel Aviv's excellent (almost beachfront) Basel Hotel starting at $50 a night per person, double occupancy. With this deal, you also get a Hertz manual transmission rental car (there is a 35¢ per kilometer charge plus insurance; an automatic transmission car can be ordered for a higher price). El Al also offers a **Sheraton Moriah Hotel Flexi package** that gives you accommodations at five-star Sheraton Hotels across Israel, including the Sheraton Plaza Jerusalem, starting at $110 per night for a double. El Al's more expensive **"Dantastic"** packages include accommodations at the luxury Dan Hotel chain at considerable savings. But look at their plans carefully. The Laromme "Combo/4" offers rather undistinguished hotels in Jerusalem, Tel Aviv, and at the Dead Sea starting at $112 per night for a double; at times, for only $124 per night for a double, the "Laromme Combo5" gives you truly excellent hotels in Jerusalem and the Dead Sea, and a good, solid choice in Tel Aviv.

Kibbutz Packages   The **Kibbutz Hotel Chain Fly and Drive Package** is especially enticing; it lets you explore the real Israeli countryside while overnighting at comfortable kibbutz holiday villages and guest houses, the equivalent of three-star hotels, that have swimming pools or beaches, and invariably lovely settings. There are minimum 7-night deals, which include a double room and breakfast for $39 to $45 per person per night, double occupancy, and a middle-grade Avis rental car beginning at $230 per week (with unlimited mileage and manual transmission). Starting at $12 per person per night more, you can book a package that gives you a choice of more luxurious kibbutz accommodations.

Although all accommodations in the kibbutz hotel and holiday village network are the equivalent of three- or four-star hotels, you'll find great variety in the general setup and character of each facility. You'll be amazed at the sheer drama of many of the kibbutz sites, from such desert retreats as Ein Gedi (set in a botanical garden of rare trees and plantings, perched above the Dead Sea near the fortress of Masada), to places like Ye'elim, adjacent to the Negev's Hai Bar Wildlife Reserve. There are semiluxury resorts such as the lovely Kfar Blum, or the hotel at the orthodox Kibbutz Lavi; there are also simpler holiday villages such as Nasholim, on the shores of the Mediterranean; or Ein Gev, on the Sea of Galilee. Many kibbutzim in the program are just a few minutes' drive from Jerusalem or within easy distance of Tel Aviv.

You can arrange for a kibbutz land package (including the **Kibbutz Association Fly and Drive** packages) independently of any airline ticket by calling the **Israel Tourism Center** (see above) at ☎ **888/669-5700** or 201/556-9669. You may add additional days to the Kibbutz Hotel Chain Plan at rates far below those you could book independently and then move on to independent arrangements for the rest of your trip. There are also single supplements and children's rates.

BED & BREAKFAST

Kibbutz Country Lodgings   Unlike the network of kibbutz hotels and holiday villages, which are really three- or four-star country hotels, and the kibbutz resorts, which are often quite separate from the actual kibbutz, this option consists of a growing network of smaller kibbutz and moshav communities that run simple guest bungalows or buildings, or kibbutz families who have guest room facilities in their own houses. With rates that can be as low as $65 to $70 per night for a double room, you get a comfortable bedroom, usually with private bathroom, in interesting countryside locations. Best of all, you have a chance to see a bit of real kibbutz life. This is an especially good option if you want to keep your accommodation expenses down and put the savings into a rental car for freewheeling independent travel. For a commission of approximately $35, the Israel Tourism Center (see above) (☎ **888/-669-5700**) will make reservations for you at affiliated kibbutz and bed-and-breakfast places. Travel agents specializing in Israel may also book packages for you at the Kibbutz Hotels or Country Lodgings; an agent who is doing other bookings for you may also waive the Country Lodgings booking fee. Local tourist information offices in the Galilee can also give you lists of moshav guest houses, on *moshavim,* or cooperative communities in the area.

City Bed & Breakfast   The Israel Tourism Center can make bed-and-breakfast arrangements through the **Good Morning Jerusalem** bed-and-breakfast rental office. There is a $35 commission for this service, but you save the expense and bother of international phone calls and faxes.

For bed-and-breakfast accommodations in Jerusalem (chapter 3) and Tel Aviv (chapter 6), there are rental services that will make note of your requirements and preferences and try to match them to a room in their listings. Reservations for these rooms, ranging in price from about $60 to $80 for a double, can be made from overseas.

At tourist information offices in Tel Aviv, Jerusalem, and many other Israeli cities, you can use a computer bank to access lists of accommodations in private homes for any area in the country. The information disbursed by these computers is rather lean—just a list of names, addresses, and phone numbers, but with a few phone calls, you can usually come up with something. If you're looking at local listings, the staff at the tourist information office may be willing to direct you to places they know to be especially good. Summers, weekends, and holidays, it is always best to reserve ahead.

YOUTH HOSTELS

The concept of youth hostels is right at home with the traditional Israeli preference for functional, practical lifestyle and congenial atmosphere in which travelers can meet freely and easily. **Israel Youth Hostel Association (IYHA)** hostels often offer the only available accommodations in remote areas of the country, or in areas along hiking routes. The IYHA hostels at Mispe Ramon, in the Negev, overlooking the Ramon Crater; and at Ein Gedi, beside the Dead Sea, provide great bases for hiking those areas. The Taylor Youth Hostel, at the foot of Masada, is the place to overnight if you want to make a predawn ascent onto Masada, and watch the sun rise over the Dead Sea before the day's tour buses start arriving. Other IHYA hostels, such as the small, rustic retreat at Poriya, on an orchard-covered hill overlooking the Sea of Galilee near Tiberias, are simply great bargain options.

In the past few years, the IYHA has been busy upgrading its network of facilities. Many hostels are set up with a maximum of four to six beds per room; a large percentage of these rooms now have private shower/bathrooms and can easily be converted into doubles or family rooms. Dining facilities now offer meals far superior to the once spartan youth-hostel fare.

Age is no barrier, nor is membership. Hostels offer rock-bottom prices and a friendly welcome to all. Only hostels bearing the triangular sign are authorized by the Israel Youth Hostels Association. It is advisable to book in advance.

Having a youth hostel membership card does give you certain advantages, such as better rates at the hostels, plus discounts at some restaurants, national parks, historical sites, museums, and on buses and trains. The IYHA also offers packages that combine car rental or bus travel with stays at its hostels. The headquarters of the **Israel Youth Hostels Association** is located in Jerusalem at the International Convention Center, P.O. Box 6001, Jerusalem Z.C. 91009 (☎ **02/655-8400;** fax 02/655-8430), where you can obtain information on present offerings of the Youth Travel Bureau.

Note: Not all youth hostels take foreign currency, and it's a good idea to check availability of space (especially in summer months) before arriving. The Israel Youth Hostels Association also has 14-, 21-, and 28-day bargain-price tours and car-rental packages. Fax, write, or inquire at the Jerusalem office for further information.

Non-IYHA–Affiliated Hostels In most Israeli cities, a number of private non-IYHA hostels flourish; they can range from decent to decrepit. In Jerusalem and Tel Aviv, not more than two independent hostels per city come even distantly close to the standards of an IYHA hostel, but they do have spirit. Most are small, less institutional, and can arrange to rent private rooms. Especially in the big projected tourism year 2000, they may be among the only budget choices available. We list one or two urban, private hostel choices for Jerusalem, Tel Aviv, and Eilat at the beginning of the accommodations sections of those chapters.

Suggested Itineraries

Without doubt, Jerusalem is the most fascinating place in Israel. If you have very limited time, plan to spend most of it there. Distances are not great in Israel, and it is possible to get a quick taste of the desert, the Mediterranean coast, and even the Sea of Galilee on day trips from Jerusalem. If you plan to visit Eilat, or get a real feel for the Galilee, then overnight trips become necessary. *Note:* These itineraries are recommended for travelers who have access to a private car. Although public transportation is an option, these itineraries would be difficult or impossible to complete within the allotted time frames.

If You Have 1 Week

Day 1   You might do well to make **Tel Aviv** your first stop, where from May to October you can recover from jet lag by beaching and swimming in the sparkling, warm Mediterranean.

Day 2   Take in the ambience of Israel's beachside metropolis. Spend at least a few hours at the unique **Diaspora Museum.** Visit **Old Jaffa** for outdoor seaside dining and a stroll.

Day 3   Move on to **Jerusalem.** Stroll through the restored **Jewish Quarter** of the Old City in the late afternoon or at twilight; include a visit to the **Western Wall,** which is fascinating at any hour. Dine in the New City.

Day 4   Take a guided tour of the **Old City,** or see it on your own. Do the **Arab bazaars** from 9am to noon. Then see the **Dome of the Rock** and the **El Aksa Mosque,** which close by 3pm (both sites are closed all day Friday). The **Holy Sepulcher Church** is best scheduled for last because it remains open until early evening.

Day 5   Take in more of the Old City and the view from the **Mount of Olives** or do the highlights of the **New City:** the Israel Museum, Yad VaShem Holocaust Memorial and Museum, Hadassah (Ein Kerem) Hospital, the Knesset, or any of the city's smaller museums.

Day 6   Rent a car or go by guided tour to the fortress of **Masada** in the Judean Desert and have a fast, superbuoyant swim in the **Dead Sea** at Ein Gedi. You can also drive up the Jordan Valley to the **Sea of Galilee,** visit **Nazareth** or the ancient, ruined synagogues around the lake, overnight in the area, swim in the lake, and return to Jerusalem the next morning.

Day 7   Free day in Jerusalem; optional morning trip to **Bethlehem,** 5 miles south of Jerusalem.

If You Have 2 Weeks

Days 1 and 2   Head for **Tel Aviv** and overcome jet lag at the beach. Kibbutz guest houses along the coast are a relaxing alternative if you have a car; swim at **Caesarea's** Roman Aqueduct Beach. Dine at Caesarea's port amid crusader ruins.

Day 3   Go north along the coast. Make **Haifa, Nahariya,** or a **kibbutz** guest house your base. Explore the walled Arabic port city of **Akko, Lohamei Ha-Getaot Holocaust Museum,** and the cliffs at **Rosh Ha-Niqra** on the Lebanese border.

Day 4   Move inland across the northern Galilee. Base in **Safed, Metulla,** or a kibbutz guest house. Visit the ancient ruined synagogue at **Baram** (perhaps the loveliest in Israel) and the **nature reserves and springs** at Baniyas and Tel Dan.

Day 5   Spend the day at the **Sea of Galilee.** Circle the shoreline of this mysterious and lovely lake with its New Testament sites at Tabgha, Capernaum, and the Mount of Beatitudes. The eastern shore south of Ein Gev has quiet beaches. Overnight at **Tiberias,** a kibbutz holiday village, or guest house along the lake.

Day 6   Use your accommodations at the Sea of Galilee as a base. Explore the **Golan Heights** or **Nazareth** and the central Galilee. Have a late swim in the lake and dine in Tiberias.

Day 7   Travel south through the Jordan Valley visiting the archeological park at **Bet Shean** or the Bet Alpha Byzantine mosaic synagogue floor at **Kibbutz Hefzibah.** Overnight at Kibbutz Kalia or Kibbutz Ein Gedi guest house along the dramatic coast of the Dead Sea.

Day 8   Explore the Herodian fortress of **Masada;** try to sink in the unearthly Dead Sea. Then head south through the Negev to **Eilat,** stopping at the national park at Timna for an off-the-main-highway view of the real **Negev.** Dine and overnight in Eilat.

Day 9   **Snorkel** the coral reef with its exotic Indian Ocean fish or view the fish at the aquarium or from a glass-bottom boat. Enjoy Eilat's busy restaurant scene and nightlife.

Day 10   Head to **Jerusalem.** Take an evening walk to the **Jewish Quarter** of the Old City and the Western Wall. Dine in the New City.

Days 11, 12, 13, and 14   Explore both the **Old and New Cities;** include a morning trip to **Bethlehem,** 5 miles south of Jerusalem.

Fast Facts: Israel

American Express   The toll-free information and refund number is ☎ **177/ 440-8694.** There are representatives in Jerusalem, Tel Aviv, Haifa, and Amman in Jordan.

Business Hours   Israel does not have a standard set of business hours. For local business hours, see "Fast Facts" for your destination area. Government offices are open on weekdays, usually from 7:30 or 8am. Some are closed to the public on Friday, and all are closed on Saturday; in summer, they are open until 1 or 3pm; in winter, they remain open until 2 or 4pm. Banks are open Sunday, Tuesday, and Thursday 8:30am to 12:30pm and 4 to 5:30pm; on Monday and Wednesday 8:30am to 12:30pm only; on Friday 8:30am to noon.

Camera/Film   Although film is cheaper in the United States, it can be bought almost anywhere in the country. Since the sun's so bright, and reflections tend to get glaring, many photographers use special filters to soften such effects. There are three restrictions on picture taking in Israel: certain military areas, which are plainly marked in several languages as no-photo territories; aerial photography over inland routes without special permission; and certain people, who use their own sign language (usually hands over their face, or in your face) to let you know they don't want to be photographed, for religious or other reasons.

Doctors/Dentists   Embassies and consulates keep lists of English-speaking doctors and dentists. Remember also that on weekends and holidays the consulate always has a duty officer on call if a real emergency arises.

Drug Laws   Drug laws are enforced in Israel. Travelers should never attempt to buy illegal drugs.

Drugstores   In Israel, pharmacists are allowed to advise about medicines and medications, and can sell you many items that would require a prescription in the United States. If you need medication at night, on Friday afternoon, or on Saturday, when drugstores are closed, check the *Jerusalem Post* for a list of pharmacies on round-the-clock emergency duty in your area.

Electricity   The electric current used in Israel is 220 volts AC (50 cycles). If you bring an electric shaver, iron, or radio, you can buy an inexpensive transformer in Israel to convert the current to the American voltage cycle. Or you can buy 220-volt equipment at special shops that can be directly used in Israel. Sockets (or power points) usually take special Israeli three-prong plugs or sockets designed for round plugs. If your appliance has two prongs on its plug, you can buy a plug adapter in Israel quite easily for 2 or 3 shekels.

Embassies/Consulates   The **American Embassy** is at 71 Ha-Yarkon St., Tel Aviv (☎ **03/519-7575;** fax 03/510-2444). The **U.S. Consulate-General** in East Jerusalem is at 17 Nablus Rd. (☎ **02/622-7200**). The West Jerusalem consulate building is at 18 Agron St. (☎ **02/622-7230;** after hours 02/622-7250), just down the hill from the Jerusalem Plaza Hotel. Both are open Monday to Friday 8am to noon. Most services are at the East Jerusalem Consulate, but call first to check.

The **Australian Embassy** is at 37 Shaul Ha-Melekh St., Tel Aviv (☎ **03/695-0451**).

The **Irish Embassy** is at 266 Ha-Yarkon St., Tel Aviv (☎ **03/930-9055**).

The **British Embassy** is at 192 Ha-Yarkon St., Tel Aviv (☎ **03/524-9171** or 03/524-9178; fax 03/524-3313). The **British Consulate-General** in West Jerusalem is at Tower House, beside St. Andrew's Church, Remez Street (near the train station) (☎ **02/671-7724**); in East Jerusalem, it's near the Sheikh Jarrah neighborhood at 19 Nashashibi St. (☎ **02/541-4100**). This consulate will also handle matters for **New Zealand** citizens.

Canadians should contact the consular section of their new embassy in Tel Aviv at 3 Nirim Beit Hasepanut, Yad Eliahu (☎ **03/636-3300**). *Beware:* Many Israelis in tourism (and tourist brochures) may still refer you to the Canadian Embassy on Ha-Yarkon Street, but that site is now a hotel.

Emergencies **Magen David Adom (Red Shield of David)** is the Jewish equivalent of the Red Cross. They provide ambulance and first-aid service in virtually every city and town. At their clinics in major cities, you can get emergency medical or dental treatment on the Sabbath or at other times when normal practitioners are unavailable. For Magen David Adom emergency ambulance service in Jerusalem, Haifa, Tel Aviv, and most other parts of the country, dial ☎ **101.** For emergencies requiring hospitalization, dial ☎ **102.** The Magen David Adom clinic in Jerusalem is in Romema, near the Central Bus Station.

Mail Post offices and mailboxes in Israel are identified by a red sign bearing a white leaping deer. English-style red-letter boxes are also used. Special yellow intracity mailboxes are found in Tel Aviv and Jerusalem. You can buy stamps at shops and news stands bearing a similar sign.

The main post offices in the large cities are usually open from 7am to 7pm Sunday to Thursday; hours for branch post offices are 8am to 12:30pm and 3:30 to 6pm. All post offices are open on Friday and eves of holidays from 7am to 1pm. All are closed on Saturday.

Post offices have current postal-rate schedules, printed in English and Hebrew, on their bulletin boards. Post offices send telegrams and telexes, and also operate overseas telephone calling centers.

The use of zip codes inside Israel is becoming more widespread, but it is not yet absolutely required for sending letters. Note that it can take 2 weeks or more for an airmail letter to travel between Israel and North America.

Newspapers/Magazines Your indispensable sources of news, entertainment, and information in Israel are the daily English-language newspaper the *Jerusalem Post,* or the daily *International Herald Tribune,* which comes with a complete copy of the English-language edition of *Ha'aretz* tucked inside (*Ha'aretz* is the country's most prestigious newspaper, known locally as *The New York Times* of Israel). If you can't find them in the business section of the town you're in, or at a newspaper kiosk, try a big tourist hotel early in the morning before it sells out.

The Friday morning edition of both the *Post* and *Ha'aretz* carry the weekly magazine section filled with features, entertainment notices, and radio and television listings.

Jerusalem Report, a very readable English-language news magazine, offers excellent coverage on Israel and Jewish issues; it is published every 2 weeks. It is sold at bookstores that carry English language items. *Eretz* magazine is a beautifully photographed journal of Israeli nature, travel, and history.

Police   Each city and town has its own municipal force, and the army keeps a vigil throughout the country. In the major cities, in an emergency, dial ☎ **100.**

Radio   Radio signals come in from all eastern Mediterranean countries, and often from Europe as well. The Voice of America and the BBC's World Service are both accessible on the AM (middle-wave) dial.

Kol Israel (The Voice of Israel) broadcasts news bulletins in English on 576 or 1170 kHz at 7am and 1 and 5pm. News in French follows these English programs. There's even a schedule of bulletins in easy Hebrew for those learning the language. Also, you can hear news broadcasts in English from Cairo and Amman at various times throughout the day.

Rest Rooms   Israeli cities and tourist sights are well provided with public toilets. Look for signs to the "WC," or "OO," or look for the various male-female symbols: pipe and fan, man and woman silhouettes, and so on.

Safety   In general, Israel is a pretty safe place, but this doesn't mean you can ignore simple, commonsense precautions. Whenever you're traveling in an unfamiliar city or country, stay alert. Be aware of your immediate surroundings, and don't leave valuables on view in a rental car. The incidence of car theft in Israel is extremely high. Watch out for pickpockets, especially in crowds, markets, in the crushes at bus stops, or in the narrow streets of Jerusalem's Old City bazaar. Muggings are rare, but they do occur.

Warning: Get away from and report any unattended objects in public places.

Taxes   A 17% value-added tax (VAT) is included in the price of everything paid for in shekels. When hotel bills are paid by foreigners in dollars, however, VAT is not applicable. Everything charged to the hotel bill—meals, room, telephone—receives the VAT exemption.

In most tourist-oriented shops, the VAT on single-item purchases of more than $50 can be refunded at the airport. To reclaim the VAT, turn over forms (you should receive these at your point of purchase) to customs as you leave Ben Gurion Airport (or by mail). You should be warned that claiming this refund may be a lengthy business, so get to the airport early if you intend to do so.

Telephones   Public pay telephones accept magnetic phone cards, good for 10, 20, or 50 units. Magnetic phone cards cost a bit less if you buy them at the post office but they are also sold at stationers, news stands, and at many hotel desks. A local call is generally one unit and permits you to speak for 3 minutes. There are also slightly more expensive pay phones that accept shekels, but they are fewer in number. Pay phones that use cards do not accept coins.

Dialing ☎ **144** will get you **directory assistance.** Directory and overseas operators speak English. The overseas operator is ☎ **188.** Toll-free numbers have prefixes of 177 and 1-800, however, when you use the 1-800 number to access AT&T, there is a charge.

Each city in Israel has an **area code:** Tel Aviv and the airport are 03; Jerusalem is 02; Haifa and the Western Galilee, 04; Netanya and Heerzlia, 09; Eilat and most of the Negev, 07; Tiberias, Nazareth, Safed, and most of the northeastern Galilee is 06. Look in the phone book for others.

When you **call from another country to a number in Israel,** you do not dial that initial "0" (zero) in the area code. Dial Israel's country code (972), Jerusalem's area (or city) code (2), then the local seven-digit number (624-1009). If you're **calling within Israel,** say from Jerusalem to a number in Haifa, you must use the initial zero of the area code.

The access code from Israel for AT&T is ☎ 1-800/949-4949; for MCI ☎ 177/150-1151; for Sprint ☎ 177/102-3412; for British Telecom ☎ 1-800/943-2744; and for Canada Direct ☎ 1-800/9494-105.

Television   Check the Friday *Jerusalem Post* or *Ha'aretz* newspapers for the week's schedule. Israel television's channels 1 and 2 offer many British and American programs. CNN news is available at many hotels. Israel's state-operated channel 1 broadcasts international and local news in English at 6:15pm. Jordan's channel 2 broadcasts an English-language evening schedule from Amman at 8:30 or 9pm, with news in English at 10pm, as well as many familiar American or British programs. Times are often an hour earlier in summer.

Time   Israel has daylight saving time in summer but only from late March to early September. The basic time difference between New York and Jerusalem is 7 hours: When it's 5am in New York, it's already noon in Jerusalem. When daylight saving times don't match, the time difference is 6 hours. Religious political parties do not support daylight saving time; the period of time allotted to daylight saving time is sometimes curtailed or canceled with little notice. For the time, dial ☎ **155.**

Tipping   In tourist spots and better-quality hotels, restaurants, and clubs, tip 10%, unless the menu states that a service charge is included. In more modest restaurants, do as the Israelis do: Leave small change in the 5% to 10% range. The person waiting on you may pick up your offering with indifference. That's probably because he or she didn't really expect a tip, rather than because the tip was too small.

You needn't tip taxi or sherut drivers unless they've performed some special service. But you should always offer a tip to a guide or caretaker (self-appointed or otherwise) who actually does help you to see some holy site or ancient ruin. If there is no admission fee, and if a man or boy comes running to unlock the gate for you, he deserves a small tip. But when he offers you a guided tour, or simply begins to guide you, you can say no. By saying nothing, you encourage misunderstanding. By saying yes, you've made a contract, and you should proceed to agree on a price.

Tip about 10% at the barber's or hairdresser's, part to the person who washes your hair, part to the one who cuts it. Tip a hat or coat checker and a lavatory attendant a few coins unless a price is posted. In hotels, tip the housekeeping staff and the bellhop.

Water   Drink lots and lots of it to prevent dehydration during the hot, dry Israeli summer. Tap water is drinkable throughout Israel, although in some areas local minerals may cause short-term upset stomach. You may prefer to be extra safe and buy the bottled water available in grocery stores. In a cafe, ask for "soda" and you'll receive a club soda.

3 Getting to Know Jerusalem

No one will ever be able to pinpoint what makes Jerusalem so special. The mountains, the wind, the extraordinary light may be part of it. Three thousand years ago, King David, the beloved warrior-psalmist of the Bible, made Jerusalem his capital. Perhaps he saw the poetry of the place as it was then. The Gihon Spring flowed through a paradise of gardens nestled at the foot of the Kidron Valley. From there a long narrow ridge rose steeply northward, filled with stone houses perched precariously on its sides. At the top of the ridge, seeming to hang in the heavens, was the threshing floor of Araunah, which David purchased as the site of the Temple his son, Solomon, would one day build. Overlooking everything were the vast groves of the Mount of Olives, an ocean of silver leaves shimmering in the sun and wind, the source of the city's wealth; over the ridge of the Mount of Olives, the sun rose each day. From its crest, the view opened onto the desert, stretching over barren mountains and down steep wadies eastward to the Dead Sea. Into this wilderness, with great ceremony, the scapegoat was released each year, carrying with it Jerusalem's sins.

For more than a thousand years after the time of King David, Jerusalem was the physical as well as the spiritual capital of the Jewish world. Jews longed for the splendid Jerusalem of King Solomon, for the Jerusalem of the great prophets, for the ruined Jerusalem of the Babylonian Captivity, for the modest Jerusalem of the early Second Temple period. For the redemption of Jerusalem during the Maccabee Revolt in B.C. 167, Jews fought and died, and were rewarded with a miraculous victory over the Hellenistic Seleucids of Syria. It was in the dazzling and legendary Jerusalem built by King Herod that hundreds of thousands of Jews perished during the great revolt against Rome in A.D. 70. Defending the ruins of Herodian Jerusalem, hundreds of thousands more died during the Bar Kochba Revolt in A.D. 135. To this day, ancient Jerusalem remains the dream at the heart of Jewish civilization; it rests at the center of Western civilization's consciousness.

Although the physical grandeur of Herodian Jerusalem long ago vanished in the ravages of warfare and time, the city's mystique has expanded far beyond anything that could have been dreamed of in ancient times. The most awesome holy places of Judaism, Christianity, and Islam have come to dot the Old City and its nearby hills. During the centuries of the Crusades, Jerusalem was the ethereal vision that moved the armies of Europe and Islam, but for almost 700 years after the Crusades ended, the actual city of Jerusalem existed as a shadowy, forgotten backwater, slowly falling into ruin and decay. Not until the 19th century did the city again begin to come alive and reemerge from behind its walls.

During the years of the British Mandate (1918–48) the current incarnation of Jerusalem developed as a quiet religious center, tourist attraction, and university town in a remarkably beautiful mountain setting. Nineteen years of division by war, barbed wire, and minefields (1948–67) brought Jerusalem's gentle renaissance to a temporary halt. With the city's reunification in 1967, however, Teddy Kollek, the city's world-renowned mayor, began a 25-year crusade to make sure Jerusalem would not merely exist or even thrive but would absolutely shine!

1 A Brief History

JERUSALEM TODAY Jerusalem today is a busy place. New construction is going on everywhere, bringing new industry, new highways, and, in the next few years, a whole new hotel scene. The constant stream of civic delights—museums, concerts, performances—developed by Teddy Kollek helped turn an austere outpost in the Judean hills into a lively, Mediterranean city with cafes, pubs, and restaurants packed to the brim with activity. The newly created pedestrian streets of the downtown center are flooded with strollers and, especially in summer, you'll find a nightly air of festive celebration.

A walled city is always a small town at heart, and for the past century, even as Jerusalem expanded beyond its walls and across the surrounding hills, it remained in spirit a small town: inward looking, personal, intensely aware of its local gossip and also with its thundering history. Now, for good or for ill, Jerusalem stands on the verge of becoming a true metropolis rather than the small city of exotic neighborhoods and religious communities the world has known for the past 70 years. What Jerusalem will be like as it enters the 21st century is a point of international interest and concern. For 3,000 years, through splendor and desolation, glory and poverty, despite all imperfections, the earthly Jerusalem has always been a place that rose to its extraordinary legend. Will the New Jerusalem be able to maintain its mystique: With a major highway system routed just 30 feet from the walls of the Old City, so that visitors have to climb a pedestrian overpass in order to enter the Jaffa Gate? With many of the eccentric, small-scale 19th-century neighborhoods of the New City, and their networks of pedestrian streets, courtyards, and Ottoman-era mansions (underappreciated in a town with Herodian, Byzantine, and Omayyid treasures to preserve) slated to be demolished and replaced with office blocks? With a new wave of 30 skyscrapers being planned for the previously low-rise center of West Jerusalem and the arrival of such worldly establishments as Pizza Hut, McDonald's, Tower Records, and Toys R Us? At what point will Jerusalem begin to seem like anywhere else?

The city is at a crossroads politically and socially as well as physically. Will it ever in some way be a shared capital for Palestinians and Israelis? Will the religious Jewish community become the demographic and ruling majority in West Jerusalem and, if so, what will happen to the museums, parks, entertainment, and cultural institutions created by the city's secular community over the past 30 years? Should developers be allowed a free hand to Manhattanize Jerusalem or should limits be placed on the future growth of the city?

Jerusalem has been a holy city for 3,000 years, far eclipsing the length of time that any other place has borne such a title. It is also a holy city for all three great religions of the Western world: Judaism, Christianity, and Islam. Optimists believe that city planners will find a way to turn a mysterious walled holy city into a fast-paced holy megalopolis. For now, in many ways, the city walks a tightrope between its legend and the rapidly encroaching world of the 21st century.

AN ANCIENT CITY   Jerusalem ranks high on a world list of continuously inhabited cities. It was in existence long before it was first mentioned in Pharonic records of the 2nd millennium B.C., or in the Bible.

Genesis relates that Abraham visited Melchizedek, "king of Salem," one of the first known references to Jerusalem. However, for the next 800 years the city played no part in biblical or Jewish history. Then, in 1004 B.C., King David, the charismatic poet-warrior, captured Jerusalem, which was a small Jebusite/Canaanite city perched on a narrow hill just to the south of the present Old City walls. The city was considered neutral territory, situated on land not controlled by any of the 12 tribes of Israel, and seemed an ideal choice for a capital that would not exacerbate tribal rivalries. David brought the Ark of the Covenant to Jerusalem from his former capital, Hebron. On the Ophel, a stretch of ascending land between the settlement of Jerusalem and the high place that was to become the Temple Mount, David built his palace and declared that henceforth Jerusalem would be the capital.

Under the reign of David's son Solomon, Jerusalem grew in importance. It was the center of a brief-lived empire that stretched from southern Syria to the Gulf of Eilat. African ivory and gold, cedar from Lebanon, spices, textiles, and pottery from distant lands adorned its houses and were bargained for in its markets. The queen of Sheba came to Jerusalem with her entourage, bearing unimaginable treasures in exchange for Solomon's wisdom; tradition says she returned to her distant homeland (possibly in Africa) bearing his child. With the aid of Phoenician architects and artisans sent by his ally, King Hyram of Tyre, Solomon built the great Temple (960 B.C.) and constructed a more magnificent palace (although the Bible records the grandeur of Solomonic Jerusalem with awe, the city would actually have been a small, densely packed Early Iron Age settlement covering no more than several acres).

Under Solomon's visionless successors, the kingdom split in two: the larger kingdom of Israel to the north and the smaller kingdom of Judah to the south, with Jerusalem remaining the capital of small, struggling Judah.

The House of David continued to reign in Jerusalem for $3^1/_2$ centuries. Some of the Davidic rulers dispensed social justice and encouraged religious revivals under the influence of the great prophets; some of the kings turned to the worship of other gods. Invaders came and retreated. The northern kingdom of Israel, ruled by a succession of non-Davidic Jewish/Israelite dynasties, fell to Assyria in the late 8th century B.C. and vanished from history, its population dispersed throughout Assyria's great empire. The Assyrian armies then stormed across Judah, destroying its towns and cities.

Only Jerusalem was able to avoid defeat and destruction, thanks to one of the most miraculous and fateful engineering feats in history. An underground tunnel was dug in 701 B.C. by King Hezikiah (with the encouragement of the Prophet Isaiah) from inside the city's walls to Jerusalem's water source, the Gihon Spring, located in a valley outside the walls. The workers, digging from each end of the proposed tunnel, frantically hacked through the bedrock of Jerusalem in a wildly curving S-shaped route, somehow managing to meet, thereby creating underground access to the Gihon Spring (which was then camouflaged) before the dreaded Assyrians arrived to lay siege to the city. With its hidden water supply Jerusalem was able to withstand the Assyrian siege and was saved. The fragile beginnings of Western monotheism, precariously taking root in 8th-century B.C. Jerusalem, were not swept away into the dustbin of

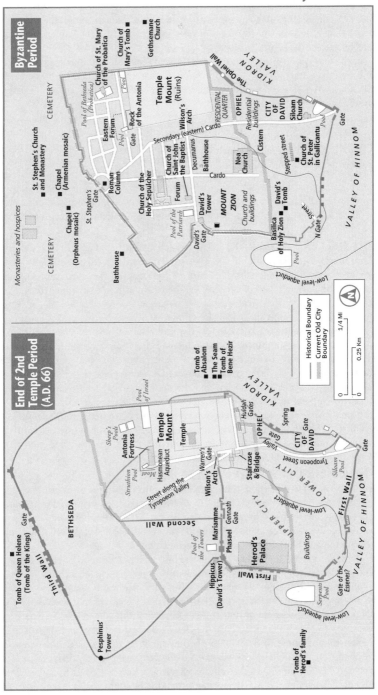

Historic Jerusalem

Byzantine Period

Monasteries and hospices

St. Stephen's Church and Monastery

Chapel (Armenian mosaic)

Chapel (Orpheus mosaic)

CEMETERY

St. Stephen's Gate

Bathhouse

Roman Column

Church of the Holy Sepulcher

Pool of the Patriarch

David's Gate

David's Tower

MOUNT ZION

Church of Saint John the Baptist

Forum

Decumanus

Cardo

Bathhouse

Nea Church

David's Tomb

Basilica of Holy Zion

Church and buildings

Secondary (eastern) Cardo

Wilson's Arch

Rock of the Antonia

Eastern Forum

Gate

Church of the Probatica

Church of St. Mary

Pool of Bethesda (Probatica)

Pool

CEMETERY

Church of Mary's Tomb

Gethsemane Church

Temple Mount (Ruins)

The Ophel Wall

KIDRON VALLEY

RESIDENTIAL QUARTER

Residential buildings

Cistern

Stepped street

Church of St. Peter in Gallicantu

OPHEL

CITY OF DAVID

Siloam Church

Gate

N Gate

Street

Pool

Low-level aqueduct

VALLEY OF HINNOM

End of 2nd Temple Period (A.D. 66)

Tomb of Queen Helene (Tomb of the Kings)

Gate

Third Wall

Psephinus' Tower

BETHSEDA

Pool of Israel

Sheep's Pools

Antonia Fortress

Struthion Pool

Moat

Hasmonean Aqueduct

Street along the Tyropoeon Valley

Second Wall

Pool of the Towers

Mariamme

Phasael

Hippicus (David's Tower)

First Wall

Gennath Gate

UPPER CITY

Herod's Palace

Buildings

Low-level aqueduct

Serpents Pool

Gate of the Essenes

Temple Mount

Temple

Warren's Gate

Wilson's Arch

Staircase & Bridge

LOWER CITY

Tyropoeon Street

Low-level aqueduct

First Wall

Tomb of Absalom

The Seam

Tomb of Bene Hezir

KIDRON VALLEY

Huldah Gates

OPHEL

Spring

CITY OF DAVID

Gate

Valley Gate

Siloam Pool

Gate

VALLEY OF HINNOM

Tomb of Herod's family

Historical Boundary

Current Old City Boundary

0 1/4 Mi

0 0.25 Km

history. Perhaps more than any other structure built by human beings, the water tunnel of King Hezikiah, which still exists today (see "East Jerusalem Attractions," chapter 4), changed the course of history.

In the next century, the messages of Isaiah and Jeremiah, and the religious reforms of King Josiah, strengthened Judean Judaism, so that unlike the religion of the Northern Kingdom of Israel, it would be able to survive both the defeats and exiles that lay ahead.

Jerusalem was conquered by the armies of Nebuchadnezzar, king of Babylon, who in 586 B.C. destroyed the temple, sacked the city, and carried most of Jerusalem's inhabitants into exile in Babylonia. But Babylonia soon fell to the Persians, and in 540 B.C. King Cyrus of Persia allowed the Jews to return to their homeland and rebuild a modest Second Temple. Only a small remnant of the exiles chose to leave what had become a comfortable, cosmopolitan Jewish community in Babylonia and resettle the ruins of Jerusalem. The next centuries were remarkably quiet, and it was during this period that many believe the core of postbiblical Jewish religion and tradition was created in Jerusalem.

THE HELLENISTIC PERIOD   The city fell under the domain of Alexander the Great in 331 B.C. Hellenistic rule later passed to the Syrian-based Seleucids, and it was against their attempts to forcibly Hellenize the Jews that the Maccabees, a priestly family from the Judean village of Mod'in, led their famous revolt between 167 and 141 B.C. The festival of Hanukkah marks the recapture and rededication of the temple during the revolt against the Seleucids.

For the next century, Jerusalem was the capital of an independent Jewish Commonwealth ruled by the increasingly Hellenized descendants of the Maccabees, the Hasmonean Dynasty. To some Jews, however, including those who gravitated toward the ascetic Essene sect, the legendary House of David remained the spiritual and eternal royal dynasty; the Hasmoneans and the priesthood they controlled were merely transient temporal authorities. In the minds of many Jews living 2,000 years ago, the dichotomy between the spiritual and earthly Jerusalem, nurtured through centuries of psalmists, prophets, and the Babylonian exile began to take on new, mystically intense meaning. This dichotomy, with its many interpretations, has remained part of the Western world's concept of Jerusalem into modern times.

THE ROMAN OCCUPATION   Pompey claimed Jerusalem for Rome in 63 B.C., and in 37 B.C. Herod (whose Idumaean father converted to Judaism) was appointed king of Judea by the Romans. Perhaps in an effort to make himself loved by his reluctant and resentful subjects, or to impress his Roman overseers with his industry, Herod rebuilt Jerusalem and designed a palatial temple area that dwarfed the original Temple of Solomon and replaced the less grand Second Temple.

Herod died in 4 B.C. The city that he had built, with its fortress, towers, aqueducts, and vast temple complex, was the Jerusalem that Jesus knew. Herod's great temple complex, initially opposed by many Jews who felt it was too Roman in its grandeur, became a symbol of Jewish national and religious aspirations and a constant flash point in Jewish opposition to Roman rule. As never before, the temple became a center for Jewish pilgrimage from Judea, the Galilee, Babylonia, Persia, and all parts of the Roman Empire; more than 100,000 pilgrims could be accommodated in Jerusalem during the great festivals of Passover and Sukkot. To a greater extent than ever, religion was Jerusalem's major industry, and it was increasingly big business. During this period, rabbinical Judaism was also developing, grounded in study, prayer, synagogue, and careful analysis of ethical and ritual rules governing Jews everywhere. This component of Judaism flourished alongside the priestly cult, which was centered on the temple in Jerusalem.

It was to the city that was a magnet for the ancient Jewish world that Jesus came to celebrate Passover, and it was in Jerusalem that under Pontius Pilate, the Roman procurator, Jesus was imprisoned and crucified. According to most Christian traditions, the Church of the Holy Sepulcher marks the site of the crucifixion and burial of Jesus, and the Via Dolorosa is the way Jesus trod, carrying the cross, from prison to Golgotha.

The Jewish rebellion against Roman rule in A.D. 66 drove the Roman occupiers from Jerusalem, and brought the Roman armies of Titus and Vespasian to reconquer Jerusalem. In A.D. 70, Rome starved out the population of Jerusalem, destroyed the city and its temple, and killed or sold into slavery most of its surviving inhabitants. The Roman Tenth Legion was stationed beside the ruins of the Jaffa Gate for more than 60 years to prevent Jews from filtering back and reestablishing their city.

There is evidence, however, that a small number of Jews and early Christians (who were considered to be a Jewish sect) may have continued to live in (or visit) the ruins of Mount Zion, where they provided services for the Tenth Legion's camp. Jews were permitted to visit Jerusalem during the years after the Roman destruction and were still able to identify the exact locations of specific holy sites among the ruins. Talmudic lore records that a group of rabbis walking on the Temple Mount noticed that a fox had made its lair in the wreckage of the Holy of Holies. Aging witnesses to Jesus' last days in Jerusalem would have been able to pass on their memories of where those events took place to a younger generation. Although the city was now desolate, the powerful charisma of Jerusalem continued to grow.

Bar Kokhba's revolt in A.D. 132, triggered by the decision of the Emperor Hadrian to rebuild Jerusalem as a non-Jewish Roman outpost, returned the ruined city to the Jews for 3 short years. The temple site was rededicated, though probably not rebuilt, and daily sacrifice was reinstated. The revolt ended in A.D. 135 with even greater military disaster for the Jews than the revolt of A.D. 70. According to some estimates, half a million civilians died in each of the revolts against Rome, numbers unheard of in ancient warfare. Hadrian leveled the ruins of Jerusalem, sowed the land with salt, and, with an entirely different city plan and arrangement of streets, built a Roman city called "Aelia Capitolina" in honor of the imperial family and the Roman god Jupiter Capitolina. Hadrian filled Aelia Capitolina with pagan temples and barred Jews from residing in the city for all time. Herod's vast Temple Mount platform, and its great retaining walls, too massive and still too politically sensitive to demolish, were among the few features from Herodian Jerusalem that remained. According to some historians, a Roman temple (or at least, an altar) may have been installed on the site of the Jerusalem temple itself. Jews were generally allowed into the city only to visit the ruins of the Temple Mount and only on the ninth day of the month of Av, the anniversary of the temple's destruction.

The building of Aelia Capitolina was an attempt to make Jerusalem into just another provincial city on the fringe of the Roman Empire. Today, you can still see elements from this alien interlude in Jerusalem's history, including a fragment of the colonnaded Cardo, Aelia Capitolina's main north-south thoroughfare, which was uncovered by archaeologists in the 1970s. The basic layout of the Old City, divided into quadrants

Impressions

Jerusalem: the city which miraculously transforms man into pilgrim; no one can enter it and remain unchanged.

—Elie Wiesel

Saints & Warriors: Caliph Omar & Saladin

Islamic forces have conquered Jerusalem twice: in A.D. 638, and again in 1187, when it was recaptured after 88 years of crusader rule. Both times, the warriors who won Jerusalem were among the most extraordinary men Islamic civilization has ever produced. In each case, Jerusalem was captured without resort to a final military onslaught, and in each case, although these leaders stayed only briefly in Jerusalem, their association with the city came to be regarded as the crowning triumphs of their lives.

Omar ibn el Khattab (d. 644), the second successor to the Prophet Muhammad, was a warrior of great saintliness who eschewed all luxuries and dressed in a simple rough-spun cloak. According to legend, when the Byzantine ambassador came to Medina to seek an audience with Caliph Omar, he was directed to a hill outside the city. There he found only a man alone, asleep on the ground under a palm tree, using his dusty sandals for a pillow. When the ambassador was told that this was the caliph, he responded, "Great Omar, you are truly a ruler of peace and justice unequaled to be able to go unprotected among your people in such a way."

Accepting the peaceful submission of Jerusalem from the Byzantine patriarch Sophronius in A.D. 638, Omar declined an invitation to pray in the Church of the Holy Sepulcher for fear that in future times, any place in which he had prayed would be turned into a mosque. According to tradition, the tolerant and visionary Omar permitted Jews to reside in Jerusalem again; initiated the cleaning of the Temple Mount, which had been used as a garbage dump for 300 years; and ordered the transformation of Jerusalem into an Islamic as well as a Jewish and Christian holy city. Omar's redemption of the Temple Mount as a holy place eventually led to the building of The Dome of the Rock, a lasting monument to his brief, radiant encounter with Jerusalem.

Saladin (1137–93), of Kurdish origin, was the sultan of Egypt, Syria, Yemen, and Palestine, founder of the Ayyubid Dynasty, and the most romantically heroic of all Islamic generals. Saladin's moral leadership and passion, rather than overwhelming tactical advantage brought his disparate forces to victory over the crusaders at the Horns of Hittin, near Tiberias, on July 4, 1187. Three months later, Jerusalem surrendered under Saladin's siege. In contrast to the massacre of Muslims and Jews that had accompanied the crusader conquest of Jerusalem in 1099, Saladin's victory was marked by chivalry and compassion. Native Christians were allowed to remain in the city; those of crusader origin were offered safe passage with their goods out of the country via Akko on payment of a ransom of 10 dinars each. As Saladin and his brother watched the wealthy, including the crusader patriarch and his retinue, depart with treasure-laden wagons, leaving thousands of unransomed poor to be sold into slavery, they announced a donation to ransom 7,000 poor Christians, thus shaming the patriarch into matching their generosity. In one of the many historical coincidences fraught with meaning to Jerusalemites, Saladin conquered the city on October 2, 1187, the anniversary of the Prophet Muhammed's Miraculous Night Journey from Mecca to Jerusalem, and his ascension from the Temple Mount to the heavens. The selfless Saladin, in the great tradition of early Islamic leaders such as Omar ibn el Khattab, eschewed personal possessions and died without even enough money to pay for his grave.

by perpendicular intersecting market streets leading from the Damascus and Jaffa gates, is inherited from this time, as is the Arabic name for Damascus Gate (Bab-el-Amud, or Gate of the Column), recalling a towering, long-lost column that once stood inside the gate to serve, in traditional Roman fashion, as a distance marker.

THE BYZANTINES   Jerusalem's 200-year stint as an ordinary town ended with the Emperor Constantine, who converted the Roman empire to Christianity and turned Jerusalem into a Christian holy city. He built the Church of the Holy Sepulcher in approximately A.D. 330, and the Byzantine emperor, Justinian, 200 years later, renovated and enlarged it. Jerusalem regained its ancient name, and again became an extraordinary destination for religious pilgrimage from all over the ancient world—this time by followers of a new religion. The city was filled with churches, monasteries, and convents, and daily religious processions. Jews were forbidden to reside in Byzantine Jerusalem, but the tradition, begun after the Bar Kochba Revolt in A.D. 135, of allowing Jews to visit the city and mourn the loss of the Temple, continued. At times, Jews were allowed only to view the city from the Mount of Olives.

ISLAM & THE CRUSADES   Caliph Omar, second successor to Muhammed, began the Muslim occupation of Jerusalem in A.D. 638. In the decades after his death, according to his wishes that the Temple Mount not lie in ruins, with its sacred rock exposed to the elements, Caliph Abd el-Malik built the masterpiece Dome of the Rock (A.D. 687–91) marking the spot from which the Prophet Muhammad, in his miraculous night journey, rose from the earth to glimpse Paradise. By A.D. 720, the Al Aksa Mosque, Islam's third holiest sanctuary, had been built at the southern edge of the Temple Mount. Under the tolerant rule of the early Muslims, Jews were allowed again to reside in Jerusalem and the Christian community continued to flourish.

Around the year A.D. 1000, the mad Caliph Al Hakim, ruling from Egypt, began a wave of anti-Christian persecution that culminated in the burning of the Church of the Holy Sepulcher. Feudal Europe responded with the Crusades, and in the wars that followed, the mystical concept of Jerusalem was burned more strongly than ever into the traditions of both Christianity and Islam. After the initial success of the First Crusade in 1099, Jerusalem changed hands several times between crusaders and Muslims (most notably under Saladin). The Crusader Church of Saint Anne (A.D. 1147), with its near miraculous acoustics, is Jerusalem's great architectural treasure from this era. Hundreds of architectural fragments from crusader buildings, in secondary use adorning Mameluke and Ottoman period buildings throughout the Old City, attest to the massive destruction inflicted on the city during these centuries. The entire Jewish population of Jerusalem was massacred when crusader armies captured the city in 1099, but by the year 1260, not long after the crusaders had been dislodged, a small Jewish community was reestablished. The Mamelukes, an Egyptian dynasty, added Jerusalem to their empire in 1244. Over the next two and a half centuries, Jerusalem was slowly filled with Mameluke mansions, religious buildings, and covered markets, all notable for tall, "stalactite"-ornamented doorways and careful stonework.

TURKISH RULE   In 1517, the Ottoman Turks, also Muslims, took control of Jerusalem. In an esthetic stroke of genius, the 16th-century Ottoman rulers faced the deteriorating exterior of the Dome of the Rock with dramatic cobalt blue and turquoise ceramic tiles from Persia and Anatolia. The Ottomans also rebuilt the magnificent walls around Jerusalem in 1538, but these largely ceremonial fortifications (gunpowder and cannon had made such defensive structures obsolete) surrounded a depopulated community devastated by centuries of crusader wars and struggling to survive. By the early 19th century, the city's population, estimated to have been close to 100,000 in Herodian times, had shrunk to less than 15,000. Only in the second half of the 19th century did the city begin to come alive again, with its Jewish, Christian, and Muslim communities spreading into neighborhoods beyond the walls of the Old City.

In the last decades of the 19th century, as the European powers vied for influence in this strategic portion of the floundering Ottoman Empire, each government planted its flag in Jerusalem under the guise of vast church-related construction projects. The number of monuments to European nationalism that date from this brief era is amazing. Germany's massive neo-Romanesque Dormition Church and Monastery on Mount Zion recalls Worms Cathedral overlooking the Rhine; the delicate, Renaissance-inspired Holy Trinity Church in the Russian Compound echoes the late 15th-century Cathedral of the Assumption in the Kremlin; St. George's Cathedral in East Jerusalem, completed in 1912, is an enclave of neo-Gothic Britain built from Jerusalem stone, with a bell tower and cloister that calls to mind an almost hallucinatory fragment of Magdalene College at Oxford. The exotically medieval Russian Church of Saint Mary Magdalene with its gilded onion-shaped domes transformed the vista of the Mount of Olives. Florentine, Ethiopian, and French architecture sprang up across the city in the form of hospitals, churches, convents, and pilgrimage facilities.

THE BRITISH ARRIVE   Turkish rule lasted exactly 400 years, until General Allenby marched through Jerusalem's Jaffa Gate at the head of a British regiment in the final year of World War I. Under the British Mandate (1918–48), the New City blossomed and much of downtown West Jerusalem took on its basic shape. Landmarks such as the YMCA, the King David Hotel, the Rockefeller Museum in East Jerusalem, the original Hadassah Hospital and Hebrew University on Mount Scopus, the art-moderne Central Post Office on Jaffa Road, Saint Andrew's Church near Abu Tor, and West Jerusalem's King George Street all stand as monuments to that era. The Rehavia neighborhood, with its streamlined buildings and curving balconies designed in the International Style by refugee architects from Germany, and the exotic mansions built for the city's leading Arabic families in the adjacent neighborhood of Talbeyeh, are also part of Jerusalem's British Mandate–era heritage.

TO THE PRESENT DAY   In November 1947, the United Nations voted to establish two states in Palestine: one Jewish, the other Arab. Jerusalem was to remain a united, international city, independent of either proposed state. In spite of this decision, by early 1948 the Jewish sector of Jerusalem found itself under siege by Arab forces and suffered shelling and bombardment for many weeks. Eventually, Israeli forces secured a narrow strip of mountainous land (the Burma Road), which connected the Jewish part of Jerusalem to the rest of Israel, and the siege was broken. The State of Israel was established in the 1948 War of Independence, but the cease-fire lines left Jerusalem split down the middle, from north to south, by a wall of concrete, barbed wire, and minefields. The modern western section of the city remained in Israeli hands, but the Old City, including the Jewish Quarter (from which all Jews had been expelled) and the modern Arab neighborhoods north of the Old City (along with the rest of West Bank), were annexed by the Kingdom of Jordan.

Impression

Jerusalem of gold, of copper, of light . . . To all your songs, I am the harp.
—Popular Israeli song

In the Six-Day War of 1967, East Jerusalem came under Israeli control and the city was reunited once again. But the distinctions left by two decades of division still remain: downtown East Jerusalem and the Old City are predominantly Palestinian (Christian and Muslim Arabs) and West Jerusalem is predominantly Israeli.

2 Orientation

ARRIVING

BY PLANE A reasonably priced way to get to Jerusalem from Ben-Gurion Airport is by **sherut,** a van shared by eight passengers with a fixed per-person rate. The current fare is NIS 42 ($9.50) per person, baggage included. The sherut stand, run by Nesher Taxi, is to the left as you exit the arrivals area of the terminal building. Confirm that the destination of the Nesher van is Jerusalem, give your luggage to the driver, and climb in. When all the seats are claimed, the van will take off. The driver must, without charging an extra *agora* (a single small-denomination coin), take you from the airport to the hotel or residential address of your choice anywhere in Jerusalem. If you're lucky, you'll be the first in your group to be dropped off at your destination. If not, you'll get to see a bit of the city. The **public Egged buses 945** or **947** (NIS 18 [$3.35]) provide the least expensive option and run from 6am to 10:30pm. Ground Information will direct you to the Jerusalem bus, which will take you to the Central Bus Station in West Jerusalem. From there, you can take a taxi or a municipal bus (NIS 5 [$1.10]) to your destination. The fixed-price rate for a **private taxi** is about $35 to $40. If you happen to have four people in your party (standard taxis take only up to four passengers), the cost for this most convenient option is really little more than that of a sherut. Agree on a definite price ahead of time. Taxi drivers do not expect tips, but if you have a number of heavy bags, the driver may quote a slightly higher fare. If your driver doesn't charge extra for help with bags, offer a 10-shekel ($2.20) tip. All major car-rental companies have offices at Ben-Gurion Airport.

For the return trip to the airport, your hotel will be glad to call in advance and make an appointment for a taxi or sherut to pick you up. If you want to make your sherut reservation in person, the office of **Nesher Taxis and Sheruts** (☎ **02/625-7227**), known for its extremely reliable airport service, is at the intersection of Ben-Yehuda Street and King George V Avenue in West Jerusalem, right across from the City Tower.

BY TRAIN At press time, train service to Jerusalem has been suspended. In the past, one or two trains a day from Tel Aviv arrive at Jerusalem's old **Ottoman Railroad Station.** The scenery as the train approaches Jerusalem is quite beautiful, but the scanty schedule can be a hassle. Municipal buses to all parts of Jerusalem leave from outside the Jerusalem Train Station. Downtown buses are across the street.

BY BUS Most buses arrive and depart from the **Central Bus Station,** which is at the western entrance to the city, right on Jaffa Road not far past the intersection with Herzl/Yirmiyahu Boulevard, and virtually across the street from Binyane Ha-Uma, Jerusalem's large convention center. *Note:* After depositing most passengers, Egged intercity buses from Tel Aviv and Haifa arriving in Jerusalem after 8pm generally continue down Jaffa Road to the center of town, making additional request stops along the way. The buses then stop at the corner of Agron Street and the beginning of King David Street, and at the corner of Agron Street and King George Street. Check with your bus driver: If you're going to the center of town, this is a convenient, free option.

However, if you are traveling by bus to Jerusalem from the south or east (Bethlehem, Hebron, or Jericho), your bus may arrive at the **East Jerusalem Bus Station** on Sultan Suleiman Street near the Damascus Gate, between Nablus Road and Saladin Street.

Note: As this edition goes to press, a **new Central Bus station** is under construction and a **temporary Central Bus station** has been set up on the south side of Jaffa Road, a quarter of a mile closer to the center of town, just west of Mahane Yehuda, Jerusalem's central vegetable market. During 2000, the new bus station may be in place. An information counter at the temporary Central Bus Station will direct you to the municipal bus you need for your destination inside Jerusalem.

BY CAR   Route 1 (Highway 1) is the main road to Jerusalem from Tel Aviv and Ben Gurion Airport; it runs right into Jaffa Road, downtown West Jerusalem's main street. Signs at the entrance of the city direct you to the downtown center, via a slightly circuitous route, since private cars are barred from the first few blocks of Jaffa Road, near the city entrance. If you're going to the Renaissance, Sheraton Four Points, or Paradise Hotels at the western edge of the city, follow signs for Herzl Blvd./Government Center.

From the Sea of Galilee, the Dead Sea, or Eilat and the Negev, the most direct route is Route 90, which follows the Jordan Valley. From Route 90, turn onto Route 1 just south of Jericho, and make the steep ascent up to Jerusalem. At the edge of the city, follow signs to the Center. This will take you to the northern walls of the Old City. Turn right if you're heading for the center of West Jerusalem, and left for East Jerusalem.

From Beersheva, it is best to avoid the West Bank, as Israeli rental cars are not insured for travel in the West Bank with the exception of Route 90, along the Jordan Valley, and Route 1 from Jericho up to Jerusalem. Drive to Kiryat Gat, and link up to Route 1 west of Jerusalem.

Parking is difficult in Jerusalem. Many hotels have very limited or no parking facilities. There are parking garages at Hillel and Yoel Solomon streets in downtown Jerusalem; outside Jafa Gate on Mamilla Street; and on Mamilla Street under the Hilton Hotel. It is much easier to use public transportation or taxis. The Old City is only accessible by foot.

All major **car-rental agencies** are clustered on two long blocks of King David Street, beginning at Mamilla Street.

VISITOR INFORMATION

There's a **Ministry of Tourism** information desk (☎ **03/971-1145**) in the Arrivals Hall of Ben-Gurion International Airport. The staff will provide city maps, brochures (which you must buy), and answer your questions. A hotel reservations desk nearby can also help you find a room for the night.

The **Municipal Tourist Information Office** (☎ **02/625-8844**) is on the right side of Safra Square, Jerusalem's Municipal Government Center at the end of Jaffa Road just west of the Old City. It's open Sunday to Thursday 9am to 4pm; Friday 9am to 12:30pm. Here you can pick up free tourist publications, travel information, lists of private rooms for rent, and advice on hotel rooms and tours.

In the Old City, there's a **Tourist Information Office** just inside Jaffa Gate, a few steps down on the left (☎ **02/628-0382**). At press time, the hours were Sunday to Thursday from 8am to 5pm; Friday from 8am to 1pm; in summer, there may be Saturday hours. This is a privately run office that sells maps and booklets, but there is a shelf with free tourist brochures. The Information Office will also rent a recorded walking tour of the Old City for NIS 40 ($8.80) per day plus a security deposit.

The **Christian Information Center** (☎ **02/627-2692**) at the far end of the square inside Jaffa Gate offers all kinds of useful information, including about tours, Christian hospices, and religious services. It's open Monday to Saturday 8:30am to 1pm.

If you're surfing the Web, the **Ministry of Tourism** is at www.infotour.co.il, and the **Municipality of Jerusalem** site is www.Jerusalem.muni.il.

MAPS & PUBLICATIONS   Maps of Jerusalem are available at the Tourist Information Office inside the Jaffa Gate and cost $3 to $5, depending on the type you choose. It also sells books on travel in Israel, but check your planned purchases carefully—I bought a book of Israeli road maps that was totally out of date (the office was kind enough to give me a refund). The office also offers a shelf of free pamphlets and information, including the always useful *Jerusalem Menus* publications, with their useful restaurant discount coupons. Most major hotels have a counter with a selection of free flyers and pamphlets, and reasonably good free maps. If your hotel doesn't have a good selection, check out the lobbies of other major hotels.

The *Jerusalem Post* has a daily listing of city events, but the Friday (weekend) edition is your best bet, with an exhaustive list of the week's activities throughout Israel. The *International Herald Tribune* contains the English-language edition of *Ha'aretz,* Israel's most respected newspaper. The Friday *Ha'aretz,* like the *Jerusalem Post,* contains a detailed section on events in Jerusalem and throughout the country. Another excellent source of information is the free monthly *Events in the Jerusalem Region,* prepared by the Tourist Office and available at the Municipal Tourism Information Offices and in hotel lobbies.

The free tourist newspaper *Your Jerusalem* contains the best bus directions in town. There are many small bookletlike free publications for visitors, ranging from *Hello Israel* to *Jerusalem Menus,* filled with current information and discount dining coupons, but keep in mind that the shopping and restaurant information in these magazines is paid advertising. At press time, the lively free student/backpacker newspapers distributed in hostels and at places like the Strudel Internet Cafe (11 Monbaz St., in the Russian Compound) have all ceased publication, but may be back again.

CITY LAYOUT

To get around Jerusalem easily, you must understand how the city grew. In the early 1800s, Jerusalem was still a walled medieval city—a tortuous maze with sewage running down the streets. After the mid–19th century, Christian pilgrims and Zionist settlers began to create neighborhoods outside the city walls. From 1948 to 1967, Jerusalem was further divided when modern West Jerusalem remained under Israeli jurisdiction while the Old City became part of the Kingdom of Jordan. Although the city has been united under Israeli control since 1967, Jerusalem is still three different cities in one: the Old City, the Israeli new city of West Jerusalem, and the Arab new city of East Jerusalem.

Due east of the Old City, the Kidron Valley lies between ancient Jerusalem and the Mount of Olives (*Et-Tur* in Arabic). On the slopes of the mount, facing the Old City, is the Garden of Gethsemane. Farther down the valley, south of the Old City walls, is the Arabic town of Silwan, where the earliest settlement of Jerusalem developed more than 5,000 years ago. This is where the Jerusalem of King David and King Solomon was located.

Neighborhoods in Brief

THE OLD CITY   The Old City is easily defined: It is the area still enclosed within the grand walls built by the Ottoman Turkish sultan, Suleiman the Magnificent, in 1538. The Old City is divided into four quarters: the **Muslim Quarter,** the **Christian Quarter,** the **Armenian Quarter,** and the **Jewish Quarter.** Seven gates provide access through the massive walls; two of these are important for the visitor. The **Jaffa Gate** (*Sha'ar Yafo* in Hebrew, *Bab el-Khalil* in Arabic), at the end of the Jaffa Road (*Derekh Yafo*), is the main access to the Old City from West Jerusalem. **Damascus Gate** (*Sha'ar Shechem* in Hebrew, *Bab el-Amud* in Arabic) is the main access from East Jerusalem (if you get lost in the Old City's labyrinthine alleys, just ask for either gate).

Except in the Jewish Quarter, the dominating motif here is Arab: The food is Arabic, the language is Arabic, and customs are Eastern.

WEST JERUSALEM   To the west and south of the Old City, this modern Israeli city is a huge area of residential, commercial, and industrial development punctuated by high-rise hotels and office towers. Extending far to the south and west, and encroaching on the east, the "New City" (as it's sometimes called) includes the Knesset and the government precinct on the western edge of town; one of Hebrew University's two large campuses; the Israel Museum; and, on a distant western hilltop, the Hadassah Medical Center. Broad avenues twist and turn along the tops of the Judean Hills to connect West Jerusalem's outlying quarters with the century-old downtown area.

Downtown West Jerusalem is centered on Zion Square (Kikar Ziyon), where Jaffa Road intersects with Ben-Yehuda Street. A few short blocks west of Zion Square is King George V Avenue (known as King George Street or Rehov Ha-Melekh George), which joins Ben-Yehuda and Jaffa Road to form a triangle. Many of the hotels, restaurants, and businesses of interest are in or near this triangle. **Ben-Yehuda Street** is now a bustling pedestrian mall filled with souvenir, jewelry, and Judaica shops, cafes, and places to grab a quick snack. Evenings, especially in good weather, Ben-Yehuda becomes a mecca for younger travelers and young Israelis. A quainter pedestrian mall network, centering on **Yoel Salomon Street,** runs off Zion Square at the foot of Ben-Yehuda Street. This area is known as Nahalat Shiva. It's renovation has transformed Jerusalem's evening ambience from that of a quiet mountain town to a lively, gregarious Mediterranean-style city where people like to stroll and rendezvous in cafes. This small enclave of old West Jerusalem is being preserved, but other 19th-century neighborhoods in West Jerusalem are slated for demolition and will be replaced by large office blocks.

EAST JERUSALEM   Not as modern and sprawling as the western part, East Jerusalem is nevertheless a bustling 20th-century cityscape lying north of the Old City. Its compact business, commercial, and hotel district starts right along the Old City's north wall on **Sultan Suleiman Street,** which runs from Damascus Gate to Herod's Gate, and then downhill to the Rockefeller Museum. **Nablus Road** (*Derekh Shechem* in Hebrew) runs northeast from Damascus Gate to the American Colony Hotel; **Saladin Street** (*Salah ad-Din* in Arabic), the area's chief shopping thoroughfare, starts at Herod's Gate and meets Nablus Road near the American Colony Hotel. The triangle formed by these streets encloses the heart of downtown East Jerusalem. This area is quiet at night, and is only beginning to recover economically from the years of the Intifada.

3 Getting Around

BY BUS   Here are some of the most important destinations, and the buses that take you there:

Abu Tor (and Railroad Station):	6, 7, 8, 21, 30, 48
American Colony (East Jerusalem):	23, 27

Bet Ha-Karem:	6, 14, 17, 18, 20, 21, 24, 27
Damascus Gate (Old City):	27
East Jerusalem:	23, 27, 99
Ein Kerem:	17
German Colony (South Jerusalem):	4, 14, 18, 24
Ge'ula Quarter:	3, 9, 39
Hadassah Hospital:	27
Israel Museum:	9, 17, 24
Jaffa Gate (Old City):	3, 19, 20, 30, 80, 99
Jewish Quarter (Old City):	1, 38
King George V Avenue	4, 7, 8, 9, 14, 31, 48
Mount Scopus:	9, 23, 26, 28
Mount Zion:	38
Railroad Station	6, 7, 8, 21, 30, 48
Yad VaShem:	13, 17, 18, 20, 23, 24, 27, 39, 40, 99
Zion Square:	6, 13, 15, 18, 20, 21

Bus drivers make change, sell single and multiple tickets and passes, and speak English.

A full-fare city bus ticket costs NIS 5 ($1.10). But if you ask the driver for a **kartisiya** (that's "kahr-tee-*see*-yah"), he'll sell you a pass good for 20 trips, plus one extra trip for free. You'll be amazed at how quickly you can use up a kartisiya. The pass is punched each time you board a bus. If two of you are traveling together, just tell the bus driver, "pamayim" (twice) as you hand him the kartisiya, and he'll punch two fares. Students pay reduced fares and can buy a special discount kartisiya as well.

There is a city bus station near Damascus Gate on Nablus Road for destinations in East Jerusalem and surrounding Arabic communities.

BY TAXI OR SHERUT   Sheruts travel the main bus route from Sederot Herzl to Jaffa Road and Zion Square on Shabbat; they charge a shekel per person more than standard bus fare. The trick is finding one with room and flagging it down. Private taxis will take you throughout the city and charge higher night and Shabbat rates. The standard initial drop is approximately NIS 10 ($2.20), but this rate is always rising. You have a right to ask that the meter (*ha-sha-on*) be turned on, or you can agree on a price before starting. Taxi drivers do not expect tips; at most, if your driver claims to have no change, round off the fare to the nearest shekel. Your driver may charge extra if he assists you with heavy baggage. If he doesn't do this, a tip of a few shekels may be warranted. Whether or not the meter is used, you may request a receipt (ka-ba-*lah*).

ON FOOT   Central Jerusalem and the Old City are compact and easy to walk. It is difficult to get to museums and the Knesset area at the Western side of town by foot, as distances are relatively far, and pedestrian facilities along the access roads are not good.

Fast Facts: Jerusalem

American Express   American Express International's office is at 19 Hillel St. (☎ **02/624-6933;** fax 02/623-1520). It's open Sunday to Thursday 9am to 5pm and Friday 9am to 1pm, and exchange rates here, especially for American Express traveler's checks, are relatively good and there is no commission charge; mail is held for American Express customers. Lost or stolen American Express traveler's checks can be reported 24 hours daily by calling toll free ☎ **1-800-943-8694.**

Area Code   The area code is 02.

Baby-Sitters   Ask at the front desk of your hotel.

Consulates   See "Fast Facts: Israel" in chapter 2.

Crime   See "Safety," below.

Currency Exchange   Banking hours are 8:30am to noon or 12:30pm; on Sunday, Tuesday, and Thursday also from 4 to 5pm. There are many banks on Ben-Yehuda Street, Jaffa Road, and King George V Avenue. **Money changers,** which are legal and offer slightly better rates than banks, will change money in less time with no commission. In East Jerusalem, a number of money-changer offices are on Saladin Street; in the Old City, these offices can be found inside Damascus and Jaffa gates; they are generally open daily from 9am to 5 or 6pm. In West Jerusalem, **Change Point,** a convenient money-changing office, has branches on the Ben-Yehuda Mall near Zion Square, open Sunday through Thursday from 9am to 8pm and on Friday from 9am to 1pm.

   ATMs connected to the CIRRUS/NYCE system can be found at Zion Square, and at the City Tower, corner of Ben-Yehuda Street and King George V Avenue.

Dentists/Doctors   Ask your hotel or consulate for a list of English-speaking doctors and dentists. For a centrally located, American-trained and -certified dentist, try Dr. Mat Weiner, 1 bar Kinora St. (☎ 02/567-1167), 2 blocks north of Jaffa Road. For Dental First Aid, call ☎ 02/625-4740. Open daily.

Drugstores   The *Jerusalem Post* lists under "General Assistance" the names and addresses of duty pharmacies that stay open nights and on the Sabbath.

Emergencies   To call the **police,** dial ☎ 100. Dial ☎ 101 for Magen David Adom (Red Shield of David), Israel's emergency first-aid **ambulance** service. Magen David Adom has a clinic in Romema, near the Central Bus Station, and also a mobile intensive-care unit (☎ 02/652-3133) on call 24 hours a day. For **medical emergencies** requiring hospitalization, dial ☎ 102.

Hospitals   Hospital emergency rooms are open daily, 24 hours. Bring your passport and have a means to pay the fees. In central Jerusalem: Bikur Holim Hospital, Straus Street near Jaffa Road (☎ 02/670-1111). At the western edge of the city: Sha'arei Tzedek Hospital, Sderot Herzl, Bayit Vegan (☎ 02/655-5111; emergency room ☎ 02/655-5508). For information on possible Blue Cross–Blue Shield coverage at Hadassah Hospital, Ein Kerem, call ☎ 02/677-6029.

Hot Lines   Helpline (Milev Center for Crisis Counseling) (☎ 02/654-1111) offers English speaking counselors for all problems and age groups. You can call the Jerusalem Rape Crisis Center at ☎ 02/625-5558 daily, 24 hours. The Mental Health Hotline (Eran) can be reached at ☎ 02/561-0303 from 8am to 11pm; if this office is closed, call ☎ 03/523-4819 in Tel Aviv. English is spoken, and visitors are welcome to call.

Libraries   The American Cultural Center Library (☎ 02/625-5755) is on Keren Hayesod Street on the block between Agron Street and the Sheraton Moriah Hotel, open Sunday through Thursday from 10am to 4pm. The British Council Library (☎ 02/628-2545) is on Nablus Road next to the East Jerusalem YMCA.

Liquor Laws   East Jerusalem is largely Muslim; Islamic law forbids the use of alcohol. Drinks are served in hotels that cater to Western visitors, but unless an East Jerusalem or Old City restaurant offers a wine list with its menu, assume that alcohol is not available. Do not attempt to drink outdoors or in public places in East Jerusalem or the Old City.

Lost Property   Unattended objects stand a good chance of being zapped by the bomb squad. Check with the local police, and try to retrace your steps.

Luggage/Storage Lockers   Bags are best stored at your hotel. Be prepared for a security check before storing.

Newspapers/Magazines   In addition to *The Jerusalem Post* and the *International Herald Tribune* (see "Maps & Publications," above) the twice-monthly *Jerusalem Report* magazine has become Israel's English-language answer to *Time* and *Newsweek. Eretz* magazine, beautifully written and photographed, focuses on nature, history, and travel in Israel.

Photographic Needs   The downtown King George Street/Ben-Yehuda area abounds with 1-hour photo-developing shops. Prices are comparable to nondiscount developing in the United States. To avoid X-ray problems at the airport, it's a good idea to develop film before leaving Israel. Photo Prisma at 44 Jaffa Rd. (☎ **02/623-4796**), just across from Zion Square, has an English-speaking staff and a good reputation for stocking fresh film. For fast developing, Take One on Ben Hillel St. between Ben Yehuda and Shamai streets is a good, middle-price-range choice.

Police   Dial ☎ **100.** Border police in military uniforms carrying highly visible weaponry patrol Ben-Yehuda Mall and other central areas. (They fine jaywalkers.)

Post Office   Jerusalem's Central Post Office (☎ **02/624-4745**) is at 23 Jaffa Rd., near the intersection with Shlomzion Ha-Malka Street. General hours for all services are Sunday to Thursday from 7am to 7pm; limited services (telephone and telegraph) are open nights and on the Sabbath. East Jerusalem had its own main post office, which is now a branch, opposite Herod's Gate at the corner of Saladin Ibn Sina and Sultan Suleiman streets.

In the Old City, the post office is a few steps from Jaffa Gate, up past the Citadel of David and next to the gate of the Christ Church Anglican Hospice. A branch in West Jerusalem is on Keren Kayemet Street half a block from the corner with King George V and the Jewish Agency.

Radio   News in English is on Israel Radio at 7am, 1pm, 5pm, and on AM 575, 1170, and 1458 kHz.

Religious Services   The Christian Information Center (P.O. Box 14308; ☎ **02/62-2692**), inside Jaffa Gate on Omar Ibn El-Khattab Square near the Christ Church Hospice and opposite the entrance to the Tower of David, has a list of all Christian services. The center is open Monday through Saturday from 8:30am to 1pm; closed Sunday and holidays. *This Week in Jerusalem,* available free at major hotels, lists Reform, Conservative, and Orthodox Jewish synagogues.

Rest Rooms   In the Old City, signs read "WC" or "OO," and indicate public rest rooms. In West Jerusalem, restaurants and cafes are the best option.

Safety   Jerusalem is a low-crime city, but be aware of pickpockets in the crowd crushes of the Old City and avoid the deserted bazaars after dark. While political demonstrations in West Jerusalem are passionate but usually safe, it is advisable to avoid demonstrations in East Jerusalem or in the Old City. Keep alert at all times. Get away from and report any unattended or suspicious object immediately.

Telegrams/Telex/Fax   There are telex and fax services at the Central Post Office, 23 Jaffa Rd. Inside the Old City, the Bookshelf, Jewish Quarter Road (☎ **02/626-0473;** fax 02/627-3889), offers excellent fax service and will even notify you after hours about any fax responses you may receive. For telegrams, dial ☎ **171.**

Telephones   See "Fast Facts: Israel" in chapter 2.

4 Where to Stay

Israel has tons of five-star hotels, but inexpensive and moderately priced hotels are in short supply, especially in Jerusalem. There are a few hotels with atmosphere and ambience in every price category, but most choices are internationally generic and bland.

A number of hotels listed here can be booked as part of El Al, Tower Air, or other packages, or through discounters, at substantially lower prices. Especially in off-seasons, there are discounts to be found in all price categories if you plan ahead through a good travel agent. Jerusalem's hotels are busiest at Passover and Easter, in September or October during the Jewish High Holidays (Rosh Hashanah, Yom Kippur, Sukkot, Simchat Torah), and at Christmas. Many hotels consider July and August regular season. *Note:* All official hotel prices are quoted in U.S. dollars. Foreign travelers are expected to pay by credit card or foreign cash; if they pay the equivalent amount in shekels, they must also pay an additional value-added tax (VAT) of 17%.

An interesting alternative to a hotel is a bed-and-breakfast accommodation in a private home or apartment. Prices are considerably lower than hotels, and you have the chance to experience the lifestyle of one of the city's many unusual neighborhoods. Hosts are often senior citizens with lovely, spacious (by Israeli standards) homes, and a genuine interest in working with visitors from abroad.

A room in an apartment that has its own private bathroom should be about $40 for a single and $60 for a double, with breakfast and service included. A small studio or private flat would be about $50 for a single and $70 for two people; really unusual places, with private entrances, gardens, views, or especially nice decor could be about $60 for a single and $85 for two.

Good Morning Jerusalem, 9 Koresh St., Jerusalem 94146 (☎ **02/623-3459;** fax 02/625-9330, e-mail: gmjer@netvision.net.il), is a bed-and-breakfast and holiday apartment rental agency. With listings elsewhere in Israel as well as in Jerusalem, they will reserve accommodations for you and try to match your requirements regarding noise, neighborhood, kashruth, and so on, to the listings they have available. (The office cannot vouch for the kashruth standards of any particular household, and accepts the claims of its participating hosts.) The office is open Sunday to Thursday from 9am to 5pm and Friday from 9am to 1:30pm. It is often possible for a tourist arriving at Ben-Gurion Airport to call and arrange for accommodations that night, but obviously, it is best to reserve ahead of time. With advance notice, the office can make arrangements to meet nighttime arrivals.

Home Accommodation Association of Israel (www.bnb-jerusalem.co.il; e-mail: hq@bnb-jerusalem.co.il) is an affiliation of home owners, many with very unusual properties and locations and provides a similar service. **Home Hospitality** (☎ **02/ 645-2198;** www.bnb.co.il), is another choice. Try all three before making a decision.

Rehavia Real Estate (☎ **02/623-2604;** fax 02/625-2519; e-mail: eshel02@ netvision.net.il) arranges short-term rentals of apartments ranging from simple studios to beautiful private houses. Studios range from $500 to $800 a month; one-bedroom apartments begin at about $1,300 a month.

The Association for Promotion of Home Accommodations (☎ 02/531-9944; fax 02/532-2929) is an organization of private home owners in the B&B market; a bedroom or studio accommodation can start as low as $40 a day in winter, or $50 a day in summer. There are reduced rates for longer stays. Contact Dan Tamir.

If you are interested in renting an apartment, keep an eye out for posters in store windows and read the classified section of the *Jerusalem Post*. You can also reserve an entire flat for yourself (rate is according to number of people; 1-week minimum stay) from Good Morning Jerusalem through the **Israel Tourism Center,** or **ITC** (☎ 888/ 669-5700 or 201/556-9669 in the U.S. and Canada; e-mail: israelhotels@ worldnet.att.net.). There is a $25 to $35 fee for this service, but you save on overseas phone bills and can discuss the neighborhood and kind of flat you would like.

Other alternatives are to stay in a Christian hospice or at the YMCA. Hospices were originally built to accommodate the pilgrims and tourists that began to arrive in great numbers in the 1880s. Many are housed in atmospheric 19th-century buildings with evocative Jerusalem architecture and style. They are open to travelers of all faiths and offer comfortable private rooms with bathrooms. Hostels also offer private rooms and good services in interesting surroundings.

THE OLD CITY

The advantage to staying in the Old City is that you feel the rhythms and hear the sounds of this extraordinary (largely car-free) place—the calls to prayer from the minarets, the medley of bells from the city's ancient churches. You'll watch the bazaars come to life in the morning and slowly close down for the night; you'll catch glimpses of street life that a visitor based in the New City would never see. You won't come across any high-rise (or even low-rise) luxury palaces in the Old City, just a few inexpensive to moderately priced hotels, hospices, and hostels. The crime rate in the Old City, as in all of Jerusalem, is low, but the streets here (except for parts of the Jewish Quarter) are deserted at night and can seem intimidating. You'll need a spirit of adventure and an enjoyment of labyrinths and Casbah-like alleyways in order for this to be the right part of town for your base.

NEAR JAFFA GATE
Inexpensive
Christ Church Guest House. Jaffa Gate (P.O. Box 14037), Jerusalem 91140. ☎ **02/ 627-7727.** Fax 02/627-7730. E-mail: christch@netvision.net.il. $46–$51 per person in double; 50% discount for child under 13 in double with one parent. Rates include breakfast and service. MC, V.

This is one of the best-located hospices, situated just inside the Jaffa Gate, next to the post office and across from the entrance to Tower of David. Through the big iron gates you'll find a flagstone courtyard with trees and benches, a century-old English-style church that now houses a Protestant/Messianic congregation, and single, double, and triple rooms with private baths in a series of beautifully maintained 19th-century buildings. The gates to Christ Church Guest House close at 11pm, and stay locked until 6am, except by special arrangement. As with most good guest houses, this one is heavily booked during the summer months and at Christian holidays—best to reserve in advance for those times. Meals cost $13 extra for lunch and dinner. This establishment also runs the nearby inexpensive Coffee Shop and organizes tours and lectures oriented toward the Protestant Messianic movement; however those guests who are not evangelical are under no pressure to join. A protected parking area is an added feature, although the management cannot take responsibility for cars parked there.

Gloria Hotel. Latin Patriarchate St. (P.O. Box 14070), Jerusalem. ☎ **02/628-2431.** Fax 02/628-2401. 94 units. A/C TEL. $80–$100 double. Discounts in off-season. Add $15 per person for Christmas and Easter. Rates include breakfast and service. AE, V. Limited free parking. About 80 feet inside Jaffa Gate, turn left on Latin Patriarchate Street; hotel is on the right. Bus: 20.

The three-star–equivalent Gloria is moderately priced, considering its location and modern facilities. The entrance is up a flight of steps; from there an elevator takes you up one more level to the hotel desk, where an English-speaking clerk awaits you. The lobby is spacious but simple, with lots of Jerusalem stone and a scattering of local crafts as decorative touches. The rooms, which were renovated in 1987, are relatively large and quiet and have either twin or double beds, and central heating. The dining room, where you'll find the breakfast buffet, overlooks the Tower of David and West Jerusalem. In 1999, a new 22-room annex was added across the street from the main building; ask to see these new rooms before deciding which you prefer. Small amenities may not be available, but the Old City ambience, good management, and excellent location are big pluses.

✪ **Saint Mark's Lutheran Guest House.** Saint Mark's Rd. (P.O. Box 14051), Old City, Jerusalem. ☎ **02/628-5105.** Fax 02/628-5107. E-mail: luthhosp@netvision.net.il. 23 units (all with bathroom or shower). TEL. High season (Easter/spring, fall, and Christmas) $80–$90 double. Regular season (June 16–Sept 14 and winter except Christmas) $78–$83 double. Prices depend on rate of exchange between U.S. dollar and German mark. Rates include breakfast. No credit cards. Bus: 20 to Jaffa Gate.

The most beautiful, atmospheric, and well-run hotel in the Old City (and perhaps all Jerusalem), this German Lutheran guest house occupies a series of lovely restored stone buildings and terraced gardens overlooking the main bazaar, just a 5-minute walk from Jaffa Gate. The location, close to the heart of the Old City, allows guests to experience the atmosphere inside the Old City walls from a secluded oasis. Rooms are simply furnished but comfortable and have small refrigerators; bathrooms are modern. Coffee and tea are available to guests. The site is shared by, but separated from, the Evangelical Lutheran Hostel. Although this part of the Old City, bordering the restored Jewish Quarter and the Jaffa Gate, is quite safe, a slight drawback for the less adventurous might be the idea of walking to the guest house at night. The staff of Saint Mark's is very welcoming to visitors from all countries and backgrounds. Call for directions before going and arrange for a porter to meet you.

NEAR DAMASCUS GATE
Inexpensive
✪ **Austrian Hospice.** 37 Via Dolorosa (P.O. Box 19600), Jerusalem 91194. ☎ **02/627-4636.** Fax 02/627-1472. 34 private units with bathrooms, plus dormitory facilities. $80–$95 double. Rates include breakfast. No credit cards.

This massive complex located in the Muslim Quarter, between the Damascus and Lions's Gates, was built in 1857, and served as a hospital from 1948 to 1985. Only in recent years was it restored to its original use as a hostel for pilgrims and visitors to Jerusalem. Beautifully managed and renovated, the Austrian Hospice's gardens, terraces, fabulous rooftop vistas of the Old City, careful security, and dedicated staff are all real pluses. The feeling here is quiet but friendly, with visitors from all backgrounds welcome. Rooms are furnished simply but are comfortable and heated in winter. Inexpensive dorms are down in the basement. A coffee shop on the premises is open through the evening and serves light meals; half-board is available for $5 per person. Call ahead for information on **wheelchair access** (unusual in the Old City). Curfew is 10pm; but late permission can be obtained.

Dollar Rates

Hotel rates in this book are quoted in dollars only, as few hotels are willing to provide room rates in shekels. Hotel bills paid in foreign currency are not subject to 17% VAT.

WEST JERUSALEM

The Zion Square/Ben-Yehuda Mall area is the place to stay if you want to be in the midst of the city's lively restaurants, cafes, and bars, and in an area where you can stroll, shop, and people watch in the evenings. A number of hotel choices are a few blocks further south, in the King George Street/King David Street triangle, within walking distance or a short bus ride of Zion Square. Farther south you'll find a number of pleasant hotels in the interesting neighborhoods of Abu Tor and the German Colony (you'll need a bus or taxi to get to Zion Square). The outlying Bus Station/Sderot Herzl area on the western side of town is the fourth major West Jerusalem hotel area. It can be a 20-minute or more bus ride into Zion Square from this area, and you'll need a taxi on the Sabbath; the better hotels offer shuttle service into town.

ZION SQUARE, JAFFA ROAD & BEN-YEHUDA MALL

Step out of your hotel and you'll be right in the heart of the downtown shopping and restaurant district, with a great variety of cafes, window-shopping, and people-watching possibilities. The area is noisy, and in summer, discos add to the roar of traffic. There is one luxury hotel here; the rest are moderate and inexpensive choices.

Expensive

Dan Pearl Jerusalem. Zahal Square, Jerusalem. ☎ **02/622-6666;** 800/223-7773 reservations from the U.S. Fax 02/622-6649. E-mail: danhtls@danhotels.co.il. 86 units. A/C TV TEL. $276 double; standard suites up to $575 double, breakfast included. Add $65 per standard room Passover, Sukkot, and Christmas. AE, DC, MC, V. Fee parking available. Bus: 19, 20.

Completed in 1996, this sparkling new, well-designed three-story addition to the Dan Chain has been fitted into a small triangle of land less than 100 feet from the walls of the Old City. In terms of luxury, this hotel is a notch below the nearby King David, but rooms here are fresh and interestingly designed, with blonde contemporary furniture, and curving veneer and stone walls that add a sense of spaciousness. The standard suites, with living room, bedroom, two bathrooms, and kitchenette are good possibilities for families; children under 18 accompanied by one adult are $10 per night. Because the hotel is not higher than the Old City's walls, rooms with the more expensive Old City view essentially face out onto a busy road and a stark wall. Sound insulation is good if windows are closed.

Dining: Restaurant and cafe.

Amenities: Indoor pool, sauna and steam room, synagogue and *mikvah,* shops, business center, 24-hour room service, concierge, travel desk.

Moderate

Haneviim 54 Inn. 54 Haneviim St., Jerusalem. ☎ **02/624-7432.** Fax 02/624-7263. 18 units. A/C MINIBAR TV TEL. $100–$120 double. Rates include breakfast. AE, MC, V. Fee parking available.

At press time still under construction (opening in summer 2000), this inn set in an old, sprawling stone mansion looked too good to leave out of this edition. Each room will be different, but all will be on par with good hotel standards—spacious, with new bathrooms and tasteful decor. The management also runs the excellent Haneviim 54 restaurant complex downstairs; breakfasts should be top rate. The location, 2 blocks from bustling Zion Square, yet a stone's throw from quiet 19th-century enclaves like Ethiopia Street and Mea Shearim, is unique, and the ambience is intriguing. Restaurant noise may be a problem, but the rooms are located behind thick walls, in various wings of the house. Worth faxing for current information.

✪ **Jerusalem Tower Hotel.** 33 Hillel St., Jerusalem. ☎ **02/620-9209.** Fax 02/625-2167. E-mail: jth@isracom.net.il. 120 units. A/C TV TEL. $136–$150 double; lower rates on El Al Sunsational 5-Night Package. Rates include breakfast. AE, DC, MC, V. Fee parking available. Bus: 18, 20, and all buses to Zion Square.

This modern upper moderate–range hotel is a comfortable place to stay. You enter through a small lobby on the ground floor of an office tower 2 short blocks from Zion Square; rooms are on the upper floors of the building and many offer sweeping views (try to get a room facing the Old City). Rooms are compact but modern and well planned, equipped with radios as well as TVs, and decorated with a colorful wall of patchwork design that frames an arabesque arch above the beds; the upper floors are well buffered against the city's street noise. Public areas are recently refurbished. Baby-sitting, laundry, and room service are offered. The 5-night El Al Sunsational Package makes this great location affordable for almost everyone; specify that you want this downtown location rather than other choices in the package.

Lev Yerushalayim Suite Hotel. 18 King George St., Jerusalem. ☎ **02/530-0333.** Fax 02/623-2432. 50 suites. A/C TV TEL. $155–$185 double plus 15% service. July, Aug, Jewish and Christian holidays $235–$275. Rates include breakfast. AE, DC, MC, V. Bus: 4, 7, 9, 14.

Lev Yerushalayim means "heart of Jerusalem," and this glistening, relatively new tower complex is indeed located in the heart of West Jerusalem, right across the street from the intersection of King George Street and the Ben-Yehuda Mall. The pleasant suites consist of a contemporary living room/kitchenette and bedroom freshly decorated in soft colors and soundproofed against the roar of downtown traffic. The suites are a good choice for families; extra sleeping space is available on convertible living-room sofas, with a surcharge of $15 per night for each additional guest. Fully equipped kitchenettes include a microwave oven. A self-service Laundromat and fitness center in the complex are available to hotel guests. There are discounts for stays of over 7 days.

✪ **Notre Dame Guest House.** P.O. Box 20531, Jerusalem. ☎ **02/627-9111.** Fax 02/627-1995. 150 units. A/C TEL. $96–$108 double. Rates include breakfast. No credit cards. Bus: 19, 20. On Paratrooper's Rd., opposite New Gate.

Located in a beautifully restored landmark just steps away from the walls of the Old City, convenient to Israeli as well as Arab municipal bus routes, the massive Notre Dame complex is a center for Roman Catholic institutions and pilgrim groups, but all travelers seeking a tranquil atmosphere with expertly managed three-star accommodations are welcome. Public areas are spacious, with Jerusalem stone architecture; rooms are simple but comfortable, and many share a terrace balcony. All have a bathroom or shower. A coffee shop, open daily from 9am to 11pm, serves light, cheap meals. La Rotisserie, a luxury restaurant patronized by savvy Jerusalemites, is also on the premises. Laundry and dry-cleaning services are available.

The hotel is at the end of Jaffa Road, across from the walls of the Old City, a block east of the Municipality Center at Safra Square.

Zion Square Hotel. 25 Shammai St., Jerusalem. ☎ **02/624-4644.** Fax 02/624-4136. 120 units. A/C TV TEL. $160 double; 20% to 30% discount Jan 10–Feb 28, June–Sept, Nov 1–Dec 7. AE, DC, MC, V. All buses to Zion Square.

Accommodations in Downtown West Jerusalem

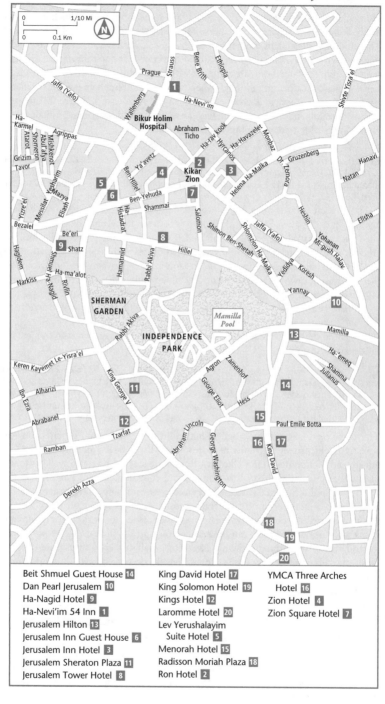

Beit Shmuel Guest House **14**	King David Hotel **17**	YMCA Three Arches
Dan Pearl Jerusalem **10**	King Solomon Hotel **19**	Hotel **16**
Ha-Nagid Hotel **9**	Kings Hotel **12**	Zion Hotel **4**
Ha-Nevi'im 54 Inn **1**	Laromme Hotel **20**	Zion Square Hotel **7**
Jerusalem Hilton **13**	Lev Yerushalayim	
Jerusalem Inn Guest House **6**	Suite Hotel **5**	
Jerusalem Inn Hotel **3**	Menorah Hotel **15**	
Jerusalem Sheraton Plaza **11**	Radisson Moriah Plaza **18**	
Jerusalem Tower Hotel **8**	Ron Hotel **2**	

Housed on the upper floors of a massive 1980s stone office tower, this hotel is liter-ally built over Zion Square, at the intersection of Jaffa Road and the Ben-Yehuda Mall. The modern, rather plain rooms have double-glazed windows that keep street noise down—even so, the noise from the Zion Square crowds at night may make this loca-tion impossible. Many rooms are equipped with small refrigerators; TVs receive CNN. Some rooms are extralarge, although when rented as doubles there is no extra charge; try for these more spacious accommodations. The hotel caters largely to European groups; a health club in the building with an exercise room, sauna, and indoor heated swimming pool is available to hotel guests for a fee.

Inexpensive

✪ **Jerusalem Inn Guest House.** 6 Ha-Histadrut St., Jerusalem. ☎ **02/625-1294.** Fax 02/625-1297. E-mail: jerinn@netvision.net.il. 13 units; 4 with private bathrooms; 9 with shared bathrooms. $45–$54 double. Visa only for payment; other cards accepted for reserva-tions. Bus: 4, 7, 9, 14.

Centrally located on a quiet street just off both King George Street and the Ben-Yehuda Mall, this guest house bridges the gap between hostel and budget hotel. Affil-iated with the sparkling Jerusalem Inn Hotel, the guest house is spotlessly clean and efficiently run. There are four newly renovated rooms with new private bathrooms, two of which have especially nice decor, air-conditioning, private safes, and are among the best deals in town: Ask about them. The nine rooms with shared bathrooms come in different sizes and are great low-budget choices. All rooms have satellite TVs, fans, voice mail, and free local calls. Breakfast can be arranged at additional charge at the Achva Cafe in the Jerusalem Inn Hotel.

The entrance to Ha-Histadrut Street is off King George Street across from Hamash-bir department store.

✪ **Jerusalem Inn Hotel.** 7 Hyrcanos St., Jerusalem. ☎ **02/625-2757.** E-mail: jerinn@netvision.net.il. 15 units. A/C TV TEL. $68–$86 double; 15% higher holidays and high season, which includes July–Aug. Breakfast $5 extra. Visa only for payment; other cards accepted for reservations. On Jaffa Rd., coming from Zion Square, turn left on Helena Ha-Malka St., then left on Hyrcanos. Bus: 18, 20 and all buses to Zion Square.

This is the best, brightest little budget hotel in town. The location is perfection—on a relatively quiet street, a lengthy block from Jaffa Road, it's a 3-minute walk to Zion Square and 10 minutes to the Old City. Rooms are reached by stairway: They're well planned, airy (most with small balconies), and contain amenities like digital safes, voice mail, and refrigerators. Rooms are decorated with framed art posters and fur-nished with comfortably firm beds (high-density foam mattresses on heavy wooden slat frames especially designed by the hotel's owner). Good for both family groups and single travelers, larger rooms can be arranged for up to four or even five people. All rooms have private bathrooms with glass enclosed stall showers (in this price category, most other hotels offer only shower sprays that flood your entire bathroom). Unlike many hotels in this price range, the Jerusalem Inn is geared totally to foreign visitors and doesn't rent rooms by the hour. For a surcharge, you can arrange breakfast at the hotel's Achva Cafe.

Menorah-Ron Hotel. 44 Jaffa Rd., Jerusalem 94222. ☎ **02/625-3311.** Fax 02/625-3313. 22 units. A/C TV TEL. $75 double. AE, MC, V. Bus: 5, 6, 13, 20, or 21 to Zion Square.

The grand doorway here, just across Jaffa Road from Zion Square, provides a small touch of old-fashioned elegance to an otherwise rather basic, functional hotel. Through its gracious portal is a tiny registration booth; up a long flight of steps are modern rooms with radiators for winter days. All but one have showers only in the

> ## ⓘ Family-Friendly Hotels
>
> To keep the little ones busy, try **Ramat Rachel** *(see page 88)*, at Kibbutz Ramat Rachel (at the southern end of the number 7 bus line), which offers a big pool and playground facilities. The **Mount Zion Hotel** *(see page 87)* has a roomy pool (visited by interesting local families with kids), and a number of its rooms are extra large and can accommodate families.
>
> **Lev Yerushalayim** *(see page 78)*, right in the center of town, is a suite hotel—all rooms include a kitchenette, and living areas containing couches that convert into beds. In the luxury category, the alcove rooms at the new **Jerusalem Hilton** *(see below)* offer extra space for families planning to bunk together; at the **Dan Pearl** *(see page 77)*, right next to the walls of the Old City, many rooms are actually suites with a separate bedroom. Both the Dan Pearl and the **Laromme Hotel** *(see page 83)* offer year-round swimming.

bathrooms. The sound of traffic on Jaffa Road and music from Zion Square at night can be a problem for some travelers, despite the insulated windows.

Zion Hotel. 10 Dorot Rishonim St., Jerusalem. ☎ **02/623-2367.** Fax 02/625-7585. 26 units. A/C TV TEL. $78–$96 double. Rates include breakfast. AE, DC, MC, V. Bus: all buses to Zion Square.

Half a block from Zion Square and Jaffa Road, set among the cafe- and restaurant-lined pedestrian streets of the Ben-Yehuda Mall, the veteran Zion Hotel was completely renovated in the mid-1990s. The result is a small centrally located hotel choice with public areas and rooms that show a bit of old Jerusalem architecture. Rooms are small, but recently decorated, with completely remodeled bathrooms; each has a shower or bathtub. Service is friendly, but, as with most moderately priced hotels, laid-back. Street noise from Ben-Yehuda Mall may be something to consider.

KING GEORGE STREET & KING DAVID STREET

A few blocks away from the Ben-Yehuda/Zion Square triangle is a group of hotels spread out along the southern reaches of King George Street, which becomes Keren Hayesod Street. About half a mile from Zion Square, Keren Heyesod runs into King David Street, and another cluster of hotels. The distance to Zion Square from most of these hotels is walkable, but in the hot sun or after a hard day's touring, many will want to take a bus or taxi. Nearby are Liberty Bell Park, Yemin Moshe, and the Cinémathèque, with its hillside of neighboring cafes and restaurants.

Very Expensive

✪ Jerusalem Hilton. 7 King David St. ☎ **02/621-1111** or (800/HILTONS for reservations in the U.S. and Canada). Fax 02/621-1000. E-mail: h_center@netvision.net.il. 384 units. A/C MINIBAR TV TEL. $310–$395 double. AE, DC, MC, V. Bus: 6, 18, 21.

This is the newest (1998) luxury hotel in Jerusalem, with only the nearby King David Hotel as its rival. Located on the corner of a busy intersection, the Hilton does not have the tranquil buffering gardens of the King David, but unlike other new hotels in town, it has a distinctive architectural style and a fabulously convenient location complete with views of the Old City. Rooms are the last word in comfortable design, all done in calm, pale beiges and natural textiles combined with sleek, elegant furnishings. Almost all have views of the Old City, and offer many extra amenities, including bathrooms containing both tubs and separate stall showers. Deluxe rooms, rooms with extra alcoves, and suites are available at higher rates. There are no-smoking rooms and rooms for travelers with disabilities. Israel's special Ahava Dead Sea soaps, shampoo, and cosmetics are used in all rooms.

Dining/Diversions: Hilton Hotels has invested carefully in the Jerusalem Hilton's in-house food and dining options, including the exceptional Le Divellec French restaurant (see "Where to Dine," below), and the beautifully appointed Sushi Bar. There are a variety of kosher dining facilities, a lobby bar, lounge, and pool restaurant.

Amenities: Heated outdoor pool, children's pool, state-of-the-art Cybex health club and spa with variety of massage and treatment programs, sauna, steam room, synagogue, shopping arcade, hairdresser, business center, executive floors and lounge, concierge, travel desk, 24-hour room service.

✪ **King David Hotel.** 23 King David St., Jerusalem 94101. ☎ **02/620-8888.** Fax 02/620-8882. E-mail: danhtls@danhotels.co.il. 237 units. A/C MINIBAR TV TEL. $380–$460 double; $453–$530 deluxe rooms. No standard rooms available Oct 4–Apr 17. Rates include breakfast. 15% service charge. AE, DC, MC, V. Bus: 6, 18, or 21.

The luxurious five-star King David is Jerusalem's status address, built in 1930 as a regional companion to the legendary Shephard's Hotel in Cairo. Shephard's was destroyed during anticolonialist riots in the early 1950s, and the King David, too, has suffered the trials of history. In 1946, its south wing, housing British military headquarters, was blown up by a Jewish terrorist organization. The entire wing of the building was subsequently rebuilt, but if you look closely, you can see differences in the stone.

The King David continues to be a perfectly maintained symbol of a bygone era (including a rather formal staff), but its reputation and list of diplomatic and celebrity guests continues to grow. The lofty Egyptianesque/Canaanite art deco public rooms should be experienced for their own sake; the view from the gardens and the terrace (where Paul Newman and Eva Marie Saint had a rendezvous in the 1960 film *Exodus*), with vistas toward the walls of the Old City, are exquisite. The gardened, country club–style swimming pool is a plus in summer.

Guest rooms were completely redone in 1997–98 with the total number reduced so that individual rooms are now larger. Furniture is contemporary, with dark-grained woods that suggest the lavish tropical veneers of the elegant 1930s; many bathrooms now sport a glass-enclosed shower as well as a tub. Higher-priced suites and superior rooms, with views of the Old City, are definitely special. The hotel is the raison d'être for a surrounding colony of expensive tourist, Judaica, and jewelry shops. The Zion Square/Ben-Yehuda Mall area is several rather lonely uphill blocks away. Discounters and package tours can get you into the King David for considerably less than the prices above.

Dining/Diversions: The gigantic breakfast buffet is famous, but the hotel's seven restaurants and cafes are average and definitely surpassed by the choice of interesting restaurants in town. There's an indoor bar and a terrace bar.

Amenities: Outdoor swimming pool, fitness and massage center, sauna, tennis court, shopping arcade.

Expensive

✪ **Dan Panorama Jerusalem.** 39 Keren Hayesod St., Jerusalem. ☎ **800/223-7773** in the U.S., 212/752-6160 in New York, or 02/569-5695 in Israel. Fax 02/625-0120. E-mail: danhtls@danhotels.co.il. 292 units. A/C TV TEL. $278–$344 double. Rates include breakfast. 15% service charge. Discounts available on 4-day Dan Hotel packages. Two children under 18 pay for breakfast only. AE, DC, MC, V. Bus: 4, 7, 8, 14, or 48.

Hotel Tip

Hotel prices in Israel are not cheap, but the eleventh commandment for travelers to Israel is: THOU SHELT NOT PAY FULL PRICE. Packages and discounters or travel agents specializing in Israel can get you into many of the most interesting Israeli hotels at prices far lower than the rack rates.

The Dan Panorama is around the corner from the King David Hotel, close to Liberty Bell Park, Yemin Moshe, and the Cinémathèque, and a walk or quick bus ride to Ben-Yehuda Mall (the bus stop is at the hotel's front door). Although carefully run, it's less fancy than the nearby King David, and lacks the King David's gardens and views, but it's centrally located, with elegant public areas that glisten. The hotel has just been added to the Dan Hotel Chain; rooms are comfortable, average size, and slated for renovation. The staff is friendly and efficient.

Dining: The in-house restaurants offer above-average hotel fare.

Amenities: Room service 7am to 11pm; secretarial services; children's activities weekday afternoons in summer and Passover; refrigerator in room on request, small rooftop swimming pool; extra fee for health club, Jacuzzi, and sauna.

Jerusalem Sheraton Plaza. 47 King George St., Jerusalem. ☎ **800/325-3535** in the U.S., or 02/629-8666. Fax 02/623-1667. 300 units. A/C TV TEL. $200–$300 double, $548–$761 suite. Club Floor rms extra; higher rates for Christmas and Jewish holidays. 15% service charge. Breakfast $18 extra per person. AE, DC, MC, V. Bus: 4, 7, 9, 14.

This 1970s 22-story tower is the top hotel closest to the Ben-Yehuda Mall area, though it's still a 10-minute walk. Always bustling, the public areas are what is expected of a hotel in this class, but not unusual. Rooms are moderately spacious and have balconies and either minibars or refrigerators; all views are good and those facing south offer spectacular views of the Old City. Club Floor rooms contain minibars, fax machines, PC outlets, and receive special staff service. The hotel's entrance plaza is below street level; to leave by foot entails climbing a hill or stairway.

Dining: Among the Sheraton's four restaurants, the Cow on the Roof, a kosher French restaurant, is excellent, under the direction of the world's preeminent kosher chef Shalom Kadosh; menus throughout the Sheraton's other restaurants reflect Kadosh's advice and influence.

Amenities: Outdoor seasonal pool, massage room, sauna, shopping arcade, hairdresser, business facilities, children's center in summer.

✪ **Laromme Hotel.** 3 Jabotinsky St., Jerusalem. ☎ **02/675-6666.** Fax 02/675-6777. E-mail: management@laromme-hotel.co.il. 308 units. A/C MINIBAR TV TEL. $187–$276 double; add $60 Jewish holidays and Christmas. Rates include breakfast. 15% service charge. AE, DC, MC, V. Free parking. Bus: 4, 8, 9, 14, 17, 48.

Originally slated to be a skyscraper, the Laromme was redesigned into a low-rise that would not clash with the city's skyline. The result is an interesting structure set at the edge of Liberty Bell Park (a plus for guests with children) and built around a balconied atrium lobby; the public areas were renovated in 1999. The Laromme has a good reputation for service. Rooms come in two sizes: the larger (Maximum) rooms are spacious, with luxurious bathrooms, and cost about $50 additional for a double room. There are 14 well-appointed suites. All rooms are light, airy, and contain well-designed contemporary furnishings. There are rooms for travelers with disabilities. The location is close to the quaint Yemin Moshe neighborhood, but a 15-minute uphill walk to the Ben-Yehuda Mall downtown area (downtown buses stop around the corner in front of the Dan Panorama Hotel).

Dining/Diversions: Three kosher restaurants, including separate meat and dairy/vegetarian facilities; the quality Bistro Restaurant, famous for its meat fondues, and a lounge/piano bar in the evening.

Amenities: Hairdresser, shopping gallery, fitness room. A roomy, newly redesigned leisure complex with heated outdoor swimming pool, children's pool and Jacuzzi (covered by an air balloon in winter) provides the best year-round swimming in the center of the city.

Moderate

Eldan Hotel. 24 King David St., Jerusalem. ☎ **02/567-9777.** Fax 02/625-2154. 76 units. A/C TEL. $150, $170, $210 double in low, regular, high seasons, respectively. Rates include breakfast. AE, DC, MC, V. Bus 6, 18, 21.

With a great location almost across the street from the King David, the Eldan opened in 1999. Public areas shine, and include a fitness room free for guests and a small business center. Rooms are average size and are up-to-the-minute in amenities and style; most have bathrooms with tubs, eight have stall showers. Run by Eldan, Israel's largest car-rental company, there are small rate discounts if you rent an Eldan vehicle.

Hanagid Hotel. 7 Schatz St., Jerusalem 94267. ☎ **02/622-1111.** Fax 02/624-8420. Reservations through Best Western International. 48 units. A/C TV TEL. $125–$140 double. Rates include breakfast. 15% service charge. AE, DC, MC, V. Bus 4, 8, 9, 19.

Opened in 1998, this is a bright new hotel on a quiet street a block and a half from the very central intersection of King George and Ben Yehuda streets. Rooms are not large, but they're new and pleasant. There is a bar lounge and coffee shop as well as business facilities. The hotel is glatt kosher. Off-season, in late fall and winter, rates can go as low as $90 for a double room.

Kings Hotel. 60 King George St., Jerusalem. ☎ **02/620-1201.** Fax 02/620-1211. E-mail: sales@prima.co.il. 187 units. A/C TV TEL. $143–$190 double. Rates include breakfast. AE, DC, MC, V. Bus: 4, 8, 9, or 48.

Location is the big plus for this hotel: right at the entrance to the prestigious Rehavia neighborhood, and a 10-minute walk to the Ben-Yehuda area (it's also next door to Hechal Shlomo, the Great Synagogue). A good supermarket is half a block away. The lobby and lounge areas were renovated in the late 1980s, and have a light, garden feel. Rooms have been more recently redone; they are functional rather than gracious, and rather small. The hotel is often used by tour groups and is available at discounts through package consolidators. You enter the hotel on Ramban Street; note that this busy intersection suffers from a high level of traffic noise. Service is marked by small economies; guest-room air-conditioning may be turned off at midday, when most guests are out. The hotel contains two restaurants and a lounge/bar.

King Solomon Hotel. 32 King David St., Jerusalem. ☎ **02/695-555.** Fax 02/624-1774. E-mail: solhotel@netvision.net.il. 148 units. A/C MINIBAR TV TEL. $135–$184 double; from $204 suite. Higher rates Sukkot and Dec 15–Jan 20. Rates include breakfast. AE, DC, MC, V. Bus: 5, 18, or 21.

Although situated at the fork of busy King David and Keren Hayesod streets, the design of this modern hotel, built in the 1980s, manages to keep street noise to tolerable levels. The main entrance is on a service driveway between the two major thoroughfares and opens to an airy, pleasant multilevel stone-floor lobby. Room furnishings are blandly modern but superior rooms and suites, available are spacious and many offer excellent views. The large rooftop pool, with a view of the Old City walls in the distance, is quite spectacular. Dining facilities in the Queen of Sheba (Middle Eastern/Continental restaurant) and the Lobby Lounge are glatt kosher. The hotel is within walking distance of Yemin Moshe, the German Colony, and the Cinémathèque, but you'll probably want to take a bus to the downtown Ben-Yehuda Mall area. In off-season, special packages offer double rooms in the $100 range. There are also rooms for travelers with disabilities.

✪ YMCA Three Arches Hotel. 26 King David St. (P.O. Box 294), Jerusalem 91002. **☎ 02/625-7111.** Fax 02/623-5192. 56 units. A/C TV TEL. $145 double; $195 suite. Rates include continental breakfast. AE, MC, V. Bus: 6, 18, or 21 to King David St.

This historic landmark, across the street from the King David Hotel, opened in 1933 and was designed in an art deco Byzantine-Islamic style by Arthur Loomis Harmon, who also did New York's Empire State Building. It is a center for lectures, performances, and classes as well as an excellent hotel. Public areas are lovely and atmospheric; all guest rooms were totally reconstructed in the early 1990s and now sport modern bathrooms and an intelligent decor designed around kilim motifs and reproductions of paintings by Israeli artists. Beds are fairly firm. The atmosphere, facilities, and location make this the best value for the money in Jerusalem.

The YMCA houses a good cafe, in addition to the Tsriff Restaurant, where the elegant terrace is one of the most popular fair-weather dining places in town. Guests may use the 1930s-style indoor swimming pool on the premises and also have free use of tennis and squash courts, jogging track, and a fitness room.

Inexpensive

✪ Beit Shmuel Guest House. 13 King David St., Jerusalem (entrance around the corner at 3 Shamia St.). **☎ 02/620-3473** or 02/620-3456. Fax 02/620-3467. 40 units. A/C. $66–$80 double; $84–$108 triple; $112–$132 quad; dorm beds $24–$29. Rates include breakfast. AE, MC, V. Bus: 6, 18, or 21 to first stop on King David St.

Affiliated with the IYHA, this guest house and cultural center, sponsored by the World Union for Progressive Judaism, has attracted visitors of every age and faith from all over the world. The large, modern complex, designed by Moshe Safdie (who also designed Montreal's Habitat), offers views of the Old City, a network of terraces, gardens, and courtyards, and a full schedule of lectures, concerts, and cultural activities on the premises. Rooms can be set up as dorms, family facilities for up to six people, private doubles, or even as singles. Despite the architecturally impressive building, the place can seem somewhat institutional, and with heavy use, decor in rooms is wearing thin. Dining hall meals run $13. From December 12 to January 4, visitors are charged higher summer rates. Early reservations are recommended. Call ahead for information on wheelchair access. Heavily booked with groups in summer.

Rosary Convent Guest House and Hostel. 14 Agron St. (P.O. Box 54), Jerusalem. **☎ 02/625-8529** or 02/623-5581. Fax 02/623-5581. 23 units (shower facilities available). $60–$70 double. Rates include breakfast. No credit cards. Bus: 4, 7, 9, 14, 19.

For spotless, simple but pleasant accommodations, you can't beat the Rosary Convent, set back from the road in a quiet garden located around the corner from the Jerusalem Plaza Hotel and across the street from the Supersol supermarket. Rooms are airy, with high ceilings, but can be chilly on very cold winter nights. The gate to the complex closes at 10pm; if you plan to be out later, you must try to make arrangements with the management ahead of time.

WESTERN EDGE OF CITY/SDEROT HERZL

Stretching from the area of Jaffa Road near the Central Bus Station to the area of Sderot Herzl that runs toward the residential neighborhood of Beit Ha-Kerem, this area offers modern expensive and moderate choices. There's not much that's interesting within walking distance of most of these hotels, and the highway system in the area does not lend itself to excursions by foot. But they are all close to major bus routes into the center of town; the better, more distant hotels offer free shuttle service to various points in the city. This area is not far from the Knesset and Government Center, the Hebrew University's Givat Ram Campus, and the Israel Museum.

Expensive

Holiday Inn Crowne Plaza. Givat Ram, Jerusalem. ☎ **02/658-8888.** Fax 02/651-4555. 397 units. A/C MINIBAR TV TEL. $258–$288 double; add $30 for deluxe rms; $90 for club level rms. 15% service charge. Two children up to age 19 stay free in parents' rm, except during high season and in Club Level rms. Rates include breakfast. AE, DC, MC, V. Fee parking available. Bus: 5, 6, 20, 21, 48, or any bus to Central Bus Station.

For more than 20 years, this landmark tower on a hill at the western edge of the city was the Jerusalem Hilton. Public areas, though spacious, are a bit jumbled. Views from the rooms, all with small balconies, are a plus; rooms themselves are unremarkable. There are no-smoking rooms and rooms for travelers with disabilities. The location is perfect for conventions at the neighboring Binyinei Ha-Uma Convention Center.

Dining/Diversions: The Kohinoor Restaurant serves splendid kosher Indian food. All hotel food services are above average. There's a bar/lounge.

Amenities: Free downtown shuttle service, business center, outdoor pool in a pleasantly sheltered garden, tennis courts, miniature golf, playground; health club (at extra charge) with sauna and Jacuzzi, quality shopping arcade.

Moderate

Four Points Sheraton Jerusalem Hotel. 4 Vilnai (formerly Wolfson) St., Jerusalem. ☎ **02/655-8888.** Fax 02/651-2266. 198 units. A/C TV TEL. $140–$180 double ($232 at Christmas, Passover, and Jewish High Holidays). lower rates on El Al Sunsational 5-Night Package. Rates include breakfast. AE, DC, MC, V. Free parking. Bus: 5, 6, 18, 20, 21, or any bus on Jaffa Rd. to Sderot Herzl.

A 15- to 25-minute bus ride into the center of town, this upper moderate price hotel is a bargain choice for El Al passengers who book it as part of an El Al Sunsational Package. Located in a major hotel strip near the Binyanei Ha-Uma Convention Center, this high-rise was built for business travelers and visitors in the 1980s. Rooms are comfortable but small and standard in decor. The big draws here are the indoor and outdoor swimming pools and exceptionally good free sports facilities. Specify if you want this location when you purchase the El Al Sunsational Package.

Park Plaza Hotel. 2 Wolfson St., Jerusalem. ☎ **02/658-2222.** Fax 02/658-2211. 217 units. A/C TV TEL. $130–$165 double. Rates include breakfast. AE, DC, MC, V. Free parking. Bus: 5, 6, 18, 20, or 48.

Formerly the Sonesta Jerusalem, this modern hotel built in the 1980s is wrapped around a light-filled atrium which, unfortunately, is only used for private functions. Public areas and facilities are skimpy, but the rooms are pleasant for this category, and equipped with small-screen TVs. The lack of a pool is a shortcoming; facilities include a restaurant and a lounge/bar.

Renaissance Jerusalem Hotel. 6 Wolfson St., Jerusalem. ☎ **02/659-9999.** Fax 02/651-1824. 625 units. A/C TV TEL. $143–$200 double. 15% service charge. Rates include breakfast. AE, DC, MC, V. Free parking. Bus: 5, 6, 14, 18, 20, 21, or 48 to Herzl Blvd. at Rupin Bridge.

There are two separate high-rise towers in this well-equipped 16-year-old Ramada International hotel; the less-expensive tower is sometimes closed during off-season, and everyone is moved into the attractive deluxe rooms. Public areas are spacious and serve as a conduit between the two sections, with hundreds of tiny starlights creating a romantic, almost sculptural effect at night.

The large indoor and outdoor swimming pools, tennis courts, and use of the excellent health club are major strong points. Restaurant facilities are glatt kosher. Except in high season, you'll often find a discount policy: stay 7 nights and pay only for 6. This is the farthest hotel from the center of town on Sderot Herzl, but there's a free downtown shuttle service; from here you can walk to Mount Herzl and Yad VaShem.

FARTHER WEST: EIN KEREM
Inexpensive

Sisters of Sion Convent. Ha-Oren St., Ezor "D," Ein Kerem, Jerusalem. ☎ **02/641-5738.** Fax 02/643-7739. 34 units (23 with private bathroom; 8 with shared bathroom). $80 double. No credit cards. Bus: 17 to Ein Kerem.

Located in the village of Ein Kerem, with its terraced hillsides, gardens, and orchards, this hospice is a quiet, atmospheric retreat a half-hour bus ride from downtown Jerusalem. Not all guests are religious; some travelers come for the tranquillity and charm of Ein Kerem, which was the birthplace of John the Baptist. Rates are slightly higher on weekends; reservations are essential. Meals are always beautifully prepared and a full pension plan can be arranged.

SOUTH JERUSALEM
South of the King George Street/King David Street area, you'll likely use buses or taxis to get to the center of town, although many will find the half-hour walk interesting. Two atmospheric hospices are located in the Abu Tor and German Colony neighborhoods. Hebron Road, with views of the Old City, also offers two hotel choices. A half-hour municipal bus ride from the center of town, you'll find a large kibbutz hotel in the Judean mountains on the edge of the desert.

MODERATE

Ariel Hotel. 31 Hebron Rd., Jerusalem. ☎ **02/568-9999.** Fax 02/673-4066. E-mail: info@@arieljrm.co.il. 126 units. A/C TV TEL. $140–$180 double; $50 extra suite. Rates include breakfast. 15% service charge. MC, V. Bus: 7,8, 21, 48.

Originally planned as a residential hotel, the modern, relatively high-rise Ariel offers a variety of room sizes (some quite large) and arrangements, which makes this a good choice for families or small groups. Many rooms have views of Mount Zion, for $20 per person extra. Public areas have been recently redone with sparkling polished stone and glitzy furniture. Decor in private rooms is utilitarian, but there may be renovations within the next 2 years. The hotel is not far from Liberty Bell Park, the Cinémathèque, and the beautiful Yemin Moshe neighborhood, with its gardens and marvelous vistas. A block away, across from the railroad station, you'll find buses to every part of town.

✪ **Mount Zion Hotel.** 17 Hebron Rd., Jerusalem 93546. ☎ **02/568-9555.** Fax 02/673-1425. E-mail: hotel@mountzion.co.il. 140 units. A/C TV TEL. $165–$235 double. Rates include breakfast. Children stay free in parents' rm. Christmas, Passover, and Sukkot $40 per room extra. Rates $10 lower per person in winter. AE, DC, MC, V. Bus: 7, 8, 21, or 48.

One of Jerusalem's newest and architecturally most interesting hotels, the Mount Zion is partly composed of renovated 19th- and early 20th-century Jerusalem stone buildings that have been carefully blended into a modern complex. The whole structure has an old-world charm, with modern conveniences. The hotel is built on a cliff facing the Old City's walls, and on a hillside shared by Jerusalem's fashionable Cinémathèque. The terraces, sprawling wings, hidden gardens, and swimming pool offer views of the Old City that rival those of the King David Hotel (the health club is set up so that treadmill runners have a dazzling panorama; it also contains a Jacuzzi and old-style

Turkish bath/steam room). Superior rooms have better views and polished stone bathrooms. Suites, with wonderful vistas, are spacious and have minibars or kitchenettes.

Manager Rachael Goldberg has offered guests who book independently and present this book, subject to availability, a room upgrade and a 10% reduction for stays of more than 3 days.

Ramat Rachel Hotel. Kibbutz Ramat Rachel, Jerusalem 90900. ☎ **02/670-2555.** Fax 02/673-3155. E-mail: resv@ramatrachel.col.il. 164 units. A/C TV TEL. $157–216 double. Jewish holidays 15% extra. Rates include breakfast. AE, DC, MC, V. Free parking. Bus: 7.

More like a resort than a hotel, this is the only kibbutz guest facility within the reach of Jerusalem's municipal bus routes. Ramat Rachel offers its visitors a vast swimming pool (heavily patronized by Jerusalemites in summer), night-lit tennis and basketball courts, a playground, fitness center, Jacuzzi, Turkish bath, sauna, and views of Bethlehem and the Judean desert. For those who want to relax as well as sightsee, or for families with children, this is a unique choice. There are 60 brand-new rooms and all rooms (including recently refurbished older rooms) are brightened with colorful textile creations by the noted artist Calman Shemi. Seven rooms are designed for travelers with disabilities, and there is wheelchair access to all hotel facilities. There are no-smoking rooms. Service is above average for a kibbutz establishment, and there is transport to Ben-Gurion Airport for guests.

INEXPENSIVE

✪ **Saint Andrew's Hospice.** Church of Scotland, P.O. Box 8619, Jerusalem. ☎ **02/ 673-2401.** Fax 02/673-1711. 20 units. TEL. $80 double. Rates include breakfast. MC, V. Bus: 4, 8, or 48 along King George V Ave. or Keren Hayesod St., or 6, 18, or 21 from Central Bus Station or Jaffa Rd.; railroad station or Khan Theater stop.

Situated on a small hill, the banner of St. Andrew waving from its tower, and surrounded by a garden with panoramic views of Mount Zion and the Old City, this hospice is only a few steps from the railroad station and the Khan Theater. Rooms are simple but spotless; five new rooms were added in 1997 and there is one handicapped-accessible ground-floor room. The building is adorned with beautiful examples of Armenian ceramic tiles from the 1930s, which were created by Jerusalem's famous Palestinian Pottery Workshop. The efficient and friendly Scottish staff offers a hearty $11 dinner. Sunbula, a nonprofit shop selling fine Palestinian embroidery and local crafts, is also on the premises. Excellent value.

NORTH JERUSALEM
EXPENSIVE

✪ **Hyatt Regency Jerusalem.** 32 Lehi St., Jerusalem. ☎ **02/533-1234.** Fax 02/581-5947. E-mail: hyattjrs@trendline.co.il. 503 units. A/C MINIBAR TV TEL. $185–$235 double. 15% service charge. Rates include breakfast. AE, DC, MC, V. Bus: 4. Free shuttle to downtown Jerusalem.

Designed by David Resnik, one of Israel's foremost architects, the Hyatt Regency opened in 1987 and has gained a reputation as one of the city's finest hotels. Set on the lower slopes of Mount Scopus, the Hyatt's seven arcaded courtyards and multilevel atrium lobby settle gracefully across the landscape, with vistas of the city in the distance. "Distance," is the one problem—there is a free shuttle bus into the center of West Jerusalem, but you're not close to anything here, and the neighborhood is not interesting for walks. Rooms are less institutional than in most Israeli hotels; those on the Regency Club floors include many special staff services. There are often special discounts such as 5 nights for the price of 4. The hotel is planning a major guest room renovation during the time span of this edition.

Dining/Diversions: Among the Hyatt's strong points are above-average food services, crowned by the top-class Valentino's Restaurant and theme buffets (Tex-Mex, Middle Eastern, Asian) 3 nights a week. There's also a choice of cafes, bars, and disco/pubs.

Amenities: Large, beautiful but mainly shallow outdoor swimming pool and two floodlit tennis courts; guests are offered discounts or free passes to the in-house fitness center, regarded as the best in town; sauna; steam room; business center; large shopping arcade; hairdresser.

EAST JERUSALEM

With the construction of the big new Olive Tree Hotel and the Jerusalem Novotel, the axis of good hotels in East Jerusalem has shifted to the extreme western edge of this part of town. For decades, most of East Jerusalem's hotels had been located in and around Saladin Street, the bustling main shopping thoroughfare of the area. These hotels, like the neighborhood in general, have not aged well, and a band of new, upper moderate hotels is being built just to the east of Highway 1, which divides the eastern and western parts of the city. This area is relatively convenient to West Jerusalem and has always been home to East Jerusalem's best and most vibrant hotels—the legendary American Colony Hotel, and the moderate Jerusalem Hotel—as well as the best Christian guest houses (Notre Dame and St. George's). East Jerusalem's best restaurants are also beginning to accumulate in this area. There are still a few good hotel choices left in East Jerusalem's downtown center, and also on the Mount of Olives, with its wonderful views. Most of East Jerusalem's hotels are within walking distance of the Damascus Gate.

The atmosphere of downtown East Jerusalem is Palestinian, and the genuine helpfulness and hospitality found in many of East Jerusalem's hotels is very much in the Arabic tradition. As a rule, East Jerusalem hotels offer good value and are somewhat less expensive than those in the western part of town. Be forewarned, however, that the area is relatively dead at night.

Most East Jerusalem hotels raise their prices by 20% to 25% during the Christmas and Easter holidays.

EXPENSIVE

✪ **American Colony Hotel.** Nablus Rd. (P.O. Box 19215), Jerusalem 97200. ☎ **02/ 627-9777.** Fax 02/627-9779. 92 units. AC TV TEL. $265–$290 double. 15% service charge. Rates include breakfast and service charge. AE, DC, MC, V. Free parking. Bus: 27.

The former home of a Turkish pasha, this romantic four-star hotel with beautiful gardens and a swimming pool is in a class by itself. Popular with international journalists, scholars, archaeologists, and diplomats, the American Colony has become almost as legendary as Rick's Cafe in *Casablanca*. Its walled courtyards are just past the top of the hill where Saladin Street and Nablus Road meet. Public areas are decorated with splendid Armenian ceramics, intricately painted antique wooden ceilings, and other authentic old Jerusalem touches; in the cloisterlike lobby above the garden, local archaeological finds are displayed in glass cases. There are some less-expensive economy rooms, as well as more costly executive "pasha" rooms and suites. In the Pasha's Style rooms and suites, you'll find antiques juxtaposed with modern bathrooms; some rooms are decorated with mother-of-pearl cocktail tables and copper trays and have ornate gold-and-blue ceilings. Many accommodations are in less-august buildings across the courtyard. The economy and some of the standard rooms are often quite ordinary, so ask to see different rooms if it's possible. Even if you can't afford this kind of luxury and ambience, you might want to treat yourself to the elegant Saturday afternoon buffet or the charming garden cafe for a light meal or dessert.

Jerusalem Accommodations & Dining

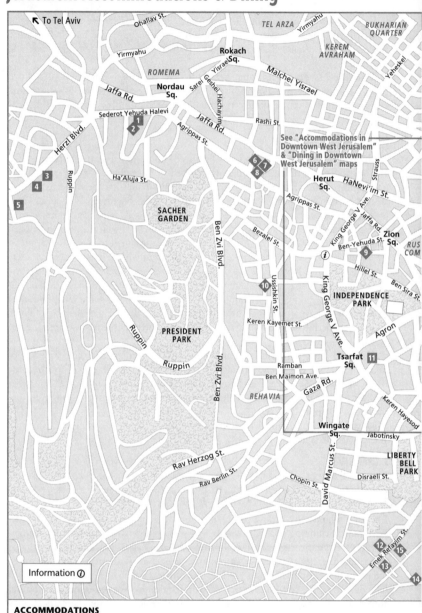

ACCOMMODATIONS

American Colony Hotel 28
Azzahra Hotel 25
Ariel Hotel 16
Four Points ITT Sheraton Hotel 4
Holiday Inn Crowne Plaza 1
Holyland East Hotel 24

Hyatt Regency Jerusalem 33
Jerusalem Hotel 26
Mount Zion Hotel 18
Notre Dame Guest House 22
Novotel 30
Park Plaza Hotel 3

Renaissance Jerusalem Hotel 5
Rosary Convent Guest House 11
Royal Plaza Olive Tree Hotel 29
Saint Andrew's Hospice 19
St. George's Hostel 27
Tulip Inn 23

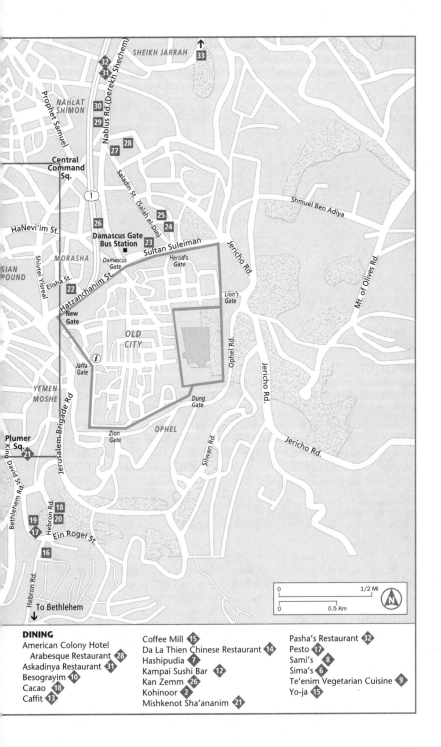

DINING

American Colony Hotel
 Arabesque Restaurant 28
Askadinya Restaurant 31
Besograyim 10
Cacao 18
Caffit 13

Coffee Mill 15
Da La Thien Chinese Restaurant 14
Hashipudia 7
Kampai Sushi Bar 12
Kan Zemm 26
Kohinoor 2
Mishkenot Sha'ananim 21

Pasha's Restaurant 32
Pesto 17
Sami's 8
Sima's 6
Te'enim Vegetarian Cuisine 9
Yo-ja 15

Dining/Diversions: Three restaurants, including the French/Continental Arabesque Room; excellent bar; pianist and live music many nights.

Amenities: Room service, baby-sitting, laundry, dry cleaning, outdoor pool, children's pool.

Royal Plaza Olive Tree Hotel. 23 St. George St., Jerusalem 46752. ☎ **02/541-0410.** Fax 02/541-0411. www.royal-plaza.com. E-mail: olivplza@netvision.net.il. 310 units. A/C TV TEL. $180–$250 double; $60–$80 extra suite. AE, DC, MC, V. Free parking. Bus: 27.

Opened just in time for the year 2000, this large eight-story structure represents a new generation in Jerusalem hotels. The planners of the Olive Tree have thought about Jerusalem and its traditions. Public areas are built around a stone-walled atrium (with an olive tree as its centerpiece); architectural touches include arabesque windows and reproductions of Herodian doorways and columns. In the mode of ancient traveler's *khans* or inns (which were also built around courtyards), hotel guests are greeted with olive oil, *zaatar* (local spices) and bread when they check in at reception. At least for the opening months, staff will be garbed in "biblical" costumes and will include fortune tellers and other exotic personnel. Rooms are new and fresh but not very interesting, with plain, inexpensive furniture. However, they're modern, with safes, hair dryers, fax modems, digitally locked doors, and voice mail (some are no-smoking). You're within walking distance of East Jerusalem restaurants and the Old City, but it's a longer walk or taxi ride to get to the downtown center of West Jerusalem.

Amenities: There is an indoor pool, Jacuzzi, free fitness room, beauty salon, and summer children's club.

MODERATE

Holyland East Hotel. 6 Harun er-Rasheed St. (P.O. Box 19700), Jerusalem 91196. ☎ **02/627-2888.** Fax 02/628-0265. 105 units. A/C TV TEL. $110–$145 double. Rates include breakfast. AE, DC, MC, V. Bus: 27.

Be sure to check out the roof—this hotel, built in the 1950s, offers stunning views of the Old City, the Dome of the Rock, the Mount of Olives, and the New City. The lobby is decorated with 1960s modern furnishings, and most bedrooms have a balcony and new, firm mattresses. Try for a room with a view toward the Old City. Rates are reduced when business is slow.

✪ **Jerusalem Hotel.** Nablus Rd. (entrance at 4 Antara Ben-Shadad St.), Jerusalem. ☎ and fax **02/628-3282;** for reservations in the U.S. 800/657-9401. www.jrshotel.com. E-mail: raed@jrshotel.com. 15 units. $95–$125 double. Rates include breakfast. AE, DC, MC, V. Bus: 27.

This increasingly popular hotel, run by the very hospitable, well-informed Saadeh family, is a real winner, housed in an old stone mansion with thick walls, high ceilings, and a garden cafe. Rooms were beautifully redone in 1997, exposing Jerusalem stone walls, and refitted with new bathrooms; extra touches include hand-crafted, traditional Egyptian furniture and a second phone outlet for Internet connection. The restaurant, under the personal supervision of Mrs. Wedad Saadeh, offers good Middle Eastern dishes in both the garden and in the traditional dining room with low tables and pillow-covered divans. On Saturday evenings, the hotel serves an excellent Lebanese buffet ($16) with salads, vegetarian dishes, and six hot dishes, plus traditional Middle Eastern oud (lute) music. On Thursday evenings, there's live western music.

The entrance at 4 Antara Ben-Shadad St. is off Nablus Road, on a side street facing the north side of the Egged East Nablus Road Bus Station. The garden and a very high Plexiglas shield screen out the small bus station, which is closed by late afternoon.

Novotel. 9 St. George St., Jerusalem. ☎ **02/532-7232.** Fax 02/532-7241. 370 units. A/C TV TEL. $162–$196 double. Rates include breakfast. AE, DC, MC, V. Bus: 27.

From the outside, this hotel, which opened in 2000, looks like a twin of its neighbor, the Olive Tree Hotel, but there are differences. The public areas have less Jerusalem personality, the swimming pool is outdoors, and the fitness room is an additional charge. Rooms are comfortable, and contain refrigerators; some are no-smoking, and there are special rooms for travelers with disabilities. The Old City and East Jerusalem's downtown are walkable, but it's a long walk or taxi ride over to West Jerusalem's center.

Tulip Inn Jerusalem Golden Walls Hotel. Sultan Suleiman St., Jerusalem 97200. ☎ **02/627-2416.** Fax 02/626-4658. E-mail: asmin@pilgrimpal.com. 103 units. A/C TV TEL. $100–$145 double. 10% student discount. AE, DC, MC, V. Bus: 27.

This conveniently located three-star hotel is on the western side of the east Jerusalem bus station, which means that rooms on that side tend to be noisier. The three-story, limestone building has views of the old city walls (across the street). It's not an opulent place, but it does have clean, comfortable contemporary rooms, both public and private, and a bar, plus in-house restaurant. Lower prices are available in the low season, which includes June 10 to August 10, but excludes Easter and Christmas and October. Rates are sometimes negotiable.

INEXPENSIVE

✪ **St. George's Cathedral Guesthouse.** 20 Nablus Rd. (P.O. Box 19018), Jerusalem. ☎ **02/628-3302.** Fax 02/628-2253. 24 units. $80–$90 double. 10% service charge. No credit cards. Bus: 27.

This well-run Anglican/Episcopal establishment offers private rooms housed in a cloister around an English garden. Accommodations are simple; they were redecorated in 1996, with new bathrooms, and the ambience is both evocative and comfortable. Rooms vary, so ask if you can have a look at a few before taking one. There's a charming Jerusalem stone bar in the basement, and the entire very British enclave seems like the setting for a chapter of *The Jewel in the Crown.* The staff is knowledgeable and very helpful.

To find it, walk up Nablus Road and you'll be approaching Saint George's Cathedral on the right. The hotel is in the cathedral compound, where Nablus Road and Saladin Street meet. Bus no. 27 comes right to the door of Saint George's (bus noise may be a problem for some).

MOUNT OF OLIVES

To the east of downtown East Jerusalem, the Mount of Olives is a bit out of things, but some returning visitors wouldn't dream of anyplace else to stay in the city. It's a downhill walk to the Old City and East Jerusalem, and there's no public transport over to West Jerusalem, so you may find yourself resorting to taxis, especially at night. But you'll be rewarded with incredible views of Jerusalem, and almost bucolic, spiritual surroundings. Women should not walk on the Mount of Olives unescorted at any time.

Mount of Olives Hotel. 53 Mount of Olives Rd., Jerusalem. ☎ **800/762-9295** in the U.S., or 02/628-4877. Fax 02/689-4427. E-mail: info@mtolives.com. 61 units. TEL. $48–$78 double. Rates include buffet breakfast. AE, DC, MC, V. At top of hill on Mount of Olives Rd., turn right and pass through Arab village of Et-Tur and continue past two hospitals. Russian church will be on left; hotel is at bend in road to left.

The distinguishing features of this friendly, family run hotel are its tentlike, red-cloth bar and its proximity to the Church of the Ascension, next door. Rooms are simply furnished, but comfortable and centrally heated. Vistas from this part of the Mount of Olives are marvelous. Ask about room 317 (the panorama room), with an especially fabulous view of the Old City. There is a TV lounge.

OUTSIDE THE CITY
MODERATE

Kiryat Anavim Kibbutz Hotel. Kiryat Anavim 90833. ☎ **888/669-5700** or 201/566-9669 in the U.S. and Canada, or 02/534-8999. Fax 02/534-8848. 50 units. A/C TEL. $106–$144 double. Rates include breakfast. AE, DC, MC, V. Bus: to Kiryat Anavim and Abu Ghosh from Central Bus Station.

This three-star choice combines the services of a comfortable hotel with a country atmosphere. Several of the rooms can be arranged to lodge a family of three or four. The hotel offers such facilities as a vast swimming pool, a children's pool, restaurant, TV room, snack bar, and cocktail bar. The rustic site, amid the Judean mountains, is lovely, although just beginning to recover from the great forest fire of 1995; there are nature trails and as an added extra, you get free admission to the kibbutz's 1960s Friday night dance. The location, so close to Jerusalem, lets you combine a tranquil resort experience with major sightseeing. Discounts are available on Kibbutz Hotel Package plans.

The hotel is near the village of Abu Ghosh, 12 kilometers (7¹/₂ mi.) west of Jerusalem, just north of the highway to the airport and Tel Aviv.

INEXPENSIVE

✪ **Neve Shalom-Wahat al Salaam Guest House and Hostel.** Doar Na Shimshon 99761. ☎ **02/991-7160.** Fax 02/991-7412. E-mail: nswasinn@trendline.co.il. 39 units. $72–$100 double. Passover and Aug 10% higher; 10% lower Nov 1–Feb 28. Rates include breakfast. AE, DC, MC, V.

This village of peace is located in the countryside near the Latrun Monastery, between Tel Aviv and Jerusalem just where the plain of Ayalon begins to rise into the mountains of Judea (the ancient borderland between the Israelites and their long-time enemies, the Philistines). The name means "oasis of peace" in both Hebrew and Arabic. The village with its sweeping vistas was founded as a place where Israeli Jews and Israeli Arabs could live together in friendship and understanding, and over the years its inhabitants have turned their community effort into a national center for learning and dialogue. The guest house, originally built for study seminars, is now open to the public, and visitors are welcome to spend a night or two here within a 25-minute drive of Jerusalem and Tel Aviv, enjoying the lovely countryside and getting a feel for this unusual project. The simple but comfortable rooms, all recently built, have private bathrooms, radios, and use of a TV room. There's also a swimming pool. A delicious home-style lunch or dinner vegetarian buffet is $16 (the talented chef originally came from Morocco), and you can join a lecture (if offered in your language) for about $5. Although not a kibbutz, Neve Shalom-Wahat al Salaam can be included as an overnight choice in the Kibbutz Hotel Chain discount packages, which can be reserved in the U.S. and Canada by calling ☎ **888/669-5700** or 201/556-9669.

Buses and sheruts between Tel Aviv and Jerusalem will let you off at the Latrun Junction. You must prearrange with Neve Shalom for a pickup near the junction.

5 Where to Dine

Jerusalem has a huge selection of restaurants, dairy bars, lunch counters, snack shops, delicatessens, and cafes.

Dining Tip

Saturday night is very big for dining out in Israel, but because kosher restaurants often prepare food for Saturday night on Thursday before closing for the Sabbath, and because nonkosher restaurants will not have received fresh fish and vegetables for 2 days, you won't find restaurants at their best. If you're going to splurge at a top restaurant, do it midweek.

In the Old City and East Jerusalem, you'll find mostly Middle Eastern cuisine. Pork is prohibited to Muslims, as it is to Jews, but you will find pork and shellfish in East Jerusalem restaurants catering to tourists or Christian Arabs. There are no kosher restaurants in East Jerusalem or in the Old City except in the Jewish Quarter. The Old City has plenty of snack stands and inexpensive Arab restaurants. Most Old City eating places are open daily from late morning to 5 or 6pm.

In West Jerusalem, the dining scene is quite different. Downtown West Jerusalem has become something of an international food festival, and most places are open until very late at night. You'll find pedestrian streets that are virtually wall-to-wall restaurants. There are pizza parlors, hamburger stands, and Viennese-style cafes. Restaurants in West Jerusalem serve American, Indian, Thai, Mexican, Italian, Central European, French, Fusion, and Middle Eastern cuisine. A majority are kosher.

SABBATH DINING Kosher restaurants usually close by 2 or 3pm on Friday. The following nonkosher restaurants, described in detail later in this chapter, have Friday evening or Saturday afternoon hours and provide a good variety of choices. Downtown West Jerusalem: Stanley's, Gilly's, Ocean, Pepperoni's, Focaccia, Le Tsriff at the YMCA, Eldad Vesayhoo, Sakura, Spaghettim, Taco Taco, McDonald's, Arcadia, Dahlia Renaud. German Colony and Baka: Da La Thien. East Jerusalem: American Colony Hotel, Askidinya, Pascha, Kan Zeman at the Jerusalem Hotel.

THE OLD CITY
NEAR JAFFA GATE
Inexpensive

✪ **Armenian Tavern.** 79 Armenian Orthodox Patriarchate Rd. ☎ **02/627-3854.** Reservations necessary Fri–Sat evenings. Main courses NIS 25–50 ($5.50–$11). AE, DC, MC, V. Tues–Sun 11am–10:30pm. ARMENIAN.

This is the prettiest restaurant in the Old City, in a newly restored room with exposed stone walls, crusader-era arched ceilings, an indoor fountain, rustic wooden tables, and panels of hand-painted Armenian tiles that are a feast for the eye. The food is prepared with special Armenian herbs and seasonings that give each dish a slightly novel taste. Inexpensive first courses are great here—delicate home-style meat pizzas (small but delicious) and a range of cold salads, soups, and stuffed vegetables. The pepper salad and the cucumber and yogurt salad are excellent. Main courses are mildly exotic and always delicious. Friday nights, special traditional dishes are brought in from the kitchen of the owner's and neighboring family's homes—you can have a fine home-style feast. Background music is Armenian and Greek; wine and beer, a rarity in Old City restaurants, is an added attraction.

After entering Jaffa Gate, turn right at the Tower of David (Citadel). Continue straight; restaurant is on the right, down a flight of stairs.

Coffee Shop. Jaffa Gate. ☎ **02/628-6812.** Soup NIS 14 ($3); soup and salad bar NIS 28 ($6.20). No credit cards. Mon–Sat 10am–6pm. SOUP/SALAD.

Spotless, wholesome, and brightly decorated with contemporary tiles designed by the Jerusalem Pottery Workshop, the Coffee Shop is one of the best bets in the Old City. It serves a thick homemade soup of the day (as much as you want) plus a simple but very fresh all-you-can-eat salad bar. Tasty home-style bread and butter comes with your meal. The Coffee Shop is occasionally closed at odd times for religious services.

When you enter Jaffa Gate, turn right just after David Citadel; it's on the left.

NEAR DAMASCUS GATE

While there are not many restaurants in this area, you can find many Arabic pastry shops, places grilling whole chickens (which can be carved and packed in aluminum foil for takeout), and fresh juice bars. Wander from Damascus Gate along Suq Khan es-Zeit Street, which bears to the right at the fork.

Inexpensive

Abu Assab Refreshments. Suq Khan es-Zeit Bazaar. No phone. NIS 5–8 ($1.10–$1.80). Daily 9am–5pm. FRESH JUICES.

The best place in the Old City for fresh orange, grapefruit, and carrot juice (often as sweet as cantaloupe juice), Abu Assab always purchases the best of the crop. Have yours at the juice bar, or follow the tiny staircase upstairs for table service. It's located three-quarters of the way from Damascus Gate to the Cardo, on the right side.

✪ **Abu Shukri.** 63 Al Wad Rd. ☎ **02/627-1538.** Main courses NIS 10–28 ($2.20–$6.20). No credit cards. Daily 8am–4:30pm, later on Sat. MIDDLE EASTERN.

This restaurant, one of the best and most affordable in Jerusalem, can be found where the Via Dolorosa and Al Wad Road meet. It's famous for hummus (mashed, seasoned chickpeas eaten with pita bread) that is so spectacular that in earlier times, people in Jordan used to send out for it, and lines of Israelis waited for tables on Saturday afternoons. Try your hummus with whole chickpeas in olive oil, or black beans, or with roasted pine nuts (my favorite) and be sure to ask for the pita bread to be served hot (included in the price). I like to order a small plate of chopped salad and mix it in with the hummus; falafel here is fresh and spicy. In 1999, Abu Shukri began to add meat to its menu—you can get excellent grilled kabobs, shwarma, and *kubbeh* (cracked wheat dumplings stuffed with meat). Mint tea is a good beverage choice.

Families Restaurant. Suq Khan es-Zeit Bazaar. No phone. Shwarma NIS 14 ($3.10); main courses NIS 16–30 ($4.50–$8.40). No credit cards. Daily 8am–6pm. MIDDLE EASTERN.

For decades, this restaurant, owned by the Abdulatif family, has been one of the few where you will see both Arabic families and tourists dining. The shwarma is probably the best in the bazaar—you can order a shwarma sandwich filled with your choice of salads at a table, or take it away. The spacious arched ceiling dining room probably goes back to the time of the Crusades. The soups and traditional oven dishes like hummus and meat casserole are good, the salads worthwhile. Light, homemade fruit ice creams, available at the take-out counter, are a specialty of the house.

Coming from direction of Jaffa Gate, it will be on the right about 100 feet after the turn for Via Dolorosa.

Jaffar and Sons Pastry Cafe. Suq Khan es-Zeit Bazaar. No phone. Items NIS 7 ($1.55). Daily 9am–5pm. ARABIC PASTRY.

People flock to Jaffar for a wonderful Middle Eastern dessert called *kanafeh,* which you will see being cut from large pizzalike trays. A recipe with origins that date from ancient times, kanafeh is mildly sweet cheese, grains, and pistachios baked in a very light honey syrup and served (optionally) with a bit more honey syrup on top. Buy a ticket at the cashier's counter for an order of kanafeh and take a table (drinking glasses are communal—you'll probably prefer a soft drink or bottled water) in the newly renovated polished gray marble cafe that has unfortunately replaced the old domed-ceiling rooms, or ask to have your order boxed for takeout (bring your own napkins and plastic forks). Absolutely delicious when warm!

From Damascus Gate, bear right at the fork in the road, and continue into the narrow bazaar. Jaffar is the second large pastry shop with glass windows on the right.

THE JEWISH QUARTER

This part of the Old City is home to a number of kosher fast-food spots, the best of which is a branch of Bonker's Bagels at the Seven Arches, near the Burnt House. On Jewish Quarter Road are two wonderful (nonkosher) old-fashioned Arabic-style bread bakeries where you can buy warm, freshly baked pita and big sesame bread rolls, which are tasty to snack on as you make your way around the Old City. Ask them for a tiny package of *zatar* (local spices) to flavor the bread in the traditional Middle Eastern style.

Expensive

Cardo Culinaria. Covered Section of the Cardo. ☎ **02/626-4155.** Reservations necessary. Set lunch NIS 115 ($25), set dinner NIS 160 ($35); 12% service added. AE, MC, V. Sun–Thurs noon–2pm and evenings by reservation only. Fri noon–2pm. FAUX ROMAN.

If you've ever had the urge to dress up in a toga and dine in a room that looks like a set from a 1950s B-movie biblical epic, the Cardo Cullinaria is the answer to your dreams. Tour groups are often booked in here, and if you let yourself go with the flow, the whole experience can be enjoyable; kids especially find this place fun. The stone furniture and dishes are modeled after Herodian artifacts dug up not 500 feet from your table, and food items that originated in the Americas and were introduced to the Middle East after Columbus, such as tomatoes, potatoes, and corn are strictly verboten. A meal starts with Iraqi pita bread, served with olive oil and *zaatar* (local herbs and spices); then comes lentil soup (with croutons). Tasty *zaatar* chicken is the main course for the budget lunch; more expensive lunch and dinner menus add a course of goose breast in plum sauce or stuffed Cornish hen. All menus offer stir-fried veggies and (naturally) Caesar salad followed by plates of fresh and dried fruits for dessert. Coffee and tea belong to a later era, and are thus unavailable, but there's wine and entertainment at the evening meal. Dinner is a spectacle, with dancing girls and (anachronistic) amplified music included in the price.

WEST JERUSALEM
NEAR ZION SQUARE
Expensive

✪ **Darna.** 3 Hyrcanos (Horkanos) St. ☎ **02/624-5406.** Reservations necessary. Main courses NIS 80–170 ($17.60–$42); complete business lunch NIS 80 ($17.60); set menu dinner NIS 200 ($37); *menu gastronomique* (tasting menu) NIS 280 ($62). AE, DC, MC, V. Sun–Thurs 12:30–3:30pm and 6:30pm–12:30am; Sat after Shabbat to midnight. MOROCCAN.

The owner of Darna, a successful Jerusalem restaurateur who came to Israel from Morocco as a youth, decided to create a fabulous, authentic Moroccan restaurant after he revisited North Africa in the early 1990s and was dazzled by the beauty of his one-time homeland. Moroccan designers and craftsmen were brought to Jerusalem to create just the right setting; top chefs were imported to supervise the intricacies of classic Moroccan cuisine prepared within the bounds of kashruth. The result is a memorable place that delights the eye and the taste buds without being hokey or touristy.

The *dechicha* (spiced barley soup) and the mezze of Moroccan salads are wonderful and very reasonably priced, as is the *pastilla*, a sweet phyllo pie usually made of pigeon, but done here with Cornish hen. These courses alone would make a fine light dinner, but the baked lamb with almonds, the couscous dishes, and the *tagines* (lamb or chicken cooked with dried fruits or vegetables in covered clay pots), are also first quality, as is the unusual stuffed sea bass, and the Safi-style sea bream. Service is in a graceful Moroccan style, and carefully chosen background music seems to echo the medinas of Fez and Marrakech. For two people, soups, the mezze and one main course or one set menu plus one main course could be more than adequate. This is one of the best dining experiences in Israel.

✪ **Haneviim 54.** 54 Haneviim St. ☎ **02/624-7432.** Reservations necessary. Main courses NIS 74–100 ($15.30–$22). AE, DC, MC, V. Sun–Thurs noon–11pm; Fri noon–3pm; Sat after Shabbat. MEDITERRANEAN FISH & VEGETARIAN.

This is a miracle—a kosher restaurant that offers one of the most lively, elegantly inventive menus in the country. Haneviim is not cheap, but it also does not go through the roof in terms of price. It's set in a renovated Ottoman-era mansion, with a dining terrace for good weather—the indoor dining room is a bit too cramped on busy nights. There are a number of fine carpaccios on the list of first courses, as well as a dynamite green salad, a house fish soup freshly herbed and aromatic with Pernod; and a tart of grouper and apple with port wine butter sauce. I adore Haneviim's spiced sweet potato soup with citron peel, but it's not often available. The daily menu keeps changing. A typical main course might be salmon on a cake of sweet potatoes with orange butter; but the kitchen can do a simple grilled fresh fish to perfection. Desserts are exquisite. Indoor dining areas can be a bit cramped on busy nights.

Moderate

✪ **Angelo.** 9 Hyrcanos (Horkanos) St. ☎ **02/623-6095.** Reservations recommended. Main courses NIS 38–68 ($8.40–$15). Complete lunch specials NIS 36 ($7). AE, DC, MC, V. Sun–Thurs noon–11pm; Sat after Shabbat to midnight. Closed Fri. KOSHER ITALIAN.

The most superb pasta in the country is served at this little place run by Angelo, a new immigrant from Rome, and his wife, Lori, a new immigrant from the United States. The ravioli is light as a cloud, the gnocchi are elegantly tender, and the risotto (a rarity in Israel) is excellent. There's also a rich cannelloni filled with ricotta and smoked salmon. Angelo's sauces are alive with flavor (I love his spicy tomato sauce, and spicy pescatora dishes), and he does special home-style favorites of the Roman Jewish community, like *spaghetti cacio e pepe* (with cheese and black pepper). If you arrange ahead of time, Angelo can prepare other Roman Jewish dishes. Focaccia and thin crust personal pizzas are made in a stone oven. Meat is not served here, but there is a fresh fish special. There are a number of Italian dessert choices. The restaurant is 2 blocks from Zion Square, parallel to Jaffa Road.

✪ **Eucalyptus.** Safra Square Municipal Center on Jaffa Road, Building 4. ☎ **02/624-4331.** Reservations recommended. Main courses NIS 55–85 ($12.10–$18.70); 10% service charge. AE, DC, MC, V. Sun–Thurs noon–4pm and 6–11pm; Fri noon–2:30pm; Sat after Shabbat. ISRAELI.

If anything could be called "Israeli cuisine," award-winning chef Moshe Basson has defined it. When his kitchen is at its best, it can turn each recipe into a work of art. The walls of this pleasant, spacious restaurant are decorated with rustic artifacts and antique farming tools. Mr. Basson knows the fields and farms around Jerusalem like the shelves of his own pantry and the vibrant flavors of herbs and spices used in Jerusalem kitchens for centuries appear in everything you order. Try an assortment of

Dining in Downtown West Jerusalem

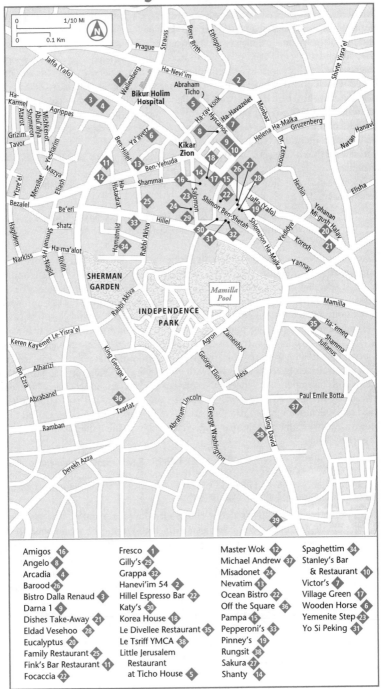

Amigos 16	Fresco 1	Master Wok 12	Spaghettim 34
Angelo 8	Gilly's 29	Michael Andrew 37	Stanley's Bar
Arcadia 4	Grappa 32	Misadonet 24	& Restaurant 10
Barood 26	Hanevi'im 54 2	Nevatim 13	Victor's 7
Bistro Dalla Renaud 3	Hillel Espresso Bar 22	Ocean Bistro 22	Village Green 17
Darna 1 9	Katy's 30	Off the Square 36	Wooden Horse 6
Dishes Take-Away 21	Korea House 18	Pampa 15	Yemenite Step 23
Eldad Vesehoo 28	Le Divellee Restaurant 35	Pepperoni's 33	Yo Si Peking 31
Eucalyptus 20	Le Tsriff YMCA 38	Pinney's 19	
Family Restaurant 25	Little Jerusalem	Rungsit 38	
Fink's Bar Restaurant 11	Restaurant	Sakura 27	
Focaccia 22	at Ticho House 5	Shanty 14	

Middle Eastern salads or an appetizer of grilled fresh forest mushrooms, and you'll begin to see that everything is unusual and delicious. Soups include sorrel, eggplant, and Jerusalem artichoke, tomato with mint, and special in-season creations like a rich, cold almond and garlic soup filled with mint leaves and grapes (the chef knows just the taste effects he wants you to experience). Chicken mahlooba, a traditional dish baked with seasoned rice, walnuts, and pine nuts, is the house specialty (normally a heavy, earthy dish, here it is prepared in a light manner—if you don't like dark chicken, order it with skewers of exquisitely grilled cubes of chicken breast). Seasonal specialties include figs stuffed with chicken and served in a date sauce. Homemade liquors and other tidbits round out the menu. For $33 per person, Eucalyptus will let you sample its entire repertoire, and have seconds on things you especially like, wine included.

It's 1 block from Zion Square parallel to Jaffa Road on the second floor of the Jerusalem Inn Guest House.

○ **Stanley's Bar & Restaurant.** 3 Horkanos St. ☎ **02/625-9459.** Main courses NIS 50–90 ($11–$19.80); luncheon specials NIS 26–39 ($5.70–$8,50). AE, DC, MC, V. Daily noon–midnight. FRENCH/SOUTH AFRICAN.

Take excellent meats, basted with South African marinades and grilled by cooks who care about what they're doing. Add a spacious dining room away from the tourist crush, a selection of good French sauces and first courses, a touch of homey South African specialties, and you have the formula for a delicious, gracious but not overly pretentious restaurant that's easy to enjoy. Appetizers include a number of fine Israeli foie gras choices; skewers of portobello mushrooms grilled with a house marinade; onion soup served in a pastry crust; and South African Boerewors sausage. Main courses include lamb spare ribs, filet mignon, Tournedos Rossini, salmon, chicken and mullard (an Israeli hybrid), all served with your choice of Dijon, pepper, port wine, cream with mushrooms, or ginger and caper sauces. The fabulous complete luncheon specials are the most elegant as well as the best deal in town, and range from a light salad and quiche to soup or salad plus sirloin steak, salmon, or chicken. Grilled fillet of ostrich may become Stanley's new hit. Cape brandy pudding filled with nuts, is the dessert of choice.

Wooden Horse. 3 Ya'avetz St. ☎ **02/624-4395.** Reservations recommended. Main courses NIS 48–115 ($12.50–$25.30); most main courses under $16; complete luncheon specials till 5pm NIS 38–52 ($8.40–$11.50). AE, DC, MC, V. Sun–Thurs noon–midnight; Fri noon–3pm; Sat after Sabbath. CONTINENTAL.

This is an informal place that's a great choice for both kosher and nonkosher diners. Excellent meats form the heart of the menu (which also includes fish and poultry), all served with generous portions of grilled sweet potatoes, zucchini and other vegetables. The hefty, flame-grilled sirloin steak is the best piece of kosher meat I've encountered in Jerusalem, and amazingly, it's available on the under $9 complete luncheon special served until 5pm. (If you want your steak rare, emphasize your request.) Soups, salads and first courses are good, headed by a number of foie gras choices. As the restaurant is kosher, there are no cream sauces, but among the three house sauces, I recommend an olive oil–based sauce filled with fried garlic and rosemary that went well with a generous, tender veal chop. There are pleasant house wines. The dessert list is short and not quite up to the main courses. At press time, for a 5 shekel surcharge, you could order the bargain luncheon specials until 8pm.

Inexpensive

○ **Little Jerusalem Restaurant at Ticho House.** Abraham Ticho St., off Ha Rav Kook St. ☎ **02/624-4186.** Light meals NIS 28–40 ($6.20–$8.80); main courses NIS 36–70

ⓘ Family-Friendly Restaurants

Moshiko's *(see page 110)* on the Ben Yehuda Mall is the best falafel and shwarma place in town—it's messy but delicious enough to entice most kids (outdoor tables only, so in winter this is a poor option). Nearby Pizza Hut, Burger King, and McDonald's do offer indoor seating. On the Yoel Salomon Mall, the **Yemenite Step**'s *(see page 105)* special Yemenite pancake dishes stuffed with chicken, meat, or veggies are exotic and delicious. The kosher **Master Wok** *(see page 112)* on King George Street is a cafeteria serving generous portions of fresh, tasty Chinese food at budget prices. You can see what you're getting and be in and out quickly. The budget **Family Restaurant,** hidden on a passageway between Shammai and Hillel streets, is also cafeteria-style, and offers a hot counter of great homemade Sephardic dishes.

($8–$15.40). DC, MC, V. Sun–Thurs 10am–midnight, Fri 10am–2pm; Sat after Shabbat to 11:45pm. VEGETARIAN & FISH.

You'll be amazed when you come upon this large hidden oasis with its gardens and terrace cafe right in the center of downtown West Jerusalem—it's especially wonderful for outdoor dining in summer. Built in 1880 as a private villa, around 1912, Ticho House became the home of artist Anna Ticho and her husband, Dr. Abraham Ticho, a legendary ophthalmologist dedicated to wiping out endemic eye disease. For more than half a century, the Tichos were at the center of Jerusalem's creative and intellectual society; after Anna Ticho's death in 1980, it was decided to keep the tradition of the Tichos' house as Jerusalem's meeting place par excellence. The building is now a downtown branch of the Israel Museum. There's a permanent exhibition of Anna Ticho's drawings, and another with Dr. Ticho's international collection of antique Hanukkah lamps. In the restaurant, indoors or out, you can order crepes, soups, sandwiches (hot cheese and herbs is a favorite), or vegetable pies and casseroles as well as a variety of more pricey fish dishes.

Saturday evenings, Ticho House offers a "Viennese Night," with a wonderful string quartet playing waltzes, and an all-you-can-eat buffet of blintzes and Viennese pastry. on Tuesday evenings, there's live jazz, and in addition to the regular menu, a wine and cheese buffet that includes soup and salad for $16. Service is friendly, and the kitchen is kosher.

Village Green. Beit Yoel, corner of Jaffa Rd. and Rivlin St. ☎ **02/625-1464.** Full meals NIS 30–42 ($6.60–$9.20). MC, V. Sun–Thurs 9am–10pm, Fri 11:30am–3pm. Closed Sat. VEGETARIAN CAFETERIA.

Until 1999, this great vegetarian choice (a Jerusalem institution) was located in cramped quarters on the Ben Yehuda Mall. Now, with its big new dining room and tables spread out onto the plaza at the Jaffa Road end of Rivlin Street, it's still sometimes hard to fit everyone in. Portions are big, delicious, and reasonably priced. Grab a tray and proceed to the counter, where English-speaking staff will explain the changing array of freshly baked vegetable pies in whole-wheat crusts, quiches, lasagnas, buckwheat burgers, and grilled tofu served with herbs or spicy peanut sauce. You can order just a cup of cold yogurt or garlic and cucumber soup beautifully flavored with dill, or a full meal with your choice of a custom-designed salad, steamed vegetables, and brown rice (all priced by weight) or hot soup, and a selection of great breads and dressings. Until 11am on weekdays, there's a top quality, all-you-can-eat breakfast

Getting Connected in Jerusalem

Jerusalem offers a wide variety of atmospheric places to get on line. Charges are usually NIS 6–7 ($1.30–$1.50) for 15 minutes. In West Jerusalem, the lively **Strudel Internet Cafe and Wine Bar**, 11 Monbaz St., in the Russian Compound neighborhood, (☎ 02/623-2101) serves great soups and takes Mastercard and Visa. Open Mon–Fri, from 10am until after midnight, and Saturday 3pm until after midnight, but by 8pm it's very much a party spot ("Strudel" is Hebrew slang for the "@" sign). The nearby **Netcafe**, 9 Helene Ha-Malka St. (☎ 02-624-6327) is quiet and serves good coffee. Open Sun–Tues 11am–10pm; Wed–Thurs 11am–11pm; Fri 10am–3pm; Sat 9pm–midnight. **Tmol Shilsom Bookstore Cafe,** 5 Yoel Salomon Mall (☎ 02-623-2758) is a writers' cafe and a thoughtful place to get online (with excellent food). Internet access here is available Sun–Thurs, 9am–3pm. Deep in the bazaars of the Old City, **Abu Assab's Internet Cafe,** above the venerable Abu Assab Orange and Carrot Juice Shop, at 172 Suq Khan es Zeit St. (the main thoroughfare running from Damascus Gate south), (☎ 02/628-2486) is open daily 9am–10pm and offers many discount plans and specials like a free, fresh-squeezed glass of orange or carrot juice (the best in town) with each hour online. In the Jewish Quarter, the little **Bookshelf Bookstore,** 2 Jewish Quarter Rd., (☎ 02-627-3889) is an interesting center of neighborhood activity, with 2 computers overseen by very helpful owners. Open Sun–Thurs 10am–6pm; Fri 10am–2pm.

buffet filled with country cheeses, yogurts, fresh juice, fruits, veggies, and eggs prepared to choice, all for NIS 36 ($8). Some macrobiotic foods are offered. Microwave ovens are used.

There is a quieter branch of Village Green with a garden terrace behind the Old Bezalel Art School building at 1 Bezalel St. (☎ 02/625-1464). Prices and menus are the same.

YOEL SALOMON STREET/RIVLIN STREET MALL & VICINITY
Expensive

Katy's. 2 Ha-Soreg St. ☎ 02/623-1793. Reservations recommended. Main courses NIS 95–150 ($21–$33); complete fixed-price gourmet meal NIS 180 ($40). Add 17% VAT and 15% service. AE, DC, MC, V. Daily 12:30–4:30pm and 6:30pm–midnight. FRENCH.

Long a favorite with Jerusalemites for an intimate, special night out, this is the very personal restaurant of Katy Ohana, who draws on French, North African, and local traditions to create her cuisine. Katy *is* the menu; what her restaurant offers can be very different each day. Her eggplant and goat cheese with basil, and her mushrooms, salmon, and seafood with caviar sauce are among her well-known first courses. Duckling with black currant sauce and her wonderful goose liver are the acknowledged main course specialties. Servings are usually bountiful.

✪ **Ocean Bistro.** 7 Rivlin St. ☎ 02/624-7501 or 02/623-3899. Reservations required. Main courses NIS 90–160 ($20–$35); fixed-price lunch NIS 95 ($21); fixed-price dinner NIS 160 ($35). AE, DC, MC, V. Daily 1–3pm and 7pm–midnight; last order at 10pm. MEDITERRANEAN SEAFOOD.

Set in the small, intimate stone rooms of a century-old building 1 block from the Yoel Salomon Mall, this is one of Israel's masterpiece restaurants, with an international reputation for excellence. Nothing from the kitchen is less than perfection, be it the freshest giant prawns with wild herbs and olive oil grilled on citrus charcoals; a grouper baked with fresh herbs in a clay oven; a heavenly focaccia served with herbed olive oil, rosemary, and antipasti; or a simple grilled tomato garnishing a plate of incredible seafood pasta. First courses may include crab risotto in grape leaves or eggplant sashimi in Sicilian olive juices; I especially recommend the delicate crab wrapped in pasta leaf with tomato seed butter. Shrimp dishes are exquisite, as is the fresh fish. Aged baby Marino lamb from the Golan is the basis for Ocean's meat menu; rack of lamb heads the list, but look for an interesting interpretation of Arabic shwarma. The kitchen's emphasis on simplicity lets the freshest, finest ingredients speak for themselves, yet the elegance and uniqueness of each dish is very clear.

The wine list and desserts are equal to the rest of the menu. I especially recommend a medley of inventive sorbets. The arched-ceiling dining room does not have the right acoustics for a quiet conversation, but like everything else in the restaurant, it has understated charm. Extra-attentive service is part of the Ocean experience.

Moderate

Gilly's. 33 Hillel St. ☎ **02/625-5955.** Reservations not accepted. Main courses NIS 75–115 ($16.50–$25.30). AE, MC, V. Mon–Fri noon–4pm and 6–11pm; Sat noon–10pm. Closed Sun. STEAK.

One of Jerusalem's biggest success stories, Gilly's for years offered the thickest, most delicious cuts of meat in town served with salad and potato au gratin at prices that, by Israeli standards were reasonable. Now Gilly's has gone in for fancy first courses as well (and raised its prices), but the arched-ceiling, 19th-century dining room is almost always busy with the hubbub of happy customers. A fillet steak with your choice of sauces runs $21; there are also upmarket first courses like goose liver or sautéed shrimp in tomato and garlic sauce. Especially recommended are the spareribs (a meal in itself), and the massive hamburger plate and the relatively affordable sirloin steak. Turnover is fast, but for lunch or dinner plan to come either early or late if you don't want to wait for a table. It's located in the last building on Yoel Salomon Street Mall, at the corner of Hillel Street.

✪ **Grappa.** 7 Ben Shetach St. ☎ **02/623-5001.** Reservations required. Main courses NIS 45–100 ($10–$22). Business lunch NIS 55 ($12.10). AE, DC, MC, V. Daily noon–3am. FRENCH/CONTINENTAL.

With its eye-catching logo and walls painted a hot 1950s coral, this small, bustling place is packing customers in and has become *the* restaurant for Jerusalemites to see and be seen. The food is generally excellent and fairly priced. Topping the ambitious main courses is the Grappa steak—a tower of filet mignon, goose breast, and foie gras (if you want your fillet rare, make it very clear when you give your order). First courses range from a plate of mussels in garlic and butter (try these on a day when the mussels are freshly arrived) to shrimp wrapped in smoked salmon on a bed of avocado. A popular selection of pastas and salads (hot mushroom salad with garlic, butter, and wine; grilled salad with smoked goose breast and ham) are good choices on the lower end of the menu.

Pampa. 3 Rivlin St. ☎ **02/623-1455.** Sandwiches and light meals NIS 14–20 ($3–$4.40); main courses NIS 45–115 ($10–$25.30). AE, DC, MC, V. Sun–Thurs noon–midnight, Fri noon–2pm, Sat after Shabbat. SOUTH AMERICAN GRILL.

With a special grill imported from Argentina, this restaurant turns out tasty barbecue meats, starting with reasonably priced take-out steak, chicken, or Argentinean sausage sandwiches on large rolls, and moving up market to barbecue chicken, salmon, delicious *asado* (roast meat; order it with bones for more flavor), and filet mignon. You can add a skewer of grilled vegetables for balance. The place is cozy, and in good weather there are outdoor tables on the mall. It's as good as the nearby Argentinean El Gaucho, which has maddening acoustics in winter. The banana tortilla with rum here is delicious.

Yo Si Peking. 5 Shimon Ben-Shetah St. ☎ **02/625-0817.** Reservations recommended on weekends. Main courses NIS 49–65 ($10.80–$14.30). AE, MC, V. Sun–Thurs noon–midnight; Sat 1 hour after Shabbat to midnight. Closed Fri. GLATT KOSHER CHINESE.

Set in a 19th-century building on a side street near Zion Square, this glatt kosher restaurant has a devoted following and offers a variety of vegetarian, chicken, fish, and meat dishes. The food is tasty, though not strongly authentic. Downstairs (entrance is from a separate door on the street) Yo Si Peking's Express offers great value with complete set meals (including good, filling soups) for $6.50 to $9 from noon to 7pm

Inexpensive

Amigos. 19 Yoel Salomon Mall. ☎ **02/623-4177.** Reservations recommended for dinner. Main courses NIS 40–70 ($8.80–$15.40). Lunch specials NIS 40 ($8.80) AE, MC, V. Sun–Thurs noon–midnight, Fri noon–3pm, Sat after Shabbat. KOSHER MEXICAN.

Kosher and Mexican may seem mutually exclusive, but Amigos serves up excellent versions of classics like tortilla soup, chili, tacos, and burritos, as well as margaritas that are works of iced sculpture. Filled with Israelis as well as Americans yearning for the taste of home, Amigos evolves into a Mexican-style bar by late evening. The flautas filled with chicken or tender, delicious steak, the sizzling fajitas, and the tortilla salad, served with chunks of chicken breast in a flaky flour tortilla, are all delightful. Salads and nonmeat fajitas make this a good place for vegetarians as well.

Korea House. 7 Ma'alot Nachalat Shiva St. ☎ **02/625-4756.** Main courses NIS 40–70 ($8.80–$15.40). AE, DC, MC, V. Daily noon–midnight. KOREAN.

With the prettiest dining garden in town, this little place, on a hidden lane between Yoel Salomon and Rivlin streets, has become one of Jerusalem's unexpected successes. The traditional Korean music emanating from garden is enticing, and the food (prepared by the grandmotherly Mrs. Oh, who is from Korea) is delicious, whether it comes to your table in authentic form, or modulated for Western tastes. The *Bul Gu Gi*, a tasty roast beef dish, always pleases; there are also great chopped roast calamari and shrimp dishes. The many fish and vegetarian choices are a real pleasure. Luncheon specials start at NIS 40.

✪ **Misadonet.** 12 Yoel Salomon St. ☎ **02/624-8396.** Main courses NIS 44–60 ($9.80–$13.20). AE, DC, MC, V. Sun–Thurs 11am–11pm, Fri 11am–3pm, Sat after Shabbat. KURDISH.

This is one of the most interesting ethnic restaurants in town, located in a quaint 19th-century building, with its kitchen supervised by a wonderful Kurdish-Israeli grandmother who truly knows her stuff. *Kubbeh,* a kind of dumpling often made with a cracked wheat crust and stuffed with meat or vegetables, is the heart of Kurdish cuisine. Here a number of varieties are served as appetizers and in homemade soups that are delicate blends of many tastes. A specialty of the house is *anjesia,* a large meat kubbeh in an apricot-raisin sauce; the dish to die for is *giri-giri,* a rich creation of lamb hearts stuffed with rice, pine nuts, walnuts, and meat, served in a slightly curried sauce of apricot, walnuts, and raisins. There's also fish, fried in the Kurdish style, with almonds, pine nuts, and garlic.

Look for the sign midway down Yoel Salomon Mall; Misadonet is in a courtyard off the mall.

✪ **Shanty.** 4 Nahalat Shiva. ☎ **02/624-3434.** Light meals NIS 20–40 ($4.40–$8,80); main courses NIS 35–65 ($7.70–$14.40). No credit cards. Sun–Thurs 7:30pm–after midnight, Fri 11am–3pm and 9:30pm–after midnight, Sat after Shabbat to after midnight. INTERNATIONAL.

Located in the heart of the city's restored 19th-century restaurant district, this popular and trendy pub restaurant keeps late hours and serves fresh, interesting food. The chef here is a master of spices, herbs, and seasonings. You can have a simple Jerusalem-style country plate of toasted pita, zatar (a mixture of local spices), fresh vegetables, and labaneh, or you can try Southeast Asian beef, chicken, or veggie pad thai, South American roast beef (*asado*) in brandy and rosemary sauce, or designer broccoli blintzes in a béchamel, garlic, and walnut sauce. Shanty's spicy pumpkin and sweet potato soup is one of my favorites; in season you'll find a dynamite mango soup as well. Salads filled with chunks of hot chicken or marinated livers mixed with mild herbs and spices clock in at under $9 and are meals in themselves. Indoors, Shanty can become rather smoky, but in good weather, tables are set in the courtyard. Shanty is always a favorite spot for wine, a salad, soup, and conversation. There is a full bar and wine list.

✪ **Yemenite Step.** 10 Salomon St. ☎ **02/624-0477.** Reservations recommended for dinner. Main courses NIS 35–55 ($7.70–$12.10). No credit cards. Sun–Thurs noon–1am, Fri noon–3pm, Sat after Shabbat to 1am. YEMENITE.

This place, which I consider among the most special of the many interesting choices on Salomon Street, offers a chance to sample home-style Yemenite cooking. You can order Yemenite meat soup, a meal in itself, with homemade Yemenite bread, or large, flaky, fried *melawach* pancakelike dishes served with spiced beef, chicken, or vegetables. The spicy meat *shaweeya,* made partly with organ meats, is fabulous. There are also vegetable dishes and delicious Yemenite teas and coffees to try with dessert. The decor is unexotic, and like most places on the mall it's cramped and often mobbed, but the food is tasty and unusual.

JERUSALEM COURTYARD

The Jerusalem Courtyard, filled with interesting restaurant selections that are a bit quieter than those on the Yoel Salomon and Rivlin Pedestrian Malls, can be reached through the gate at 31 Jaffa Rd. or via the lane to the left side of the Ocean Restaurant on Rivlin Street.

Moderate

Barood Bar Restaurant. Jerusalem Courtyard. ☎ **02/625-9081.** Main courses NIS 38–60 ($8.40–$13.20); lunch specials (till 5pm) NIS 40 ($8.80). AE, DC, MC, V. Mon–Sat 12:30pm–1am. CONTINENTAL/SEPHARDIC HOME-STYLE.

This cozy, friendly little place with a few additional tables out in the courtyard offers hefty choices like pork spare ribs with barbecue sauce rosemary or goose breast in an oyster sauce, but the Balkan/Sephardic home-style dishes are what's most interesting. Look for leek stew with meat and plums, or an oven-baked casserole of spicy meatballs with eggplant. There are also interesting first courses like pickled quail eggs or *pastelikos* filled with meat and pine nuts, eaten with hard-boiled egg and spiced salad. There's live music and a party atmosphere, often with Bulgarian Sephardic music Fridays at 4:30pm; Saturdays from 5:30 to 8:30pm there's jazz. There is a full range of alcoholic and nonalcoholic drinks.

✪ **Eldad Vesehoo.** Jerusalem Courtyard. ☎ **02/625-4007.** Dinner reservations recommended. Main courses NIS 46–95 ($10.20–$21); lunch specials (till 5pm) NIS 30–44

($6.60–$9.60); fixed-price dinner NIS 70 ($19.50). AE, DC, MC, V. Daily noon–1am or later. FRENCH/MEDITERRANEAN.

Tucked away in a lane leading into the restaurant-filled Jerusalem Courtyard, this little restaurant with a few extra tables outside in summer has the feel of a place in southern France. The food, too, can vie with French standards. The filet mignon is superb and you can enjoy a leisurely paced meal with fine first courses and wines. Appetizers include goose liver done to perfection, shrimp soup, and salads. Main courses range from tarragon chicken or sautéed mussels to wonderful grilled trout served with your choice of sauces. The thick sirloin steak is especially recommended. Beyond belief are Eldad's complete luncheon specials. The choices are written in Hebrew only on the place mats (ask your waitress for a translation). They include chicken, steak, and fish choices served in a variety of fine sauces; along with Stanley's (see above) Eldad offers the most elegant as well as the best lunch deals in town! In summer, the cold yogurt, cucumber and dill soup is fabulous.

✪ **Pinney's.** Jerusalem Courtyard. ☎ **02/625-9270.** Reservations recommended for dinner. Main courses NIS 40–88 ($8.80–$19.50); business lunches from NIS 36 ($8). AE, DC, MC, V. Daily noon–11:30pm. MIDDLE EASTERN.

The first restaurant on the left as you enter the courtyard from Jaffa Road, Pinney's is admired for excellent meat served with interesting Middle Eastern salads and side dishes. Pinney (who also owns Eldad Vesayhoo, see above) has cornered the market on top quality meat, and he serves it at prices that are amazingly low, considering what you get. Luncheon specials center on grilled skewered meats, breast of chicken, and nicely seasoned kabobs (ground meat), each offered with something special, like home-style Persian rice or an interesting hearty soup. Each lunch comes with hot pita bread and three beautifully made traditional salads per person. Ask your waitress about possible salad choices (avoid something ordinary, like plain techina), and about the ever-changing list of special oven baked meat dishes offered each day—they're exceptionally good, but not written on the English menu.

✪ **Sakura Japanese Restaurant.** Jerusalem Courtyard. ☎ **02/623-5464.** Sushi and sashimi platters NIS 10–85 ($2.20–$18.70); main courses NIS 60–75 ($13.20–$16.50). AE, DC, MC, V. Daily noon–midnight. JAPANESE.

Designed to suggest a typical, small-town restaurant in Japan, Sakura is believed by many to be the best Japanese restaurant in Israel, with standards that outdistance anything available in trendier Tel Aviv. The menu varies according to the seasonal availability of sushi fish, which is flown in almost daily from New Zealand, the Pacific Northwest, and the North Atlantic. There are traditional first courses like miso soup and wakame salad, and a selection of main courses that includes very fresh shrimp or calamari tempura, soba noodle dishes, salmon teriyaki, mussels in a sweet and sour sauce, and mixed sushi and sashimi platters. There's also a special fresh dinner fish of the day as well as moderately priced lunch specials.

ON & OFF THE BEN-YEHUDA STREET MALL
Inexpensive
✪ **Family Restaurant.** 23 Hillel St. ☎ **02/623-1590.** In the pedestrian passageway that connects Hillel St. and Shammai St. Main dishes NIS 25–40 ($5.50–$8.80). MC, V. Sun–Thurs 8am–8pm, Fri 8am–2pm. Closed Sat. ISRAELI HOME-STYLE.

The best no-frills restaurant in town looks from the outside like another hole-in-the-wall selling shashliks and mixed grill at its front window. Inside, you'll find a hot counter filled with a wonderful array of home-style dishes (designed by a talented

Israeli grandmother) that are a mixture of both East European and North African Jewish traditions. The best choices include fluffy fried potato patties filled with meat or mushrooms; artichoke hearts stuffed with meat and served in a creamy lemon sauce; schnitzel stuffed with mushrooms; spicy Moroccan-style fish; and house rice with raisins, pine nuts, and walnuts. Busiest at lunchtime when it may be hard to grab a table, you may find many items sold out by evening. Come at off-hours, ask for Itzik (show your Frommer's) and he'll let you put together a full meal with whatever seems most interesting to you for $9, coffee or tea included. The reasonably priced grilled meats are also quite good. Takeout is 20% less.

Focaccia Bar. 4 Rabbi Akiba St. ☎ **02/625-6428.** Main courses NIS 28–45 ($6.20–$10). AE, DC, MC, V. Daily 9am–2am. ITALIAN/MEDITERRANEAN.

A 19th-century cottage with a large dining garden is the setting for this easy, informal meeting place. In a corner of the garden, a brick taboon (oven) turns out focaccia and pizza. You can order generous hot salads filled with stir-fried veggies and chicken or goose breast, plus soups, pizzas, pastas, or stylish appetizers like fried calamari, or a plate of smoked salmon with quail eggs, cream cheese and raw vegetables. The clientele ranges from professors to families to teenyboppers, the atmosphere is lively, and the place gradually becomes an al fresco bar late on summer nights.

Hillel Espresso Bar. 8 Hillel St. ☎ **02/624-7775.** Light meals NIS 15–30 ($3.33–$6.66). MC, V. Sun–Thurs 7am–1am; Fri 7am–2pm. SANDWICHES.

Along with its neighbor Aroma, this is a stylish hangout for Jerusalem's coffee drinkers but it's also famous for terrific, Mediterranean-style sandwiches made with great breads, wonderful cheeses, herbs, spices and other ingredients. The "Hillel" sandwich consists of sun-dried tomato, fried eggplant, feta cheese, basil, and nuts; other interesting combos include salmon and smoked tuna or omelette, goat cheese, tomato, and scallion. There are also salads, good cakes, and a soup of the day. As the place is kosher, there's no meat. Takeout makes this a good choice for picnics or a meal on a run.

Nevatim. 10 Ben Yehuda St. ☎ **02/625-2007.** Complete meal specials NIS 32–42 ($7–$9.20); á la carte NIS 17–30 ($3.70–$6.60). AE, DC, MC, V. Sun–Thurs 11am–10pm; Fri 11am–3pm. VEGETARIAN CAFETERIA.

With tables out on the Mall in good weather, this small, friendly veggie cafeteria offers soups, salads, plates of steamed vegetables, tofu, stuffed or stir-fired vegetables, quiche, lasagna, veggie pies, veggie burgers, stuffed baked potatoes, and spaghetti. Here, unlike at Village Green, salads and steamed vegetables are sold not according to weight, but according to the size of the plate—the staff is usually generous in piling on your requests. There are delicious desserts and natural juices.

✪ Spaghettim. 8 Rabbi Akiva St. ☎ **02/623-5547.** Main courses NIS 23–52 ($5.80–$11.60). AE, DC, MC, V. Daily noon–1am. ITALIAN.

This bustling restaurant (one of my favorites) holds forth in the spacious arched-ceiling rooms of one of the city's great 19th-century mansions. Antipasto, salad, and soups here are hefty and filled with fresh herbs. The al dente spaghetti served with your choice of more than 50 sauces that are divided into three categories based on tomatoes, olive oil, or cream. Each sauce is filled with fresh herbs and vegetables. My favorites are *pollo zingara* (sliced breast of chicken, peppers, fresh mushrooms, garlic, hot chile, and red wine); *bianco* (peas, lemon, dill, garlic, and hot chile); the mild and peppery Alfredos; and *pollo coriander,* almost Indian in its exotic richness. Ostrich meat in a red wine hunter's sauce of fresh mushrooms and cream is among the more unusual choices. As a first course, I strongly recommend the minty salad Panzanella,

Coffee & People Watching

The Ben-Yehuda Street Mall is great for people watching and full of cafes that keep late hours. You can order giant, eminently shareable salads as well as quiches, pasta dishes, soups, rich desserts, pastry, and of course, coffee. If you just want coffee, make sure there are no minimum charges. **Cafe Chagall** and the **Riveria Cafe,** at the lower end of the Mall, are the best spots for people watching. Further up Ben Yehuda, on the left, you'll find **Cafe Atara,** the first Viennese cafe in Jerusalem, founded in 1938 by refugees from Austria who dazzled Jerusalem with their lavish pastries. Over the years, the Atara became a local legend—during the siege of West Jerusalem in 1948, it never shut, even when it had nothing to offer but water and a mimeographed copy of the *Jerusalem Post.* In 1996, the beloved cafe was driven out of its original home by Pizza Hut, but has made a brave comeback at its new location. Its clientele includes artists, journalists, and politicians as well as the usual tourist crowd.

A great cup of coffee, probably the best in town, can be found 2 blocks south of the Ben Yehuda Mall, at **Aroma,** on the corner of Hillel Street and Rabbi Akiva Street. It's a counter and a few tables, but in the past few years it has become a Jerusalem institution. It's open daily round the clock. **Cafe Achva,** at 7 Horcanos St., is a quieter place for very good coffee and a snack. It's manager, Olga, is a recent Russian immigrant always trying out new specialties in preparation for enlarging the cafe's menu of light, very fairly priced meals.

Kapulski's, for decades the foremost pastry cafe in Tel Aviv, has added a Jerusalem version at the Hillel Street end of the nearby Yoel Salomon Street Mall (again great for people watching). A second **Kapulski's** can be found at 46 Emek Refaim St., in the German Colony. **Tmol Shilshom Bookstore Cafe,** 5 Yoel Salomon Mall (rear courtyard), is an atmospheric retreat, its walls lined with books, where patrons read and browse, write letters, log on to the internet, or just linger over coffee, soup, salad, wine, or cake. Full meals and desserts here are truly excellent. Owner David Erlich arranges a marvelous calendar of evening readings in Hebrew, English, and other languages. To find it, walk down the Yoel Salomon Mall; turn left into a covered alleyway beside the 8 Together Ceramics Gallery. Once in the courtyard, the cafe is at the far left and up a flight of outdoor stairs. In the Russian Compound area, you'll find **Strudel Internet Cafe and Wine Bar** at 11 Monbaz St. (e-mail: strudel@ inter.net.il). A friendly place to get online, there's great homemade Kurdish soup here as well as salads and sundaes; it's closed Sunday. Party atmosphere in the evenings.

easily sharable. For dessert, or as a meal in itself, you might want to try one of the sweet spaghettis, ranging from *arancio* (fresh orange, butter, cream, and liqueur) to chocolate or poppy seed. Imported and Israeli wines are available, and there is a garden terrace for dining in good weather, as well as a no-smoking section.

Moderate

✪ **Pepperoni's.** 4 Rabbi Akiva St. ☎ **02/625-7829.** Dinner antipasti buffet plus main course NIS 60–70 ($13.20–$15.40); lunch antipasti buffet plus main course) NIS 40–48 ($8.80–$10.60); lunch antipasto buffet NIS 30 ($6.60). AE, DC, MC, V. Daily noon–midnight. ITALIAN/MEDITERRANEAN.

As you enter this rustic 19th-century Jerusalem stone building, you are greeted with a bountiful selection of more than 20 wonderful appetizers and salads that are brought to your table (as much as you like) by your waitress, along with a cutting board filled with sausages, cheeses, breads, and fresh vegetables, all included in the fixed price of your meal. The ever-changing choices on the antipasti table are done with a fine touch and lots of fresh herbs: potato salad in a cold yogurt and dill dressing; spicy Sephardic-style carrot salad; roasted pepper with chickpeas, parsley, and onion; or baked and smoked eggplant casseroles. After grazing on these robust country starters, it's hard to believe the main course is yet to come. You choose from at least a dozen interesting daily specials, or, for a surcharge, select from some extraspecial choices. An apèritif on the house starts out your feast. Though it's often busy, this is a great place for a leisurely meal.

ON & OFF KING GEORGE V AVENUE
Expensive
✪ **Arcadia.** 10 Agrippas St. ☎ **02/624-9138.** Reservations recommended. Main courses NIS 100–150 ($22–$33); lunch fixed-price menu NIS 110 ($24.20). AE, MC, V. Mon–Fri 12:30–3pm and 7–10:30pm; Sat 1–3pm and 7–10;30pm. Closed Sun. In the lane between 63 Jaffa Rd. and 10 Agrippas St. FRENCH/MEDITERRANEAN RIM.

This little hideaway has understated, minimalist decor, a dining garden, and top reviews from Israeli and foreign food writers. The content of the French/Mediterranean Rim menu constantly changes and is done with a light touch that matches the decor. Among first courses, you may find a terrine of salmon served with a dill sauce based on fragrant, home-pressed olive oil, or a heavenly goose liver sautéed in balsamic vinegar and onion jam. Baby saddle of lamb on a bed of ratatouille with blackened roasted garlic and thyme flowers heads the list of main courses, which always includes simple, carefully prepared fresh fish. The wine list is especially good, drawing on boutique choices from Israel's Castel, Bustan, and Margolit wineries as well as imports. In my own experience, the serving staff has not been strong in explaining details of menu choices, and pigeons can make dining under the trees in the garden fraught with danger. Arcadia is away from the bustle of the downtown restaurant district, and is reached through an offbeat little lane.

Fink's Bar Restaurant. 2 Ha-Histadrut St. ☎ **02/623-4523.** Reservations recommended evenings. Light meals and appetizers NIS 25–70 ($5.50–$15.40); caviar NIS 260 ($57.20); main courses NIS 70–210 ($15.40–$46.20). AE, V. Sat–Thurs 6pm–after midnight; closed Fri. CONTINENTAL.

This is a Jerusalem legend, the oldest of all West Jerusalem's restaurants. A quick early evening visit may make you wonder what all the fuss is about; however, what appears to be a small middle-class American bar with a few tables on the side offers an amazingly lengthy, beautifully prepared menu and knowledgeable service that has kept its clientele of political leaders, artists, and writers coming back for more than half a century. A recent addition to Fink's legend was Peter Arnett and the CNN news team, who decided to celebrate the end of the Gulf War here, and phoned in by satellite from Baghdad to make the reservation. You can order Russian caviar, a sliced avocado salad, or chateaubriand for two; whatever you want, Fink's will provide. The bar is the best stocked in the country, and can be an interesting spot for evening encounters. It's located off King George V Avenue near Ben-Yehuda.

Moderate
Besograyim. 45 Ussishkin St. ☎ **02/624-5353.** Main courses NIS 45–75 ($10–$16.50). AE, DC, MC, V. Sun–Thurs 9am to after midnight, Fri 9am–3pm, Sat after Shabbat to midnight. VEGETARIAN & FISH.

Street Meals

Falafel & Shwarma   My favorite falafel is on the corner of Agrippas Street and the wide uncovered pedestrian street of the Mahane Yehuda market (on your right as you walk up Agrippas Street from King George: It's the first broad market street past the covered market area). Here you'll find two side-by-side **Yemenite falafel counters** serving well-spiced falafel fritters, and all kinds of salads, pickled vegetables, sauces, and condiments. For a bit extra, you can ask for your falafel to be wrapped inside an enormous Iraqi pita instead of a plain pocket pita, which makes for a very filling meal. Best of all, you can carry your sandwich across Agrippas Street, and through one of the entrance portals to the old Nahalot neighborhood, where you'll find a small playground with benches. There, under the scrutiny of the local cats, you can sit down and enjoy your meal (bring your own napkins). This park is also a good place to bring a take-out mixed-grill sandwich from **Sima's** or **Sami's** farther down Agrippas Street. I always like to slice a few little plum or cherry tomatoes from the market into my takeout sandwiches.

At the corner of Agrippas and King George streets, you'll find a large and very busy **falafel and shwarma place** with mountainous displays of chopped salads. Here you'll have to eat standing on the sidewalk like a normal Israeli, but without the local skill of not dripping falafel sauce all over yourself and having half your sandwich land in the gutter. The falafels are average, but the spot is convenient, open until 10pm or later from Sunday to Thursday (till 2pm Fridays), and the turnover is fast, which ensures freshness. **Moshiko's** at the lower end of the Ben-Yehuda Mall does Jerusalem's best shwarma sandwiches. The quality is tops, the portions excellent, and if you can nail down one of Moshiko's outdoor tables, you can people watch and not lose half your sandwich on the ground.

On the north side of Hanevi'im Street, opposite its intersection with Havatzelet Street, you'll find two places selling what many Jerusalemites consider the **best falafel** in town. See if you agree with the experts. A favorite with students, these counters offer no place to sit down, but you can shelter indoors in bad weather.

The Gate Cafe, just inside the Damascus Gate, on the left, serves fabulous extra spicy "hand-built" shwarma, a kind of shwarma not made on a spit.

Bagels   Bonkers Bagels, 41 Jaffa Rd. (☎ 02/624-4115), right at Zion Square, sells a variety of freshly made bagels ranging from onion, garlic, and whole wheat

Located a few blocks from the Ben-Yehuda triangle, in a late-Victorian stone bungalow surrounded by a shady dining terrace, this vegetarian and dairy restaurant has real charm and wonderful food. I recommend the soups, including Argentinean gazpacho; the very hefty, inventive salads; vegetarian pies served with salad; and the special salmon steak served in a creamy house sauce. For dessert, you can choose from a variety of homemade cakes and pastries. There is often live music on Wednesday and Thursday evenings.

✪ **Bistro Dalia Renaud.** 10 Agrippas St. ☎ **02/625-7647.** Reservations necessary for dinner. Light meals and quiche NIS 35–52 ($7.70–$11.40); dinner courses NIS 70–100 ($15.40–$22). AE, DC, MC, V. Daily noon–11pm. Down a pedestrian lane beside 10 Agrippas St. or 63 Jaffa Rd. NORTHERN FRENCH.

to cheese for approximately (60¢) each. They're more breadlike than traditional American bagels, but they're tasty. They also sell bagel sandwiches made with a wide choice of cream cheeses, lox, and other fillings. It's open Sunday to Thursday 24 hours, on Friday until 2pm, and on Saturday after Shabbat. There are Bonkers Branches in the Jewish Quarter of the Old City at the Seven Arches, and on King George Street, between Jaffa Road and the Hamashbir Department Store. Friday mornings, Bonkers sells fresh baked loaves of challah for Shabbat.

Burekas   The block of shops on Hanevi'im Street opposite Havatzelet Street includes a **bakery with a sidewalk window** counter where you can order fresh-from-the-oven potato, spinach, or cheese burekas, as well as miniature cheese or fruit Danish-style pastries. You can find burekas throughout the city, but they're always more of a treat when fresh. The Mahane Yehuda market is another good place for freshly baked burekas.

Fresh Roasted Nuts   Yaavetz Street, a small pedestrian passageway running between Jaffa Road (half a block east of King George Street) and the Ben Hillel Street section of the Ben-Yehuda Mall complex, has two shops selling absolutely the best fresh-roasted nuts in town. My favorite is the shop at the far end of the street from Jaffa Road, just at the foot of the steps leading up to the Ben-Yehuda Mall. Prices on the signs are usually quoted for 1 kilo; divide by 10, and you'll have the price for 100 grams, which is a reasonable-size bag for one person to carry around for fortification on a day's sightseeing.

Take-Home Meals   Dishes, a storefront with no street number (and at press time, with no sign) on Jaffa Road across from Safra Square, is a little place with card tables covered with fresh-off-the-stove pots of homemade Iraqi kubbeh, soups, couscous, wonderful meat, chicken and fish patties, stuffed vegetables, and many other foods from Middle Eastern Jewish cuisines. Point to what looks interesting, put together a meal, and take it back to your hotel room. Everything is delicious and authentic; a very full meal rarely tops $5 to $7.

Ice Cream   Conus, a wonderful Israeli choice, is on a passageway facing the side of the Hamishbir Department Store on King George Street. The American **Ben and Jerry's** is at the top of Hillel Street 1 block down from King George; it's self-service with tables. There's an American **Carvel** on King George Street, in a row of shops set back from the road to the side of Bank Ha-Poalim.

Belgian Waffles   Babette's at Shammai Street near Yoel Saloman Street is a Jerusalem legend—each waffle is custom made.

With a fabulous pastry chef in its kitchen, this little informal place offers the richest, most wonderful desserts and quiches in Israel, all prepared in true Alsatian tradition. Ingredients as well as skill are evident in every gourmet morsel—Dutch butter, superb cheeses, the finest herbs, vegetables, and meats. The Alsatian torte is a house specialty, filled with fillet of beef, pork jambon, and marinated in white wine; dinner courses might include breast of mullard or fillet steak in creamed mushroom or red wine and port sauce; the fabulous breads, great with the house pâté, are all in-house. For dessert, try the fruit tarts of homemade jam, the crème brûlée, or the lavish truffle made with black Belgian chocolate, Kahlua, and Grand Marnier. There are fixed-price luncheon specials starting at NIS 82 ($18).

✪ **Fresco.** 59 Haneviim St. ☎ **02/537-8225.** Reservations necessary. Main courses NIS 50–90 ($11–$19.80). AE, DC, MC, V. Mon–Sat 1pm–1am. Take Wallenberg St. from Jaffa Rd.; Fresco is near the top of Wallenberg, on the left-hand side of the street. MEDITERRANEAN.

This 19th-century mansion was once the home of the Navon family (Yitzak Navon, Israel's president during the 1980s, was a scion of this old Jerusalem family). Today, with its lovely dining garden, intimate rooms, and arched windows, *Beit Navon* (the Navon mansion) houses Fresco, a quiet, charming hideaway that serves wonderful food, some of which has its origins in French, Spanish and Italian tradition; some drawing on local ingredients and traditions. There's a wide range of interesting tapas—meatballs filled with herbs and spices and served in a frothy saffron/almond sauce, is a gourmet version of an old Jerusalem recipe. Among the main courses, the lamb cutlets flavored with a consume of ginger and louisa (a local herb) also has roots in Jerusalem's cuisine. The constantly changing menu abounds with rustic, skilled presentations of foie gras, fish, seafood (including calamari, four kinds of crab, shrimp, mussels, and lobster) as well as steaks.

Despite the entrance through an ugly parking lot, Fresco is the kind of hidden enclave that nurtures slow, romantic meals. Spanish, Italian, Israeli, and California wines are served.

Inexpensive

Marvad Haksamim. 16 King George St. ☎ **02/625-4470.** Main courses NIS 22–50 ($6.20–$14); most under $10. No credit cards. Sun–Thurs 10am–11pm; Fri 10am–3pm. EUROPEAN/ISRAELI.

Well known for heaping plates of freshly made home-style food, this is a bustling no-frills place where it's hard to get a table at lunch- and dinnertime. Turnover is fast, however, and you'll be rewarded for waiting. Your meal comes with Yemenite tomato puree and a large freshly baked loaf of flat, flaky Yemenite *salouf* bread (1 shekel charge and very worthwhile). Main-course offerings include healthy portions of goulash, schnitzel, chicken, brisket, or grilled meats served with your choice of potatoes, rice, pasta, vegetables, or salad. You probably won't need a first course to fill up, but in case you want a light meal, you can have a plate of five kinds of house salads for NIS 18 ($5) or stuffed vegetables for NIS 16 ($3.50). There are also rich Yemenite calf's foot, or pumpkin, potato, and meat soups as well as Kurdish-style koubeh soups and European blintzes (including liver blintzes) that make the menu a bit exotic. Service is attentive and speedy. This is an extremely good value.

Master Wok. 17 King George St. ☎ **02/625-2730.** Main courses and combo plates NIS 18–35 ($4–$7.70). MC, V. Sun–Thurs 11:30am–10pm; Fri 11:30am–2pm. CHINESE (KOSHER LEMEHEDRIN).

At this self-service cafeteria, which serves Chinese food as good as any in Jerusalem, you can choose tasty chicken, beef, tofu, or vegetable stir-fried dishes, as well as delicious sesame, sweet and sour, or spicy General Tsao's chicken, all in generous portions and reasonably priced. The food is good, but to ensure you have the best possible meal here, my advice is to go with what looks most freshly cooked; ask them not to dip into the bottom of the serving trays (where draining oil accumulates). Also, don't be shy about asking them to scoop into your plate a little more of whatever you like if your helping looks smaller than what's being doled out to locals (the staff sometimes scrimps on portions for reticent tourists). A quick, economical place to have a fun meal.

Off the Square. The Mill Shopping Center, 8 Rambam St. ☎ **02/566-5956.** Main courses NIS 34–55 ($7.50–$12.10). AE, DC, MC, V. Sun–Thurs 9am–11pm, Fri 11am–3pm, Sat after Shabbat to midnight. GLATT KOSHER/DAIRY VEGETARIAN.

This restaurant has become a Jerusalem institution, with an ever-expanding menu of vegetarian, dairy, and fish choices all prepared within the bounds of strict glatt kosher standards. Now in a new location at the Windmill Shopping Plaza down the block from the King's Hotel, the restaurant's good values and family friendly atmosphere continue to prevail. You can have a vegetarian pie, pasta, a salad, or soup for a modest price or fish, cheese fondue, and wine, for two or three times as much. Great desserts include cheesecakes and apple and pecan pies. There are special low-cholesterol dishes and no MSG is used. Beer and wine are served as well as milkshakes and herbal teas.

AGRIPPAS STREET & MAHANE YEHUDA

Walk up Agrippas Street a few blocks and you'll reach Mahane Yehuda, Jerusalem's lively fresh-produce market. You'll find yourself surrounded by no-frills restaurants and holes-in-the-walls serving generous portions of grilled meats, *shashlik* (chunks of meat on a skewer), and kabobs (which in Israel consist of ground meat on a skewer).

Inexpensive

Hashipudia. 6 Ha-Shikma St. ☎ **02/625-4036.** Main courses NIS 26–70 ($5.70–$15.40); complete lunch specials noon–5pm NIS 40 ($8.80). AE, DC, MC, V. Sun–Thurs noon–midnight. MIDDLE EASTERN.

Shipudia means "skewer," and this restaurant specializes in skewers of beef or lamb, chicken hearts and livers, chicken or goose breast, and that pièce de résistance of skewered meats: goose liver. Most of the skewers are in the $3 to $7 range, and come with your choice of two side dishes. You can put together the combination of your choice, and as an added treat, Hashipudia makes wonderful fresh Iraqi pita bread each evening in a traditional oven. A lunch special of salad or soup, main course, baklava, and tea or coffee is offered for under $10. A full range of economically priced soups, and stuffed vegetables, as well as more expensive steaks, chops, and fish makes this one of the best restaurant choices in the Agrippas Street neighborhood. Not to be confused with Shipudei HaGefen, on Agrippas Street.

To find it, head west on Agrippas Street; Ha-Shikma Street is a right turn after the market.

Sami's. 80 Agrippas St. ☎ **02/625-0985.** Main courses NIS 23–55 ($5–$12.10). AE, DC, MC, V. Sun–Thurs 11am–midnight, Fri 11am–3pm, Sat after Shabbat to midnight. MIDDLE EASTERN.

Sami's is the recently opened challenger to longtime Sima's, its across-the-street neighbor (see below). There are partisans on both sides as far as taste: Sami's, with its polished marble floors and walls and adequate seating, has certainly elevated *me'orav Yerushalmi* (Jerusalem mixed grill) to a new standard of elegance. You may even be allowed to order a hefty small-size mixed-grill sandwich and eat it at a table, although the rule of Agrippas Street is that unless you order a meal, you don't get a plate (your sandwich comes in a paper bag). Steaks, kabobs, schnitzels, and salads are all excellent. Prices include pita, olives, and pickled vegetables.

✪ **Sima's.** 82 Agrippas St. No phone. Main courses NIS 23–55 ($5–$12.10). No credit cards. Sun–Thurs 9am–11pm, Fri 9am–1pm, Sat after Shabbat to midnight. MIDDLE EASTERN.

Sima's is one of my favorite places on the street, justly admired for its wonderfully seasoned legendary mixed grill, which comes with chips (french fries), salad, bread, and condiments for about $11. Sima's is often mobbed, so the take-out mixed-grill sandwiches are a good bet. It has recently been modernized and expanded in response to its upstart competition (Sami's, see above) across the street. You must order a platter meal rather than a sandwich in order to qualify for table service at busy times.

NEAR THE YMCA & KING DAVID HOTEL
Expensive

✪ **Le Divellec Restaurant at the Hilton Hotel.** ☎ **02/621-1111** daytime; **02/621-2020** evenings. Reservations necessary. Main courses NIS 117–135 ($26–$30) plus 17% VAT for nonguests of Hilton Hotel. AE, DC, MC, V. Sun–Thurs 7–10:30pm. FRENCH.

The spacious, tranquil Le Divellec takes Israeli restaurants in general, and hotel and kosher restaurants in particular, to new levels of excellence. The restaurant is guided by Jacques Le Divellec, whose Paris restaurant has received two Michelin stars, but exacting chef de cuisine Eric Attias is responsible for the day-to-day success of the kitchen. Hilton Hotels has given Attias the support and resources to maintain a menu few places in Israel can attempt. Truffles are flown in from France; only fish from the sea, rather than farmed fish, is used. As an Israeli, Attias is at home with local herbs and olive oils, and a master of sauces that are both light and exquisite; his way with Israel's already-notable foie gras is sublime. The menu changes day to day and according to season, but among first courses look for panfried foie gras escallop with a confit of root vegetables, and caramelized goose liver with Jaffa oranges. The menu is dominated by a marvelous array of fish, but there are also poultry, fillet of beef, and lamb choices, all served with generous portions of beautifully prepared vegetables. There are also occasional forays into the traditions of the Middle East, like an elegant Moroccan tagine of fish with chickpeas and saffron. Deserts and the wine list are excellent; service is pleasant and unpretentious.

✪ **Michael Andrew.** In the Zionist Confederation House, 12 Emile Botta St. ☎ **02/624-0090.** Main courses NIS 70–110 ($15.40–$24.30), including a 12.5% service charge. Set lunch menus NIS 72–82 ($15.80–$18). AE, DC, MC, V. Sun–Thurs noon–2:30pm (last orders) and 7–10:30pm (last orders); Fri noon–2:30pm. From King David St., follow Emil Botta St. past parking lot. Look for sign on right to Zionist Confederation House. BELGIAN.

A nonmeat (kosher) Belgian new cuisine restaurant that has received rave reviews since its opening in 1996, Michael Andrew's menu is dominated by elegantly prepared fish and vegetarian courses. Come here for an exciting gourmet dinner within the bounds of kashruth and for the romantic view overlooking the Old City. First courses may include stuffed zucchini flowers or ravioli of eggplant confit served beside a sauce touched with coriander. Fresh sea bass, bream, and other fish of the day, beautifully presented, are among main course choices. Desserts are splendid, and the wine list is very careful and complete. To make your meal special, reserve one of the few window tables. A tiny balcony, reached through the kitchen, has a single table for two with sweeping vistas—it's probably the most private, romantic spot to have a fine meal in all Jerusalem (bring something warm for windy Jerusalem evenings).

Mishkenot Sha'ananim Restaurant. Yemin Moshe (below the Windmill). ☎ **02/625-1042** or 02/625-4424. Reservations recommended. Main courses NIS 100–180 ($22–$39.60); business lunch $29; add 15% service. AE, DC, MC, V. Daily 11am–1am. Bus: 5, 18, or 21 to Liberty Bell/Bloomfield Garden; take staircase street from the Yemin Moshe Windmill. FRENCH/CONTINENTAL.

Located in the beautifully restored 19th-century Yemin Moshe neighborhood, this restaurant is on the itinerary of most official VIP visitors who are not kosher. Moise Peer has created a classic French restaurant that derives extra pomp from its inspiring views of the Old City walls, its formal service, museum-like wine cellar, and culinary standards. Duckling and foie gras are mainstays; the duckling Paradise with figs is recommended, as are the tournedos Rossini (cuts of fillet steak on a bed of artichoke hearts with truffles and a Madeira-based sauce) and the exotically flavored salmon trout. Tables are not really set up to take advantage of the view, which is wonderful by day, but somewhat lost at night. The wine list is extensive.

Moderate

Le Tsriff Restaurant at the YMCA. 26 King David St. ☎ **02/623-1154.** Reservations recommended evenings. Main courses (which include a first course) NIS 70–100 ($15.40–$22). AE, DC, MC, V. Daily 8am–midnight. CONTINENTAL.

The gracious dining room here is decorated in the Islamic art deco style of the British Mandate, with an Ottoman Turkish fireplace and French doors leading out to the terrace. The menu ranges from lower priced vegetable, meat, and shrimp pies to very pricey fish and steak dinners. There is also a complete wine list. In good weather, dining on the terrace is a Jerusalem tradition. A less-expensive breakfast, light lunch, and dessert and coffee menu is served only on the outdoor terrace.

Rungsit. 2 Jabotinsky St. ☎ **02/561-1757.** Reservations recommended. Main courses NIS 50–115 ($11–$25.30). AE, DC, MC, V. Sun–Thurs noon–midnight; Fri 11:30am–3pm; Sat after Shabbat to midnight. GLATT KOSHER THAI/JAPANESE.

If you're looking for something exotic within the bounds of kashruth, this is an excellent choice. The menu is mostly Thai, strongly modified for Israeli taste, which means most dishes come in somewhat sweet rather than highly spiced hot sauces. Main courses shine with top quality ingredients. The boned crispy duck in mildly piquant sauce and the curried lamb may not be totally authentic, but they *are* heavenly. Appetizers are not the strong points here, but the Thai coconut and chicken soup spiced with coriander and lemon is wonderful.

Inexpensive

Giora's. 10 King David St. ☎ **02/624-1015.** Main courses NIS 30–55 ($6.60–$12.10); Fri night Shabbat dinner and Sat lunch NIS 65 ($14.50). AE, DC, MC, V. Sun–Thurs noon–11pm; Sat after Shabbat to 11pm. VEGETARIAN.

Located in a newly renovated 19th-century building, Giora offers a delicious, creative vegetarian menu that's eminently affordable. The shareable chef's platter combines a number of Giora's specialties, including inventive moussaka, and pancakes stuffed with spicy "Indonesian" rice. The quiches are somewhat like soufflés; the zucchini, leek, and pumpkin quiche is especially tasty. You can also order grilled or baked fish with potato and salad. Inventive desserts and wine served by the glass make this a nice place for a leisurely meal and conversation. Because Giora is part of a guest house, its kashruth certificate allows the serving of meals on the Sabbath, if prearranged and paid for. The Friday night dinner with wine and challah is an excellent choice for kosher travelers who are vegetarian.

THE WESTERN EDGE OF THE CITY

Moderate

✪ **Kohinoor.** In the Holiday Inn Crown Plaza Hotel. ☎ **02/658-8867.** Reservations recommended. Main courses NIS 30–68 ($6.60–$15); lunch buffet NIS 55 ($12.10) plus 10% service. AE, DC, MC, V. Sun–Thurs noon–4pm and 6pm–midnight, Fri noon–4pm, Sat after Shabbat to midnight. KOSHER INDIAN.

With its black-lacquered Queen Anne chairs, decorative Southeast Asian artifacts, and attentive service, this kosher branch of Tel Aviv's famous Tandoori Restaurant creates a graceful atmosphere of Anglo-Indian elegance. The sumptuous and affordable luncheon buffet is an unusual chance for travelers who are kosher to become acquainted with one of the world's great cuisines. You might want to start your meal with *zafrani lassi,* a refreshing, chilled "yogurt" drink. The boneless tandoori chicken dishes are a favorite main course, succulent and flavorful. I was amazed by the fine *nawabi korma,* a boneless chicken prepared in lightly creamed and seasoned saffron sauce based on soy instead of milk in order to conform to kashruth regulations.

Everything is authentic and of very high quality, but for those who are not accustomed to Indian food, the staff will be happy to adjust the seasonings to moderate levels.

SOUTH JERUSALEM
GERMAN COLONY & BAKA
Inexpensive

Caffit. 35 Emek Refaim St. ☎ **02/563-5284.** Light meals and main courses NIS 30–55 ($6.60–$12.10). DC, MC, V. Sun–Thurs 7am–1am; Fri 7am–2pm; Sat after Shabbat. Bus: 4, 14, or 18. CAFE.

With its busy garden terrace, this is the main watering hole for the gentrified German Colony. Breakfasts are served, and the large salads with a basket of rolls and herb butter are popular. Pastas, crepes, bagels and lox, and vegetable pies round out the menu. People come here just to sit and talk over a piece of cake, crepes, or ice cream, along with a glass of wine or other alcoholic beverage.

Coffee Mill. Emek Refaim 23. ☎ **02/672-5491.** Coffees and teas NIS 10–15 ($2.20–$3:30); pastries and sandwiches NIS 9–16 ($2–$3.50). AE, MC, V. Sun–Thurs 7:30am–8pm (till 10pm in summer); Fri 7:30am–3pm. Bus 4, 14, 18. COFFEE.

One of the many little neighborhood places that make the German Colony special, the Coffee Mill's walls are lined with 70 kinds of beans and tons of teas. They'll prepare a cup of Guatemalan, Ethiopian, Sumatran, mint chocolate, almond, or butterscotch coffee for you, as well as exotic teas. Sandwiches are rather plain; the homemade cakes and pies are quite nice.

Da La Thien Chinese Restaurant. 34 Derekh Bet Lehem (Baka). ☎ **02/673-2432.** Main courses NIS 32–90 ($7–$19.80). MC, V. Mon–Fri noon–3pm and 6:30–11pm, Sat noon–10pm. Closed Sun. Bus: 21 to first stop on Derekh Bet Lehem, then walk back 2 long blocks toward the town center; Da La Thien is opposite a service station. NONKOSHER CHINESE.

This bungalow, from the British Mandate period, is considered by some to house the best nonkosher Chinese restaurant in town. It is open on Shabbat, and there is a wide selection of chicken, seafood, pork, and beef dishes. Calamari and shrimp are at the higher priced end of the menu; most dishes are under $12.

Kampai Sushi Bar. 20 Emek Refaim St. ☎ **02/563-1170.** Main courses NIS 36–55 ($8–$12.10); business lunch NIS 40 ($8.80). AE, DC, MC, V. Sun–Thurs 12:30pm–midnight; Fri noon–3pm; Sat after Shabbat. Bus: 14, 18. SUSHI.

This charming little place, serving meals prepared according to kashruth, but without a kashruth certificate, feels like a tiny piece of Japan. The food is delicious and the visual presentation is delightful. Try the miso soup dotted with scallion, inari (tofu dumplings stuffed with fish, shiitake mushroom, and scallion), a variety of gyoza (pastry dumplings), and quality, fresh sushi and sashimi combination plates. There's a choice of Japanese and European beer, Israeli wines, and sake. In good weather, a few tables are set outside.

Te'enim Vegetarian Cuisine. 21 Emek Refaim St. ☎ **02/563-0048.** Main courses NIS 32–50 ($7–$11). AE, DC, MC, V. Sun–Thurs 8am–11pm, Fri 8am–2pm. INTERNATIONAL VEGETARIAN.

Owner Patrick Melki, who comes from the south of France, has designed the menu of this neighborhood vegetarian restaurant with real style. Each night of the week, in addition to the standard fare, there is a special dinner from a different part of the world. The numerous salads range from Mediterranean classics to Chinese. Tofu dishes are house specialties. Desserts are homemade and each choice just a bit original.

Yo-ja Asian Bar-Restaurant. 25 Emek Refaim St. ☎ **02/561-1344.** Main courses NIS 35–62 ($7.70–$13.60). AE, DC, MC, V. Sun–Thurs noon–11pm; Fri noon–3pm; Sat after Shabbat. CHINESE.

This kosher Asian-style restaurant specializes in noodle and dim sum dishes, although it offers meat, poultry, and vegetarian dishes as well. There is an open kitchen, so you can watch the Chinese cooks at work, and a dining terrace in a rear garden. Always delicious, Yo-ja's noodles are a chewy earthy in-house interpretation of Asian noodles, served in Thai, curried, Szechuan, and other styles. The doughy dim sum are tasty, as are the soups. The kitchen will do authentically fiery Szechuan and Hunan spicing on request.

HEBRON ROAD

The magnificent hillside overlooking the Old City has developed a number of lively restaurants and cafes. The beautiful stone Haas Promenade, or Tayelet, that winds along the hillside comes with its own cafeteria and a new, elegant restaurant, as well as out-of-the-way spots on the grass where you can bring your own picnic. Just before twilight is an especially nice time to come, when the Old City and the Judean Hills sink into a powdery mysteriousness. To get to this neighborhood, take bus no. 5, 6, 7, 8, 21, or 48 to the railroad station, or bus no. 4, 14, or 18 and ask for the stop nearest the Cinémathèque.

Inexpensive

✪ **Cacao at the Cinémathèque.** Hebron Rd. ☎ **02/671-0632.** Main courses NIS 35–70 ($7.70–$15.40). Add 13% service charge. AE, DC, MC, V. Daily 10am to after midnight. ITALIAN/MEDITERRANEAN.

With dazzling views of the Old City walls, Mount Zion, and the ancient City of David, the terrace of this restaurant is an absolute must for a meal or coffee and dessert, from late April until November (and whenever the weather is warm enough in winter). The staff lets the freshest vegetables, the finest herbs, and wonderful breads and cheeses speak for themselves. You can feast on a large country salad, an order of freshly baked focaccia bread (served with fresh herbs and olive oil, and highly recommended), or try the soups, elephantine bagels, homemade pastas, and excellent peasant sandwiches. Fresh salmon and trout, very moderately priced, are among the real gems of the menu. Desserts here are refined rather than hardy, and include a thick, pure, flourless chocolate cake. Jazz players and other musicians perform on Fridays from 5 to 9pm; Mondays from 6 to 9pm there's a chamber quartet. There's a full bar with a good array of wines. All Saturday, there are complete meal specials for under $10. *Note:* Reserve if you want a table on the terrace!

Pesto. Khan Bldg., Remez St. ☎ **02/671-9602.** Reservations recommended. Main courses NIS 36–68 ($8–$15). AE, DC, MC, V. Daily noon–midnight. Bus: 4, 7, 8, 14, 18, 21, or 48 to Khan/Train Station stop. ITALIAN.

Located on the upper floor of an old stone caravanserai (a caravan inn) from Ottoman time, this good, nonkosher Italian restaurant is open on Shabbat, and can mix milk and meat, so you can order traditional dishes like chicken parmigiana and lasagna with meat. Pastas are served with traditional sauces as well as such house creations as a liver, cream, and vodka sauce. In good weather, the restaurant spills out onto a broad terrace overlooking the khan's courtyard; it's a picturesque spot for a leisurely meal.

Promenade Café. Haas Promenade (Tayelet). ☎ **02/673-2513.** Main courses NIS 30–45 ($6.60–$10). No credit cards. Daily 9am–midnight. Bus: 8 or 48 from Jaffa Rd. CAFETERIA.

The Tayelet's own cafeteria-restaurant is not up to the view, but you'll find light meals and less-expensive main courses at the self-service section, plus desserts, beer, and wine.

EAST JERUSALEM
EXPENSIVE

⭐ **American Colony Hotel Arabesque Restaurant.** Off Nablus Rd. ☎ **02/627-9777.**
Reservations recommended. Main courses $17–$30 plus VAT; Sat luncheon buffet $34 plus
VAT; AE, DC, MC, V. Daily noon–3pm, 6:30–10:30pm; Sat noon–3pm. CONTINENTAL/
MIDDLE EASTERN.

The legendary Saturday luncheon buffet here at the atmospheric American Colony
Hotel is a truly marvelous feast. The meal includes as much as you like of the soup,
salads, fish, chicken, lamb, and beef dishes (as well as coffee and desserts). A whole
chilled salmon, rich and beautifully prepared, is often the masterpiece of the spread,
but there are surprises each week, like fresh calamari or Brittany mussels. This is a great
place to dine after spending Saturday morning in the bazaars of the Old City. The
ambience, simple yet mildly exotic, harks back to a romanticized British Empire. For
other meals, the Arabesque Restaurant runs from above average to interesting, with
such unusual touches as curried banana soup or spicy South African ostrich stew.
There is always a menu of fine traditional Middle Eastern dishes. The moderately
priced Courtyard Café offers American Colony atmosphere and light meals in the $5
to $12 range. A weekday lunch in the courtyard, somewhat less lavish than the Satur-
day buffet, clocks in at under $20, including the service charge.

MODERATE

Askadinya Restaurant Bar. 11 Shimon Hazadik St. ☎ **02/532-4801.** Reservations recommended. Main courses NIS 35–80 ($7.70–$17.60). AE, DC, MC, V. Wed–Mon noon–
midnight; Tues 7pm–midnight. One block east of Highway 1, and 4 long blocks north of the
new Olive Tree Hotel. CONTINENTAL.

With a courtyard for summer meals, and a cozy stone dining room for colder weather,
Askadinya offers one of East Jerusalem's most inventive menus filled with dishes that
are fun and delicious. Start with spiced pumpkin soup filled with herbs and shrimp or
a large, interesting salad. Main courses include lamb cutlets in a sauce of mustard,
capers, and sliced palm hearts; turkey steak Parmesan; and steak fillet medallions in
raisin and carmel sauce topped with crumbled banana and apricot. There are also traditional choices, like veal cordon bleu, as well as a good array of pastas, poultry, and
fish. You can come for light meals, coffee and dessert, or for the pleasant outdoor bar.
On Thursday evenings, there's live classical music.

⭐ **Pasha's Restaurant.** 13 Shimon Hazadik St. ☎ **02/582-5162.** Reservations recommended evenings. Main courses NIS 38–48 ($8.50–$10.70). AE, DC, MC, V. Daily noon–
midnight. One block east of Highway 1, and 4 long blocks north of the new Olive Tree Hotel.
ARABIC.

This is the best Arabic restaurant in Jerusalem, offering many homemade specialties
that just aren't offered elsewhere. Among the appetizers are wonderful lamb spleens
stuffed with parsley, garlic, and meat; great kubbeh (cracked wheat dumplings fried
and filled with meat or vegetables); fried goat cheese; sautéed lamb brains; as well as
hummus flavored with thin slices of fried lamb. The perfectly grilled skewers of cubed
lamb, chicken breast, and liver are moist and tasty, but the traditional oven dishes such
as mansaf (seasoned lamb cooked with pine nuts and almonds, served on rice with an
earthy Bedouin yogurt) and musakhan (chicken baked with onion, local spices, and
served on special fresh baked flat bread) are worth trying. The assortment of mezze salads is good, and the Arabic pastries are homemade. After dining, you can order a
nargeila (hookah) to smoke in a number of flavors. Pasha's is located in a charming
1920s stone bungalow with a dining garden that is closed and heated in cold weather.
The building is shared with the interesting Al Wasiti Art Gallery.

INEXPENSIVE

Kan Zeman. In the Jerusalem Hotel, 4 Antara Ben Shadad St. ☎ **02/628-3282.** Main courses NIS 25–50 ($5.50–$11). MC, V. Daily 11am–11pm. On a side street off Nablus Rd. facing the north side of the Egged East Bus Terminal. MIDDLE EASTERN.

In good weather, the vine-covered garden here is one of the most pleasant spots for a leisurely meal in East Jerusalem. The Jerusalem Hotel has become one of the city's savviest meeting places; Jerusalemites and travelers from both sides of the city come to enjoy the ambience. Highly recommended is the Saturday night all-you-can-eat Lebanese buffet filled with an array of salads, hot appetizers, meat courses, and desserts for $16, with live classical Arabic music. The buffet's centerpiece is the barbecue: skewers of tender steak fillet, chicken breast, and seasoned kabob (ground meat) are constantly basted over the fire (never overcooked) and served moist and juicy. The daily menu includes Arabic and western salads, an interesting home-style shwarma, grilled meats, and a few traditional oven baked specialties. In cold weather, the garden restaurant moves indoors to a Bedouin-style dining room.

IN THE COUNTRYSIDE WEST OF JERUSALEM
MODERATE

Kela David. Highway 38 (Beit Shemesh-Beit Guvrin Hwy.), Givat Yishaiahu. ☎ **02/999-4848.** Main courses NIS 32–90 ($7–$19.80). AE, DC, MC, V. Mon–Sat 10am–10pm. MEDITERRANEAN.

Set in a vineyard, Kela David (David's Slingshot) is a wonderful place for country appetizers and wine, and also for a major meal. For a light repast, the plate of cheese and peppers toasted in olive oil, garlic, and rosemary, served with fabulous homemade bread and kalamata olives are sharable and under $8 (the olive, onion, and health breads are sensational). Herbed lamb or chicken, slow roasted on hot stones in a taboon oven for 12 hours head a list of main courses that also includes goose liver in white wine sauce, as well as trout, pastas, and steak. Salads, desserts, and coffees are excellent; virgin olive oil (not importable into the United States) and local wines are for sale. Look for a pink house in a vineyard to the left of Highway 38 as you travel southward toward Beit Guvrin.

✪ **Mitspe Massua Restaurant.** Ranger's Station, Massua Forest, Beit Shemesh-Beit Guvrin Highway. ☎ **02/991-2464** or 050/306-084. Main courses NIS 36–60 ($10–$16.80). DC, MC, V. Sun–Thurs 11am–midnight and Sat after end of Shabbat. RUSTIC.

The country-style stone terrace and stone walled pavilion of this restaurant provide fabulous views, and the food, prepared by owners Yakki and Miri Cohen, is wonderful. This is one of the very few kosher restaurants in the country with kashruth certificates for both meat and dairy meals. If you give at least 2 days notice and bring a large enough party, the Cohens can prepare a complete shepherd's feast of lamb cooked with wild thyme, rosemary, hyssop, basil, and oregano for $55 per person. Otherwise, the ever-changing menu might start out with homemade bread, an assortment of Middle Eastern salads, fresh vegetables, and country cheeses, followed by a sumac- and dill-covered baked trout with vegetables and stuffed baked potato. A smaller meal of soup and salad combined with the view will be very affordable and memorable. As everything is cooked slowly on coals, allow at least 1½ hours for chicken or fish. You can call ahead to get your meal started, or, while you wait, enjoy the views of the Cohens' fabulous herb garden, or take a donkey ride around the area for around $15 for the hour.

4

Exploring Jerusalem

Jerusalem possesses much that is striking and beautiful, but more than most great destinations, it demands a sense of vision as well as eyesight. In the Hebrew language, you do not say you will "go to Jerusalem." The idiom is to "ascend" or "go up" to the city. It is not merely the city's altitude that is alluded to in this phrase.

Jerusalem today is adorned with an enticing network of museums, concerts, and performances, as well as with the archeological treasures of its past, almost miraculously rediscovered and displayed in ways that interact with the daily life of the city. There are three main sightseeing areas in Jerusalem: inside the Old City's walls, downtown East Jerusalem, and West Jerusalem, the "New City."

1 The Old City

The Old City is enclosed by a 40-foot-high wall built in 1538 by Suleiman the Magnificent, the greatest of the Ottoman Turkish sultans (some portions of the wall, in fact, are more than 2,000 years old). The existence of this wall, which gives unity and magnificence to the Old City, is something of a miracle. According to legend, Sultan Suleiman, who never visited Jerusalem, had a dream that he would be devoured by lions unless he rebuilt the walls that had lain in ruins around Jerusalem since the crusader wars of the early 13th century. So disturbing was this dream to the sultan, that he sent his architects from Istanbul to reconstruct Jerusalem's walls. Either through ignorance, or because the architects hoped to keep some of the building funds for themselves, the new walls did not include the southern part of Mount Zion, which had been inside Jerusalem's defenses in earlier times. When the sultan learned of the architects omission, he had them beheaded.

There are eight gates in the Old City fortress wall. The main gates are the **Jaffa Gate,** entered from Mamilla-Agron Street or Jaffa Road, and the **Damascus Gate,** entered from Ha-Nevi'im Street or Nablus Road. Israelis call Damascus Gate Sha'ar Shechem; the Arabic name is Bab el Amud. On the eastern side of the Old City, the **Golden Gate,** traditional entrance point for the Messiah, has been walled up for centuries.

The Old City itself is divided into five sections: the **Christian Quarter,** the **Armenian Quarter,** the **Muslim Quarter,** the **Jewish Quarter,** and **Temple Mount** (Mount Moriah), the latter including the Western (Wailing) Wall, the Dome of the Rock, and El Aksa Mosque. The Dome of the Rock and the El Aksa Mosque were built from A.D. 690 to 720, six hundred years after the Temple was destroyed by Rome. Throughout the Islamic world, this complex is called **Haram es Sharif,** or The Noble Sanctuary.

THE JAFFA GATE

The citadel tower, beside the Jaffa Gate, is called the **Tower of David,** although historically, this site was developed 800 years after David had died. Three massive towers built by Herod on the foundations of Hasmonean fortifications originally stood on this spot. After the destruction of Jerusalem by the Romans in A.D. 70, the foundations of the towers guarding the Jaffa Gate were among the few structures not deliberately obliterated on orders from Rome. They were left standing to show there had once been a city that had been no pushover to subdue. Each of the subsequent rulers of Jerusalem, from Romans and Byzantines to Muslims, crusaders, and Ottoman Turks, has rebuilt the fortifications beside Jaffa Gate, though none have come close to the scale of Herod's Towers.

Today, the citadel is the **Tower of David Museum of the History of Jerusalem** (☎ 02/627-4111), showing well-chosen temporary exhibits and an array of permanent dioramas and multimedia presentations about Jerusalem and its history. Although some of the permanent exhibits look like illustrations from a school textbook, they are useful teaching tools. The structure of the citadel itself, with its great views of the New and Old cities, is fascinating. It's a good setting for an interactive teaching performance for visitors called "The Great King Herod Murder Mystery," during which the audience is invited to untangle a web of intrigues and murders that actually occurred in the Herodian court 2,000 years ago. The court of the citadel has been the venue for concerts and for performances of plays by contemporary Israeli writers. The museum is open Sunday to Tuesday and Thursdays 9am to 7pm; Wednesday 9am to 10pm; Friday 9am to 4pm; and Saturday from 9am to 7pm. Admission is NIS 30 ($6.60) for adults. "The Great King Herod Murder Mystery" is performed in English on Saturday nights at 9pm in winter and 10pm in summer, but check for current times; admission is NIS 28 ($7.80). From April to October, a sound-and-light show that narrates Jerusalem's history in 40 minutes is presented in English on Saturdays at 9pm, and on Mondays and Wednesdays at 9:30pm. Admission is NIS 30 ($6.60). There are admission discount packages to the museum, the mystery performance, and the sound-and-light show for children, students, and seniors.

A breach in the city walls beside Jaffa Gate was made for the visit of Kaiser Wilhelm II and his entourage in 1898. Here the leader of the British forces, General Allenby, liberating Palestine from Ottoman rule, entered Jerusalem in 1917. Today, this breach allows automobiles to penetrate into the area of the Old City just inside the Jaffa Gate.

If you head straight into the **bazaar** (the suq) from the Jaffa Gate, you'll enter David Street, bustling with shops selling religious crafts and souvenirs, maps, and household items. On your left, just past the entrance to David Street, is the **Petra Hotel,** which in its day (more than a century ago) was Jerusalem's most elegant accommodation for visitors. The view from the roof is one of the most spectacular in Jerusalem, with the Dome of the Rock perfectly centered in front of you, and the entire Old City at your feet. Ask to visit the roof at the money-changer's desk just inside the door; the fee is NIS 5 ($1.10) per person. After this overview, you'll have a better idea of where things are in the maze you're about to enter.

If your first destination is the Church of the Holy Sepulcher, then take the first left off David Street, called Christian Quarter Road. But if the Western Wall and the Temple Mount are your first goal, continue straight along David Street. It makes a quick jog to the right and then to the left in the heart of the covered bazaar, where it changes its name to Street of the Chain (Silsileh, Shalshelet). Follow the street downhill as the bazaar continues. Eventually, a right on a small side street marked Ha-Kotel leads to the Western Wall. If you go straight down the Street of the Chain, however, you arrive at the Gate of the Chain, an entrance to the Temple Mount, otherwise known as the Noble Enclosure (Haram es-Sharif), with the Dome of the Rock and El Aksa Mosque its main attractions.

ARMENIAN QUARTER

As you enter Omar Ibn el Kattab Square on David Street, you'll see a road heading off to the right, past the moat. This route is the Armenian Patriarchate Road, leading into the Armenian Quarter, a quiet residential area centered around Armenian religious structures. Armenia was the first nation to adopt Christianity, predating Emperor Constantine's conversion of the Roman Empire by several decades. From that time on there has always been an Armenian presence in Jerusalem.

In the Armenian Quarter are many hidden enclaves and ancient buildings, including the **Church of the Holy Archangels,** from the early medieval period, and the **Gulbenkian Library,** containing more than 4,000 illuminated manuscripts, some of which can be seen during special exhibits. Access to these sites is variable.

The splendid **St. James Cathedral,** entered through the Armenian Monastery on Armenian Patriarchate Road, dates from the 11th and 12th centuries and is built on the site of earlier churches. It commemorates the place where James the Elder, son of Zebedee, was put to death by order of Herod Agrippas I in A.D. 44 (Acts 12: 2). The cathedral also contains the tomb of James, the oldest brother of Jesus and first bishop of the Jerusalem Christian community. This James was the author of the Epistle of James and was stoned to death in A.D. 62. The cathedral, with its rich interior of hanging lamps, censers, and ceremonial objects, may be visited for services daily from 3 to 3:30pm.

The **Helen and Edward Mardigian Museum of Armenian Art and History** (☎ 02/628-2331) displays a magnificent collection of artifacts and religious objects as well as a chronicle of Armenian history. It is open Monday to Saturday from 10am to 5pm; admission is NIS 5 ($1.10).

The Armenian Patriarchate Road follows the inside of the Old City wall and winds around to the left, passing the Zion Gate, the Jewish Quarter parking lot (inside the Old City walls) and eventually leading downhill to the Western Wall and above the Western Wall, the Dome of the Rock.

THE JEWISH QUARTER

Let's take a detour through the Jewish Quarter on our way to the Western Wall and Temple Mount. By doing so, you'll save an uphill walk, as the wall lies well below most of the quarter. But first, some history and information about this part of town and its relationship to the other parts of the Old City.

The Jewish Quarter lies directly west of the Temple Mount and sits on a higher hill than the Temple Mount itself. With the exception of the sacred Temple Mount, the entire original city of Jerusalem from the time of David was outside and to the south of the walls of the present Old City. Over the centuries, ancient Jerusalem spread northward, up the slope. In the time of King Hezekiah, around 700 B.C., much of the uphill area now occupied by the Jewish Quarter had become a new addition to the city, surrounded by the Broad Wall. But the wall and its many towers were not strong enough to keep out Nebuchadnezzar of Babylon, who conquered and laid waste to Jerusalem in 586 B.C.

Jews returned to Jerusalem after the Babylonian Captivity, but it took centuries for the city to regain its former size and grandeur. In the late Second Temple period, Jerusalem again expanded uphill and the area that is now the Jewish Quarter developed into the aristocratic and priestly residential neighborhood, with many luxurious mansions overlooking the Temple Mount. The main market street of Herodian Jerusalem developed at the bottom of the Tyropoean (Cheesemakers') Valley, which separates the heights of the Jewish Quarter from the Temple Mount. So that thousands of religious pilgrims could make their way to the Temple Mount without becoming entangled in the crush of the market, massive pedestrian overpasses were constructed. By the 1st century A.D., Herodian Jerusalem had expanded northward, beyond the present city's northern wall and the Damascus Gate. A new, bustling upper market developed where the present Suq Khan el Zeit market leads toward the Damascus Gate. The original City of David, the oldest part of town, came to be known as the Lower City.

Jerusalem was again leveled in A.D. 70 by Roman armies (the remains of houses burned in that conflagration have been uncovered in what is now the Jewish Quarter); 65 years after the Romans destroyed Jerusalem, they (and later their Byzantine successors) rebuilt the city. You can visit several recently uncovered vestiges of Byzantine times in the Jewish Quarter, including the Nea Church, and the southern end of the city's major north-south thoroughfare, the Cardo Maximus. Jews were forbidden to reside in Jerusalem during the long Byzantine period, which began in A.D. 326, and many Jewish inhabitants of the area allied themselves with the then pagan Persians, who conquered and occupied the city from A.D. 614 to 629. The Muslims were Jerusalem's next conquerors in A.D. 638, and under their more tolerant rule, a permanent Jewish community was reestablished in the northeast quadrant of the Old City, on the site of the present Muslim Quarter. The Crusaders conquered Jerusalem in 1099 and celebrated their triumph by massacring most of the city's Jewish population as well as thousands of Muslims.

In 1267, after the Crusaders were driven from Jerusalem, a small Jewish community reestablished itself in the ruins of what is now the Jewish Quarter. This area has been the center of the Jewish community in the Old City ever since.

The Jewish Quarter's most recent destruction came during and after the 1948 war with Jordan, when all the synagogues and most other buildings in the quarter were severely damaged, and over the next 2 decades fell into almost total ruin; many were systematically demolished. Since the Israeli conquest of the Old City during the 1967 War, the quarter has been rebuilt and revitalized. Although some buildings have been carefully re-created, and many new structures were designed to blend in with them, the basic nature of the current Jewish Quarter is quite different from the impoverished, densely populated neighborhoods that existed here before 1948.

Following St. James Road (a left turn off Armenian Patriarchate Road) to where it becomes Or Hayim Street, you'll come to the **Old Yishuv Court Museum,** 6 Or Hayim St. (☎ **02/628-4636**). This museum displays artifacts and crafts typical of Ashkenazi and Sephardic communities in the Jewish Quarter from the middle of the 19th century to the end of Turkish rule in 1917. Admission is NIS 14 ($3), and it's open Sunday to Thursday from 9am to 2pm.

The **Cardo Maximus** is a recently excavated 2nd- to 6th-century street that was Roman and Byzantine Jerusalem's main market and processional thoroughfare, once bordered by stately columns and lined with portico-shaded shops. What you see now, some 8 feet beneath the level of the bordering Jewish Quarter Road, dates from the Byzantine period. The original street is said to have been laid out by the Roman Emperor Hadrian (A.D. 117–38) when he rebuilt the city as Aelia Capitolina after the

Old City Jerusalem

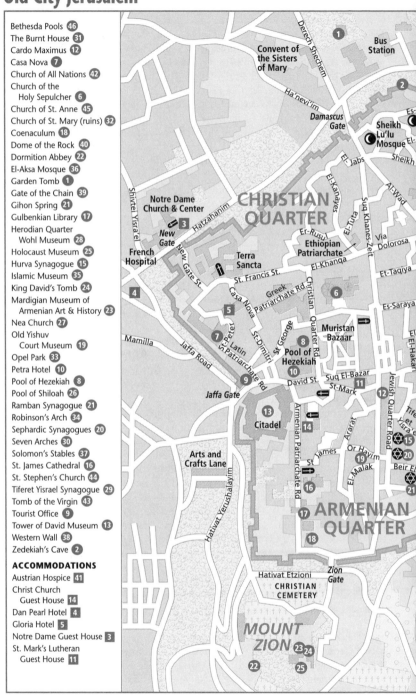

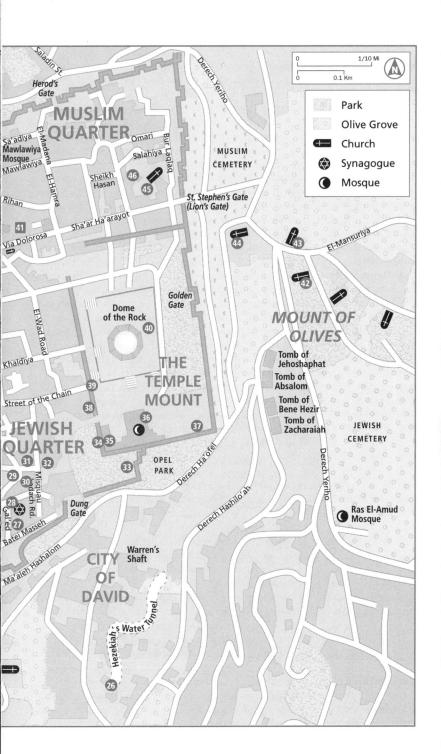

125

Bar-Kokhba Revolt of A.D. 132–35. In late Byzantine times, the Cardo was extended southward and served as the processional route between the Holy Sepulcher and the Nea, Jerusalem's two largest churches of that era.

The southern portion of the Cardo is open to the sky; the rest is beneath the modern buildings of the Jewish Quarter. At the end of Or Hayim Street, you can visit the open area of the Cardo; its imposing columns, found by archaeologists, have been reerected. As you walk northward along the reconstructed Cardo, where modern tourist shops have been installed, you can see on your right the walled-up facades of crusader-era shops built into arches. In this restored section you can look down well-like structures that reveal how far above the original level of the land the city has risen in its constant rebuilding on the ruins of each wave of destruction. You'll also see fragments of the city's defensive walls dating from the First Temple period, about 700 B.C.

Parallel to the Cardo is the Jewish Quarter Road. At the far side of the parking lot at the southern end of Jewish Quarter Road are the ruins of the **Nea Church,** long sought by archaeologists and only recently uncovered. The Nea (or "New" in Greek) was Byzantine Jerusalem's largest and second most important church after the ✪ **Church of the Holy Sepulcher.** Built by Justinian in A.D. 543, it was destroyed either by an earthquake in the late 6th century, or during the Persian conquest of A.D. 614. So complete was the Nea's eradication that its precise location was only discovered during excavations in the 1980s. Some historians theorize that the many marble columns needed to build the vast Nea may have been salvaged from the ruins of the Herodian temple, which had lain abandoned after its destruction in A.D. 70. (Procopius, a contemporary Byzantine historian, reports a bit skeptically that the columns needed to build the Nea had magically appeared near the construction site as if from heaven.) If the Nea's columns had indeed been taken from the Temple Mount, then outraged Jews who aided the Persians in their conquest of the city in A.D. 614, may have made a special effort to demolish a building constructed from pieces of their ruined Temple. Ironically, these building materials may have returned to the Temple Mount in the 7th century when the Islamic conquerors of Jerusalem reused material from the city's many ruined Byzantine structures to build the El Aksa Mosque and the Dome of the Rock. To the untrained eye, unfortunately, there is not much to see, but these few recently discovered fragments of the long-lost Nea provide a physical basis to one of Jerusalem's great and elusive legends.

Many Jewish Quarter buildings from other times are today recalled by only a single arch, doorway, or minaret. You can inspect the haunting arches, altar, apse, and ruined cloister from the once lost **Crusader Church of Saint Mary of the Teutonic Knights** (1128) on Misgav Ladach Street. If you enter the ruins, walk back to the apse, where the windows frame a wonderful view of the Temple Mount. Across from the entrance to the church is a small covered square known as the **Seven Arches.** In the pre-1948 Jewish Quarter, the Seven Arches was the heart of a lively market packed with vegetable vendors and customers. Rebuilt in its original form after 1967, the Seven Arches no longer host a market, and seem to perform no function. To the west, you'll see the minaret from the **Sidnah Omar Mosque,** and beside it a single broad, graceful arch, rebuilt from the remains of the **Hurva Synagogue,** which was once the Great Synagogue of the Jewish Quarter. Its name, meaning "ruin," recalls its difficult and unfortunate history. The original Hurva was built in the 16th century with Ottoman permission, but was soon destroyed by Ottoman decree; over the centuries, the name "hurva" became attached to the desolate site that had been built with so much hope and pride. In the 1850s, a new synagogue was authorized and built. Heavily damaged in the 1948 war, it was destroyed after the Jordanians captured the

Jewish Quarter. Since 1967, there have been a number of movements and plans (including one by the visionary American architect, Louis Kahn) calling for a new Hurva, but for now, the arch, marking the line of the building's domed roof, stands as a memorial to the synagogue that once was.

Between the minaret and the Hurva Arch is the **Ramban Synagogue** of Rabbi Moshe Ben-Nahman, who helped reconstitute the Jewish community of Jerusalem in 1267, after it had been obliterated by the crusaders. You'll also want to take a look at the complex of four small **Sephardic synagogues** named for Rabbi Yohanan Ben-Zakkai, whose school, according to tradition, occupied this site during the Second Temple period. One of the four is named for the rabbi himself, another for Eliyahu Ha-Nevi (Elijah the Prophet); the other two are the Central Synagogue and the Istanbuli Synagogue. During Muslim rule, no church or synagogue was allowed to exceed the height of the nearest mosque, so to gain headroom, the floors of these synagogues were laid well below ground level. The synagogues are open Sunday to Thursday from 9:30am to 4pm, and Friday from 9:30am to noon. Admission is NIS 12 ($2.60).

The **Tiferet Israel (or Yisrael) Synagogue** (Ashkenazi) was founded by Nisan Bek and inaugurated in 1865. Dedicated to the Hasidic Rabbi Israel Friedmann of Ruzhin (the synagogue's name means "Glory of Israel"), it was destroyed after the War of Independence and recently restored.

Moving eastward across the Jewish Quarter in the direction of the Western Wall, you can visit two remnants of the neighborhood's elegant Herodian past.

The **Herodian Quarter Wohl Museum** (☎ 02/628-3448) contains archaeological excavations, done in the 1970s, of the wealthy residential quarter of Herodian Jerusalem. It includes remains of a palatial mansion with painted faux marble walls, mosaic floors, an atrium pool, and ritual bath installations indicative of the prevailing standard of living and religious observance in this affluent quarter. Admission is NIS 14 ($3), or by combined ticket NIS 16 ($3.50) with the Burnt House (see below). It's open Sunday to Thursday from 9am to 5pm, on Friday from 9am until 1pm.

The **Burnt House** (☎ 02/628-7211) is a remnant of the destruction of Jerusalem by the Romans in A.D. 70. The wealthy Upper City, site of the present Jewish Quarter, held out for a despairing month after the Lower City and Temple Mount fell. From these heights, the inhabitants of the Upper City had stood on their roofs and watched with horror as the temple went up in flames. When the Romans finally decided to storm the Upper City, they found little resistance; much of the population was near death from disease and starvation. The Burnt House chillingly brings to light the day when the Romans burned the Upper City. In the 1970s, when archaeologists excavated what was the kitchen or workroom of this building, they found the forearm bones of a young woman amid the debris. As diggers continued to excavate the area of the room that lay where the arm pointed, they uncovered a wooden spear, almost as if the young woman had been reaching for this weapon when she met her death. Most tantalizing of the household artifacts found on this site is a set of weights marked with the name "Bar Kathros," a priestly family mentioned in the Talmud (and also in an ancient folk song as one of the wealthy families that oppressed the poor). Historians know the House of Bar Kathros was responsible for the manufacture of incense for the temple. The excavated house, now preserved beneath modern buildings, is a museum with a brief slide show about the site. The entrance to the house is marked on a modern door in the Seven Arches off Misgav Ladach Road (ask if you have difficulty finding the door). The house is open Sunday to Thursday from 9am to 5pm, on Friday from 9am until noon. Admission is NIS 14 ($3); a combined ticket to Burnt House and Herodian Quarter can be purchased for NIS 16 ($3.50).

THE WESTERN WALL

This is the Ha-Kotel Ha-Ma'aravi. It was formerly called the "Wailing Wall" by European observers because Jews for centuries came here to bewail the loss of their temple. It is the holiest of Jewish sites, a remnant of the Herodian retaining wall that once enclosed and supported the Temple Mount.

For centuries the wall stood 60 feet high and 91 feet long, towering over a narrow alley 12 feet wide that could accommodate only a few hundred densely packed worshipers. In 1967, immediately after the Six Day War, the Israelis bulldozed the Moors Quarter facing the wall to create a plaza that could accommodate tens of thousands of pilgrims. They also made the wall about 6½ feet higher by digging down and exposing two more tiers of ashlars (squared stones) from the Second Temple Plaza's retaining wall that had been buried by accumulated debris for centuries. At the southern end, away from the area reserved for prayer and worship, archeologists since 1967 have uncovered spectacular remains from various periods.

At the prayer section of the Western Wall, grass grows out of the upper cracks. The lower cracks of the chalky, yellow-white blocks have been stuffed with bits of paper containing prayers. Orthodox Jews can be seen standing at the wall, chanting and swaying. Visitors of all religions are welcome to approach the Wall and to pray silently beside it. Men who would like to go to the wall must wear a hat or take a head covering, at no cost, from a box beside the entrance to the prayer area. Women may borrow shawls and short-skirt coverings. A separate section at the extreme right of the Western Wall is reserved for women, who are not allowed into the men's section in keeping with Orthodox Jewish tradition. Services are held here daily; no photography or smoking is permitted on the Sabbath.

The exposed lower courses of the Western Wall are composed of enormous rectangular ashlars, or carefully carved stones, each dressed only with the recessed borders typical of Herodian era stonework. The sides of these monumental ashlars have been carved with such precision that they rest perfectly against and on top of each other, without mortar. Over the centuries, the fine straight lines and margins of some of the ashlars have eroded away.

The Wall was built by King Herod just before the time of Jesus and is part of a structure that retains the western part of Temple Mount and the vast, artificial ceremonial plaza Herod created on the Temple Mount itself. These retaining (as well as defensive) walls surround the western, southern, and eastern sides of the Temple Mount; the largest of the ashlars is 11½ feet high and 47½ feet long and weighs approximately 400 tons. According to Josephus, the Roman Jewish historian, construction of the walls took 11 years, during which time it rained in Jerusalem only at night, so as not to interfere with the workers' progress.

In the right hand corner of the Women's Prayer Area, beside a protruding newer building, you can see an area of the Wall composed of small, rough stones. These stones block a fragment of a Herodian era gate to the Temple Mount, today called Barclay's Gate after the 19th-century American consul who first identified it. To the south of the earthen ramp leading up the Temple Mount, you can see a fragment of large stonework protruding out of the Wall. This is **Robinson's Arch,** all that remains of a great stairway, set on arches, that passed over the busy market street at the foot of the Western Wall, and led directly into the Great Stoa on the southern side of Temple Mount.

The Western Wall is actually much higher and longer than the portion you can readily see today. For an idea of how high the original construction was, enter the doorway located between the men's rest rooms and the public telephones on the plaza's northern side. Both men and women can enter free upon request, Sunday, Tuesday, and Wednesday from 8:30am to 3pm, Monday and Thursday from 12:30 to 3pm, and on Friday from 8:30am to noon; closed Saturday. Enter the dark labyrinth of vaults and chambers, pitfalls (now rendered safe by lamps, grates, and barriers), and passages. Inside, the continuation of the Wall is clearly visible. Shafts have been sunk along the Wall to show its true depth. The arches in this artificial cavern date from various eras, ranging from Herodian (37 B.C.–A.D. 70) to crusader (1100–1244). The platform is behind a prayer room filled with Orthodox worshippers. The prayer room is off-limits to women, except in the viewing area.

A special walk into recently excavated tunnels alongside the Western Wall can be arranged by making an appointment with the **Western Wall Heritage Foundation** (☎ **02/627-1333**). Admission is NIS 20 ($4.40); special tours will be extra.

TEMPLE MOUNT (HARAM ES SHARIF)—DOME OF THE ROCK

Take the rising pathway to the right of the Western Wall, which leads to the Temple Mount, Mount Moriah. In the Islamic world, this is the Haram es-Sharif, the Noble Sanctuary, and one of its crowning architectural achievements. After David conquered Jerusalem, he purchased the flat rock at the top of Moriah from Arunah the Jebusite, who had used it as a threshing floor. Some historians theorize that the name Arunah, a dialect variation of Aron, may indicate that Arunah was a Canaanite priest, and the site a Canaanite holy place. The Bible (2 Chronicles 3) relates that "Solomon began to build the house of the Lord at Jerusalem on Mount Moriah." The more modest Second Temple (Solomon's was destroyed by Nebuchadnezzar in 586 B.C.) was originally built by returnees from the Babylonian Captivity between 525 and 515 B.C., and later, shortly before the time of Jesus, Herod enlarged and rebuilt it into the most massive religious complex in the eastern Roman Empire. The vast Temple Mount you see here is an artificially created, flat, stone-paved platform, about 30 acres in area, built by Herod to accommodate vast numbers of pilgrims in ancient times. Herod's temple complex was destroyed by the Romans in A.D. 70. All structures on the Temple Mount today, including the Dome of the Rock and the El Aksa Mosque, are Islamic holy places and religious institutions built after the Muslim conquest of A.D. 638.

There is no charge to enter the Temple Mount compound. You must not, however, wear shorts or "immodest" dress in the compound. (If your outfit is too revealing, guards may be willing to provide you with long cotton wraps, or they may ask you to return another time with more modest clothing.) Visitors are allowed on the Temple Mount by permission of the Islamic religious authorities, and are asked to obey instructions given by the guards.

There is an admission fee of NIS 38 ($8.40) to go inside the two mosques and the Islamic Museum. I highly recommend that you invest in the combined admission ticket, which may be purchased from a stone kiosk between El Aksa and the Dome of the Rock. Visiting hours are 8:30am to 3pm. You may usually remain on the Temple Mount, but cannot enter the Dome of the Rock or the El Aksa Mosque, during the midday prayers. The Temple Mount is not open to visitors on Friday or Muslim holidays, or during the Islamic holy month of Ramadan.

○ **El Aksa Mosque,** after Mecca and Medina, the third holiest place of prayer in the world for Muslims, is the first shrine you'll reach. Completed in A.D. 720, it is among the oldest mosques in existence and also among the most beautiful—a vast broad basilica originally nine naves wide. It was in front of the graceful porticos of the El Aksa that King Abdullah of Jordan was assassinated in 1951, by gunmen who felt he was attempting to create a basis for eventual peace in the area. He died here in the presence of his then 15-year-old grandson, the late King Hussein of Jordan.

A mosque is a sacred enclosure open to air and light (as opposed to the dark interiors of pagan-era temples). Because a mosque is a sacred precinct, you must remove your shoes before entering. This tradition is very ancient, going back to the time when Moses, approaching the Burning Bush in the Sinai, heard the voice of God telling him to put off his shoes. You must also leave handbags and cameras outside, so you might want to come with a partner who can watch these things for you.

After passing through the portico, you will enter a broad open hall hung with chandeliers and covered with oriental rugs. The mosque's lofty ceilings, supported by a forest of varied columns, are embellished with early Islamic and Byzantine design. Up front, past rows of great marble pillars, is a wood-partitioned platform reserved for the Jordanian royal family. The extraordinary wooden stair pulpit of the El Aksa Mosque, one of Islam's great artistic treasures for more than 7 centuries, was commissioned by Saladin for the rededication of El Aksa as a mosque after the crusader occupation. Originally built by master artisans from Syria, it was destroyed when a mentally disturbed Australian tourist set fire to the El Aksa in 1969, and has been painstakingly reconstructed by craftspeople retrained in techniques that have not been used for hundreds of years. A separate women's prayer chamber, in blue, is at the right. As you enter the El Aksa, you face south, in the direction of Mecca. **Mihrabs,** or prayer niches on the southern wall, remind worshippers of the **qibla,** or direction they must face during prayers, which are performed five times a day. During the five daily prayers, the El Aksa is filled with worshippers who in unison perform the rituals of prostration that accompany Islamic prayer. Non-Muslim visitors are not permitted inside mosques at these times. In between prayers, when visitors are allowed to enter, you will find a large, serene space, with perhaps a few individual worshippers at various places on the floor. Unlike most churches and synagogues, a mosque contains no pews or chairs. Visitors are invited to view the architecture and design details of the building; however, they are requested not to engage in any prayers.

Leave El Aksa, reclaim your shoes, and turn right. You will only be permitted to walk to the end of the building, but at the far end of the vast pavement is a corner in the city walls. Some say this is the "pinnacle of the Temple" where Satan took Jesus to tempt him (Matthew 4:5). In the distance, you can get a marvelous view of the Mount of Olives and the Kidron Valley.

A stairway leads to the so-called **Solomon's Stables,** perhaps first misidentified by the Crusaders. Today, these subterranean chambers filled with pigeons are popularly believed to have been the stables for King Solomon's thousands of horses. The "stables" are actually the substructure supporting this portion of Herod's vast, artificially created ceremonial platform that is the present surface of the Temple Mount. To add to the confusion about the site, many Muslims believe the "Solomon" referred to is the Ottoman Sultan Suleiman (Solomon) the Magnificent, who rebuilt the walls that surround the present Old City and did extensive repair work on the Dome of the Rock during his reign in the mid-1500s. (For security reasons, this area will probably be closed to visitors.)

Heading straight across the temple plaza toward the Dome of the Rock, you'll pass **El-Kas,** the fountain where Muslims perform their ritual ablutions before entering the holy places. It is equipped with a circular row of pink marble seats, each of which has a faucet. The fountain is not for the use of non-Muslims.

The exterior walls of the dazzling **Dome of the Rock** are covered with a facade of Persian blue tiles, originally installed by the Ottoman Sultan Suleiman the Magnificent in the mid–16th century. In 1994, under the auspices of Jordan's King Hussein, the great dome was completely reconstructed and regilded with 80 kilograms of 24-karat gold. The Dome of the Rock is reached by climbing the broad ceremonial stairs

Temple Mount (Haram es Sharif)

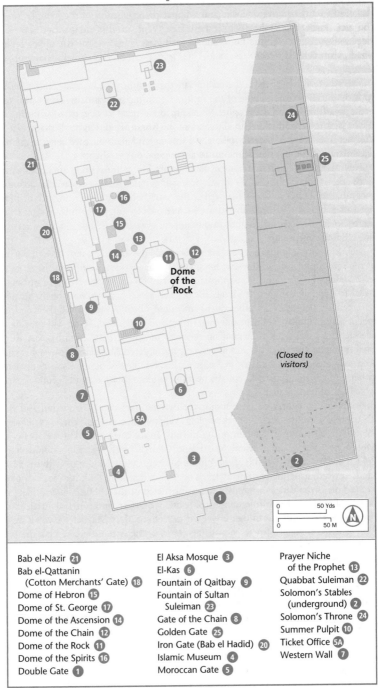

Bab el-Nazir 21
Bab el-Qattanin
  (Cotton Merchants' Gate) 18
Dome of Hebron 15
Dome of St. George 17
Dome of the Ascension 14
Dome of the Chain 12
Dome of the Rock 11
Dome of the Spirits 16
Double Gate 1

El Aksa Mosque 3
El-Kas 6
Fountain of Qaitbay 9
Fountain of Sultan
  Suleiman 23
Gate of the Chain 8
Golden Gate 25
Iron Gate (Bab el Hadid) 20
Islamic Museum 4
Moroccan Gate 5

Prayer Niche
  of the Prophet 13
Quabbat Suleiman 22
Solomon's Stables
  (underground) 2
Solomon's Throne 24
Summer Pulpit 10
Ticket Office 5A
Western Wall 7

that lead to a decorative archway and a raised center portion of the Temple Mount complex. The Dome of the Rock's interior is every bit as lavish and intricate as the outside. Plush carpets line the floor, and stained-glass windows line the upper ceiling. Again, visitors must remove their shoes and leave them on shelves before entering the shrine.

Everything in this beautiful Muslim sanctuary, built in A.D. 691, centers on the rock that occupies the middle of the shrine. According to Islamic tradition, this rock is the spot from which the Prophet Muhammad ascended to view paradise during the Night Journey described in the 17th Sura of the Koran. Tradition holds that when the Prophet rose, the rock tried to follow, and although it failed, the cave beneath the rock was formed. Footprints of Muhammad are pointed out on the rock.

Next to the rock, a few strands of the Prophet Muhammad's hair are kept in a latticework wooden cabinet. A stairway leads under the rock to a cavelike chamber; according to tradition, this is the Well of the Souls, where it is said the souls of all the dead are gathered. Glass partitions have been erected to stop pilgrims from eroding the sacred rock—for centuries it has been chipped away by the faithful who wanted to bring home a memento.

Jewish tradition holds that on this rock occurred the supreme act of faith that stands at the very foundation of the Jewish religion: Abraham's near sacrifice of Isaac. Genesis 22 relates how Abraham, in approximately 1800 B.C., followed God's instructions to go to Moriah and sacrifice Isaac, his beloved son. Isaac, unaware of the dreadful command, followed in his father's steps and asked, "Behold the fire and the wood, but where is the lamb for a burnt offering?" Abraham responded, "God will provide for the sacrifice," as he built the altar on the rock and prepared to bind his son. At the final moment, the voice of God intervened and ordered Abraham to lower his knife. Approximately 900 years later, in 960 B.C., the temple of Solomon was constructed either on or beside this rock. For the next millennium, the First and Second Temples were located on this site.

From the flat courtyard surrounding the two mosques you have a wonderful view. To the south are the Valley of Jehosaphat (Valley of Kidron) and the U.N. Government House (Mount of Contempt) on the hill. To the east on the lower slopes of the Mount of Olives, the Russian Magdalene Church, with its many onion-shaped golden domes, and the Tomb of the Virgin. Midway up the Mount of Olives is a large modern white structure with many levels of arcades that seem built into the side of the slope. This is the vast Mormon Center, constructed in the 1980s, and considered to be one of the most beautiful examples of contemporary architecture in Jerusalem. On the crest of the Mount of Olives, above the Church of Mary Magdalene, you'll see the high-steepled Russian Monastery and the Dome of the Ascension, marking the place from which Jesus ascended to heaven. Farther to the right and a bit downhill is the gray, tear-shaped dome of Dominus Flevit, which commemorates the spot where Jesus wept as he saw a vision of Jerusalem in ruins. Indeed, from the time of the city's destruction in A.D. 70, until the building of the Dome of the Rock in A.D. 691, Jews traditionally stood near this spot and viewed the actual ruins of the Temple Mount. To the right, on the southern crest of the ridge, is the modern Seven Arches Hotel, built during Jordanian times on the ancient Jewish cemetery of the Mount of Olives.

Your combined entrance ticket also admits you to the **Islamic Museum,** in the southwest corner of the Temple Mount complex, to the right of the El Aksa Mosque. The museum is filled with architectural details, including capitals and carved stonework from earlier structures on the Temple Mount as well as ornamental details from earlier periods of the El Aksa Mosque's existence.

DUNG GATE, SILWAN (THE CITY OF DAVID) & OPHEL PARK

The gate in the city wall near the Temple Mount is Dung Gate, which leads to the Ophel Park and the ancient City of David. It was originally just a small doorway in the wall, but over the years it has been widened to accommodate cars and buses. Jerusalemites claim that the Gate is named for the debris from each consecutive destruction of Jerusalem that was dumped out into the valley below. Beyond Dung Gate is the Valley of Kidron and the Arab neighborhood of Silwan, where the original settlement of Jerusalem developed in prehistoric times beside the Gihon Spring. This is where the walled city of Jerusalem existed in King David's time, where the prophets walked, and the events of First Temple Jerusalem took place.

By the 2nd century B.C., the growing city of Jerusalem was expanding uphill and northward, onto the site of the present Old City. The newer Upper City was the more affluent part of town; the older Lower City was densely populated and poor. In the centuries after the Roman destruction of Jerusalem in A.D. 70, the population of Jerusalem had so greatly decreased and the technology of warfare had progressed to such a point that the original City of David was no longer militarily defensible. It was left outside the walls of the city and by medieval times had sunk to the status of a small, sporadically settled village known as Silwan. So completely forgotten was the site of the original city that until late in the 19th century, most historians and visitors believed the Jerusalem of the First Temple period had been located on the site of the present Old City.

In Silwan you can visit the underground water tunnel and the collection **Pool of Siloam** (in Hebrew, *Shiloah*) built by King Hezekiah in 701 B.C.; this remarkable structure hid Jerusalem's water supply from the Assyrians and saved the city from destruction. At the southern end of Silwan (which takes its Arabic name from the biblical pool of Siloam), just beyond where the walls of old Jerusalem would have been, are ancient overgrown gardens of pomegranates and figs still watered by the **Gihon Spring.** These gardens, originating in prehistoric times, most likely occupy the site of the gardens of the Kings of Judah, and may be the site of the walled gardens that inspired the Song of Songs. It was to a tent beside the Gihon Spring that David initially brought the Ark of the Covenant, the pivotal first step in Jerusalem's transformation into a holy city. Here the ark had rested until the Temple of Solomon was built to house it. The Bible also records that King David was buried inside this city; if so, his tomb should be somewhere in Silwan, rather than at the site on Mount Zion that has been venerated since at least medieval times. Normally, under Judaic law, burials are not permitted within the walls of a city, but an exception was apparently made for King David. Archaeologists are still searching for evidence of the Davidic burial site, but the Lower City was extensively quarried for building stone in the centuries after the Roman destruction, and the true location of David's Tomb, legendary for its powers, remains one of Jerusalem's mysteries.

You can enter daily from 9am to 5pm, for free, and follow the paths along the steep hillside past the excavation site. However, under current political conditions, it is best to visit this area with an organized tour. **Zion Walking Tours** (☎ 02/652-2568; fax 02/628-7866) offers tours that depart from the Tower of David inside the Jaffa Gate; ask at the tourist office for information. **Archeological Seminars Ltd.** (☎ 02/627-3515) and **SPINI** (☎ 02/625-2357; fax 02/625-4953) lead guided tours of the City of David. See "Organized Tours," below, for more information.

OPHEL ARCHEOLOGICAL PARK

South of the Western Wall, near the Dung Gate, but not as far down into the valley as the City of David, is the entrance to the Ophel Archeological Park. The park transports visitors back 3,000 years, to the time of the Book of Kings. It was here, between the temple and the walled city below, that King David built his palace. Here Solomon built his House of the Cedars of Lebanon, a palace for his many wives and concubines, as well as a government complex from which he ruled his empire. Here the Prophet Isaiah advised King Hezekiah—perhaps Isaiah lived in a house built on one of the foundations recently excavated and restored. Archaeologists have even found physical evidence of the backsliding into pagan religions the prophets once railed against. Under the floor of a First Temple period house, within sight of the temple itself, excavators in the 1980s uncovered a hidden cache of pagan gods. The park is being expanded for the millennial celebration in the year 2000.

The park is open Sunday to Thursday from 9am to 5pm, on Friday until 1pm; closed Saturday. Tours, given hourly, begin at the excavations inside the Old City walls at the foot of the Temple Mount and exit through the Dung Gate to the section of the park that lies outside the south wall of the Old City. Admission is NIS 16 ($4.50), half price for children.

THE MUSLIM & CHRISTIAN QUARTERS

✪ **Church of Saint Anne.** The Lion's Gate (Saint Stephen's Gate). Admission NIS 10 ($2.20). Mon–Sat 8am–noon and 2–5pm (until 6pm in summer); closed Sun.

Coming from the Lion's Gate, on the right, 200 feet inside the gate, is a wooden doorway leading to a hidden garden enclave where you'll find this beautiful 12th-century crusader church, erected in honor of the birthplace of Anne (Hannah), the mother of Mary. It is built next to the Bethesda Pool, the site where Jesus is believed to have healed a paralytic. As the church is just a few hundred feet east of the Sanctuaries of the Flagellation and the Condemnation, at the beginning of the Via Dolorosa, you might want to visit it before following the stations of the cross. Saint Anne's acoustics, designed for Gregorian chant, are so perfect that the church is virtually a musical instrument to be played by the human voice. Pilgrim groups come to sing in the church throughout the day, and you, too, are welcome to prepare a song of any religion—only religious songs are permitted. The church's acoustics are most amazing when used by a soprano- or a tenor-range solo voice.

VIA DOLOROSA

This is the **Way of the Cross,** traditionally believed to be the route followed by Jesus from the Praetorium (the Roman Judgment Hall) to Calvary, which was the scene of the crucifixion. Over the centuries, millions of pilgrims have come here to walk the way that Jesus took to his death. Each Friday at 3pm priests lead a procession for pilgrims along Via Dolorosa (starting in the Monastery of the Flagellation at the tower of Antonia, not far from the Lion's Gate). Large wooden crosses are carried by some of those in the procession and prayers are said at each of the 14 stations of the cross. The Via Dolorosa begins in the Muslim Quarter, in the northeast corner of the Old City, and winds its way to the Church of the Holy Sepulcher in the Christian Quarter.

You can enter the **Sanctuaries of the Flagellation and the Condemnation,** where Jesus was scourged and judged. In the sanctuaries are some of the original paving stones of the Lithostrotos. Hours are daily from 8am to noon; 2 to 6pm from April through September, 1 to 5pm from October through March.

The Sanctuary of the Condemnation marks the first station of the cross. As you leave the sanctuary to follow the Via Dolorosa, keep in mind that each station of the cross is marked by a small sign or a number engraved in the stone lintel over a door. Paving stones on the Via Dolorosa itself have been set in a semicircular pattern to

Church of the Holy Sepulcher

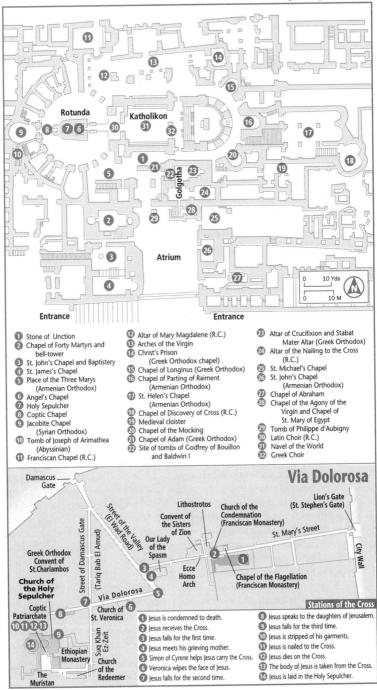

Rotunda

Katholikon

Golgotha

Atrium

Entrance   Entrance

0   10 Yds
0   10 M

1. Stone of Unction
2. Chapel of Forty Martyrs and bell-tower
3. St. John's Chapel and Baptistery
4. St. James's Chapel
5. Place of the Three Marys (Armenian Orthodox)
6. Angel's Chapel
7. Holy Sepulcher
8. Coptic Chapel
9. Jacobite Chapel (Syrian Orthodox)
10. Tomb of Joseph of Arimathea (Abyssinian)
11. Franciscan Chapel (R.C.)

12. Altar of Mary Magdalene (R.C.)
13. Arches of the Virgin
14. Christ's Prison (Greek Orthodox chapel)
15. Chapel of Longinus (Greek Orthodox)
16. Chapel of Parting of Raiment (Armenian Orthodox)
17. St. Helen's Chapel (Armenian Orthodox)
18. Chapel of Discovery of Cross (R.C.)
19. Medieval cloister
20. Chapel of the Mocking
21. Chapel of Adam (Greek Orthodox)
22. Site of tombs of Godfrey of Bouillon and Baldwin I

23. Altar of Crucifixion and Stabat Mater Altar (Greek Orthodox)
24. Altar of the Nailing to the Cross (R.C.)
25. St. Michael's Chapel
26. St. John's Chapel (Armenian Orthodox)
27. Chapel of Abraham
28. Chapel of the Agony of the Virgin and Chapel of St. Mary of Egypt
29. Tomb of Philippe d'Aubigny
30. Latin Choir (R.C.)
31. Navel of the World
32. Greek Choir

Via Dolorosa

Damascus Gate

Lithostrotos   Church of the Condemnation (Franciscan Monastery)

Lion's Gate (St. Stephen's Gate)

Convent of the Sisters of Zion

St. Mary's Street

Street of the Valley (El Wad Road)

Our Lady of the Spasm

City Wall

Greek Orthodox Convent of St.Charlambos

Street of Damascus Gate

(Tariq Bab El Amud)

Ecce Homo Arch

Church of the Holy Sepulcher

Via Dolorosa

Chapel of the Flagellation (Franciscan Monastery)

Coptic Patriarchate

Church of St. Veronica

Stations of the Cross

Suq Khan Ez-Zeit

Ethiopian Monastery

Church of the Redeemer

The Muristan

1. Jesus is condemned to death.
2. Jesus receives the Cross.
3. Jesus falls for the first time.
4. Jesus meets his grieving mother.
5. Simon of Cyrene helps Jesus carry the Cross.
6. Veronica wipes the face of Jesus.
7. Jesus falls for the second time.

8. Jesus speaks to the daughters of Jerusalem.
9. Jesus falls for the third time.
10. Jesus is stripped of his garments.
11. Jesus is nailed to the Cross.
12. Jesus dies on the Cross.
13. The body of Jesus is taken from the Cross.
14. Jesus is laid in the Holy Sepulcher.

mark those stations directly on the street. Other stations are behind closed doors; knock and a monk or nun will probably be there to open up for you. There's a rest room opposite station 3.

The following is a quick guide to the stations of the cross:

Station 1: Jesus is condemned to death. **Station 2:** Jesus receives the cross (at the foot of the Antonia). **Station 3:** Jesus falls for the first time (Polish biblical-archeological museum). **Station 4:** Jesus meets his mother. **Station 5:** Simon the Cyrene helps Jesus carry the cross. **Station 6:** Veronica wipes Jesus' face. **Station 7:** Jesus falls the second time (at bazaar crossroads). **Station 8:** Jesus consoles the women of Jerusalem. **Station 9:** Jesus falls the third time (Coptic Monastery).

The five remaining stations of the cross are inside the Church of the Holy Sepulcher (see below). **Station 10:** Jesus is stripped of his garments. **Station 11:** Jesus is nailed to the cross. **Station 12:** Jesus dies on the cross. **Station 13:** Jesus is taken down from the cross and given to Mary. **Station 14:** Jesus is laid in the chamber of the sepulcher and from here is resurrected.

CHURCH OF THE HOLY SEPULCHER AT GOLGOTHA

The church is divided among the six oldest Christian sects: Roman Catholic, Armenian Orthodox, Greek Orthodox, Egyptian Coptic, Ethiopian, and Syrian Orthodox. Each denomination has its own space—right down to lines drawn down the middle of floors and pillars—and its own schedule of rights to be in other areas of the church at specific times. The decor, partitioned and changed every few feet, is a mixture of Byzantine and Frankish crusader styles.

You can observe the various stations inside the church—the marble slab at the entrance is the Stone of Unction, where the body of Jesus was prepared for burial; the site of Calvary on the second floor; the early 19th-century marble tomb edifice enclosing the actual cave of the sepulcher.

After the Roman Emperor Constantine converted to Christianity and made Christianity the religion of Rome in A.D. 326, his mother, Queen Helena, made a pilgrimage to the Holy Land and located what was believed to be the tomb from which Jesus rose. Further excavation nearby uncovered the True Cross, which became the most sacred relic of the Christian world until it was carried off by the Persians in A.D. 614. It was over this tomb that Constantine built the first Holy Sepulcher Church, a complex of classical structures, which was enlarged by Justinian 200 years later. Fire, earthquake, the 7th-century Persians, and a mad 11th-century Muslim caliph destroyed much of the church, but the crusaders rebuilt it in the 12th century. The church has been restored many times and is currently being renovated. In 1997, the renovated interior of the great dome covering the Sepulcher was unveiled. It is bright, fresh, and to some a bit incompatible with the antiquity of the place. Its design motifs had to be neutral, avoiding incorporating any of the special traditions of the branches of Christianity that control different areas of the building.

If you're in Jerusalem during Easter week, you can attend many of the fascinating services, based on ancient Eastern church traditions, that are held at the church. Most notable are the Service of the Holy Fire, the dramatic pageant called the Washing of the Feet, and the exotic midnight Ethiopian procession on the part of the church under Ethiopian jurisdiction—the roof. No admission fee; modest dress required.

Lutheran Church of the Redeemer. Between Muristan Bazaar and Suq Khan es Zeit Bazaar (☎ **02-627-6111.** Admission to tower NIS 4 (90¢). Mon-Sat 9am – 1pm; 2pm– 5pm. English services Sun 9am.

Kaiser Wilhelm II of Germany made a pilgrimage to Jerusalem in 1898 to dedicate the Church of the Redeemer, a Protestant Church just outside the gates to the Church of the Holy Sepulcher. Ottoman Turkish permission to allow construction of a Protestant church at such a prestigious location symbolized the growing alliance between Germany and the Ottoman Empire, one that would continue through World War I. The Church has become a venue for concerts and performances of organ music; the view from the tower (no elevator) is exceptional.

DAMASCUS GATE & THE BAZAARS

The Damascus Gate, largest and most magnificent of all the entrances to the Old City, is the main route into the Old City from East Jerusalem. Once you are inside the gate, cafes, shops, and market stalls line a wide-stepped entrance street going downhill; Arabs sit inside and out smoking water pipes and watching you as you watch them. The game they're playing is shesh-besh, a sort of backgammon. Music emanates from coffeehouses and shops. Whether you take **El-Wad Road** to the left, or **Suq Khan es-Zeit** to the right, the way becomes very narrow and confusing. Unlike the markets near the Jaffa Gate, which cater primarily to visitors, this part of the bazaar is an authentic market used by the people of East Jerusalem. You'll see stalls of spices and coffees, blacksmiths, craft shops, pastry and bread bakeries, shops selling sneakers and children's wear, butcher stalls, tiny one-chair barber establishments, shoe stores, and fruit and vegetable stands.

Suq Khan es-Zeit becomes **Suq el Attarin,** the Bazaar of the Spices, now mostly a clothing bazaar. In other centuries, this covered market was lined with open sacks of curry, cocoa, sesame, pepper, saffron, and all kinds of beans, dried herbs, medicines, and vegetables. Parallel and to the right of this central market street is the covered Suq El-Lahhamin (the Butchers' Bazaar), its pavement often slippery with puddles of blood.

If you continue walking straight, eventually Suq El Attarin will cross David Street and soon thereafter, it becomes the renovated Cardo, which runs through the restored Jewish Quarter. The area, incidentally, is well patrolled by police officers.

THE OLD CITY RAMPARTS

A good place to explore is the walk on the **Old City walls.** You can enter the wall route at Damascus Gate, although you can also enter at Zion Gate or Jaffa Gate. The views are thrilling and an entire circuit of the walls is about $2^{1}/_{2}$ miles, or less than an hour's walk. Underneath the present Damascus Gate, the Roman-era gate, to the left and below, has been excavated. Within this classical, triple-arched gate (which may have been extant in Jesus' time) there's a small museum, displaying laser reconstructions of the original gate, and worth a quick visit. Again, notice how much lower ground level was before 2,000 years of destruction and rebuilding.

Note that it's not a great idea for anyone to walk alone on the ramparts at any time of day. The ramparts are at times patrolled by groups of unruly local kids and unsavory illegal "guides."

The entry ticket costs NIS 14 ($3.10) for adults, NIS 8 ($1.80) for students, and is good for 2 days (3 days if you buy on Friday). The ramparts are open Saturday to Thursday from 10am to 4pm, and on Friday from 9am to 2pm.

STREET OF THE CHAIN

Perpendicular to the Suq El Attarin–Cardo market is the Street of the Chain, which runs gently downhill to the **Gate of the Chain,** the most important entrance to the Haram es Sharif or Temple Mount. This was the great residential street of medieval Islamic Jerusalem. It starts out as a typical market passageway, but as you get closer to the Haram, you'll begin to notice monumental, richly ornamented doorways of

Schindler's Grave

With the making of the film *Schindler's List*, Oscar Schindler, the German busi-nessman who fervently worked to save the lives of Jewish slave laborers during the Holocaust, has become world famous. His final resting place, arranged by those who owed their lives to him, is in a graveyard on Mount Zion. Exit the Zion Gate, turn left, cross the road, and continue downhill around to the right to a Christian cemetery (many of the graves have Arabic inscriptions). The grave of the often puzzling but heroic Oscar Schindler is in the lower tier, marked by many stones left on it, in Jewish tradition, by visitors.

Mameluk period mansions and buildings decorated with carved stonework in "stalac-tite" patterns over the entranceways. You can only surmise this area's affluent past; like much of the Old City, the neighborhood is overcrowded and has not yet benefited from programs of restoration and renovation.

MOUNT ZION

This important location can be easily spotted as you approach the walls of the Old City from the west or the south. The building with a round squat tower is the Dor-mition Abbey, and near this site is King David's Tomb and the Room of the Last Sup-per (Coenaculum) above it. To reach **King David's Tomb,** walk out Zion Gate, proceed down a narrow alley bounded by high stone walls, and turn left. Although this place has been venerated as the site of David's burial, the tradition can only be traced back to early medieval times; many believe the tomb would have been located in the ancient City of David, south of the present Old City. The building is open daily, including the Sabbath, from 8am to 5pm, until 2pm on Friday. Cover your head when you enter the room.

Near King David's Tomb (in fact, in the same building) is a doorway and flight of stairs leading to the **Coenaculum (Upper Room),** where Jesus sat with his disciples to celebrate the Passover seder, the Last Supper. Again, the room's authentic-ity is based on many centuries of veneration; however, some question this tradition. It is open daily from 8:30am to 4pm.

In the cellar of a building (71) near King David's Tomb is the **Chamber of the Holocaust,** an eerie room lit by candles and dedicated to the memory of the six mil-lion Jews slain by the Nazis. The chamber, a private memorial, is open for visits Sun-day to Thursday from 9am to 4pm and on Friday to 1pm.

Close by is the graceful **Dormition Abbey** (☎ 02/671-9927), built in the early 20th century on the spot where, according to tradition, Mary fell into sleep before her burial and assumption into heaven. Inside the church are an elaborate golden mosaic, a crypt containing interesting religious artwork, and a statue of Mary, around which are chapels donated by various countries. From the tower of the church there's a good panoramic view. It is open daily from 8am to noon and 2 to 6pm. The Dormition Abbey at times is a dramatic venue for public concerts.

2 West Jerusalem Attractions

MUSEUMS

Ammunition Hill Memorial and Museum. ☎ **02/582-8442.** Admission NIS 14 ($3); half price for students and children. Sun–Thurs 9am–5pm; Fri 9am–1pm. Bus: 4, 9, 25, 28, or 99.

At the top of Givat Ha-Tachmoshet (Ammunition Hill), between Sheikh Jarrah and Ramot Eshkol, the site of a bloody battle in 1967, this museum is dedicated to the reunification of Jerusalem and to those who died in the Six-Day War. You can walk through bunkers and trenches, and five exhibition halls full of weapons, maps, battle plans, and more.

✪ **The Bible Lands Museum.** 25 Granot St., beside the Israel Museum. ☎ **02/561-1066.** Admission NIS 28 ($6.20); discounts for students. Sun–Tues and Thurs 9:30am–5:30pm; Wed 9:30am–9:30pm; Fri 9:30am–2pm; Sat 11am–3pm. Call ahead for a schedule of English-language tours.

This museum, opened in 1992, was founded by Dr. and Mrs. Elie Borowski, who donated an incomparable private collection of ancient Near Eastern artifacts as the nucleus of an institution that would survey cultures surrounding the ancient Judeo-Israelite world.

This is an art lovers' museum: Visitors will be amazed by the beauty of the objects on display. In the words of Dr. Borowski, a noted Near Eastern scholar and adviser to museums, who carefully built his collection over a period of 40 years, "Each of the objects has its time in history, its location in space, its meaning in religion and daily life, and last but not least, its beauty and artistry."

The museum is arranged chronologically: Artifacts from differing cultures that existed at the same time are displayed side by side. Themes such as religious worship, trade, communication, and transportation are examined in ways that bring the objects to life, and give us a personal, human insight into life in the times they represent.

Museum highlights: the Assyrian ivories from Nimrud (ca. 800 B.C.), including a masterpiece winged griffin delicately grazing on foliage; the 4th-century A.D. sarcophagus of Julia Latronilla, with its bas-relief depiction of the life of Jesus (among the earliest known representations of Jesus and of elements of Christian theology). Other objects catch the eye with their charm, vitality, or mysterious beauty: an Egyptian cosmetics container in the shape of a swimming girl (ca. 1550 B.C.); a Minoan terracotta sarcophagus, freely painted in bright colors with folk motifs; a 1st-century A.D. Roman painted linen shroud with the ethereal, serene image of a woman covering its length. A special section of the museum is devoted to cylinder seals and scarabs; a remarkable computer/video program brings these minute works of art to life with detailed, fascinating explanations. There are also visiting exhibitions and new donations.

The Bible Lands Museum hosts a program of Saturday evening concerts (including wine and cheese) that often features many of the country's most talented new immigrants (NIS 45 [$10]; discounts for students).

Bloomfield Science Museum. Rupin St. at Givat Ram. ☎ **02/561-8128.** Admission NIS 26 ($5.70); students NIS 18 ($4). Mon, Wed–Thurs 10am–6pm; Tues 10am–8pm; Fri 10am–1pm; Sat 10am–3pm. Bus: 9, 24, or 28.

Another of the city's brand-new attractions, this is a hands-on museum with many state-of-the-art exhibits that can be of special interest to children and young adults.

✪ **Israel Museum.** Ruppin St. ☎ **02/670-8811.** www.imj.org.il. Admission NIS 33 ($7.20); special two-time and multiple-entry tickets available. Sun–Mon and Wed–Thurs 10am–5pm; Fri, eve of holidays, and holidays 10am–2pm; Sat 10am–4pm; main building only open Tues 4–10pm. Bus: 9, 17, 24, or 99.

Opened in May 1965, this complex is an outstanding example of modern Israeli architecture. There are five main components: the Bezalel Art Museum, the Samuel Bronfman Biblical and Archeological Museum, the Billy Rose Art Garden, the Shrine of the Book, and the always lively and fascinating Children's Wing.

Jerusalem Attractions

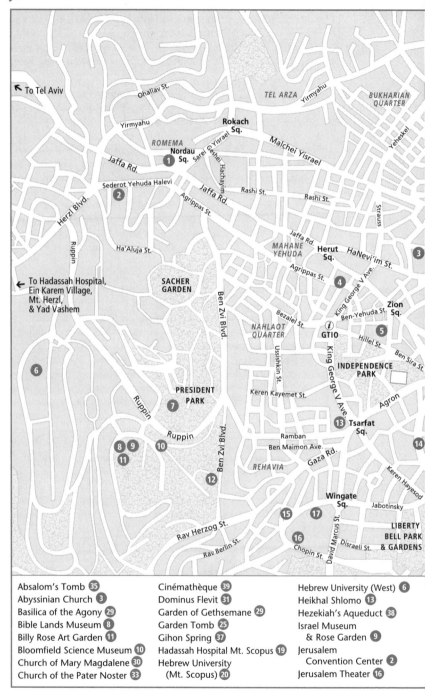

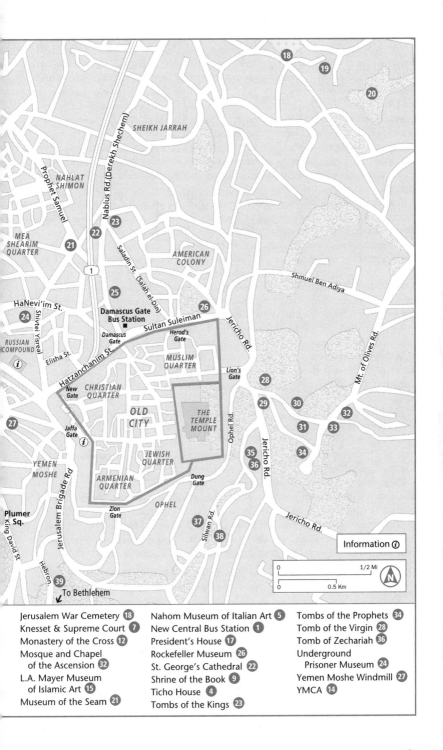

Jerusalem War Cemetery	18	Nahom Museum of Italian Art	5	Tombs of the Prophets	34
Knesset & Supreme Court	7	New Central Bus Station	1	Tomb of the Virgin	28
Monastery of the Cross	12	President's House	17	Tomb of Zechariah	36
Mosque and Chapel of the Ascension	32	Rockefeller Museum	26	Underground Prisoner Museum	24
L.A. Mayer Museum of Islamic Art	15	St. George's Cathedral	22	Yemen Moshe Windmill	27
Museum of the Seam	21	Shrine of the Book	9	YMCA	14
		Ticho House	4		
		Tombs of the Kings	23		

The **Judaica Wing** is composed of ceremonial artifacts from Jewish communities throughout the world, including manuscripts from Iran, Italy, and Poland. In one room, there are dozens of Hanukkah lamps, silver Torah ornaments, serving trays, and shofars; other rooms contain a vast exhibit of costumes worn by Jews in the lands of the Diaspora, all displayed among the artifacts and elements of architecture that surrounded the daily life of each community. There is a reconstructed 17th-century Italian synagogue as well as a German one from the 18th century. The recently transferred interior of a synagogue from Cochin, India, is one of the museum's newest treasures. The museum shows the work of Israeli contemporaries and also contains period rooms. The **Archeology Wing** contains the world's largest collection of objects found in Israel.

The **Bronfman-Bezalel complex,** in the main building and adjoining wings, houses a bookstore and gift shop in its lower level, as well as a snack bar and auditorium. Outside, to the right of the stairs, is the museum cafeteria (moderate prices).

Three important new pavilions have been added in recent years. One contains a beautifully chosen collection of **pre-Colombian Central American art** from 2000 B.C. to A.D. 1550; another is a separate building housing ancient glass; and the third is the **Walter and Charlotte Floersheimer Pavilion for Impressionist and Post-Impressionist Art** with works by Corot, Monet, Renoir, Degas, Gauguin, Matisse, and others. The new **Weisbord Pavilion,** just across the walk from the museum's entrance building and gift shop, houses a small collection of Rodin as well as visiting exhibits of modern art.

Another remarkable part of the museum is an archaeological garden between the Shrine of the Book and the Youth Wing complex. It contains classical Greco-Roman sculptures, sarcophagi, and mosaics, most of which were discovered and excavated in Israel.

The **Billy Rose Art Garden,** on a 20-acre plot, has been impressively landscaped by the renowned Japanese American artist, Isamu Noguchi. In the garden of semicircular earth-and-stone embankments is a 100-piece sculpture collection, which contains both classical and modern European, American, and Israeli works—Rodin, Zorach, Henry Moore, Picasso, Maillol, and Channa Orloff.

Then there's the **Shrine of the Book,** with its distinctive onion-shaped top, contoured to resemble the jar covers in which the Dead Sea Scrolls were discovered. In addition to housing the prized Dead Sea Scrolls and the Bar Kokhba letters, the underground shrine is the exhibition site for additional finds from Masada.

On Saturday or holidays, you have to buy your tickets just outside the museum, from a local ticket agent. The museum is located south of the Knesset.

✪ **L. A. Mayer Memorial Museum of Islamic Art.** 2 Ha-Palmach St. ☎ **02/566-1291.** Admission NIS 16 ($3.50). Sun–Mon and Wed–Thurs 10am–3pm; Tues 10am–6pm; Fri–Sat 10am–2pm.

This is another jewel of a museum very worth visiting, with a strong permanent collection of Islamic art, and consistently superb visiting exhibitions. A wonderful collection of Palestinian costumes and embroidery, the great national folk craft of the region, tops the exhibits of local art; the Islamic jewelry gallery is an additional pleasure. The museum also houses a large and fascinating international collection of clocks, including the famous Salomons collection of Bruquet watches from Paris dating from 1769 to 1823. A new collection of Islamic carpets was added in 1999.

Nahon Museum of Italian Jewish Art. 27 Hillel St. ☎ **02/624-1610.** Admission NIS 10 ($2.80). Sun–Wed 9am–2pm; Thurs 9am–1pm. Services Fri evening and Sat morning.

This museum contains the transported interior of the beautiful 18th-century synagogue of Conegliano Veneto, near Venice, which is open for services on Friday evenings and on Saturday mornings. The exhibits cover the scope of Italian Jewish life and contain ritual objects from medieval times to the present; you may be able to visit the on-site workshops of a special team of Italian and Israeli artisans working to restore and preserve these treasures of Jerusalem's Italian Jewish community. The garden and plaza in front of the complex seem to be a small piece of Italy itself.

✪ **Sir Isaac and Lady Edith Wolfson Museum.** In Heikhal Shlomo, King George St. ☎ **02/624-7112.** Admission NIS 10 ($2.20). Sun–Thurs 9am–1pm. Bus: 4, 7, 8, 9, or 48.

One of the city's hidden treasures is this outstanding international collection of antique Hanukkah menorahs, paper cuts, kiddush cups, wedding contracts, and mezzuzot, all displayed in intimate, accessible rooms. Although mostly composed of antique objects, the collection also includes works of contemporary Judaica by craftspeople like Oded Davidson and Danny Azulai, whose shops can be visited in downtown Jerusalem; there are well-chosen temporary exhibits of antique and contemporary Judaica coordinated to the time of year.

Skirball Museum of Biblical Archeology. Hebrew Union College, 13 King David St. ☎ **02/620-3333.** Free admission. Sun–Thurs 10am–4pm; Sat 10am–2pm.

For archaeology buffs, this handsomely displayed collection, largely of objects discovered at Tel Dan in the north, is a worthwhile stop.

Museum of the Seam. Shivtei Israel, Saint George St. and Nablus Rd. (Route 1). ☎ **02/628-1278.** Admission NIS 25 ($5.50). Sun–Thurs 4–8pm. Bus: 1, 11, or 27.

Right on what had been the no man's land between East and West Jerusalem, this old Turkish-era mansion was turned into a fortress and used as an Israeli command post during the 1948 War of Independence and up until 1967. Until 1999, the museum was dedicated to the history of divided Jerusalem. Now the Museum has become an Israeli institute, attempting to establish dialogue, understanding, and coexistence between Israelis and Palestinians, using lectures, art exhibits, and state-of-the art media displays. From 9am to 3pm, the museum hosts special education groups.

To get there, from East Jerusalem, continue up Nablus Road; you'll pass East Jerusalem's American consulate building. Nablus Road goes to the right of the consulate. Detour left across the busy Route 1 highway to Tourjeman Post on the highway's western side. From West Jerusalem, it's on the edge of Mea Shearim.

The Museum of Taxes. 32 Agron St. ☎ **02/625-8978.** Free admission. Sun, Tues, and Thurs 1–4pm; Mon, Wed 10am–noon. Bus: 5, 18, 19, or 21.

This museum is devoted entirely to aspects of taxation and collection in ancient Israel, during the Diaspora, and in Israel today; it's one of a handful of museums dealing with taxation in the world.

Underground Prisoners Museum. Russian Compound. ☎ **02/623-3166.** Admission NIS 8 ($1.75). Sun–Thurs 8:30am–4pm.

Housed in the 19th-century Russian pilgrimage hostels that later served as British Mandate Jerusalem's Central Prison, this museum documents the prison conditions suffered by many who fought for Jewish immigration to British Mandate Palestine, and for the establishment of a Jewish state.

MEMORIALS
Mount Herzl. Free admission. Park Apr–Oct daily 8am–6:30pm (Nov–Mar close at 5pm); museum Sun–Thurs 9am–5pm, Fri 9am–1pm. Bus: 17, 17A, 18, 20, 21, 23, 24, 26, 27, 39, 40, or 99 to Herzl Blvd.

Mount Herzl is located at the end of the Bet Ha-Kerem section. It is the memorial for Theodor Herzl, who predicted and worked for the founding of Israel until his death in 1904. A large black monolith marks Herzl's interment. Herzl's wife and his parents are buried there, too. The cemetery also contains the graves of Golda Meir, Levi Eshkol, and other important leaders. The final resting place of Yitzhak Rabin is also here.

Down the road from the Herzl cemetery, inside an entrance made of orange stone, is a military cemetery for those who have fallen in the country's many wars.

The **Herzl Museum** (☎ 02/651-1108), exploring the life and work of the founder of modern Zionism, contains a replica of Herzl's Vienna study with his own library and furniture. No admission fee.

✪ **Yad VaShem Memorial and Holocaust Museum.** ☎ **02/675-1611** for information. No admission fee. Sun–Thurs 9am–4:45pm; Fri 9am–1pm. Hall of Names Sun–Thurs 10am–2pm; Fri 10am–1pm. Archives and Library Sun–Thurs 9am–3pm. Closed Sat and Jewish holidays. Bus: 17, 18, 20, 21, 23, 27, or 99.

Down the road from Mount Herzl is a ridge called Har Ha-Zikron (Mount of Remembrance). The **Avenue of the Righteous Among the Nations,** lined with trees planted in tribute to each individual gentile who helped save Jewish lives during the Nazi era, leads into the memorial.

The heavy entrance gate to the **Hall of Remembrance,** designed by two of Israel's leading sculptors, Bezalel Schatz and David Polombo, is an abstract tapestry of jagged, twisted steel. Inside is a huge stone room, like a crypt, where an eternal flame sheds an eerie light over the plaques on the floor: Bergen-Belsen, Auschwitz, Dachau.

The building to the left has a permanent exhibition of photographs and effects relating to the Holocaust. Other exhibits include works pertaining to the Holocaust, and the **Hall of Names,** which contains more than three million pages of testimony, as well as the names, photographs, and personal details of as many of those who perished in the Holocaust as Yad VaShem has been able to gather. Visitors are invited to contribute information about relatives and friends in order that no victim will be forgotten.

On the crest of the western slope of the **Mount of Remembrance** stands a 20-foot-high monument dedicated to the 1¹/₂ million Jewish soldiers among the allied forces, partisans, and ghetto fighters. Below the monument one can see the **Valley of the Destroyed Communities,** commemorating the 5,000 European Jewish communities that disappeared during World War II. There is a special memorial to the **Children of the Holocaust** commemorating more than 1¹/₂ million murdered children.

Across the hill is an archive building that has possibly the most complete library dedicated to this topic.

CHURCHES & MONASTERIES

Rehov Ha-Nevi'im (Street of the Prophets) was the "Christian street" of 19th-century West Jerusalem, and still has a variety of churches and missionary societies. From Zion Square, in the heart of downtown Jerusalem, cross Jaffa Road and go up the hill on Rav Kook Street. Opposite the intersection of Ha-Rav Kook and Ethiopia streets is the entrance to the narrow, high-walled Ethiopia Street with its 19th-century stone mansions. Here you'll find the splendid **Abyssinian (Ethiopian) Church.** The elegant building with the Lion of Judah carved into the gate above the courtyard is the spiritual home of the Coptic Ethiopian clergy. The lion symbolizes the meeting of the Queen of Sheba, the Ethiopian empress, and King Solomon, from whom she traditionally received the emblem. The interior of the turn-of-the-20th-century circular church is filled with a wonderful array of icons and paintings; although none are in the Ethiopian tradition, many were chosen for their charm and native beauty. Bungalows for clergy and pilgrims from Ethiopia surround the church enclave.

Notre Dame de France is on Shivtei Israel Street at Zahal Square, just opposite New Gate in the Old City walls. The Assumptionist Fathers built this monastery in 1887 to serve as a pilgrim's hostel. The monumental buildings of the complex, on the old border between East and West Jerusalem, were badly damaged during heavy fighting in the 1948 war. Part of the complex, restored in the 1970s, serves as a hospital, a restaurant, hotel, and pilgrimage center.

Saint Andrew's Church of Scotland was built by the people of Scotland in 1929 and was dedicated by General Allenby, who had liberated Jerusalem from the Ottoman Empire in 1917. This Presbyterian church is situated on a hilltop near Abu Tor and the Jerusalem railroad station. Also at the top of Abu Tor, and built over the foundations of a medieval church, is the **Greek Orthodox Monastery,** called the "Church of Evil Counsel." It contains catacombs and crypts. Private cottages on the grounds are rented to fortunate Jerusalemites, including one of the country's most talented and respected poets.

The **Russian Orthodox Holy Trinity Cathedral** is just off Jaffa Road. This white multidomed architectural gem in the Renaissance style was originally constructed after the Crimean War for pilgrims of the Russian Orthodox faith (see "Russian Compound," below).

There are also a number of interesting churches and monasteries in Ein Kerem and Rehavia (see "Exploring West Jerusalem Neighborhoods," below), and in Abu Ghosh (see section 10, below).

MORE ATTRACTIONS

Beit Ticho (Ticho House). Off Harav Kook St. ☎ **02/624-5068.** Free admission. Exhibit rooms Sun–Thurs 10am–5pm (Tues till 10pm); Fri 10am–2pm; Sat after Shabbat to 5pm. Restaurant Sun–Thurs 10am–midnight; Fri 10am–3pm; Sat after Shabbat.

You'll be amazed when you come upon this large hidden oasis with its gardens and terrace restaurant/cafe right in the center of downtown West Jerusalem—it's especially wonderful for outdoor dining in summer. Loved by Jerusalemites, both for its beauty and its history (and also as a meeting place), Ticho House was built in 1880 as a private villa for the Aga Rashid Nashishibi; later it became the home of artist Anna Ticho and her husband, Dr. Abraham Ticho, a legendary ophthalmologist who maintained his surgery there. The building is now a downtown branch of the Israel Museum, complete with a handy museum gift shop. There's a permanent exhibit of Anna Ticho's controlled, powerful drawings, as well as visiting exhibitions arranged by the museum. Upstairs, Dr. Ticho's consulting office is preserved, filled with his international collection of antique Hanukkah lamps. Especially moving are the notes to Dr. Ticho, preserved under glass on his desk, from members of the Arab, Jewish, and British communities after he was seriously wounded during the political unrest of 1929. Ticho House hosts poetry and fiction readings, intimate theater and music performances, and a Friday morning concert series.

Chagall Windows at Hadassah Medical Center. Ein Kerem. ☎ **02/641-6333.** Admission and tour of Chagall windows: NIS 14 ($3); discount for students and seniors. Sun–Thurs 8am–1:15pm and 2–3:45pm; Fri and eves of holidays 8am–12:30pm. Bus: 19 or 27 from Jaffa Rd.; 19 from Jaffa Gate, Agron St., King George V Ave., or Bezalel St.

The largest medical center in the Middle East, the Hadassah Hebrew University Medical Center stands on a hilltop several miles from downtown Jerusalem. The center contains a medical school, nursing school, hospital, dental and pharmacy schools, and various laboratory buildings. The hospital's synagogue contains Chagall's 12 exquisite stained-glass windows depicting the blessings that Jacob, on his deathbed, bestowed to each of his 12 sons (Genesis 49:1-27). The sons of Jacob became the founders of the Twelve Tribes of Israel.

Call for information about complete 5-hour tours of the Medical Center, including the Chagall windows.

Hebrew University. Givat Ram Campus (West Jerusalem). ☎ **02/688-2819.** Free University tours Sun–Thurs 11am from Visitors Center in the Sherman Building. Bus: 9, 24, or 28 to modern Givat Ram campus.

Surrounded by rolling hills, the Hebrew University is one of Israel's most dramatic accomplishments, with over 18,000 students on this and the Mount Scopus campus. Built to replace the university's original Mount Scopus campus, which was cut off from West Jerusalem from 1948 to 1967, the Givat Ram Campus now houses the university's science departments.

Take special architectural note of the Belgium House Faculty Club, La Maison de France, the Physics Building, and the huge National and University Library (partly inspired by LeCorbusier's Villa Savoye in Poissy, France) at the far end of the promenade. And don't miss the mushroom-shaped synagogue behind the library or the futuristic gym. The synagogue, with its dome supported by eight arches, was designed by Heinz Rau (one of the designers of Brasilia) and the important Israeli architect, David Reznik; Reznik's imprint dots the city—he designed Jerusalem's Hyatt Regency Hotel, and codesigned the Mormon Center on Mount Scopus.

You can stop for lunch in the cafeteria of the Administration Building, or in the Jewish National and University Library, which contains a vast stained-glass window depicting images of Jewish mysticism.

Heikhal Shlomo. 58 King George V Ave. No phone. Free admission; Wolfson Museum NIS 10 ($2.20). Tours Sun–Thurs 9am–1pm; Fri 9am–noon. Bus: 4, 7, 8, 9, or 48.

Facing the large main park, Gan Ha-Atzma'ut, this imposing complex includes the Great Synagogue and the former Seat of the Rabbinate, designed in a rather vague imitation of what was believed to be King Solomon's Temple. Weekly programs—religious and folk songs, lectures, and readings—mark the end of Shabbat and the beginning of the new week. For times of traditional religious services, check at Heikhal Shlomo, your hotel, or the tourist information office. The Wolfson collection of Judaica (see museums, above), one of the world's finest, can be seen on the fourth floor.

Jerusalem Artists' House and Old Bezalel Academy of Arts and Design. 12 Shmuel Ha-Nagid St. ☎ **02/625-3653.** Free admission. Sun–Fri 10am–1pm and 4–7pm; Sat 10am–1pm. Bus: 4, 7, 8, 9, 19, or 48.

Many cultural activities center on the Jerusalem Artists' Association. Exhibitions of art, evenings of chamber music, concerts, readings, jazz, and art lectures are scheduled each year (for specifics, check with the tourist office or at the office here); there's an expensive restaurant (Cezanne) and a very good, affordable vegetarian restaurant (the Village Green). On the main floor, paintings and sculptures of more than 500 artist members are sold (if you buy, they'll ship your purchases). Upstairs and throughout the building are general exhibitions in August and the spring; special exhibitions, featuring about three artists at a time, change every 3 weeks during the rest of the year. Note the beautifully carved outside doors, the crenellated roof and dome, and the garden sculpture. The present Bezalel School is at the Hebrew University.

Model of Ancient Jerusalem. Holyland Hotel, Bayit, Vegan. ☎ **02/643-7777.** Admission NIS 18 ($4). Sun–Thurs 9am–5pm; Fri 9am–1pm; summer daily 9am–8pm (Fri–Sat until 5pm). Bus: 21 or 21A from downtown.

Created by the late archaeologist Michael Avi-Yonah, and constantly updated with new discoveries, this is a perfectly scaled-down model of Jerusalem as it was in the time of the Second Temple, with palaces, mammoth walls, and elegant towers.

To get there, take the road opposite Mount Herzl and follow signs pointing to Holyland Hotel. The garden is a short walk from the hotel's entrance.

Parliament (Knesset). Government Quarter—Kiryat Ben-Gurion, Kaplan St. ☎ **02/675-3333.** Free guided tours on Sun and Thurs 8:30am–2:30pm; viewing of Knesset sessions Mon or Thurs 4–9pm, Wed after 11am. Closed Jewish holidays. Bus: 9, 17, 24, 28, or 99.

This modern landmark—called by some West Jerusalem's Acropolis, by others an airport terminal with no runway—houses mosaics and tapestries by Chagall, as well as Knesset sessions that run the gamut from funereal to the most rowdy in the democratic world. The entranceway, a grillwork of hammered metal, is the work of the Israeli sculptor David Polombo, who did the dramatic doors at Yad VaShem. You must have your passport with you, and you may be subject to a careful security search. Always call ahead to check current schedule.

Russian Compound. Off Jaffa Rd. near Zion Square.

Once this 19th-century series of structures surrounding the beautiful Russian Orthodox Holy Trinity Cathedral was the world's largest "hotel"; it could accommodate 10,000 Russian pilgrims at one time (until World War I, Russians composed the largest block of pilgrims in the Holy Land). Today, this neglected but architecturally striking enclave serves as a municipal parking lot and an Israeli lock-up; at visiting times, families of prisoners can often be seen huddling outside the police barricades. Around the back, near the entrance to the prison, a low iron fence surrounds a monumental Herodian-era column abandoned in the process of being carved directly from bedrock—it cracked. Underground Prisoners Museum (see above) is housed in part of the Russian Compound complex. There are plans to restore the pilgrimage buildings, and turn the parking lots into gardens and the complex into luxury and moderate hotels—it could create an oddly romantic touch of Saint Petersburg right in the heart of Jerusalem.

As you walk along Jaffa Road from Zion Square, look up to your left (north), before the main post office, and you'll see the Russian Orthodox Cathedral.

Sanhedrian Tombs. Sanhedria. Free admission. Gardens daily 9am–4 or 5pm; tombs Sun–Fri 9am–4 or 5pm. Bus: 2 from Jaffa Gate.

Go up Shmuel Ha-Navi, off Shivtei Israel Street, to northeast Jerusalem's beautiful public gardens of Sanhedria. Here you look at the Tombs of Sanhedria or the Tombs of the Judges, where the judges of ancient Israel's "Supreme Court" (during the 1st and 2nd centuries) are buried. The three-story burial catacomb is intricately carved from rock.

Supreme Court Building. Next to Knesset. ☎ **02/675-9612.** Sun–Thurs 8:30am–2:30pm; free tours in English Sun–Thurs at noon. Bus: 9, 17, 24, 28, or 99.

In a country starved for good modern architecture, the new Supreme Court Building, opened in 1992, is a major hit with Israelis and visitors alike. The contemporary design of the building incorporates traditional Middle Eastern motifs of domes, arches, and passageways, all set up to create interesting interplays of shadow and light.

YMCA. 24 King David St. ☎ **02/625-7111.** Free admission; small donations for the tower. Tours Mon–Sat 9am–3pm. Bus: 5, 6, 18, or 21.

One of the most outstanding landmarks in the city, the YMCA was built in the early 1930s with funds donated by a Montclair, New Jersey, philanthropist named James Jarvie. Designed by the architectural firm that did New York City's Empire State Building, the building is an interesting mixture of art deco, Byzantine, and Islamic styles. This is probably the most amazing YMCA in the world. On the first floor, you'll find a replica of the London room in which the YMCA was founded in 1844. The 152-foot tower (open Monday to Saturday from 9am to 2pm) offers one of the most dramatic panoramas of the city. Notice the six winged bas-relief seraph that ornaments the center of the tower's facade; the tower also houses the only carillon in the Middle East. Concerts played on the tower bells, especially at midnight on New Year's Eve, are among the city's little-known pleasures. Built by Christian, Jewish, and Muslim workers and artisans, the YMCA is a meeting place for all the city's communities. The complex includes a swimming pool, tennis courts, athletic fields, lecture and concert halls, a gymnasium, restaurant, and one of the best hotels in Jerusalem.

3 Exploring West Jerusalem Neighborhoods

YEMIN MOSHE   In the 1850s, British philanthropist Sir Moses Montefiore, with the help of Judah Touro from New Orleans, built the nucleus of this residential quarter, the first outside the walls of the Old City, in an effort to bring indigent Jews from the Old City into a more healthful environment. The project included the now famous windmill for grinding flour. Despite its magnificent view and graceful architecture, the neighborhood remained poor for more than a century.

Today, Yemin Moshe is a picturesque, beautifully restored neighborhood—an architectural treasure and one of the most elegant addresses in town. There are no shops, but the views are spectacular. It's a fascinating place for an early evening or winter afternoon stroll; however, a noontime walk in the hot July sun is not recommended. The steep pedestrian-street staircases of Yemin Moshe may make it a bit difficult for those with walking problems.

Down one of the first flights of staircases is the **Yemem Moshe Windmill,** which houses a museum dedicated to Sir Moses Montefiore. It is open Sunday to Thursday from 9am to 4pm, and until 1pm on Friday. Below the Montefiore Windmill is the original row of **old stone buildings (Mishkanot Sha'ananim),** built by Sir Moses Montefiore in 1854. Ornamented by Victorian ironwork porches, the buildings are used as a residence for visiting artists and diplomats.

A replica of the Liberty Bell in Philadelphia stands in the center of Jerusalem's **Liberty Bell Garden,** not far from the windmill. The 7-acre garden has a picnic area, vine-covered trellises, and a large children's playground and an entertainment area. You may wonder why a copy of the Liberty Bell has been made into the centerpiece of a Jerusalem park. The words inscribed on the American original were spoken by one of Jerusalem's most famous inhabitants, the Prophet Isaiah, more than 2,500 years before the Declaration of Independence: "Proclaim liberty throughout the land, and to all the inhabitants thereof." It was with these words that Israel's independence was announced in 1948.

MEA SHEARIM   This area, a few blocks north of Jaffa Road, is populated by Hasidic and ultra-Orthodox Jews of East European origin. It is a world unto itself and a visit here is like going back in time to the world of religious eastern European Jewry that existed before the Holocaust. Originally built in the late 19th century as a semifortified agricultural community in what was at that time open countryside, about a mile beyond the walls of the Old City, the neighborhood consists of numerous courtyards designed to be defended against unruly Bedouin marauders. In the 20th century, the area came to be inhabited by Hasidic rabbinical courts and followers of the many Hasidic sects that emigrated to Jerusalem from Europe. Some married women in this area, according to strict East European Orthodox tradition, wear wigs and scarves over their shaved heads. A number of residents speak only Yiddish in conversation, as Hebrew is considered too sacred for daily use. Some don't even recognize the laws of the Israeli government, believing that no State of Israel can exist before the coming of the Messiah. Demonstrators protesting such issues as medical autopsies, driving on Saturday, and coed swimming pools have clashed with the police. The neighborhood is filled with synagogues, yeshivas, and small workshops and shops selling religious objects.

Architecturally, Mea Shearim has the feel of an 18th-century Polish ghetto, the more so because of the traditional dress and lifestyle of its residents. Visitors to this area are requested to dress modestly (no shorts, short skirts, uncovered arms or shoulders for women; slacks for men). Men and women are advised not to walk in close proximity (certainly not hand in hand!) and visitors are advised to stow away cameras and to be very discreet in taking photographs. No inhabitant of Mea Shearim will voluntarily pose for snapshots, and there have been incidents in which improperly dressed visitors have been spat upon or stoned.

GERMAN COLONY & BAKA   One mile south of downtown West Jerusalem, these two picturesque neighborhoods, filled with overgrown gardens, are undergoing a process of gentrification. For many years, the old cottages and mansions (built at the start of the century by German Protestants and affluent Arabic families) housed Israelis from exotic places like Kurdistan and Morocco, but more recently, members of Jerusalem's American, British, and Latin American immigrant communities have been moving in. The two charming neighborhoods offer family run restaurants and shops that tend to reflect the area's ambience. **Emek Refaim Street** (a southern continuation of King David Street) is the German Colony's main artery; a walk down **Yehoshua Ben Nun Street,** which runs parallel to Emek Refaim 1 block to the west beginning at **Rachel Immenu Street,** gives you a better idea of the neighborhood's interesting residential architecture. Because of the area's newfound popularity, modern apartment buildings are being squeezed into every possible garden and empty lot. Much of the area was saved from demolition through efforts lead by Sara Fox Kaminiker, who came to Israel from the United States and served on the city council under the administration of Teddy Kollek (Sara Fox Kaminiker's book of walking tours, *Footloose in Jerusalem,* which includes this neighborhood, is highly recommended).

In Baka, the main street is **Derekh Bethlehem.** On many of the narrow side streets running off this thoroughfare, you'll find eccentric examples of Arabic mansions and 1930s bungalows. For those who like architecture, the quiet back streets of both neighborhoods are good places to meander by bike.

REHAVIA-TALBEYEH   A turn to the west from King George V Avenue, either at the Jewish Agency compound or at the Kings Hotel, will bring you into Jerusalem's most beautiful residential section, with its middle- and upper-class, tree-lined streets. Rehavia's glory is its collection of 1930s International Style apartment buildings and houses. Talbeyeh, just to the south, is filled with elaborate villas and mansions built mainly by Jerusalem's Arab Christian community in the 1920s and 1930s. Abandoned when their original owners fled in 1948, these houses are now inhabited by Israelis. **Hovei Zion Street** is lined with examples of these gracious homes.

Sights in the area include the **prime minister's residence,** at the corner of Balfour and Smolenskin; and the **Alfasi grotto** (also called the "Tomb of Jason"), on Alfasi Street, a frescoed and inscribed tomb discovered by builders while they were digging foundations (open from 10am to 4pm). The medieval **Monastery of the Cross,** in the Valley of the Cross outside Rehavia was built by Gregorian monks in the 11th century and is now maintained by the Greek Orthodox Church. According to tradition, the beautiful monastery is located on the spot where the tree stood from which the cross was made. If you don't want to walk down the rocky hillside from Rehavia to the monastery, take bus no. 9 or 17. The monastery is open Monday to Friday from 9am to 4pm. Admission is NIS 5 ($1.10). At the southern edge of Rehavia, in Kiryat Shmuel, is **Bet Ha-Nassi,** the president's residence. You can look through the gates, but except for receptions, it is not open to the public.

EIN KEREM   This ancient village, in a deep valley at the western edge of Jerusalem, is traditionally regarded as the birthplace of John the Baptist. Now incorporated into Jerusalem, you can reach it in less than a half hour by bus 17 from King George Street or Jaffa Road. The lanes and gardens of Ein Kerem (Well of the Vineyard) are lovely; the old Arabic style houses have been grabbed up and renovated by some of the city's most successful and famous inhabitants; and high above the area, on the crest of the mountains, is the vast Hadassah–Ein Kerem Medical Center (not accessible from Ein Kerem itself). Ein Kerem contains a number of 19th-century European churches, convents, and monasteries. Most important is the **Church of Saint John** in the center of town, marking John the Baptist's birthplace (open daily from 6am to noon and 2 to 5pm); on request you can see the grotto beneath the church with its Byzantine mosaic. On Ma'ayan Street, you'll find the **Church of the Visitation** (open daily 8 to 11:45am and 2 to 5pm), commemorating the visit of Mary to her cousin Elizabeth, the mother of John the Baptist. It was often depicted in medieval and early Renaissance paintings as a scene in which the two expectant women touch each other's stomachs, and according to legend, the two infants jumped for joy inside their mothers' wombs when Mary and Elizabeth met. Below the Youth Hostel off Ma'ayan Street is a mosque and minaret marking the well from which Mary drew water; farther along the ridge is the Russian Convent, known as the **Moscobiyah,** a fascinating enclave of 40 Jerusalem stone buildings scattered among a wooded area of pines and cypresses. The nuns live in small ocher-painted houses reminiscent of wooden cottages in Russia. You can make an appointment to visit by calling ☎ **06/625-2565** or 02/541-2887. Bring a snack or canteen along, or you can pick up something in the grocery at the center of town. Restaurants here look appealing, but meals are expensive and nothing special. The times for return to Jerusalem should be posted at the bus stop in the center of Ein Kerem; you may have to wait in downtown Jerusalem for up to 30 minutes until the infrequent bus 17 to Ein Kerem picks you up.

MAHANE YEHUDA   The Old Market Quarter—liveliest on Wednesday and Thursday—is off Jaffa Road, half a mile west of Zion Square. In a square off Mahane Yehuda and Jaffa Road, there is a war memorial commemorating the "Davidka," an improvised weapon used in the defense of Jerusalem.

4 East Jerusalem Attractions

You can probably cover the major sights of East Jerusalem in half a day. As you go along **Saladin Street** from the north, toward the Old City walls, you'll pass the **Ministry of Justice,** on the right. Farther down, across the street in a tree-shaded compound, is the famed **Albright Institute of Archeological Research.** Just past it on the left, you'll find **Az-Zahra Street,** a modern thoroughfare of clothing and appliance stores, bookshops, restaurants, and hotels, leading to the Rockefeller Museum.

The Garden Tomb. Conrad Schick St. ☎ **02/628-3402.** Free admission (donations accepted). Mon–Sat 8am–12:15pm and 2:30–5:15pm; Protestant service in English Sun 9am. Bus: 27.

The 1st-century tomb, discovered in 1867 by Dr. Conrad Schick, is very similar to the biblical description of the tomb of Jesus. In 1883, General Gordon, hero of China and Khartoum, visited the tomb on his way to Egypt, and in a fit of pique over the exclusion of Protestant services from the Church of the Holy Sepulcher, had a vision that this site outside the Damascus Gate was the real tomb of Jesus. The tomb was finally excavated in 1891, and whether it is "the place" or not, it certainly meets some of the specifications: near the site of the crucifixion, outside the walls of the city, hewn from the rock, a tomb made for a rich man, and situated in a garden. As late as the early 20th century, the hill Gordon identified as Golgotha (Calvary), or according to the New Testament, "The Place of the Skull," was indeed eerily shaped like a skull, but construction and quarrying have obscured this impression.

To get there, head up Nablus Road (Derekh Shechem), opposite Damascus Gate. Look for the side street named Conrad Schick Street on the right.

✪ **Rockefeller Archeological Museum.** Sultan Suleiman St. ☎ **02/628-2251.** Admission NIS 26 ($6). Sun–Thurs 10am–5pm; Fri and eves of holidays 10am–2pm. Bus: 1 or 2.

Located near Herod's Gate, and named for John D. Rockefeller, who financed its construction with a gift of $2 million in 1927, the Rockefeller is a treasury of regional archaeological materials ranging from the Stone Age to the 18th century. The museum's eclectic 1930s design is a Jerusalem landmark that combines elements of Byzantine, Islamic, and art deco, and includes a beautiful, recently renovated cloister garden set around a reflecting pool. The building was damaged during the Six-Day War, but the museum's displays were barely affected, and there was no damage at all to the many Dead Sea Scrolls kept for study in the museum at that time, under Jordanian control.

Much of the collection was excavated in Acre and Galilee by American and English archaeologists during the first half of this century. Pottery, tools, and household effects are arranged by periods—Iron Age, Persian, Hellenistic, Roman, Byzantine. Among the museum's special treasures are 9th-century carved wooden panels from the El Aksa Mosque; crusader stonework that once adorned the entrance to the Church of the Holy Sepulcher; and richly ornamented early Islamic architectural details from the 8th century Hisham's Palace near Jericho. There is also a special gallery of Egyptian Antiquities; in the south gallery's Paleolithic section are the bones of Mount Carmel Man.

Saint George's Cathedral. Nablus Rd. Free admission. Daily 9am–4pm. Bus: 27.

Neo-Gothic towers adorn this compound, which also includes an excellent travelers' guest house and the headquarters for the Anglican archbishopric, with jurisdiction extending as far across the Middle East as Sudan. It's a rare architectural enclave for this part of the world, recalling the courtyards of Oxford or Cambridge. Feel free to pass through the courtyard for a look. The complex also contains a religious college, a school, a small garden, and residences. There is a small exhibit of beautiful Palestinian textiles on display as well.

Tombs of the Kings. Saladin St. Admission NIS 5 ($1.10). Mon–Sat 8am–12:30pm and 2–5pm. Bus: 27.

Behind Saint George's, on the left side as you head down Saladin Street, is a gate marked "Tombeau des Rois." About 20 feet down a stone stairway, you'll see a hollowed-out courtyard, with several small cave openings. Inside one are four sarcophagi, covered with carvings of fruit and vines. Despite the name, the tomb is for the family of Queen Helena of the Mesopotamian province of Adiabene, who converted to Judaism in Jerusalem around A.D. 50.

Zedekiah's Cave. Near the Damascus Gate. Admission NIS 10 ($2.20). Daily 10am–4pm. Bus: 27.

Follow the Old City walls to the east of Damascus Gate and you'll soon come to the entrance leading under the walls into Zedekiah's Cave, or Solomon's Quarries, which tradition calls the source of the stones for Solomon's Temple. Because of this, the cave is of special importance to the worldwide Order of Masons, which claims spiritual descent from the original builders of the First Temple. Jewish and Muslim legends claim that tunnels in those caves extended to the Sinai Desert and Jericho. The quarries got their name because King Zedekiah was supposed to have fled from the Babylonians through these tunnels in 587 B.C., only to be later captured near Jericho. An illuminated path leads you far back into the caves and under the Old City.

MOUNT SCOPUS, MOUNT OF OLIVES & VALLEY OF KIDRON

You can reach the Mount of Olives Road either by driving north up Saladin Street or by taking a left turn at the wall, just past the Rockefeller Museum. For Hebrew University Mount Scopus campus, take bus no. 4A, 9, or 28 from downtown West Jerusalem.

MOUNT SCOPUS   From Sheikh Jarrah (on Nablus Road), the road heads past the Mount Scopus Hotel and proceeds, gradually curving, past Shepherds Hotel. At the bend in Mount Scopus Road, to your left, you'll see the **Jerusalem War Cemetery,** the resting place for British World War I dead. You are now on Mount Scopus–Har Hatsofim, which means "Mount of Observation." It was here that the Roman armies of Titus and Vespasian camped in A.D. 70 and observed the city under siege as they planned their final attack.

About 100 yards down the ridge, you will find the **Mount Scopus Hadassah Hospital** on the left. The **Hebrew University on Mount Scopus,** which opened on April 1, 1925, is now one of the largest institutions of higher learning in the Middle East. It is mostly housed in a vast fortresslike megacomplex designed by David Resnik. The design seems to reflect the university's past experience. At the end of the War of Independence in 1949, the cease-fire lines found Israeli defenders still holding out at the Hebrew University and Hadassah Hospital, two important Jewish institutions deep in the heart of Jordanian-controlled East Jerusalem. For the next 19 years, these two bastions were resupplied by monthly Red Cross convoys, and a new Hadassah Hospital and Hebrew University had to be built in West Jerusalem. Since 1967, the hospital and campus have been restored to their original functions and greatly enlarged. From the Truman Research Institute (a pink stone building) there's a sweeping view of both the New and Old cities. Tours are Sunday to Friday at 11am from the Sherman Building.

VIEWS OF JERUSALEM   The road skirting the ridge proceeds past the high-towered Augusta Victoria Hospital—an Arab Legion bastion during the Six-Day War—the Arab village of Et-Tur, the Mount of Olives, the Jewish Cemetery, and the Seven Arches Hotel. The best views of Jerusalem are from the Hebrew University on Mount Scopus, the Jewish graveyard on the Mount of Olives, and the Seven Arches Hotel. For optimum viewing and photographs, come in the morning, when the sun is behind you.

AT&T Direct® Service

AT&T Access Numbers

Aruba	800-8000	Czech Rep. ▲	00-42-000-101
Australia	**1-800-551-155**	Egypt●(Cairo)†	510-0200
Austria ●	**0800-200-288**	**France**	**0-800-99-0011**
Bahamas	1-800-872-2881	**Germany**	**0800-2255-288**
Barbados+	1-800-872-2881	**Greece●**	**00-800-1311**
Belgium ●	**0-800-100-10**	Guam	1-800-2255-288
Bermuda+	1-800-872-2881	**Hong Kong**	**800-96-1111**
Cayman Isl +	1-800-872-2881	**Hungary**	**06-800-01111**
China, PRC▲	10811	India ✗,➤	000-117
Costa Rica	0-800-0-114-114	Ireland ✓	1-800-550-000

AT&T Direct® Service

AT&T Access Numbers

Aruba	800-8000	Czech Rep. ▲	00-42-000-101
Australia	**1-800-551-155**	Egypt●(Cairo)†	510-0200
Austria ●	**0800-200-288**	**France**	**0-800-99-0011**
Bahamas	1-800-872-2881	**Germany**	**0800-2255-288**
Barbados+	1-800-872-2881	**Greece●**	**00-800-1311**
Belgium ●	**0-800-100-10**	Guam	1-800-2255-288
Bermuda+	1-800-872-2881	**Hong Kong**	**800-96-1111**
Cayman Isl +	1-800-872-2881	**Hungary**	**06-800-01111**
China, PRC▲	10811	India ✗,➤	000-117
Costa Rica	0-800-0-114-114	Ireland ✓	1-800-550-000

Israel	1-800-94-949	Philippines●	105-11
Italy●	172-1011	Portugal▲	0800-800-128
Jamaica●	1-800-872-2881	Singapore	800-0111-11
Japan●▲	005-39-111	Spain	900-99-00-11
Malaysia	1800-80-0011	Switzerland●	0-800-89-0011
Mexico●▽	01-800-288-2872	Thailand✆	001-999-111-11
Neth.Ant.○	001-800-872-2881	Turkey●	00-800-12277
Netherlands●	0800-022-9111	U.K.	0800-89-0011
New Zealand●	000-911	U.K.	0800-013-0011
Panama	800-001-0109	Venezuela	800-11-120

FOR EASY CALLING WORLDWIDE

L₂ Just dial the AT&T Access Number for the country you are calling from.
Z Dial the phone number you're calling.   3 Dial your card number.

For access numbers not listed ask any operator for **AT&T Direct**℠ Service.
In the U.S. call 1-800-331-1140 for a wallet guide listing all worldwide AT&T Access Numbers.

Visit our Web site at: www.att.com/traveler
Bold-faced countries permit country-to-country calling outside the U.S.

- ● Public phones may require coin or card deposit to place call.
- + Outside of Cairo, dial "02" first.
- ▲ May not be available from every phone/payphone.
- ✆ Public phones and select hotels.
- ✓ Use U.K. access number in N. Ireland.
- ○ When calling from public phones, use phones marked "Lenso."
- ▽ When calling from public phones, use phones marked "Ladatel."
- ✗ Not available from public phones.
- ▼ Available from phones with international calling capabilities or from most Public Calling Centers.
- ○ From St. Maarten or phones at Bobby's Marina, use 1-800-872-2881.

When placing an international call *from* the U.S., dial 1 800 CALL ATT.

© 1/2000

Israel	1-800-94-949	Philippines●	105-11
Italy●	172-1011	Portugal▲	0800-800-128
Jamaica●	1-800-872-2881	Singapore	800-0111-11
Japan●▲	005-39-111	Spain	900-99-00-11
Malaysia	1800-80-0011	Switzerland●	0-800-89-0011
Mexico●▽	01-800-288-2872	Thailand✆	001-999-111-11
Neth.Ant.○	001-800-872-2881	Turkey●	00-800-12277
Netherlands●	0800-022-9111	U.K.	0800-89-0011
New Zealand●	000-911	U.K.	0800-013-0011
Panama	800-001-0109	Venezuela	800-11-120

FOR EASY CALLING WORLDWIDE

L₂ Just dial the AT&T Access Number for the country you are calling from.
Z Dial the phone number you're calling.   3 Dial your card number.

For access numbers not listed ask any operator for **AT&T Direct**℠ Service.
In the U.S. call 1-800-331-1140 for a wallet guide listing all worldwide AT&T Access Numbers.

Visit our Web site at: www.att.com/traveler
Bold-faced countries permit country-to-country calling outside the U.S.

- ● Public phones may require coin or card deposit to place call.
- + Outside of Cairo, dial "02" first.
- ▲ May not be available from every phone/payphone.
- ✆ Public phones and select hotels.
- ✓ Use U.K. access number in N. Ireland.
- ○ When calling from public phones, use phones marked "Lenso."
- ▽ When calling from public phones, use phones marked "Ladatel."
- ✗ Not available from public phones.
- ▼ Available from phones with international calling capabilities or from most Public Calling Centers.
- ○ From St. Maarten or phones at Bobby's Marina, use 1-800-872-2881.

When placing an international call *from* the U.S., dial 1 800 CALL ATT.

© 1/2000

Go halfway around the world.
Sound like you're halfway around the block.

A Peoples' Princess

Among the thousands of people who have found their final resting place on the Mount of Olives, one of the most recent and unusual is Princess Alice of Greece, mother of Prince Phillip, duke of Edinburgh, and mother-in-law of Queen Elizabeth II. Born in Windsor Castle in 1885, the great-granddaughter of Queen Victoria, Princess Alice at an early age was diagnosed as being almost totally deaf. Carefully trained in lip reading, she was fluent in both English and French; later in life she also mastered Greek.

In 1903, Princess Alice married Prince Andrew, son of King George of Greece, and devoted her life to helping others. During the 1912 Balkan War, she worked as a nurse close to the battlefront, caring for sick and wounded Greek soldiers. During this time, both the princess and her father-in-law, King George, stayed in the home of the family of Haim Cohen, in the northern Greek city of Trikkala, near the war zone. Their friendship continued when Cohen later became a member of the Greek parliament. By the late 1930s, the Greek royal family was no longer in power, but Princess Alice remained in Athens, wearing the habit of a nun as she became increasingly committed to a life of religion and charitable work. In 1943, during the Nazi occupation of Greece, Princess Alice learned that the widow and children of Haim Cohen were in hiding near Athens, trying to escape deportation to the death camps in Poland. At the risk of her life and with the help of two servants, Princess Alice hid her Jewish friends on the grounds of the royal palace for 13 months, until Athens was liberated. Princess Alice died at Buckingham Palace in 1969, and in 1988, in accordance with her dying wish, was reinterred at the **Church of Saint Mary Magdalene** on the Mount of Olives. In 1994, Prince Phillip and his sister, Princess Sophie, traveled to Jerusalem to receive Yad Vashem's Medal of Honor of Righteous Among the Nations, awarded to their late mother. A tree in memory of Princess Alice has been planted at Yad Vashem.

✪ **MOUNT OF OLIVES**   Here you'll find a half dozen churches and one of the oldest Jewish cemeteries in the world. It was this cemetery that religious Jews had in mind when they came to die in the Holy Land. Start down the path on the right and you'll come to the **Tombs of the Prophets,** believed to be the burial place of Haggai, Malachi, and Zechariah. Many Jews have believed, and perhaps still do, that from here the route to heaven is the shortest, since God's presence is always hovering over Jerusalem; others have held that here, on the Mount of Olives, the resurrection of the dead will occur.

Farther up the road, on the southern fringe of Et-Tur, stands the **Mosque (and Chapel) of the Ascension** (ring the doorbell for admission), marking the spot where Jesus ascended to heaven. Interestingly enough, this Christian shrine is under Muslim control. Muslims revere Jesus as a prophet. However, they do not believe Jesus to be the son of God, nor do they believe that Jesus died on the cross.

Just a few steps away is the **Church of the Pater Noster,** built on the traditional spot where Jesus instructed his disciples in the Lord's Prayer. Tiles along the walls of the church are inscribed with the Lord's Prayer in 44 languages. The Carmelite Convent and Basilica of the Sacred Heart are on the adjoining hill.

From up here you can see a cluster of churches on the lower slopes of the Mount of Olives. All can be reached either from here or from the road paralleling the fortress wall, diagonally opposite Saint Stephen's Gate (Lion's Gate).

If you head down the path to the right of the Tomb of the Prophets, you'll come to **Dominus Flevit** (open daily 8am to noon and 2:30 to 5pm), which is a relatively contemporary Franciscan church that marks the spot where Jesus wept over his vision of the future destruction of Jerusalem. Next, the Russian Orthodox **Church of Mary Magdalene,** with its onion-shaped spires, was built in 1888 by Czar Alexander III (open Tuesday and Thursday from 10 to 11:30am). Call ☎ **02/628-4371** for more information.

The Roman Catholic **Garden of Gethsemane** (open 8:30am to noon and from 3pm to sunset, April to October; 8:30am to noon and from 2pm to sunset in winter) adjoins the **Basilica of the Agony (Church of All Nations)**; it's in the courtyard where Jesus supposedly prayed the night before his arrest. The church's gold mosaic facade shows God looking down from heaven over Jesus and the peoples of the world. The church was built by people from 16 different nations in 1924. Next door, past beautifully tended gardens of ancient olive trees and bougainvillea, is the **Tomb of the Virgin,** which is a deep underground chamber housing the tombs of Mary and Joseph. The tomb is open daily 8am to noon; 2:30 to 5:30pm.

VALLEY OF KIDRON   The Valley of Kidron is between the Mount of Olives and the Old City walls. It runs south, between Mount Ophel (where David built his city) and the Mount of Contempt. Just under the wall here, roughly in front of El Aksa Mosque, are two tombs: **Absalom's Tomb** and the **Tomb of Zechariah.** At one time, religious Jews would throw stones at Absalom's tomb (Kever Avshalom), in condemnation of Absalom, who rebelled against his father, King David. Scholars attribute Absalom's Tomb to Herodian times—it is Jerusalem's only relatively intact structure from before the Roman destruction in A.D. 70.

The Valley of Kidron is also known as the Valley of Jehoshaphat. The Book of Joel records that the judgments will be rendered here on resurrection day: "Let the heathen be awakened, and come up to the Valley of Jehoshaphat, for there will I sit to judge all the heathen round about." Muslims hold to a similar belief. They believe Muhammad will sit astride a pillar under the wall of the Dome of the Rock. A wire will be stretched from the pillar to the Mount of Olives, opposite, where Jesus will be seated. All humankind will walk across the wire on its way to eternity. The righteous and faithful will reach the other side safely; the rest will drop down in the Valley of Jehoshaphat and perish.

About 200 yards down the valley is the **Fountain of the Virgin,** at the Arab village of Silwan. Water from the spring (the Gihon) anointed Solomon king and served as the only water source for ancient Jerusalem. During the Assyrian and Babylonian attacks (8th century B.C.), King Hezekiah constructed an aqueduct through which the waters could be hidden inside the city, an extraordinary engineering feat at the time. **Hezekiah's Aqueduct** is still there (underneath the church commemorating the spot where Mary once drew water to wash the clothes of Jesus). It's about 1,600 feet long, and the depth of the water is 10 to 16 inches. The walk takes about 40 minutes; take a flashlight or candles with you. You can walk through from Sunday to Thursday between 8:30am and 3pm, on Friday and holiday eves until 1pm. Entrance is free, but give the caretaker a tip. It is best to visit Silwan and Hezekiah's tunnel with a tour group (see section 6 for information). Above the **Gihon spring** lie the ruins of King David's city (See "Dung Gate, Silwan (The City of David) & Ophel Park," above.)

5 Especially for Kids

The **Train Puppet Theater** in Liberty Bell Park offers programs (in Hebrew, but nonetheless interesting) for children and hosts an International Puppet Theater Festival every other year. Call ☎ **02/561-8514** for information or check the listing in Friday's *Jerusalem Post*. See "Jerusalem After Dark," below. The **Israel Museum's** lively **Children's Wing** has great exhibits, many of them hands-on, workshops in recycled materials, and a library of fabulous children's books you can sit and read. See "Museums" in section 2, above.

The Time Elevator. Beit Agron, Hillel and Rivlin sts. ☎ **02/625-2227.** Admission NIS 44 ($9.70). Sun–Thurs 10am–8pm.

This is a 30-minute multimedia semivirtual reality history of Jerusalem presented in a former auditorium refitted with special chairs and a floor that provides special motion effects. It's not good for younger children or for those who do poorly on roller coaster rides. The presentation itself is interesting, but expensive for what you get. The show is repeated about every 40 minutes.

The Tisch Family Zoological Gardens. Manahat, Jerusalem. ☎ **02/675-0111.** Admission NIS 35 ($7.70) adults; NIS 25 ($5.50) children. Sun–Thurs 9am–6pm (until 5pm in winter); Fri 9am–6:30pm; Sat 10am–6pm. Bus: 26, 33, 99.

Jerusalem's Biblical Zoo has recently moved into this new, beautifully landscaped site at the western edge of the city, with a state-of-the art open design that blends into the surrounding countryside. Emphasis is on creatures mentioned in the Bible or native to Israel. Children will enjoy the friendly waterfowl and the camel encampment (camel and pony ride facilities are planned). There is a pleasant safari-style refreshment facility on the grounds. In summer, during the heat of the day, most animals are inactive; the zoo is at its best in cooler weather. Prepare for a 10-minute walk from the bus stop.

Walking Tour: The Old City

Start: The Jaffa Gate
Finish: The tour has three options: The first will take you to the Jewish Quarter and the Western Wall, the second to the Islamic shrines and mosques on the Temple Mount, the third to an unusual Christian enclave on the roof of the Church of the Holy Sepulcher.
Best Times: Sunday to Wednesday from 8am to 3pm.
Worst Times: Shabbat, Muslim holidays, Friday, or after 3pm when the Dome of the Rock is closed.

This is a meandering walk that will get you to some major sites, offbeat vista points, and authentic refueling stops, but the Old City is a vast, intricate Chinese box of experiences, as unplanned and exotic as the 4,000-year history of Jerusalem itself. One way to enjoy the texture of this sublime hodgepodge is simply to plunge in and wander, chancing upon hummus parlors and holy sites, ancient bakeries and antique Bedouin embroideries. I will clue you in to a bit of Jerusalem's history and local lore as we move along.

FROM THE JAFFA GATE TO THE CARDO   The first part of the walk takes you to the Cardo, where the walk divides into three possible options. We begin at:

Walking Tour—The Old City

1. The Jaffa Gate
2. Government Tourist Information Office (GTIO)
3. New Imperial Hotel
4. The Petra Hotel
5. The view from the Petra Hotel roof
6. Suq El Hussor
7. Stone rooftop
8. Cardo
9. Hurva Synagogue
10. Herodian Quarter Excavations
11. Crusader Church of St. Mary
12. Western Wall
13. Archeological excavations at the southern foot of the Temple Mount
14. Southern wall of the Old City
15. The Temple Mount
16. El Aksa Mosque
17. Dome of the Rock
18. Islamic Museum
19. Suq El Attarin Bazaar
20. Suq Khan Es Zeit
21. Ethiopian Compound and Monastery
22. Crafts shop
23. Ethiopian Chapel
24. Chapel of the Archangel Michael
25. Church of the Holy Sepulcher

Walking Tour Routes

- –·–·– Option 1
- ·········· Option 2
- – – – Option 3

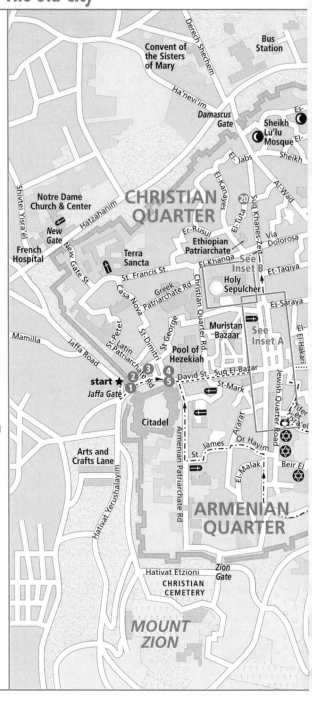

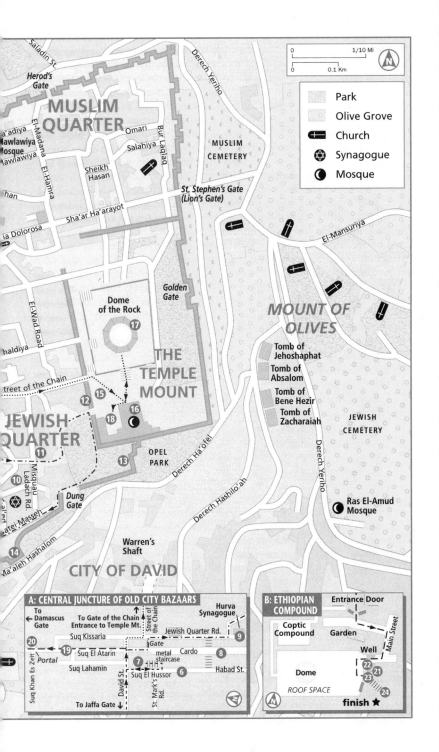

Herod's Gate

Saladin St.

MUSLIM QUARTER

Omari

Salahiya

Bur Lailad

a'adiya
Mawlawiya
Mosque
Mawlawiya

El-Madana

El-Hamra

Sheikh Hasan

han

ia Dolorosa

Sha'ar Ha'arayot

Derech Yeriho

MUSLIM CEMETERY

St. Stephen's Gate (Lion's Gate)

El-Mansuriya

0   1/10 Mi
0   0.1 Km

Park
Olive Grove
Church
Synagogue
Mosque

El-Wad Road

haldiya

treet of the Chain

Dome of the Rock
17

Golden Gate

THE TEMPLE MOUNT

MOUNT OF OLIVES

Tomb of Jehoshaphat
Tomb of Absalom
Tomb of Bene Hezir
Tomb of Zacharaiah

JEWISH CEMETERY

12   15
18   16

JEWISH QUARTER

11

10

13

OPEL PARK

Derech Ha'ofel

Derech Yeriho

Misgau Ladach Rd.

a'er Masseh

Dung Gate

Derech Hashilo'ah

Ras El-Amud Mosque

14

Ma'aleh Hashalom

Warren's Shaft

CITY OF DAVID

A: CENTRAL JUNCTURE OF OLD CITY BAZAARS

To Damascus Gate ←

To Gate of the Chain Entrance to Temple Mt.

Street of the Chain

Hurva Synagogue

Jewish Quarter Rd.

Suq Kissaria

20

19   Suq El Atarin

Suq Lahamin

Suq Khan Es Zeit

Portal

Gate

Cardo

metal staircase

7

Suq El Hussor

6

David St.

St. Mark's Rd.

To Jaffa Gate ↓

9

8   Habad St.

B: ETHIOPIAN COMPOUND

Entrance Door

Coptic Compound

Garden

Well

Main Street

Dome

ROOF SPACE

22   21

23

24

finish ★

1. Jaffa Gate. Before you enter Jaffa Gate, which is the traditional entrance to the city for visitors from the West, check out the stones from many eras that make up the present Old City wall, which was erected by order of the Ottoman Turkish Sultan Suleiman the Magnificent in 1538. Some stones have been dressed with carefully cut flat borders surrounding a raised, flat central area (the boss), in the style of King Herod's stone cutters, and probably dating from 2,000 years ago. You will see this style again in the monumental stones of the Western Wall, a retaining wall for the vast artificial platform that Herod constructed to surround the original Jerusalem Temple site with room for the thousands of Jews who made the pilgrimage from all over the ancient world. You will notice other kinds of stones with flat borders and rougher raised bosses, in the pre-Herodian style of the Hasmoneans (the Maccabees) who were the last Jewish rulers of Jerusalem until modern times with the exception of Bar Kokhba, who conquered the ruins of the city during the Second Jewish Revolt against Rome in A.D. 132–35. You will also see rough ashlars of the Byzantine era, as well as the virtually undressed stones of Crusader and medieval times. In each of the upper corners of the closed decorative archway to the left of the Jaffa Gate, notice stones carefully carved into a leaf design, which are believed to have come from a long-destroyed crusader church. The walls of Jerusalem, like the city itself, are composed of stones used again and again, just as many of the legends and traditions of the city reappear and are reassembled by each successive civilization and religion.

Inside the gate, on the left, is:

2. The Tourist Information Office. Here you can pick up free maps, information, and tourist publications.

Enter the archway on the left to the arcade of:

3. The New Imperial Hotel, built in the 1880s ,was in its time the most luxurious hotel in Jerusalem. In the 19th century, the now largely deserted arcade was a private bazaar for hotel guests, where the beggars, lepers, cripples, and "riffraff" of Jerusalem could be neatly excluded. Slightly uphill and in the center of the arcade is a broken street lamp mounted on a cylindrical stone that was uncovered when the foundations for the New Imperial were being dug. The Latin lettering, "LEG X" records a marker for the camp of the Tenth Legion Frentensis, which conquered and destroyed Jewish Jerusalem in a.d. 70. Flavius Josephus wrote that after the temple and the buildings of Jerusalem were systematically razed and the surviving inhabitants led off to slavery, death, and exile, the Tenth Legion encamped beside the ruins of the Jaffa Gate for 62 years to guard the ruins against Jews who might try to filter back and reestablish the city. The discovery of this marker in proximity to the Jaffa Gate confirms Josephus's account. The once-elegant New Imperial, as it drifted into seediness, became a spot for romantic assignations during the British Mandate period. Characters played by Bogart (if not Bergman) would have felt at home.

Next door is the:

4. Petra Hotel. The first modern hotel built in the Old City in the 1870s, the once elegant Petra, now undergoing restoration, is largely a backpacker's hostel. Herman Melville and Mark Twain probably stayed in an earlier structure on this site (the old Mediterranean Hotel) during their visits to what was then a decrepit warren of ruins filled with lice-covered beggars and crazed religious fanatics. Neither Melville nor Twain found Jerusalem a pleasant place to stay.

Enter at the far right as you face the building, climb the stairs to the second floor lobby of the Petra, and ask the person at the desk for permission to see:

5. The view from the Petra Hotel's roof. Be sure to show this book; admission is about NIS 5 ($1.10) per person. From the lobby, climb two more long flights of stairs, and emerge from the creaky wooden attic stairs onto the roof with its strange series of curved stone domes. Turn left, up a few steps and left again, and you will face one of the Old City's great panoramas—perfectly aligned, with the golden Dome of the Rock (site of the First and Second Temples) in the exact center of the vista, with the roofline of the city spread out below you. This is where photographers come for postcard views. The roof used to be a quiet, contemplative spot, but guests of the Petra Hostel have made the roof into a wall to wall sleeping bag encampment in summer.

As you look eastward toward the Temple Mount, you'll see the Mount of Olives across the horizon behind the Dome of the Rock. In ancient times, this now barren ridge was a natural olive grove, and its cultivation was one of the sources of ancient Jerusalem's wealth. The green area of the ridge, just behind the Dome of the Rock, is the Garden of Gethsemane (Gethsemane is the anglicized version of the Hebrew word for "olive press"), where Jesus was arrested after the Last Supper. This is the western side of the Mount of Olives ridge. On the eastern side, out of view, is the site of the village of Bethany where Lazarus, who was raised from the dead by Jesus, and his sisters, Mary and Martha, lived. Jesus may have been making his way to their house after the Passover dinner at the time of his arrest.

The Dome of the Rock was built in A.D. 691. According to legend, the saintly warrior Omar Ibn El Khattab, who conquered Jerusalem for Islam in A.D. 638, was greeted by the Christian Archbishop Sophronius at the Jaffa Gate. Sophronius surrendered the city peacefully to Omar, and then offered to lead the new ruler on a tour of his conquest. The first thing Omar Ibn El Khattab asked to see was "the Mosque of Suleiman," or the place where Solomon's Temple had once stood. The vast ceremonial platform surrounding the site of the ancient Jewish temple was one of the few architectural landmarks of Herodian Jerusalem that the Romans had found too difficult to eradicate when they destroyed the city in A.D. 70. Three hundred years later, as Christianity triumphed over Roman paganism, the Temple Mount was one of the places in the city left purposely in ruins (perhaps symbolically) by the Byzantine Christians. By the time of the Muslim conquest, the Temple Mount had become the garbage dump for Jerusalem and the surrounding area. Omar Ibn El Khattab was so saddened by the sight of the ancient holy place defiled and in ruins that he removed his cloak and used it to carry away debris. Sophronius prudently followed Omar's example. Later Muslim authorities ordered the most beautiful building to be placed over the rock. The silver-domed El Aksa Mosque, on the southern edge of the Temple Mount, also commemorates this event.

Just below the Petra's roof is a large rectangular empty area, the Pool of Hezekiah, misnamed centuries ago for the Judean king whose hidden water system saved ancient Jerusalem from Assyrian onslaught in 701 B.C.; the pool is actually a disused reservoir for a water system constructed in Herodian and Roman times. To the north, you will see the great silver dome of the Church of the Holy Sepulcher, built over the site venerated for almost 2,000 years as the place of Jesus' crucifixion and entombment. In the far distance, beyond the walls of the Old City, on the northern part of the Mount of Olives ridge, the small city is the complex of the Hebrew University and Hadassah Hospital on Mount Scopus. To your right (south), inside the walls of the Old City, are the domes of the

Armenian Cathedral of Saint James, the roofs of the Armenian and Jewish quarters of the Old City, and 5 miles to the south, beyond the hill of Abu Tor (believed to have been the Hill of Evil Counsel as well as the site of the Blood Acre purchased for a potters' field with Judas Iscariot's 30 pieces of silver) is Bethlehem, birthplace of King David and of Jesus.

Leave the Petra Hotel and continue down David Street to the bazaar:

6. **Suq El Hussor,** now a rather small basket market. Turn right. (Among the many imported baskets from Asia, you'll still find some rustic examples of local olive twig baskets.)

About 60 feet on the left side of Suq El Hussor, you'll notice an open metal staircase. Climb up the staircase, and you'll be on:

7. **The stone rooftop of the covered markets.** Here you'll discover a different world above the bustling labyrinths of the bazaars. The broad rooftop area straight ahead covers the exact center of the Old City, where the four quarters meet. At the right time of day, if you listen carefully, you will hear emanating from the large dome on your right the unmistakable sound of a game of billiards; this dome at the very heart of the Holy City covers a billiard parlor. In crusader times, this large structure housed the city's bourse or exchange. From this rooftop, you can clearly see the architectural distinctions among the four quarters of the walled city: the orange-tile-roofed Christian Quarter to the northwest; the dome-roofed Muslim Quarter with its many television antennas to the northeast; the new stonework of the Jewish Quarter to the southeast, rebuilt by the Israelis after they reoccupied the Old City in 1967 (this area is devoid of antennas; its inhabitants receive cable); and, to the southwest, the older stone buildings of the Armenian Quarter. Again, through the maze of TV antennas, you get an interesting chance to photograph the lavish Dome of the Rock.

Descend the metal staircase, and backtrack on Suq El Hussor to David Street. Turn right onto David Street. The next right on David Street leads to the:

8. **Cardo,** the restored and renovated section of Roman and Byzantine Jerusalem's main market street, now filled with stylish modern shops.

At this point you have three choices for the rest of your tour.

THE FIRST OPTION: THE JEWISH QUARTER   You could easily wander the streets of this beautifully reconstructed area for a number of hours. Walk south on the Jewish Quarter Road to the:

9. **Hurva Synagogue** (see under "The Jewish Quarter," above, for more information).

☕ **TAKE A BREAK**   A slice of kosher pizza, a falafel, a light meal, or wonderful Arabic bread fresh from the bakery oven are all available on the section of the Jewish Quarter Road beyond the Hurva Synagogue.

Walk across the square behind the synagogue and you'll see signs for the:

10. **Herodian Quarter excavations** in the center of the Jewish Quarter.

Take Tiferet Israel Street, which runs from the northeastern corner of the big square to the end, where you will come upon the:

11. **Crusader Church of Saint Mary.** Turn right at the church and make a left to the great staircase, which descends down to the:

12. **Western Wall.** Between the Western Wall and the Dung Gate, you can enter the area of the:

13. **Archeological excavations** at the southern foot of the Temple Mount.

From the excavations, take the road inside the City Wall uphill to the:

14. **Southern wall of the Old City** with its lovely view down into the valley below, which was the site of the original City of David 3,000 years ago.

    You will see a parking lot inside the city walls; cross it and turn right into a pathway that becomes Habad Road. Follow Habad Road to the far end. Or Hayim Street is a left turn off Habad Road. Continue uphill until the road ends at the Armenian Patriarchate Road. A right turn onto this road will get you back to the square inside the Jaffa Gate.

SECOND OPTION: THE TEMPLE MOUNT   From the Cardo, if it is not a Friday, and not after 12:30pm, continue straight onto where David Street seems to end. Turn right, then quickly take the first left, a continuation of David Street called the Street of the Chain. Continue down this road to the great green door (the Gate of the Chain) at the end, which leads directly onto the:

15. **Temple Mount.** The Temple Mount (in Arabic, Haram es Sharif) is open for visitors until 3pm. Give yourself ample time to walk around the ceremonial plaza and enjoy the views of the Mount of Olives. Non-Muslims must buy admission tickets (approximately NIS 30/$6.60, well worth the fee) from a small stone kiosk to the right of the El Aksa Mosque, which will admit you to both mosques and to the museum (you may be asked to wait outside during noonday prayers). It is permissible to take photographs outdoors on the Temple Mount, but you cannot bring a camera into mosques or shrines.

    Walk diagonally to the right after entering the Gate of the Chain to the southern end of the Temple Mount to:

16. **El Aksa Mosque.** This is the main Islamic prayer hall on the Temple Mount.
    In the center of the Temple Mount is the:

17. **Dome of the Rock.** You can't miss its lavish exterior tiles and its golden dome.
    At the southwest corner is the:

18. **Islamic Museum,** with a collection of Islamic artifacts from earlier periods on the Temple Mount.

THIRD OPTION: THE BAZAARS & THE CHURCH OF THE HOLY SEPULCHER   This walk begins at the intersection of David Street and the Cardo. Turn left into the narrow, covered:

19. **Suq El Attarin Bazaar,** the Spice Market. Covered during the time of the crusaders, who perhaps could not bear the blazing summer sun of the region, it's actually an additional segment of the Cardo, once the great Roman north-south market and ceremonial street. The Roman Cardo, originally broad and colonnaded, evolved over centuries into the present warren of narrow, parallel bazaars (including the Butcher's Bazaar, with its dangling skinned sheep heads and gutters of blood, parallel just to the left) that runs all the way north to the Damascus Gate. El Attarin is now mostly clothing and sneaker shops.

    Follow it until you exit from the covered portion, through a nondescript portal, and continue straight on. The next section of the street, no longer roofed over, but covered by shop awnings is:

20. **Suq Khan es-Zeit,** the Market of the Inn of the Olive Oil. Probably since Herodian-Jewish times this area has been a major food market—the Frankish Crusaders called this the **Malcuisinat,** or Street of Bad Cookery, unhappy with the many Middle Eastern specialties sold here. You will notice pastry shops displaying mysteriously radiant mountains of baklava arranged on top of glowing lightbulbs and flashlights; the peanut baklava filling is sometimes dyed green to approximate the more costly pistachio. There are also chewy rolled pancakes filled with nuts or sweet cheese, served in a honey syrup; other shops sell dried

fruits or dark globs of fruit- and nut-filled nougat. There are also hibachis cooking kebabs and shashliks, and rotisseries of chickens to go. Any of these places are good bets for snacks.

☕ **TAKE A BREAK   Abu Assab Refreshments,** a busy Old City landmark, sells fresh orange, grapefruit, and carrot juice, and is the least expensive and best of its kind in town. A good place to stave off dehydration and fill up on vitamins, you can order these juices straight, or in any combination. You can stay downstairs for a quick break, or go upstairs where there is table service. Mike, the British-educated manager, who is often at the downstairs carrot juice counter, will translate the Arabic price list.

A short way along the same side of the street is a stone staircase. Climb the staircase to the top, turn left, and follow the lane to the end, turn right, follow the street around through the Coptic Convent and onto the:

21. Ethiopian Compound and Monastery, on the Church of the Holy Sepulcher's roof with the protruding dome in the center. Through the windows of the dome you will be able to see the **Chapel of Saint Helena** inside the Holy Sepulcher Church below; you'll even be able to smell the church incense, and at times, hear services and prayers.

The Ethiopians use this roof area each year on the Saturday midnight eve of Easter Sunday for one of the city's most exotic religious processions. The Ethiopian Patriarch, with a great ceremonial African umbrella, circumambulates the dome, followed by monks beating ancient drums—so large that they must be carried by two men—and by chanting white-robed pilgrims. The procession then retires to a leopard-skin tent (nowadays made of canvas in a leopard skin pattern) to chant and pray through the night. This very moving ceremony is open to the public, and many Jerusalemites make it a point to attend each year.

The Compound is spread across the sprawling segments of the roof of the Church of the Holy Sepulcher. Note that here on this ancient roof entire trees and gardens grow, among them the olive trees (or offshoots of olive trees) in which Abraham supposedly found the ram he offered in sacrifice after God freed him from the commandment to sacrifice Isaac. Beside the expanse of the roof surrounding the dome, are the living quarters of the tiny, walled, fortresslike monastery. Visitors may not enter this monastery compound, but you can look into the lane at the entrance to the monastery: the low round-walled buildings and trees offer a distinctly African feeling. For centuries, the Church of the Holy Sepulcher has been divided among the six oldest factions of Christianity, and in the most recent division, the Ethiopian Church, with roots dating from the 4th century A.D., got the roof. Both Ethiopian monks and a lay community have inhabited this location for centuries (you can often smell the wonderful spicy cooking of the communal kitchen). Note the church bells hanging in the ruined gothic arches of the crusader-era church structure to the right and above the tiny main street.

To the left of the doorway into the monastery lane, you will find the community's well, with a shaft running down through the Holy Sepulcher Church (running water has obviated the need for the well, but the Ethiopians still have the right to a certain amount of water from it each day).

Opposite the well is a small, sometimes open door leading to a:

22. **Crafts shop.** It's usually closed, but at times you can find Ethiopian crafts and hand-painted icons for sale.

From this door continue around the corner to the large ancient wooden door leading to the:

23. **Ethiopian chapel,** a structure probably built in medieval times. Here, if a monk is in attendance, you will be shown crucifix-shaped holy books written in ancient Ge'ez (the sacred language of Ethiopia), and you will have time to take in the paintings (unfortunately done by European religious painters rather than by traditional Ethiopian religious artists) that depict the Queen of Sheba visiting King Solomon in approximately 940 B.C. Charmingly, the artist has decided to depict an anachronistic group of 18th-century Hasidic Jews among King Solomon's entourage. From the traditionally believed union of the queen and King Solomon, the royal Ethiopian family is said to have descended (one of the emperor of Ethiopia's titles was "the Lion of Judah"), and in 1935, when Emperor Haile Selassie was forced to flee the Italian invasion of his country, he took up residence in Jerusalem, "the land of my fathers." There is a tray for contributions at the back of the chapel.

Continue to the rear of the chapel and down the staircase to the:

24. **Chapel of the Archangel Michael.** In this ancient chapel, with its carved and inlaid wood paneling, the community of Ethiopian monks gathers in late afternoon for prayers (4pm in winter; 5pm during daylight saving time). It is sometimes possible for visitors to sit in the rear of the chapel and listen to the traditional Ethiopian chanting, which is extremely beautiful.

The ancient wooden door of the chapel leads outside to the main entrance plaza in front of the:

25. **Church of the Holy Sepulcher.** Now that you've seen the roof, you are ready to journey through the very special interior. (See "The Old City," above, for a detailed description of the church.) After visiting the church, make your way back through the bazaars to David Street and the Jaffa Gate.

6 Organized Tours

As a general rule of thumb, make certain that your tour guide is officially licensed by the Ministry of Tourism. Also, on any guided tour that includes holy places, you must dress modestly. This means no shorts (men or women), no sleeveless shirts or blouses, and women should have a head covering.

BUS TOURS   The **Jerusalem Circular Line Egged bus no. 99** (☎ **02/624-8144**) stops at 34 of the most visited sites throughout the city, from the Mount of Olives to Yad VaShem. The bus leaves the Jaffa Gate terminus at 10am, noon, 2pm, and 4pm Sunday to Thursday; on Friday the 4pm run is omitted. There are no Saturday buses. A single tour ticket is NIS 18 ($5). This is a great way to get a quick rundown of what the city has to offer and where things are. You can also buy a full-day ticket, or a 2-day ticket—with these you can get off and back on the bus as many times as you like during the validity time of your ticket. It is always wise to check with the tourist information office inside Jaffa Gate for the latest information on bus 99's timetable and route.

GUIDED WALKING TOURS   Free municipal walking tours in English are offered Saturdays at 10am from 32 Jaffa Rd.; check with the **Tourist Information Offices** at Jaffa Gate (☎ **02/628-0382**) or Safra Square (☎ **02/625-8844**) for current information. The Jaffa Gate office also rents recorded, self-guided walking tours for approximately 45 NIS ($10) per day. The Sheraton Jerusalem Plaza Hotel, 47 King George V Ave., at Agron Street (☎ **02/629-8666**), sponsors tours of various areas. Drop by the hotel to pick up a schedule, or check "Events in the Jerusalem Region," issued by the GTIO. Meet in the lobby of the hotel at 8:50am for any tour.

The ✪ **Society for the Protection of Nature in Israel (SPNI),** 13 Helene Ha-Malka St. (☎ **02/624-4605** or 02/625-2357), sponsors excellent and fascinating walking tours within Jerusalem as well as hikes and tours of the surrounding countryside. A 1-day tour is approximately NIS 180 ($40).

Various commercial concerns will take you on guided tours of the city that emphasize its history and archaeology. **Archeological Seminars Ltd.,** 34 Habad St. in the Jewish Quarter (☎ **02/627-3515**), will guide you through the Jewish Quarter, Temple Mount, the Temple Mount excavations, the City of David (Ophel), or the Christian and Muslim quarters of the Old City. Tours run Sunday to Thursday and cost around $18 per person for a 3-hour itinerary. For information on schedules, various itineraries, and the chance to "dig for a day" at an archaeological site, phone or stop at the office.

Zion Walking Tours (☎ **02/628-7866**) will show you the historical and archaeological highlights of the Old City or the Mount of Olives. Half day tours depart from the Tower of David and cost NIS 54 to 81 ($12 to $18), with senior and student discounts. **Walking Tours Ltd.** (☎ **02/652-2568**) also offers 3- to 4-hour itineraries in the same price range.

7 Outdoor Pursuits & Sports

BIKING   The **Jerusalem Bicycle Club** (☎ **02/643-8386,** ask for Gershon; or 02/561-9416, ask for Benni) is an informal group that can arrange outings, help plan routes throughout the country, and give advice to those interested in bicycling and renting bikes. The club often does rides starting at 7am on Saturdays.

HEALTH CLUBS   **Samson's Gym** is centrally located at the Lev Yerushalayim Hotel, 18 King George St. (☎ **02/530-0333**). The **Hyatt Regency** (☎ 02/532-2906), offers some of the best health club facilities in town.

JOGGING   Jerusalem, with its many hills, is not the easiest place for unplanned jogging; a very useful paperback, *Carta's Jogger's Guide to Jerusalem,* by Morton H. Seelenfreund (available at Steimatzky's Bookstores for around $7), maps out many good possibilities.

SWIMMING   You have a choice of many pools. One of the cheapest (but also most crowded) is the **Jerusalem public pool,** 43 Emek Refaim St. (☎ **02/563-2092**). On Saturday and holidays, Israelis pack the pools. Admission is NIS 32 ($9). It is open from 8am to 5pm.

A more convenient, although more expensive, option is to pay the visitors' rate to use a pool at one of the city's hotels. In central Jerusalem, try the **Dan Pearl Hotel** (☎ **02/622-6666**), and the **Laromme Hotel** (☎ **02/675-6666**); at the western edge of the city there's the **Four Points Sheraton Hotel** (☎ **02/655-8888**), and the **Jerusalem (Ramada) Renaissance Hotel** (☎ **02/659-9999**). All the above hotels have swimming facilities throughout the year, with indoor or indoor and outdoor pools. Admission policies vary according to time of year and rate of occupancy, but could be in the NIS 72 to 90 ($16 to $20) range.

In good weather, the outdoor pool at the **Mount Zion Hotel** (☎ **02/568-9555**), and the outdoor pool at the **King David Hotel** (☎ **02/620-8888**) offer pleasant gardens and spectacular views of the Old City's walls.

TENNIS   Reservations are always needed to secure a court. The **YMCA,** King David Street (☎ **02/569-2692**), is a good, central place to play if you have your own equipment. Open Monday to Saturday 8am to sunset; approximately $7 per hour. The **Hebrew University at Mt. Scopus** (☎ **02/581-7579**) has 10 lighted courts and rents equipment. Open Sunday to Thursday 7am to 10pm at $7 per hour; and Friday and Saturday 7am to 5pm at $8.50 an hour.

8 Shopping

THE SHOPPING SCENE

Jewelry, Judaica, and local Israeli crafts and art objects are the most interesting items for shoppers. Many shops in the Ben-Yehuda area, as well as in the Jewish Quarter of the Old City, sell reproductions of cast bronze antique wall menorahs from North Africa, medieval Italy, and Eastern Europe. The designs are authentic and decorative. There is no lack of modern menorahs, mezuzahs, dreidels, candle holders, and embroidered yarmulkes, as well as objects for Passover, Sukkot, Shabbat, and synagogue services. *Note:* It is possible to bargain a bit at most tourist shops in West Jerusalem. Very few of the stores on Ben Yehuda Street or King David Street will allow you to return an item if you see something nicer or at a better price elsewhere, so shop carefully. Shops in Mea Shearim often have a better selection and better prices.

There are also many outstanding individual shops that sell original art, jewelry, glass, and ceramics. Most of our listings are for places where you can find handmade items, and purchase them directly from the artisans who make them.

HOURS, SALES TAX & SHIPPING   Tourist shops are generally open Sunday to Thursday from 9am to 7pm, although some shops close from 1 to 4pm for siesta. On Friday, shops are open from 9am to 2pm.

There is no sales tax; however, unless otherwise stated, the value-added tax (VAT) of 17% is included in the price. Always ask about VAT exemptions when paying in foreign currency. Some expensive tourist shops will give you voucher forms, good for VAT refunds on items costing more than $50 when presented at Ben-Gurion Airport just before you leave the country. See "Fast Facts: Israel" in chapter 2.

Merchants are generally cooperative about packing your purchases securely for shipping or for the plane ride home. If you decide to mail purchases home, remember to bring strong tape with you to the post office, as all packages must be inspected for security and customs before they can be sealed. You must also bring your passport to the post office for identification when you mail packages.

SHOPPING A TO Z
ART

Israel Museum. Ruppin St. ☎ **02/670-8811.**

An exciting selection of posters are on sale here. Also, check out reproductions of Anna Ticho's charcoal and pen-and-ink landscapes and Shalom of Safed's vibrant primitive paintings, as well as high-quality reproductions of Judaica and antiquities at reasonable prices.

Jerusalem Artists' House Gallery. 12 Shmuel Ha-Nagid St. ☎ **02/625-2636.**

Housed in the Ottoman Turkish buildings of the original Bezalel Academy of Art and Design (the school has now moved to the Hebrew University campus), this remarkable cooperative gallery, sponsored by the Jerusalem Municipality and the Israeli government, represents more than 500 juried Israeli artists, ranging from the famous and established to the newest and most promising. Upstairs, you'll find a changing array of one-person and group exhibits. The staff of the Artists' House can put you in touch with any artist whose work interests you, and they will arrange for the shipping of your purchase. The gallery is open Sunday to Thursday from 10am to 1pm and 4 to 7pm; on Friday 10am to 1pm; Saturday 11am to 2pm.

BASKET WARE

Suq El Hussor. Old City.

With the death in 1996 of the next to last vendor of traditional basketry, Jerusalem's once roaring basket market has fallen victim to bamboo import items, but you can still find a few locally made, primitive olive-twig baskets, a Jerusalem tradition that is thousands of years old. Rough, almost bird's nestlike in texture, these baskets look great when filled with dried flowers, fresh fruit, yarn, or almost anything else. Don't pay more than NIS 22 to 27 ($5 to $6) for a basket with a handle, the kind used by country women to collect fresh grapes or figs. Bigger traylike baskets, the kind women in the markets carry on their heads, should cost NIS 45 to 58 ($10 to $13). One of the few places where real olive twig branch baskets can be found is a small hole-in-the-wall shop on the right side of Christian Quarter Road in the Old City, between David Street and St. Helena Street. The owner, a small man with a small mustache, is one of the toughest bargainers in town.

BOOKSTORES

Most bookstores carrying a selection of books in English are within 2 blocks of Zion Square. Look for the following stores: **Librairie Franççaise Alcheh,** 30 Jaffa Rd. (☎ 02/625-7058), between Zion Square and the central post office; the well-stocked **Steimatzky** chain, with its large main branch at 39 Jaffa Rd. and smaller branches at 9 King George St. and on the Ben-Yehuda Pedestrian Mall. Steimatzky's maintains very small branches in many major hotels and sells a good selection of English- and foreign-language periodicals, books, and guidebooks to various regions of the country.

For used books try **Sefer Ve Sefel Bookshop,** 4 Yavetz St. (☎ 02/624-8237), where you'll find the largest selection of English language fiction in Israel, and used but current guidebooks; **Clal Center Bookstore,** 97 Jaffa Rd. (ask directions to their affiliate, **Moffit,** also in the Clal Center); and **Yalkut Bookstore,** in the rear plaza of the Redjwan Building on King George St. **Tmol Shilshom Bookstore Cafe** in a rear courtyard off 5 Yoel Salomon St.(☎ 02/623-2758), has a small eclectic collection of new and used books and magazines, and remains open until midnight on Sunday through Thursday; it's mainly a cafe with a wonderful program of readings and live music. **The Bookshelf,** 2 Jewish Quarter Rd. (☎ 02/627-3889), in the Jewish Quarter of the Old City, has an especially helpful management and an influx of good reading material, often shipped from Princeton, New Jersey. It also offers fax and Internet service and does photocopying; it is open from Sunday through Thursday from 10am to 6pm, and on Friday from 10am to 2:30pm. **Stein Books,** 52 King George St. (☎ 02/624-7877), is well known for Jewish Studies and rare books; **Stein on Schatz,** Schatz St., a new, well-stocked less academic affiliate of Stein—it will be open for browsing (but not for buying) on Saturdays. The little **Gur Arieh** bookshop at 8 Yoel Salomon is worth checking out and a good place to pick up the *Jerusalem Post* or *Herald Tribune.* The **SPINI** bookstore, with lots of detailed maps and hard-to-find books about Israel, is at 13 Heleni Ha-Malka St. (☎ 02/624-4605). The **American Colony Hotel Bookshop,** at the American Colony Hotel in East Jerusalem, stocks work by many Middle Eastern writers.

CHOCOLATE

Hand Made Chocolates by Max Brenner. 23 Emek Refaim St., German Colony. ☎ **02/ 561-2123.**

The creamy bonbons in this jewel of a shop look like contemporary art, and are imbued with uniquely Israeli flavors like mint leaf, lavender flower, and assorted spice, as well as blueberry liqueur and zesty lemon. You'll also find heavenly truffles and cocoa beans rolled in fabulous chocolate concoctions. Prices begin at NIS 3 (66¢) per piece, with gift boxes (you select each piece) ranging from NIS 27 to 97 ($6 to $22). Items are kosher (dairy).

CRAFTS

Contemporary Crafts

Cadim Gallery. 4 Yoel Salomon Mall. ☎ **02/623-4869.**

This cooperative gallery displays the work of the award-winning Meira Una, as well as Mark Yudell's ceramic creatures and a range of excellent functional pottery and inventive Judaica by some of the country's best ceramists.

Darian Armenian Ceramics. 12 Shlomzion Hamalka St. ☎ **02/623-4802.**

This shop is the creation of Arman Darian, a recent immigrant from the former Soviet Armenia where he studied traditional calligraphy and design. Here you'll find wonderful soup tureens, cups and plates, tiles, and lamp bases, all hand-painted in the Armenian tradition, but with graceful designs that are uniquely Arman's. There are sometimes experiments and bargain seconds on the shelves, but you'll find beautiful first-quality pieces as well. Arman will also design to your specifications.

8 Ceramists Altogether. 11 Yoel Salomon Mall. ☎ **02/624-7250.**

For contemporary handmade ceramics, this pottery cooperative in West Jerusalem will give you a good idea of the current Israeli ceramics scene. Look for beautiful ceramic Hanukkah menorahs and Passover seder plates as well as functional and decorative pottery made by the cooperative's artists.

Guild of Ceramists. 27 Salomon St. ☎ **02/624-4065.**

Eleven ceramists are represented in this cooperative shop at the Hillel St. end of the Yoel Salomon Mall. Among other things, many of these artisans will custom design tiles.

House of Quality. 12 Hebron Rd. Bus: 4, 5, 6, 7, 8, 18, 21, or 48, and walk to Hebron Rd.

Across the street from and midway between the Mount Zion Hotel and the Cinémathèque, this conglomeration of craft workshops offers all sorts of delights. I especially admire the witty, unique ceramic Judaica of Gaya Smith, and the silver creations of Oded Davidson (see individual listings below), whose studios are here, but all of the craftspeople at this center are of very high caliber. Craftspeople are in their workshops at varying times. Just around the corner, in Saint Andrew's Guest House, you can visit **Sunbula,** which sells traditional Palestinian crafts and embroidery.

Sarachin Ethiopian Center for Art and Crafts. 20 King Solomon St. ☎ **02/625-2678.**

This nonprofit store sells embroidery, baskets, clay figurines, and Judaica made by recent immigrants from Ethiopia. You'll find a selection of yarmulkas, clay Hanukkah menorahs, embroidered dolls, and clothing made from the beautiful hand-woven embroidered cloth of Ethiopia. Prices range from NIS 22 to over 450 ($5 to over $100) for some of the figurines done by famous artisans. Menorahs start at NIS 126 ($28). Call ahead, as volunteers don't always make it in for their shifts.

Traditional Ceramics

The outer walls of the Dome of the Rock are covered with turquoise and cobalt-blue ceramic tiles in the Persian tradition. Two Armenian pottery workshops, Jerusalem Pottery and Palestinian Pottery, listed below, were brought to Jerusalem at the start of the British Mandate in order to maintain the Dome of the Rock's lavish facade. They are internationally acknowledged masters of traditional Anatolian hand-painted ceramics. These two workshops now produce items for sale to the general public. After a quick survey of the showrooms here, you'll appreciate the difference between their hand-painted folk ceramics, tiles, and bowls, and the mass-produced work available in the bazaars; the rich colors are unmatched anywhere else.

✪ **Jerusalem Pottery.** 15 Via Dolorosa. No phone.

Near the sixth station of the cross in the Old City, this shop, run by the renowned Karakashian family, is notable for individual plates and tiles decorated with lovely traditional bird, animal, and floral designs, as well as for its interpretations of ancient Jewish and Christian motifs, many taken from ancient manuscripts or mosaic floors. Standards of craftsmanship are the highest, with the most careful hand painting (tile designs are incised) and the richest colors. I've seen this shop's magnificent and varied tiles used to face a colonial fireplace in Massachusetts and also to ornament a poolside garden wall in South Florida. The designs were equally at home in each environment. Jerusalem Pottery is open Monday to Saturday from 9:30am until 5pm; a bit later in midsummer.

✪ **Palestinian Pottery.** 14 Nablus Rd. ☎ **02/628-2826.**

This workshop's chief artist, Marie Balian, is most famous for her multitile ceramic panels, which are richly hand-painted visions of Persian gardens, desert oases, and Middle Eastern motifs. In 1992, the Smithsonian Museum in Washington, D.C., mounted "Views of Paradise," a special exhibit of 22 of Mrs. Balian's creations; her panels also adorn the Sukkot Patio at the home of the president of Israel. Palestinian Pottery produces a steady stream of traditional plates, bowls, name and address tiles, and smaller panel compositions in floral designs that can be used as tabletops or as stunning architectural details. Ask to see the display of Palestinian Pottery's work spanning the past 70 years. The workshop is near the American consulate in East Jerusalem, and is open Monday to Saturday from 9am to 4pm; it is always a good idea to call ahead and check on hours.

GIFTS

Brinn and Berohm. 10 Shlomzion Hamalka St. ☎ **02/623-4617.**

Jerusalem has one old-fashioned European-style shop packed full of Romanian and Hungarian embroidery, and plenty of bric-a-brac. Run by the charming and venerable Emma Berohm, it's located just near the intersection of Jaffa Road and Shlomzion Hamalka Street, 2 blocks east of Zion Square. Like most good haunts for treasure hunters, it's hard to see the shop's sign, but you'll find an eclectic, intriguing, and unplanned show window.

Chaim Peretz. 2 Rabbi Ariye St. ☎ **02/625-0859.**

In this little workshop, Chaim Peretz makes attractive, very reasonably priced stained glass art and Judaica, sold for considerably higher prices at stores elsewhere in the city. The walk to his shop, in the quaint, labyrinthine Nahlaot neighborhood south of Agrippas Street near Mahane Yehuda, is always interesting (you'll inevitably have to ask the locals for directions). Once there, you'll find an array of charming menorahs, mezzuzot, Hands of Fatima, candle holders, and mirrors. If your stay in town is long enough, you can order your selection in the colors and designs you prefer. The shop is on a pedestrian lane off one of Nahlaot's neighborhood commons. If no one is around, ask along the street. A phone call ahead of time can be useful.

Charlotte. 4 Koresh St. ☎ **02/625-1632.**

Founded in 1938, this store, on the street just behind the Central Post Office on Jaffa Road, is the oldest gift shop in West Jerusalem. The secret of its longevity is a carefully chosen mix of modern Israeli jewelry and crafts, handmade Bedouin objects, old pieces of copper ware, and unusual antiquities, all at very reasonable prices. Jerusalemites have never ceased to be delighted with Charlotte's selections, and if you stop by, you'll see the difference between this place and many of the less personal tourist shops on the Ben-Yehuda Mall.

Lifeline for the Old. 14 Shivtei Israel St. ☎ **02/628-7829.**

This shop sells toys, needlework, clothing, jewelry, Judaica, and crafts handmade by Jerusalem's senior citizens, and is a **mitzvah** (blessing) for both craftspeople and customers. Sales and donations keep this remarkable institution afloat. The workshops, which help provide a meaningful creative outlet for Jerusalem's elderly, can be visited Sunday to Thursday from 8:30am to 11:30pm. The gift shop is open Sunday to Thursday from 9am to 4pm and Friday from 9am to 11am.

Shlomo Mishaly Metal Work. 8 Yoel Salomon St. ☎ **02/625-7856.**

Decades before the Yoel Salomon Mall became a center for trendy restaurants and craft galleries, Shlomo Mishaly had his neighborhood shop here, where he turned out handmade metal items and Judaica in designs of his own imagination. There are one-of-a-kind handwrought boxes, inexpensive Hands of Fatima, mezuzzot, lamps, and menorahs that use oil, candles, or electricity. I especially admire Mr. Mishaly's noise-makers for Purim in the shapes of fish.

GLASS
✪ **Nekker Glass Company.** 6 Bet Israel St. ☎ **02/582-9683.**

It was this store, near the Mirrer Yeshiva on the northern fringe of Mea Shearim, that revived the ancient glassblowing traditions that began in this part of the world more than 2,000 years ago. The Nekker family arrived in Jerusalem from Baghdad in the early 1950s and quickly set up a small glass factory employing both Arab and Jewish glassblowers. Slowly the factory began to experiment with designs and techniques from ancient times, and has even developed ways to reproduce soft, ancient patinas in a variety of colors. At Nekker's tiny workshop, you are invited to watch the glassblowers at work. Yehuda Nekker, the patriarch and chief designer, virtually dreams in glass. The stock is on sale for a fraction of what it costs in retail shops. A special line of museum-style reproductions is higher in price. The Nekker staff will pack your purchases securely for travel.

JEWELRY
✪ **Hedya Jewelers and Sarah Einstein's Collection.** 7 Maalot Nachalat Shiva (in the network of lanes between Yoel Salomon and Rivlin sts.). ☎ **02/622-1151.**

For unusual antique jewelry, visit this near legendary shop where you'll find a dazzling collection of jewelry made from the exquisite component pieces of antique objects like Yemenite wedding necklaces or tribal Persian headdresses. They have been taken apart and combined with rare beads into smaller compositions that modern women can wear with flair and elegance. Among the extraordinary creations made by Sarah Einstein, her staff, and Hedya, you'll find a choice of one-of-a-kind necklaces and earrings that range from delicate to dramatic and encompass every tradition in the Middle East. Hedya, an Israeli jeweler, designs accessories such as earrings to coordinate with each of Sarah's unique pieces. Special orders are welcome here; Hedya's own custom-made Hands of Fatima and Judaica are exquisite.

Ophir. 38 Jaffa Rd. ☎ **02/624-9078.**

Many Jerusalemites and visitors have become fans of this shop's delicate jewelry designs that echo Victorian, Edwardian, art deco, and Middle Eastern styles, and are made by the owner, Avraham, himself. Prices are extremely reasonable, and Avraham's stock is augmented by many unusual antique and semiantique items. There's a small glass display case beside the doorway. Enter the building, and you'll find Ophir's tiny studio at the back of the ground floor. A second, tiny branch of Ophir, packed with wonderful things, is on the Ben Yehuda Mall, between Moshiko's Shwarma and Burger King. Open Sunday, Monday, Wednesday, and Thursday from 9am to 1pm and 4 to 7pm; Tuesday and Friday from 9am to 1pm only.

JUDAICA

Archie Granot, Papercuts. 1 Agron St. ☎ **02/625-2210.**

Traditional Jewish paper cuts began to develop as a folk art in Europe and North Africa. In many homes it was the custom to hang a delicately cut piece of paper (called a *mizrach,* from the Hebrew word for "east") on the eastern wall of a room, to indicate the direction of Jerusalem. There are a number of excellent practitioners of this craft in Israel, but Archie Granot has raised this folk tradition to new levels. Working with multiple layers and colors, he creates works of amazing beauty and intricacy, ranging from *mizrachs* in traditional and contemporary styles to wedding contracts and mezuzzot. Prices can range from a few hundred dollars to several thousand dollars. Granot's works are in the collections of the Israel Museum, the Victoria and Albert Museum, the Jewish Museum of New York, and the Philadelphia Museum of Judaica. To find his workshop/gallery, proceed down Yoel Salomon Street from Jaffa Road; turn left just after the last building on Yoel Salomon; look for his sign at the top of an old outdoor staircase on the left.

Avi Biran, Silversmith. Jerusalem House of Quality, 12 Hebron Rd. ☎ **02/672-6242.**

Award-winning Avi Biran specializes in his own brand of contemporary Judaica—the designs have elegance, but also have a sense of humor and insight that that makes you think about the rituals and customs these objects are meant to accompany. Prices range from several hundred dollars for a mezuzzah or dreidle, to thousands for a major Hanukkah menorah.

Danny Azoulay. 5 Yoel Salomon St. ☎ **02/623-3918.**

A highly skilled craftsperson who came to Israel from Morocco as a small child, Danny Azoulay specializes in porcelain and fine ceramic Judaica, and his tiny shop is filled with hand-painted Hanukkah menorahs, charity boxes laced with brass or silver designs, mezuzzot, spice boxes, and dreidels. One of my favorite designs is a tiny porcelain Hanukkah lamp (too small for the strictly observant) that sells for about NIS 540 ($120). Mr. Azoulay's creations delicately blend Florentine, Islamic, central European, and contemporary motifs into a style that is unique. At times you may be able to purchase seconds at a discount, either at this shop, or at Mr. Azoulay's studio, not far from Mahane Yehuda. A number of Danny Azoulay's pieces can be seen at the

Wolfson Museum in Hekhal Shlomo. The shop also sells hand-calligraphed illuminated manuscripts and **ketubbot** (marriage contracts) by some of Israel's finest scribal artists like Amalya Nini and Aden Halter.

Gaia Smith, House of Quality. 12 Hebron Rd. No phone.

Gaia Smith takes the long tradition of using architectural motifs in the back plates of Hanukkah menorahs and goes delightfully wild. Her extraordinary hand-built menorahs and items of Judaica are designed around cottages in the Galilee with vistas of the hills, apartments on Central Park West with views of the Manhattan skyline, a child's toy-strewn bedroom on a wintry Hanukkah night—all filled with wit, charm, and a touch of mystery. You might even bring photographs of the interior and exterior of your house and commission a menorah, charity box, or mezuzzot based on it. Ms. Smith's reputation among collectors, as well as her prices, are on the rise.

✪ **Oded Davidson, House of Quality.** 12 Hebron Rd. ☎ **02/679-1082.**

One of the country's most interesting Judaica silversmiths, Oded Davidson combines skill and vision to create unique designs delicately engraved with personal whimsy and charm. Davidson's silver dreidels, menorahs, spice boxes, and other creations (ranging in price from several hundred dollars to over $1,000) have been bought by many collectors and museums, including the Wolfson Museum at Hekhal Shlomo. You may arrange to see Oded's remarkable portfolio by visiting his workshop; Oded's in-person explanations of his work are always fascinating. Open Sunday to Thursday from 9am to 4pm (to noon on Tuesdays).

Shlomo Ohana. 20 Ein Yaakov St., Mea Shearim. ☎ **02/582-9996.**

Some of the best loved and most beautiful objects of Judaica have been created over the centuries by neighborhood metalsmiths working with humble materials such as tin, copper, and brass. In Shlomo Ohana's workshop, this tradition absolutely soars. You'll find amulets, *hamsas* (Hands of Fatima), and Shabbat candle holders, moderately priced. Shlomo Ohana, who was born in Morocco, also makes the simple glass-enclosed Hanukkah lamps traditionally mounted beside doorways in Jerusalem's 19th-century neighborhoods; his davvening Hassidim are a popular tourist item, and more expensive at the few shops that carry his creations. The experience of visiting this workshop, deep in Mea Shearim's Ein Yaacov market, is always fascinating; in deference to Mea Shearim's ultraorthodox community, women should dress modestly, and men should avoid shorts. If the shop is closed, ask one of the neighbors when it will reopen.

Shulamit Noy Dunievsky. 18 Shivtei Israel St. ☎ **02/628-1987.**

In her busy ceramic workshop, Shulamit Noy designs hand-built contemporary Hanukkah menorahs glazed in pastel colors, with motifs of oasis gardens, birds, starry desert nights, flowers, and pastoral creatures that ornament the back plates. A few designs are done by mold and run under NIS 450 ($100), but Shulamit's beautiful one-of-a-kind menorahs are the real collectors' items. Interesting and very reasonably priced contemporary kiddush cups and other items of Judaica are on display in an always changing array of inventive designs.

PALESTINIAN EMBROIDERY

You'll notice antique Palestinian embroidered robes hanging from the doors of many shops in the Old City bazaar. Red, rose, and scarlet on hand-woven black cloth are the preferred colors, stemming from a tradition that goes back almost 3,000 years, to the centuries when the prophets warned against women who sewed with scarlet threads of vanity. Many of the current embroidery designs can be traced back to patterns introduced by the crusaders almost 1,000 years ago. You can find interesting scraps of embroidery suitable for framing for anywhere from NIS 23 to 125 ($5 to $30). Complete caftans, especially those with long, pointed medieval sleeves, if not worn, can be hung or mounted as dramatic decorative focal points. A beautifully photographed book, *Traditional Palestinian Embroidery and Jewelry,* by Abed Abu Omar, is sold for approximately NIS 90 ($20) at his Bedouin antiques and embroidery shop on the Christian Quarter Road near the Greek Patriarchate Road, or at the shop of Mr. Abu Omar's nephew (also named Abed Abu Omar) just next to the fountain in the Muristan Bazaar. The shop of **Maher Natsheh,** 10 Christian Quarter Rd., also carries a good range of antique and old textiles.

In addition to the many shops in the Old City markets selling caftans and antique or semiantique embroidery, three church-supported nonprofit shops (two in the Old City and one in West Jerusalem) offer a dazzling array of freshly made, top-quality embroideries all done by specially trained women who are working to support their families. Quality is assured, and prices at these shops are extremely fair.

Benevolent Arts Society of the Holyland. Sixth Station of the Cross, Via Dolorosa, Old City. ☎ **02/628-4367.**

This shop is managed by the legendary Ms. Frayda Hanna, who by teaching the skills necessary to create the best-quality traditional Palestinian crafts, has helped three generations of women to support their families. Freshly embroidered tablecloths, napkins, and traditional items are to be found here, as well as embroidered vestments and chasubles, and a selection of inexpensive gift items.

✪ **Melia.** Arab Orthodox Society Art and Training Center. Frere's St., inside the New Gate, Old City. ☎ **02/628-1377.**

The newest of the nonprofit embroidery shops, Melia offers many beautiful traditional pieces, as well as some imaginative decorative items. In addition to the classic divan pillowcases, I especially liked a dramatically embroidered mirror frame as well as designer-embroidered women's jackets and embroidered T-shirts. There is also a selection of Western-style tablecloths and embroideries. Here, as in the other shops, the pieces with naturally dyed thread are the richest and most beautiful.

✪ **Sunbula.** Saint Andrews Hospice, King David and Remez sts., West Jerusalem. ☎ **02/672-1707.**

This nonprofit shop sells a magnificent collection of densely embroidered divan pillowcases, wall hangings, and shawls, all alive with traditional motifs and colors. Many fabulous pieces are less than NIS 450 ($100). There are also heavy woven Bedouin tent rugs, embroidered linen tablecloths and napkins, and a good selection of inexpensive handmade crafts and gift items. Custom-tailored jackets and other fashion items can be ordered. The shop is run with an excellent eye for beautiful things. It is open Monday to Saturday from 9am to 6pm as well as Sunday from 11am to 1pm. The shop is in the Saint Andrew's complex, on a hill between the train station and the Cinémathèque, and is close to Gaia Smith, House of Quality (see above).

THE OLD CITY MARKETS

A major attraction for visitors, the Old City markets have many shops offering such local products as olive wood chess and nativity sets, rosaries, carved camels, boxes, and (a great buy at three for $1) Christmas tree ornaments. You'll also find heavy, hand-blown glassware from Hebron, inlaid wooden boxes from Egypt and Syria, mother-of-pearl objects from Jordan, new and inexpensive Yemenite and Bedouin-style jewelry, and locally made leather goods.

The Art of Bargaining

Under normal conditions, Middle Eastern shopping is supposed to take a good deal of time, with lots of theatrics and diplomacy. But these days many merchants are willing to get down to the nitty-gritty with fewer rituals. However, if you find something you like, you must bargain for it. The main rule is, be courteous and keep your cool. Appear politely unsure the object is something you really want. It often helps if you're with a friend who pretends you're late for a bus or an appointment—you might even pretend to walk away. If a merchant doesn't come down on his price, don't panic and pay full price. The chance is that you'll find the same thing or something similar close by, and if not, if you leave gracefully, you can always come back and try again. Much depends on how badly the merchant needs to convert some of his stock to cash on the day of your visit. If nothing else, after a few hours of browsing and bargaining, perhaps you'll have a new appreciation for the intricacies of the Middle East peace process.

Many shops sell suede and shearling mittens, slippers, and jackets of varying quality (the lace-up shearling baby slippers are a practical gift idea). The leather shop of **Mr. Abd El-Karim Sharabati** (no sign) at 100 Christian Quarter Rd. (on the left, three shops in from the corner of David Street), is known for the largest selection of these items, and also for well-designed sandals and women's shoes commissioned from local factories. You'll also find fair starting and final prices (although you must always comparison shop and bargain).

A few shops in the Arab bazaar around the Christian Quarter Road often carry **tribal Bedouin flatweave rugs and weavings** made of wool, goat, or camel hair—one of the world's great remaining national crafts. In older, more expensive pieces, look for bold diamond patterns and rich, subdued reds, browns, yellows, and oranges made from natural dyes of henna, pomegranate, saffron bark, and leaves from desert plants. Newer pieces often tend to bright reds and other hard colors, but are still very attractive. The shop of **Mr. Maazen Kaysi** (no sign), with a plate-glass show window and a recessed entrance on the right side of the Christian Quarter Road (just past the first pedestrian turning on the right as you come from David Street), has the finest and largest selection of Bedouin weavings and rugs. He also often obtains interesting kilims bought from new Israelis immigrants from Central Asia as well as hand-embroidered Romanian peasant blouses bought from Romanian pilgrims. Prices start high, but bargain.

The shops dealing in ancient antiquities are fascinating, but judge any object you may want to purchase in terms of its decorative value rather than its alleged age or rarity. **Barakat,** an ancient antiquities shop on David Street opposite the archway leading to the Church of the Redeemer, is the Old City's best-known dealer, with branches in many places, including Rodeo Drive in Los Angeles.

Interesting old-looking metal trays and other metal objects abound—they're decorative, but seldom real antiques. Some shops on the Street of the Chain (a continuation past the Cardo of David Street), are wonderful small caves selling copper and brass trays and pots, as well as old door knockers and reproductions of centuries-old menorahs.

The **Ashab Ceramic Workshop** on Via Dolorosa near the first station of the cross (☎ 02/627-2967) does custom-designed orders for tiles and specializes in many traditional Islamic and Armenian motifs, and is always a pleasure to visit.

In the Jewish Quarter of the Old City, one of my favorite shops for old objects and Judaica is **Mansour Saidian** (no sign), opposite the Mizrachi Bank on the corner of Tiferet Israel Street. There's always a selection of 19th-century European and Iranian kiddush cups and old menorahs stashed away among the cases of newer objects and jewelry. Bargain!

Colors of Jerusalem, 43 Jewish Quarter Rd. (☎ 02/628-3493), is a retail and consignment shop selling arts and crafts made by recent and relatively recent immigrants and ranging in price from a few dollars to several hundred dollars. You'll find items here like handmade puppets, Ethiopian basketry and ceramics, and hand-painted wooden Russian eggs. The owner of the shop, an immigrant from Los Angeles, is himself a craftsman, with a collection of his own Judaica designs. There is also a selection of Zionist and Israeli poster art.

The Old City Oil Press Art Gallery, 33 Jewish Quarter Rd., is interesting for its large, unusual collection of jewelry and other objects that incorporate old pieces of Roman glass. There's also contemporary Judaica, paintings, sculpture and prints.

The markets are also filled with all kinds of shops selling Arabic desserts, spices, and snacks, all of which should be part of the Old City shopping experience.

PHOTOGRAPHS

Vision Gallery. 18 Rivlin St. ☎ **02/622-2253.**

Neil Folberg, noted for his landscapes and photographs of the Jewish world, is the owner of this quality gallery that handles the works of international contemporary photographers, and represents artists including Micha Bar Am, David Harris, Tom Baril, and Marc Riboud. Vintage photographs of the Middle East and of Jewish subjects are also featured. Prices begin at NIS 380 ($85) for Middle Eastern prints and continue to hundreds or thousands of dollars. Israel's other gallery of note specializing in photography is the Silver Print Gallery in Ein Hod (see chapter 7, section 5).

9 Jerusalem After Dark

Israel has long been known for the high quality of its musicians, and the recent wave of Russian immigrants has led to an even greater embarrassment of riches. Classical music lovers will discover new and remarkable artists performing everywhere, from concert halls and clubs to street corners and pedestrian malls. Be on the lookout for performances by the **Rishon-le-Zion Symphony Orchestra;** this group from a suburb of Tel Aviv is filled with many remarkable musicians recently arrived in the country. The **Israel Museum** (☎ 02/563-6321 for the box office) hosts a full program of music, dance, theater, and film performances. Its Ticho House branch holds a Friday morning series of recitals, readings, and other cultural events. The **Bible Lands Museum** has a Saturday evening series of classical, jazz, and folk music; wine and cheese are served before each performance. Also watch for **English Theater productions** listed in the Friday editions of the *Jerusalem Post* and *Ha'aretz* newspapers, with actors and audiences drawn mainly from Israel's English-speaking immigrant community. You'll sometimes find translations of topical Israeli plays and revues, which can be especially interesting to visitors. The jazz and blues scene is surprisingly excellent.

To find out what's going on, look in the Friday edition of the *Jerusalem Post, Ha'aretz,* and in the monthly **Calendar of Events,** which you can pick up free at Tourist Information Offices. Lectures, readings, films, concerts, and English-language and Hebrew performances will be listed. If you have a student card, bring it; at times you may be given a discount.

PERFORMANCE CENTERS

Al Hakawati Palestinian National Theater. Nuzha St., East Jerusalem. ☎ **02/ 628-0957.** Tickets about NIS 22 ($5). Bus: 27.

At this theater you'll find cabaret-style productions and plays that are usually strongly political. From time to time, a specific production may be censored or unexpectedly shut down by the authorities, but both Israeli and foreign visitors are welcome, and English synopses are usually available. For those interested in the Palestinian movement, a visit here can be interesting, regardless of what is being performed. Nuzha Street runs off Saladin Street just to the south of the American Colony Hotel.

Beit Shmuel/Center for Progressive Judaism. Shama'a St., off King David St. ☎ **02/ 620-3456.** Tickets NIS 68–90 ($15–$20). Bus: 6, 18, 21.

Performances here billboard the best in contemporary and popular Israeli singers and musicians. In summer, concerts are held in the outdoor courtyard; always bring something warm.

Binyane Ha-Uma. Opposite Central Bus Station. ☎ **02/655-8558.**

This convention center is host to performances by the renowned **Israel Philharmonic Orchestra,** which gives frequent concerts in Jerusalem.

Jerusalem Theater/Sherover Theater/Rebecca Crown Hall/Henry Crown Auditorium. 20 David Marcus St. ☎ **02/560-5755** for information. Bus: 15.

Located near the corner of Chopin (in the Rehavia District near the president's house), this modern complex opened its doors in 1975 and houses the Jerusalem Theater (Sherover Theater), Henry Crown Auditorium, and the smaller, more intimate Rebecca Crown Hall. Original Israeli plays and Hebrew translations of foreign classics and modern works are performed in the theater's main hall; visiting troupes also use the main hall for performances in foreign languages. The theater is the home of the **Jerusalem Symphony Orchestra** and the **Israel Chamber Ensemble,** and the Israel Philharmonic also performs here. From October through early June, the Henry Crown Auditorium hosts the **Etnacha Concert Series,** produced by Israel Radio's classics station. The Etnacha performances are free; call ☎ **02/561-7167** for schedule information.

The Khan Theater. 2 Remez St. ☎ **02/671-8281** (bar). Bus: 4, 7, 8, 14, 18, 21, or 48, anywhere along King George V Ave. going south, or eastbound on Jaffa Rd.

Located across from the railway station, this Ottoman Turkish caravansary was refurbished and opened in 1968 as a nightclub, catering mostly to visitors. In the last few years, it has upgraded its program to include concerts of chamber music or jazz, Hebrew repertory theater, and occasional performances in English. Besides the theater, the building includes the Pesto Italian restaurant on the upper terrace, and a bar for drinks, dancing, and many cultural events. There are still tourist programs of Israeli folksingers, traditional dances, and audience sing-alongs.

Mount Zion Cultural Center. Outside Zion Gate, near King David's Tomb. ☎ **02/ 671-6841.** Bus: 1,38.

Many Saturday nights after Shabbat you'll find a busy evening of Klezmer and Hassidic-style dancing and music starting around 8pm in winter; 9pm in summer. This section of Mount Zion houses Yeshivas and Jewish outreach programs and many of the participants are students, but all are welcome. Call for information; prices vary by event.

Targ Music Center. Ein Kerem. ☎ **02/641-4250.** Bus 17.

Located in the rustic village of Ein Kerem, at the far western edge of Jerusalem, the Targ Music center hosts a variety of Friday late morning/early afternoon concerts, as well as other events. Allow at least 1¹/₂ hours by public transportation from downtown Jerusalem.

Ticho House. Harav Kook St. ☎ **02/624-5068.** Bus: any bus to Zion Square.

A block away from Zion Square, Ticho House maintains a busy schedule of events and performances, including poetry readings, events for children, and Friday morning concerts.

Train Puppet Theater. Liberty Bell Park. ☎ **02/561-8514.** Bus: 4,14,18.

Jerusalem has become a center for puppetry, and delightful, inventive performances are held here throughout the year. In October, Jerusalem hosts an International Puppet Theater Festival.

YMCA. 26 King David St. ☎ **02/569-2692.** Bus: 6, 18, 21.

Concerts and performances of Israeli music and folk dancing are held here throughout the year, usually on Monday, Thursday, and Saturday evenings. As there are no reserved seats, come early to nail down a spot. Always call to verify schedules and performances.

MORE ENTERTAINMENT
Son et Lumière. Jaffa Gate. NIS 28 ($6.20).

During the warmer months, a sound-and-light show combined with slides about the history of Jerusalem is featured in the Citadel of David at Jaffa Gate. Performances are in English at 8:45pm, from April to October, but check on times and tickets in advance. Be prepared for the chill created by the stone fortress and the night breezes. A free twice-weekly outdoor concert series consisting of local music groups was begun at the Citadel during the summer of 1995; if it continues, it is a pleasant opportunity to enjoy performances ranging from ethnic to classical. Check with the Tourist Information Office for details.

Sultan's Pool. In a valley beneath the Old City walls between Jaffa Gate and Mount Zion.

This dramatic setting is great for major outdoor classical, rock, and jazz concerts in warm weather; a typical month might include concerts by Sinead O'Connor or Bob Dylan, and a performance of *Carmen*. Check with the Tourist Information Office for schedules.

CLUBS & BARS
Israelis (especially Jerusalemites) are not really a drinking people—an evening at a cafe over a meal, or wine and snacks is more the local style. The cafes on **Ben-Yehuda Street** offer outside tables where patrons come to see and be seen. Saturday nights are teenage mob scenes. You can also try the more intimate **Rivlin Street,** and the neighboring **Salomon Street Mall,** which form the heart of the cafe/pub scene in West Jerusalem. **The Russian Compound** neighborhood, up Helene Ha-Malka Street from Jaffa Road, centered on Monbaz Street, is home to a number of constantly changing pubs and bars that offer live music and dancing on various evenings; Friday and Saturday nights they're throbbing.

Of the major hotels, the cavelike bar at the **American Colony** in East Jerusalem is by far the most atmospheric, visited by locals and international journalists as well as travelers in the know. You can also have drinks, good food and atmosphere at the hotel's **Courtyard Cafe/Bar,** set in the hotel's inner garden. In West Jerusalem, the **King David Hotel's bar** offers the most style. All the large hotels have bars, but with the exception of The Khan Theater (see above), the nightclub scene barely exists outside the hotel circuit.

✪ **Fink's.** 2 Ha-Histadrut St. ☎ **02/62-4523.**

Probably the best-stocked bar in the country, this tiny, unexotic-looking bar/restaurant may also be the Middle East's most politically savvy drinking spot (*Newsweek* has rated Fink's one of the 50 best bars in the world). Prices are reasonable, and the range of choices astonishing. It's open from Saturday to Thursday, 6pm to midnight. Closed Fridays.

Mike's Place. 7 Helene Ha-Malka St. (corner of Horkanos St.), Russian Compound. ☎ **051/233-761** (mobile phone).

The Russian Compound is filled with pubs and bars that come and go. Mike's Place is the most long-lived and friendly in the area, with a great nightly program of live blues, folk, and current musicians from the local rock scene. The crowd is an easy mix of Israelis, students, tourists, professionals, and occasionally Palestinians (from age 18 to 50); in good weather, tables move out to the broad sidewalk. Affordable pizzas, focaccia, and grilled meat and fish are served day and night. No decor, no one dresses up, no bouncers and no cover charge, but a two-drink minimum. Open daily 10am till at least 2am; music starts around 10pm.

Pargod. 94 Bezalel St. ☎ **02/623-1765.** Cover: usually NIS 23 ($5); no charge on Fri afternoon (Fri night cover must be paid in advance).

This club features local musicians most nights, from 9:30pm to 12:30am. Wednesday and Friday afternoons are reserved for jazz (1:30 to 5:30pm).

The Underground. 1 Yoel Solomon St.

The Underground is an enormously popular pub/disco with Israelis and foreigners under 21. Frenzied during the summer student tourist season. NIS 15 ($3.30) minimum to enter inner sanctuary.

Zanaibar. 13 Shammai St. ☎ **02/623-4510.**

A stylish bar for 20- and 30-something Israelis and travelers, this is a place where English is widely spoken. The bar offers more than 200 choices; great roast beef, and mixed cheese plates are house specialties. Monday is house party night, with dancing to electronic and live music. Open daily, 7pm to 3 or 4am.

FILMS

West Jerusalem shows the latest European and American films, almost always in the original language with Hebrew subtitles. In the eastern part of the city, the films come mostly from Arab countries and are in Arabic without subtitles. The Friday *Jerusalem Post* carries film listings and times, but seldom the address or phone number of the cinemas.

The most prominent theater is the world-famous **Cinémathèque** (☎ **02/672-4131**) or Israel Film Archive, which is the scene of nightly screenings of the classics, the best of the current international scene, rarely shown international films, and the experimental and the arcane. Films are usually in the original language, with Hebrew and (often) English subtitles. Members of the Cinémathèque get the first seats, but a half hour before screening time tickets go on sale to the public. Besides the movie houses, there are other places that screen films, such as the Jerusalem Theater, Binyane Ha-Uma, and the Israel Museum.

The Cinémathèque is located near the railway station. Go to the traffic intersection between the railway station and Hebron Road. Walk down the slope to the northeast, toward the Old City, and soon you'll come to the Cinémathèque, built into the hillside below the Hebron Road.

Other well-known cinemas and venues for film are **G. G. Gil,** Jerusalem Mall, Malha (**☎ 02/678-8448**), and the **Jerusalem Theater,** 20 Marcus St. (**☎ 02/560-5755**).

10 Side Trips Outside Jerusalem

KENNEDY MEMORIAL   Seven miles from downtown Jerusalem, in the same general direction of Hadassah Medical Center, Yad Kennedy is reached by following the winding mountain roads past the Aminadav Moshav. Opened in May 1966, the 60-foot-high memorial to Pres. John F. Kennedy is designed in the shape of a cut tree trunk, symbolizing a life cut short. The mountaintop memorial is encircled by 51 columns, each bearing the emblem of a state of the Union, plus the District of Columbia. The city bus no. 20 stops quite a distance away. Be prepared to take a cab and have the driver wait.

To the west is the village of Batir, site of a stronghold that witnessed the last Jewish revolt against the Romans, in A.D. 135, by Bar Kokhba. The view from the parking lot is breathtaking—a never-ending succession of mountains and valleys. The monument and adjoining picnic grounds are part of the John F. Kennedy Peace Forest.

ABU GHOSH   In the Israeli Arab town of Abu Ghosh (biblical Kiriath Jearim), 13 kilometers (8 mi.) west of Jerusalem, are two sites that can be reached by bus. Abu Gosh's great treasure is the 12th-century **Crusader Church of the Resurrection,** acquired by the French in the late 19th century and now under the guardianship of the Lazarist fathers. Like the Crusader Church of Saint Anne in Jerusalem's Old City, the Church of the Resurrection was designed with marvelous acoustics for Gregorian chant, but it's less heavily restored and more atmospheric. It is built over an ancient cistern and well that was in use from early Canaanite times. It's open Monday to Wednesday and Friday and Saturday from 8:30 to 11:30am and 2:30 to 5:30pm. The 20th-century **Church of Notre Dame of the Ark,** built on the site of a Byzantine church, marks the last place the Ark of the Covenant rested before it was brought to Jerusalem by King David. It is open daily from 8:30 to 11:30am and 2:30 to 5:30pm. Abu Ghosh is an Arab village that decided to side with the Israelis in the 1948 War of Independence. Now that many Israelis feel uneasy about wandering the Old City of Jerusalem, they flock to Abu Ghosh, especially on Saturdays, to enjoy hummus and other Arabic-style foods. (A number of hummus places call themselves "Abu Shukri"; they're okay, but have no connection to the **real** Abu Shukri in Jerusalem's Old City).

NEOT KEDUMIM BIBLICAL LANDSCAPE RESERVE   The reserve is in the Lod District between Jerusalem and Tel Aviv on Route 443(**☎ 08/977-0770**). Neot Kedumim is a kind of living museum of the farming, harvesting, and shepherding techniques of ancient times laid out across 625 acres of land carefully planted with flora of the biblical period. An explanatory text brings the landscape vividly to life and relates it to accounts in the Old and New Testaments and the Talmud. Guides are expert at explaining references to nature in Judeo-Christian scriptures; you'll find an olive press, a *sukka* (harvesters' shelter), and see how ancient ink was made from a

Wineries in the Hill Country

West of Jerusalem are a number of interesting small wineries. The **Latrun Monastery** (☎ 08/922-0065) is a gardened enclave founded by Trappist monks in 1890 just where the Judean hills begin to rise from the coastal plain 20 kilometers (12 mi.) west of Jerusalem. A shop at the entrance gate sells Domain de Latroun wines, liqueurs, and spirits as well as honey and olive oil produced at the monastery. Visitors are welcome to explore the gardens, vineyards, and orchards. It's open Monday to Saturday from 9am to 1pm and 2 to 5pm. From Highway 1, the Tel Aviv-Jerusalem Highway, get off at the Latrun interchange. Follow Highway 3 briefly in the direction of Ashkelon and you will come to the Laturn Monastery, opposite the large Armoured Forces Monument. No entrance fee.

The **Soreq Winery** (☎ 08/934-0542) is a new boutique winery located 40 minutes south of Tel Aviv at Kibbutz Tal Shahar. Opened in 1994, the Soreq winery produces Cabernet Sauvignons, Chardonnays, and Merlots. Call ahead to arrange a private tour of the winery. You can buy wine and cheese at the winery shop, and there is a picnic area on the premises. Open Sunday to Thursday from 10am to 5pm. From Highway 1, the Tel Aviv–Jerusalem Highway, exit at the Latrun interchange. Take Highway 3 south toward Ashkelon for approximately 9 kilometers. The winery is located 2 kilometers after the Nachshon interchange. No entrance fee.

The **Tzora Winery** (☎ 02/990-8261) is a boutique winery with a rising reputation for Cabernet Sauvignon, Sauvignon Blanc, and Chardonnay wines. It is located on Kibbutz Tzora in the mountains between Beit Shemesh and Jerusalem, and will arrange private tours if you call ahead. There is a wine and cheese store and picnic area on the premises. Open Sunday to Thursday from 9am to 5pm; Friday from 9am to 2pm; Saturday from 10am to 5pm. From Highway 1, the Tel Aviv–Jerusalem Highway, exit at the Beit Shemesh (Sha'ar Hagai) interchange and take Route 38 south toward Beit Shemesh. From Route 38 (about 8km from Highway 1) take Route 3835 to Kibbutz Tzora. No entrance fee.

The **Cremesan Winery** is run by members of the Italian Salisian monastic order. The beautiful winery can be visited daily at Beit Jalla, near Bethlehem on the West Bank, but the interesting, Italian-style wines produced at Beit Jalla can also be purchased at the **Bet Jimal Monastery** (☎ 02/991-7671), inside Israel, near the town of Beit Shemesh (see below). Open Monday to Saturday 8:30am to 5pm. There are picnic tables overlooking a fine view behind the monastery, where you may visit until dusk. Bet Jimal Monastery is located 2 kilometers south of Beit Shemesh, left turn off Route 38.

powder composed of resin, ground pomegranates, and oak gallnuts. With an advance reservation, you may be able to join a group of 15 or more for a vegetarian buffet of reconstructed ancient recipes (American food critic Mimi Sheraton found the food delicious). Admission is NIS 32 ($7), last admission 2 hours before closing. Open Sunday to Thursday from 8:30am to sunset; Friday and holiday eves from 8:30am to 1pm. Telephone for driving or bus instructions. Guided tours in English are given Friday at 9:30am; reserve ahead to arrange other times. There are also self-guided tours; trails are wheelchair accessible, and electric carts and wheelchairs are available on advance reservation.

SOREQ STALACTITE CAVES   Located 20 kilometers (12 mi.) west of Jerusalem along the road out of Ein Kerem (☎ 02/991-4833), this place is a favorite excursion for tour groups. Set in the limestone region, the caves are full of incredible formations. The scenery along the road from Ein Kerem to the moshav of Nes Harim, a mile from the caves, is by itself worth the pleasant excursion. Admission is NIS 18 ($4), and includes a lecture with slides and a tour. Hours are Sunday to Thursday from 8:30am to 3:30pm, Friday from 8:30am to noon. Direct service is by tour bus only. Egged will take you on a tour to the caves and nearby sights for about NIS 90 ($20).

Driving Tour: The Mountains West of Jerusalem

When Highway 1 from Tel Aviv to Jerusalem ascends into the Judean Mountains at Sha'ar Ha Gai (the Gate of the Valley) you can catch a few glimpses of the true magnificence of the Judean landscape. Sadly, this is all of the Judean Mountains that most visitors to Israel ever see. Intensive construction of communities along this corridor to Jerusalem, the widening and straightening of the highway, and a forest fire in 1995 that destroyed 70 years of reforestation have all diminished the wonders of this once dramatic route. But "the secret places of the hills" (to quote *The Song of Songs*) still exist untouched in the countryside just to the south of Highway 1, filled with forested mountains, ancient terraced hillsides, and dramatic ravines and vistas. Most visitors who rent cars in Israel take off for the mountains of the Galilee and Golan, or the Negev Desert. This drive, starting just minutes from Jerusalem will pass vistas as dramatic as any in Galilee, and introduce you to some of the simple pleasures of the hills.

   From Sderot Herzl in West Jerusalem, take the right turn to Ein Kerem, and follow the road downhill to:

1. Ein Kerem, the birthplace of John the Baptist and now a semirustic village that has been incorporated into the city of Jerusalem. Although this is not part of the hidden countryside route that lies ahead, you might want to explore the churches of the town, and walk down some of the local streets, where old Arabic cottages and villas are being renovated and gentrified into one of Jerusalem's most sought after communities. Follow the main road through Ein Kerem, and around to the left out of town. At the beginning of Route 386, which is the main road we shall follow, take a right turn at the sign to Mevasseret and follow this side road (which becomes Route 395) for a brief detour to:

2. Sataf, a small nature reserve, busy on the weekends when the cheese cave is open, but wonderfully tranquil the rest of the week. The Judean countryside is filled with springs that run through soft strata of limestone; these springs provide the basis for many of the communities in the region. Although Sataf is now a reserve, for thousands of years, the spring here supported the villages that arose with each wave of civilization. You can visit the spring in a cave created over the eons, and crawl through a short man-made tunnel to a water collection pool. It is not hard to imagine that the ancient Jewish concept of the *mikvah,* or ritual and spiritual purification in a pool fed by flowing water, originated with such life-giving springs in the Judean hills. Swimming in the pool is supposed to be prohibited, but on both quiet and busy days, I've seen people try out the water. From the pool, you can follow pathways downhill to where Jerusalemites are allowed to rent plots of land and plant organic gardens watered according to traditional irrigation techniques. At press time there is no admission fee to Sataf.

Driving Tour—The Mountains West of Jerusalem

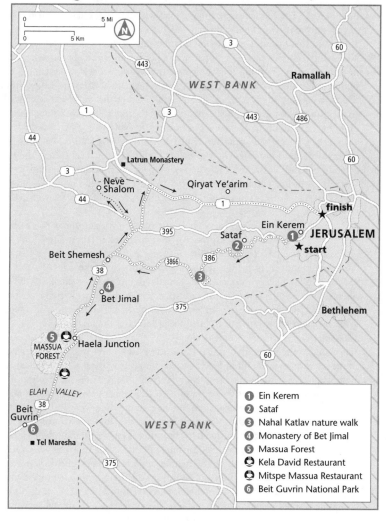

From the parking area near the spring, it's a short drive or a 45-minute walk (look for signs with the symbol of a picnic table) to visit the cave of **Shai Selzer,** goatherd and cheese maker par excellence. Here you can buy a variety of excellent goats' milk cheeses produced by three families that have permission to live on this mountain. There are Italian-style Parmesans, Swiss-style cheeses, blue cheeses reminiscent of the South of France, and local varieties like *avitia* (made to be eaten with watermelon!) or mild soft cheeses wrapped in grape leaves—great with fresh bread and fruit as you travel. Open in summer on Friday from 4 to 7pm and Saturday from 11am to 7pm; in winter, Saturday only 11am to 4pm.

After exploring Sataf, return to the Mevasseret turn-off, and turn right onto Route 386. You will pass the Monastery of St. John the Baptist of the Wilderness uphill on the left and continue along a road with dazzling vistas. Don't hesitate to pull off the road and enjoy the quiet and the views. Watch for an orange sign and a very small parking area on the right indicating the:

3. **Nahal Katlav nature walk.** This pathway takes you into a richly forested valley; in late winter/early spring the whole area is alive with rockrose, cyclamen, red buttercups, broom, wild licorice, and garlic. There are also Katlav Tulips, from which, according to local belief, all tulips throughout the world are descended. In the distance to the lower right, hidden amid the forest, look for a lone, domed building, the "tomb of the sheik." According to Muslim legend, hundreds of years ago a mysterious wanderer visited a nearby village. When he hung his clothes on a dead pomegranate tree before bathing in the local spring, the tree came to life and blossomed. His tomb was a pilgrimage destination until 1948, when the Muslim population was forced to leave the area. The Katlav nature walk can take 1 to 2 hours depending on your pace and how far you decide to go.

After the Katlav walk area, at a "T" in the road, turn right onto 3866 to Beit Shemesh. The road continues through a Jewish National Forest named for the late vice president Hubert Humphrey, a strong supporter of the State of Israel. There are a number of picnic areas and vista points along the way. At a fork in the road, follow the sign to the left, eventually leading into the small city of Beit Shemesh. You will pass through an industrial part, and eventually come to a traffic light at a "T" intersection. Turn left onto Route 38 to Beit Guvrin. After about 4 kilometers, turn left, where an orange sign indicates the road to the:

4. **Monastery of Bet Jimal,** founded, along with an agricultural school, by the Salesian order in the late 19th century. It's surrounded by orchards that have an air of medieval otherworldliness. For years, the monks have pleaded with the city of Beit Shemesh not to develop areas adjacent to or in direct view of this beautiful enclave; in most directions they have succeeded. For many visitors, the highlight of a stop at Beit Jimal is a chance to purchase homemade wine and take in the exceptional view from the monastery roof. At the adjacent Convent of the Assumption of the Virgin (to the left), beautiful ceramics (among the best folk art in the country) are for sale, hand-painted by the sisters (most of whom have taken a vow of silence). Walk to the right, around to the back of the monastery, and you will find pieces of a mosaic floor from the 5th- and 6th-century Byzantine Church of the Tomb of St. Stephen. Discovered in 1915, they are displayed alongside a small chapel. Further behind the complex are picnic tables with a view down to the coastal plain—a wonderful place from which to watch the twilight. This site is believed to have been Kfar Gamla, the village of the great talmudic leader, Rabbi Gamliel.

According to Christian tradition, Rabbi Gamliel, who headed the Sanhedrin in Yavneh after the destruction of Jerusalem in A.D. 70, was the teacher of Saul, who later became St. Paul. The Salesian school, closed for many years when it was cut off from its potential students on the West Bank, is again functioning. You may visit the monastery and its extensive countryside Mondays to Saturdays from 8:30am to dusk. The wine and ceramics shops and monastery buildings are open until 5pm.

From Bet Jimal, you can turn left back onto Route 38 south, and visit:

5. **The Massua Forest,** with its excellent restaurant and beautiful vistas overlooking the coastal plain; it's a right turn off Route 38.

☕ **TAKE A BREAK** **Mitspe Massua Restaurant,** Ranger's Station, Massua Forest, Beit Shemesh-Beit Guvrin Highway (☎ **02/991-2464** or 050/306-084), a country-style restaurant with fabulous views, is one of the few kosher restaurants with kashruth certificates for both meat and dairy meals and an excellent and affordable cuisine. The Mitspe Massua Restaurant is not open from late Friday afternoon until the end of Shabbat. Further south on the Beit Shemesh–Beit Guvrin Highway, as it passes through the Elah Valley, where the young David fought the Philistine Goliath with a slingshot, you'll find another good country dining choice, **Kela David,** a vineyard, winery, and restaurant/cafe at Givat Yishiahu (☎ **02/999-4848**). Traveling south on Highway 38, look for a pink house in the fields to the left; access is via a dirt road on the left just past what looks like a junkyard. Kela David is not kosher, and is open Monday to Saturday from 10am to 10pm. (In chapter 3, "Getting to Know Jerusalem," see "In the Countryside West of Jerusalem," under "Where to Dine," for a full description of both restaurants.

A good add-on to this drive would be to continue further down Route 38 to the fascinating:

6. Beit Guvrin National Park, which includes the Beit Guvrin caves, the ruins of Beit Guvrin, and the ruins of Maresha, a Judean town during the time of the First Temple. After the Babylonian destruction, Maresha was settled by Edomites, then Phoenicians. Eventually it evolved into a Hellenistic town that was conquered by the Hasmonean Jewish dynasty in the 1st century B.C. and forcibly converted to Judaism. Beit Guvrin was a strongly Jewish city from the Second Temple period through the time of its destruction during the Bar Kochba Revolt of A.D. 132–35. Ruins of a 3rd-century synagogue have been found here, as well as artifacts from a 12th-century crusader fortress destroyed by Saladin in 1191. Most of these finds are displayed in the collection of the Rockefeller Museum in Jerusalem (see "East Jerusalem Attractions," earlier in this chapter). The Arab village of Beit Jibrin stood here until the 1948 war; in 1949, the modern kibbutz of Beit Guvrin was built on the site. The ruins and vistas from the top of Tel Maresha (2km from Kibbutz Beit Guvrin) are extremely beautiful. Some of the easiest caves to explore are the caves right at Tel Maresha. The 800 caves at Beit Guvrin are thought to be partly the product of natural erosion, and largely the result of centuries of quarry activity by a number of different civilizations. Many are bell shaped, with light streaming in from quarrying holes on the ceilings. The caves have been used as animal pens, water cisterns, and even as shelters for religious hermits; most recently they were a locale for Sylvester Stallone's movie *Rambo III*. In summer, the National Parks Authority has minibuses and guides to convey visitors to the best sites in this 1,250-acre site. It's open Saturday to Thursday from 8am to 4pm and on Fridays from 8am to 3pm. Admission is NIS 20 ($4.40), with a NIS 5 ($1.10) discount for students.

From Beit Guvrin, take Route 38 back through Beit Shemesh and on to Highway 1, from which you can return to Jerusalem or drive northwest to Tel Aviv.

5

The Palestinian Authority/West Bank

The West Bank is must-see territory. Jesus was born in Bethlehem; Abraham entered the land of Canaan in Samaria; the patriarchs are buried at Hebron; and Mount Gerizim at Shechem (modern Nablus), sacred to the Samaritan sect, is the place where the Twelve Tribes of Israel were convened by Joshua.

The character of this area is different from what you see in Israel. About 95% of the population is Palestinian; about 5% are Israelis who live in settlements created since 1967, when Israel occupied the West Bank in the Six-Day War. The countryside in the West Bank is less intensively developed than inside Israel, and the landscape is dotted with bucolic Arabic villages that bring biblical scriptures to mind. In many places you will see veiled Arab women walking by the roadside balancing great loads on their heads. Donkeys, urged on by old men or little boys, groan under their burden of olive-wood twigs. On the other hand, in many places the countryside is sliced by modern highways and bypass roads to new Israeli settlements.

The older neighborhoods of the West Bank's major cities (Hebron, Bethlehem, and Nablus) contain small but fascinating Casbahs and old markets, but their sprawling newer sections are rather jumbled, busy urban communities that developed without much planning. Downtown Ramallah (a 10- or 15-minute sherut ride from Jerusalem's Damascus Gate) is one of these newer centers, but it's abuzz with lively restaurants and cafes that are packed with locals, East Jerusalemites, and travelers. As the peace process has begun, it's even become trendy among younger Israelis to dine and dance in Ramallah!

Palestinians hope that the area of the West Bank, awarded to them by the 1947 United Nations vote to partition Palestine (which both Palestinians and the Arab world in general rejected at that time) will form the territorial nucleus of a Palestinian state. However, the many smaller, outlying Israeli settlements, with their access roads, security areas, and checkpoints, tend to limit Palestinian hopes for a homeland. Travelers should understand that until the peace process hammers out a solution to this situation, the West Bank remains politically charged.

Despite ongoing negotiations about the future of the area, both Israelis and Palestinians welcome tourism with great enthusiasm and do everything to facilitate the itineraries of visitors. For the year 2000, Palestinians, with massive international aid, have been sprucing up their cities, building hotels, and updating their long neglected tourism infrastructure. Jericho now sports a brand-new international casino, and a cable car up to the New Testament's Mount of Temptation. Jericho has a new desert resort hotel, and both Jericho and Bethlehem will soon be home to five-star Intercontinental hotels, the first world-class hostelries ever to be built in the West Bank. Guided tours are the best way to visit the West Bank. If you want to strike out on your own, shared vans and taxis leaving from near Jerusalem's Damascus Gate provide transportation to major West Bank towns. Remember that with the exception of Highway 1 to the Dead Sea, and Highway 90 running along Jordan Valley through the outskirts of Jericho and along the Dead Sea, Israeli rental cars are *not insured* in the West Bank. If you want to drive through the West Bank independently, you must rent a car from a Palestinian agency in East Jerusalem.

Palestine Authority Tourism Offices have been established in Bethlehem and at the Allenby Bridge at the Jordanian border and green-and-white signposts are set up, in English, to guide you to all the major sites.

Around Jericho, the "No Entry" signs are clearly posted. Past these signs, you may find yourself an unwelcome guest in a military zone beside the Jordanian border.

If you have questions or concerns while in the area, stop in any local police station. In my own experience, West Bankers have been extremely kind, but you must be courteous and follow a few commonsense rules. Male visitors should not approach or ask women or young girls for directions unless there is no one else around to give information. No visitors should take photographs without permission, or display alcoholic drinks. This is also not a place to try to practice your Hebrew; unless you are visiting a Jewish settlement or speaking to an Israeli army patrol, stick to English or what Arabic you might know, and make it clear that you are a tourist.

For current information on travel conditions in the West Bank, check with the American Embassy in Tel Aviv (☎ **03/519-7575**), or the American Consulate General in Jerusalem (☎ **02/623-4271**).

Publications: *This Week in Palestine,* a free pamphlet for visitors, comes out twice a month. It's filled with detailed listings for events, sites, activities and restaurants throughout the West Bank, and can be picked up at many East Jerusalem Hotels and often at the Tourism Information Office inside Jaffa Gate in Jerusalem's Old City. *This Week in Palestine*'s Web site is www.jmcc.org

TOURS OF THE AREA

Egged Tours, 244 Jaffa Rd. (☎ **02/530-4422**), offers a complete range of half- and full-day tours from Jerusalem to places in the immediate area as well as a half-day tour of Jericho, the Dead Sea, and Qumran. **United Tours,** 23 King David St. (☎ **02/625-2187**), offers similar tours. Tours begin at $24 per person half day; $55 per person full day. The price usually includes pick up and drop off at your hotel. Most hotels will be happy to book Egged or United tours for you. The **Christian Information Center** inside Jaffa Gate (☎ **02/627-2692**) can also direct you to tours, especially of Bethlehem. Most travel agencies in East Jerusalem can book tours to the West Bank and Bethlehem; the Arab companies even run tours on Saturday. **Alternative Tours** (☎ **052/864-205** or 02/628-3282; e-mail: raed@jrshotel.com) is a Palestinian company that offers a 3-hour tour of Bethlehem ($10); a 6-hour tour of Hebron ($15); trips to Jericho, Nablus, and Ramallah ($18 to $20) as well as more political tours, including a Palestinian-oriented walking tour of the Old City of Jerusalem; and tours to the Galilee, to a refugee camp, and to Gaza. Alternative Tours originate at the Jerusalem Hotel in East Jerusalem. **PACE (Palestinian Association for Cultural**

Exchange) offers a program of full- and half-day guided bus tours throughout the West Bank. All tours originate and end in Ramallah; prices range from $14 to $40. Amani Tours in Ramallah (☎ **02/298-7013**) and the PACE Center (☎ **02/ 298-6854**) arrange these excursions. **Heartland Christian Biblical Tours** (☎ **02/ 940-0422**) does a variety of 1-day tours of the West Bank for $40 to $60. The **Society for Protection of Nature in Israel (SPNI),** 13 Helene Hamalka St., Jerusalem (☎ **02/624-4605**), offers 1-day and overnight nature hikes and tours of the region.

Note: As administration of the West Bank is turned over to the Palestinian Authority, Israeli-based tour organizations and agencies may no longer be permitted to conduct tours to the area. New Palestinian agencies will open as the political situation develops.

1 From Jerusalem to Jericho & the Dead Sea

The trip from Jerusalem to Jericho and the Dead Sea is only a 45-minute ride. Take Highway 1 from the Damascus Gate to North Jerusalem, turning east to the Dead Sea. From the Dead Sea you can drive south along the shore to Qumran, Ein Gedi, and Masada. For Jericho, turn north. The main road takes you to the Oasis Casino, with its adjacent Intercontinental Hotel, and skirts Jericho itself to take you to the new Mount of Temptation Cable Car, Tel Jericho, the mosaic floors of Jericho's two ruined, Byzantine-era synagogues, and the extraordinary ruins of the 8th-century early Islamic Hisham's Palace. From there, you can continue to the Jordan Valley, and up to Bet Shean and the Sea of Galilee (approximately a 2-hour drive if you don't make stops).

Drivers should check with their car-rental agencies concerning permission to drive to the West Bank and Jericho and for explicit directions for the road to the Dead Sea via North Jerusalem near French Hill.

SIGHTS ALONG THE ROAD

INN OF THE GOOD SAMARITAN   To the right, within sight of the main road, is what is known as the Inn of the Good Samaritan, supposedly the site where Jesus' parable of the Good Samaritan took place. What is definitely known is that this site has been an important landmark since ancient times. A Roman road once passed here, as did others even before that, including an ancient caravan route. The present inn is of Turkish construction and is some 400 years old. At press time, the inn is not accessible to the public.

WADI KELT   Further on the main road, follow the sign pointing left to the **Saint George Monastery** (Greek Orthodox), where communities of monks have lived since the 6th century A.D. A place of mysterious beauty, it's perched in isolation on the side of a dramatic desert gorge near the spring of Wadi Kelt. According to tradition, it was here that the Old Testament prophet Elijah was fed by ravens. The waters of the Wadi Kelt spring once ran through the aqueducts built by King Herod (late 1st century B.C.); today the spring continues to irrigate part of Jericho. Park your car (lock all bags in the trunk) and walk over to the wadi, for a view of the monastery hanging on the side of the opposite cliff. You can follow a path and make the very steep ascent to the monastery (bring water, and do not try this in the heat of a summer day). The monastery has some frescoes and architectural fragments from Byzantine times, and can be visited Monday to Saturday from 8am to 4pm. Although the monks will point out the tomb of Saint George, most traditions hold that the patron saint of England is buried at the Church of Saint George in Lod, near Ben-Gurion Airport. Late afternoon and at twilight, with birds swooping above the monastery, is an evocative time to visit.

The mainly downhill, several-hour hike through Wadi Kelt to the outskirts of Jericho is dramatic and manageable for most people in winter; in the heat of summer, it should be approached with caution. Organized hikes will have vehicles waiting at the end of the itinerary. The Wadi is especially lovely in late winter, when it is filled with wildflowers. On the banks of Wadi Kelt near Jericho, are the remains of winter palaces of the Hasmonean and Herodian dynasties. In past years, the SPNI has offered 1-day downhill walks through Wadi Kelt toward Jericho. The future of SPNI's programs in the West Bank is not certain at this time. *Warning:* Only hike the Wadi Kelt–Jericho route in a supervised group with a vehicle waiting at the Jericho terminus. Lone hikers have been attacked in the isolated wadi, or swept away by flash floods.

NEBI MUSA   Near here, the main road curves down more steeply, and a right turn (follow the signs) will lead you to a cluster of ancient buildings. According to Muslim belief, this site, called Nebi Musa, is the "Tomb of Moses" (the Bible cites Mount Nebo, in Jordan, as Moses' burial place). This was also the destination of an annual Muslim pilgrimage, the festival of Nebi Musa, which has been suspended under the Israeli occupation. The are discussions about the future of this dramatic place: The complex may be developed as a Palestinian heritage center.

As you return to Highway 1 and continue driving, you'll descend into the Jordan Valley, from which you'll make a left off the main highway to go to Jericho. As you travel toward Jericho, you'll notice the crumbling, sand-brick huts of a large Palestinian refugee camp across from the new casino complex. Most of the refugees who lived here fled to Jordan during the 1967 war.

2 Jericho

35 kilometers (22 mi.) E of Jerusalem; 181 kilometers (121 mi.) S of Tiberias.

Jericho is one of the most famous biblical sites—where the walls "came tumbling down" when the Israelites, led by Joshua, made their reentry into the Promised Land after the Exodus from Egypt. This miracle is one of the most powerful stories in the Bible, but Jericho's claims to fame extend far beyond the Battle of Jericho. At 850 feet below sea level, it is by far the lowest city on the face of the earth. It is also the world's oldest known city, with its origins dating from the dawn of human existence. The Jordan Valley, a northern extension of the Great African Rift, has been a migration route for birds and land creatures for eons. Jericho is on the route early humans would have taken as they moved out of Africa to populate the rest of the world. Permanent human habitation began here well over 15,000 years ago, nourished by the mild, below-sea-level climate and the plentiful waters of the Ein es Sultan spring. More than 11,000 years ago, a permanent settlement developed—its inhabitants were among the first human beings to engage in settled agriculture. By 8,000 B.C., Jericho had become a walled community—perhaps the first recognizable city on the face of the earth! The inhabitants of Neolithic Jericho built a round tower structure uncovered by archaeologists at Tel Jericho; it survives to a height of 8 meters. More than 25 strata of civilizations can be seen at the tel of Jericho, among them the city of approximately 1200 B.C. that Joshua and the returning Israelites would have conquered. According to the Bible, the tribes approached from the Jordan River, sent in spies, who were sheltered by the harlot Rahab, and to the blasts of trumpets blown by priests, the city was attacked and captured. But according to archaeologists (in one of the few instances when the evidence gathered at excavations has not matched biblical accounts), there is no evidence of a great destruction or even of walls that came tumbling down from Joshua's time period! Most archaeologists who have worked at the site believe that during the general time period when the Israelites entered the Promised Land, Jericho was at a low point in its history, and was not surrounded by defensive walls. Still, new archaeological evidence is always being uncovered.

For the next thousand years, Jericho remained a small agricultural center surrounded by its famous oasis of date palms. During the Hasmonean and Herodian dynasties, Jewish kings built winter palaces in the Jericho oasis as retreats from Jerusalem's raw, chilly winters. Jericho's balsam plantations became the source of rare perfume and incense, prized throughout the Roman empire; its date groves provided income for the royal families. Because Jesus spent 40 days in the wilderness among the cliffs overlooking the Jericho region, Byzantine times brought dozens of monasteries and small churches to the city; caves in the cliffs above Jericho became the abodes of hundreds of monastic hermits. In A.D. 724, Caliph Hisham, an early Islamic ruler, continued the tradition of the Jewish royal families, and built a palatial winter hunting lodge at Jericho, but the area slowly fell into decline, accelerated by the crusader wars. Baedeker's 1876 guidebook to the Holy Land describes Jericho as "a collection of miserable huts inhabited by sixty families." Only in Turkish and British Mandate times, with the reconstruction of irrigation systems, did Jericho begin to revive. Prominent Arab families from Jerusalem built winter residences in the oasis, but the town remained a quiet backwater. In 1994, Israeli forces withdrew from Jericho, and this ancient city (politically the most placid in the West Bank) became the first area to come under control of the Palestinian Authority.

If you visit Jericho from Jerusalem in the fall, winter, and spring, you'll be amazed at how comparatively warm the weather is, and delighted by the roadside stands selling dates, bananas, and oranges. In summer, Jericho and the Jordan Valley are unbelievably hot (an old Jerusalem saying warns: "Jericho is heaven in winter, and hell in summer"). With the construction of new hotels, resorts, and a casino at the edge of the city, Jericho hopes to revive its long lost tradition of being a lushly gardened winter retreat.

ESSENTIALS

GETTING THERE   Under present conditions, group tours are recommended rather than individual travel. You must carry all your travel documents with you, although you may not be asked to show them.

By Car   It's a 35-minute drive on the main highway from Jerusalem.

VISITOR INFORMATION   There's a **Tourist Information Office** in Jericho's Old City (☎ **02/992-2935**), and a tourist desk in the town center at the Municipality Building open Saturday to Thursday from 8am to 2pm.

SEEING THE SIGHTS

The interesting archaeological sites are outside the modern town. Coming from Jerusalem from Highway 1, make a left turn onto the road to Jericho. You'll soon pass Jericho's new state-of-the-art **Oasis Casino** (☎ **02/231-1111**) open daily around the clock (it's the only casino in the world across the road from a refugee camp). If you want to try your luck, you must have a foreign (not a Palestinian or Jordanian) passport with you to enter the casino; a dress code bans sandals, jeans, hiking shoes, shorts, and T-shirts. Israelis, who have no legal gambling inside their own country, lose a million dollars a day here. Next door, a luxury Intercontinental Hotel will be opening during the year 2000.

Continuing north, the road becomes Ein es-Sultan Street (the main road to Beit Shean and the Galilee that skirts downtown Jericho). After passing a number of garden restaurants, you'll finally come to a fork in the road. Just along the right-hand road is **Tel es-Sultan,** also called **Tel Jericho,** which is a mound covering the many-times-ruined city of ancient Jericho. Across the street from Tel Jericho is the new Jericho Tourist Center, filled with souvenir shops, and upstairs, the entrance to the new **Jericho Cable Car** (☎ 02/232-1590), open daily from 8am to 7pm; to 8pm in summer. Fare is $5 or its equivalent in shekels. This 5-minute cable car ride takes you up to the Mount of Temptation (site of the temptation of Jesus) and offers a spectacular view of the entire region. From the panorama cafe at the Mountain terminus, you can make the further climb up to the **Greek Orthodox Monastery of the Temptation and the Qarantal,** built on the traditional site of Jesus' 40 days in the wilderness. Once accessible only by foot after an arduous climb, the monastery is now visited by hundreds of tourists, both religious and nonreligious, who after taking the cable car ride, feel obliged to knock at the monastery door. The present monastery, built into the side of the cliff in 1896, houses four monks in permanent residence, and a chapel built into one of the caves believed to have sheltered Jesus. If you come on a day without many tourists, this is a spiritual, atmospheric place, especially toward evening, when the vistas are filled with swooping birds. Officially, the monastery is open to visitors Monday to Saturday from 8am to 2pm and 3 to 7pm, but the monks, overwhelmed by the flood of tourists, sometimes shorten visiting hours.

ANCIENT JERICHO   The artificial hillock of **Tel es-Sultan,** or Tel Jericho, covers the remains of 25 strata of civilization. Many of the objects unearthed here, such as plaster-covered human skulls from the New Stone Age, are displayed at the Rockefeller and Israel Museums. The structures excavated in the tel may not seem to be especially impressive, but because of their extreme antiquity, they provide invaluable glimpses into the dawn of civilization. Among the most interesting structures is Jericho's Neolithic defensive wall, about 10,000 years old. It is a landmark in psychological as well as architectural history; for the first time a structure defined those who belonged to the community and those who did not. The famous round tower, from the same early time period, is also visible. Located within the city instead of along its walls, this structure does not seem to have been part of city's defense system. Some scholars speculate the tower may have been a kind of silo, although at this primordial stage of agricultural history, there would have been few crop surpluses. Others theorize the tower may have been a cult structure—perhaps like the legendary Tower of Babel, an attempt to rise to the level of the heavens and the gods. The archaeological park at Tel Jericho is open from 8am to 6pm in summer, till 4pm in winter. Admission is NIS 14 ($3.10).

Across the road from Old Jericho is the cool, shady oasis of **Ein es-Sultan,** the Sultan's Spring, also called Elisha's Fountain. According to the story, when Elisha cast salts into Jericho's water source, the bitter water turned to sweet.

Signs back on the main road indicate the turnoffs for two ruined, Byzantine era synagogues. The Na'aran Synagogue is first (a left turn) then the "Shalom al Yisrael" synagogue (a right); Caliph Hisham's Palace is about 4 kilometers (2¹/₂ mi.) along the right fork, past Old Jericho.

THE SYNAGOGUES   A sign for the **Na'aran Synagogue** indicates a left turn just off the main highway near the Mount of Temptation. This 5th- to 6th-century synagogue was one of the first excavated in the Holy Land; it was uncovered by accident during World War I when the Ottoman Turks shelled a British army unit camped here. The synagogue's mosaic floor depicts the cycle of the Zodiac, a tableau of the Jerusalem Temple and its sacred objects, and the story of Daniel in the Lion's Den, all carefully labeled with mosaic inscriptions in Hebrew. At some point after the floor was laid, the iconoclastic movement became powerful, and representations of living beings in the mosaic were carefully gouged out (presumably by Jewish zealots, as they avoided defacement of the Hebrew inscriptions). Although mutilated, the mosaic was the tantalizing forerunner of the many beautiful, intact mosaic synagogue floors that would be discovered in Israel and Palestine throughout the 20th century. The synagogue was most likely destroyed by Byzantines in the 7th century. The site is open daily from 8:30am to 3pm. Check with tourist information in Jerusalem before visiting. Admission is free.

For the **Shalom Al Yisrael Synagogue,** look for a sign on the right after the Na'aran Synagogue turnoff. Probably dating from the 6th century, the ruins of this synagogue contain a beautiful, well-preserved mosaic floor with a menorah and the inscription, "Shalom al Yisrael" ("Peace unto Israel") at its center. Because this mosaic, dating from a slightly later time than the Na'aran synagogue, does not contain representations of living creatures, it was spared the wrath of iconoclasts. The mosaic floor was protected beneath the structure of a private Arab house; Jewish visitors at times use the site for prayer. Open daily from 8:30am to 3pm; admission is free. Check with tourist information in Jerusalem before visiting.

CALIPH HISHAM'S PALACE   To reach Caliph Hisham's Palace, take the right fork at the northern end of Ein es-Sultan Street, and pass between Tel Jericho and the Cable Car terminal. After 2^1/$_2$ kilometers (1^1/$_2$ mi.) you'll come to a sign pointing toward the palace. Turn right, as the sign indicates, and follow the little road 1^1/$_2$ kilometers (1 mi.) to the ruins.

The palace, begun in A.D. 724, and destroyed by an earthquake in A.D. 747, is a fantastic blend of Romanesque and Arabic architecture, decorated with fine mosaics as well as carved stone and plaster reliefs. At this early point in Islamic history, the use of decorative images of animals and human beings seems to have been permissible; niches and recesses in the interior walls once housed statuary. The fine abstract mosaic of the bath house, perhaps suggesting the ripples and reflections of water and sunlight, is one of the largest uncovered in the region; the proximity of the bathhouse to the throne room may indicate it was used, in Roman/Hellenistic fashion, as a relaxing venue for official meetings and government discussions. Perhaps the most magnificent find in the palace is the hauntingly mysterious mosaic of the Reception Hall, depicting two gazelles feeding under a pomegranate tree (or tree of life), while a lion attacks a third gazelle (climb the stairs behind the guest hall, which takes you inside for a better view). When you get back to Jerusalem, visit the Rockefeller Museum, where you can see the best of the carved stone and stucco work from this palace, plus a model of the entire site. Open daily 8am to 5pm (until 4pm in winter). Admission is NIS 14 ($3.10).

WHERE TO STAY

Jericho Resort Village. P.O. Box 162, Jericho, Palestinian Authority. ☎ **02/232-1255.** Fax 02/232-2189. E-mail: reservation@jericho-resort.com. 104 units, all with bathtubs. A/C MINI-BAR TV TEL. $120 double; bungalows for 4 people $150. Rates include breakfast. V.

Opened in 1998, this bright, new resort consists of 56 rooms in a central five-story building, and 46 bungalow units set around the gardened swimming pool. Summer and weekends, families with children can make this a lively but noisy place. At other times, this can be a quiet retreat; the extradry, warm weather can make you feel great on a winter day. There is a rooftop fitness/health center with fabulous views of the oasis, as well as an oxygen room, dry and wet saunas, tennis and volleyball courts, and freshwater, Dead Sea water, and children's pools. Middle Eastern and Continental buffets are served in the hotel's restaurants when occupancy is high. Although this is a four-star-type hotel, with pleasant but not luxurious decor, there are important amenities like safes in all rooms and 24-hour room service.

WHERE TO DINE

The **Mount of Temptation Restaurant** (☎ 02/232-2614), across the street from the lower terminal of the Cable Car is the largest restaurant in Jericho, with seating for over 1000 possible tourists passing through, as well as an emporium of gift shops. It is standard Middle Eastern fare, with a buffet for $10 to $12. A pleasant continental/Middle Eastern restaurant, with great vistas, will open on the upper terrace of the Cable Car's Mount of Temptation Terminal during 2000.

There are many garden restaurants and cafes on the main road between the center of town and Old Jericho. Lunch here can be very pleasant, well away from the tourist bus crowds next to the Old Jericho site. The busier restaurants are more likely to have fresh supplies and a varied menu. **Seven Trees Garden Restaurant** (☎ **02/232-2781**), on Ein es-Sultan St. is one of the better choices. Complete meals are in the $10 range, with light, à la carte Arabic dishes around $5 to $6. You can also buy supplies of dates, bananas, and oranges from roadside stands.

3 The Dead Sea & Qumran

45 kilometers (30 mi.) SE of Jerusalem.

Coming from Jerusalem, after turning onto the road running along the Dead Sea in the direction of Qumran, you'll see old Jordanian military encampments. As you drive by, you can't help but notice the calmness of the Dead Sea. The mountains along this stretch are sand-colored with black, fierce-looking peaks. When the mountains turn to a reddish hue, you're near the **Qumran Caves.** A side road leads up to the ruins of Qumran. In a nearby cave, the Dead Sea Scrolls were found in 1947 by a Bedouin shepherd boy. These are the oldest existing copies of the Torah and other parts of the Bible: they also include previously unknown ancient Jewish writings.

ESSENTIALS

GETTING THERE   By Bus   Buses will take you to Qumran from Egged's **Central Bus Station** in Jerusalem. Check with Egged and United Tours, as this area may come under Palestinian Authority jurisdiction.

By Car   From Jerusalem, bypass Jericho and turn right (south) onto Highway 90, the main road along the coast of the Dead Sea. Continue following the signs to Qumran and Ein Gedi.

EXPLORING ANCIENT QUMRAN

This ancient site, excavated in the 1950s by a team headed by Père Roland de Vaux, has become the subject of a major archaeological controversy in recent years. Père de Vaux initially postulated that Qumran had been inhabited since the 8th century B.C., and that sometime in the 2nd century B.C., it had become the monastic desert retreat of the Essenes, an ascetic, mystical Jewish sect of the Second Temple period that may have influenced early Christianity. Père de Vaux and most archaeologists theorized that the Dead Sea Scrolls, found in nearby caves, were portions of the Essene community's library, hidden from the approaching Roman armies at the time of the First Revolt Against Rome (A.D. 66–70). Qumran itself was destroyed by the Romans in A.D. 68. Structures uncovered at Qumran were interpreted in terms of the Essenes' collective religious community life as recorded by Flavius Josephus and the Roman historian Pliny the Elder, who wrote of an Essene settlement near the Dead Sea, "above Ein Gedi." In neither of these writings is the precise location of the Essene community named.

Although most scholars accept the theory that Qumran was an Essene monastic community, and that the Dead Sea Scrolls are part of the Essenes' library, recent reinterpretations of Qumran's location and structures have led a few scholars to postulate that Qumran may have been a traders' inn and military and customs outpost rather than the communal settlement of a religious sect. Qumran lies at a strategic point in an ancient trade route: Goods from Arabia and Africa were shipped up the Red Sea to Eilat, and then overland through the Arava Valley to the southern tip of the Dead Sea, where they were floated across to Qumran. At Qumran, the cargoes were unloaded and sent along the ancient Salt Road to Jerusalem. According to this theory, the otherworldly Essenes would not have settled at the crux of a major commercial route, but in a more remote location such as the caves in the mountains "above Ein Gedi." If this interpretation is correct, then the previously unknown writings found among the Dead Sea Scrolls may not be those of the Essenes at all, but a more mainstream sampling of extra biblical literature from the time of the Second Temple, brought to the caves for safekeeping from Jerusalem. This heated debate is an example of the very partisan passions with which Israelis follow archaeological discoveries.

The excavated settlement includes trenches, pottery sheds, step-down baths, cisterns, bakery sites, and cemetery plots. You will also see the long, flat, tablelike structures that Père de Vaux believed were the desks of the community's "scriptorium," where the Dead Sea Scrolls were written. Israelis love to debate whether these structures could or could not have been used as desks for ancient scribes of any normal human size. See what you think. You can view all the excavations from the top of the village tower. Near the ruins, signs direct you to the caves where some of the scrolls were found. It's a 10-minute walk, and you are permitted to visit the closest and most accessible cave. High above, you'll notice the mountains are dotted with many more caves. The **National Park at Qumran** (☎ 02/994-2235) is open daily from 8am to 4pm and includes an air-conditioned snack-bar facility. Admission is NIS 14 ($3).

BEACHES ON THE DEAD SEA

You can swim at **Einot Zuqim** (Ein Feshcha, ☎ 02/994-2355), a large park with trees, picnic tables, freshwater pools, and a beach on the Dead Sea just 3 kilometers (2 mi.) south of Qumran. Saturdays are packed, but fewer visitors come on the weekdays. The freshwater pools, fed by local springs, can get murky and sometimes have a fish or two swimming around. You can also take a dip in the lifeless Dead Sea, cover yourself with mineral rich Dead Sea mud, or walk on the beach. Admission of NIS 30 ($6.60) includes use of the shower facilities. Open March to November daily from 8am to 5pm; winter hours are variable.

A SIDE TRIP TO RACHEL'S TOMB

The direct route from Jerusalem to Bethlehem for independent travel is 8 kilometers (5 mi.) south on Hebron Road. Your tour bus, however, may take the more scenic route via Bethany.

Tour buses usually stop at the shrine marking the site of Rachel's Tomb, on the Jerusalem-to-Bethlehem road about 1½ miles from the northern entrance to Bethlehem. It was built in 1840 by Moses Montefiore, a noted British philanthropist, and leader of the British Jewish community. Rachel, wife of Jacob and mother of Joseph and Benjamin, is revered by Jews, Muslims, and Christians. The outer room is empty; the inner room, the cupola, contains the tomb. Rachel, the beloved second wife of Jacob, was barren for many years, and her despairing cry, "Give me children or else I die," (Genesis 30:1) touches the hearts of those who read the Bible to this day. After many years, Rachel bore Joseph, who became the favorite son of Jacob. She died at this place, giving birth to her second child, Benjamin. In Jewish folklore, the spirit of Rachel weeps for her motherless children and for the tragedies of the Children of Israel; dozens of women, many of whom have not been able to have children, come here daily to pray. Men need a head covering to enter the shrine. The site is heavily guarded by both Palestinian and Israeli soldiers. You can also get here from Jerusalem by taking Arab sherut vans or minibus parked across the street and a block west of Damascus Gate in the Old City. Hours are Sunday to Thursday from 8am to 5pm (until 6pm in summer), and on Friday until 1pm. From Rachael's Tomb, it is about a 25-minute walk up busy Manger Street, with its many shops and restaurants, until you get to the Old Town of Bethlehem, with Manager Square and the Church of the Nativity. If you're coming to Bethlehem on a minibus from near the Damascus Gate in Jerusalem, the start of Manger Street, near Rachael's Tomb, is the best place to ask the driver to let you off.

4 Bethlehem

8 kilometers (5 mi.) S of Jerusalem.

Pilgrims have come to the birthplace of Jesus to see the traditional cave and manger for more than 17 centuries. In the Bible, Bethlehem is mentioned several times, first in connection with Rachel, who died there after giving birth to Benjamin (Genesis 35:19). The Book of Ruth records that Bethlehem was the place where Ruth, the loyal Moabite widow of an Israelite, married Boaz in one of history's most famous love stories. King David, a descendant of Ruth and Boaz, was born in Bethlehem and tended his sheep in the hills of Judea. From Bethlehem he went out to fight Goliath; later he was summoned from Bethlehem by the Prophet Samuel to become king of Judah. To Israelis, Bethlehem is Bet Lechem, "house of bread"; to Arabs, Bet Lahm means "house of meat." Much of the Manger Square area and the Old City of Bethlehem have been cleaned and renovated with the aid of international contributions in preparation for the year 2000. A walk up Old Bethlehem's main street (running off Manger Square opposite the Church of the Nativity) is a good introduction to this area.

ESSENTIALS

GETTING THERE   By Sherut   At press time, public buses no longer run from Jerusalem to Bethlehem, as Bethlehem is now in Palestinian Authority territory. You can grab a seat in an Arabic sherut—shared vans and minibuses to Bethlehem are parked along the north side of Sultan Suleiman Street, midway between the Notre Dame Pilgrimage Center and the Damascus Gate. The fare is NIS 3.5 (75¢). These vans will let you off at the checkpoint on the Israeli–Palestinian Authority border, where you might be able to find a waiting taxi: A fair fare from there to Manger Square in the center of Bethlehem should cost no more then NIS 10 ($2.20). Negotiate the fare in advance.

Alternatively, you could take your minibus a bit farther down the road to Rachael's Tomb. After visiting the Tomb, it's a half hour walk to Manger Square. A direct private cab from Jerusalem to the Check Point could run around NIS 25 ($5.50). Some cabs waiting at the Damascus Gate may be able to do the direct route to Manger Square. Agree on all fares in advance. Under present conditions, guided tours are the best choices for visiting Bethlehem (see below).

VISITOR INFORMATION   Tourism Information, run by the Palestinian Authority, is in a little yellow booth on Manger Square. Another office, just off Manger Square, in under the Al Andalus Hotel (☎ **02/647-7050**). Here you can get a free map, and information on hotels and home accommodations and tours, both political and historical. Open Monday to Friday from 8am to 3pm; Saturday from 8am to 1pm.

The **Alternative Tourism Program** (☎ **02/277-2151;** fax 02/277-2211; e-mail: atg@mail.p-ol.com) has been set up by educators and professionals from the Bethlehem-Beit Sahour community to introduce foreign visitors to this ancient community, and acquaint them with current political and social conditions. Headquartered in Beit Sahour's Raprochment Center (which also hosts twice monthly dialogue meetings between Israelis and Palestinians), the organization sponsors tours of cities and towns throughout the West Bank, visits to educational, cultural, and religious institutions, and refugee camps as well as opportunities to do volunteer work in community projects, along with study tours and accredited courses for overseas students. Alternative Tourism also arranges B&B home stays in Bethlehem starting at $25 per person, and is an unusual opportunity to have personal contact with an informed, relatively moderate segment of the Bethlehem community.

CHRISTMAS PILGRIMAGES TO BETHLEHEM

There are actually three Christmases celebrated in Bethlehem: Catholics and Protestants hold their services on December 24 and 25, the Orthodox churches on January 6, and the Armenians on January 17 and 18. Visitors must have their passports with them when going to Bethlehem on Christmas Eve. On the evening of December 24, choirs from all over the world assemble and sing in front of Saint Catherine's Church near Manger Square.

Walking to Bethlehem from Jerusalem has been a tradition that pilgrims have followed for centuries. The traditional 2- to 2¹/₂-hour walk (best undertaken with an organized group) begins at the Jerusalem railway station at Abu Tor, continues on Derekh Hevron, the main road near the Talpiot section, past Jerusalem's industrial area to farming country. The road passes the Greek Monastery of Elias. Here the road takes a sharp turn, and is lined with olive trees. In the low hills beyond the trees to the right is the Arab village of Bet Jallah (biblical Gilo), birthplace of the prophet Nathan. The road enters the northern edge of Bethlehem.

Admission to the Church of the Nativity on Christmas Eve is restricted to those holding special tickets that can be obtained for free from the **Franciscan Pilgrim's Office,** Jaffa Gate (next to the Christian Information Office), P.O. Box 186, Jerusalem 9100 (☎ **02/628-2621**). There are special telephone booths for tourists to phone Christmas greetings home with the bells of Bethlehem pealing in the background. Restaurants and coffeehouses stay open all night during the season, and some banks operate until midnight. Rates in Bethlehem, Nazareth, and even some Jerusalem hotels go up during the holiday period, so be sure of your accommodations before you arrive. The weather can get very cold, and it might even snow. The tourist office will have a schedule of processions and activities.

EXPLORING BETHLEHEM

THE MAJOR SHRINES   Facing Manger Square, the ✪ **Church of the Nativity** is the principal shrine of Bethlehem and the oldest church in the country. The construction of the church (A.D. 326) dates from the time of Queen Helena, the mother of the Roman emperor Constantine the Great, who made a pilgrimage to the

Holy Land in the early part of the 4th century. She searched out the grotto of Christ's birth, and ordered a church to be built over the spot. The Emperor Justinian, 200 years later, found the original church heavily damaged (probably by an earthquake), and built a renovated, larger church on the old site. A restoration of the two previous churches was carried out by the crusaders, which explains why the church looks like a fortress.

You'll enter through a low doorway that was, according to legend, designed to prevent unbelievers from riding into the church on horseback. Another legend records that the low door was installed by the Muslims after the crusaders were driven from Bethlehem to remind Christian travelers that they were humble guests, allowed to visit the site by the sufferance of their Muslim hosts. It is also probably not a coincidence that the doorway makes one pause and bow.

The basilica of the church is divided into five naves by four rows of Corinthian pillars. Every pillar bears the ancient, faded picture of an apostle. Several dozen gilded lamp fixtures hang from the oak ceiling. The floor is stone and wood, with occasional trap-door openings that reveal the original Byzantine mosaic floor beneath. Up front, beyond a magnificent silver-and-gold chandelier, is the Altar of the Nativity, equally ornate with gold-and-silver decoration. The Greek Orthodox occupy the area to the right of the altar, the Armenian denomination the area to the left. Armenian, Greek, and Franciscan priests are responsible for the preservation of the church.

On either side of the altar, narrow stone staircases lead down to the manger, supposedly the scene of Jesus' birth. Simply lit by hanging lights, the grotto is in the wall of the cave, marked by a silver star.

If you find your way to the grand, shiny **Franciscan church** just north of the Church of the Nativity, you'll see a small stairway on the right at the back of the nave. Down the stairs here is a maze of rock-hewn rooms and chambers, part of which is supposedly a portion of the original stable where Jesus was born. Later used as catacombs for martyred innocents, the stable rooms look much more "authentic" than the marble portion under Greek Orthodox control. Also down beneath the church is a cavelike chamber where Saint Jerome translated the Bible from Hebrew into Latin.

Back upstairs, exit through the courtyards of cloisters and convents. Notice the difference in dress of the various priests who administer the church—the bearded Greeks in long black robes with their long hair tied into a bun; the Armenians in purple- and cream-colored long robes; and the Franciscans in brown.

The Milk Grotto is the place where Mary, in nursing the infant Jesus, is said to have dropped some milk that promptly turned the rocks of the cavern chalky white. Visits made here by nursing mothers are supposed to help their lactation, and packets of the powdered stone are sold as souvenirs. The grotto, run by the Franciscans, is open daily from 8 to 11:45am and from 2 to 5pm.

SEEING THE TOWN   If you want to explore more of Bethlehem, walk out of Manger Square to the right of the mosque that is at the opposite end of the square from the Church of the Nativity. This is Paul VI Street, Bethlehem's main drag, although it is more a pedestrian street than a throughway. The street goes uphill past cobblers' shops, a smithy, coffeehouses, hole-in-the-wall stores both ancient and modern, people buying supplies, and children playing.

Up the hill, you'll come to the striking Evangelical Lutheran Christmas Church, with a very handsome minaret-like steeple.

Off Manger Square, near the Bethlehem Hotel, you'll find the **Palestinian Heritage Center** (☎ 02/274-2642), a shop where the traditional crafts and household objects of the Bethlehem area are exhibited; inexpensive local crafts are sold here, with the money going to the actual craftspeople. The **Bethlehem Museum**

The Shepherds, the Professor & the Scrolls

On your left as you walk on the main market street uphill from Manger Square, not far up the road, look for a seemingly empty shop with the sign "Kando" above it—this was a shoe repair and antiquities shop where the first Dead Sea Scrolls to be discovered were brought by Bedouin shepherds in 1947. Kando himself had no idea of the meaning and value of what the Bedouin had brought him. Prof. E. L. Sukenick, of the Hebrew University in Jerusalem, noticed broken fragments of the scrolls and was shown some complete scrolls while browsing at Kando's. Acting on a feeling that the scrolls might just be far older than any others known to be in existence, Prof. Sukenick risked his life to return to Bethlehem and purchase as many of the Scrolls as he could afford on the very day in November 1947, when the United Nations in New York was voting to partition Palestine into a Jewish and an Arab State. Rioting had erupted throughout Palestine, and West Jerusalem was virtually under siege. According to his journal, when he stepped off the bus in Jerusalem clutching the Scrolls in a paper bag, Prof. Sukenick said the prayer one recites on escaping death. He was probably the last Jew to visit Bethlehem until after the Six-Day War in 1967. When Israel's War of Independence ended, the fragile Scrolls were unraveled, in some cases using surgical instruments. Only then was it learned that the only Scrolls of the Bible to survive from the time when the Temple stood in Jerusalem, had been restored, both to the Jewish people and to the world.

(☎ 02/274-2589), housed in a 19th-century edifice in the Old Town on Star Street, exhibits exquisite examples of Bethlehem embroidery, costumes, and other traditional crafts. It is open Monday to Saturday from 8am to 2pm (call to reconfirm); admission is NIS 3 (60¢).

THE SHEPHERDS' FIELDS   This is where it is traditionally believed that the shepherds were told of Jesus' birth by angels. Actually, there are two Shepherds' Fields—the ones maintained by the Roman Catholic Church and others maintained by the Greek Orthodox Church. Both are east of Bet Sahur, where the road forks. The right fork leads to the Greek Orthodox fields, the left to the Roman Catholic.

By heading back toward Jerusalem for a few blocks, and taking a sharp right at the appropriate sign, you can make your way to the Shepherds' Fields along either Shepherds' Street or Bet Sahur Road. You can walk from Manger Square to either set of fields, visit for half an hour, and walk back, and the entire expedition on foot will last about 2 hours. *Warning:* Take this walk *only* in a group.

WHERE TO STAY

Bethlehem has a good, if small, collection of hotels. Be aware that rates may sky-rocket during the year 2000–01 celebrations. The hotels listed are only a short walk from Manger Square along Paul VI Street. A new, five-star Intercontinental Hotel is due to open near Rachael's Tomb, at the northern end of the city, during the year 2000. The **Alternative Tourist Program** (☎ 02/277-2151) also arranges B&B home stays in Bethlehem, renting rooms with private families that start at $25 per person.

Al Andalus Guest House. Manger Square (P.O. Box 410), Bethlehem. ☎ **02/274-1348.** Fax 02/274-2280. 10 units (all with shower). $70 double. 25% increase at Christmas. Rates include breakfast. AE, DC, MC, V.

Set on the south side of the square in the arcade, this hotel with a pleasant family style management, is one of the best places to stay on Manger Square. The centrally heated rooms are clean and cheerful, with tile showers and colorful curtains and spreads, and look out either on Manger Square or to the hills of Judea. Guests of the hotel receive a 10% discount at the Al Andalus restaurant.

Bethlehem Star Hotel. Al-Baten St. (P.O. Box 282), Bethlehem. ☎ **02/274-3249.** Fax 02/274-1494. 72 units (all with shower or bathtub). $60 double. Add 30% for Christmas and Easter seasons. Rates include breakfast and service. DC, MC, V.

Conveniently located at the corner of Freres Street, the Bethlehem Star is quiet, friendly, and modern. The hotel has an elevator, and some triples that are perfect for families with children. A few rooms have city views.

To reach the hotel, walk out of Manger Square on Paul VI Street and keep looking for Al-Baten Street at side streets on the right; the hotel is about a block away uphill.

Grand Hotel Bethlehem. Paul VI and Freres sts. (P.O. Box 18), Bethlehem. ☎ **02/274-1440.** 50 units (all with bathtub). A/C. $65–$80 double. Rates include breakfast. MC, V.

Bethlehem's most comfortable, modern hotel contains a snappy lobby, restaurant, and cocktail lounge. The bright, colorful rooms have large windows, scarlet spreads, and wall-to-wall carpeting.

✪ **Orient Palace Hotel.** Manger Square, Bethlehem. ☎ **02/277-7766.** 27 units (all with bathroom). TEL. $100 double. Add 30% or more for Christmas and Easter. Rates include breakfast. MC, V.

Set in an atmospheric garden courtyard to one side of Manger Square, this hotel underwent major refurbishing in 1997 and provides good, fresh accommodations for the price. Built by the Greek Orthodox Committee, the hotel is right next to the church, and often surrounded by the sound of tolling bells. It has a large dining room; when there is enough business, dining facilities are open 24 hours, with a self-service buffet featuring 12 Middle Eastern salads. The hotel also sports a colorful sitting room with a view of the city from its bar. Some of the attractive, centrally heated rooms have balconies and views of the Judean Hills.

WHERE TO DINE

Al Andalus Restaurant. Manger Square. ☎ **02/274-3519.** Main courses NIS 30–45 ($6.60–$10); lunch special NIS 36 ($8). AE, DC, MC, V. Daily 8am–5pm (after 5pm with special reservations). ARABIC.

Al Andalus caters to tourist groups with a set meal consisting of soup or grapefruit (depending on the season), salad, a main course of meat or chicken with vegetable and potatoes, and dessert. There are traditional Arabic main courses, international choices, and also hamburgers, salads, omelettes, and other light fare. Local style meat-filled pastries are a house specialty. Service of 10% is added to the bill. Air-conditioned.

Saint George Restaurant. In the Municipality Building, Manger Square. ☎ **02/674-3780.** Main courses NIS 30–45 ($6.60–$10). MC, V. Daily 8am–11pm or midnight. ARABIC.

Another place for something substantial is the Saint George, next door to the Government Tourist Information Office. Out front are umbrella tables for al fresco dining; within, the cream-colored walls are adorned with murals of Bethlehem, and tables are covered with red cloths and graced with flowers; background music further enhances the ambience. Choices are mainly well-prepared grilled chicken and meat dishes. If you're daring, try the roast pigeon stuffed with rice, meat, and almonds; or a platter of six different kinds of vegetables. Main courses include salad and potato.

SIGHTS BETWEEN BETHLEHEM & HEBRON

Under present circumstances, check with tourist information in Jerusalem about tours and visits to this area of the West Bank. *Note:* Israeli rental cars may not be insured for travel to this part of the West Bank.

The twisting southward road between Bethlehem and Hebron (distance: 33km/20 mi., about a 30-min. drive) is wide and in good repair. Beautiful villas line the road on the outskirts of Bethlehem; the road then dips close to the picturesque village of Bet Jalla, to the right in the nearby hills. Farther along come rich fields, more villas, and new homes. Soon you pass a big archway (on the right) spanning a road leading to the nearby villages of Husan and Nahhalin. The archway honors Saint George, depicted on horseback in the arch's center. This is the road David took from Bethlehem to carry his brother's food to the battle area in the Valley of Elah, where he subsequently met up with Goliath.

THE HERODION   Herod the Great had ambitious plans for this dry mountaintop in the barren hills of Judea. He reshaped the entire mountaintop into a perfect cone, and then built a lavish palace fortress on top, complete with a synagogue (one of the few that can be dated to the time of the Second Temple), *mikve* (ritual bath), storerooms, and 200 marble steps leading down the mountainside. He even piped in water, for swimming pools and hot baths at enormous expense.

The Herodion, finished in the 1st century B.C., was only one of Herod's grand palace-fortresses (another was atop Masada). Herodion is cared for by the Society for Protection of Nature in Israel (SPINI), and at press time is still part of the Israel National Parks system, although it is located in the Palestinian Authority (☎ **037/762-251** [mobile phone]). Call ahead to verify hours and other regulations. Open daily from 8am to 5pm (until 4pm on Friday). Admission is NIS 18 ($4). Independent travelers touring Bethlehem can visit Herodian by taxi from the center of town. Round-trip fare, including waiting time, should be NIS 30 to 40 ($6.60 to $8.80).

SOLOMON'S POOLS   Soon you'll see signs, and a left turn takes you to Solomon's Pools. There's been some quibbling about the exact origin of the pools. Most hold that they're really the work of Herod, who brought the water here by aqueduct from springs near Hebron. Others argue that these pools were indeed built by Solomon as part of his grand scheme for supplying Jerusalem with water.

Whatever the case, it's clear that these pools were a source of water for the Herodion, and more important, for Jerusalem, from at least the time of Herod the Great (37–4 B.C.) to the time of modern Israel. The Romans kept the pools and aqueducts in good repair, the Ottoman Turks built a fort (now in ruins) to defend them, and the British kept the system in good working order until the end of the mandate.

Nature hikes can be arranged in the beautiful Judean countryside between Solomon's Pools and the lovely cliff-side village of Artas. Contact **Alternative Tourism** (☎ **02/277-2151**) (see above) for information about these walks to Artas. The walks terminate at a charming, restored village house, the Artas Heritage Museum, where organized groups are brought for tea, or meals with a talk about traditional village life and a performance by traditional musicians.

The country road eventually joins the main highway at the town of Halhoul. Turn left to get to Hebron, which is roughly 26 kilometers (15¹/₂ mi.) from the Herodion.

5 Hebron

37 kilometers (23 mi.) S of Jerusalem.

Of the biblical sites in the Holy Land, none is more affecting than the Tomb of the Patriarchs in the Cave of Machpelah, where Abraham and Sarah, Isaac and Rebecca, and Jacob and Leah are buried. (You can read all about it in Genesis, starting with chapter 23). This is significant history for adherents of all three great religions, a direct link between us and the Middle Bronze Age. Sadly, Hebron's modern history has been marred by the acts of extremists that continue to cast a pall over the city. In 1929, the small, ancient Hebron Jewish community that had lived peacefully among its Arab neighbors for centuries, was suddenly attacked; at least 63 were killed, many more were wounded and mutilated, and the surviving Jewish community fled. In 1994, an Israeli settler opened fire on Muslim Hebronites at prayer in the mosque at the Tomb of the Patriarchs. Again, the number of dead and wounded, including children, was appalling.

Today, Hebron is the most socially conservative and religious of the West Bank's major cities. Tensions are constant between Hebron's Arab citizens and Israeli settlers who have returned to live in houses in the center of town that had been inhabited by Jews before the massacre of the city's Jewish population in 1929. The nearby Israeli settlement at Kiryat Arba is among the most militant in the West Bank; both sites are occasionally a flash point for violence. Check with the Government Tourist Information Office on the current situation before you go.

Depending on conditions, here's how you should visit Hebron: If conditions are very tense, don't! If there's been a minor flare-up of tensions, go on an organized tour. The bus tours do not run if the situation is known to be dangerous. About the worst way to visit Hebron is by rented car. With Israeli license plates, it will be assumed that the driver is an Israeli, too; rental car insurance often does not cover glass breakage.

ESSENTIALS

GETTING THERE   Under present conditions, it is best to visit Hebron in a guided tour from Jerusalem. Consult with tourist information about tours that will best suit your interests. *Note:* Israeli rental cars may not be insured for travel to this area of the West Bank.

VISITOR INFORMATION   There is no information office in Hebron.

SEEING THE SIGHTS

Taking the main road through Hebron, you'll first pass lovely villas and a few shops and grocery stores. At one point, islands of trees, flowers, and greenery divide the highway lanes, after which the archaeological Museum of Hebron will be on your left (nearby are several places for cool drinks).

When you see a glass factory, a pottery factory, and a woodwork factory side by side in a huge three-story building on your left, you'll be in the shopping district (photo shops, tailors, tiny clothing stores, shoe stores, grocery stores). In this area you'll see a roadside pillar pointing to Abraham's Tomb; when the road forks, bear left toward the tombs. Shortly after there's another sign, a red one, pointing out the **Jewish Cemetery.** Dating back many centuries, this cemetery was almost entirely destroyed during the 1929 attack on Hebron's Jewish community, but people still come here to pray and stand in awe. Hereabouts the road narrows until it is just barely two lanes and leads by shops of shoemakers, carpenters, leather workers, and saddle makers (who outfit camels and donkeys). Coming into the vegetable area, the road widens and the Muslim

Cemetery is to the right. Here there's an open expanse and a sign guiding you left to Abraham's Tomb.

✪ **TOMB OF THE PATRIARCHS**   Enclosing the Cave of Machpelah, the tomb is what gives Hebron its designation as one of the four "Holy Cities"—the others being Jerusalem, Tiberias, and Safed. To religious Jews who now can worship at the sacred Tomb of the Patriarchs, the holy experience is second only to worshipping at the Western Wall in Jerusalem. Genesis tells how Abraham bought his family burial cave for 400 silver shekels. From this purchase comes the tradition that Hebron is thus one of three places in Israel that Jews can claim by virtue of having purchased the property; the same claim is made for the Jerusalem Temple and the Tomb of Joseph. As Abraham is traditionally regarded as the father of the Arabic as well as of the Jewish people, and as Islam regards Abraham as the first Muslim, the site is also sacred to Muslims.

The tombs of Abraham, Isaac, and Jacob (and their wives) are housed in a fortress built by Herod. The walls, resembling the massive walls Herod built around the Temple Mount enclosure in Jerusalem, range from 40 to 60 feet high. You may visit the tombs between 7:30 to 11:30am and 1:30 to 4 or 5pm. From 11:30am to 1:30pm devout Muslims worship inside, and no other visitors are allowed. No non-Muslim visitors are permitted on Friday, the Muslim Sabbath, or on Muslim holidays. *Note:* Visiting hours are determined by strict security considerations; it is best to reconfirm the hours before a visit.

Inside the walls, the Muslims built a mosque around the tombs. The square main basilica is richly decorated with inlaid wood and ornate mosaic work reminiscent of the Dome of the Rock. Inscriptions from the Koran run along the walls. In the main section you will see the tombs of Isaac and Rebecca, red-and-white stone "huts" with green roofs. Looking inside, you'll see the richly embroidered drapes covering the cenotaphs. (The real tombs are underground, beneath the cenotaphs.) In an adjoining courtyard are the gold-embroidered tapestries covering the cenotaphs of Abraham and Sarah, behind a silver grating. Just opposite is the tomb of Jacob and Leah, with a 700-year-old stained-glass window. A shrine to Joseph is right next door, but the authentic tomb of Joseph is generally thought to be near Nablus.

6 A Tour to Ramallah, Nablus (Shechem) & Samaria

We now explore the areas north of Jerusalem, biblical Samaria. This was the land of Canaan that Abraham first saw more than 4,000 years ago, the scene of great events involving Jacob, Joseph, Joshua, and the rulers of the northern kingdom of Israel.

Check with the Tourist Information Office in Jerusalem on current conditions in these towns. At press time there were no organized tours to this region.

FROM RAMALLAH TO NABLUS

Arabic for "the Heights of the Lord," **Ramallah** is a cool, high town—during the years when Jordan occupied the West Bank (1948–67), Ramallah was the most popular summer resort in Jordan ("the Switzerland of Jordan"). You will see elegant villas on hillsides green with pine groves. At 2,900 feet, Ramallah sits some 300 feet higher than Jerusalem. A Christian and Muslim city, Ramallah is prosperous; the downtown center is lively and filled with modern restaurants and shops, but it's unplanned and not very graceful. As social life and a new tradition of stepping out at night begins to develop in Palestine, Ramallah is becoming *the* center of things. Among the local favorites are **Rukab's Ice Cream,** on Main Street, open daily from 8am to midnight;

Angelo's Pizza, 3 blocks from Manara Circle, open daily 9am to midnight; **BBQ Za'rour,** popular for grilled meats and chicken in generous portions for well under $10 on the fifth floor of the Farah Building on Main Street, entered from the back of the building; open daily 9am to midnight. For fancier meals, try **Al Barduni** (☎ **02/295-1410**), with its dining terrace, on Jaffa Street, not far from the Manara Circle; open daily noon to midnight. **Rumours,** off Main Street, near the Post Office, is a very large place with a stage at its center and place for dancing. The menu runs from Arabic to Continental and even Asian dishes; there is a bar, Western and Arabic music, and dancing on Saturday nights. Open Sunday to Thursday noon to midnight and Saturday until 2am.

Should you stop for a while in Ramallah, make sure to see the town's large, beautiful park, which contains a well-equipped children's playground. You might also want to see King Hussein's former palace, a pleasant but unostentatious building.

Once past Ramallah, a road on your left will take you on a shortcut to **Jericho** (34km/20¹/₂ mi.), via the Arab village of Taiybah. You'll see a large compound on your right as you continue; it was once a Jordanian hospital.

Two miles farther is the Arab village of Betin, the biblical **Bethel.** It was to Bethel that Abraham and Lot returned from Egypt. Later, as described in Genesis, the Lord appeared to Abraham's grandson, Jacob, in a dream: "... and behold a ladder set up on the earth, and the top of it reached to heaven: and behold the angels of God ascending and descending it. And, behold, the Lord stood above it, and said, I am the Lord God of Abraham thy father, and the God of Isaac; the land whereon thou liest, to thee will I give it, and unto thy seed." The hill today is called Jacob's Ladder, but unless you have a guide to point it out, you'll never find it.

After passing through a countryside of olive groves, orchards, and pastures, the next village you'll see is **Bir Zeit,** which means "the Oil Well," and from the main road, you'll see the sign for Bir Zeit University, the West Bank's most famous institution of higher learning. A bit farther along on the left is the village of **Ein Sinya,** with its cluster of old and new buildings, some dating from Turkish times. Farther along, high in the hills, is the town of **Sinjil,** the Arab name for the settlement of the French monk Saint Giles, who lost his life here.

Now the road twists and turns through low hills covered by groves of olive trees. Soon you'll see a 5-foot stone pillar pointing to the ruins of ancient **Shiloh** on the left: Shiloh is where the Tabernacle and the Ark of the Covenant were housed in the centuries between the time of Joshua and King David. It is also the place where the men of Benjamin's tribe, short of women, carried away the daughters of Shiloh who were innocently dancing in their vineyards.

As you pass Shiloh, note the natural Canaanite agricultural terraces still being worked in the hills. The steep winding road here was constructed originally by the British. It snakes down toward the village of Lubban, and the rich fields in the **Valley of Dotan.** Pull over before you descend and take in the magnificent view of the valley and Lubban.

As you continue on, keep an eye out for the small villages that dot the surrounding hills. The Valley of Dotan was where Joseph was sold into slavery.

ANCIENT SHECHEM & NABLUS

Just before you reach Nablus, the largest town in the West Bank, you'll want to stop on its southern outskirts for **Jacob's Well, Joseph's Tomb,** and biblical **Shechem.** At Shechem, Abraham first entered the land of Canaan. The town had been founded, according to biblical sources, by Shechem, Hamor's father. By the period of the Patriarchs, early in the 2nd millennium B.C., it had become a major Canaanite city and cult center. In pre-Davidic times it was a far more important Canaanite city than Jerusalem. Jacob sojourned nearby, built an altar, and dug a well. After the Exodus from Egypt, Joshua also built an altar at Schechem and summoned the tribes together. Here Joshua united the tribes in a covenant ceremony that is considered the beginning of the history of the Israelite nation in their own land. Archaeological remains of ancient Shechem show that it was a large city; some of the most important finds from Shechem are displayed in the Rockefeller Museum in East Jerusalem. Archeologists have long puzzled over why Shechem, if it was such an important place, was situated in such a vulnerable position, in a pass between the two mountains, Ebal and Gerizim.

Mount Gerizim was the site of the Samaritans' ancient temple. The origins of the Samaritans are complex. After the death of King Solomon in 920 B.C., his kingdom was divided into two separate nations: Judah, with its capital at Jerusalem, and the larger, more powerful Kingdom of Israel in the north, composed of the descendants of the 10 northern Israelite tribes. The division probably reflected old cultural and religious differences between the northern Israelites and the southern tribe of Judah.

The Samaritans are believed to be descended from the few Israelites who remained behind when the Assyrians carried off most of the population of the northern Kingdom of Israel in the 8th century B.C. For all practical purposes, the 10 northern tribes of Israel disappeared from history at that time; the Assyrians resettled other subject peoples on the land that had been Israel. The Jews in the southern kingdom of Judah survived in their homeland for another 135 years, until they were carried off into the Babylonian Captivity in 586 B.C. When the Persian king Cyrus released the Jews from the Babylonian Captivity and they returned to Judah after a 60-year absence (around 530 B.C.), the Samaritans wanted to help them to rebuild. The Jews refused their help, declaring that the Samaritans were no longer Jews; that they had intermarried with foreign peoples who had settled into the land, and had adopted pagan customs. (Despite these ancient accusations, the Samaritan tradition observes Torah regulations with great rigor.)

The factions split and remained split down through the centuries, the Samaritans claiming that they and only they have continuously inhabited Israel and kept the traditions pure. They also are the keepers of a Pentateuch (the first five books of the Old Testament), which they say came to them from Aaron, brother of Moses. The Samaritan Bible does not include the Books of the Prophets or any of the later books of the Jewish Holy Scriptures. By the second century B.C., the split between the two people had widened. The Samaritans, in the tradition of the northern Israelite tribes, maintained their Temple on Mount Gerizim beside Shechem; the Jewish Temple, following the Davidic monarchy tradition, remained steadfast in Jerusalem. The Samaritan Temple was destroyed by the Jewish Hasmoneans, and again during revolts against the Romans and Byzantines. In ancient times, the Samaritan population numbered at least in the hundreds of thousands. Today, approximately half the present Samaritan population of the world (which numbers only in the hundreds) lives in Nablus; the rest are Israeli citizens and reside in Holon, a suburb of Tel Aviv. Despite the ancient rivalry, relations between Jews and Samaritans in modern times are very cordial and cooperative. Samaritan families, for centuries isolated and inbred, now have begun to marry into Jewish families.

MOUNT GERIZIM   Mount Gerizim is holy to the Samaritans, who believe it to be the true site ordained by God for the building of the temple, as well as the site of Abraham's Altar, where he prepared to sacrifice his son, Isaac. To this day, the entire 500-strong Samaritan community gathers at Mount Gerizim on Passover. They do not hold a seder, but they sacrifice lambs for the Passover feast on the site of Abraham's Altar, observing the holiday, they say, as their forebears did 25 centuries ago. The present-day local Samaritans will show you the altar, between the rocks at the summit of Gerizim, and will be glad to point out altars built by Adam and Noah. About 275 Samaritans live in the Nablus region these days, calling themselves children of the tribes of Manasseh, Aaron, and Efraim, but all of the Samaritans gather on Mount Gerizim for their festivals and holidays, and many have built homes for holiday use on the slopes of the mountain. The right of the Samaritans to keep their holy place on Mount Gerizim has been guaranteed by agreements between the Israelis and the Palestinian Authority.

JACOB'S WELL   You'll recognize the **Convent of Jacob's Well** by its two large metal doors. Ring the electric buzzer to notify the convent's sole monk that you'd like to enter the locked gate. As the doors open, you see a beautiful cluster of well-tended small gardens. To the right is a tiny station for prayer, housing a picture of Jesus and the Woman of the Well, another name for this convent. Directly ahead are two blue pillars, mounted with ancient Roman capital stones that support a new ceramic arch leading to the shrine and the huge unfinished church. In 1912, the Russian Orthodox Church began building this enormous basilica, but work stopped with the onset of World War I. Later, this and all other Russian Orthodox holy places were turned over to the Greek Orthodox Church, which still maintains them.

The outside walls were part of a Byzantine church that once stood on this site. Inside the basilica area, with its three separate nave sections, the larger and central section is sheltered with tentlike fabrics and contains a cross atop a broken Roman pillar. Here the Feast of the Samaritan Woman is held. Two painted cement buildings, looking much like guard stations, cover and secure two 18-step passages leading down to the chapel and well. Although the small, beautiful chapel looks older, it was built in 1910 on the site of the earlier chapel from the time of Queen Helena, mother of Constantine. Rich and intimate, the chapel is hung with shining incense burners and paved with painted tiles; its walls are covered with old paintings and icons, most depicting Jesus and the Woman at the Well. In the center is Jacob's Well, with wrought-iron fixtures and a metal pail—a bit incongruous amid so much elegance.

MODERN NABLUS

The name Nablus is the Arabic contraction of the Greco-Roman city that was once here, Neapolis. It was founded by Titus, who named it Flavia Neapolis in honor of his father, Flavius Vespasian. Now the largest West Bank town, with modern buildings climbing up the surrounding steep hillsides, Nablus in some ways has the feel of Haifa without the sea. Nablus is in fact a business center, home of the local soap-making industry and equally known for the sweet baklava pastries and heavenly *kanaffeh* made here—the best in all the Middle East. You'll find interesting olive twig basketry and other country crafts at the old market inside the Casbah. The Casbah, or Old City of Nablus, is architecturally very interesting and beautiful: If the political situation stabilizes, Nablus's Old City could develop into a wonderful visitor site.

SAMARIA

The road to Samaria curves downward, and you'll note the many caves in the area and the small houses built into the hillsides. Women sit in front of their houses near the road working with stitchery or wool, and you may also see a group of them working together to sift or grind grain beside the road. On the hill to the right is Samaria (in ancient times, Sebastia).

The entire region of Samaria was occupied by the tribes of Ephraim and Manasseh, the children of Joseph, in biblical times. Samaria was once the capital of the Kingdom of Israel, the northern of the two Jewish nations. Inside the village a **mosque** has been built within the ruins of an old crusader cathedral. Beneath it, reputedly, is the tomb of Elisha, the prophet, and also the head of John the Baptist, brought here by Herod Antipas at the request of Salome. The hills bear witness to the Roman city that once stood here: ruins of a hippodrome, columns, towers, a theater, palace walls.

At an earlier time, however (around 876 B.C.), Omri founded the capital of the Kingdom of Israel here. His son, Ahab, married Jezebel, daughter of a Phoenician king. She brought Baal and other idolatrous pagan gods to the people of Israel. The prophets fought her, particularly Elijah, who challenged the priests of Baal in the famous cliff-side battle on Mount Carmel, and gave Jezebel such bad press that her name is synonymous with that of an evil woman even today. Samaria remained the capital under Jeru and Jeroboam, but in 725 B.C. the Assyrians plundered Samaria, ending the Kingdom of Israel, and carried off 25,000 of its inhabitants.

The road from Nablus moves on past Dotan (traditionally the city where Joseph was sold into slavery by his brothers), to Jenin. Take a left at the square in the middle of this little town and follow the road north. From here you can head north to Afula and from there to Nazareth and Haifa, or east to the Jordan Valley and the Sea of Galilee.

6 Tel Aviv

Tel Aviv is everything Jerusalem is not. The city began with a gorgeous strip of beach along the Mediterranean and went on from there to become the bold and busy city that never sleeps. Known locally as the Big Orange, Tel Aviv has no holy sites and until its founding in 1909 it had no history. It does have oyster bars, nightclubs, samba sessions at the beach on summer evenings, and miles and miles of massive medium-rise apartment buildings. In summer, the heat and humidity can put New York to shame. Tel Aviv is the country's commercial center, and also the cultural capital; the nation's newspapers and most books are published here (excepting the *Jerusalem Post*); concerts are frequent, and the Hebrew-language theater thrives. Here you can find an art scene in the many galleries around the Gordon Street neighborhood, and there are top-flight clothing stores scattered throughout the city. A look at the back of some of the free tourist magazines distributed throughout town, and you'll figure out that the city also hosts a thriving sex industry. To an idealistic kibbutznik, an Arab Israeli from Nazareth, or an observant Jew from Jerusalem's Mea Shearim District, the mere mention of Tel Aviv can conjure up an image of Gomorrah in its worst depravity.

Tel Aviv today is riding the wave of the country's high-tech economic boom, and it shows everywhere. In the past few years, the city's hotels and stock exchange have begun to buzz with the energy of high-powered business deals from all over the world. Glass skyscrapers and new hotels dot the city's landscape; more are under construction. Optimism and signs of new prosperity abound. If the promise of the peace process is allowed to develop, many envision 21st-century Tel Aviv as the Singapore of a new Middle East.

As always, Tel Avivans love to play. In the 1980s, the city's beaches were beautifully renewed, and are now among the cleanest and most easily accessible urban beaches in the world. The Tel Aviv Museum of Art has just received the important Jaglom Collection of Impressionist and Post-Impressionist Art; the Diaspora Museum of Jewish History is one of the most inventive learning experiences in the world. The 1990s have seen the construction of an opera house, new performing arts centers, and the development of a rarefied luxury restaurant scene.

At the same time, Tel Avivans are thinking about the nature of their city's personality and have begun to preserve and gentrify neglected landmarks and neighborhoods that delineate the city's 90-year history.

Impressions

Matzoh is like Israel. . . . It may be dry and noisy, and sometimes it's hard to swallow . . . but it's ours.

—Kirschen, "Dry Bones" (Israeli cartoon)

Restored Old Jaffa is a must for evening dining and strolling, loved by visitors and Israelis alike.

Elsewhere in Tel Aviv, you'll notice exotic Arabesque/art deco structures from the 1918–30 period and wonderful 1930s and early 1940s International Style buildings that once defined the city's ultramodern image. In the 1930s, many refugee architects and designers from Germany sought shelter in Palestine. For them, the sands of Tel Aviv provided an opportunity to create a dazzling metropolis of the future based on the clean, functional lines of International Style. By the beginning of World War II, Tel Aviv had burgeoned into an urban garden of ultramodern white concrete architectural wonders—the curvilinear balconies and rounded corners of Tel Aviv's building boom were featured in architectural journals throughout the world.

But despite its architectural pizzazz, 1930s Tel Aviv close up was not the sleek, perfectly planned utopia it appeared. Many of the dazzlingly photographed buildings admired by the outside world were filled with old-fashioned workshops. In summer, the broad, futuristic streets (designed by architects whose hearts were still in pre-1933 Berlin) sweltered under the Palestinian sun, and blocked whatever evening breezes might blow in from the sea.

After Israeli independence, Tel Aviv mushroomed, first with refugee camps and temporary housing for hundreds of thousands of Jewish survivors of the Holocaust who poured into the country; later with vast, drab housing projects. During the austere 1950s, Tel Aviv, although a young city, became run-down, especially around its downtown center at Moghrabi Square. The beach, one of Tel Aviv's strong points, piled up with garbage and was neglected. The modern buildings of the 1930s and early 1940s, built of sand bricks, began to crumble. The city offered little in the way of museums, hotels, or restaurants, and word was out that Tel Aviv was a hot, humid concrete heap, ungainly and uninteresting.

In the past 25 years, however, Tel Aviv has undergone a slow, carefully nurtured revolution. The beach, only a few blocks from anywhere in the city center, has made a spectacular comeback. Performing groups, ranging from the Israel Philharmonic Orchestra and the Cameri Theater to the New Israel Opera, have put Tel Aviv on the cultural map.

Tel Aviv now incorporates the once-separate city of Jaffa, which *does* have a history going back thousands of years (the Prophet Jonah lived in this seaport before his encounter with the whale). If you climb the hill of Old Jaffa and look northward toward Tel Aviv's shoreline, you'll see a city that is coming of age and that actually stands on the threshold of majesty. It's an amazing achievement for a city not yet 100 years old.

1 Orientation

ARRIVING

BY PLANE   Flights arrive at Ben-Gurion International Airport at Lod, on the outskirts of the city. There is a fixed standard daytime taxi fare of approximately NIS 90 ($20) from Ben-Gurion to central Tel Aviv. This fare includes one suitcase per passenger; additional suitcases are NIS 3 (66¢) each. After 9pm and on Shabbat, the fixed fare is NIS 105 ($23). To get to Tel Aviv by public transportation, take bus 475 (fare is NIS 10/$2.20) from Ben-Gurion to the Central Bus Station in southern Tel Aviv (far from most hotels). For the Tel Aviv Hotel district, take the **United Tours Airport Shuttle Service** bus no. 222 for NIS 20 ($4.40) that departs at least once an hour (usually every 40 minutes), between 4am and midnight (on Saturday, from noon to midnight). It leaves the airport, stops at the El Al Terminal at the Central Railway Station, the B'nei Dan Youth Hostel, then travels all along the waterfront boulevard named Ha-Yarkon Street, stopping at each cluster of hotels. The trip from the airport to your hotel should take an hour or less.

BY TRAIN The **Central Railway Station** (sometimes called North Railway Station because it's in the northern reaches of the city) stands at the intersection of several major arteries—Petah Tikva Road, Haifa Road, and Arlosoroff Street. From here, municipal buses will take you throughout the city.

BY BUS From the **Central Bus Station** into town, take bus no. 4, which runs along Allenby Road and then up Ben-Yehuda Street. As you ride along Ben-Yehuda, you'll be parallel to and a block away from Ha-Yarkon Street, where many hotels are located. Ask the driver for the stop closest to your hotel. Take the no. 5 bus to Dizengoff Square.

BY CAR Major highways connect Jerusalem, Haifa, and Ashkelon with Tel Aviv.

VISITOR INFORMATION

The **Tourist Information Office** (☎ **03/639-5660**) is at store no. 6108 near platform 630 on the sixth floor of the New Central Bus Station in South Tel Aviv, at the terminus of bus no. 4 and 5, and unfortunately far from the hotel and tourist areas. It is open from 9am to 5pm Sunday through Thursday; on Friday and holiday eves the hours are 9am to 1pm. This office can provide a list of rooms for rent with private families. If your hotel doesn't have piles of different free tourist publications, the shelf at the Sheraton Hotel and Towers is usually well stocked.

CITY LAYOUT

Tel Aviv and Jaffa (Yafo in Hebrew) together form a large urban area. But the Tel Aviv–Jaffa you'll get to know is actually the downtown seafront section, extending east only to the thoroughfare of Ibn Givirol Street. This is a 6-kilometer (4-mi.) strip at least 1 kilometer (1/2 mi.) wide, but only certain sections are of interest to us as the commercial, cultural, and entertainment centers. The rest of the turf is residential or industrial.

MAIN ARTERIES & STREETS

Moghrabi Square is where **Allenby Street,** a major shopping artery (named after the British general who took Palestine from the Turks in 1917) meets **Ben-Yehuda Street.** Between Moghrabi Square and the waterfront is a short section of Allenby Street, which ends in **Allenby Square** at the water's edge. Here Tel Aviv's original opera house once stood (in which the very first Knesset sessions were held in 1948); it's symptomatic of Tel Aviv's short, intense existence that 6 decades provided ample time for the beachside Opera House to be built, to thrive, to decline into decrepitude, to be pulled down, to be long forgotten, and then commemorated by a luxury skyscraper and shopping mall: the Opera Tower. At the side of Allenby Square, facing the sea, the Hotel Metropole (1920s–30s) with its art-deco ground-floor arcades, hints at the waterfront Doge's Palace and Piazza San Marco in Venice. More like Venice, California, it became the crux of Tel Aviv's red-light district as the neighborhood declined over the decades. Recently, it was saved from demolition and renovated.

Dizengoff Square (actually a circle) is the very heart of Tel Aviv. Its 1930s design— "the Etoile of Tel Aviv"—was altered in the 1970s when it was covered with an elevated pedestrian plaza perched above busy Dizengoff Street near the intersection of Pinsker and Zamenhoff streets. There are proposals to return Dizengoff Square to its original state.

Running north from **Allenby Square** along the seafront is the Herbert Samuel Esplanade, and half a block inland, parallel to the Mediterranean, is **Ha-Yarkon Street,** where most of the better and middle range hotels are located. On Ha-Yarkon, overlooking the beach, you'll also spot the big brown U.S. Embassy building (the United States and most other countries have not recognized Jerusalem as Israel's capital and maintain their embassies here in Tel Aviv).

North of the Dan Hotel, the huge hotels march along the beach: the Sheraton, the Ramada, the Holiday Inn, the Sheraton Moriah Plaza, and the Hilton. Right next to the Sheraton Moriah Plaza Hotel, where Ben-Gurion Boulevard joins Ha-Yarkon Street, is Namir, or Atarim, Square (Kikar Namir), a modern multilevel plaza with inexpensive restaurants, outdoor cafes, and views of the sea.

South of Moghrabi Square, off Allenby Street, you'll find a number of interesting enclaves. At the intersection of Allenby and King George streets, the vast, outdoor **Carmel Market** is filled with stalls selling vegetables, fruits, and meat, interspersed with bargain clothing, pastries, and all kinds of oddities. Colorful and full of life, it's an interesting place to observe Tel Avivans on the hunt for their daily bread. Just south of the Allenby–King George Street entrance to the Carmel Market, you'll find the **Nahlat Binyamin Pedestrian Mall,** which hosts a wonderful outdoor crafts market on Tuesdays and Fridays. This neighborhood contains many architecturally interesting buildings from the 1920s and 1930s. Still farther south is the **Neve Zedek** area, Tel Aviv's oldest neighborhood, with the new **Suzanne Dellal Center for Dance and the Performing Arts** at its heart. This was a dilapidated, partly demolished region of cottages and workshops from Tel Aviv's first decade of existence; it is just now beginning to fill up with interesting boutiques, cafes, and shops for designer furnishings and accessories. At the inland side of the intersection of Allenby and King George streets, opposite the entrance to the Carmel Market, is Tel Aviv's archetypal **Sheinkin Street:** Tel Avivans love its cafes and general ambience; visitors either adore its authenticity or find it too typical to be of much interest.

All the way at the northern end of Tel Aviv, just south of the Yarkon River, is a section of small streets filled with restaurants and clubs, popular with a youngish tourist crowd as well as Tel Aviv's yuppies. Crossroads for this area is the intersection of Dizengoff and Yirmiyahu streets. The northern blocks of Dizengoff (and to some extent, Ben-Yehuda) Street is increasingly filled with top-of-the line clothing shops, and stores devoted to interior design, a concept unknown in Israel until a few years ago.

Just north of the Yarkon River, you'll find **Ha-Yarkon Park,** the city's major park, with walks through botanical gardens, artificial lakes and boat rental facilities, an outdoor amphitheater, and an ecology center and museum. Further north, in the suburb of Ramat Aviv, is **Tel Aviv University,** with the famous Diaspora Museum (Beit Hatfutsot) on its campus.

Inland, at the center of town, is Malchei Israel Square, recently renamed **Itzhak Rabin Square,** where Ibn Givirol Street, Ben-Gurion Boulevard, and Frishman Street meet. It is dominated by Tel Aviv's city hall and a great plaza. Although this is merely the Tel Aviv Municipal Government complex rather than a national center, the plaza competes with sites in Jerusalem as the focus of many national political demonstrations and marches. It was here that Prime Minister Rabin was assassinated in 1995 after addressing a peace rally. Another important inland location is **Tzimoret Square,** with the Ha-Bimah National Theater and Mann Auditorium (home of the Israel Philharmonic). Tzimoret Square is bounded by Dizengoff, Tarsat, Ahad Ha-Am, Rothschild, and Marmorek streets. A few blocks to the south, down Carlebach Street, is the **Tel Aviv Cinémathèque.** Slightly to the east, on Shaul Ha Melech Boulevard, is the **Tel Aviv Art Museum complex** and the **Golda Meir Center for the Performing Arts.**

Finally, there's **Jaffa (Yafo),** a large working class community. Visitors come mostly to enjoy the picturesque hilltop section overlooking the sea known as Old Jaffa and the nearby, Fellini-esque flea market district on the inland side of Yefet Street near the Clock Tower.

SUBURBAN NEIGHBORHOODS

Within half an hour of Tel Aviv are some eight or so suburban residential communities, many of which were born when Tel Aviv ran out of elbow room.

Bat Yam   Meaning "Daughter of the Sea," Bat Yam is 3¹/₂ miles south of Tel Aviv, right on the beach. Popular in summer, the community is famous for fine wide beaches, cleaner than those in Tel Aviv itself.

Ramat Gan   Ramat Gan, or "Garden Heights," is located, gardens and all, 2 miles east of Tel Aviv. Also an industrial community, Ramat Gan is the upper-middle-class suburbia of Tel Aviv, with many private houses, flourishing gardens, and a population of 150,000.

In Ramat Gan, the "village" of **Kfar Ha-Maccabia,** which looks like a group of college dormitories, was built by sports enthusiasts to accommodate the international athletes who participate in the Maccabee Games. But since the games are held once every 4 years, the rooms are rented out between games, the swimming pool remains in use, and the dining room offers first-class service and kosher meals.

Also in Ramat Gan is Bar Ilan University, which emphasizes religious Judaic studies in conjunction with major academic subjects. Take bus no. 43, 45, 64, 68, 70, 164, or 400 from Tel Aviv.

B'nei Brak   This one's an Orthodox Jewish community founded in 1924, located 1 mile east of Ramat Gan. The town houses a cluster of yeshivas and other religious institutions. If you visit, both men and women must wear modest attire.

Kfar Habad   Thirteen kilometers (7.8 mi.) Southeast of Tel Aviv, this is a Lubavitch Hassidic community. Although other Hassidic groups are inward looking, the Lubavitcher sect is known for its outreach programs to Jews throughout the world. The community contains a completely furnished replica of the late Lubavitcher rabbi's redbrick Tudor-style Brooklyn apartment house, which can be seen in the distance on Highway 1 if you are traveling from Tel Aviv to Jerusalem. Look to the right after passing a sign that reads: "Ben Shemen 11 kilometers." The replica is a building with a triple gabled roof among the surrounding white structures. The Lubavitcher rabbi never visited Israel in his lifetime, but his followers wanted him to feel totally at home if he did.

Petah Tikva   Meaning "Gate of Hope," Petah Tikva was begun as a moshav in 1878, and was built with the help of Baron Benjamin Edmond de Rothschild. A stone archway commemorates Rothschild's influence on this town of 115,000. The Petah Tikva

Getting Connected in Tel Aviv

Tel Aviv is one of the most superconnected places on earth. You will never want for places to get on-line. Convenient to the hotel district, **Web Stop Internet Lounge,** 28 Bogroshov St. (☎ **03/620-2682;** www.webstop.co.il), is a home away from home for anyone who needs to feel connected. There's a coffee bar and a real bar (though limited) on the premises, as well as classy computer desks that seat two, log-on sites for laptop users, red velvet sofas, a computer with a mini-cam (and all the possibilities that entails) and snacks that don't exactly say "tech-head" (like sun-dried tomato and brie sandwiches). It's the kind of place with lots of regulars, where everybody knows your name.

synagogue was the first to be built in a Jewish village in Israel in modern times. Seven miles east of Tel Aviv and highly industrial, Petah Tikva is surrounded by about 1,500 acres of orange groves.

Savyon   Originally organized by a South African group, Savyon is a posh community, 8 miles southeast of Tel Aviv. Many expensive villa-type houses are found here—also a tennis club, swimming pool, and gardens of iris, tulip, and gladioli.

2 Getting Around

BY BUS   From the new **Central Bus Station** into Tel Aviv, bus no. 4 goes to Allenby Road, Ben-Yehuda Street; on Ben-Yehuda, you will be running parallel to and a block inland from Ha-Yarkon Street; take bus no. 5 to go to the Mann Auditorium, Dizengoff Square, Dizengoff Street, and the IYHA youth hostel B'nei Dan. *Note:* No. 4 and 5 sheruts run the 4 and 5 bus routes 7 days a week, and are slightly cheaper than the buses (see "By Taxi/Sherut," below). From the Central Bus Station to Jaffa, take bus no. 46, and get off near the Clock Tower on Yefet Street.

To get to **Jaffa** from Tel Aviv, take bus no. 10, 25, or 26 heading southward. Bus 10 runs along Ben Yehuda Street, a block inland from Ha-Yarkon Street, and takes you to Jaffa's Clock Tower on Yefet Street, close to Old Jaffa and the Flea Market. Bus 25, which you can pick up on King George Street near Dizengoff Street, runs through Jaffa on Jerusalem Street, a very long block parallel to and inland from Yefet Street. If you're walking, simply head south along the waterfront promenade, which eventually runs into Jaffa. Bus 25 running northward will get you to the Diaspora Museum and Tel Aviv University. For **intercity Egged bus information,** call ☎ **03/537-5555.** For information on **Dan Bus service,** which operates in the Tel Aviv/Sharon region, call ☎ **03/639-4444.**

BY TAXI/SHERUT   Seven-passenger vans run along the bus 4 and 5 lines. They even run on a reduced schedule on Shabbat. If a van comes along, by all means take it rather than wait for the bus. Prices are a drop lower than bus fares on weekdays; on Shabbat there is a small surcharge.

When taxis are scarce, your best bet is to try at one of the major hotels. You have the right to demand that the meter (*ha-sha-on*) be used, but many drivers will negotiate a fixed nonmetered fare to your destination, which may or may not be to your advantage. There are legal surcharges above the metered fare on Shabbat and after 9pm. If you use the meter, ask for a receipt (*ka-ba-lah*).

Fast Facts: Tel Aviv

American Express   American Express International is at 32 Ben Yehuda St. (☎ **03/526-8837;** for lost traveler's checks, call 800/943-8694). Mail is held for American Express cardholders. Open Sunday to Thursday from 9am to 5pm and Fri 9am to 1pm.

Currency Exchange   Especially convenient is Bank Ha-Poalim on Ha-Yarkon Street across from the Dan Hotel (near Mendele Street), which has a street-side ATM connected to Visa, Cirrus, and NYCE. There are numerous currency exchange offices along Ha-Yarkon and Ben Yehuda streets. They usually have exchange rates comparable to the banks, are open longer hours and involve less waiting in line. Tel Aviv does not have Jerusalem's option of Old City money changers open every day, but it does have shady people offering to change money on the streets. Avoid them no matter what rate they quote.

Doctors/Dentists   You can get a list of English-speaking doctors and dentists from the embassy, and often from your hotel's front desk. There is an Emergency Dental Treatment Center at 18 Reines St. (☎ **03/523-9241**).

Drugstores   The *Jerusalem Post* lists under "General Assistance" the names and addresses of duty pharmacies that stay open nights and on Shabbat for the current week.

Embassies/Consulates   Many countries do not accept Jerusalem as Israel's legal capital, and so their embassies remain in Tel Aviv. See "Fast Facts: Israel" in chapter 2 for a list of embassies and consulates.

Emergencies   For police, dial ☎ **100.** In medical emergencies, dial ☎ **101** for Magen David Adom (Red Shield of David), Israel's emergency first-aid service and ambulance. For fire, dial ☎ **102.** Medical Help for Tourists (toll free) ☎ **177/022-9110.**

Hospitals   For visitors with Blue Cross–Blue Shield insurance, call ☎ **03/ 579-0081** or 03/755-3546 for information.

Hot Lines   For the Rape Crisis Center, dial ☎ **03/523-4819;** Drug Counseling ☎ **03/546-3587.**

Laundry/Dry Cleaning   Try 63 Ben-Yehuda St., near Bograshov, which advertises "6 Hour Cleaning and Laundry." Hours are 7am to 1:30pm and 3:30 to 6pm. If you want to do it yourself, 51 Ben-Yehuda St. has coin-operated machines. Figure $5.50 for washing, soap, and adequate drying.

Libraries   British Council Library 140 Ha-Yarkon St., near Gordon St. (☎ **03/522-2194**). Hours are Monday to Thursday from 10am to 1pm and 4 to 7pm; Friday from 10am to 1pm.

Newspapers/Magazines   See the special Tel Aviv events supplement published on Friday in the *Jerusalem Post* (available only in the Tel Aviv region).

Post Office   Tel Aviv's Central Post Office is at 132 Allenby Rd. General hours for all services are Sunday to Thursday from 7am to 7pm, though limited services (telephone and telegraph) are open nights and on Shabbat. Branch post offices are on Ha-Yarkon at Trumpeldor, at 3 Mendele St., next to the Hotel Adiv between Ha-Yarkon and Ben-Yehuda, and just off Dizengoff Square on Zamenhoff Street. Telegrams can be sent at all post offices or by phoning ☎ **171.**

Radio   Israel Radio news can be heard at 576, 1170, and 1458 kHz at 7am, 1pm, 5pm, and 8pm. BBC World Service broadcasts at 1322 kHz.

Safety   Israel's largest city has less crime than most cities its size, but there is still enough that you must observe the normal precautions. Don't walk in deserted areas, especially the beaches, after dark.

Telegrams/Telex   See "Post Office," above.

Television   There are three Israeli State channels and one English-language channel from Lebanon specializing in American reruns. Commercial channels and cable service have arrived in Israel over the past few years, and a selection of cable channels is usually available at better hotels.

Useful Telephone Numbers   For all flight arrival and departure schedule information, including last-minute changes, call ☎ **03/973-1111;** For train information, call ☎ **03/693-7515.**

3 Where to Stay

Most of Tel Aviv's hotels are on Ha-Yarkon Street, which runs along the beach from Mograbi Square northward. The five-star hotels are on the sea side of Ha-Yarkon. Most of the four, three and two star choices are on the inland side of Ha-Yarkon, or on Ben Yehuda Street, which parallels Ha-Yarkon 1 block inland. Tel Aviv can be a very noisy city. If you're looking for a moderate or budget hotel, don't take a room facing on a main street, unless it has air-conditioning and soundproof windows. Get off the heavily trafficked streets or take a room in the back; Tel Aviv hoteliers charge the same rates for front and back rooms.

PRIVATE ROOMS & APARTMENTS   The Government Tourist Information Office, New Central Bus Station, 6th Floor (☎ **03/639-5660**), compiles and prints a list of agencies and individuals who rent rooms and apartments. Though they will not make a contact or reservation for you, and they cannot guarantee the quality of service or accommodations, the tourist office staff will give you a copy of the list for free.

ALONG HA-YARKON STREET

Ha-Yarkon Street runs along the Mediterranean. The five-star hotels are all on the sea side of the street and either have direct access to the beach, or are across a small but busy road. The southern end of Ha-Yarkon is run down, but new construction is upgrading this area. Just before the Dan Hotel, the street becomes more upscale; north of Atarim Square, Ha-Yarkon becomes a pleasant residential thoroughfare, but not as interesting for strolling. Near Gordon Street, Ha-Yarkon becomes a wider thoroughfare with divider barriers; guests staying in moderate hotels on the inland side of the street can't just dash across the road and down to the beach.

VERY EXPENSIVE

Crowne Plaza. 145 Ha-Yarkon St., Tel Aviv. ☎ **800/HOLIDAY** in the U.S. and Canada, or 03/520-1111. Fax 03/520-1122. 239 units. A/C MINIBAR TV TEL. $358–$418 double. 15% service charge. Rates include breakfast. AE, DC, MC, V. Bus: 4 on Ben-Yehuda St.; ask for stop closest to Gordon St.

The high-rise Crowne Plaza shares a long block just north of Gordon Street with the Sheraton Moriah and Ramada Hotels, all of which offer direct access to the beach. Other pluses include a stylish early '90s decor that has not yet worn thin, a highly praised business center, and better-than-average in-hotel restaurant services. No-smoking rooms and rooms with handicap access are available; all rooms have balconies. The inventive, upper-bracket Pacific Grill serves a continental menu with interesting Pacific Rim/Asian touches.

Dining/Diversions: Restaurant, English-style pub, lounge, and poolside cafes.

Amenities: Business center, business lounge, Crowne Plaza Club floors with special services and snacks. Indoor and outdoor swimming pools, health club (additional charge), sauna, massage, steam room, valet parking (fee).

✪ **Dan Tel Aviv Hotel.** 99 Ha-Yarkon St., Tel Aviv. ☎ **800/223-7773** in the U.S., or 03/520-2525. Fax 03/524-9755. E-mail: dantelaviv@danhotels.com. 286 units A/C MINIBAR TV TEL. $294–$472 double. Add 15% service charge. Rates include breakfast. Family plans for children under 18. AE, DC, MC, V. Bus: 4 on Ben-Yehuda St.; ask for stop near Dan Hotel.

With an outstanding central location right on Gordon Beach, the Dan started out as a small hotel in the 1950s, and in a series of expansions and upgradings, was lovingly developed into today's modern megacomplex. Service is very strong, decor in the deluxe rooms rivals the Hilton's as the best in Tel Aviv, and a beautiful, efficient business center as well as a Jacuzzi, sauna, health club with steam bath, and shopping arcade mark the hotel's latest renovations. The new, sparkling indoor pool, overlooking the sea, offers the best winter swimming of any hotel in town). Because the hotel was built in many sections over 4 decades, the layout is a bit complicated—many of the lower-category rooms (Superior) with older furniture face courtyards; upper-category rooms (Deluxe) are divided into those facing busy Ha-Yarkon Street and those facing the sea; there are no balconies. You must walk across the road to access the beach. The expensive La Regence Grill Room is a solid but predictable dining choice, the small Bedouin-style lounge/bar is most attractive.

Dining/Diversions: Three restaurants, lounge/bar.

Amenities: Business lounge, special services and lounge for guests in deluxe rooms and suites. Indoor and outdoor swimming pools, health club, sauna, steam bath, solarium, children's activities summer and holidays; use of golf facilities at Dan Accadia Hotel in Herzlia, 15 miles north of Tel Aviv.

✪ **Tel Aviv Sheraton Hotel & Towers.** 115 Ha-Yarkon St., Tel Aviv 63573. ☎ **800/325-3535** in the U.S. and Canada, or 03/521-1111. Fax 03/523-3322. 346 units (all with bathroom). A/C MINIBAR TV TEL. $295–$350 double; add $90 for Tower floors. Rates include breakfast only on Tower floors; $25 extra for other rooms. Add 15% service charge. AE, DC, MC, V. Bus: 4 to Ben-Yehuda and Gordon sts., walk down Gordon St. to Ha-Yarkon.

This is the most fun of Tel Aviv's five-star hotels: right on Gordon Beach (across the road) with its interesting mix of visitors and locals, just steps from the Ha-Yarkon Street restaurant and cafe district and the art galleries of the Gordon Street area. Unlike more isolated comparable hotels farther north, the Sheraton is an easy walk to Dizengoff Square, Allenby Street, the Yemenite Quarter, and the Carmel Market. In addition, the Sheraton's dining facilities are the best of any hotel in the country starting with its top-of-the-line Twelve Tribes Restaurant. By paying your hotel bill in foreign currency, you avoid the 17% value-added tax (VAT). Rooms are spacious; on the deluxe Tower Floors, all were beautifully renovated in 1998 with light furniture and bright, cheerful spring colors. On one standard floor, rooms have not been redone at press time. Sheraton, of all the high-rise beachfront hotels, has many rooms facing squarely out onto the Mediterranean. Try for these rooms; the view of the sunset, or of rolling waves on a stormy winter night will be worth the extra price. Because of noise considerations, avoid rooms with adjoining doors. Personal attention in the Executive Towers is outstanding, and a full range of business facilities is available on the premises.

Hotel Dining

Most in-house hotel restaurants in Israel are bland and overpriced; all are kosher. With a few exceptions, such as the fabulous Le Divellec at the Jerusalem Hilton (see chapter 3), and the Twelve Tribes at the Sheraton in Tel Aviv (see above), you do much better stepping out and enjoying the lively, fascinating restaurant scene (kosher and nonkosher and in every price range) that thrives in all of Israel's major cities.

Dining/Diversions: A variety of top-quality restaurants, cafes, lounge/bar, disco/nightclub.

Amenities: Business center, Executive Tower floors with special services and snacks. Outdoor pools, health club (additional charge), parking (fee).

EXPENSIVE

Carlton Hotel. 10 Elizier Peri St., Tel Aviv. ☎ **800/223-0888** in the U.S., or 03/520-1818. Fax 03/527-1043. E-mail: request@carlton.co.il. 282 units. A/C MINIBAR TV TEL. $230–$284 double; add $70 for executive club rms. Rates include breakfast. AE, DC, MC, V. Bus: 4.

The entrance to this carefully run hotel built in 1981 is through a covered highway section of Ha-Yarkon Street, so you feel as if you are at an airport, but once inside, the place is calm and comfortable. A large marina complex separates the building from the beaches, and although views from many guest rooms are nice, the Carlton feels more like a city hotel than most of its other five-star neighbors. Guest rooms are especially well insulated from traffic noise and have modern decor, balconies, relatively soft beds and TVs that offer 43 channels. There are dazzling vistas from the small rooftop swimming pool and the hotel has an in-house synagogue. In addition to tourists, the hotel has a clientele of business travelers and religious guests. There is a business center and lounge, 24-hour room service, and a sauna and massage room. There are special services for club rooms, two restaurants and no-smoking guest rooms available.

Mercure Marina Hotel. 167 Ha-Yarkon St., Tel Aviv. ☎ **800/Mercure** in the U.S. and Canada, or 03/521-1777. 160 units. A/C TV TEL. $180 double. Rates include breakfast. AE, DC, MC, V. Bus: 4.

Opened in 1996, this hotel is in the Atarim Square–Marina complex and does not have direct access to the beach—you go through the complex and down a staircase to the beach. Entrance is through the sunken covered highway section of Ha-Yarkon Street and an elevator takes you up to the reception level. Guest rooms are modern and bright, set around a large indoor atrium and offer safes, voice mail, and hair dryers; no-smoking rooms and rooms for travelers with disabilities are also available. Perhaps because of the entrance, the hotel seems impersonal, but its facilities are new and fresh and the rates are a relatively good deal.

Amenities: 24-hour room service, business services, and business lounge. Swimming pool and Jacuzzi with great beach views on the roof.

Renaissance Tel Aviv. 121 Ha-Yarkon St., Tel Aviv. ☎ **03/521-5555.** Fax 03/521-5588. E-mail: reservation@renaissance-tlv.co.il. 340 units. A/C MINIBAR TV TEL. $185–$250 double. Breakfast $18 extra. AE, DC, MC, V.

The southernmost and best located of three beachfront tower hotels just north of Gordon Street, the Ramada shares this prime spot with the Crowne Plaza and Sheraton Moriah Hotels. There is a pleasant terrace cafe overlooking the sea in good weather, and an indoor heated pool ensures the opportunity to do a bit of swimming, even in

Tel Aviv Accommodations & Dining

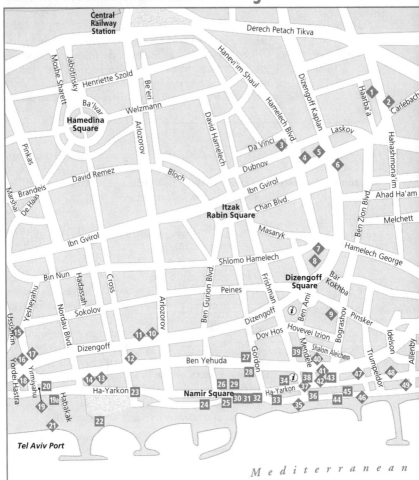

ACCOMMODATIONS

Adiv **39**
Armon Ha-Yarkon **20**
Astor Hotel **35**
Basel Hotel **29**
Best Western Regency Suites **45**
Carlton Hotel **24**
Center Hotel **8**
City Hotel **34**
Dan Panorama **65**
Dan Tel Aviv **36**
David Intercontinental Hotel **64**
Gordon Inn **27**
Grande Deborah Hotel **28**

Holiday Inn Crowne Plaza **31**
Maxim Hotel **43**
Melody Hotel **14**
Mercure Marina Hotel **25**
Olympia Hotel **26**
Ramada Continental **32**
Shalom Hotel **23**
Sheraton Moriah Plaza **30**
Tal Hotel **19a**
Tel Aviv Hilton **22**
Tel Aviv Sheraton **33**
Top Hotel **47**
Yamit Towers **44**

DINING

Abu Nasser Restaurant **76**
Ali Oli **58**
Aladin **71**
Apicus **52**
Barbunya **13**
Batya **9**
Bebale **11**
Brew House **59**
Cafe Kazzeh **57**
Cafe Nordau **10**
Capot Tmarin **53**
Chicago Pizza Pie Factory **46**
Chimney Pub **38**

Dim Sum Restaurant 7
Erez Lehem 5
Forel 37
Giraffe 6
Hungarian Blintzes 15
Itamar 60
Keren 66
Kimel 61
Lilith 49
Maganda 62
Manta Ray 75
Mika 56
Mongolian Grill Bar 47
Movenpick 4

Mul Ha-Yam Restaurant 21
Muscat 73
Osteria da Fiorella 12
Pappagaio 1
Paradiso 2
Pastalina 67
Picasso 42
Red Chinese Restaurant 17
Roshfeld 3
Said el Abu Lafia 69
Shangri La 35
Shao Lin Dim Sum 55
Shaul's Inn 63
Shirat Hayam 72

Shtsupak 19
Spaghettim 54
Taboon 74
Tandoori 8
Taste of Life 31
Twelve Tribes 29
Victor & Margaret Tayar's 70
Whitehall Steakhouse 41
Yakimono 18
Yin Yang 50
Yoe' ezer Wine Bar 68
Yo Si Peking 16
Yotvata in Town 48

winter. Rooms are comfortable and recently freshened up, but not exceptional; all have balconies. There are often special promotional rates.

Dining: Restaurant, two cafes, bar.

Amenities: Business club, indoor pool, children's pool, fitness room, sauna, Jacuzzi, children's program in summer, parking (fee).

✪ **Sheraton Moriah Tel Aviv.** 155 Ha-Yarkon St., Tel Aviv 63453. ☎ **800/221-0203** in the U.S. and Canada, or 03/521-6666. Fax 03/527-1065. 346 units. A/C MINIBAR TV TEL. $220–$300 double. Rates include breakfast. AE, DC, MC, V. Bus: 4 to Gordon St.

In 1996, the Sheraton Moriah's public areas and most guest rooms were beautifully refurbished employing a scheme of natural textures and materials such as stone, unglazed pottery, and silvered iron. The result is some of the best hotel interior design in the country—elegant and unpretentious. Guest rooms on the Business Floors (10 to 17) are understated, with blonde Biedermeier-influenced furnishings set against off white and soft cream-colored walls, textured carpets, and tailored textiles of navy and cream. Located directly on the beach, not far from the heart of the Ha-Yarkon Street restaurant district, the Gordon Street neighborhood of art galleries, and a pleasant stroll to Dizengoff, this is good value in the five-star category.

Amenities: Business center, children's programs in summer. Outdoor pool, parking (fee).

Yamit Park Plaza Hotel. 79 Ha-Yarkon St., Tel Aviv. ☎ **03/519-7111.** Fax 03/517-4719. 120 units. A/C TV TEL. $157–$200 double; $176–214 studio; $248–$296 one-bedroom suite; $372–$440 two-bedroom suite. Breakfast included for standard and studio rooms. AE, DC, MC, V. Bus: 4 to Ben Yehuda St.; ask driver for closest stop.

A possible option for families that want better-quality accommodations and more privacy, the totally (1999) renovated rooms and suites in this beachfront (across the road) high-rise are most attractive. There are standard rooms; larger studio rooms; and one- and two-bedroom suites with kitchenettes. There are also two restaurants. Rates include service charge and are for one to two people in the rooms, one to two people in one-bedroom suites, and one to four people in two-bedroom suites. You can add up to two additional people in suites for $20 per person; breakfast can be arranged for an additional charge.

Amenities: Room service 8am to 11pm; outdoor swimming pool; fitness room (fee); Jacuzzi; sauna; self-service laundry (fee); free parking; business center opening in 2000.

MODERATE

✪ **Adiv.** 5 Mendele St., Tel Aviv 63907. ☎ **03/522-9141.** Fax 03/522-9144. E-mail: iladiv01@1bh.net. 71 units. A/C TV TEL. $100–$110 double; $120–$135 junior suite. Rates include breakfast. AE, DC, MC, V.

With gleaming, newly redesigned public areas faced with polished, rose-colored stone, and freshly spruced-up single and double rooms, the Adiv has become one of the most attractive moderately priced hotels in town. The location is excellent, on a side street half a block from Ha-Yarkon Street and the beach, convenient to many restaurants and window-shopping areas. Most rooms are toward the back of the building, where the blare of traffic is somewhat muffled. Rooms have refrigerators; there is free parking and free coffee in the lobby. Readers' letters attest to the staff's attentiveness.

✪ **Basel Hotel.** 156 Ha-Yarkon St., Tel Aviv. ☎ **03/524-4161.** Fax 03/527-0005. 120 units. A/C TV TEL. $145–$157 double. Rates include breakfast. 15% service charge added. AE, DC, MC, V.

Located on the inland side of Ha-Yarkon Street, between Gordon Street and Atarim Square, from the outside this convenient, well-run seven-story hotel looks smaller than it really is. Given four stars under the now-suspended hotel rating system, the Basel offers a functional lobby larger than that of most hotels in this class, with shops and a small bar, an outdoor swimming pool, and comfortable rooms with medium firm beds, many of which are in the depths of the building, away from street noise. Rooms have cable TV, electric kettles, and refrigerators. The staff is quite good, and 12-hour room service is available. The Basel is a fabulous deal on El Al's Sunsational package—a double room can run from $40 to $60 a night. Higher rate is for July and August. Though the Basel is in the heart of the swanky beachfront hotel district, you have to detour a long block around the divided Ha-Yarkon Street underpass if you're going to the beach by foot. Parking is free, but very limited.

Best Western Regency Suites Hotel. 80 Ha-Yarkon St., Tel Aviv 63432. ☎ **03/517-3939.** Fax 03/516-3276. E-mail: bestwest@netvision.net.il. 20 units. A/C TV TEL. $184–$207 suite; $20 additional person. AE, DC, MC, V.

Just a few years old, with its polish not yet worn thin, this Best Western Hotel consists of up-to-date one-bedroom suites with small living room areas and fully equipped kitchenettes. It offers discounts to long-term visitors, and is ideal for families or business travelers who want to prepare some of their own meals. It is located on the inland side of Ha-Yarkon Street, across from the beach, just where the neighborhood becomes markedly better. Breakfast is not included, but can be arranged at the small in-house coffee shop.

City Hotel. 9 Mapu St., Tel Aviv. ☎ **03/524-6253.** Fax 03/524-6250. E-mail: atlashot@netvision.net.il. 96 units. A/C TEL TV. $100–$130 double. Rates include breakfast. AE, DC, MC, V.

Well located, on a side street close to Ha-Yarkon, the City Hotel has pleasant, recently renovated public areas; guest rooms are simple but comfortable but, along with the bathrooms are in the process of being redone at press time. All rooms have electric kettles and safes (fee per day). Corner rooms, markedly roomier and only a bit more expensive, are a good deal here, especially if there's an extra person in the room. The City Hotel is part of the well-run Atlas Chain; the buffet breakfast here is a cut above most in this category.

Olympia Hotel. 164 Ha-Yarkon St., Tel Aviv. ☎ **03/524-2184.** Fax 03/524-7278. E-mail: olympia@infolink.net.il. 52 units. A/C TV TEL. $100–$135 double. Rates include breakfast. AE, DC, MC, V.

This modern three-star-equivalent hotel a half block south of Ben-Gurion Street was completely renovated in 1997. Guest rooms are fresh and bright, equipped with refrigerators; some have views of Namir Square and of the Mediterranean. Across the street and past Namir Square, you have staircase access down to the beach. There are business services, and room service from 7am to 11pm. No pool or fitness room, but for a fee, hotel guests can have access to these facilities at a hotel nearby.

INEXPENSIVE

Maxim Hotel. 86 Ha-Yarkon St., Tel Aviv 63903. ☎ **03/517-3721** or 03/517-3222. Fax 03/517-3726. 59 units (52 with bathroom, 7 with shower). A/C TV. $95–$100 double. Rates include breakfast. AE, DC, MC, V.

Near the corner with Bograshov, just where Ha-Yarkon Street begins to be a bit classier, the modern Maxim Hotel offers sea views from its front-facing rooms. Guest rooms are small but were redecorated in 1998; refrigerators are available on request.

There is a smoky bar/cafe in the lobby. The slightly higher rates are for the rooms that have glimpses of the sea. Free parking is a plus.

NORTHERN TEL AVIV
VERY EXPENSIVE

✪ **Tel Aviv Hilton.** Independence Park, Ha-Yarkon St., Tel Aviv. ☎ **03/520-2222.** Fax 03/527-2711. 595 units. A/C MINIBAR TV TEL. $335–$400 double; from $620 suite. Breakfast included only with Executive Floor deluxe rms. Service charge included. Breakfast $24 extra per person. AE, DC, MC, V.

The massive Hilton is set far back from Ha-Yarkon Street in a small park overlooking a quiet, sheltered area of Tel Aviv's beachfront. Public areas and guest rooms here were completely redone in 1998–99. The skilled staff here is probably the best in the city; restaurant facilities are good, spacious, and varied; the hotel's superb state-of-the-art business center, meeting rooms and conference facilities are the best in Israel, and always buzzing (the Hilton's kosher sushi bar and option of a Japanese-style breakfast are indicative of the hotel's role as a focal point for business ties between Israel and Asia). The Hilton is also well attuned to vacationers, and offers a full range of recreational facilities. Better-category rooms are the best in Tel Aviv, decorated with tasteful accessories and classic fruit-wood furniture; a variety of stylishly designed suites are offered (one has a Jacuzzi and bathroom corner window with spectacular views of the sea). All rooms have balconies; lower-category rooms are also well designed and have been freshly redone. The location is a bit of a hike to interesting streets; the sheltered Hilton Beach gives you the feel of being away from the city; the downside is that the water here at times can trap seaweed and garbage swept in by the tides. The large saltwater swimming pool, refilled each day, is a real plus, and unique among Tel Aviv hotels.

Dining/Diversions: Five restaurants (including the top-quality King Solomon Grill; the Yakimono Sushi Bar (kosher); buffet and light meal restaurants; two bars.

Amenities: Business center, special service for Executive Floors and Club Room, in-house doctors and complete medical clinic, airport shuttle. Outdoor saltwater pool, CYBEX fitness center, sauna, massage, steam bath, two tennis courts, access to marina, shopping arcade, parking (fee).

MODERATE

Melody Hotel. 220 Ha-Yarkon St., Tel Aviv. ☎ **03/527-7711.** Fax 03/527-7750. E-mail: atlashot@netvision.net.il. 34 units. A/C TV TEL. $137–$157 double high and low seasons. Rates include continental breakfast. AE, DC, MC, V.

Located just across the road from the Hilton Hotel, the Melody is the gem of the Atlas Hotels Chain. Formerly the Canadian Embassy, in 1998, it was made into a hotel, with sleek, beautifully designed and furnished rooms equipped with Internet and fax outlets, good work desks, refrigerators, and soundproof windows; those facing the street have panoramic views of Independence Park and the grounds of the Hilton, with glimpses of the sea. There are handicapped-accessible rooms. The lobby is small, and doubles as a coffee bar for breakfast. The staff is attentive, and a good beach is just across the street. Free parking.

Shalom Hotel. 216 Ha-Yarkon St., Tel Aviv. ☎ **03/524-3277.** Fax 03/523-5895. 48 units. A/C TV TEL. $120–$140 double; off-season and student discounts available. Rates include breakfast. Bus: 4 or 5. AE, DC, MC, V.

The Shalom Hotel is a modern, five-story structure with a bright new lobby. All the front rooms have balconies with views of the Mediterranean and Independence Park. Guest rooms are functional, with refrigerators, but not special. In front of the hotel is the Stagecoach Restaurant and Pub with Wild West decor and live music every evening.

Tal Hotel. 287 Ha-Yarkon St. ☎ **03/542-5500**. Fax 03/542-5501. E-mail atlashot@ netvision.net.il. 120 units. $137–$157, breakfast included. AE, DC, MC, V.

The Tal's location, up near the northern edge of Tel Aviv, is a drawback, but in another location, this 11-story hotel would surely be more costly. Guest rooms are very spacious, with pleasant, contemporary decor, and newly rebuilt, polished stone bathrooms. Amenities include hair dryers, voice mail, safes, refrigerators, and electric kettles. There are also connecting rooms and rooms with kitchenettes that make this a good choice for families. Business facilities are on the premises; there are rooms especially designed for business travelers, and rooms for travelers with disabilities.

NEAR DIZENGOFF SQUARE
MODERATE

Center Hotel. 2 Zamenhoff St. at Dizengoff Sq., Tel Aviv. ☎ **03/629-6181**. Fax 03/629-6751. E-mail: atlashot@netvision.net.il. 56 units. A/C TEL. $100–$112 double. Rates include breakfast. AE, DC, MC, V.

Recently remodeled with a modest but spiffy '90s look for its small public areas, the Center Hotel, part of the well-managed Atlas Hotel chain, is a modern choice right at the heart of the busy Dizengoff Square area, but not close to the beach. Many of the rooms are toward the back of the building and are buffered against the neighborhood's high level of street noise. There are radios, kettles for making tea or coffee, and safes (fee) in the rooms.

ALONG BEN-YEHUDA
INEXPENSIVE

✪ **Gordon Inn.** 17 Gordon St., Tel Aviv. ☎ **03/523-8239**. Fax 03/523-7419. E-mail: sleepin@inter.net.il. 31 units (18 with shower). A/C. $47–$56 double without bathroom, $60–$71 double with bathroom. $17 per person for 5 or more people in a room with bathroom; summer surcharge. Rates include continental breakfast. AE, DC, MC, V. Bus: 4 on Ben Yehuda St. to Gordon St.

Opened in 1995, this well-managed guest house bridges the gap between hostel and hotel. Continental breakfast is served in a pleasant dining room; small private rooms are spartan with metal frame beds and thin mattresses; half have private bathrooms. There are also larger group or family rooms, each equipped with wardrobes and bedside reading lamps; most have private bathrooms. The location, on Gordon Street with its many art galleries, adds a touch of class, but its spot on the corner of Ben-Yehuda Street means heavy bus and traffic noise. Add 15% for single and double rooms whenever high season is declared. Lockers are $2 a day extra. No charm, but in this price category it's by far the best choice.

MODERATE

Grand Hotel Deborah. 87 Ben Yehuda St. ☎ **03/527-8282**. Fax 03/527-8304. E-mail: atlashot@netvision.net.il. 60 units. A/C TV TEL. $129–$150 double. Rates include breakfast. AE, DC, MC, V.

A block inland from the beach, the Grand Deborah is located on the 5th to 11th floors of a building that towers above its immediate neighbors, so all rooms have sweeping views of the city. Rooms are spacious, renovated in the mid-1990s, and, like the lobby, unusually formal in furniture and decor. Each room has a safe, refrigerator, hair dryer, electric kettle for coffee or tea and medium-firm beds. This is an Atlas Hotel, and guests can use the small pool at Atlas's nearby Basel Hotel.

ℹ️ Family-Friendly Hotels

Two all-suite hotels right on the beachside Ha-Yarkon Street are good bets for families with children: **Best Western Regency** (*see page 219*), and the **Yamit Park Plaza Hotel** (*see page 218*). Both have kitchenette facilities. If you have a car, and are willing to drive 25 minutes north of Tel Aviv, **Kibbutz Shefayim's Hotel** (*see page 264*), with its adjacent water park (including a swimming pool with waves), is fun for younger children, and a very pleasant base for exploring the Tel Aviv/Coastal region.

Top Hotel. 35 Ben Yehuda St. ☎ **03/517-0941.** Fax 03/517-1322. E-mail: atlashot@ netvision.net.il. 64 units. $100–$129 double. Rates include breakfast. AE, DC, MC, V.

A bit less expensive than the other hotels in the Atlas Chain, the cheerful, well-run Top has a very central location a block inland from the beach. Rooms are compact, all with newly rebuilt bathrooms; a redecoration of guest rooms is planned during the time span of this edition. Amenities include voice mail, safes, electric kettles, and, on request, small refrigerators.

SOUTH TEL AVIV
EXPENSIVE

Dan Panorama Hotel. 10 Kaufman St., Tel Aviv. ☎ **03/519-0190.** Fax 03/517-1777. 500 units. A/C TV TEL. $235–$295 double. Add 15% service charge. Rates include breakfast. AE, DC, MC, V. Bus: 10.

Across the road from the sea (but a 2-block walk to a swimming beach) in the southern part of Tel Aviv within walking distance of Old Jaffa, this modern high-rise held forth by itself $1^1/_2$ miles south of the main hotel district for more than 10 years. Now it has been joined by an InterContinental Hotel. Rooms are small, but all have balconies. There is a convention center next door, as well as a high-rise textile industry center, giving the Dan Panorama a business ambience, but this may change as more hotels are built in the neighborhood. There are no nearby streets for strolling; rates here are lower than for a comparable hotel in a more central location. Higher rate is for Passover and July 25 to August 25.

   Dining/Diversions: Two restaurants, lobby bar.

   Amenities: 24-hour room service, business center, business lounge. Outdoor swimming pool and sun terrace, fitness center (fee), synagogue, lobby shops, parking (fee).

David Intercontinental Hotel. 12 Kaufman St., Tel Aviv. ☎ **03/795-1111.** Fax 03/795-1112. www.interconti.com. E-mail: telaviv@interconti.com. 600 units. A/C MINIBAR TV TEL. $315–$360 double regular and holiday seasons. Rates include breakfast. AE, DC, MC, V. Bus 10 from Ben Yehuda Street stops near hotel door.

This 24-story tower, completed in 1999, is the first luxury megahotel to open in Tel Aviv in over a decade. It's indoor public areas are enclosed by a soaring, balcony-lined atrium that dwarfs the lobbies of any other hotel in Tel Aviv, but the Intercontinental's public areas do not catch vistas of the Mediterranean across the divided highway, and the hotel does not have the feeling of an urban beachfront resort offered by other top rank Tel Aviv hotels. Guest rooms do have views of the sea, and the higher you go on the elevator (and in price) the more dazzling vistas of Tel Aviv you get. Rooms are spacious and up to date in all ways, though flowered textiles in the decor are surprisingly passé. There are nice touches throughout the hotel: duvet covers over the blankets; an Internet cafe that includes cake and coffee in its rates; ecologically correct cosmetics in all guest bathrooms. The location, in an area still under development and away from most of the city's hotels and restaurants, is a minus; the stretch of beach directly across the divided highway from the hotel is not suitable for swimming, and you must walk a bit south to find a guarded beach.

Dining/Diversions: The inventive, kosher Aubergine Restaurant; a kosher sushi bar; a cigar bar, as well as cafes and a buffet restaurant.

Amenities: Medium-size heated outdoor pool and deck; lap pool with massage jets; children's pool; business center, lounge, and meeting rooms; fitness room for fee, hairdresser; synagogue, parking for fee; largest convention facilities of any hotel in the country.

JAFFA
INEXPENSIVE

Beit Immanuel Hostel. 8 Auerbach St. ☎ **03/682-1459.** Fax 03/682-9817. $12 per person in single sex-dorms; $50–$60 double. No credit cards.

This is a lovely, atmospheric, church hospice with newly renovated rooms located in a commercial/industrial neighborhood on the Tel Aviv Jaffa border. It's beautifully maintained in a garden enclave and within walking distance of Old Jaffa. There's no lockout, an 11pm curfew, no smoking, a self-service laundry room (fee), and a nightly dinner is offered for $8 ($11.50 for Friday nights). Take bus 46, which runs from the New Central Bus Station to Old Jaffa and ask for the Beit Immanuel Auerbach Street stop.

4 Where to Dine

OFF & ON HA-YARKON STREET
EXPENSIVE

✪ **Twelve Tribes.** In the Sheraton Hotel, 115 Ha-Yarkon St. ☎ **03/521-1111.** Reservations recommended. Main courses NIS 105–126 ($23–$28); complete fixed-price dinners $45; add 17% VAT. AE, DC, MC, V. Sun–Thurs 7pm–midnight. FRENCH.

The Sheraton Hotel's food preparation staff constantly stretches to create remarkable and ever-changing meals within the bounds of kashruth. At the Twelve Tribes, which wins my award as the most elegant and inventive kosher restaurant in Tel Aviv, the style is inventive, done with a light, fresh touch. The current executive chef, Hans Lelie, from the Netherlands, plans to emphasize the natural taste and texture of the food he presents. Fois gras tops the list of appetizers, but there's also a choice of lighter, more original creations that are sure to please. Then you might go on to a cream of trout soup with almonds, or orange and carrot soup, and then for a main course, have a roast Cornish hen with a house ratatouille and fried polenta in rosemary; or veal chop stuffed with nuts and fresh herbs served in a sauce of wild Maine blueberries and wine. A mildly Cajun steak fillet is always a strong point of the menu. Each evening there is a special choice of fresh fish, beautifully prepared. For business and health-conscious travelers, a menu of low-calorie, healthful but nonetheless fascinating dishes has been put into place. The wines are overseen by a sommelier. A dessert cart is lavish and worthwhile, especially for those guests who are kosher. Service is included in the prices; guests of the Sheraton Plaza who pay in foreign currency are exempt from the 17% VAT.

MODERATE

✪ **Forel.** 10 Frishman St. ☎ **03/522-2664.** Reservations recommended. Main courses NIS 60–100 ($13.20–$22). AE, DC, MC, V. Daily noon–midnight. Business lunch noon–5pm. SEAFOOD.

Forel means "trout," and the owner of this sparkling little place handy to the hotel district, has patented a special grill with delicate rollers to charcoal this fish to perfection. Try the trout stuffed with garlic and eggplant or with mushrooms and almonds on your first visit here. Another time you might try charcoal grilled Nile perch in Provenççal sauce or the magnificent (and extremely expensive) fish and seafood soup. First courses range from house pâté, or matjes herring to selections from the antipasto table. Business lunches run from NIS 45 to 75 ($10 to $16.50) and include first and main courses plus coffee or tea. There is also a selection of steaks and poultry, and for $60, you can even order a lobster.

Mongolian Grill Bar. 62 Ha-Yarkon St. ☎ **03/517-4188.** Reservations recommended. Lunch NIS 69 ($15.20); dinner NIS 85–100 ($18.70–$22). AE, DC, MC, V. Daily noon–1am; lunch served noon–4pm. MONGOLIAN.

Meat is becoming more and more popular among the formerly vegetarian Israelis, and the idea of this unusual grill is derived from the times when warriors set their shields over fires out in the open fields, and cooked up vegetables and freshly hunted meat with fiery spices and oil. There is a large buffet table of uncooked chunks of steak, lamb, chicken, liver, and other choices as well as vegetables, spices, herbs, and oils. You gather your choices for a mixed-grill combination into a bowl and hand it to one of the cooks, who spreads it out on the restaurant's central grill. You don't have to duplicate Mongolian cuisine's hot spices, but my advice is not to be shy about seasonings and vegetables; if you're hesitant, your dish will be bland. At dinner, you can repeat as often as you like with new concoctions; at the less-expensive lunch price, you only get one try. The more expensive dinner buffet includes a slightly more unusual selection of ingredients. All menus come with rice and baked noodles. The place seems like an outpost in the Northeast Asian desert, especially when busy.

✪ **Picasso.** 88 Ha-Yarkon St. ☎ **03/510-27845.** Reservations recommended evenings. Light meals NIS 32–54 ($7–$11.80); main courses NIS 52–95 ($11.40–$21). AE, DC, MC, V. Daily 7am–3am. CONTINENTAL.

Located in a yellow-and-white International Style building from the late 1930s, Picasso offers a view of the sea, stylish but affordable food, and a '90s Tel Aviv ambience that is hard to beat. Great for light meals, elegant but hefty salads, and fine main courses, Picasso also becomes the quintessential yuppie meeting place for drinks, coffee, dessert, and talks late into the night. The best choices include goose liver terrine with sugared ginger; breast of mullard with spicy Thai sauce; and a variety of fresh grilled fish brushed with garlic, olive oil, and rosemary. Fresh mussels are flown in Mondays and Thursdays; you can have them Provenççal or Thai style with fan and button mushrooms, lemongrass, garlic, and soy sauce.

Shangri La. In the Astor Hotel, 105 Ha-Yarkon St. ☎ **03/523-8913.** Reservations recommended for evenings. Main courses NIS 45–85 ($10–$18.70); lunch special NIS 70 ($15.40). DC, MC, V. Sun–Thurs 12:30–midnight; Fri 12:30–4pm; Sat after Shabbat. KOSHER THAI.

This spacious restaurant, adorned with columns and capitals that hint at art deco Canaanite and with vistas that overlook the Mediterranean, is the setting for a menu prepared with lightness and elegance. You can order your dishes mild, hot, or fiery—mild does not mean you lose out on carefully prepared, exotic seasonings. Me krob crispy noodles with scallions; the tam yum soup filled with fried mushrooms, and onions in a garlic and lemongrass seasoning; the steamed bass in coconut milk; and the all-you-can-eat appetizer buffet set up for the lunch special, are real delights, as are the Thai desserts.

Whitehall Steakhouse. 6 Mendele St. ☎ **03/524-9282.** Main dishes NIS 55–114 ($12–$25); lunch specials NIS 55–90 ($12–$20). AE, DC, MC, V. Daily noon–midnight. STEAKS.

A modern, air-conditioned retreat near Ha-Yarkon Street in the heart of the tourist district, Whitehall's luncheon specials, which include salad bar, soft drink, beer or wine, bread, french fries or baked potato, your choice of sauces, and coffee or tea (served Sunday to Friday noon to 6pm), are an excellent value. Appetizers range from shrimps to pâté de foie gras and main courses from baby back ribs to shish kebabs, steaks, and prime ribs, all grilled on charcoal fires. An extra NIS 22 ($5) at dinner allows you to add the bottomless salad bar. There is also a dessert menu.

INEXPENSIVE

The Chicago Pizza Pie Factory. 63 Ha-Yarkon St. ☎ **03/517-7505.** Pizzas (for two people) NIS 45–85 ($10–$18.70). AE, DC, MC, V. Sun–Thurs 6pm–1am; Fri noon–3am; Sat noon–1:30am. PIZZA.

Chicago Pizza is a smash success among Israelis, and a natural attraction for visitors and international students because of its location in the Ha-Yarkon Street hotel area near the American embassy. It's a strange mix of seafront 1930s—modern Tel Aviv cement structure adorned with a touch of neon, and an interior that is a shrine to the history of Chicago. The restaurant also sports current sports videos, 1960s music, and upmarket deep-pan pizzas that are heavy on toppings but sometimes light on the seasonings and the color of the tomato sauce. People come for the scene as much as the pizza. There are salads, pastas, and doggie bags, in case you're alone and can't finish a two-person pizza at one sitting.

✪ **Yotvata in Town.** 76 Herbert Samuel Promenade. ☎ **03/510-4667.** Light meals NIS 22–35 ($4.65–$7.70); main courses NIS 33–75 ($7.20–$16.50). AE, DC, MC, V. Daily 7am–4am. DAIRY/VEGETARIAN.

The kind of restaurant Israelis loved best 30 years ago was a little place doing simple, freshly made salads, and good-quality dairy dishes. Popular Yotvata has carried this concept into the '90s and turned it into a bustling, high-powered, multistory emporium on the beachfront. Everything is made from the best-quality produce bought directly from kibbutzim and from the famous dairy kibbutz at Yotvata. For under $10 there are salads, cheese platters served with fresh herbs and vegetables, blintzes, pancakes, vegetable pies, pastas, and pizzas. At the upper end of the price range, you'll find a selection of fish, chicken, pasta, and hamburgers as well as bagels and lox. The mixtures of natural fruit juices are famous, as are Yotvata's many ice-cream parlor desserts.

ALONG BEN-YEHUDA STREET
MODERATE

Barbunya. 163 Ben-Yehuda St. ☎ **03/527-6965.** Reservations not accepted. Fixed-price meals NIS 56–68 ($12.30–$15). AE, DC, MC, V. Sat–Thurs noon–midnight; Fri noon–6pm. FISH.

Up near the Hilton Hotel, this no-frills restaurant serves fried and grilled fresh fish, and although the sign may not be in English, at lunch and dinnertime, you can often spot the place by the line of dedicated customers that extends out to the street. Once

> ## ⓘ Family-Friendly Restaurants
>
> **Spaghettim** *(see page 231)*, with its 60 spaghettis (including chocolate!), heads the list of good family choices, followed by the trendy **Yotvata** (a favorite of Tel Aviv teenagers and students *(see page 225)*, with its menu of delicious dishes and fruit drinks made from farm fresh products. No-frills **Barbunya** *(see page 225)*, near the hotel district, offers good fresh fish and very speedy service, with appetizers and seltzer included— get there early at dinnertime, before the lines form out to the street. **Abu Lafia**'s *(see page 238)* bread bakery in Jaffa sells wonderful Arabic pizzas and stuffed breads—bring lots of napkins and do a picnic in the nearby gardens of Old Jaffa.

inside, you'll find paper tablecloths and a choice of fish and shrimp, depending on the day's catch. There's a slightly higher price for red snapper, shrimp, and grouper. Fish is either grilled or fried in garlic and lemon, or butter, and comes with an array of Middle Eastern salads and club soda. Substitutions are not possible, but you do have the option of ordering dessert for an extra charge. Half a block north, across the street at 192 Ben Yehuda, Barbuna has a second, smaller location.

Osteria da Fiorella. 148 Ben-Yehuda. ☎ **03/527-4750.** Main courses NIS 36–75 ($8–$16.50). AE, DC, MC, V. Sun–Thurs noon–4pm and 7pm–midnight; Fri noon–3:30pm; Sat after Shabbat. ITALIAN.

This excellent nonkosher restaurant serves *"vera cucina italiana"* (authentic Italian cuisine) prepared by a family that immigrated to Israel from Rome in the early 1980s. There are two sparkling floors divided into cozy dining areas. The menu has most of the traditional Italian dishes, plus special Roman-Jewish home-style treats like straccotto—veal slowly cooked for Shabbat. The house Fiorella sauce is a wonderful creation.

INEXPENSIVE

Bebale. 177 Ben-Yehuda St. ☎ **03/546-7486.** Main courses NIS 30–45 ($6.60–$10). AE, DC, MC, V. Daily noon–midnight. EUROPEAN JEWISH.

Unlike many of its decades-old competitors (such as Batya over on Dizengoff), Bebale is new to the Yiddish cuisine just-like-Grandma-made game. Located near trendy North Tel Aviv, it has developed a discerning and devoted following of young professionals. Decor is simple, in keeping with the style of older establishments in this market, but the food is genuine and contains all the classics, with a tiny pinch of the '90s tossed in. Appetizers include pickled herrings, jellied calves' feet, and kreplach and matzoh-ball soups; on Saturdays, a Sabbath cholent of potatoes, meat, vegetable, and kishke is offered for $10. Main courses come with no side dishes—you'll pay extra for vegetables or a potato. The thick, fluffy, nongreasy potato-zucchini latkes ($2.50) are light, filling, and make a good minimeal or take-out snack.

Cafe Nordau. 145 Ben Yehuda St. ☎ **03/524-0134.** Main courses NIS 25–60 ($5.50–$13.20). Business lunch Sun–Thurs NIS 36 ($10). AE, DC, MC, V. Sun–Wed 8am–2am; Thurs–Sat 24 hours. CONTINENTAL.

A long-time landmark among local cafes, with round-the-clock weekend hours, this is a popular meeting place and draws part of its clientele from the gay community. The menu is not entirely vegetarian—you'll find items like schnitzel among the salads, soups, and pasta dishes. There are sidewalk tables and pets are permitted. You can stop in just for pastries (NIS 18 to 22/$5 to $6.20) and coffee.

✪ **Taste of Life.** 60 Ben-Yehuda St. ☎ **03/620-3151.** Main courses NIS 16–45 ($3.50–$10). MC, V. Sun–Thurs 9am–11pm; Fri 9am–2pm; Sat after Shabbat. VEGETARIAN.

You'll be amazed by this tiny no-frills restaurant's tasty natural vegetable meals: soy sausages, vegetarian shwarmas, wheat burgers, tofu falafels, vegetarian faux steak sandwiches, and soy ice creams. My favorite is the barbecued twist on whole wheat pita served with medium spicy sauce and homemade mustard. Founded by the Hebrew Israelites, an African-American religious group whose dietary laws prohibit milk or meat products, The Taste of Life uses no milk or meat, nothing is fried, there is no cholesterol, and almost no salt, yet everything tastes great. Other delicious choices here are steamed vegetables and veggie stir-fries, tofu cheeses in assorted flavors, and okira sticks that seem a bit like fish sticks! Drinks include juices, veggie coffee, and carob milk. For dessert there's soy ice cream and carob cakes and candies.

ALONG ALLENBY STREET & SOUTHWARD

This area, stretching from the beginning of Allenby Street south to the Tel Aviv–Jaffa border, is away from most tourist hotels, but it contains some of the best restaurants in the country. Some fine upper-bracket restaurants are located near the booming Tel Aviv stock exchange in the area between Ahad Ha-Am Street and Rothschild Boulevard. These places can be very busy at lunchtime, but in the evening, the mood is more relaxed.

EXPENSIVE

✪ **Capot Tmarim.** 60 Ahad Ha'Am St. ☎ **03/566-3166.** Reservations required. Dinner main courses NIS 120–140 ($26.40–$31). Complete fixed-price dinner NIS 200–250 ($44–$55). Complete fixed-price lunch NIS 75–125 ($21–$35). AE, MC, V. Sun–Fri 12:30–3:30pm; 7:30pm–last order taken at 10:30pm. FRENCH/MEDITERRANEAN RIM.

Dining here is an experience that is special to Tel Aviv. Ofer Gal has carefully set his restaurant in an enclave that evokes the feel of 1930s Tel Aviv design—a mix of International Style with Arabic floor tiles, hand-painted Armenian plates, and Biedermeirer-derived chairs that might have been brought by immigrants from Germany. The menu creations also encompass Tel Aviv's roots—sophisticated, international, but with Middle Eastern–inspired flourishes. The menu changes daily. In summer, you may find refreshing watermelon soup with feta cheese and mint; in winter, look for an earthy hummus soup with baked bread crust. First courses range from eggplant with mild Safed goat cheese, basil, and cherry tomato in pastry to veal sweetbreads and celery in pasta with cream capers sauce; the flambéed quail in salad with pâté is especially fine, and there is always a rich, fascinating foie gras choice. Saddle of lamb in red wine sauce served with remarkable miniature stuffed eggplants is done to perfection, with the meat rare and tender, the herbed skin crisp and flavorful; a sirloin of lamb with polenta and pesto lavishly blends traditions. There is a constantly changing array of fresh fish and poultry choices, all prepared with a light, inventive hand (delicately smoked mullard with balsamic vinegar and meat sauce is recommended). Desserts run around $10, and can be rich (vanilla cheesecake with fresh mango); light (fresh figs and sweet tomato with kitaif biscuits and anise sherbet); or creations steeped in local traditions, like a heavenly interpretation of Arabic mahalabi (thickened milk, rosewater, and cornflower) served with peanut and coconut ice cream, or a splendid date brioche. A careful wine list is served by the glass and bottle. Desserts cost around $10; main courses at lunch are less expensive than at dinner. A 12% service charge is added to each bill.

❍ **Keren.** 12 Eilat St., Jaffa. ☎ **03/518-1358** or 03/681-6565. Reservations required. Dinner main courses NIS 120–140 ($26.40–$31); fixed-price lunch NIS 115–140 ($25.30–$31). AE, DC, MC, V. Daily 7pm–midnight and Mon–Sat noon–4pm. FRENCH.

Perhaps the most charming of Israel's elegant dining establishments, Keren is housed in a restored antique wooden building with second-floor verandas, resembling a Caribbean planter's house. Brought by ship from America to the sand dunes of Jaffa in the 1860s, the building is even more incongruous today in the commercial and industrial neighborhood that has grown up around it. Step inside, however, and you are transported to a place of vision with an exceptional, constantly changing menu. Among Keren's famed first courses are a seafood salad heavy with calamari; calamari and yogurt on wild marrow; a delicate ravioli of calves' brains in a lemony veal consommé; and zucchini flowers stuffed with seafood. Foie gras is a specialty—the goose liver with techina on oven-roasted tomatoes is done with a nod to local flavors. Black olive soup with pita bread bruschetta is another twist on the tastes of Israel. Main courses could include sea bass in crab sauce, steak fillet with goat cheese in hot vinaigrette sauce, or fresh hake prepared with okra in a hyssop pesto. Desserts (included in the fixed-price lunch—a very good value) are magnificent. A dinner tasting menu is $73.

❍ **Mika.** 27 Montifiore St. ☎ **03/528-3255.** Reservations advised. Main courses NIS 62–110 ($13.60–24.20); fixed-price lunch NIS 75 ($16.50). DC, MC, V. Daily noon–2am. FUSION.

Mika's space is designed with an understated, minimalist style that creates a New York/SoHo kind of setting for its stylish, Asian-influenced menu—a menu that has taken Israeli food critics and restaurant goers by storm. There's an inventive sushi list, followed by remarkable appetizers that range from blue crab sautéed in sake, coconut milk and chili to arugula salad with tempura goat cheese in a miso balsamic vinaigrette. Main courses include seafood fettuccini in saffron and vegetable broth; barbecued spare ribs; seared foie gras with caramelized pear, Merlot, and blueberry sauce; sea bass in tamarind sauce; and five-spice breast of mullard (a duck/goose hybrid) with scallion pancakes. Desserts include a passion-fruit flan; a dynamite warm chocolate cake with vanilla ice cream; and tempura ice cream with caramel, chocolate sauce, and roasted almonds. An extensive bar and wine list keeps Mika going late into the night.

❍ **Yin Yang.** 60 Rothschild Blvd. ☎ **03/560-6833.** Reservations advised. Light meals or dim sum NIS 20–40 ($4.40–$8.80); main courses NIS 45–90 ($10–$20). Daily 12:30–11:30pm. AE, DC, MC, V. CHINESE.

This excellent Chinese restaurant could compete with the best of them in cities like New York, Paris, or San Francisco. Owner Israel Aharoni, at the forefront of Israel's restaurant revolution, has designed a menu more authentic and inventive than is usually found in a Chinese restaurant for Westerners. For a first course, sliced pork in spicy garlic sauce is recommended by Aharoni; I enjoyed the spicy cucumber salad. Duck dishes are famous here; try duck in honey garlic sauce. Among other dishes you won't find at most Israeli Chinese restaurants are calamari Szechuan style, beef in anise, and crab done in a number of interesting styles. You can come for dim sum daily from 4 to 6pm. Special dishes, like smoked duck, must be ordered in advance and are in the $40 price range.

MODERATE

❍ **Ali Oli Bar Restaurant.** 2 Brenner St. ☎ **03/528-1378.** Reservations recommended at night. Tapas and light meals NIS 25–70 ($5.50–$15.50); main courses NIS 75–115 ($16.50–$26.30). AE, DC, MC, V. Mon–Sat noon–2:30am. MEDITERRANEAN RIM.

This easygoing place looks like a small, simple restaurant with a large rear garden for dining in good weather, but it serves up the freshest calamari, mussels, and shrimps in town, singing with flavor and prepared to pure perfection with just the lightest touch of herbs, garlic, and olive oil. Culinary skill shows throughout the menu, which also includes heavenly meat empanadas, foie gras, and steaks as well as well as inventive vegetable tapas and antipasti. A paella for two that must be preordered is recommended. Monday to Thursdays there are complete lunch menus for $12 to $16. The spirit of Ali Oli is friendly and fun-loving, with a wide-ranging clientele enjoying exquisite food served without pretentiousness. A well-stocked bar includes a special "dream list" of wines carefully selected by Antonio, Ali Oli's Spanish owner/chef, who planned and created this Tel Aviv gem.

Apicius Restaurant-Bistro Wine Bar. 60 Rothschild Blvd. ☎ **03/560-5902.** Reservations useful. Main courses NIS 42–75 ($9.20–$16.50). AE, DC, MC, V. Sun–Fri 12:30pm–2am; Sat 7pm–2am. FRENCH/MEDITERRANEAN RIM.

Housed in an old Rothschild Boulevard mansion, with a dining veranda facing the shady street, and with a menu designed by Yuval Amirav, who has worked at Tel Aviv's gourmet Keren Restaurant (see above), Apicius is one of the most special but unpretentious choices in the city. By day, this is high-powered banking territory, but at night the clientele changes and the mood of Apicius is relaxed. There is always an array of superb tapas to be grazed upon slowly, and many dishes can be ordered as either first or second courses: shrimp in butter and crab sauce can be $5.50 or $8.80; goose liver in apple Calvados can be $9 or $15. The constantly changing menu offers divine reinterpretations of Eastern Mediterranean traditional dishes, like grape leaves stuffed with goat cheese, almonds, and confit of tomato; or lamb kebab with grape leaves and rich Arabic labeneh (yogurt). Order a main course done with the special Apicius sauce, an enticing, mysterious combination of caramel, orange, and meat stock. Belgian chocolate terrine and crème brûlée are desserts of choice. The restaurant slowly evolves into a wine bar during the late hours of the night.

Itamar. 12 Rothschild Blvd. ☎ **03/517-7403.** Reservations useful. Main courses NIS 44–85 ($9.70–$18.50). AE, DC, MC, V. Daily noon–3am. BISTRO.

A small, cozy place with a sidewalk terrace, this bar/bistro is a tiny, quiet slice of France tucked away among the glitzy dining and night spots along Rothschild Boulevard. The menu is traditional—well prepared and not compulsively inventive as the menus of so many Israeli French restaurants are—and the chef does not go lightly on butter and wine. House pâté of foie gras with mango is a recommended first course, and the rabbit in wine sauce or the herbed crepe filled with duck in cassis sauce are good main course choices, many of which are served with a puree of potato popular among Tel Aviv's French restaurants that I find bland and unappealing. The desert menu is filled with crepes and interesting varieties of mousse.

Kimmel. 6 HaShahar St. ☎ **03/510-5204.** Reservations necessary. Main courses NIS 55–100 ($12–$22). AE, DC, MC, V. Daily noon–after midnight (kitchen closes at 11pm). COUNTRY MEDITERRANEAN.

An old Tel Aviv building in the shadow of the Shalom Tower skyscraper houses this delightful place. At lunch, it's high-paced and filled with business people, but in the evenings, it becomes a cozy rustic retreat. The menu starts with earthy house bread and is flavored with lots of zataar (local spices) as well as dill, garlic, lemon and olive oil, and interesting sauces of wild berry/pepper, lemon/honey, fig, pistachio, or raisins. First courses include mushrooms stuffed with goose liver in plum and fig sauce; bouillabaisse; or calamari stuffed with risotto and seafood. Main courses range from tongue prepared in a sauce of tomato and meat stock to lamb chops in spicy barbecue sauce; ostrich fillet in curry, lemon and garlic; fillet mignon served with saffron and buttered shrimp or in a blackberry/pepper sauce; and trout, shrimp, sea bass, and Norwegian salmon, all prepared in inventive ways.

✪ **Lilith.** 42 Mazeh St. ☎ **03/629-8772.** Reservations recommended. Lunch main courses NIS 40–75 ($11.20–$21); dinner main courses NIS 50–115 ($14–$32.20). AE, DC, MC, V. Sun–Thurs 10am–midnight, Fri 10am–5pm, Sat 7pm–midnight. CONTEMPORARY MEDITERRANEAN RIM.

Every object in this sleek, glass-walled restaurant was chosen for its natural textures and clean, strong shapes and design. The menu is a perfect match: natural artistry that enhances the textures and superb quality of the ingredients. Lilith's owners are perfectionists who searched for years to find the right supplier for their succulent lamb chops; even the tiniest olive served here must be exquisite. Karen Hendler-Kremerman, one of the owners, is author of *The Art of Gourmet Grilling* (Multimedia Books, 1991), and her standards of exquisite simplicity shine in light first courses like salmon carpaccio served with cucumbers and fennel/mustard sauce, or the delicate squid salad, as well as in main courses like herb-crusted New York steak, sea scallops in rice vinegar sauce, and the fabulous salmon grilled with olive oil and herbs. There are also easy, unpretentious choices for a light meal here—the best grilled hamburger in the country; a hearty sandwich of avocado and marinated turkey breast, or a simple late-summer fig salad. A choice of excellent desserts and carefully selected wines round out Lilith's charms. Designer furniture, tableware, and other items are sold in a corner of the restaurant.

Pastalina. 16 Elifellet St. ☎ **03/683-6401.** Reservations required. Fixed-price menu NIS 100 ($22). AE, DC, MC, V. Sun–Fri 7pm–midnight; Sat noon–midnight. ITALIAN.

Located in an out-of-the-way spot on the Tel Aviv–Jaffa border, Pastalina, with its sleek glass-brick decor, is the trendy place to go for exciting pasta. The fixed-price menu, which changes daily, includes a splendid, inventive antipasti buffet, and a main-course choice of pasta, chicken, or fish. Always relaxing, worthwhile, and delicious.

INEXPENSIVE

Brew House. 11 Rothschild Blvd. ☎ **03/516-8666.** Light meals NIS 22–52 ($4.80–$11.50). Main courses NIS 50–90 ($11–$19.80). AE, DC, MC, V. Daily noon–1 or 2am. INTERNATIONAL.

Set in a microbrewery on a trendy section of Rothschild Boulevard, this is a bustling, snazzy place with live jazz, swing, and blues on Friday afternoons and Sunday evenings. Glistening brewery paraphernalia winds its way like a sculptural installation through the multilevel space and provides dark, alelike designer beers with 4.7% to 6% alcohol content. You can have a hot dog with mustard, a hefty $11 hamburger, assorted pub snacks, sausages with sauerkraut, or a pile of spicy buffalo wings (two sizes), spare ribs in hoisin sauce, Malaysian chicken, or a lettuce and goat cheese salad in sesame vinaigrette. Business lunches are NIS 30 to 40 ($6.60 to $8.80); beer runs NIS 10 to 24 ($2.20 to $5.30).

Shao Lin Dim Sum and Noodle Restaurant. 31 Montefiore St. ☎ **03/566-5870.** Dim sum (by the piece) NIS 5–8 ($1.10–$1.76); noodles and main courses NIS 23–NIS 40 ($5.10–$8.80) AE, DC, MC, V. Daily noon–11pm. CHINESE.

This inexpensive, fun place is the brainchild of Israel Aharoni, owner of the nearby and more upmarket Yin Yang. You can sample from among 20 exquisitely presented cold salads (about $1 per 100 grams) and 25 different kinds of steamed or fried dim sum, or choose from a wide range of noodles served with vegetables, chicken, pork, or seafood. Sunday to Thursday from noon 6pm, a "Business Lunch" of salad, dim sum, and noodles is offered for just under $7; evenings and weekends the menu expands to

An Ethnic Dining Experience

If you want to sample Tel Aviv's most authentic Middle Eastern food at bargain prices and are willing to take a 15-minute bus ride, **Etzel Street** in the **Hatikvah District of South Tel Aviv** is the place to explore. Pick up southbound bus no. 16 on Allenby Street near Moghrabi Square, and ask the driver to let you off at Rehov Etzel in Hatikvah. Probably Tel Aviv's best-kept restaurant secret, Hatikvah is a vast area inhabited by Israeli families from countries like Yemen and Iraq, and lengthy Etzel Street is virtually wall-to-wall with restaurants serving skewered meats, oriental salads, and delicious Iraqi pita breads that the waiters obtain straight from the ovens of the many bakeries that dot the street—one of Etzel Street's mottoes is that Iraqi pita more than 3 minutes old is stale. Here you can purchase your meals by the skewer, which means you can put together a skewer of beef and a skewer of turkey breast (about $3.50 each in most places) plus a salad and chips (french fries) ($2 each), and come up with a tasty, filling meal for less than $10. Or you can be more daring and order breast of goose and chicken hearts and livers for the same price per skewer. The pièce de résistance of Etzel Street restaurants is the enormously rich but delicate goose-liver skewer, barbecued to perfection and going for $6 to $7. The street is like a food festival; just pick out a place that looks busy and interesting (preferably next door to a bread bakery) and grab yourself a table.

include a wide range of chicken, duck, pork, beef and vegetarian main courses, each prepared with Aharoni's special touch, and all very reasonably priced. Desserts range from steamed chocolate dumplings and fried wonton stuffed with dates to lotus cakes and coconut balls. Asian beers, wines, and sake are served.

✪ **Spaghettim.** 18 Yavne St. ☎ **03/566-4479.** Reservations recommended. Spaghetti NIS 22–55 ($5–$12.10). AE, DC, MC, V. Daily noon–1am. ITALIAN.

This is a restaurant that can make you fall in love with spaghetti. There are more than 50 kinds of interesting sauces, ranging from traditionals like carbonara and all'arrabbiata to unusual creations like an olive oil–based sauce filled with breast of tender, fresh sautéed chicken, dill, garlic, and lemon; or a salmon and asparagus sauce with white wine and nutmeg. Soups and salads, like the spaghetti dishes, are filled with fresh herbs and vegetables and are hefty in size. For dessert, there's a choice of pannecotta, Italian ice creams, and al dente spaghetti with dark chocolate, ice cream, and brandy sauce, or poppy seeds. Delicious, filling, imaginative, and with many choices under $8, the restaurant's charge of $2 for home-style bread, does not seem unfair. A selection of Israeli and imported wines are available.

YEMENITE QUARTER & CARMEL MARKET

Walk along Allenby Street from Moghrabi Square. At 54 Allenby St., turn right and walk to the grid of little streets at its far end. This is the Yemenite Quarter (Karem Ha-Teimanim), a favorite of Tel Avivans and visitors alike. Don't let the neighborhood's appearance rattle you—the people here are honest and respectable, and it's a perfectly safe area to traverse. Built in 1909, this is one of the oldest parts of the city. Its tangled streets harbor many restaurants; they are not especially Yemenite, but that serve some of the tastiest Middle Eastern food. Some restaurants in the quarter have become pricey and tourist oriented; below are some of the best.

MODERATE

Maganda Restaurant. 26 Rabbi Meir St. ☎ **03/517-9990.** Reservations recommended. Main courses NIS 30–70 ($6.60–$15.40). No credit cards. Sun–Thurs noon–midnight; Sat after Shabbat. YEMENITE/MIDDLE EASTERN.

The Maganda has recently been remodeled, and is now airy, modern, and very attractive. The cuisine is Yemenite Middle Eastern, strictly kosher, and includes grilled meats such as lamb shashlik, kabob, and skewered duck. The menu is in English and Hebrew. In summer, the restaurant offers rooftop dining.

To get there, enter the Yemenite Quarter, turn right at the end of the alley, then left onto Najara Street.

Shaul's Inn. 11 Eliashiv St. ☎ **03/517-7619.** Reservations recommended. Main courses NIS 30–70 ($6.60–$15.40). AE, DC, V. Sun–Thurs noon–midnight; Fri noon–3pm; Sat after Shabbat. MIDDLE EASTERN.

The remodeled, enlarged blockbuster of this neighborhood, with heavy wooden chairs, flagstone floors, and a large photomural of a Yemenite wedding on one wall, this kosher restaurant at the corner of Eliashiv can get packed to the street on Saturday nights. Stick to the main room on the ground floor; downstairs, where there is an intimate restaurant and bar, the prices go up by more than 100%. English is spoken here, and the waiters will help you choose from the Middle Eastern specialties. The "Specialty of the Inn" is the lamb's breast stuffed with rice and pine nuts—deliciously tasty. Have a Turkish or Greek salad, or a gorgeous stuffed eggplant, cabbage, or pepper.

To get there, go west down Ge'ulah Street off Allenby; half a block down Ge'ulah, make a diagonal left turn onto Ha-Ari Street; turn right onto Rabbi Meir Street, then left onto Kehilat Aden Street.

SHEINKIN STREET

Beginning on the west side of Allenby Street, across from the Carmel Market, Sheinkin Street is sometimes called Tel Aviv's Greenwich Village. It's a mix of cafes, unusual to offbeat shops, and family stores—a stroll and a meal here lets you sample a slice of Tel Aviv life away from the Hotel District and the beaches. King George Street, which makes a "V" with Sheinkin Street at Allenby, is home to a number of excellent and reasonably priced bakeries if you'd like a snack to take back to your hotel room.

Cafe Kazzeh. 19 Sheinkin St. ☎ **03/629-3756.** Light meals NIS 24–50 ($5.30–$11); fish courses up to NIS 75 ($16.50). AE, DC, MC, V. Sun–Thurs 8:30am–midnight, Fri 8:30am–4pm; Sat after Shabbat. VEGETARIAN/CAFE.

The most famous of the cafe/restaurants on Sheinkin Street, from the outside Cafe Kazzeh looks small, but it stretches back to a hidden rear garden. The small high-ceiling rooms offer a homey sense of intimacy and perhaps remind yuppies from North Tel Aviv of their grandparents' British Mandate–era apartments. There are salads, pastas, vegetable pies, and a popular dish of vegetable couscous as well as coffees and cakes on the menu (the orange-chocolate cake is a specialty). Wine by the glass is $3.50; by the bottle $18 to $22. People come here for conversation and the mildly bohemian ambience, but the cafe would not be so successful without food that's a cut above the rest.

IN & AROUND DIZENGOFF SQUARE
MODERATE

✪ **Tandoori.** In the Dizengoff Square Hotel, 2 Zamenhoff St. ☎ **03/629-6185.** Reservations recommended. Main courses NIS 25–64 ($5.50–$14.10; all-you-can-eat lunch buffet

NIS 55 ($12.10) plus 10% service charge. AE, DC, MC, V. Daily 12:30–3:30pm and 7pm–1am. INDIAN.

Why visit an Indian restaurant in Israel? Only for some of the best food, most relaxing but elegant ambience, and pleasant service in Tel Aviv. Tandoori is serenely presided over by Vinod Pushkarna and his wife, Reena, whose Jewish Bombay heritage helped to create the restaurant's special atmosphere. Try the ever-changing all-you-can-eat daily luncheon buffet, one of the best values in town, or share a succulent plate of boneless tandoori chicken with rice and side dishes. Two can easily dine in the $15 per person range. You can also have an extensive multicourse feast. I especially like the chicken dishes served in skewered chunks, like the boneless breast of chicken marinated in mint and herbs; the fabulous chicken tikka masala; the giant prawns in ginger, and a dry sautéed vegetable dish so light and elegant it almost seems to herald an Indian nouvelle cuisine. The homemade dessert dumplings and Indian ice creams made of thickened milk and dried fruits and nuts are very interesting. Ask about lassi, Tandoori's refreshing chilled yogurt and fruit drink.

INEXPENSIVE

○ **Batya.** 197 Dizengoff St. ☎ **03/527-3888.** Main courses NIS 23–39 ($5–$8.60). V. Daily 11am–10pm. EUROPEAN/JEWISH.

Strangely enough, trendy Tel Aviv remains Israel's center for East European Jewish cooking, and Batya, presided over by the wonderful Batya Yom Tov, is one of the oldest restaurants specializing in this tradition. You'll step into a delicious, precholesterol-conscious world of kreplach, golden chicken soup, chopped liver, stew, duck with Polish mustard sauce, baked Shabbat pudding, and brisket with potatoes. Decor is no-frills, and a good part of Batya's clientele has probably been patronizing the restaurant since it was established in 1941.

NEAR IBN GIVROL STREET, HA-BIMAH & MANN AUDITORIUM

Ibn Givol Street runs through Tel Aviv's center of culture, from the Cinémathèque at the corner of Ibn Givrol Street and Rehov Ha-Arba'a northward to Shderot Shaul Ha Melekh where you'll find the Tel Aviv Museum of Art and Golda Meir Performing Arts Center; the Ha Bima National Theater and Mann Auditorium are just 2 blocks west of Ibn Givrol on Dizengoff. This area is lined with restaurants, including choices for fine dining as well as places for quick meals and after performance coffee and cake.

EXPENSIVE

○ **Roshfeld.** 23 Shaul Ha Melekh Blvd. ☎ **03/609-4666.** Reservations recommended. Main courses NIS 95–150 ($21–$33); business lunch NIS 90–120 ($19.80–$22). AE, DC, MC, V. Daily 12:30–3pm and 7:30pm–midnight. Last order taken at 11pm. FRENCH.

The latest of Tel Aviv's elegant places to dine, this is a showcase for the talent of Jonathan Roshfeld, acclaimed by many as the best chef in the country, with a resume that includes Israel's most sublime restaurants. Roshfeld's ever-changing menu follows a path that runs between classic and nouvelle cuisine, but it always stays close to perfection. Appetizers include carpaccio of grouper, enhanced with balsamic vinaigrette and sliced razor thin; or a rich foie gras with green apple puree. Among main courses, Roshfeld's meat, seafood, and poultry dishes are prepared with fine olive oil, wines, herbs, and butter. The delicate, flavorful "Seven Hours" lamb falls off the bone and melts in your mouth; grilled shrimps in herb butter, or sea wolf in herbs with white wine are simple yet perfect. Dessert chef Eran Shwartzbard provides a menu unequalled in Israel and the broad wine list and sommelier rounds out the formal, professional service. The restaurant's minimalist, white-on-shades-of-white design is restrained and formal, but enlivened by an open kitchen. A complete gourmet tasting menu is NIS 300 ($66). A meal for two could run from $100 to $150, ordering modestly from the wine list. A 12% service charge is added to each bill.

MODERATE

Papagaio. 14 Ha'arba'a St. ☎ **03/562-6888.** Reservations recommended. Dinner NIS 100 ($22). Lunch NIS 66 ($14.70). AE, DC, MC, V. Sun–Fri noon–4pm and 7pm–midnight; Sat 12:30pm–midnight. SOUTH AMERICAN MEAT GRILL.

Israelis love this all-you-can-eat meal grill where you pay a fixed price and take whatever you like from skewer-carrying waiters, or roasts and steaks fresh off the fire. The meats are done in Argentinean style, seasoned with salt, pepper, and served with chimichanga sauces as well as with a table full of interesting salads, tapas, and vegetables. At dinner, the choices include 10 to 12 kinds of meats as well as fish, chicken, and chorizo; the lunch menu is limited to seven choices, and the popular grilled salmon is available only at dinner. Drinks and dessert are extra; there is a 10% service charge. On Wednesday, Thursday, and Friday evenings there is live entertainment starting around 9:30pm.

INEXPENSIVE

❖ **Erez Lehem.** 52 Ibn Givrol St. ☎ **03/696-9381.** Sandwiches NIS 16–26 ($3.50–$5.70). Business lunch NIS 30–35 ($6.60–$7.70). AE, DC, MC, V. Daily 8am–1am. SANDWICHES/SALADS.

Erez Komarovsky's wonderful gourmet bread bakery/restaurant in upmarket Herzlia has become a local legend, and although you have to go up to Herzlia to try the complete Erez restaurant, a number of Erez Lehem (Erez Bread) bakery cafes have opened throughout the Tel Aviv area. At press time, this one is the most accessible to travelers. Indoors, there are a few pocket-size tables beside the inviting bread counter, but there's also a wide, covered sidewalk filled with roomier tables. There are constantly changing lists of sandwiches designed by Erez, all made with top-quality ingredients, the contents richly herbed and drizzled with olive oil (a salami, fig, arugula, and buffalo-milk cheese sandwich was delicious); there are also platters and salads, but who could pass up Erez's bread? Erez's dessert list is also legendary, with chocolate fondant, ice creams, muffins, cheese cakes, lemon tart, and decadent brownies among the rich creations. The business lunch, served from 11am to 5pm, includes a sandwich, salad, hot or cold drink, and dessert! The menu is in Hebrew, but the waitresses will patiently translate. A great place for an after-performance coffee and dessert. Takeout is available.

Giraffe Noodle Bar. 49 Ibn Givrol St. ☎ **03/691-6294.** Main courses NIS 33–55 ($7.25–$12.10) AE, DC, MC, V. Daily noon–1am. ASIAN.

Stylish but casual, with sidewalk tables in good weather, Giraffe serves up a variety of delicate, quality gyoza (dumplings), Asian salads, dim sum, and sushi. The spicy egg noodles with chopped shrimp, pork, and goose breast is the house specialty, but you'll also find a range of Japanese, Thai, and Chinese noodle dishes. French-style desserts here are extremely good, and add a touch of elegance, especially if you're combining a meal here with a concert or performance.

Movenpick Marché. 2 Shaul Ha Melekh Blvd. ☎ **03/609-2387.** Main courses NIS 35–70 ($7.70–$15.40). AE, DC, MC, V. Daily 11:30am–midnight. Espresso Bar and Bakery Sun–Fri 5am–midnight or later; Sat 9am–midnight. INTERNATIONAL.

The Movenpick Marché is a Swiss phenomenon spreading to many countries, including the United States. You'll find a vast market area filled with stalls of fresh produce, breads, cheeses, fish, and meats, all of which are turned into salads and stir-fries, or grilled or baked before your eyes. There are stalls for pizza, pasta, Far Eastern foods, grilled or fried fish, sautéed shrimps and calamari, and barbecued meats as well as bakeries, desserts, and a booth selling Movenpick's famed Swiss ice cream. You take your choice, cafeteria-style, to your table—in some ways it's like an inventive, quality food court in a shopping mall. There are business lunch specials until 4pm priced in the $7 to $10 range. Try the Espresso Bar Bakery with a sidewalk cafe at the entrance to the complex: here you can have coffee and a fine dessert or a light meal after catching a performance or visiting the nearby Tel Aviv Museum of Art.

NORTH BY THE YARKON RIVER

The neighborhood, just south of the Yarkon River, sometimes called Little Tel Aviv, is centered on Yirmiyahu Street, a short street near the point where Ben-Yehuda and Dizengoff streets meet, a block from the bend in the Yarkon. Take a bus or a cab north on Ha-Yarkon, Ben-Yehuda, or Dizengoff all the way to Yirmiyahu.

EXPENSIVE

✪ **Mul Yam.** Tel Aviv Port. ☎ **03/546-9920.** Reservations necessary. Main courses NIS 85–180 ($18.70–$40). AE, DC, MC, V. Daily 12:30–3:30pm and 7:30–10:30pm. Bus: 4 or 5. SEAFOOD.

The name of this cutting-edge new seafood restaurant/oyster bar is a Franco-Hebrew pun: "Mul Yam" means "facing the sea." The moules (mussels) are flown in several times a week from Brittany, becoming moules au gratin or moules and pasta with garlic and fresh herbs. Here you can watch fresh-off-the-plane oysters being consumed by Tel Aviv's nonkosher elite. You may not have come to Israel for French shellfish, but the kitchen is excellent, inventive, and written up in the *New York Times.* Main courses include a dynamite cold lobster salad, pumpkin and ricotta ravioli with shrimp and clams in lobster sauce, and grilled red mullet on black (squid ink) pasta. Whole grilled Nova Scotia lobster starts at $40.

MODERATE

Red Chinese Restaurant. 326 Dizengoff. ☎ **03/546-6347.** Reservations recommended evenings. Main courses NIS 35–80 ($7.70–$17.50). AE, DC, MC, V. Daily 1pm–midnight. Bus: no. 4 or 5 to end of Dizengoff or Ben-Yehuda. CHINESE.

With the exception of the world-class Yin Yang in South Tel Aviv (see above), this is the best Chinese restaurant in town and has thrived for years in one of the city's most sophisticated, affluent neighborhoods. It's a bit more affordable than Ying Yang, with the kind of menu familiar to those who frequent Chinese restaurants in England or America. Not kosher, it offers shrimp and calamari dishes as well as a wide range of duck, fish, pork, chicken, and vegetarian choices. There is also a small Thai-style menu. Wine and beer are served.

Yakimono. 5 Yodei Ha'sira St. ☎ **03/544-3864.** Reservations useful. Main courses NIS 33–65 ($7.20–$14.30). AE, DC, MC, V. Daily noon–1:30am. JAPANESE/SUSHI.

With a 22-year run, Yakimono is the oldest sushi restaurant in Tel Aviv—other places come and go, but no one else has mastered the long-term logistics of obtaining and serving the freshest fish possible for sushi and sashimi. You'll always find a changing selection of fresh sushi and sashimi of the day, as well as shrimp, cuttlefish, octopus, and eel, along with tempuras and ramen noodle soups. The restaurant is justly proud of its seaweed, cucumber-skin, and salmon-skin hand rolls. There is an authentic sushi counter as well as tables in a large enclosed sidewalk veranda. A kosher Yakimono has been set up at the Hilton Hotel, where not only must requirements of kashruth be maintained, but also a demanding Japanese clientele must be satisfied.

Yo Si Peking. 32 Yirmiyahu St. ☎ **03/544-3687.** Main courses NIS 40–80 ($8.80–$17.60). AE, DC, MC, V. Sun–Thurs noon–midnight, Fri noon–3pm, Sat after Shabbat to midnight. GLATT KOSHER CHINESE.

Although by no means a budget restaurant, this busy establishment usually comes in a few shekels less than the other kosher Chinese choices in town. There's an extensive selection of dishes done in a variety of styles that are tasty, if not high on either Chinese American or Chinese authenticity. Soups here are rich and filling. Chicken, vegetarian, and noodle dishes are in the lower price range; beef, duck, fish, and veal choices are at the more expensive end.

INEXPENSIVE

Hungarian Blintzes. 35 Yirmyahu St. ☎ **03/605-0674.** Main courses NIS 30–40 ($6.60–$8.80). AE, DC, MC, V. Sun–Thurs 12:30–1am; Sat after Shabbat. Bus: 4. BLINTZES.

Blintzes, or doughy crepes filled with either sweet or savory ingredients, are a well-loved East and central European tradition. At this long-running blintz paradise, the dozens of choices are all nonmeat, and run from mushroom goulash in paprika blintzes to sweet cheese or apple and cinnamon, all served with a dollop of sour cream if you choose. There are good soups and salads to round out a meal. At the holiday of Shavu'ot, when dairy dishes are traditionally eaten, you'll need a reservation just to get near the place.

Shtsupak Fish Restaurant. 256 Ben Yehuda St. ☎ **03/544-1973.** Reservations recommended evenings. Complete meals NIS 55–75. ($12.10–$16.50). AE, DC. Mon–Sat noon–midnight. FISH/SEAFOOD.

Well worth a trek or taxi ride from the hotel district, the bustling Shtsupak serves wonderful fresh fish and is a bit better and more atmospheric than its rival down Ben Yehuda Street, Barbunya, which is closer to most hotels (see above). Both places are functional, no frills, and serve excellent fresh grilled or fried fish and shrimp that comes with a big mezze (selection of Middle Eastern salads) included in the price; Shtsupak has a sidewalk dining terrace, a somewhat more leisurely pace, and usually comes out ahead of Barbunya in its salads, sauces, and size of its portions.

ON ALMAH BEACH NORTH OF JAFFA
MODERATE

✪ **Manta Ray.** Almah Beach Near Dan Panorama Hotel. ☎ **03/517-4774.** Reservations recommended; necessary summer evenings. Main courses NIS 65–90 ($14.30–$19.80). DC, MC, V. Daily 9am–midnight. Bus: 10 from Tel Aviv to Jaffa; get out at the Intercontinental Hotel stop. SEAFOOD.

The quintessential beach restaurant, Manta Ray is an open air pavilion that looks out on the rolling surf of an empty stretch of Tel Aviv's coast, and is perfectly positioned to catch the sun setting over the Mediterranean. The food is simply prepared, but full of flavor and inventiveness. Manta Ray is famous for its plate of 12 ever-changing small appetizers at 11 shekels apiece. It's always an interesting combination of traditional Middle Eastern as well as very contemporary or exotic dishes and comes with wonderful bread. This platter can easily be shared, and allows you to sample the kitchen while enjoying the view (discuss what the selection will be with the waiter). Main courses come with green salad, and a pile of delicious sliced, grilled sweet potatoes. Among my favorites are the grilled shrimp; the sage-scented sea bass fillet, and the fried calamari, but it's virtually impossible to go wrong with any of the main courses. There are good, $4 to $7 breakfasts here in the morning, and showers on the beach, in case you'd like to use this as your swimming beach. Note that unlike Tel

Aviv's more northern beaches, Almah beach is not protected by stone breakwaters, and although there are lifeguards, the sea here is treacherous, especially in the afternoon. The atmosphere here is informal, and you can feel as comfortable ordering a light meal as with a major feast.

JAFFA
EXPENSIVE

✪ **Margaret Tayar's.** 4 Retsif Ha-Aliyah Shenei St. ☎ **03/682-4741.** Reservations recommended. Always call to check opening hours. Main courses NIS 60–95 ($13.20–$21). No credit cards. Oct 1–May 31, Mon–Sat 1–7pm; June 1–Sept 30, Mon–Fri noon–4pm, 7pm–midnight, Sat noon–7pm. Closed Sun. Bus: 10 to Jaffa Clock Tower. SEAFOOD.

This fish restaurant, a landmark for Jaffa and Tel Aviv locals, has regularly made the top of the Ten Best Restaurants in Israel list put out each year by *Ma'ariv*, one of the country's largest newspapers. In the worst of winter, it's a four-table affair with a seafaring interior, but as soon as the warmer weather arrives, the restaurant expands its easygoing spirit into a large covered terrace overlooking the sea. Whatever the season, you know you are in the presence of an inspired cook who loves to see people enjoying her creations. Portions are enormous, and everything is delicious, whether you choose deep-fried fillet of fish stuffed with "caviar"; rolled grape leaves filled with rice, nuts, and raisins served in yogurt and herbed olive oil; baked artichoke stuffed with a smooth, creamy ground lamb filling; superb couscous; or masterfully seasoned whole grilled fish. Margaret Tayar makes everything herself each day, from the marinated North African salads and spicy fish sauces (which you might want served on the side) to the strudel filled with Middle Eastern fruits (order the strudel at the start of your meal, so it will be fresh from the oven in time for dessert). She is always whipping up masterpiece tidbits and she'll be happy to help you put together a dinner that displays the wonders of her kitchen for NIS 115 to 160 ($25 to $35) per person (although portions here are so large that two can easily share this kind of feast).

Shirat Hayam. 33 Hatzorfim St. ☎ **03/681-3271.** Reservations recommended. Main courses NIS 65–90 ($14.30–$20). MC, V. Sun–Thurs noon–midnight; Sat evening from 1¹/₂ hrs after the end of Shabbat to midnight. Closed Fri. Bus: 10 to Jaffa Clock Tower. GLATT KOSHER FISH & MEAT.

Set in an evocative, restored building in the gardens at the top of the hill of Old Jaffa (near the Hammam), this restaurant offers wonderful views, and fish and meat dishes all done with a special touch. Among the first courses you'll find kosher "shrimp" in sesame, and salmon pâé; excellent fresh fish that can be ordered in a number of different ways is a major attraction here, but the Shirat Hayam baked duck is also quite famous. Most main courses come with a big mezze of 14 salads and side dishes. There is a large selection of interesting desserts and kosher ice creams.

✪ **Taboon.** Inside Jaffa Port. ☎ **03/681-6011** or 03/681-1176. Reservations recommended. Main courses NIS 75–140 ($8–$31). AE, DC, MC, V. Daily 12:30pm–midnight. Bus: 10 from Tel Aviv. SEAFOOD.

White minimalist decor is the setting for a menu filled with fish and seafood that are breathtakingly light and fresh, prepared in a special taboon oven that preserves moisture and enhances flavor. There are many inventive appetizers served as small mezze dishes, so you have a chance to try a number of unusual creations. I've found these first courses to be fascinating but at times uneven; don't go overboard with first courses, but put your money on the more dependable entrees. Among those, you'll find fresh shrimps or fish, taboon-baked with fresh herbs and served in a variety of sauces (simple olive oil and balsamic vinegar is recommended); spicy seafood ragout; and excellent salmon ravioli. Grouper here is excellent in all forms and meats are also available. There's live classical music or jazz on varying afternoons and evenings.

If you come by bus, ask the driver for the Old Jaffa (Yafo Atik) stop closest to Jaffa Port; if you're coming to Jaffa Port after a stroll through Old Jaffa, it's a 10-minute walk south of the restored area of Old Jaffa.

✪ **Yoe'ezer Wine Bar.** Yefet St. opposite the Clock Tower. ☎ **03/683-9115.** Reservations advisable. Main courses NIS 50–100 ($11–$22). AE. DC, MC, V. Daily 1pm–1am. CONTINENTAL.

The creation of Shaul Evron, an Israeli journalist and food writer, Yoe'ezer Wine Bar is a gourmand's dream tucked under the cavernous arches of a building that goes back to Crusader times. Here you can sit for hours talking and sampling excellent wines and brandies as well as fine breads and cheeses, a rich pâté de campagne, a confit de fois gras, antipasti as beautiful as a still life, exquisite veal liver (usually fresh on Mondays), and oysters flown in from Brittany at the week's end. You can keep things simple, or go on to main course choices that include prime ribs and a memorable beef bourguignonne, or a fine, thick heart of entrecôte steak. Quality and skill show in everything, and prices are reasonable enough that you can put together a virtual banquet. A plate of fine Israeli cheese and bread is NIS 32 ($7), and the wine list runs from expensive imports to well chosen and very reasonably priced Israeli wines. Desserts are splendid, starting with Belgian chocolate cake.

The wine bar is on the inland (east) side of Yefet Street, a few feet down an alley opposite the Clock Tower.

INEXPENSIVE

Aladin. 5 Mifratz Shlomo St. ☎ **03/682-6766.** Reservations not accepted. Main courses NIS 44–75 ($9.70–$16.50). AE, MC, V. Daily 11am–1am. MIDDLE EASTERN/EUROPEAN.

The food here is average, but you couldn't ask for a more wonderful setting in which to dine: a 600-year-old building with covered terraces overlooking the sea and a spectacular view of the Tel Aviv coastline. The building's interior (at one point in its long history a Turkish bath) is decorated with exotic metalwork. This is the place to order a selection of Middle Eastern salads with pita bread, or have a slow unhurried meal of grilled fish or meat while watching the sunset. The atmosphere is informal and congenial and there's a good selection of wines, teas, and coffees.

✪ **Said el Abu Lafia and Sons Pita Bakery.** 7 Yefet St. ☎ **03/683-4958.** Baked goods NIS 8–16 ($1.75–$3.50). Mon–Sat 8am–10pm. Bus: 10 to Clock Tower. BREAD BAKERY.

Near the Clock Tower, this bakery is a Tel Aviv institution and offers fresh-from-the-oven breads, delicious one-person Palestinian pita-bread pizzas, and peasant-style cheese, potato, and vegetable bourekas and stuffed breads any one of which is a meal in itself. Everything is takeout and the parks and vista points of Old Jaffa across the street and up the hill are ideal for picnics. Don't confuse Abu Lafia's with neighboring imitations. Bring lots of napkins.

JABALYA BEACH

A mile and a half south of Old Jaffa and the Port Area is Jabalya (in Hebrew sometimes "Givat Aliya") Beach. You need a car or a taxi to get to this out-of-the-way area. Tel Avivians in the know patronize the excellent seafood restaurants here, enjoying the unobstructed views of the sunset. Long neglected, this neighborhood is starting to become a piece of prime residential real estate. Don't try swimming here—its all rocky ledge.

MODERATE

✪ **Abu Nassar On The Hill Fish and Seafood Restaurant.** 130 Kedem St., Donolo area, Jabalya (Givat Aliya) Beach, Jaffa. ☎ **03/507-5539** or 03/506-7132. Reservations necessary Thurs–Sat. Main courses NIS 70–100 ($15.40–$22). AE, DC, MC, V. Daily noon–midnight. FISH.

The venerable Abu Nassar restaurant now holds forth in a large modern glass pavilion with a thatch-roofed terrace for dining and taking in the sunset. Here you can be sure of fresh fish and good portions for a fair price. Early in the evening, you'll find both Israeli Arab and Jewish families enjoying everything on their plates. Later, the atmosphere is more leisurely. To start the meal there's a traditional mezze of excellent Arabic salads at NIS 16 ($3.50) per person for six selections, served with a basket of toasted garlic pita. As a first course, or as a larger main course, the fresh calamari stuffed with shrimps, pine nuts, and parsley in garlic and butter sauce is exquisitely rich and succulent. Grilled sea bass usually tops the list of fresh fish selections, all served with chips (french fries) and vegetables; you can also have grilled shrimp or even steak if a non-fish eater is in your group.

5 Attractions

THE TOP ATTRACTIONS
MUSEUMS

Ben-Gurion House. 17 Ben-Gurion Blvd. ☎ **03/522-1010.** Free admission. Sun, Tues–Thurs 8am–3pm; Mon 8am–5pm; Fri 8am–noon; first Sat of each month 11am–2pm. Bus: 4 or 5.

The house and personal items remain as they were when Paula and David Ben-Gurion lived here. Ben-Gurion's impressive personal library, comprising some 20,000 books, bears witness to his knowledge and scholarship. Most of the signs in the museum are in Hebrew only, but this will not detract much from your visit. In the bedroom, there is a blocked-in window that was used as a bomb shelter.

Bet Bialik Museum. 22 Bialik St. ☎ **03/525-4530.** Free admission. Sun–Thurs 9am–4:30pm; Sat 11am–2pm. Closed Sat in Aug and Fri year-round. Bus: 4.

From 1925 to 1933 this was the home of the first great modern Hebrew poet, Haim Nachman Bialik. The 94 books he wrote, with translations in 28 languages, are here, as are articles, correspondence, paintings, photographs, and an archive of hundreds of his manuscripts. If you understand Hebrew or Yiddish, the guides can tell you many interesting stories about the famous writer. The decor and atmosphere of the house gives you a feel for the world of the cultured, European-oriented Tel Aviv community of the 1920s. A wonderful collection of paintings by Jewish artists from the pre–State of Israel era, filled with visions of the life and landscape of British Mandate Palestine, is an additional pleasure at this gem of a museum. Combine this stop with a visit to the neighboring Rubin Museum (see below).

✪ **Bet Hatfutzot.** The Nahum Goldmann Museum of the Jewish Diaspora. Tel Aviv University campus. ☎ **03/646-2020.** www.bh.org.il. Admission NIS 30 ($6.60). AE, DC, MC, V. Discounts for students and seniors. Sun–Tues and Thurs 10am–4pm; Wed 10am–6pm; Fri 9am–1pm. Bus: 7, 24, 25, 45, 49, 74, 86, or 274.

This extraordinary museum in Ramat Aviv, off Klausner Street inside the Matatia Gate (University Gate 2), was the brainchild of Dr. Nahum Goldmann, founder and first president of the World Jewish Congress. In the huge, strikingly modern building are countless artful exhibits that chronicle the 2,500-year history of the Jewish Diaspora.

The collection contains no objects from the past, but is rather a multimedia history lesson: Here is what happened to the Jewish people, and what they accomplished, between the time when they were driven from Israel and the time when they returned. Photographs, documents, replicas of artifacts, films, music, maps, and scale models vividly bring to life the communities, synagogues, households, and workshops of Jews living in dozens of countries. There is an introductory Chronosphere (slide projection lecture) about the Diaspora for an extra fee (if you already know the basics of Jewish history, skip it). Among the highlights are a model of a 13th-century Jewish community with more than 100 tiny figurines clad in period dress and engaged in various occupations; and fascinating scale models of famous synagogues, including one in China in 1653.

Most rewarding, especially for those who have time for a return visit, is the archival film collection of dozens of Jewish communities throughout the world, and the extraordinary collection of Jewish music. If you're ancestor-hunting, for a small fee you can get a computer printout on any of 3,000 Jewish communities, and look for information on record in the museum's genealogy research center. Jewish visitors can also record information about their families. (The research center can be time-consuming, since the office is understaffed, and the archives, which depend totally on material given to them by visitors, are by no means complete.) There's a dairy cafeteria on the premises, or you can lunch at any of the many university campus cafeterias. The small museum/bookshop is very worthwhile.

✪ **Eretz Israel Museum Complex.** 2 Chaim Levanon St., Ramat Aviv. ☎ **03/641-5244.** www.eimuseum.co.il. Admission NIS 30 ($6.60). AE, MC, V. Discount for students and seniors. Sun–Thurs 9am–2pm; Wed 9am–6pm; Sat 10am–2pm. Bus: 24, 25, 27, 45, or 74, 86, 274.

This museum complex lies within a large enclosure that also encompasses **Tel Qasile,** an ancient mound in which 12 strata of past civilizations have been discovered. Selected artifacts from Tel Qasile are displayed in the museums, but especially fascinating is the archaeological site, where you can enter and explore a rebuilt typical house from the pre-Israelite Canaanite period.

Besides Tel Qasile, Eretz Israel has eight attractions. The **Kadman Numismatic Pavilion** has exhibits chronicling the history of coinage and monetary systems. The ✪ **Glass Pavilion** has a fine, rare collection of glass vessels spanning 3,000 years of civilization, from 1500 B.C. to A.D. 1500, the largest collection of ancient glass in Israel. The **Ceramics Pavilion** shows how pottery was made, decorated, and used throughout the ages, and has a reconstructed dwelling from biblical times complete with pots. The **Ethnography and Folklore Pavilion** holds a wealth of Jewish ethnic art and handcrafts—household and religious items, jewelry, and costumes, set in scenes from daily life. A special feature is a wall of antique Hanukkah menorahs from all over the world. The **Nechushtan Pavilion** is devoted to mining and metallurgy as practiced during biblical times in the Timna Valley, Arava, and Sinai. The **"Man and His Work" Center** holds truly fascinating displays showing how men and women have earned their daily bread in Israel since ancient times. In the **Mosaic Square,** you can see the mosaic floor of a Samaratan synagogue (discovered in situ on the grounds of the museum) as well as mosaic floors brought from a Roman villa in Bet Guvrin, a synagogue from Tiberias, and a mosque from Ramla. For astronomy shows, the **Lasky Planetarium,** also displays its collection of moon rocks. An especially pleasant addition to the complex is a park called **Landscapes of the Holy Land.** The museum shop is well stocked with reproductions, jewelry, crafts, and other great gift choices. A kosher cafeteria is open from 11am to 2pm.

⊘ Frommer's Favorite Tel Aviv Experiences

Restored Old Jaffa. Wandering on a summer evening in this seaside old city, and dining at one of the nearby restaurants overlooking the water.

The Beaches. My favorite is Gordon Beach, a quick dash from the many galleries in the Gordon Street area, handy to many dining spots.

Jaffa Flea Market. Magnet for some, too scuzzy for others, the market is now swamped with used jeans and Indian cotton blouses. You can still find objects from British Mandate and Early State periods, plus reproductions of antique Moroccan menorahs. Bargain mercilessly.

Hagana Museum. 23 Rothschild Blvd. ☎ **03/560-8624.** Admission NIS 10 ($2.20). Sun–Thurs 9am–3pm, Fri 9am–noon. Bus: 4 or 5.

Established beside the home of Eliyahu Golomb, a former Hagana general, this is a fascinating place, well worth the visit. The museum records the history of the Israeli military from the time of the farm-field watchmen at the beginning of the century down through the War of Independence. On the third floor, you see the various ways the Israelis hid arms inside farm machinery to escape British detection, and how they stealthily manufactured hand grenades and Sten guns in clandestine kibbutz workshops. There's one homemade grenade with the letters *USA* stamped on it, so that had a Hagana soldier been caught with the bomb, the British wouldn't have suspected that it had been made locally. But the joke here was that *USA* were the first letters of three Yiddish words meaning "Our piece of work."

Almost all of the explanatory captions in this four-story museum are in Hebrew— but never fear, the museum has a group of English-speaking interpreters.

Helena Rubinstein Pavilion. 6 Tarsat Blvd. ☎ **03/528-7196.** Admission NIS 30 ($6.60); includes admission to Tel Aviv Museum of Art nearby. Bus: 5, 18, or 25.

Here you'll find ever-changing exhibitions of works by Israeli and foreign artists. It's open the same hours as the Tel Aviv Museum of Art, with which it is affiliated.

Museum of Antiquities of Tel Aviv Jaffa (Jaffa Museum). 10 Mifratz Shlomo St. ☎ **03/682-5375.** Admission NIS 12 ($2.65); half price for seniors, students and children. Sun–Thurs 9am–1pm.

This beautiful museum building was actually a Turkish administrative and detention center during the 19th century. Displays in the five halls are of objects excavated from 30 sites within the city, covering a time span beginning in the 5th millennium B.C. and ending with the Arab period.

To get there, at the top of the hill in Old Jaffa, walk from Kikar downhill on Mifratz Shlomo Street. The museum will be on your right.

Museum of the History of Tel Aviv Jaffa. 27 Bialik. ☎ **03/517-3052.** Free admission. Sun–Thurs 9am–2pm. Bus: 4.

This museum, housed in Tel Aviv's former City Hall, uses photographs, models, a film (in English), and documents to tell the story of the city's founding and early history. The museum was newly renovated in 1997.

⊘ **Tel Aviv Museum of Art.** 27 Shaul Ha-Melekh Blvd. ☎ **03/695-7361;** box office 03/696-1297. www.tamuseum.co.il. Admission NIS 30 ($6.60); includes admission to Helena Rubinstein Pavilion. Discounts for students. Sun, Mon, Wed–Thurs 10am–6pm; Tues 10am–10pm Fri–Sat 10am–2pm and 7–10pm. Bus: 9, 18, 28, 70, 90, 111.

Tel Aviv Attractions

Ben-Gurion House ④

Bet Bialik Museum ⑩

Bet Hatefutzot, The Nahum
   Goldmann Museum of the
   Jewish Diaspora ①

Carmel Market ⑬

Clock Tower ⑱

Eretz Israel Museum Complex ②

Great Synagogue ⑭

Ha-Bimah National Theatre ⑧

Hagana Museum ⑯

Helena Rubinstein Pavilion ⑦

Independence Hall ⑮

Kerem Ha-Teimanim
   (Yemenite Quarter) ⑫

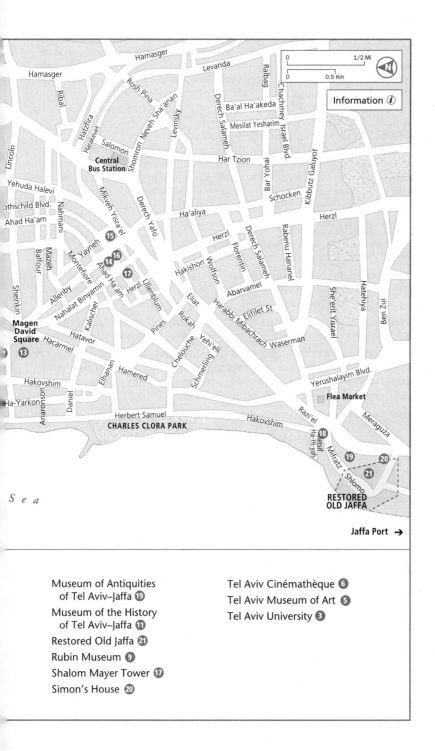

Museum of Antiquities
of Tel Aviv–Jaffa ⑲

Museum of the History
of Tel Aviv–Jaffa ⑪

Restored Old Jaffa ㉑

Rubin Museum ⑨

Shalom Mayer Tower ⑰

Simon's House ⑳

Tel Aviv Cinémathèque ⑥

Tel Aviv Museum of Art ⑤

Tel Aviv University ③

This museum houses temporary as well as permanent exhibitions—paintings, drawings, prints, sculpture, photography of both Israeli and international artists from the 16th century to the present. The collections of modern and impressionist art are especially good and not long ago was augmented by the addition of the Jaglom Collection of Impressionist and Post-Impressionist Art, including works by Pisarro, Matisse, Modigliani, and Chagall. Check out the mural by Roy Lichtenstein in the entrance lobby. Gallery talks in English are offered Wednesdays at 11:30am.

The Friday *Jerusalem Post* lists the museum's lively and well-attended films, concerts, and lectures. Call for information about the museum's shuttle bus, which sometimes gives an interesting historical and architectural tour of Tel Aviv, and is included in the price of your admission ticket. The Museum Shop is open Sunday, Monday, and Wednesday from 10am to 6pm; Tuesday 10am to 10pm; Thursday 10am to 9pm.

MORE ATTRACTIONS

Independence Hall. 16 Rothschild Blvd. ☎ **03/517-3942.** Admission NIS 12 ($2.65). Sun–Tues, Thurs 9am–2pm; Wed 9am–5pm; Fri 9am–1pm.

Meir Dizengoff, the first mayor of Tel Aviv, lived here, and it was in this historic house that the independence of Israel was declared on May 14, 1948. Exhibits here detail Israel's declaration of independence.

Rubin Museum. 14 Bialik St. ☎ **03/525-5961.** Admission NIS 12 ($2.65). Sun–Mon and Wed–Thurs 10am–2pm; Tues 10am–1pm and 4–8pm; Sat 11am–2pm. Closed Sat July–Aug.

Israeli painter Reuven Rubin captured on canvas the spirit and the sights of Mandate Palestine. Though the holy cities of Jerusalem and Safed were among his favorite subjects, he also painted scenes of Tel Aviv, his home city. The Rubin Museum hosts temporary exhibits, usually of modern Israeli artists.

Safari Park (Zoological Center). Ramat Gan. ☎ **03/631-2181.** Admission NIS 40 ($8.80) adults, NIS 32 ($7) children. Sun–Thurs 9am–4pm; Fri 9am–1pm. Bus: 30 (Yona Ha-Navi St.), 35 (Central Bus Station), or 67 (Central Ramat Gan).

The park is a wide-open plain (250 acres) where African animals roam free. For obvious reasons, visitors must remain in closed vehicles while traversing the 5-mile trail, but there is a shorter walking trail as well. You will have the opportunity to see lions, elephants, rhinos, giraffes, gazelles, impalas, zebra, ostriches and storks, and many more. There is also a newly designed monkey enclosure, as well as an aviary and reptile area. Across the street is the Ramat Gan National Park (free admission), with more animals, as well as its new Man and the Living World Museum.

Simon's House. 8 Shimon Ha-Burski St. ☎ **03/683-6792.** Free admission. Daily 8–11:45am and 2–4pm (until 6:30pm in summer).

Christian tradition places the house of Simon the Tanner next to the lighthouse of the port, at the site of a small mosque. Acts 10 recalls Saint Peter's visit to Simon's house in "Joppa."

To get there, walk south through Kikar Kedumim, the main square of restored Old Jaffa. At the end of the square, turn right to the steps.

Tel Aviv University. Ramat Aviv.

The handsome, multifaceted campus has architecture and landscaping reminiscent of a branch of the California State University system. Thirty-five buildings house the widest spectrum of studies of any university in Israel and its enrollment of 18,000 students is the largest. Courses for English-speaking students are given here. You can combine a stroll around the grounds with a visit to Bet Hatfutzot (see above), which is on the university's grounds.

MONUMENTS

At the center of the plaza suspended above the roadway in Dizengoff Square is a huge sculpture-fountain by Yaacov Agam named *Water and Fire.* Five large concentric metal rings are painted so that when the rings turn, the painted surfaces produce differing effects of light and color. At the same time (when everything is functioning), jets of water shoot upward from the rings, and at the top of the sculpture, in the midst of the shooting water, rises a jet of flame! Music accompanies the whole display in a show that lasts for 20 minutes. Agam's computerized sculpture begins to play at the beginning of each hour starting at 11am and continuing until 10pm. If you arrive a few minutes early, you may be able to get a seat on one of the benches surrounding the sculpture.

To the south along Rothschild Boulevard, in the center of the island at Nahalat Benyamin Street, is the impressive **Founder's Monument,** depicting the three phases of Tel Aviv's history. The bottom shows the workers of 1909 digging and planting, while snakes and animals form a lower border. The middle level shows the Herzlia Gymnasium (which was demolished in 1959); the uppermost section is modern Tel Aviv, showing the Ha-Bimah Theater, Bialik's home, and many modern houses.

ESPECIALLY FOR KIDS

The **Eretz Israel Museum** is great for kids: It has demonstrations of traditional crafts, a planetarium, a reconstructed Canaanite period house, and a nature exhibit. The **Bet Hatfutzot/Diaspora Museum** is a real learning experience for all ages. Many exhibits are especially geared to the young.

Safari Park is especially good for older children, who will enjoy this park where wild animals of all kinds roam free. Children of all ages will enjoy the **World of Silence Sea Aquarium** sea creatures and will be thrilled by the reptiles.

The 34-story shopping center, the **Shalom Mayer Tower (Migdal Shalom),** has an observatory with a magnificent view, with telescopes set out for a closer look. Take the glass elevator to the top where there is a cafe. The complex also houses **Mayerland,** an amusement park with many kinds of rides, and the typical goodies such as cotton candy, ice cream, and popcorn. There is also a **Wax Museum** (admission $3.60) that depicts events and personalities in Israeli history. The amusement park, observatory, and wax museum are open Sunday to Thursday from 9am to 7pm, on Friday and holiday eves until 2pm.

JAFFA

Now an integrated component in the sprawling Tel Aviv–Jaffa complex, Jaffa has a long and colorful history, dating back to biblical times. This is the port, the Bible tells us, where King Solomon's ally, the Phoenician King Hiram of Tyre, landed cedars of Lebanon for the construction of Solomon's temple; from here Jonah embarked for his fabulous adventure with the whale. The Greeks were here too, and they fostered the legend that a poor maiden named Andromeda, chained to a rock and on the verge of being sacrificed to a sea monster, was rescued by Perseus on his winged white horse. Today, visitors are shown this rock, a tourist attraction since ancient times.

The crusaders also came this way. Richard the Lion-Hearted built a citadel here that was promptly snatched away by Saladin's brother, who slaughtered 20,000 Christians in the process. Napoléon passed through 600 years or so later; a few Jewish settlers came in the 1890s; and Allenby routed the Turks from the port in 1917.

One Jewish legend has it that all the sunken treasure in the world flows toward Jaffa, and that in King Solomon's day the sea offered a rich bounty, accounting for the king's wealth. According to the legend, since Solomon's time, the treasure has once again been accumulating—to be distributed by the Messiah on the Day of the Coming "to each man according to his merits."

Today, Jaffa still shows traces of its romantic and mysterious past. The city is built into a kind of amphitheater on the side of a hill. The old section of the city has become the starlit patio of Tel Aviv, providing an exceptional view, fine restaurants, and the most beautifully restored old city in Israel. The flea market district, near the Clock Tower, is ramshackle but has real personality.

The streets from Tel Aviv run into Jaffa's Jerusalem Avenue and Tarshish Street where a great stone tower and the Turkish mosque, Mahmudiye (1812), reminds you of the city's continuing Arab community.

A STROLL AROUND OLD JAFFA

The reclamation of Old Jaffa—only a short time ago a slumlike area of war ruins and crumbling Turkish palaces—has proven to be one of the most imaginative of such projects in all Israel. Atop the hill and running down in a maze of descending streets to the sea are artists' studios and galleries, outdoor cafes, fairly expensive restaurants, and gift shops, all artfully arranged among the reconstructed ruins. Climb to the top of the hill and wander through the lanes (named for the Hebrew signs of the zodiac). At the summit is **Kikar Kedumim,** the central plaza, and at one side of it, the **Franciscan Monastery of Saint Peter,** which was built above a medieval citadel. You can visit the church for prayers on Sunday. Opposite the church is an excavation area, surrounded by a fence, where you can inspect remnants of a **3rd-century B.C. catacomb.** Facing the catacomb is a hilltop garden, **Gan Ha-Pisgah,** atop which, surrounded by trees, is a white monument depicting scenes from the Bible: the conquest of Jericho, the near-sacrifice of Isaac, and Jacob's dream.

Past the church gardens, on the sea side of the hill, is a small and charming cafe. Wander through the elaborately decorated dome-roofed room and out onto the deck, for a superb all-encompassing view of Tel Aviv and the Mediterranean coastline. Incidentally, **Andromeda's Rock** is traditionally the most prominent of those blackened stones jutting up from the floor of the bay. The view is brilliant in the morning sunlight. At night, it takes on more of a fairy-tale aura.

Returning to Kikar Kedumim, near the Muscat Restaurant, you enter the restored maze of Old Jaffa's market streets, filled with interesting antique and souvenir shops to explore. For those interested in art and interior design, **The Ilana Goor Museum,** the beautifully renovated mansion of one of Israel's successful sculptors, is a delightful stop. Over the centuries this building has been put to many uses, including a long stint as a caravansarai for 19th century Jewish pilgrims. Now each room is like a page out of *Architectural Digest,* filled with Ilana Goor's own wonderful works, and her private collection of art. There's a rooftop cafe with good food and sweeping views as well as a one-of-a-kind museum shop. Open Monday to Saturday from 10am to 10pm (4pm closing on Friday), admission is NIS 20 ($4.40).

A short (quarter-mile) stroll south of Old Jaffa brings you to the disused port of **Jaffa Harbor,** now a fenced-in area of dockside restaurants.

6 Organized Tours & Special Events

ORGANIZED TOURS The **Association for Tourism of Tel Aviv–Jaffa** leads a free walking tour of Old Jaffa starting at the Clock Tower on Yefet St. (bus 10 from Tel Aviv) on Wednesday mornings at 9am. Call the Tel Aviv Tourist Information

Office (☎ **03/639-5660**) or the Jaffa Visitors Center for current information. The new **Jaffa Visitors Center** (☎ **03/682-6796**) in Kikar Kedumim, right at the center of the restored section of Old Jaffa, gives out detailed free maps of Old Jaffa accompanied by historical information that makes it easy to do a self-guided tour of the area. The helpful center is open Sunday to Thursday from 9am to 6pm. The **Tel Aviv Municipal Tourist Information Office** (6th floor, New Central Bus Station) also gives out free Jewish municipal maps with four **"Orange" self-guided walking tour routes** of Tel Aviv, marked on the map. Signs along the routes mark the way as you go. Some of the routes are too long to undertake on a sweltering summer day, but if you break them up into smaller units, they are a good basic itinerary of what to see in different neighborhoods.

Another good source of guided tours is the **Society for the Protection of Nature in Israel (SPNI),** 3 Ha-Shfela St. (☎ **03/368-8674**). Call ☎ **03/510-0337** for information on the society's English-language walking tours in the Tel Aviv area. These are group tours that individuals can join; days tours cost $40 to $60 per person. Highly recommended.

Boat Tours from Jaffa Port to the Tel Aviv Marina and back run on Saturdays and cost NIS 22 ($5). Call Kef (☎ **03/682-9070**) or Sababa (☎ **03/681-6739**) in Jaffa Port for schedules and reservations.

SPECIAL/FREE EVENTS   Many evenings after 8pm, in the summer, there is often free samba dancing on the Herbert Samuel Esplanade, beside the beach in South Tel Aviv. There is also music and dancing at other points along the beach on evenings throughout the week. Check with the Tourist Information Office (☎ **03/639-5660**) for current information.

There are free evening outdoor concerts in the Yarkon Park and in Old Jaffa during the summer. Check the newspapers or the government tourist office for dates.

Nahalat Benyamin Pedestrian Mall, has an outdoor craft bazaar and street performers every Tuesday and Friday from 10am to 5pm. Take bus no. 4.

7 Outdoor Pursuits & Sports

BEACHES   Tel Aviv's seashore is within walking distance of Dizengoff Square. A promenade runs the entire length of the beach. Most beaches have free showers and facilities for changing. The cleanest beaches are behind the Dan and Sheraton hotels (Frishman to Gordon streets) and at the Hilton Hotel.

In a slightly more remote location, the **Bat Yam Beach,** 3 miles south of Jaffa, is wide and sandy, and gets crowded only on hot Saturdays in summer; the sea here is usually a bit cleaner than in downtown Tel Aviv. From Ben-Yehuda Street, you can take bus no. 10, which begins its run at the City Hall. June to September there is an admission fee of NIS 12 ($2.60)

Facing Kikar Namir and the Hilton is the **Hof Hadarim (Orange Beach).** Entrance and use of changing rooms are free; you can rent lockers and deck chairs. A snack bar and restaurant are also at this beach.

A word of caution: Swimming at Israeli beaches can be dangerous. The problem is a totally unpredictable undertow that can be hazardous even for a strong swimmer. It's safe, however, to swim at beaches where guards are stationed. Pay attention to the safety symbols along the beaches in the form of small flags. The color of the flag tells the story: Black means absolutely no swimming in the area, red warns you to be especially cautious, and white indicates that the water's fine. Tel Aviv's city beaches are protected in many places by a system of breakwaters and are the safest in the area.

JOGGING   The long beachfront promenade, running several miles from the northern end of Jaffa to the Hilton Hotel, provides an excellent stretch for urban jogging, without the inconvenience of cross streets and traffic lights. It's busy, which adds an element of safety, and you can stop for a dip in the sea or cool off at the public showers that dot the beaches at various intervals. There is a jogging track at **Sportek, Rokach Boulevard,** at the northern entrance of Tel Aviv (☎ **03/699-0307**). Admission to the track is free.

SAILING   Small motorboats, pedal boats, and rowboats are available to rent by the hour on the lake at **Yarkon Park,** near Yehoshua Gardens (☎ **03/642-0541**) at the northern end of the city, daily from 9am to 6pm. Motorboats are $20 per half hour; pedal and rowboats are $14 per full hour. At the **Tel Aviv Sea Center,** in Marina Atarim (☎ **03/522-4079**), in front of Namir (Atarim) Square between the Carlton and Hilton hotels, you can rent a sailboat by the hour, with or without skipper. Windsurfers are $18 per hour; small boats $30 per hour; and catamarans $42 per hour. You can also hire a boat with instructor, captain, or crew. The marina is open from 9am to 5pm daily. An alternative is merely looking—and it's a pretty sight too, seeing those bright white and striped sails on the waves.

SWIMMING   There's a salt water Olympic swimming pool open year-round at Gordon Street (☎ **03/527-1555**), on the beach facing Namir Square. The pool is open daily from 6am to 7pm; admission is NIS 45 ($10) Sunday to Thursday; on Saturday NIS 216 ($48).

8 Shopping

SHOPPING STREETS & MALLS

Allenby Street is full of furniture stores, lower price clothing shops, bakeries, bookstores, kiosks—a typical Tel Avivan street, with its hustle and bustle. The **Opera Tower** is a brand-new upscale mall, right where Allenby Street meets the sea and a short walk from the Ha-Yarkon Street hotel district (it takes its name from the municipal Opera House that was located near here during British Mandate times). Well stocked with cafes, galleries, and shops of interest to visitors, the mall is developing into something of a center for fashionable clothing, and is the centerpiece for the revival of a neighborhood, once an architectural and social dazzle in the 1930s and 1940s. It is open standard business hours, with some cafes remaining open later in the evening.

Two blocks south of Dizengoff Square, toward King George Street, you'll find the enormous indoor **Dizengoff Center Shopping Mall,** located on the lower floors of a megaoffice complex. This modern, jam-packed, multilevel shopping center is filled with houseware shops, a large array of clothing shops and boutiques, and specialty shops. You'll find branches of American stores popular with teenagers here. There are many fast-food counters, including the American Pizza Hut. It is open Sunday to Thursday from 9:30am to 9pm; Friday from 9:30am to 2pm. You can take a pleasant dip in the Mediterranean at one of the city's best beaches when you finish making your rounds.

SHOPPING A TO Z
ART

Tel Aviv's Gordon Street district is the center for the sale of serious art in Israel. Gordon Street and the cross streets, from Ha-Yarkon to Dizengoff streets, are almost wall-to-wall galleries and unusual shops. The shady, once-grand Rothschild Boulevard, with its superb restaurants, is also becoming a bit of an art district. Most galleries are open Sunday to Thursday from 10am to 1pm and 5 to 8pm.

Heading the list of places to check out is the new **Sotheby's Auction Gallery,** 46 Rothschild Blvd. (☎ **03/560-1666;** fax 03/560-8111), with exhibitions of important Israeli and international art as well as Judaica. The **Stern Gallery,** 30 Gordon St. (☎ **03/524-6303**), specializes in Israeli and foreign Jewish artists of international renown, ranging from Kadishman, Lea Nickel, and Reuvin Rubin to works by Marc Chagall. They also have special exhibitions of younger artists and occasional block-busters like "Four Generations of Pisarros." Other notable galleries include the **Givon Gallery** (contemporary works), 35 Gordon St. (☎ **03/522-5427**); the Mabat Gallery, 37 Gordon St. (☎ **03/532-6863**), with the newest art; **Nelly Aman,** 26 Gordon St. (☎ **03/523-2003**), contemporary, with many special exhibits; **Julie M.,** Glickson St. near Dizengoff (☎ **03/629-5475**), contemporary. In Old Jaffa, look for the **Horace Richter Gallery,** 24 Simhat Mazal Arie St. (☎ **03/682-5842**), with beautifully mounted, carefully chosen exhibitions.

BOOKSTORES

There are many Steimatzky branches in Tel Aviv, including those at 107 Allenby Rd. (☎ **03/566-4973**), 109 Dizengoff St. (☎ **03/523-3415**), and 4 Tarsat Ave., near Ha-Bimah Theater (☎ **03/528-0806**). For antiquarian, rare, and used books, try **Pollack's,** 36 and 42 King George St. (☎ **03/523-8613**), with its sidewalk-browsing terrace and unusual selection inside; open Sunday to Friday from 9am to 1:30pm and Tuesday only from 4pm to 7pm. If you're desperate for English reading material, especially fiction, **Halper's Quality Used Books,** 87 Allenby St. (☎ **03/629-9710**), is the mother lode, with at least a quarter of a mile of packed bookshelves winding through its premises.

CRAFTS

Cad Al Hayam. 1 Allenby St. ☎ **03/517-1423.**

A contemporary ceramics gallery on the second floor of the Opera Tower Shopping Arcade, this shop carries the work of a number of top-quality ceramists.

Contemporary Crafts Market. Nahlat Binyamin Pedestrian Mall.

This outdoor craft market, held every Tuesday and Friday, is filled with ceramics, jewelry, hands of Fatima, menorahs, and interesting gift items. This is one of the best weekly craft markets I've encountered, and prices are both fair and affordable. At the edge of the market, you'll often find a group of Druze women from the Galilee making delicious, freshly baked Druze-style bread.

Dervish. 21 Dov Hoz St., Tel Aviv. ☎ **03/524-8852.**

Two sisters from South Africa have made this craft shop into a local institution, constantly changing one of a kind items the owners personally collect on their unending travels. Their eye for beautiful objects is excellent, and their bargaining abilities must be extraordinary. They also make museum-quality reproductions of ethnic jewelry and serve free exotic coffee and Yemenite tea while you browse. There are receptions with delightful snacks whenever a new caravan load of goods comes in; ask if any of these gatherings are coming up and if you can have an invitation. The receptions are a good opportunity to buy collector items and to mingle with Israelis who share an interest in ethnic art and exotic travels. Prices range from under $5 to over $1,000. It's open Sunday to Thursday from 9am to 1pm and from 4pm to 7pm. Dov Hoz Street runs off the section of Gordon Street that's between Ben-Yehuda and Dizengoff streets.

DEPARTMENT STORES

Hamashbir Lazarchan. 115 Allenby St. ☎ **03/528-5136.**

This department store is a part of a chain throughout the country. It offers a huge assortment of merchandise, from the basement with kitchenware, a milk bar, and a supermarket, on up through its escalated levels. Goods are serviceable (some items come from Marks and Spencer in the United Kingdom) but this is not Bloomingdale's. It's a good place to pick up basics you might not have brought with you. Open Sunday to Thursday from 8:30am to 7pm, Friday until 2pm.

FASHION

North Tel Aviv is the country's center for quality women's clothing and custom-designed lines. Considering that style was almost considered sinful in the early Zionist movement, there has been a revolution in Israeli attitudes, especially in the past few years. **Kikar Ha Medina** in the northern part of Tel Aviv is a large, poorly kept square, but it's the heart of the city's high-rent neighborhood, and the retail shops around the square are filled with the best stuff in the country. The northern stretch of Dizengoff Street, starting around Gordon Street, is wall-to-wall high-style clothing shops. Among the many and varied places to explore elsewhere in the northern part of town, are **Gideon Oberson's** stylish designer showroom at 36 Gordon St. (☎ **03/524-3822**)—Oberson has moved from bathing suits to custom fashion; **Dorin Frankfurt** (www.dorinF.com) at 40 Ben Gurion St., near 164 Dizengoff (☎ **03/527-9915**), an acclaimed Israeli whose designs tend to natural textiles and easy, elegant lines; **Gottex** has an outlet shop at 148 Dizengoff. A stroll through the upper reaches of Dizengoff and Ben-Yehuda streets will reveal many additional shops and designer showrooms.

JEWELRY & JUDAICA
Yemenite Jewelry & Judaica

Ben Zion David Yemenite Silver Art. 3 Mazal Dagim St. Old Jaffa. ☎ **03/681-2503.**

You can see Yemenite-style silver jewelry, with its intricate filigree patterns, at shops throughout Israel; at Ben Zion David's workshop and showroom, in the heart of the beautifully restored Old Jaffa bazaar, you'll find some of the best examples of craftsmanship and design in this tradition created by more than 1,000 years of Yemenite Jewish silversmiths. The many branches of the David family have been skilled silver workers for generations; perhaps because of the family's long reputation for quality and fairness, prices here are quite reasonable, despite the upmarket tourist location. There's an enormous selection of earrings, bracelets, rings, and necklaces, as well as delicate mezuzzot, candlesticks, and Hanukkah dreidels, all ornamented with fine filigree designs. The showroom is generally open Sunday to Thursday from noon until late in the evening, Friday from 11am to 3pm, and on Saturday evenings after Shabbat. Credit cards are accepted.

MARKETS

Carmel Market (Shuk Ha-Carmel). Magen David Square.

At this six-sided intersection you enter the throbbing open-air market where vendors hawk everything from pistachios and guavas to sun hats and memorial candles on open tables lining the many shopping streets. Many vendors have their own songs, which tell you all about the price and quality of what is being sold. Sometimes one vendor sings against another in a competitive duet. The market runs into side streets, large and small, one side favoring dry goods, and the other dried beans, fruit, nuts, and spices in all colors and fragrances, sold from sacks. The market is open Sunday to Thursday from 8am until dark and on Friday from 8am to 2pm. Tuesdays and Fridays from 10am to 5pm, there's an arts and crafts market, complete with street performers at **Nahalat Binyamin,** off Allenby Street at the edge of the Carmel Market.

Jaffa Flea Market. East of the Clock Tower at foot of Old Jaffa.

Tradition has it that you can get the best buys here early Sunday morning. If you are the first customer on the first day of the week, the seller hopes a quick sale will bring him luck through the week. You can weave your way through a mixed array of treasures and junk. Merchandise varies, but copper, brass, and jewelry are always to be found. Bargaining is the order of the day; feel free to indulge in lengthy haggling. Even if there is a little language problem, you can get a lot understood with your hands. It's great fun even if you don't buy anything.

The flea market is open Sunday to Thursday from 10am to 6pm and on Friday from 10am to 2pm. Take bus no. 10 from Ben-Yehuda Street in Tel Aviv.

9 Tel Aviv & Jaffa After Dark

No matter what season, Tel Aviv throbs with activity after sundown. Strollers are out on the boulevards, people watchers crowd the cafes, clubs and discos throb and crash, and restaurants are packed.

The most popular form of nighttime entertainment in Tel Aviv is to stroll around and people watch. Two areas that are traditionally devoted to this pastime are Dizengoff Street and the Herbert Samuel Esplanade–Ha-Tayelet—which runs along the sandy beach. Outdoor cafe life on Dizengoff Street starts near Dizengoff Square, and works northward. The scene is pretty packed most nights, but its real crescendo is reached on Saturday nights after the cinemas let out. Pick out your seat at one of the sidewalk cafes and order a coffee, or, if it's hot, cool off with a coffee ice-cream soda (one of the most popular Israeli drinks) or the tasty apple cider.

To find out what's going on in the city, buy the *Jerusalem Post* Friday-morning edition, which contains the weekend magazine that lists everything there is to do and see and an additional, informative "In Tel Aviv" section. Also pick up *Events in the Tel Aviv Region* and other free tourist publications from the travel desk of your hotel (or check out the Sheraton's well stocked information shelves just to the left of the main entrance.

In addition to the listings below, **Hayarkon Park** (☎ **03/642-2828**), at the northern edge of Tel Aviv, hosts large outdoor concerts; there are also concerts in Hayarkon Park's Wohl Amphitheater (☎ **03/521-8210**).

THE PERFORMING ARTS

While Jerusalem has many cultural offerings, Tel Aviv is the true cultural center of Israel. Mann Auditorium is the home of the Israel Philharmonic, and there are many other musical groups. The Israel Ballet is also centered in Tel Aviv. Major ticket outlets are **Le'an,** 101 Dizengoff St. (☎ **03/524-7373**); **Hadran,** 90 Ibn Givrol St. (☎ **03/527-9955**); and **Castel,** 153 Ibn Givrol St. (☎ **03/604/4725**).

CONCERTS, OPERA & DANCE

Israel Philharmonic Orchestra. Huberman St. ☎ **03/528-9163.**

The **Mann Auditorium,** which can seat 3,000 concert-goers, is the home of this prestigious orchestra, founded in 1936 by Bronislaw Huberman. Zubin Mehta is music director. Even now that the magnificent concert hall has been built, the orchestra continues to give performances in other towns, carrying on a tradition that began during the War of Independence, when it played just behind the lines for the troops near Jerusalem and Beersheva. The orchestra is on vacation during August, September, and October until after the Jewish holidays.

New Israeli Opera. 28 Leonardo Da Vinci St. ☎ **03/692-7700.** Fax 03/695-4886. www.israel-opera.co.il. E-mail: opera@netvision.net.il. Ticket prices NIS 115–255 ($32.20–$72). AE, DC, MC, V.

Housed in the **Tel Aviv Center for the Performing Arts,** recently completed and both architecturally interesting and controversial, the New Israeli Opera is the country's newest cultural gem, performing a lively program of classic and modern opera. The company draws heavily on the talent of new immigrants from the former Soviet Union.

Suzanne Dellal Center for Dance and Theater. 6 Yehieli St. ☎ **03/510-5656.**

This new complex, built in postmodern style, is the venue for visiting dance groups as well as Israel's contemporary **Bat Sheva Dance Company,** and the **Inbal Dance Theater,** which often draws upon Israel's ethnic traditions for its style. The Dellal Center hosts interesting modern and experimental productions, as well as a wide range of concerts and music events, and has become the heart of the effort to revive and restore the old, potentially quaint Neve Tzedik neighborhood of Tel Aviv. Buses 10 and 25 pass nearby.

Tel Aviv Museum of Art. 27 Shaul Ha-Melekh Blvd. ☎ **03/696-1297.**

The museum hosts a wide range of afternoon and evening events, including music recitals, performances of chamber orchestras and ensembles, visiting choirs, theater and dance performances, and film screenings. There is a cafe on the premises for refreshments.

THEATER

Cameri Theater. 101 Dizengoff St. ☎ **03/523-3335.**

This theater presents both repertory classics and new Israeli plays. Tuesday evenings there are simultaneous translations in English. Orchestra and mezzanine seats generally cost about NIS 115 ($25); balcony seats are NIS 90 ($20). Earphone rental is an additional NIS 7 ($1.50).

Ha-Bimah National Theater. Kikar Ha-Bimah. ☎ **03/526-6666.**

Founded in Moscow in 1918 by the renowned Stanislavsky, and moved to British Mandate Palestine in 1928, the Ha-Bimah National Theater is the nation's first and best-known repertory theater. While performances are Hebrew, some productions offer simultaneous translations. This theater was the first to present Hebrew translations of plays by Shakespeare, Molière, Shaw, and O'Neill. Ticket prices vary, depending on the company performing.

THE CLUB & MUSIC SCENE

Tel Aviv and Jaffa are the nightlife centers of Israel. Their clubs have been the breeding ground for almost all Israeli singers who have gone on to international careers. The scene, especially the disco scene, changes so frequently, that only the few long-term landmarks are listed here. Some discos are on rather tacky-looking streets, but that's no indication they'll be cheap; the atmosphere can be very different inside.

Late Night Tel Aviv, 14a Pinsker St. (☎ and fax **03/525-6484**) is a company that specializes in nightlife tours of the city for groups or individuals. It's run by Maia Hoffman and Shira Skolnik, who always know the latest places and what's happening. Prices vary according to the number of people in the group and the itinerary.

LIVE MUSIC & DISCO

Bet Lessin. 34 Weizmann. ☎ **03/694-1222.**

This club hosts jazz groups many nights as well as contemporary and folk musicians. If your Hebrew is snappy, there are also stand-up comedy nights.

Camelot. 16 Shalom Aleichem St. ☎ **03/528-5222.**

Upstairs, there's a bar, downstairs live jazz and blues. Near Ben Yehuda Street, it's popular with both Tel Avivians and visitors. Open nightly 10pm to after 3am.

Caravan Night Club. 10 Mifratz Shlomo, Old Jaffa. ☎ **03/6828-255.**

The tourist-oriented Caravan offers a magnificent view of the Tel Aviv–Jaffa area. At 10:30pm there's a show of international artists (including striptease). Dancing is resumed after the show. Open Monday to Saturday from 8pm to 2am. Admission may be charged, depending on the performer. Visa is the only credit card accepted. Bus 10 to Old Jaffa.

Colosseum. Namir (Atarim) Square, Ha-Yarkon St. (between Moriah and Marina Hotels). ☎ **03/527-1177.** Disco and live music, with a cover charge of NIS 27–30 ($6–$8) for men (no charge for women).

Filled with a large, young crowd of visitors and with Israelis who want to pick them up. Your first three drinks are often free.

Lemon. 17 Hangarim St. ☎ **03/681-3313.**

There are special nights here for the over-28 crowd (usually on Thursdays) and gays (often on Monday nights after midnight). Friday is the big night, and the place really gets going after 1:30am, so you'll need to take a taxi. Cover charges vary. It's always best to phone ahead for information.

Rendez-Vous Supper Club. 77 Ben Yehuda St. ☎ **03/524-8034.**

A favorite of the Russian community, this basement restaurant has a midnight-in-Moscow feel of either melancholy, vodka-laden nostalgia, or dressed-to-kill celebration. The place only comes to life on weekends or if a group comes in to celebrate. Chicken Kiev and other Russian dishes are served while a four-piece band and singer perform Russian and popular music, and the dance floor fills up with a mixture of Israeli Russians and visitors. Dinner and dancing is from 8pm to 2am; the food is in the moderate price range ($20 per person excluding drinks).

Soweto. 6 Frishman St. ☎ **03/524-0825.**

Conveniently located in the Ha-Yarkon Street hotel district, Soweto is the place for reggae and rap and is open Monday to Saturday from 10pm until near dawn. Monday to Wednesday, the crowd is generally mid-20s or older; Thursday to Saturday, the age level drops to the upper teens. There is usually an interesting mix of Israelis, visitors, Ethiopians, and other Africans here. Entrance fee, including a beer, can be NIS 36 ($8) on weekdays and NIS 54 ($12) on Friday and Saturday nights, depending on performances.

Tzavta. 30 Ibn Gevirol St. ☎ **03/695-0156.**

This club specializes in Israeli music, both folk and popular.

Yoel Sharr's Omar Khayam. Kedumim Square, Old Jaffa. ☎ **03/682-5865.**

This club, mainly for visitors, is actually a huge room in an old Arab mansion, with lofty vaulted ceilings and stone walls. Top Israeli singers and pianists appear nightly. The show starts at 10:45pm; come earlier to get good seats. Open 9:30pm to 1:30am. Admission, including one drink, may be charged. Bus 10 to Old Jaffa.

BARS & PUBS

Singers and pianists appear nightly at the bars in the major five-star hotels such as the Dan, Hilton, Ramada, Sheraton, and Sheraton Moriah.

Hamisba'a. 344 Dizengoff St. ☎ **03/604-2360.**

At press time, it was very popular and packed, with occasional dancing on the tables. Open daily from 10pm to 5am. Cover charge of about NIS 50 ($14).

Il Barbarescco. 226 Dizengoff St. ☎ **03/524-1616.**

A small wine bar/restaurant right in the heart of trendy North Tel Aviv, serving fine cheeses, rustic salads, breads, and other tidbits and full meals to go with your wine. In good weather, most tables are on the sidewalk. "*Vino, panino e compagnia*," is the motto. Open until 1am most nights; until the wee hours on Fridays.

Joey's Bar. 42 Allenby St. ☎ **03/517-9277.**

An American-style bar run by Americans, Joey's well-stocked place is a haven for yuppie travelers. Music is American: rock from the sixties, seventies, and eighties; beer starts at NIS 14 ($3). Open daily from 5pm to 8am.

M.A.S.H. 275 Dizengoff St. ☎ **03/605-1007.**

More Alcohol Served Here is small, crowded, full of visitors and sixties and seventies music. The bar is well stocked in this local landmark. There's pub-style food for the hungry and daytime cable TV for those who want to keep up with the news. Happy hour, with 25% discount on drinks, is 5 to 8pm.

Pandora. 22 Ben Yehuda St. ☎ **03/620-0313.**

A new, stylish place near the hotel neighborhood, Pandora opens at 8pm, and offers a well-stocked bar, calm, friendly ambience, and inventive, reasonably priced snacks and light meals—a shot of Irish whisky is NIS 29 ($6.40); a portion of chicken strips with dynamite cream and mustard sauce, salad and sweet potato slices runs $9. The crowd is 25-plus.

Punch Line. 6 Ha'arba'a St. ☎ **03/561-0785.**

At Tel Aviv's singing waiter pub/music/theater club, most evenings start out with the future Minelli's, Streisands, and Joel Grey's of Israel doing stuff from *Les Misérables* and *Phantom of the Opera.* As the night goes on, they move onto rock, and later, Israeli pop and ethnic music. Visitors dance on stage and on the dance floor, and the drinks and food, though pricey, are good. Ha'arba'a Street, near the Cinémathèque, has many trendy night spots, and is a good place to pub hop.

Rose. 147 Yehuda Ha-Levi St. ☎ **03/685-0340.**

Off the tourist track, this is a stylish bar with good music and an over-30 clientele.

Terminal. Corner of Gordon and Ha-Yarkon sts. ☎ **03/544-0585.**

On the ground floor of the Gordon Youth Hostel, facing the sea, this is one of Tel Aviv's busiest pubs, crowded with conversation by late afternoon, throbbing with music, and overflowing onto the street with activity on summer nights. The crowd is part Tel Avivan, part international, and part backpacker.

Yoe'ezer Wine Bar. 2 Yoe'ezar Ish Habira St., Jaffa. ☎ **03/683-9115.**

A connoisseur's wine bar, run by one of Israel's great gourmets. Here your wine can be accompanied by exquisite food (see "Where to Dine," above). It's hidden down a little alley on the inland side of Yefet Street, just opposite the Clock Tower.

GAY & LESBIAN BARS/MEETING PLACES

Cafe Nordau. 145 Ben Yehuda St. ☎ **03/524-0134.**

Cafe by day, open till dawn some nights, the Nordau, long popular with many Tel Avivans, has also traditionally been a meeting place for members of the city's gay community.

Minerva Bar Gallery. 98 Allenby St. ☎ **03/566-6051.**

This always interesting basement art gallery with its adjacent bar is an easygoing meeting place for the lesbian community; both bar and gallery open at 8pm and the bar has a cover charge of about $11.

Zman Amiti. 22 Eilat St., Jaffa. ☎ **03/683-7788.**

The Israeli Society for Protection of Personal Rights often organizes Thursday-night events at this disco. Call for information about these nights, and special gay/lesbian nights that are arranged at other bars and clubs.

FILM

Tel Aviv has at least two dozen cinema houses; the films scene, as in New York, is a popular one. English and American films aren't dubbed, as they are in Europe, so you can sit back and enjoy the English soundtrack while the Israelis crane their necks to read the Hebrew subtitles. First-run shows cost around NIS 25 to 35 ($7 to $10). The commercial shorts that accompany many films are fascinating.

Tel Aviv Cinémathèque. 2 Sprinzak St. ☎ **03/691-7181.**

Located not far from the Mann Auditorium, the Cinémathèque, with an ever-changing daily program, screens three or four films each day ranging from international classics to rarely seen and experimental films. The Cinémathèque also hosts an annual International Film Festival, as well as special festivals of Israeli films throughout the year.

7

The Golden Coast

Like the rest of the country, the shore strip combines the old and the new in a uniquely Israeli juxtaposition. Neon and chrome exist side by side with biblical and even prebiblical ruins. And there's much to see and do on the beaches of sand, pebbles, or rocks: Sports enthusiasts can swim, fish, dive, boat, ski, or surf.

SEEING THE AREA   It's best to see the Golden Coast in sections: the southern and central coasts are convenient to Tel Aviv and can also be visited from Jerusalem; the north-central and northern coasts are easily accessible from Haifa and the Galilee. The water can be almost bathtub-warm in summer and swimming is possible from April until November. In fact, in a February heat wave, some visitors from northern climes may find the Mediterranean near Tel Aviv as warm as the North Atlantic ever gets in August.

Warning: On many days undertows and whirlpools develop that not even the strongest swimmer can fight. Obey the lifeguards! Be extremely wary about swimming in unguarded areas if there is any wave activity.

1 Ashkelon

56 kilometers (36 mi.) S of Tel Aviv.

Ashkelon is the southernmost tourist stop along Israel's Mediterranean shoreline, although beautiful beaches stretch farther south. This thriving seaside town has grown up over the ruins of civilizations buried in its sands for 25 centuries. One of the five Philistine city-states (the others were Gath, Gaza, Ekron, and Ashdod), Ashkelon was an important caravan stop. This is where Delilah supposedly snipped Samson's hair and strength, and where Herod was born.

Exactly what happened at Ashkelon over the last 4,000 years is a chapter of history still waiting to be written, since ancient Ashkelon is only now being archaeologically explored in depth. Many civilizations and sand-covered cities of antiquity lie buried here. Recent finds include perhaps the oldest arched gateway in the world, and a Philistine winery and bazaar. One of the most mysterious archaeological discoveries made here in recent years is an enormous cemetery for dogs. Ashkelon was not primarily a Jewish city, and the significance of dogs to the ancient non-Jewish population is presently being pondered. At one point along the shore, you'll see where a tentative longitudinal slice has been made into the cliff, revealing a network of pillars and caves several strata deep. Perhaps the most exciting object recently uncovered is a tiny Canaanite silver calf, probably a cult object, now on display at the Israel Museum. Further excavations will most certainly reveal important historical treasures, because the Bible mentions Ashkelon frequently.

After the crusaders and Muslims fought over the city, Ashkelon, like so many other places, fell into utter ruin. Later, builders took the remains of Roman staircases, Hellenistic pillars, and Crusader stonemasonry for building materials in Jaffa and Acre.

Ashkelon is not a big town, but it's very spread out. A large part of its population is composed of Jewish families that came to Israel from North Africa in the 1950s and 1960s. Today, the city is undergoing a major building boom as it absorbs thousands of recent immigrants from the former Soviet Union. Ashkelon has the perfect climate, blessed by cool breezes from the sea, but modified by the dryness of desert winds. Because Ashkelon is at the southern end of the coast, you have the best chance of getting in some early spring or late fall swimming here.

ESSENTIALS

GETTING THERE   By Bus   Egged bus no. 300 and 301, from Tel Aviv, arrives at the Central Bus Station on Ha-Nitzahon in the newer part of town (time: 1 hour). Frequency is about every half hour; last bus is 9pm, or 2 hours before Shabbat on Friday. Your bus will come into town passing by Migdal, the old city of Ashkelon (an Arabic town before 1948) on your right.

By Car   There are direct main highways from Tel Aviv and Jerusalem.

VISITOR INFORMATION   The **Government and Municipal Tourist Office** (☎ 07/677-0173 or 07/673-2412) is in the City Hall, Afridar Center, behind the Bus Station. It's open Sunday and Tuesday from 8am to 1pm and 4 to 6pm; Monday, Wednesday and Thursday from 8am to 2pm. You can obtain up-to-date information on everything from picnicking and camping in the beachside national park to seasonal events, such as the Arts and Crafts Fair in July or August. At the **Zephania Square branch of the Tourist Office,** 2 Ha-Nassi St. (☎ 07/671-4575; www.ashkelon. gov.il; or www.ashkelon.muni.il, you can arrange for local tours, activities, and excursions of the area.

GETTING AROUND   Municipal **bus 5** serves Zepahania Square, the Afridar Center, Bus Station, and the Pedestrian Mall in Migdal. **Bus 6** serves Afridar, the Ashkelon National Antiquities Park (near the beach) and Migda; it runs once an hour.

EXPLORING ASHKELON

The part of town you must get to know is Afridar. In **Afridar Commercial Center,** with its conspicuous Clock Tower, you will find the Municipal Tourist Office, banks, shops, restaurants, cafes, a cinema, and the small Ashkelon museum. Early on during your stay in Ashkelon, check out Afridar Commercial Center.

National Antiquities Park. ☎ **07/673-6444.** Free admission; cars: NIS 18 ($4). Apr–Sept, daily 8am–7:30pm; Oct–Mar Sat only 9am–4pm.

The highlights here are archaeological sites. Walk south along the sea, and you'll see bits and pieces of pillar and column poking through the sand. Toward the end of the public beach, a staircase leads into a park; walk through the park, and you'll soon come upon the sunken arena ("Sculpture Corner") that houses Ashkelon's handful of finds: a headless Winged Victory supported on the shoulders of a childlike Atlas, Isis and child, and grouped pieces of colonnade from Herod's collection of carved capitals, "Stoa of a Hundred Columns." There's also a refreshment stand here.

Painted Roman Tomb. Free admission. Daily.

Practically hidden in the sand dunes, this Roman burial cave is just north of the Shulamit Gardens Hotel, on the beach. The paintings hold romance and eternal springtime—nymphs reclining, marsh birds nesting in a stream thick with fish. On the ceiling are nude children playing, greyhounds and gazelles, birds, and clusters of grapes. The gods Apollo and Demeter look down between the vines, assuring that the deceased's physical, if not spiritual environment, would be Elysian.

THE BEACHES

Ashkelon's main recreational attraction is the beach, and there are several public beaches. Swim only if there is a lifeguard present or at very shallow depths, since on all but the calmest days the water can hide tricky currents. All beaches are free and seldom crowded. My favorite beach areas are about a quarter of a mile north of the Antiquities Park.

WHERE TO STAY

Ashkelon charges its highest rates from mid-July to the end of August, and during Passover and the September holidays. This all has to do with Ashkelon's weather, a commodity that local residents discuss with fanatic possessiveness. You may even be offered rain insurance: For every day it rains, beginning on the second day of your stay, you get to stay a day free—breakfast included!

An inexpensive alternative to hotels is to stay in a private home. Generally, this costs about $30 to $40 per night per person, but can double during Jewish holidays and high-season weekends. To find out about home accommodations, contact the tourist office, in **Afridar Commercial Center** (☎ 07/673-2412).

EXPENSIVE

Holiday Inn. 9 Yekutiel Adam St., P.O. Box 944 Ashkelon 78100. ☎ **07/674-8888.** Fax 07/671-8822. 215 units. A/C MINIBAR TV TEL. $155–$190 double ($240 Jewish holidays, July–Aug). Rates include breakfast. AE, DC, MC, V.

Opened in 1999 and situated on a low cliff beside the Mediterranean, this is the best hotel for enjoying Ashkelon's wonderful beaches. Architecturally, the hotel is dominated by two large white igloo-shaped wings that at press time were awaiting proper landscaping. Rooms are contemporary, up to the minute, and because of the curved design of the hotel, all have views of the sea. There are also eight duplex and garden chalet suites as well as rooms for travelers with disabilities.

Dining: Giraffe Noodle Bar, a branch of the excellent Giraffe Noodle Bar in Tel Aviv, serving Asian-style cuisine; breakfast, lunch, and dinner buffets, Viennese coffee house, sandwich bar.

Amenities: Medium-size outdoor pool, Jacuzzi, tennis and basketball court, fitness room with wet and dry saunas for fee, massage, hairdresser, children's playground, business center and services.

INEXPENSIVE

Samson's Gardens (Ganei Shimshon). 38 Sonnebend (Ha-Tamar) St., Afridar, Ashkelon. ☎ **07/673-4666.** Fax 07/673-9615. 26 units (all with bathroom or shower). A/C TEL. $66–$75 double. On Jewish holidays, add $25 to higher rates plus mandatory full board. No credit cards.

Rooms here are very basic, but have terraces overlooking the garden. Guests can use the pool at a nearby hotel at reduced rates. The clientele is often composed of seniors on vacation, but this is the budget place in a town with few hotel options. Kosher

The Golden Coast

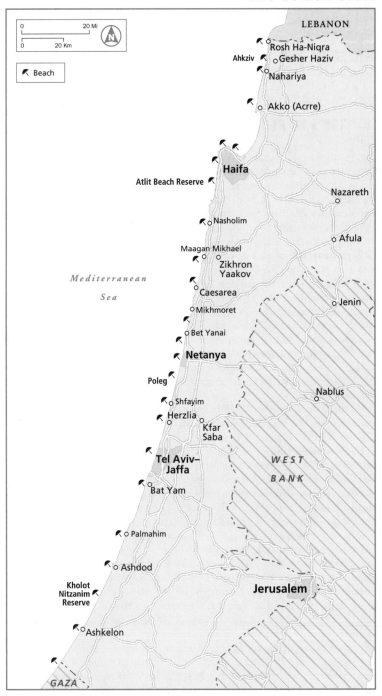

meals are available. Ha-Tamar Street is right off Darom Africa Boulevard, near the Municipal Gardens.

WHERE TO DINE

Down in Migdal, the old section of town, are various lunch counters, and there's one at the Central Bus Station as well. With such limited dining possibilities, it's not difficult to see why so many visitors arrange for half or full board at their hotels.

SIDE TRIPS TO REHOVOT & ASHDOD
REHOVOT

There are two ways of heading north from Ashkelon. The easier and faster way is along the coastal road, which intentionally misses several of the population centers in the region. The inner road, however, connecting with Gedera—once the northern tip of the Negev until Israeli farmers pushed the desert back beyond Beersheva—is well worth the extra effort and time. You can reach Rehovot from Gedera, and there's also a connecting road directly off the coastal highway.

Either way, it's a short drive to Israel's foremost scientific establishment, the ✪ **Weizmann Institute of Science** (☎ **08/934-4500** Visitor's Center). You enter through a gateway on Rehovot's main street, and as soon as you're inside the grounds you'll feel as if you've stepped into another world. This is a beautiful compound of futuristic buildings, lawns of the deepest golf-course green, lily ponds, and colorful gardens—all apparently, for the spiritual satisfaction of the hundreds of scientists from all over the world at work here.

Dedicated in 1949 in honor of Israel's first president (himself an important chemist), the institute grew out of the Daniel Sieff Research Institute, established in 1934. Conducting both fundamental and applied research, the Weizmann Institute also has a graduate school where about 700 students work for their masters degrees and doctorates.

On the grounds are the **Wix Library,** where there is an exhibition on Dr. Weizmann's life, and the **Wix Auditorium,** which presents audiovisual shows on the institute's activities at 11am and 3:15pm daily (at 11am only on Friday).

The **Weizmann House** was built by Dr. and Mrs. Weizmann as their residence in the 1930s, and is a wonderful example of International Style domestic architecture. It is a dazzling, streamlined interpretation of a Roman/Mediterranean atrium house, the masterpiece of the German refugee architect, Eric Mendelsohn, who also designed the original Hadassah Hospital and Hebrew University on Mount Scopus in Jerusalem. The interior of the house is marked by an airy, sinuous staircase set in a stair tower lit with narrow vertical windows; private living and reception wings with French doors lead to a central pool patio. Another 1930s element, round porthole windows, brings light into the house from exterior walls. The furnishings were carefully designed by Mendelsohn, who involved Dr. and Mrs. Weizmann personally in the project. The house itself (like Washington's Mount Vernon and Jefferson's Monticello) reveals much about the personality of Dr. Weizmann, the world in which he lived, and the international visitors he entertained. The Weizmann House is open Sunday through Thursday from 10am to 3pm; there are guided tours in a number of languages. At press time, tours of the Weizmann House have been suspended; to inquire about a house tour, call the Visitor's Center at the Weizmann Institute before your planned visit. Near the residence is a simple tomb marking the Weizmanns' resting place and a Memorial Plaza dominated by a Holocaust Memorial depicting the Torah being snatched from flames. A number of cafeterias at the institute serve light dairy/vegetarian meals.

Chaim Weizmann: Statesman & Scientist

Chaim Weizmann (1874–1952), biochemist, statesman, and first president of Israel, was born in a small village near Pinsk, in Russia. At the age of 11 (a decade before Herzl turned to Zionism), Weizmann wrote, "Why should we look to the kings of Europe for compassion that they should give us a resting place? In vain, all have denied . . . to Zion! Jews to Zion let us go!" A brilliant student, Weizmann gave lessons to earn his tuition at Berlin's Institute of Technology in Charlottenburg and at Fribourg University in Switzerland; in 1901, he began to teach at Geneva University. In 1903, in response to pogroms in Russia, the British foreign secretary proposed a Jewish homeland in a 5,000-square-mile area of British East Africa (Uganda). Herzl seemed willing to accept the offer; the young Weizmann sided with those who would not accept Zionism without Zion. He married Vera Chatzman, a Russian Jewish medical student, in 1906, and that year accepted a teaching position at Manchester University. In 1906, Weizmann met with Prime Minister Balfour, who wanted to interview an anti-Ugandist; Weizmann's charm and energy impressed Balfour and won him access to the highest circles of British society. He was lionized in 1916, after developing a production process for synthesizing acetone that was crucial to the British war effort. (In his professional career, Dr. Weizmann received patents for more than 100 processes and inventions.) Moving to London, he continued to build support for a Jewish homeland in Palestine. At the end of 1917, the Balfour Declaration was issued.

In the 1920s and '30s, as leader of the Zionist movement, Weizmann worked to build the infrastructure of a modern society in Palestine "house by house and dunam by dunam." Without romantic illusion and with a passion for fairness, Weizmann warned the Zionist movement to understand "the truth that 600,000 Arabs live there [in Palestine] who, before the sense of justice of the world have exactly the same right to their homes in Palestine as we have to our National Home." In 1937, addressing a Royal Commission on the Partition of Palestine, he prophetically explained the plight of European Jewry: "There are 6 million people . . . for whom the world is divided into places where they cannot live, and places which they cannot enter."

Weizmann's eloquence could not alleviate the vast tragedy that World War II brought to his people. In 1942, his own son was killed in action with the Royal Air Force over the British Channel. Struggling through the breakdown of his health and a hostile postwar British government, Weizmann's final achievement was winning American support for the incipient Jewish State in 1948. In February 1949, he was elected president of Israel, a position he held until his death. The title of Vera Weizmann's memoirs, *The Impossible Takes Longer*, summarizes the philosophy behind her husband's heavily burdened but determined optimism.

Where to Dine

Pundak Ha'Osher Ha Sheshi (The Inn of the Sixth Happiness). 53 Herzl St. ☎ **08/941-7477.** Main courses NIS 35–60 ($7.70–$13.20). DC, MC, V. Sun–Thurs 11am–9pm (last guests served). YEMENITE ISRAELI.

Rehovot is not strong on fancy restaurants, but this unpretentious place run by Mrs. Hannah Damari and her daughters offers good home-style cooking with some exotic Yemenite touches. There are well-prepared Middle Eastern salads as well as a choice of hearty Yemenite vegetable and meat soups. Main courses are grilled meats, fish, and poultry, but there may also be specials, like oven roasted lamb. Yemenite *l'huckh,* a delicious, slightly rubbery flat bread that's good with main courses, soups, and with jam and honey, is on the menu, as is regular pita.

ASHDOD

If you're traveling directly along the coast between Tel Aviv and Ashkelon, you'll pass Ashdod, now surpassing Haifa as Israel's largest and busiest port. Ashdod was one of the main Philistine coastal cities, and it was to Ashdod that the Philistines carried off the Ark of the Covenant in the period of the Judges, before the time of King Saul (1 Sam. 5:1–6). The Ark of the Covenant turned out to be a hot potato for its Philistine captors: its mere presence in Ashdod caused the idol of the Philistine god, Dagon, to fall on its face and smash to bits inside its temple during the night. Disease broke out in the city; in panic, the people of Ashdod sent the Ark to the inland Philistine town of Gath (modern Gat), and after misfortunes struck that community, the Ark was sent back to the Israelites.

   Present-day Ashdod is about 2 miles north of the ancient site. It's a planned, sprawling city of 140,000, (and growing by leaps and bounds with housing projects for recent immigrants), filled with factories and apartment blocks. Located as it is, along a glorious strip of coastline, Ashdod is scheduled to develop a tourist infrastructure sometime in the future, but for now the main tourist attraction is Idi's, one of the most famous seafood restaurants in Israel.

Where to Dine

✪ **Idi.** 6 Bosem St., Light Industrial Area, Ashdod Port. ☎ **08/852-4313.** Reservations necessary; 3 weeks in advance for Thurs evening; 1 week in advance for Fri–Sat. Complete dinner NIS 130–150 ($28.50–$33); complete lunch NIS 130 ($28.50). No credit cards. Daily noon–midnight. SEAFOOD.

People come to Idi (David Israelovits, chef and proprietor) from as far away as Jerusalem and Herziliya for his fabulous fixed-price gustatory menu of fresh fish and seafood. Travelers in this area who love seafood, or have a car, will find Idi's a very worthwhile excursion. You'll have many choices, but it is best to go with Idi's recommendation of the day. The salad mezze, accompanied by home-baked Georgian bread, is a wonderful collection of creations. The fish and seafood bouillabaisse is famous, as are the deep-fried calamari rings and sautéed shrimp served in a pan of garlic sauce. For a main course you'll be offered a selection of grilled or broiled fish and also be served additional treats from the kitchen, like calamari stuffed with mushrooms and shrimp in a rich butter, garlic, and dill sauce or steamed crab. Chocolate sorbet, halvah parfait, hot walnut pie, and a heavenly black-and-white chocolate mousse are some of the possible desserts. Decor is nautical, dress is informal. Thursday nights feature live Greek music. The exact price of a meal varies according to the catch of the day (and Idi's mood).

2 Herzlia

15 kilometers (10 mi.) N of Tel Aviv.

Herzlia is one of Israel's most famous beach resorts. It was founded in 1924 as an agricultural center, but has changed dramatically with the unexpected growth of Tel Aviv. As that large Israeli metropolis grew northward, the beaches of Herzlia suddenly became much more accessible and desirable.

   Today, when you're talking about Herzlia, you're talking about luxury. The waterfront area is studded with fine hotels and some of the country's most expensive villas;

very good restaurants abound (mostly inland). A disproportionate number of foreign diplomats reside in Herzlia; their neighbors are airline captains and other high-income earners. Swimming here is better than in Tel Aviv, and many Tel Avivans, as well as visitors, come up for a day of beaching and a pleasant meal.

ESSENTIALS

GETTING THERE   By Bus   An Egged bus ride from Tel Aviv to Herzlia takes about 45 minutes; a special bus service run by United Tours connects the Herzlia hotels with downtown and north Tel Aviv. From Herzlia you take another bus to the beach. (If you tell the bus driver that you want to go to the beach, he'll let you out at the connecting bus stop near the highway, saving you a trip into town.)

By Car   Herzlia is on a main highway, 20 minutes north of Tel Aviv.

VISITOR INFORMATION   Herzlia's sprawling layout is confusing for the first-time visitor. The luxury Sharon Hotel, right on the beach, is a major landmark. Inland just a block is De Shalit Square (Kikar De Shalit), around which you'll find several moderate hotels and inexpensive to moderate restaurants. Many fine restaurant choices will be found inland at the New Industrial Center.

THE BEACHES

This whole beachfront section of town is known as Herzlia Petuah, to differentiate it from the inland city, on a hill to the east. The Herzlia beach is lovely, but expensive by Israeli standards. The best beaches are the **Zebulun;** the **Sharon,** next to the Sharon Hotel; and the **Accadia,** between the Dan Accadia and Daniel hotels. Remember that a dangerous undertow exists, and swimming is strictly prohibited when a lifeguard is not on duty.

WHERE TO STAY
EXPENSIVE

Dan Accadia Hotel. Herzlia on the Sea 46851. ☎ **09/959-7070.** Fax 09/959-7090. 207 units. A/C MINIBAR TV TEL. $244–$380 double. 15% service charge. Rates include breakfast. Family plan and children's rates. AE, DC, MC, V.

Located on the beach in the far southern part of town, this relatively low rise resort hotel, built in 1956 and heavily renovated in 1999, is set among lawns and gardens that center on the pool area. Standard rooms are a bit small, but all have balconies and the fresh new room decor is most inviting. There are also deluxe "chalet" rooms in the pool garden, as well as very comfortable suites. There are activities for children on weekends and during the summer, poolside barbecues and dancing, and the management can arrange horseback riding and access to the golf course of the Dan Caesarea Hotel a half-hour drive to the north. Discounts are available on the Dan Hotels 7-day plan.

   Dining/Diversions: Two restaurants, snack bars, coffee shop, bar.
   Amenities: 24-hour room service, massage, hairdresser. Outdoor pool, six tennis courts, Jacuzzi, wet and dry sauna, health club, shopping arcade, free parking.

MODERATE

Tadmor Hotel. 38 Basel St., Herzlia 46660. ☎ **09/952-5000.** Fax 09/957-5124. 58 units (all with bathroom or shower). A/C TV TEL. $90–$136 double. Off-season discounts. Rates include breakfast. AE, DC, MC, V.

The Tadmor Hotel, a 5-minute walk to the beach, is an Israeli institution. Hotel staffs from all over the country train here, and chefs are cultivated and launched from the Tadmor. To this end, the hotel has two in-house restaurants and a good lunch buffet.

The building has character; it looks a bit like a desert fortress. Rooms are well maintained and comfortable, but bathrooms are small. Large gardens, an outdoor swimming pool, and a fine park with a children's playground are additional highlights.

To find the hotel, walk three blocks east of Shalit Square. Driving from Tel Aviv, look for Basel Street to the left off the main road.

OUTSIDE HERZLIA

Kibbutz Shefayim Guest House. Kibbutz Shefayim. ☎ **09/959-5595.** Fax 09/959-5555. 166 units (110 with bathtub, 56 with shower). A/C TV TEL. $86–$166 double. AE, MC, V.

Right on the sea, a 10-minute drive north of Herzlia, the location of this low-rise, modern kibbutz guest house has put it in great demand with both Israelis and visitors. A children's playground and a busy water park containing a swimming pool with waves and slides, open to the public, is another attraction, especially for families with children; it's open mid-April to mid-October. The grounds of the kibbutz are especially extensive, and include wild, sandy paths along the top of cliffs overlooking the sea, and a beach that's good for bathing on calm days—when the sea is even mildly rough, the presence of rocks in the water makes for hazards. Always check for the hours when lifeguards are on duty. At times, a kibbutz tractor brings guests up and down the cliff to the beach, a welcome aid on hot summer days. Rooms are simple but comfortable; there are rooms for travelers with disabilities.

It's on the main Tel Aviv–Haifa highway; look for exit sign for Shefayim.

WHERE TO DINE

The best place to look for inexpensive meals is in **De Shalit Square** (Kikar De Shalit), a pleasant little plaza surrounded by snack shops, ice-cream parlors, and small restaurants catering to locals and the beach crowd alike. You'll find more expensive, inventive restaurants in the building complexes of Herzlia's New Industrial Center, inland from the beach, near the Tel Aviv–Haifa highway. In fact, people from all over Israel come here for some of the best dining experiences in the country! All of our restaurant choices here are worth a star and, with the exception of Tandoori and Picasso (which have branches in Tel Aviv), they're all worth a trip from Tel Aviv.

EXPENSIVE

✪ **Ginadi on the Sea.** Promenade South of Sharon Hotel. ☎ **09/954-9958.** Reservations recommended. Main courses NIS 80–100 ($17.60–$22). AE, DC, MC, V. Daily 12:30–4pm and 7pm–midnight. SEAFOOD.

For many years, Ginadi was sous-chef at Jerusalem's elysian Ocean Restaurant; now (perhaps to the chagrin of his former employer—see Ocean, below) he's taken his superb skill with fish and seafood to this informal pavilion open to the rolling waves and the evening sunset. A meal here should begin with Ginadi's paradisiacal focaccia with rosemary and olive oil, served with antipasti (I'd request slightly fewer olives in the antipasti and more of the spectacular *hatselem,* or garlic and eggplant puree if possible). Appetizers are wonderful (in the $7.50 to $11 range) and along with the focaccia and antipasti, could make a pleasant meal. The shrimp grilled on salt; crabmeat wrapped in pasta leaf; and calamari grilled in olive oil and herbs are simple perfection. For main courses, choose from among grilled whole or fillet fish, or beautifully prepared lamb served with portions of fascinating vegetables. When Ginadi is not in-house to perform his magic with grilled fish, meals here can be merely good instead of sensational. The atmosphere is informal and waiters are friendly but not too knowledgeable or stylish; time may develop more definite standards. A large, careful wine list and worthwhile desserts are available.

✪ **Ocean.** 7 Shenkar St., Bldg. 3, Herzilia Petuach. ☎ **09/957-2270.** Reservations necessary. Main courses NIS 80–140 ($17.60–$30). AE, DC, MC, V. Daily noon–3pm; 7–11pm. Entering Herzlia from main highway, Shenkin St. is a left at the Office Depot Center. NOUVELLE MEDITERRANEAN.

Opened in late 1999, this may develop into one of Israel's more spectacular restaurants. Eyal Sheni, chef and owner of Jerusalem's legendary Ocean restaurant has decided to move closer to his natural clientele of well-heeled, worldly restaurant-goers, and has put everything into this new Herzlia endeavor. Like its Jerusalem predecessor this Ocean does not face the sea—instead, the focal point of the restaurant is Sheni's personally designed open kitchen. Everything is prepared over special citrus wood fires in the style that Eyal Sheni made famous. The restaurant specializes not only in (unfarmed) fish, but also in a menu of game meat that changes each day. Among its promises are quality prime rib of beef; citrus fire baked rack of lamb; pigeon; free range Negev chicken, as well as a superb roast grouper, all served with tiny herbed, stuffed vegetables cooked alongside main courses in the citrus wood ovens. The best of Sheni's Jerusalem masterpieces have been transferred here: heavenly grilled shrimps; seafood ravioli and crab wrapped in pasta leaf; and his signature foccaccia and antipasti. Look for delightful desserts, like a gourmet version of the traditional Middle Eastern baked cheese and honey dessert, *kanafe,* here done with a mixture of buffalo mozzarella and goat cheese roasted with orange blossom honey. The wine list is up to the menu's standard of lively excellence.

✪ **Taverna.** Dan Accadia Hotel Beach Promenade. ☎ **09/959-7107.** Reservations recommended. Main courses NIS 63–130 ($14–$28.60). AE, DC, MC, V. Sun–Thurs 6pm–midnight; Fri–Sat noon–midnight. CONTINENTAL.

Right on the beach, with an outdoor dining terrace and a beautiful view of the sunset, this is a pricey but easygoing restaurant with ceiling fans and sea breezes and a wide selection of seafood, fish, and meat. For appetizers, try the interesting Greek/Mediterranean array of small salads (mezedes) for about $3 to $5 each. You can also have light courses like goat cheese mousse, a plate of little fried fishes, or foie gras in onions and raisins, all in the $7 to $12 range. Among main courses, you'll find a changing daily menu including items like fried mullet in chili and lemon sauce, salmon trout in coriander and cream, fried mussels, or prawns diablo. There's also a selection of lamb, beef, and chicken. With its fine view, this is a good place to come off-hours just for coffee and dessert or evening drinks.

MODERATE

Black Steer Grill House. 3 Yohanan Ha Sandlar St., Herzlia Industrial Area. ☎ **09/955-7464.** Reservations necessary. Main courses NIS 50–130 ($11–$28.50); business lunches NIS 50–65 ($11.20–$14.30). AE, DC, MC, V. Daily noon–midnight. SOUTH AFRICAN STEAKHOUSE.

The best steak restaurant in the Tel Aviv area, the Black Steer is part of a famous South African chain with branches in Zimbabwe, Indonesia, and Australia. Choose from a variety of grilled steaks, spare ribs, and chicken, all served with tasty South African–style marinades. The business lunches, served from noon to 5pm are unbeatable deals; whenever you dine, you'll have excellent value and a filling meal. There are vegetarian choices. Free parking.

Coconut. Mercazim Building, 32 Maskit St. ☎ **09/956-8989.** Reservations necessary. Main courses NIS 28–70 ($6.20–$15.40). AE, DC, MC, V. Daily noon–3:30pm; 7pm–1am. THAI.

The best Thai restaurant in the Tel Aviv area, Coconuts is very reasonably priced, and offers a very large menu of well-prepared first and main courses. The fresh fish, steamed or fried, and the unusual tofu dishes are excellent, and you can ask for the curries and Thai sauces to be either toned down, or served at authentically fiery levels.

Erez. 52 Berekit St. ☎ **09/955-9892.** Reservations useful. Main courses NIS 43–80 ($9.50–$17.60). AE, DC, MC, V. Sun–Fri 8am–midnight; Sat 9:30am–midnight. BREADS & MEDITERRANEAN RIM.

First known for its fabulous breads (the best in Israel) and Mediterranean sandwiches filled with flavor, this restaurant, the creation of owner Erez Komarovsky, has expanded in recent years and become a testing ground for Komarovsky's intelligent, personal talent as a chef. Lunch and dinner offer a changing menu of inventive dishes: Always begin a meal here with one of the house focaccias—like *bianca,* spread with spices and chives and served with peeled roasted peppers, grilled zucchini, and earthy, Arabic-style labaneh (yogurt); or a focaccia of local prosciutto ham, covered with sprigs of sage and rosemary. Main courses might include sea fish with tomatoes and *za'atar* (local spices) baked on olive wood fires in a stone oven; fillet of pork baked in a sweet/bitter pomegranate syrup flavored with cumin and coriander and served on a bed of arugula and dill; chicken grilled with mustard seeds, Szechuan pepper and dill; or fried calamari in herbed olive oil with a seafood sauce. There are pastas, seafood bisques, foie gras, country salads and cheeses, stuffed steamed and baked rolls, all done with the unique Erez twist. Many dishes take risks and may not please everyone.

Picasso. 1 Ha-Etzel St., Herzliya Pituach. ☎ **09/956-6888.** Reservations recommended. Light meals NIS 33–55 ($7–$12); main courses NIS 55–95 ($12–$21). AE, DC, MC, V. Daily 8am–2am. CONTINENTAL.

This branch of Tel Aviv's quintessentially stylish but moderately priced restaurant offers an exciting, intelligent menu. Seafood, poultry, fish, and meat dishes, as well as enormous hot and cold salads, all presented in unusual ways, have made this a smash hit. New surprises are always being added to the menu including a line of healthful low-calorie choices. The large rooftop bar is an additional evening draw.

✪ **Tandoori.** Mercazim Building, 32 Maskit St., New Industrial Center. ☎ **09/954-6702.** Reservations recommended. Main courses NIS 28–65 ($6.20–$14.30). 10% service charge. AE, DC, MC, V. Daily 12:30–3:30pm and 7pm–1am. INDIAN.

This is the most opulent of the fine restaurants in the Tandoori chain, with twin curved marble staircases leading to the upper dining area, and decorative silver and enamel work imported from Jaipur. As in all the Tandoori/Kohinoor restaurants, the traditional Indian dishes you'll find here are prepared with a special lightness and elegance. I especially liked the sabzi jalfrezi, a very modestly priced dish of vegetables lightly steamed and then quickly dry-sautéed with ginger, garlic, cumin seeds, and fresh mustard. The boneless tandoori chicken dishes are my favorites, especially chicken tikka masala, but the whole range of lamb and fish choices is also superb. It's worthwhile trying the traditional Indian home-style desserts. The Tandoori chain is also famous for its cocktails. The entire experience is one of tranquillity and elegance, yet the price is reasonable.

INEXPENSIVE

Crocodile. Kikar De Shalit. ☎ **03/957-0762** or 03/957-5026. Reservations recommended. Main courses NIS 50–95 ($11–$21); salad bar NIS 44 ($10); fixed-price dinner NIS 65 ($14.30). MC, V. Daily noon–midnight or later. AMERICAN/ISRAELI.

In an expensive town like Herzlia, Crocodile is an attractive oasis of good, reasonably priced food; I place it in the inexpensive range because of the salad bar and fixed-price dinner options. The luxurious salad bar includes a selection of 25 interesting fresh salads, plus four hot vegetable dishes that range from a daily Asian stir-fry to a Saturday vegetarian bean cholent, or Sabbath casserole. The fixed-price Deal of the Week includes the salad bar, soup, your choice of one of five main courses, and coffee or tea—one of the town's great bargains. The place has a garden feel, with style enhanced by green tablecloths, candles, and tables that offer a more private ambience. The specials bring Crocodile into the inexpensive range, but those ordering à la carte will find this restaurant more in the moderate range. There's an NIS 36 ($8) complete children's meal.

3 Netanya

34 kilometers (21 mi.) N of Tel Aviv.

Netanya is regarded as the capital of the Sharon Plain, the rich and fertile citrus-grove area stretching from the outskirts of Tel Aviv to Caesarea. Perched on verdant cliffs overlooking the Mediterranean, it is also the center of Israel's diamond industry.

Founded in 1929 as a citrus center, the seaside town has for many years been a popular holiday place for Israelis. Over the years visitors (especially long-term visitors and senior citizens) have been joining them, for they've discovered that Netanya is quiet and convenient, geared to service, and in easy reach of several areas, including Tel Aviv and Caesarea. It's a sizable city, with all sorts of cafes, hotels, and shops—but the real appeal remains the sunny beach and easygoing pace. (*Note:* Those with walking problems may find the stairs up and down the cliff to Netanya's beaches something of an obstacle.) Those who decide to rent an apartment and stay in Netanya for a month or more will find the local English-speaking community extremely well organized. The population of Netanya has grown by more than a fifth in recent years with an influx of new immigrants from eastern Europe and the former Soviet Union, so Netanya has more of a European flavor than other Israeli cities.

A handsome park parallels the beach—and the coast itself has become popular with Scandinavian visitors who take dips in December and January. Most everybody else waits until April or May, when the weather is almost perfect.

ESSENTIALS

GETTING THERE   By Bus   Several express buses operate between Netanya and Jerusalem. Connections are available from Haifa, and there is regular bus service from Tel Aviv. Netanya buses (no. 601 or 605) leave Tel Aviv about every 15 minutes during the day until 7pm. The last bus to Tel Aviv departs at 11pm.

By Car   There is a main coastal highway that connects Tel Aviv and Haifa.

VISITOR INFORMATION   The **Tourist Information Office** (☎ 09/882-7286) is in a little modern kiosk at the southeastern corner of Independence Square. Hours are 8:30am to 6pm on Sunday to Thursday; from 9am to noon on Friday. Winter hours may be shorter. This office is especially helpful, and will answer questions about Netanya or other places in Israel. Be sure to pick up a copy of the monthly booklet listing special events, entertainment, and services in Netanya. If you're traveling by bus, you might also want to pick up their bus timetable, which you might find clearer than the information you'll get at the station.

Netanya closes down between 1 and 4pm every day, so plan to shop or go to the bank before or after the afternoon siesta.

SOCIAL CLUBS   Many international social clubs hold regular meetings in Netanya, including Rotary, Lions, Hadassah, Freemasons, International Toastmistress, Pioneer Women, and B'nai B'rith. Ask at the tourist office, or see the listings in the free guides to Netanya for times and places. Open House for Visitors is held every Monday, Tuesday, and Wednesday from 9:30 to 11:30am, at the British

Olim Society, 7 Ha-Matmid St., and also on Wednesday at 4pm at the **WIZO House,** 13 MacDonald St. (☎ **09/882-3192**). **The Association of Americans and Canadians in Israel (AACI),** at 28 Shmuel Ha-Naziv St. (☎ **09/833-0950**), offers a good schedule of lectures and other social activities.

If you'd like to meet an Israeli citizen, apply 3 days in advance at the tourist office and you'll soon find yourself invited to a home for a friendly chat and a cup of coffee.

SPECIAL EVENTS   In late July, there is a 1-week art exhibit on Ha-Atzma'ut Square (Sunday to Thursday from 5:30 to 11pm; closed Friday; Saturday from 8:30pm to midnight). The city sponsors free evening concerts and events throughout the summer. A **chess tournament** is held in Netanya yearly during May and June; every 2 years there's an international match. Games start at 3:30pm and last until 10pm. For further information, contact the tourist information office.

During Sukkot (Feast of Tabernacles), there are 4 free evenings of **folklore** in Ha-Atzma'ut Square, featuring the various ethnic groups living in Israel, with dance, song, and typical traditional snacks.

CITY LAYOUT   Netanya is a big town, but it's not really difficult to find your way around. The main coastal highway is known as the **Haifa Road.** Coming north on Haifa Road from Tel Aviv, you will see the exit for Netanya, which will get you onto **Herzl Street,** Netanya's main east-west boulevard. At the beginning of Herzl Boulevard, not far from the coastal highway, you'll pass the large **Kanion** (indoor shopping mall).

About 6 blocks down the street is the **Central Bus Station,** where Herzl meets Weizmann and Benyamin boulevards. Another six blocks along Herzl and you're in the great expanse of **Ha-Atzma'ut Square,** by the sea in the very heart of Netanya. Most of the hotels and restaurants recommended below are within a few blocks of the square.

The square, the town's pedestrian promenade, has been enlarged in recent years, and now extends up Herzl Street all the way to Dizengoff Street.

Around Ha-Aztma'ut Square you'll find everything you need, including the Tourist Information Office, banks, ATM machines, places to change money, a post office, and eateries of many kinds as well as pubs, discos, cinema, hotels, and more. Be warned that since the center of Netanya was not designed for a population of almost 200,000, parking is a serious problem, and parking regulations are enforced with draconian rigor!

BEACHES, SPORTS & OTHER OUTDOOR PURSUITS

BEACHES & WATER SPORTS   The main attraction at Netanya is, of course, the lovely beach, and you'll have perfect beach weather here more than 75% of the year. The water is great for swimming—you can go out pretty far before it starts to get deep. There's a lifeguard on duty, and do swim in the approved area; it's posted not to swim beyond a certain point. In addition to sand, swimming, and sun, you can enjoy the attractions in the beach complex, with restaurants and snack shops, beach chairs, large public umbrellas, a basketball court, and a gymnastics field. You'll see people **fishing** up on the rocky breakwater. **Surfing** and **sailboarding** can be arranged at the Kontiki Club down on the Netanya beach—lessons, too—open daily from 8:30am until sunset.

Of course it's beautiful to see the sun set into the Mediterranean, and in the high tourist season, student patrols keep watch to make sure everything is okay. The lifeguards leave the beach in the late afternoon. Still, be cautious at night here; stay where you see other people, especially if you're a woman alone. During the winter when the student patrols are not around, it's not a good idea to hang around the beach or the parks on the cliffs at night.

The Anglo-Saxon Connection

Visitors to Israel from English-speaking countries are often amazed at how easy it is to get around using their native language, especially in light of the fact that Israel's two official languages, Hebrew and Arabic, don't even share alphabets that remotely resemble our own. In major cities, signs, traffic instructions, and restaurant menus are almost always in both English and Hebrew. Israeli entrepreneurs have become adept at designing shop signs and logos that blend English and Hebrew lettering (which are written in opposite directions) into interesting compositions, and the chance is good that your 20-something waitperson, the sales clerk where you take your film to be developed, or the elderly Palestinian owner of a grocery shop will be able to shift into fluent English at a moment's notice. And unlike many European countries, which dub English-language films and television programs, in Israel you won't have to watch Julia Roberts, Tom Hanks, or Jerry Seinfeld bantering away in Hebrew.

Of course, the British were here from 1918 to 1948, but 30 years of the British Mandate are only one part of the formula that has made Israel so user-friendly to the English-speaking world. Immigrants to Israel from English-speaking countries, though less than 2% of the general population, have had an impact far beyond their numbers. Known locally (and to their own bemusement) as Anglo-Saxons, these Israelis have provided two of the nation's eight presidents—**Chaim Weizmann,** a British subject whose scientific discoveries were crucial to the Allied victory in World War I; and Dublin-born **Chaim Herzog,** whose father served as chief rabbi of Ireland. **Golda Meir,** a former schoolteacher from Milwaukee, held many important positions in Labor Party governments, including that of prime minister from 1969 to 1974. Former Prime Minister **Benjamin Netanyahu** was raised and educated in America. Israel's most famous and eloquent diplomat, South African–born Cambridge-educated **Abba Eban,** served as ambassador to the United Nations and was foreign minister for many years; the American-born **Moshe Arens** was foreign minister in the Likud governments of the 1980s and early 1990s. **Henrietta Szold,** the Baltimore-born first president of Hadassah, held the social welfare portfolio of the National Council of Palestine Jewry in the 1930s and was responsible for developing many elements of the emerging nation's system of health, education, and social services. South Africans, Britons, and Americans were heavily involved in creating the Association for Civil Rights in Israel, and are in the forefront of the women's rights, religious rights, and ecology and peace movements. Americans are also strongly represented in the West Bank and Gaza Settlement movements. Despite their extraordinary contribution, Anglo-Israelis are regarded by many of their fellow countrymen as something of a people apart.

The Association of Americans and Canadians in Israel (AACI) and the **British Olim Society** (for British, South African, and Australian immigrants), with branches in most main cities, offer busy schedules of lectures, get-togethers, activities, tours, and legal advice for seniors, singles, and families, and are a terrific resource for English-speaking visitors who plan to stay in Israel for an extended period of time.

If you have a car, you might want to drive to sheltered ✪ **Mikmoret Beach,** about 7 or 8 miles north toward Caesarea. It goes on for miles, and is a great place for walking.

There are lifeguards, and other facilities; parking is NIS 22 ($5) per car, but the fee is deducted from your bill if you eat a meal at the beach's restaurant.

HORSEBACK RIDING & OTHER SPORTS   Riding is available at two locations. **The Ranch** (☎ **09/866-3525**), in northern Netanya, has horseback riding daily from 8am until sunset; take bus no. 17 or 29 from the Central Bus Station. There's also the **Cactus Ranch** (☎ **09/865-1239**), open daily from 8am until sunset. Rates are approximately $20 per hour. It's always wise to reserve ahead.

Bicycle rentals can be arranged at the Hotel Promenade (☎ **09/862-6450**).

Paragliding off the sandy bluffs along the Israeli coast has become a major sport in Netanya. Lessons and equipment can be arranged through **Dvir Paragliding** (☎ **09/899-0277;** fax 09/899-1705). For other Israeli paragliding sites, contact AGUR, the Israel Hang-gliding and Paragliding Club, Sea Palace Beach, P.O. Box 1035, Bat Yam 59110 Israel; or Sky Paragliding LTD. 4 Hacharuv St., Rishpan 46915, Israel (e-mail: sky-pg@inter.net.il).

NATURE WALKS & HIKING   The **Poleg Nature Reserve,** 8 kilometers (13 mi.) south of Netanya, offers an interesting hike along the Poleg River, upstream from the point where it meets the sea. The riverbanks are lined with giant eucalyptus trees, planted almost a century ago to help drain the swamps that had developed throughout the plain of Sharon (eucalyptus seedlings were imported from Australia by early Jewish settlers, who valued their ability to withstand drought). In winter and early spring, the wildflowers along the route have made the Poleg Reserve a favorite destination for botanists. Unfortunately, the Poleg River has become seriously polluted, a situation not unusual in the intensively developed coastal plain. Recently, the Mediterranean beach has been closed to swimming, and the river water itself will probably be off-limits to visitors.

The **Iris Nature Reserve,** at the southern edge of Netanya, is a sanctuary for wild and cultivated irises. There is an adjacent pond that attracts seaside birds and waterfowl. In February and March, the Reserve is carpeted with wild, dark blue irises—pathways let you immerse yourself in this paradise that few travelers know about.

SPORTS CENTERS   **Elitzur Sports Center** (☎ **09/865-2931**) has a heated swimming pool and features squash and tennis. The center is at the end of Radak Street (take bus no. 8 from the Central Bus Station). It is open daily from 6 or 8am until 5 to 10pm (call to check which hours are on what days). The **Wingate Institute** (☎ **09/863-9523** or 09/863-9521) also has a swimming pool, as do many Netanya hotels.

VISITING A DIAMOND FACTORY

Israel is the number-one spot in the world for cutting and polishing diamonds, and Netanya is Israel's number-one diamond center, with two large factories. If you're in the market to buy, you can probably save about 20% by buying here. Even if you're not interested in buying, a visit to the **National Diamond Center,** 90 Herzl St. (☎ **09/862-0436**), could still be an unusual experience. Telephone for information about the center's interesting and pressure-free tours. The Tourist Information Office can direct you to additional diamond industry tours in Netanya.

WHERE TO STAY

In most cases, you needn't go far out of Ha-Atzma'ut Square to find a hotel. Netanya is oriented toward warm-weather vacationers and prices are seasonal. Even inexpensive hotels can charge moderate to expensive rates during high season. Generally speaking, high season is from early July to the end of August, plus Jewish holidays, and low season is November to February; between these times the prices will be somewhere between the high- and low-season rates.

In winter, be sure to check for heating—days can be balmy but nights can get chilly. All of Netanya's hotel kitchens are kosher.

NORTH OF HA-ATZMA'UT SQUARE

Rehov Ha-Melekh David is the main street going north out of Ha-Atzma'ut Square, close to the beach.

Expensive

Mercure Blue Bay Hotel. 37 Hamelachim St., Netanya. ☎ **09/860-3603.** Fax 09/833-7475. 196 units (all with bathtub or shower). A/C TV TEL. $125–$170 double. Rates include breakfast. Add 15% service charge. AE, DC, MC, V. Bus: 29.

The most northern of the town's hotels, the Blue Bay offers hourly shuttle service into the center of Netanya. Away from the sometimes busy tempo of Ha-Atzma'ut Square, this Mercure hotel is one of the largest in town. Much renovation has been done over the past few years; avoid those rooms that have not been upgraded. Facilities include a swimming pool (heated in winter), a new fitness room with sauna and Jacuzzi, restaurant, disco, bar, and a floodlit tennis court. There's a resort feel here; rooms have video players, and you can arrange bicycle rentals and in-room massage.

✪ **Seasons Hotel.** Nice Blvd., Netanya. ☎ **09/860-1555.** Fax 09/862-3022. E-mail: seasons@internet-zahav.net. 85 units (all with bathtub). A/C TV TEL. $140–$260 double standard rooms; add $150–$200 for deluxe units and suites. Rates include breakfast and service. AE, DC, MC, V.

Until the advent of the Carmel Hotel at the southern edge of Netanya, the 30-year-old Seasons was the city's top hotel. Guest rooms are large, with balconies and sea view; suites are very comfortable. Much of the hotel was totally renovated in 1994–95. Facilities include a heated outdoor swimming pool, fitness room, Jacuzzi, sauna, night-lit tennis court, three restaurants, a hair salon, and free parking. A refrigerator/minibar is available on request.

Moderate

Maxim Hotel. 8 King David St., Netanya 42264. ☎ **09/862-1062.** Fax 09/862-0190. 90 units (all with bathroom). A/C TV TEL. $70–$140 double. Rates include breakfast. AE, DC, MC, V.

The Maxim Hotel is the equivalent of a four-star establishment, and has a swimming pool and bar. Over half the guest rooms are extrasized, and at the top of the price range. Major renovations in 1997 have spruced up and freshened the facilities.

Inexpensive

Hotel Ginot Yam. 9 King David St., Netanya 42264. ☎ **09/834-1007.** Fax 09/861-5722. 54 units (all with bathroom or shower). A/C TV TEL. $58–$104 double. Rates include breakfast. AE, DC, MC, V.

On the left as you stroll up King David Street, this three-story building near the Bialik intersection is literally a stone's throw from the sea. Rooms have heat, wall-to-wall carpeting, and radios among other amenities, and there are rooms for the disabled. There's a small snack bar/restaurant.

SOUTH OF HA-ATZMA'UT SQUARE

On the south side of Ha-Atzma'ut Square, several main streets and side streets will lead you to hotel choices that are only a short walk from the beach and from the busy square.

Expensive

La Promenade Apartment Hotel. 6 Gad Machnes St., Netanya. ☎ **09/862-6450.** Fax 09/862-6450. 15 apts (all with bathroom or shower). A/C TV TEL. $140–$230 double. Up to 5 people, add $15–$25 per person. Rates include breakfast. 15% service charge. AE, DC, MC, V.

Built in the early 1990s, this is the best of Netanya's apartment hotels. Apartments are sleek, with polished marble floors and contemporary decor; all have kitchenettes and balconies. There is an indoor swimming pool and Jacuzzi, room service, and free parking. The location is in the center of things, close to Ha-Atzma'ut Square and the beach. Monthly rates are available.

Moderate

Residence Hotel. 18 Gad Machnes St., Netanya. ☎ **09/862-3777.** Fax 09/862-3711. www.inisrael.com/zyvotels. 96 units (all with bathroom or shower). A/C TV TEL. $70–$150 double. Rates include breakfast. AE, DC, MC, V.

Billing itself as "Netanya's most luxurious three-star hotel," the Residence is building its clientele by offering cut-rate prices for people staying a 1-week minimum. Most of the rooms have balconies and spectacular views of the sea. Since the hotel is eight stories tall, if you get an upper room you'll really have a bird's-eye view. There are special reduced rates for June, September, and November 1 to 15. The Residence Hotel is part of the Zyvotel Chain, with a number of properties in Netanya; guests can use the nearby Blueweiss Hotel's spa and health club for an $8 fee; or the Jacuzzi and sauna at the nearby Hotel Galil.

Inexpensive

Margoa. 9 Gad Machnes St., Netanya 42279. ☎ **09/862-4434.** Fax 09/862-3430. 64 units (all with bathroom or shower.) A/C TV TEL. $70–$110 double. AE, MC, V.

Just a short distance from the information kiosk is the Hotel Margoa—actually two Hotel Margoas, the Margoa "A" on your left and the Margoa "B" on your right, by the sea. For either hotel, the reception, as well as the dining, are done at the Margoa A. Rooms come with heat, air-conditioning, and wall-to-wall carpeting. Some of the rooms in Margoa A have balconies.

SOUTH NETANYA
Expensive

✪ **Carmel Hotel.** Jabotinsky St., Netanya. ☎ **09/860-1111,** or 09/860-1170 reservations. Fax 09/860-1166, or 09/860-1171 reservations. 190 units (all with bathroom). A/C TV TEL. $145–$255 double; additional $50–$70 for deluxe rms and suites. Rates include breakfast. 15% service charge. AE, DC, MC, V.

Built in 1994, this high-rise hotel on a now quiet stretch of beach (slated to become a luxury resort center) 2 miles south of downtown Netanya, is the city's only five-star-equivalent hotel; it has set a new standard for luxury in Netanya. Public areas are busy, rooms are fresh and attractive. Like much of Netanya, the hotel is located on a cliff above the beach—getting down to the beach can be a problem, although an elevator service is planned. Facilities include a large swimming pool, heated in winter, a health club, sauna, steam bath, Jacuzzi, children's programs in summer and holidays, and a variety of restaurants and pubs. There are ample parking facilities (always at a premium in Netanya); refrigerators and minibars are available on request. There are rooms for travelers with disabilities.

PRIVATE ROOMS & APARTMENTS

One of the best ways to save money on accommodations, particularly if you plan to stay in Netanya for some time, is to rent a private room or apartment. The actual rental arrangements will generally be handled by local agents, and you'll have to pay an agent's fee, which is a flat 10% of the total rental (no extra charge if meal arrangements are made).

Room rentals are available for at least 3 to 4 days, apartments for a week or more. Most of them are within walking distance of the sea. Rooms in private homes come with sheets and blankets, and no meals are served, though guests may use the refrigerator and stove. The cost is about $30 to $40 per person in summer; prices go up on weekends and holidays and are lower off-season.

Apartments are provided with basic furniture. The place is cleaned up before you arrive, but upkeep is on you for the length of your stay. A studio or what is known as a two-room flat (living room, one bedroom, kitchen, bathroom, balconies) costs about $900 to well over $1,000 per couple per month. A three-room flat (two-plus bedrooms) costs more than $1,500 per month. Deluxe accommodations, of course, could be more. Bear in mind that these are summer rates, and that demand will probably drive these prices up during the lifetime of this edition. The supply of apartments may also be a problem.

Consult the **Municipal Tourist Information** desk at Ha-Atzma'ut Square (☎ **09/882-7286**) for listings of private room and apartment rental agents.

WHERE TO DINE

Most of the town's cafes and restaurants line Ha-Atzma'ut Square.

EXPENSIVE

Lucullus. 2 Jabotinsky St. ☎ **09/861-9502.** Fixed-price lunch $19; fixed-price dinner $26. MC, V. Daily noon–3pm and 6pm–midnight. FRENCH/SEAFOOD.

This is probably the best and most stylish restaurant in town, and the place for a special meal. Tables are candlelit and decorated with fresh flowers, there's dance music on Fridays, and often a pianist at the bar in the evenings. Bernard Gabai, the owner of Lucullus, was born in Tunisia, and he has created a menu heavily influenced by French tradition. First courses include choices like mousse of salmon and shrimp or pâté de foie gras; main course choices include fresh fish, calamari, shrimp, and lobster as well as filet mignon, goose liver, duck, and even chateaubriand. If you choose from the à la carte menu, a complete dinner with wine could run well over $35 per person. Lucullus is located in the southern part of town, somewhat away from Ha-Atzma'ut Square. When you call for reservations, ask about the restaurant's free taxi service policy.

MODERATE

Apropo Netanya. Gan Ha Melech. ☎ **09/862-4482.** Reservations recommended for summer and holiday evenings. Main courses NIS 30–75 ($6.60–$16.50). 12% service charge. AE, DC, MC, V. Sun–Thurs 9am–midnight; Fri 9am–2pm; Sat after Shabbat to midnight. EUROPEAN/INTERNATIONAL.

In a modern, glass pavilion overlooking the sea at the far end of Ha-Atzma'ut Square, this restaurant serves the most cosmopolitan menu in town, ranging from large salads to pastas, blintzes, bagels and lox, and a list of appetizers and main courses prepared with a tasty, Thai-style touch. You can order salmon trout steamed with fine herbs, in a mildly Thai fashion, or have a traditional Thai soup, or kosher fried sesame-coated faux "shrimp." A selection of lavish kosher pastries and cakes makes this a good stop for coffee and dessert.

Pundak Ha-Yam Grill. 1 Ha-Rav Kook St. ☎ **09/861-5780.** Main courses NIS 32–60 ($7–$13.20). MC, V. Reservations not accepted. Sat–Thurs noon–midnight; Fri noon–3:30pm. GRILL.

A plain, no-nonsense grill with meats sizzling, hard-working waiters, and a minimum of decor, it is nonetheless a top favorite with locals. Reasons? The grilled meats are prepared to your order, right before your eyes; service is quick, portions are good, and prices are moderate. Order shashlik, steak, heart, or liver, and you'll get a salad, french fries, a plate of spaghetti, and several rounds of flat bread, too. For noncarnivores, there are interesting salads.

✪ **Yotvata.** Ha-Atzma'ut Square ☎ **09/862-9141.** Light meals NIS 22–32 ($5–$7); main courses NIS 32–75 ($7–$16.50). AE, DC, MC, V. Daily 8am–1am. DAIRY VEGETARIAN.

One of the best-quality dairy and vegetarian restaurants in the country, Yotvata has everything brought in fresh from the famous Yotvata Kibbutz down in the Negev. Giant servings of natural juices made from your choice of 15 different kinds of fruits are available as well as blintzes, vegetable pies, pasta dishes in cream sauces, cheesecakes, and great ice cream, all done with style. Saint Peter's fish rounds out the top end of the menu's price range.

NETANYA AFTER DARK

There's no problem finding plenty of things to do around Netanya after a day at the beach. Everything in Ha-Atzma'ut Square is open until around midnight or later, and the square is alive with strollers, sippers, diners, and people-watching cafe-sitters on a warm evening.

Be sure to check with the Tourist Information Office and the weekly calendar in the Tel Aviv section of Friday's *Jerusalem Post* for special events, performances, and activities of all kinds, including the weekly activities at the AACI, the Women's International Zionist Organization (WIZO), and the British Olim Society. There's quite a lot going on, especially during the summer months. Each week, in the amphitheater in **Gan Ha-Melekh Park,** which runs along the beachside cliffs just north of the square, there are community sings, screenings of free full-length feature films, and classical and light music (performed Sunday to Thursday from 5:45pm until sunset). There's also entertainment in **Ha-Atzma'ut Square** by top Israeli singers and folklore groups as well as community folk dancing every Saturday, beginning at 8pm. Weekly programs for children start at 6:30pm, with magicians, clowns, and so on.

Since Netanya is a resort town, with a seasonal turnover in clubs and discos, it's best to check about current choices with the well-informed tourist office at Ha-Atzma'ut Square. **Bridge** is often sponsored by WIZO on alternate Wednesday evenings; **Bingo evenings** at the Association of Americans and Canadians in Israel, 28 Shmuel Ha-Naziv St. (☎ **09/833-0950**), are Sunday at 8pm.

4 Caesarea

40 kilometers (25 mi.) N of Tel Aviv; 49 kilometers (30 mi.) S of Haifa; 16 kilometers (10 mi.) N of Netanya.

This is one of my favorite places in Israel. It has recently been the scene of a lot of activity and development—a luxury hotel, a golf course, and a country club, as well as archaeological digs.

Caesarea's beautiful excavations give you a real feeling for the tide of history that has washed Israel's shores. Located about a third of the way from Tel Aviv to Haifa, behind a cluster of banana groves, Caesarea is the spectacular city of Herod the Great (37–4 B.C.), who set out to construct a port to rival Alexandria. It was Herod who enlarged and beautified the town, adding a spectacular harbor and naming the city in honor of his Roman suzerain and benefactor, Augustus Caesar. By the time of Herod's death, Caesarea was one of the grandest port cities of the eastern Mediterranean.

Caesarea was the headquarters of Roman rule in Israel, and figures prominently in the story of the apostle Paul: He was warned not to go to Jerusalem; he went anyway, returning to Caesarea in chains to stand trial for heresy. The Jews increasingly resented the Roman domination of their land, and tensions came to a head in A.D. 60–70 when pogroms against the Jewish population began, culminating in the brutal massacre of 2,000 Jews in the Caesarea amphitheater. All Judea subsequently rose in revolt and the Romans retaliated by destroying Jerusalem in A.D. 70 and conquering Masada in A.D. 73. In A.D. 132, the rebellion of Bar Kokhba brought another massacre, and the greatest sages of the time, including Rabbi Akiva, were brought to the amphitheater of Caesarea, tortured in public, and burned alive.

Under the Byzantines, the city's history was less grisly. Caesarea was home to a succession of important church scholars, who codified the church laws, and was the seat of a metropolitan bishop responsible for all the Christian communities of the eastern Mediterranean. A small but significant Jewish community thrived throughout this time. The Arab conquest, in A.D. 640, put an end to this period.

In 1101, Baldwin I and his crusader army landed in Caesarea and slaughtered the entire Arab population. Among the treasures Baldwin's troops discovered after this conquest was a green crystal vessel reputed to be the famous Holy Grail. It was taken to Italy, where it is preserved today, known as the *Sacro Catino,* in the Cathedral of San Lorenzo in Genoa. Caesarea changed hands several times during the following century, even though Saint Louis of France had fortified its walls in 1252. Most of the crusader ruins we see today date from Saint Louis's 13th-century fortress. When Muslim armies took the town (1265 and 1291), they did their best to pull down the defenses, remembering that this had been Baldwin's beachhead, and for the next 500 years Caesarea's impressive structures slowly became covered by sand.

In the 1700s, Ahmed Jezzar Pasha, Ottoman governor of the province, sent his workmen to Caesarea to reclaim its Carrara marble, columns of decorative stone, and finely carved capitals for use in the reconstruction and beautification of his provincial capital at Acre (Akko).

An Arab village survived here, but it was abandoned by its inhabitants during the 1948 war. Caesarea's modern history really begins in 1940, when Kibbutz Sedot Yam was founded. Its members discovered the unexpected richness of Caesarea's archaeological remains, and a full campaign of restoration followed. Today, the city is one of Israel's most impressive archaeological sites.

ESSENTIALS

GETTING THERE   By Bus   Public transportation to Caesarea is poor and very time-consuming (which makes an organized tour a good option). To get to Caesarea by bus, you must first take a bus to Hadera from Tel Aviv, Netanya, or Haifa. Buses to Hadera from all these towns run roughly every 30 to 45 minutes. From Hadera, buses leave six times a day for Caesarea, departing Sunday to Thursday. Check with Egged information in Haifa for current timetables both ways. On Friday, the last bus leaves Hadera at 12:40pm, and no buses run on Saturday. Return buses to Hadera leave Caesarea about 20 minutes after each inbound arrival. You can also take one of the intercity Egged buses between Tel Aviv and Haifa, and ask to be let off on the main highway near the road to Caesarea, but from there, it's a desolate hike of about an hour to the national park.

By Car   There is a main coastal highway between Tel Aviv and Haifa, with the exit to Caesarea clearly marked.

VISITOR INFORMATION   The remains of Caesarea (Qesari or Qesarya, in Hebrew) are spread along a 3-kilometer (2-mi.) stretch of Mediterranean beach. There are two separate entrances: To the Roman theater, and ¹/₂ kilometer (¹/₄ mi.) north, to the walled crusader city. Just inland from the crusader city entrance is a small snack restaurant and a shady parking lot. Be sure to wander behind the restaurant for a look at the ruins of a Byzantine street (described below). Finally, about a kilometer (¹/₂ mi.) north of the city, a 10- or 15-minute walk along the beach, is the impressive Roman aqueduct.

EXPLORING CAESAREA
✪ CAESAREA NATIONAL PARK

Admission to the National Park is good for both the Crusader city and for the Theater. You'll arrive at either the Roman theater or the Crusader city, which are in fact right next to each other, though the entrance gates are ¹/₂ kilometer (¹/₄ mi.) apart. You can enter the city to visit restaurants or stroll the ruins for free after hours, but special exhibits are closed.

You can get a map showing the details of the succession of cities that have arisen at this site, both on land and in the water—the cities and harbors of Straton's Tower (the earliest settlement at the site of Caesaria), as well as the Herodian, the Roman, the Byzantine, and the crusader incarnation of Caesaria. I recommend that you do this, since it will give you a much better idea of the scope of the place. The excavations you see are only a very small part of what's actually there, waiting to be discovered; new finds are constantly being unearthed. During the summer of 1995, a massive temple dedicated to Roman gods was uncovered and attributed to the great builder, King Herod; it may be open for public viewing during the time span of this edition. I'll assume you're going to see the ruins from south to north, starting with the theater.

The Roman Theater, capable of seating 5,000 spectators, was constructed in the time of Jesus and Pontius Pilate, and has been restored. You may be lucky enough to visit when a summer concert or other performance is planned, and sit on the warm, pale limestone seats with the Mediterranean as a backdrop. Test the acoustics by sitting in the stands and listening to someone speak on stage or clap hands.

You enter the **crusader city** on a bridge across the deep moat, then through a gatehouse with gothic vaulting. Emerging from the gatehouse, you find yourself in the large fortified town, which covered a mere fraction of the great Herodian/Roman city. Sites within the fortified town are marked by signs in Hebrew and English. Especially noteworthy are the foundations of the Crusader Church of Saint Paul (1100s), down toward the sea, near the little Turkish minaret (1800s). The citadel, next to the group of shops and restaurants, was badly damaged by an earthquake in 1837, as was most of the crusader city.

The **Port of Sebastos,** a quay, part of the crusader port, extends from the crusader city into the sea, but King Herod's harbor at Caesarea, completed in 10 B.C. and also named Sebastos, extended at least three times as far as what you see today. It curved around to the right, where a separate northern breakwater extended to meet it, roughly where the northern Crusader fortification walls meet the sea.

The breakwater was also a wide platform, with room for large quantities of cargo, housing for sailors, a lighthouse, colossi (gigantic statues), and two large towers guarding the entrance gates to the harbor. The harbor could be closed off by a chain stretched between the two towers, preventing ships from entering; it was big enough and protected enough to permit ships to winter over, allowing the departure of ships laden with cargo from the East just as soon as winter ended.

Herod's harbor was one of the largest harbors of the Roman world, mentioned by historian Flavius Josephus as an especially amazing feat of engineering because it was a total creation—built without the usual benefit of a topographical feature such as a bay or cove. Historians did not find the harbor until 1960, when a combination of aerial photography and underwater archaeological explorations revealed the ruins sunken offshore.

We don't see more evidence of this fantastic port structure because two geological fault lines are just off the coast running below the Herodian port. Historians and archeologists believe that the harbor structure probably sank vertically downward shortly after its construction—by the 3rd century A.D. at the latest—in response to an earthquake.

The excavation of the underwater ruins is an important international project, one of the major endeavors of the Center for Maritime Studies at Haifa University. At the **Caesarea Diving Center/Gal Mor Diving Center,** Old City 38900, Caesarea (☎ **06/636-1787;** fax 06-636-0311), at the site of the ancient harbor, you can join a guided dive with equipment supplied for $50 for 1 hour. The dive explores ruins of the ancient harbor, and passes by ancient shipwrecks, classical statues, and fragments of a once-great lighthouse. Usually the center requires a minimum of three people for a tour, but for a surcharge, one- or two-person tours can be arranged. All major credit cards are accepted; reserve ahead, although dives can not be guaranteed if sea conditions are not good. An abbreviated version of the tour is available for snorkelers.

Admission (including Roman theater and crusader city) is NIS 22 ($5) for adults, half price for children. Hours are Saturday to Thursday 8am to 4pm (until 5pm April through September), and Friday from 8am to 3pm. Call ☎ **06/636-1358** or 06/228-983 for information.

THE BYZANTINE STREET

Fifty yards east of the Crusader city entrance, behind the little snack shop, is the Byzantine Street, or Street of Statues, actually part of a forum. The statues depict an emperor and other dignitaries. Much of the stone for construction of the forum was taken from earlier buildings, as was the custom at the time.

THE HIPPODROME

Head east from either the Byzantine Street or the Roman Theater to reach the ruined hippodrome, in the fields between the two access roads. Measuring 80 by 320 yards, the hippodrome could seat some 20,000 people. Some of the monuments in the hippodrome may have been brought from Aswan in Egypt—expense was no object when Herod built for Caesar!

THE JEWISH QUARTER & ROMAN AQUEDUCT

Caesarea's Jewish Quarter is outside the walls of the Crusader city, near the beach directly north. The community that flourished here during Roman times was well within the boundaries, and the walls, of Herod's city.

The great aqueduct north of the Jewish Quarter is almost 9 kilometers (6 mi.) in length, though most of it has been buried by the shifting sands. There was an earlier aqueduct here, but the present construction dates from the A.D. 100s. The southern part of the aqueduct is exposed to view, and you can see it.

THE AQUEDUCT BEACH

Swim at the white, sandy lagoons beside the romantic Roman aqueduct. Even off-season (late spring, early autumn) the sea is warmer than the North Atlantic and the Pacific ever get in the States. Some days the sea is lake-calm, but at other times, as everywhere on the coast, beware of rocks and severe undertows.

THE NEW CITY

Largely residential, the new city of Caesarea is notable for its very worthwhile museum of Spanish and Latin American Art, the **Ralli Museum,** located on Rothschild Blvd. (☎ **06/626-1013**). The museum contains a large collection of works by Latin American and Spanish artists (including artists of Sephardic origin), is housed in a spacious, beautifully designed new building and is one of Israel's unexpected and little publicized surprises. The gems of the collection include sculptures by Dali and Rodin, but the works of Latin American surrealists, representing artists from Mexico to Uruguay, are powerful and impressive. The museum is open daily 10:30am to 3pm and closed on Sunday and Wednesday. Admission is free. Children under 6 are not allowed to enter.

WHERE TO STAY

Dan Caesarea. Caesarea 30600. ☎ **06/626-9111.** Fax 06/626-9122. E-mail: danhtsl@danhotels.co.il. 114 units (all with bathtub). A/C MINIBAR TV TEL. $156–$390 double. Add 15% service charge; $78 per rm surcharge Thurs–Sat. Rates include breakfast. Family plan and children's rates. AE, DC, MC, V. Free parking.

Promoting itself as a golf hotel, the Dan Caesarea offers a full array of sports activities. The hotel is a modern four-story complex set amid acres of gardens and archaeological ruins. All rooms have balconies and vistas of the Mediterranean (some distance away) or the countryside. As with many of the older Dan Hotels, deluxe rooms have been beautifully renovated and contain luxurious polished stone bathrooms; furnishings in standard rooms show their age. There is a large outdoor swimming pool, and the hotel is adjacent to Israel's only 18-hole golf course, which guests can use for a fee. Horseback riding, fishing, diving, bicycling, and other country activities can be arranged, and there is a full program of in-hotel sports. The hotel is not close to many restaurant choices, and guests depend on in-house dining facilities, which are adequate, but no more than average.

Dining/Diversions: Restaurant, snack bar/cafe, bar.

Amenities: Outdoor pool, fitness center, Jacuzzi, sauna, two day/night tennis courts, access to golf club.

WHERE TO DINE

While there are few overnight facilities in Caesarea itself, there are pleasant restaurants, especially among the ancient ruins. Few visitors realize that these places stay open after the archaeological park has officially closed; you can enjoy extensive or light meals on their waterfront terraces as well as fabulous sunsets and starry nights.

✪ **Caesaria Cellars Winery and Restaurant.** Caesaria Park. ☎ **06/626-4644.** Reservations necessary. Main courses. NIS 35–92 ($7.70–$20.20). AE, DC, MC, V. Mon–Sat noon–midnight; Sun 6pm–midnight. In the National Park just north of the Crusader Walls, on the road to the Aqueduct Beach. CONTINENTAL.

This restaurant has the best kitchen in Caesaria and is an enjoyable place to sample local wines amidst a menu especially designed to complement wine tasting. You can order a platter of fine cheese and breads for around $8, or a "worldwide tour gourmet dinner" with six kinds of wines tied to each course or dish in the meal. Or, you can choose one main dish prepared in one of nine house sauces, created for compatibility with different wines—for example, the Fisherman sauce of lemon and garlic goes with Sauvignon Blanc; the Herod sauce of ginger, honey, and chile complements Emerald Riesling. There are quality appetizers and light meals, as well as fine desserts, and wine tasting lessons. You can buy wine by the bottle direct from the winery; sadly, the restaurant offers no view of the ruins or the sea.

Charlie's. Old Caesarea. ☎ **06/636-3050.** Reservations recommended. Main courses 50–110 ($11–$24.20). MC, V. Daily 10:30am–1am. INTERNATIONAL.

Charlie's rambles over its site among the ruins inside the crusader walls, offering you large and small whitewashed arched-ceiling dining areas and a covered harbor-side terrace. People come here for the atmosphere and views. There's a wide variety of salads, first-course fish, seafood and grilled meat choices; the food, though good, is not exceptional. A very complete bar offers wines beginning at $15 a bottle for long on-the-terrace evenings overlooking the sea. Friday evenings often include folklore performances and sing-alongs; large tour groups often book here, so reservations are imperative.

Herod's Palace. Old Caesarea. ☎ **06/626-3012.** Reservations recommended. Main courses NIS 45–85 ($10–$18.70). MC, V. Sun–Thurs 9:30am–1am; Fri 9:30am to before Shabbat; Sat after Shabbat. INTERNATIONAL.

This is the only kosher restaurant in Caesarea, beautifully situated in a restored building at the southern end of Crusader ruins inside the crusader walls. It has a large upstairs terrace overlooking the sea. A romantic place to spend balmy evenings, Herod's Palace serves a selection of grilled fish, meats, and desserts. A 10% service charge is added to each bill.

5 Israel's Wine Country

The hills northeast of Caesarea contain a pretty area that could be called Israel's "wine country." **Zichron Yaakov,** the main town in this region, was founded in 1882 under the special patronage of Baron Edmond de Rothschild, and has the distinction of being one of the first agricultural towns to be developed in Israel in modern times. With sweeping vistas of the Mediterranean from its vantage point on the Carmel Mountain Range, Zichron Yaacov has undergone a major renovation in the past few years. It's main street, the quaintest in Israel, is dotted with cafes, craft shops, and restaurants—for some it is beginning to have the feel of places like Carmel, on the Pacific coast of California, or the Hamptons, on Long Island.

Zichron Yaacov means "memorial of Jacob," and was named for the Baron's father, James de Rothschild (in Hebrew, *Jacob*); these days, many just call it "Zichron." Of interest here are the Carmel Mizrachi Winery in Zichron Yaacov, and the Baron and Binyamina Wineries in nearby Binyamina (see below).

Inland from the coastal highway is the artists' village of **Ein Hod.** Road signs point the way for drivers, and from 10am to 5:30pm there is Egged bus service from Haifa all the way up the mountainside to this famous colony. You can also take bus no. 921 to the Ein Hod roadway that intersects with the older, more inland Tel Aviv–Haifa highway, and hitchhike up the mountainside from there. (True hikers will find the half-hour uphill trek a simple one, but for others, it can be hard, especially in the heat of summer.)

Ein Hod (Well of Beauty) was built over an abandoned Arab village in 1953 by Israeli sculptors, painters, and potters, under the guidance of Marcel Janco.

The village now includes a museum of surrealist art, several workshops, and an outdoor theater. It's a picturesque place, tranquil and rugged looking, with a view of sloping olive groves and the distant Mediterranean that can inspire even the nonartistic. Crumbling archways and Moorish vaults are relics of the past that have been incorporated into the homes of the village. Most of Ein Hod's full-time residents are artists or craftspeople, and sell their work in a large, cooperative gallery. But many also sell things in their own houses and workshops, so it's worthwhile to take time and stroll through the lanes of the village (some of the best artisans' houses are in outlying areas) and enjoy the gardens and eccentric homes of this charming enclave.

Cooperation is emphasized: the village members have their own council of elders. The handyman is employed by the entire community; the gallery takes a much smaller percentage on sales than do other galleries. Many workshops are shared; and the proceeds from the amphitheater's shows and concerts, which range from folk and classical to hard rock (summer weekends only), are used for the welfare of the village. Call **04/984-3152** or **984-2029** for information.

The **Janco-Dada Museum** (☎ **04/984-2350**) is open Saturday through Thursday 9:30am to 5pm and Friday 9:30am to 5pm. Admission is NIS 8 ($1.76). The village has a modest but pleasant snack bar/cafe for visitors.

The **Ein Hod Gallery** (☎ **04/984-2548**) carries a good selection of the village's work—silver jewelry, lots of ceramics, lithographs, etchings, oil paintings, watercolors, tapestries and shawls, sculpture, and woodwork. The gallery staff will box your purchases and mail them to you wherever you live. Admission to the gallery is by a small donation for adults. It's open Saturday through Thursday from 9:30am to 5pm and Friday from 9:30am to 4pm; Open every day except Yom Kippur. All major credit cards are accepted. Among Ein Hod's many artisan's shops, check out the **Silver Print Gallery** (☎ **04/984-1067**), near the Ein Hod Square and entrance to the village. It's one of the best places in the country for photographs of pre-1948 Israel, as well as photographs from the early years of Israel's existence and works by Israel's foremost photographers. Artisan's homes and personal workshops exhibit a wide range of artwork and quality, custom designed furniture, clothing, ceramics, silk-screenings, clothing, and jewelry.

Hameyasdim Street, old Zichron's main thoroughfare, is lined with the town's original houses, some of which have been restored. Stop in to see the **Aaronson House,** 40 Hameyasdim St. (☎ **06/639-0120**), where a small museum commemorates the heroic and tragic Aaronson family. The Aaronsons' story is a national legend that has grown more romantic and poetic with time. Aaron Aaronson (1876–1919) was an agronomist of international repute who received his training in France under the aegis of the Rothschilds. He discovered and studied an ancestor of modern wheat that grows in the vicinity. He and his sisters, Sara and Rebecca, and his assistant, Absolom Feinberg, with whom he had set up an experimental farm at Athlit, were at the center of NILI, an anti-Turkish spy ring that supplied the British with intelligence during World War I (Palestine at that time was part of the Ottoman Empire, an enemy of Britain, France, and America). Feinberg was killed while traveling through Gaza on a desperate mission to contact the British army in Sinai. After the Six-Day War 50 years later, when a search was made so he could be reburied in Jerusalem, the site of his grave in Gaza was identified by a palm tree that sprouted from dates he had been carrying in his pocket when he was ambushed. Both Sara and Rebecca had been in love with Feinberg; Sara was arrested and committed suicide after being tortured by the Turks. Aaron Aaronson himself, one of the most promising and admired members of the Jewish community in Palestine, died in a plane crash on his way to the Paris Peace Conference at the end of World War I. The house, with its period ambience and display of historical mementos, is open Sunday to Thursday from 8:30am to 1am; Tuesday from 3:30 to 5:30pm and Friday from 9am until noon. Admission is NIS 14 ($3).

Opened in 1999, the **First Aliyah Museum,** 2 Hanadiv St. (☎ **06/621-2333**), is a multimedia exhibit of life in the 19th-century Jewish agricultural centers, especially those such as Zichron Yaacov, founded under the patronage of the Rothschild family. The attempts to reenact elements of 19th-century life are sometimes didactic or heavy-handed, but the methods of presentation are interesting. Wheelchair accessible. Sunday and Monday, Wednesday and Thursday 9am to 4pm; Tuesday 9am to 7pm; Friday 9am to 1pm; Saturday 10am to 2pm. Admission is NIS 16 ($3.50).

You can also visit **Ramat Ha-Nadiv,** or the Heights of the Benefactor, containing the tomb of the Baron Edmond de Rothschild (1845–1934) and his wife, Baroness Adelaide de Rothschild, set in handsome gardens filled with all the varieties of plantings the Rothschilds helped to develop in Israel. Near Ramat Ha-Nadiv's vista point, overlooking Caesaria and the Mediterranean, you'll see a stone map marking the many towns and agricultural settlements developed under Rothschild sponsorship. The Rothschilds were reinterred here, according to their wishes, after the establishment of the State of Israel.

Opposite Zichron Yaakov, on the coast, is **Kibbutz Maagan Michael,** whose beautiful carp ponds at the edge of the sea also serve as a **bird sanctuary**. Depending on the season, bird watchers can find herons, cranes, and storks and exotic birds, including (at rare times) flamingos.

The **Hof Ha-Carmel Field School at Maagan Michael** (☎ **06/639-9655;** fax 06/639-1618) is an important bird-watching center. November through February, during migrations between Europe and Africa, is an especially rich time for sightings at this station. You can arrange a private guided tour of the sanctuary through the Field School; the rate is approximately $130 for the day. If you want to visit on your own, the Field School can supply you with advice and printed material in English. Kibbutz Maagan Michael produces plastic products and also has a livestock center featuring in-residence Israeli cowboys and herds of Brahman-type cows.

Carmel Mizrachi Winery. Zichron Yaacov. Ha-Nadiv St. ☎ **06/639-1241** or 06/629-0280. Reservations recommended for tours. NIS 16 ($3.50). Sun–Thurs 9am–3pm and Fri 9am–12:30pm.

The sister winery of Carmel Mizrachi in Rishon LeZion, south of Tel Aviv, this is the largest winery in Israel; founded in 1906, it produces 60% of all wine exports. There are organized tours, wine tasting, and a shop on the premises with a complete selection of Carmel Mizrachi products sold at about 15% below standard retail price. Among notable choices are the Cabernet Sauvignon 1985 from the Rothschild Series, and the Merlots from the Estate Series. Also look for a fruity red wine called *Hilulim,* the first wine produced after the grape harvest. Check to see if there will be any of the winery's occasional evening parties, with all-you-can-eat buffets and live music.

Baron Wine Cellars. Binyamina, south of Zichron Yaacov. ☎ **06/638-0434.** Tours by appointment. NIS 16 ($3.50). Sun–Thurs 9am–4pm; Fri 9am–2pm.

This midsize winery produces wine under the Tishbi, Tishbi's Cellar, and Baron labels. Its reputation for white wines (Sauvignon Blanc, Chardonnay, and Emerald Riesling) is very good; it also produces Champenoise, a sparkling wine. Signs throughout Benyamina direct you to the winery.

Binyamina Winery. Binyamina, south of Zichron Yaacov. ☎ **06/638-8643.** Tours by appointment only. NIS 7 ($1.50). Sun–Thurs 8am–4pm; Fri 8am–1pm.

Another midsize winery, Binyamina offers the visitor a tour of its production center and the vineyards. There is wine tasting, and a shop on the premises. Investment in new staff and equipment here in the early 1990s promises to make this a very interesting though less prestigious stop. Signs throughout Binyamina direct you to the winery.

WHERE TO STAY

Carmel Gardens Hotel. 1 Etzion St., Zichron Yaacov 30900. ☎ **06/630-0111.** Fax 06/639-7030. 112 units (all with bathtub). A/C TV TEL. $120–$145 single; $120–$190 double. AE, DC, MC, V.

This contemporary, sprawling low-rise hotel, with beautiful gardens overlooking the countryside at the edge of Zichron Yaacov, was originally built in the 1970s as one of the country club–like retreats for trade union members in the days when Zionist socialism was still in full swing. It's comfortable and very attractive, but not deluxe— guest rooms are simple and offer fine views of the countryside. The hotel is a pleasant base for exploring Caesarea, Megiddo, the artists' colony at Ein Hod and the beaches of the Mediterranean coast. There is an outdoor swimming pool, lobby bar, restaurant, coffee bar, and children's play area.

WHERE TO DINE
EXPENSIVE

✪ **Picciotto.** 41 Hameyasdim St. ☎ **06/629-0646.** Reservations necessary. Main courses NIS 60–120 ($13.20–$26.40). Business luncheon specials NIS 82 ($18). AE, DC, MC, V. Mon–Sat noon–4pm and 7–11pm. INVENTIVE FRENCH.

Set in a renovated 19th-century cottage on the main street of Zichron, Picciotto is one of the best new restaurants in the country and offers an ever-changing menu that is delightful and satisfying. A meal starts with bread served with an olive tapanade. Foie gras heads the list of admired first courses that also includes skillfully prepared soups (orange sweet potato soup is a special pleasure). Main courses usually include a hearty beef or pork fillet grilled with olive oil and balsamic vinegar; quail breast in rosemary sauce, seafood and fish dishes that are original and delicious, and interesting poultry or fowl, such as mullard (a duck-goose hybrid). Desserts, whether somewhat restrained or exotically lavish, are phenomenal.

Shuni Fortress. Jabotinsky Park, Zichron Yaacov–Binyamina Road (Route 652). ☎ **06/638-0227.** Reservations recommended. Main courses NIS 67–126 ($15–$28) range. DC, V. Mon–Sat lunch and dinner. Closed Sun. One km north of Binyamina. COUNTRY FRENCH.

Set in the arched, whitewashed rooms of a renovated ancient fortress, this restaurant is the special creation of Chef Antoinne Taub, who has been an important force in shaping the traditional haute cuisine scene in Israel. There is no menu: Everything depends on what the chef is doing on the day of your visit, but you may encounter mushrooms Provencçale or goose liver pâté among the first courses, and honeyed breast of mallard or beef bourguignonne among the main courses. Classic preparation and sauces are the general rule, but there is a rustic feel to the menu here, with home-made breads, and wines from the area as well as from Chef Antoinne's own vineyard. In good weather, the few patio tables, with lovely vistas, are in demand and must be reserved ahead of time. Desserts are worthwhile.

INEXPENSIVE

Ha Temanyia Shel Santo. 52 Hameyasdim St. ☎ **06/639-8762.** Main courses NIS 25–45 ($5.50–$10). AE, DC, MC, V. Sun–Thurs 11:30am–10pm; Fri to 2pm. YEMENITE.

You may have to search a bit to find this long time mainstay from the days before Zichron became gentrified—it's in a rear garden courtyard behind number 52. The home-style food is superb. Start with hummus, salad, and bread, followed by grilled chicken or stuffed vegetables. It's the side dishes, like kabobs of meat flavored with cilantro, or Yemenite potato cakes that make this restaurant stand out.

A SIDE TRIP TO DOR

On the highway skirting the beach, road signs announce Nasholim, a kibbutz located on one of Israel's most beautiful bathing beaches, **Dor Beach.** A wide expanse of sandy beach, it is beautified by natural lagoons. Looming nearby is **Tel Dor,** a mound containing the remains of the ancient city that was inhabited since Bronze Age times by Phoenicians, Israelites, Greeks, and Romans. The ruins of a massive Greco-Roman temple dedicated to Zeus add drama to the site. Farther to the north at modern Dor is a picturesque area of caves eroded by the sea to form a natural tunnel at the water's edge.

WHERE TO STAY

Nasholim Kibbutz Holiday Village. Carmel Beach 20815. ☎ **06/639-9533.** Fax 06/639-7614. www.nahsholim.co.il. E-mail: info@nahsholim.co.il. 80 units (all with shower). A/C TV TEL. $82–$96 double. Rates include breakfast. Aug and Jewish holidays add 50%. Discounts available if booked on Kibbutz Hotels Plan (☎ 800/552-0141). MC, V.

This kibbutz-operated vacation village is about an hour's drive from Tel Aviv, and within easy access to Caesarea and Haifa. It's a great place to spend the day, or several days. The islets around the beach make for sheltered, warm swimming, even during the autumn or spring seasons, and the recreation facilities include a children's play area and tennis courts and a video television room as well as a disco/club for younger guests. Rooms are simple, lined up like rows of cabanas with small terraces in front; they include small kitchenette units. There are antiquities around this recreation village, and it's a good base for sightseeing tours. Nasholim is justly proud of its meals, among the best in the kibbutz guest-house system, which are served in the air-conditioned no smoking dining room; in summer, there are outdoor barbecues twice a week. The place is mobbed with Israeli families and kids in the summer school vacation program and on Jewish holidays; at other times it's more relaxed and quieter.

Note: There is no exit from the coastal highway to Nasholim. To reach Nasholim, leave the main coastal highway and use the parallel inland road between Binyamina and Faradis.

6 Acre (Akko)

23 kilometers (14 mi.) N of Haifa, 56 kilometers (37 mi.) W of Tiberias.

Acre (also Akko or Acco), with its romantic minarets, massive city seawalls, and palm trees framed against the sky, has had a long, eventful history. It was first mentioned in the chronicles of Pharaoh Thutmose III, about 3,500 years ago. It was a leading Phoenician port, and although it was allotted to the tribe of Asher, the tribe was never able to conquer it. The town is mentioned as part of David's kingdom, and was given by Solomon to Hiram, king of Tyre, in return for his help in building the temple.

Alexander the Great conquered Acre in 332 B.C., and later, in 280 B.C., it was captured by the Ptolemies, and renamed Ptolemais. Under this name it is mentioned in the New Testament as a stopping place of Saint Paul. Julius Caesar stayed here in 48 B.C.

From the time of Acre's allocation to the tribe of Asher, Jews had lived in relative peace with the other local inhabitants, but during the Bar Kokhba revolt many Jews were killed by the Romans. Still, remnants of the Jewish population continued to live here.

When the Arabs conquered Ptolemais in A.D. 636, the town reverted to the name of Acre, and it was known by that name until the crusaders took the town in 1104 and renamed it Saint Jean d'Acre. The town became the regional seat of Crusader government, and it expanded to include an entire underground city, which you still can visit today. Except for one 4-year period, the crusaders held Acre until the 13th century, when they were defeated by the Mamelukes, who sacked the town. The fall of Acre ensured the doom of crusader dominion in the Holy Land.

It was not until 1749, when Bedouin Sheik Daher el-Omar conquered the town, that Acre experienced a resurgence, but his plans for a serious rebuilding program came to a sudden end when he was murdered in 1775 by the notoriously cruel Ahmed El-Jezzar Pasha. Under the impetus of El-Jezzar, the town's most important rebuilding took place, including the Jezzar Pasha Mosque, the Khan El-Umdan, the Turkish bathhouse now housing the Municipal Museum, the massive stone walls, and the aqueduct to the north. These structures still stand today.

Acre's decline as a major port was sealed by the advent of the steamship and modern naval technology, with shipping activities gradually transferred to the larger port at Haifa across the bay, which remains Israel's primary port. On May 4, 1947, Acre was the scene of the largest prison break in history when 251 prisoners escaped from Acre Fortress with the help of Jewish underground fighters.

ESSENTIALS

GETTING THERE   By Bus Buses no. 262 and 272 (express) and 271 (local) leave the Haifa bus station every 10 minutes, bound for Acre; the schedule is less frequent on Saturday.

By Car Independence Road in Haifa port runs north out of the city past a heavily industrial area. At a crossroads called the "checkpost," bear left, following the signs, over the railroad tracks, and you'll be on the northern coastal road to Acre and Nahariya.

VISITOR INFORMATION Directly across from the Mosque of Jezzar Pasha is the **Tourist Information Office** (☎ 04/991-1764), open from 8:30am to 4pm Sunday to Thursday, closing early on Friday. Here—or next door, at the entrance to the Subterranean Crusader City—you can buy a large, wonderfully detailed map of the entire city of Acre for only NIS 5 ($1.40). In conjunction with this office is the **Western Galilee Tourist Society,** 1 Weitzman St., Old Akko (☎04/981-7419; fax 04/981-7423), which distributes information on touring, local festivals, and lodging throughout the entire Western Galilee.

A note for women: Medieval Acre is fascinating, but women unaccompanied by men, even in pairs or in groups, attract a lot of attention around the labyrinthine Old City.

GETTING AROUND Coming into town by car, you can simply follow the signs for the Old City. There is a small parking lot on the left ($3), just inside the city walls.

If you arrive from Haifa by bus, city buses no. 1, 2, 61, 62, 63, and 65 all make stops at the entrance to the Old City. You can also walk from the bus station: Turn left as you exit and walk 1 long block to the traffic lights on Ben-Ami Street. Turn right (west) onto Ben-Ami and walk 4 long blocks to Haim Weizmann Street. Make a left

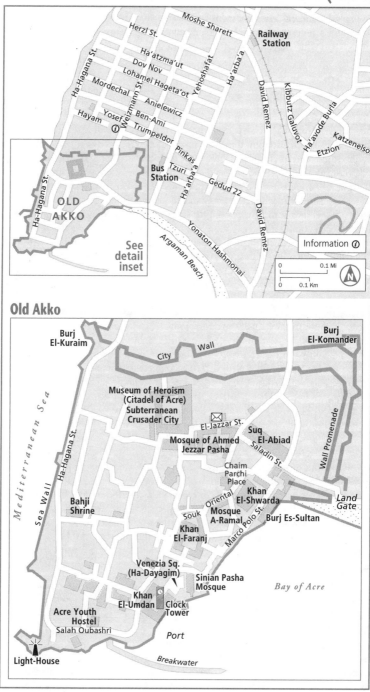

Acre (Akko)

Railway Station

Moshe Sharett

Herzl St.

Ha'atzma'ut

Dov Nov

Lohamei Hageta'ot

Mordechai

Anielewicz

Ben-Ami

Hayam

Yosef

Trumpeldor

Pinkas

Weizmann St.

Ha-Hagana St.

Yehoshafat

Ha'arba'a

David Remez

Kibbutz Galuyot

Ha'avode Burla

Katzenelson

Etzion

Bus Station

Tzuri

Ha'tapat

Gedud 22

David Remez

Yonaton Hashmonai

Argaman Beach

OLD AKKO

Ha-Hagana St.

See detail inset

Information ⓘ

0   0.1 Mi
0   0.1 Km

Old Akko

Burj El-Kuraim

City   Wall

Burj El-Komander

Museum of Heroism (Citadel of Acre) Subterranean Crusader City

El-Jazzar St.

Suq El-Abiad

Mosque of Ahmed Jezzar Pasha

Saladin St.

Chaim Parchi Place

Khan El-Shwarda

Oriental

Mosque A-Ramal

Marco Polo St.

Burj Es-Sultan

Land Gate

Wall Promenade

Mediterranean Sea

Sea Wall

Ha-Hagana St.

Bahji Shrine

Souk

Khan El-Faranj

Venezia Sq. (Ha-Dayagim)

Sinian Pasha Mosque

Bay of Acre

Khan El-Umdan

Clock Tower

Acre Youth Hostel

Salah Oubashri

Port

Light-House

Breakwater

onto Weizmann and you'll see the walls of the ancient Turkish fortress about 2 blocks ahead. Soon the minaret and dome of the Jezzar Pasha Mosque will come into view.

CITY LAYOUT   Today, Acre comprises two distinct parts. There's the modern city of Acre, with about 40,000 residents, and a number of large industrial plants (including Steel City) and immigrant housing projects. Then there's the Old City, still surrounded by high, thick stone walls on all sides, situated on the tip of land jutting out into the sea, forming the protected Bay of Acre.

EXPLORING OLD ACRE

Allow yourself a half-day to wander through Old Acre's medieval streets. Unlike the restored Old City of Jaffa, which is filled with tourist shops, Old Acre is genuine, charming, and its streets teem with real life. The best place to start your tour is at the **Mosque of Ahmed Jezzar Pasha.** Right across the street from Jezzar's mosque is the marvelous **Subterranean Crusader City,** and just a few steps farther is the **Municipal Museum** (exhibits sometimes closed for renovations) housed in Ahmed Jezzar Pasha's Turkish bath.

Next you'll wander through the pleasant and colorful streets of the **bazaar.** Be sure to see the most picturesque shop in the bazaar, **Kurdy and Berit's Coffee and Spices,** at no. 13/261 (ask around, it's deep in the market). If you make a purchase at Kurdy and Berit's, the very hospitable owner may invite you to try a cup of thick Arabic coffee. Acre's "formal" market is **Suq El-Abiad,** but numerous streets within Old Acre serve as shopping areas. You'll pass the **El-Zeituneh Mosque** to **the Khan El-Umdan** caravansary, marked by a tall, segmented tower. A **caravansary,** or khan, was a combination travelers' inn, warehouse, banking center, stable, and factory, traditionally built around a lightly fortified courtyard to house caravans, pilgrims, and other visitors.

The market streets, filled with delicious Arabic bakeries and hummus restaurants, are an excellent area to find snacks. Just beyond is the port, a good place to stop for lunch (see "Where to Dine," below). At the port, you can also hire a boat to take you on a **sea tour** of the city walls (about $5 per person). Don't be afraid to bargain. Many boat operators will be glad to take you on a motor or fishing boat cruise around Old Acre. Settle on a price in advance (about $14 to $17 for an hour is the average), and get a boat that looks comfortable. A large tourist boat, the *Princess,* takes visitors on a 20-minute ride around the Old City walls, but only when enough people are waiting to make the run profitable. The fare is $3 per person.

In Venezia Square (Ha-Dayagim in Hebrew), facing the port, is the **Sinian Pasha Mosque,** and behind it the **Khan El-Faranj** caravansary. Yet another khan, named **El-Shwarda,** is a short distance to the northeast. A few steps back is the Ahmed Jezzar Pasha Mosque. You'll also want to visit the **Museum of Heroism** and **El-Jezzar's Wall** on Ha-Hagana Street.

THE TOP ATTRACTIONS

Mosque of Armed Jezzar Pasha. Admission to mosque complex and subterranean crusader vaults NIS 5 ($1). Open 8am–noon; 1:15–4pm and 4:45–6pm. Modest dress required. No entrance during prayers (exact times vary according to the time of the year).

Ahmed al Jezzar ("the Butcher") Pasha was the Ottoman Turkish governor of Acre during the late 1700s, and notorious for his habit of mutilating both those in his government and those he governed. According to legend, on al Jezzar's whim, faithful chamberlains and retainers were ordered to slay their own children as signs of loyalty to the Pasha, and the Pasha rewarded government officials and loyal subjects with amputations of hands, arms, eyes, and legs. When Napoléon invaded Egypt, the English joined the Ottomans in trying to drive him out. Jezzar Pasha marshaled the defenses of Akko, and the city withstood Napoleon's assault in 1799. Napoléon's forces never recovered from this impasse and Napoléon's dream of conquering Egypt died outside the walls of Akko. The Pasha died in Acre in 1804, to the great relief of the city's inhabitants.

Ahmed Jezzar's contributions to Acre included building fountains, a covered market, a Turkish bath, and the harmonious mosque complex that bears his name. Begun in 1781, it is an excellent example of classic Ottoman Turkish architecture and stands among the pasha's most ambitious projects. Every great man in the empire wanted to endow a mosque in his own name, an act that not only added to his glory on earth but also gained points for him in heaven. A number of charitable institutions were usually constructed around the mosque, and shops were built into the walls, the rent from the shops paying for the mosque's maintenance. Though the greatest of these complexes were in Constantinople, the Ottoman capital, the one in Acre is a graceful provincial example of the exotic style of Ottoman architecture (rooted in both Byzantine and Persian traditions); it also illustrates how the traditional mosque complex worked.

As you approach the mosque area, El-Jezzar Street turns right off Weizmann Street. The mosque entrance is a few steps along El-Jezzar Street on the left. Before you mount the stairs to the mosque courtyard, notice the ornate little building to the right of the stairs. It's a *sabil,* or cold-drinks stand, from which pure, refreshing drinking water, sometimes mixed with fruit syrups, was distributed—a part of the mosque complex's services. Note especially the fine tile fragments mounted above the little grilled windows just beneath the sabil's dome. Tile-making was an Ottoman specialty.

Up the stairs, you enter the mosque courtyard. Your ticket will enable you to explore the complex of Crusader buildings, including a church (now flooded and used as cisterns) over which the mosque was built. Just inside the entry, mounted on a pedestal, is a marble disc bearing the *tughra,* or monogram, of the Ottoman sultan. It spells out the sultan's name, his father's name, and the legend "ever-victorious."

The arcaded courtyard around the mosque can be used for prayers during hot days of summer, as can the arcaded porch at the front of the mosque. The *shadirvan,* or ablutions fountain, opposite the mosque entry, is used for the ritual cleansing of face, neck, hands, and feet five times a day before prayers. You must slip off your shoes before entering the mosque proper. This is not merely a religious rule, but a hygienic one: Worshipers kneel on the carpets during prayer, and want to keep them clean.

Inside, you'll notice the *mihrab,* or prayer niche, which indicates the direction of Mecca, toward which worshipers must face when they pray. The galleries to the right and left of the entrance are reserved for women, the main area of the floor for men. The *minbar,* a sort of pulpit, is that separate structure with a curtained entry, stairs, and a little steeple. Around to the right are a mausoleum and a small graveyard that hold the tombs of Ahmed Jezzar Pasha and his successor, Suleiman Pasha, and members of their families. The mosque is still used by Acre's Muslim population, so when it's in service for prayer (five times a day), you must wait until the prayers are over to enter the mosque (about 20 minutes).

Subterranean Crusader City. Admission NIS 12 ($3.40) adults, discount for students and children. Admission includes entrance to Municipal Museum. Sun–Thurs 8:30am–6pm; Fri 8:30am–2pm; Sat 9am–5pm; closings are 1 hour earlier in winter.

Virtually across the street from the Mosque of Ahmed Jezzar Pasha is the Subterranean Crusader City. In the entrance is a tourism information kiosk, where you can buy a city map and an entrance ticket.

The crusaders built their fortified city atop what was left of the Roman city. The Ottomans, and especially Ahmed El-Jezzar Pasha, built their city on top of the largely intact buildings of the Crusaders. In Ottoman times, the cavernous chambers were used as a caravansary until Napoleon's attack. In preparation for the defense of his city, Jezzar Pasha ordered the walls heightened, and the Crusader rooms partially filled with sand and dirt, to better support the walls. Today, you get a good look at how the crusaders lived and worked in the late 1100s.

The bottom of the hall was built by the crusaders, the top by the Ottomans. The next hall you enter once held an illegal (in Muslim times) wine press. Next comes the courtyard, with the 125-foot-high walls of **Acre Citadel,** which was used by the British as a prison during the mandate and now houses the Museum of Heroism (see below).

Beyond the courtyard, through a huge Ottoman gate, are the **Knights' Halls,** once occupied by the Knights Hospitalers of Saint John. In the ceiling of the hall, a patch of concrete marks the spot where Jewish underground members, imprisoned by the British in the Citadel (directly above the hall), attempted to break out.

Back through the courtyard, you now head for the **Grand Maneir,** or center of government, in the Crusader city. Past it, through a narrow passage, is the **Crypt,** so named only because of its present depth; it was actually the knights' refectory, or dining hall. Beyond the refectory is a longer tunnel leading to **the Post (El-Posta),** a series of rooms and a courtyard similar to a caravansary, the precise use of which is not known.

Municipal Museum (Turkish Bath). Admission NIS 12 ($3.40) for adults, reduction for students and children. Includes admission to Crusader City. Sun–Thurs 8:30am–6pm; Fri 8:30am–2pm; Sat 9am–5pm; closings are 1 hour earlier in winter.

Down at the end of El-Jezzar Street, just around the corner, is the Municipal Museum, originally the *Hammam,* or Turkish Bath, built by Ahmed Al Jezzar Pasha as part of his mosque complex in the 1780s. The museum's collection, including antiquities, an exhibit on Napoléon's attack, and a folklore exhibit are often closed as the building undergoes repairs, but the building itself is fantastic.

Turkish baths were modeled after the Roman plan, with three distinct rooms. The first was the entry and dressing room, the next was the tepidarium (its Roman name), with warm steam, and the last was the caldarium, with hot steam. The hot room was always the most ornate.

As you walk through the first two rooms, note the tiny glass skylights in the domes. The third room, the one for hot steam, is rich in marble and mosaic work. In the center is a circular platform for steam bathing. The heat source was beneath it. Some Turkish baths have a small swimming pool here instead. Four private steam cubicles occupy the four points of the compass.

Museum of Heroism. ☎ **04/991-8264.** Admission NIS 8 ($2.20) for adults, with discount for children and students. Sun–Thurs 9am–5pm.

The museum is in the Citadel of Acre. This complex of buildings was used as a prison in Ottoman and British Mandate times. Part of the prison has been set aside in honor of the Jewish underground fighters imprisoned here by the British. With the help of Irgun forces, 251 prisoners staged a mass escape in May 1947. If you saw the movie *Exodus,* that was the breakout and this was the prison. The prison is also revered by Arab Israelis and by Palestinians, whose own national fighters were detained and, in many cases, executed here during the British Mandate.

Among the exhibits are the entrance to the escape tunnel and displays of materials showing the British repression of Zionist activity during the mandate. Not all prisoners were lucky enough to escape, however. Eight Irgun fighters were hanged here in the 10 years before Israel's independence. You can visit the death chamber, called the Hanging Room, complete with noose.

Inmates here included Zeev Jabotinsky and Dov Gruner, among other leaders of Zionism and Israel's independence movement. Before the mandate, the prison's most famous inmate was Baha' Allah (1817–92), founder of the Baha'i faith (see below).

EL-JEZZAR'S WALL

To appreciate the elaborate system of defenses built by Ahmed Jezzar Pasha to protect against Napoleon's fleet and forces, turn right as you come out of the Museum of Heroism onto Ha-Hagana Street and walk a few steps north. You'll see the double system of walls with a moat in between. Jutting into the sea is an Ottoman defensive tower called the Burj El-Kuraim. You're now standing at the northwestern corner of the walled city. Walk east (inland) along the walls and you'll pass the Citadel, the Burj El-Hazineh (Treasury Tower), and cross Weizmann Street to the Burj El-Komander, the strongest point in the walls. The land wall system continues south from here all the way to the beach.

At the entrance to the Old City on Weizmann Street, near the Walls of El-Jezzar, is a sunken children's playground bordered by the Dahar El-Omer Walls. Dahar El-Omer (or Daher El-Amar) was the sheik who rebuilt the city walls after capturing Acre from the Mamelukes.

THE KHANS & THE PORT

Make your way south through the city, toward the port, and if you need a point of reference, ask a local to point you toward the **Khan El-Umdan.** The khan, a market and inn complex for visiting merchants and caravans (dating from 1785), is much older than its tower, which was built as a clock tower in 1906 to celebrate the 30th year of the reign of the Ottoman Sultan Abdul Hamid II. El-Umdan means "The Pillars," and when you enter this vast colonnaded court you'll know how it got its name. Another of Ahmed Jezzar Pasha's harmonious works in the public service, this caravansary served commerce. It was built on the site of a crusader monastery of the Dominican order.

Just to the east of Khan El-Umdan is Venezia Square (Ha-Dayagim) and the **Sinian Pasha Mosque.** The port is to the southeast and industrious fishers are still at work here. Behind the port are two more caravansaries. The **Khan El-Faranj** (Afranj), or the Inn of the Franks, is a few steps north of the Sinian Pasha Mosque. This complex began in 1729 as a Franciscan convent, but some of the building was apparently rented to French and Italian merchants.

Northeast of the Khan El-Faranj is the **Khan El-Shwarda,** right next to a tower in the city walls called **Burj Es-Sultan.** The Burj is famous because it is the only structure erected by the crusaders that remains intact. At the tower's base is one of Napoléon's cannons, cast in Liège and captured by the Ottoman and English forces.

Walk up Marco Polo Street to your next stop. Marco Polo, by the way, was one of several famous visitors to Acre in medieval times; another was King Richard the Lion-Hearted. The **Khan El-Shwarda,** at the northern end of Marco Polo Street, occupies the site of a convent of the nuns of Saint Clare that closed in 1291 when Acre fell. There's not a lot to look at today.

The **Mosque A-Ramal** (or El-Ramel), the former "Sand Mosque," on Marco Polo Street, was built in 1704–05. A crusader inscription was found on the southeast wall of this mosque, which today forms part of the back wall of the fourth shop on the left from the mosque entrance. The Latin inscription reads, "Oh, men who pass along this street, in charity I beg you to pray for my soul—Master Ebuli Fazli, builder of the church." The mosque is now used as a scout house, and it's open daily from 4 to 6pm (admission is free).

An old **lighthouse,** still in use, stands atop the Crusader fortification of Burj Es-Sanjak, on the extreme southwest point of land at Acre. From here you get a marvelous view, both north and south. Just north of the lighthouse, you'll notice a large space in the seawall. This stretch of the wall was destroyed during the heavy earthquake of 1837, the same earthquake that leveled several cities in the mountains.

BAHJI

To Baha'is, this shrine to their prophet Baha' Allah is the holiest place on earth. Baha'i followers believe that God is manifested to men and women through prophets such as Abraham, Moses, Jesus, and Muhammad, as well as the Bab (Baha' Allah's predecessor) and Baha' Allah himself. The Baha'i faith proclaims that all religions are one, that men and women are equal, that the world should be at peace, and that education should be universal. Baha'i followers are encouraged to live simply and to dedicate themselves to helping their fellow men and women. They look forward to a day when there will be a single world government and one world language.

The Baha'i faith grew out of the revelation of the Bab, a Persian Shiite Muslim teacher and mystic who flourished from 1844 to 1850, and was executed by the Persian shah for insurrection and radical teachings. In 1863, Mirza Husein Ali Nuri, one of the Bab's disciples, proclaimed himself Baha' Allah, the Promised One, whose coming had been foretold by the Bab. Baha' Allah was exiled by the Persian government in cooperation with the Ottoman leaders to Baghdad, Constantinople, Adrianople, and finally to Acre, where he arrived in August 1868. He and several of his followers were imprisoned for $2^1/_2$ years at the Acre Citadel. The authorities later put him under house arrest, and he was eventually brought to Bahji, where he remained until his death in 1892. He is buried here in a peaceful tomb surrounded by magnificent gardens. Baha'is are still persecuted, especially in Iran where the faith was born; the Shiite Muslims in authority today look upon them as blasphemers and heretics.

You can visit the shrine at ✪ **Bahji (Delight),** where Baha' Allah lived, died, and is buried, on Friday, Saturday, and Sunday only, from 9am to noon. The house's beautiful gardens are open to visitors every day, from 9am to 4pm. Catch a no. 271 bus heading north toward Nahariya, and make sure it stops at Bahji.

Going north from Acre, you'll see an impressive gilded gate on the right-hand side of the road after about 2 kilometers (1 mi.). This gate is not open to the public. Go past it until you are almost 3 kilometers (about 2 mi.) from Acre, and you'll see a sign, SHAMERAT. Get off the bus, turn right here, and go another short distance to the visitors' gate. The Ottoman-Victorian house holds some memorabilia of Baha' Allah, and the lush gardens are a real treat.

ARGAMAN BEACH

The favorite local spot for swimming is the Argaman Beach, just south of town by the Argaman Motel. This is one of Israel's most beautiful Mediterranean beaches, with the view of Haifa on one end of the bay, and the old seawalls of Acre on the other. Lifeguards are here in summer. Unfortunately, like other beaches along the northern coast, Argaman often suffers from serious pollution.

Off-season, visitors are usually welcome for a day-use fee to enjoy the facilities at the **Palm Beach Hotel and Country Club** (☎ **04/981-5815**) on Argaman Beach. These include an outdoor Olympic-size swimming pool plus a heated indoor pool, tennis, volleyball, basketball, and squash courts, Ping-Pong tables, a health club, a Finnish sauna, and a private beach with lounge chairs and shades. Call ahead to make a reservation and ask the price.

WHERE TO STAY

If you're not up for staying in the youth hostel, which is the only choice inside the walls of the Old City, there are some fine hotel choices just a short ride from Old Acre, especially for travelers with private cars.

Palm Beach Hotel and Country Club. Acre Beach 24101. ☎ **04/987-7777.** Fax 04/991-0434. 119 units. A/C TV TEL. $126–$162 double, regular and high seasons (July–Aug). Add 20% for off-season weekends. Rates include breakfast. AE, MC, V.

A high-rise with sweeping views, the hotel is located a mile south of the Old City on the coastal road to Haifa. The greatest benefit of staying here, in addition to the wonderful beach and view, is the free use of the country club and other facilities. While nonguests may be able to use the country club when it's not too busy, staying at the hotel guarantees the privilege. On the hotel's premises are heated indoor and outdoor swimming pools, a piano bar, a Jacuzzi, squash, basketball, and tennis courts, a beach, a discotheque, self-service restaurant, and an evening terrace cafe as well as a playground area for children. All restaurant facilities are kosher. There is a bus into town.

WHERE TO DINE

✪ **Abu Christo.** Near the Old Port. ☎ **04/991-0065.** Reservations recommended on weekends. Main courses NIS 40–90 ($9–$20). AE, DC, MC, V. Daily 10am–midnight. SEAFOOD/MIDDLE EASTERN.

This well-known restaurant is particularly nice in good weather, when you can sit out on the terrace under reed shades and enjoy the delightful waterfront view, which often includes local daredevils diving from the ancient ruins. For appetizers, a round of Middle Eastern salads is especially good here. Most main courses are straightforward dishes like steak, grilled skewers of lamb, or grilled fish (the fresh grouper is expensive but delectable) all served with french fries; there are also Greek-style specialties and house dishes like skewered shrimp in sesame garlic sauce cooked on an open fire. Abu Christo often features special low-price treats, like tiny fresh fish fried in garlic, which you eat, bones, heads, and all! Full bar.

Oudeh Brothers Restaurant. Old City market area. ☎ **04/991-2013.** Reservations recommended weekends. Main courses NIS 40–90 ($9.25–$20). Higher prices for lobster. MC, V. Daily 9am–midnight. SEAFOOD/MIDDLE EASTERN.

This clean, pleasant restaurant has four large, airy dining rooms (alas, no waterfront view) and a large patio dining area beside the courtyard of the Khan El-Faranj (or Afranj), described above. It offers a wonderful 25-salad mezze, lamb shashlik with rice and salad, meat with hummus, pickles, and pita, and lots of seafood including lobster and shrimp. Turkish coffee is on the house if you've ordered a meal.

Ptolemais Restaurant. Fisherman's Quay. ☎ **04/991-6112.** Appetizers NIS 7–20 ($2–$5.60); main courses NIS 40–90 ($9–$19.80). DC, MC, V. Summer daily 10am–1am; winter daily 10am–8pm. SEAFOOD/MIDDLE EASTERN.

This restaurant, near the Abu Christo, dishes up terrific fish main courses and meals like beef with hummus at reasonable prices. Watermelon makes a refreshing dessert. Students get a 10% reduction. Here, too, there's a full bar, and you can sit either inside or on the waterfront patio, with the boats in the harbor bobbing up and down just a few feet away.

✪ **Uri Buri.** 93 Haganah St. ☎ **04/955-2212.** Reservations necessary. Main courses NIS 50–90 ($11–$19.80). AE, MC, V. Wed–Mon noon–11pm. Near the lighthouse (Midal Or) in the Old City. FISH.

Set in an old Turkish house with one room heavy on traditional Arabic decor, this restaurant's secret ingredient is owner/chef Uri Yirmias himself, who has an exceptional talent for preparing fish. Ask what's freshest and best to order. Among the specialties are tiny, tender calamari with kumquats and pink grapefruit; fresh fish with marvelous mustard/honey sauce; excellent gravlax, and wonderful chowders.

ACRE AFTER DARK

One of Acre's most enjoyable evening activities is strolling around through the tiny Arabian Nights streets, past the old khans and the towering minarets framed by moonlight and stars, gazing from the old port out across the bay toward the sparkling lights of Haifa and Acre's little lighthouse on duty. On a quiet night, moonlight shining in, you can stand in the courtyard of Khan El-Umdan and imagine all the people, animals, activities, and human dramas that have passed through here. Another atmospheric moonlight walk is around the city's seawalls.

Exotic Arabic music fills the air day and night all around Old Acre. Light and music pour out into the streets from the open doors of billiard parlors, and you're welcome to come in and shoot a few games.

You can sip a beer or cocktail at one of the waterfront restaurants, at the Burj's rooftop nightclub during the warm months, or at the other Burj meeting places. But if you're ready for a real live striptease act, head for the Burj's **Han A-Sultan** restaurant and nightclub on a Friday or Saturday evening, open until 4am. Everyone is welcome.

The **discotheque** at the Palm Beach Hotel and Country Club (☎ **04/991-2892**) is open to everyone nightly in summer months; only on Friday in winter. Music and dancing and one drink are included in the NIS 26 ($5.80) cover charge. Also at the Palm Beach is the outdoor **Pundak Cafe,** open in summertime only, from 8:30pm to 1am, with live music on the terrace, food, and drinks.

SIDE TRIPS FROM ACRE

The main highway between Akko and Nahariya parallels fragments of a stone **aqueduct** built by Ahmed Jezzar Pasha in 1780 over the ruins of a Roman aqueduct. The aqueduct originally supplied Acre with water from the Galilee's springs. Its picturesque ruins include many archways framing sabra plants. Before you reach Nahariya, you will pass two communities, just across the road from each other, that are well worth a visit.

Kibbutz Lohammei HaGetaot, the Ghetto Defenders' Kibbutz, 2 miles north of Akko, was founded in 1949 by a small group of survivors of Jewish ghettos in Poland and Lithuania. Initially scattered in towns and refugee camps throughout Israel, they felt they could best rebuild their lives among others who had similar tragic memories as former partisans and participants in Ghetto uprisings. The kibbutz flourished, and today their children and grandchildren manage the orchards, schools, and factories of this very symbolic community.

The **Ghetto Fighters' House** (☎ **04/995-8080**), a Museum of the Holocaust and Resistance, and **Yad La Yeled,** the Memorial and Museum of Children, document Jewish life in communities throughout Europe before and during the Holocaust. The complex contains a museum of writings, diaries, and artwork from the ghettos and concentration camps, and these detailed, very personal exhibits vividly inform us about the ghetto uprisings and the destruction of Jewish communities, including those in Holland, Saloniki, Vilna, and Hungary. Among the many models and installations is a replica of the Anne Frank House in Amsterdam. Especially moving are the paintings and drawings done by children. The museum is the center for an international education program designed to teach about the Holocaust, in the hope that such knowledge will help prevent such cruelties from being permitted in the future. It's open Sunday to Thursday from 9am to 4pm; Friday from 9am to 1pm; and Saturday and Jewish holidays from 10am to 5pm. There is no admission fee, but contributions are accepted for the guided tours. Bus 271 (midday frequency: every 30 minutes) from Haifa to Nahariya will make request stops at the Kibbutz.

Just across the Akko-Nahariya Highway from Lohammei HaGetaot, a sign points to **Hatzrot Yatsaf,** an absorption center for the thousands of new Ethiopian Jewish immigrants who continue to arrive in the country. This vast caravan-trailer community-by-the-sea affords you a glimpse of the most recent and perhaps most exotic *aliyah,* or wave of immigration, to Israel. The stately, graceful immigrants, some still wearing traditional white robes, are invariably courteous and kind. After the road crosses the train tracks, Hatzrot Yatsaf begins.

Things are always changing here, but after approximately 3 blocks a sign on the right should direct you to **Beit Hayotzer,** the artisans' workshop, where black low-fire terra-cotta ceramics and other crafts are produced for sale. (If there is no sign, just keep asking.) As you turn down this side road, Beit Hayotzer will be about 500 feet down on the left. The ceramic crafts on display at the **Beit Hayotzer Hatzrif Yasaf Ethiopian Craft Center** (☎ **04/991-6325**) have their roots in traditional Ethiopian pottery, but the designs also draw on the artisans' encounter with a new society. There are miniature ceramic tableaux depicting Ethiopian scenes and myths. There are handmade Hanukkah menorahs incorporating Ethiopian motifs—although because Ethiopian Jews were separated from the mainstream of Judaism too early to have had knowledge of the 2,200-year-old festival of Hanukkah, they did not celebrate this holiday until they came to Israel. Look for tiny, charming frogs, praying Ethiopian peasants, and rough ceramic "marriage boxes" in which you will find a naive representation of a couple involved in amorous activity. The boxes are used as a kind of household signal, according to the artisans—a slightly open box is meant to convey that at least one marriage partner is ready for lovemaking.

A number of the craftspeople have developed personal followings among customers and collectors. Prices range from $1 or $2 to several hundred dollars, and are about half what they would cost at galleries in the main cities. Salespeople here will often point out "seconds." I bought an exotic lion's head menorah for $42—if perfect, it would have been a $150 design. Proceeds go directly to the artisans. The workshop will pack purchases for carrying, but transport them with care: terra-cotta is highly fragile. Open Sunday to Thursday from 8am to 4pm. No credit cards are accepted.

WHERE TO STAY

Nes Ammim Guest House. Mobile Post, Ashrat 25225. ☎ **04/995-0000.** Fax 04/995-0098. 48 units (all with bathtub). A/C TV. $100–$142 double. Discount on Kibbutz Package Plan. Rates include breakfast. AE, DC, MC, V. Drive north along highway to signs pointing east to Nes Ammim and Regba; turn here and go 4km (2 mi.) inland.

Another short drive from Acre, to the north and through an enchanting avocado forest, is a 200-member Christian village organized in 1963 for the purpose of bringing Jews and Christians into closer contact. This community is famous for growing flowers. While here, you can enjoy the large outdoor swimming pool, bar, the wonderful greenhouse creations, the botanical gardens, and get a free tour of the community. Guest rooms were redone during 1995–97. There are 13 family size rooms; rooms for travelers with disabilities are also available. Although not a kibbutz, the hotel is part of the Kibbutz Guest House Association, and can be booked through their packages. Study tours on the subject of Jewish-Christian relations can be arranged through Nes Ammim.

If you're not staying here, but are interested in the community, call ahead and arrange for a tour. The Nes Ammim community is especially interested in making the land alive again, and you will be amazed by its efforts and dedication. Coming by bus is a bit more of a challenge, but it can be arranged; call ahead and they'll tell you the best way to do it.

7 Nahariya & North to the Border

Nahariya: 33 kilometers (20 mi.) N of Haifa.

Founded by German Jews in the mid-1930s, Nahariya is a popular summer resort with Israelis, but visitors are catching on. On the Lag b'Omer holiday in the spring (the only day a Jew can marry during the 6 weeks between Passover and Shavuot holidays), Nahariya is packed with honeymooners. Maybe there's a connection between Nahariya's honeymoon attractions and the fact that archaeologists dug up a Canaanite fertility goddess on its beach.

This holiday town has an unusual main street: A stream shaded by breezy eucalyptus trees runs down the middle. There is a low-key, pleasantly small-town feeling to Nahariya. Horse carts will take you around town; settle on a price before you start out.

ESSENTIALS

GETTING THERE   By Bus   From Acre, take the no. 271 or 272 Haifa-Acre-Nahariya bus. The ride is less than 25 minutes.

By Car   From Acre, Nahariya is a 15-minute drive north on the coastal highway.

VISITOR INFORMATION   When you leave the Central Bus Station, turn left and walk down about half a block on Ha-Ga'aton. On the left you'll see a small square, and at the far end of the square, a seven-story edifice with flags waving in front. This is the Municipal Building, where you'll find the **Tourist Information Office** (☎ **04/ 987-9800**), open Sunday to Thursday from 9am to 1pm and 4 to 7pm, on Friday from 9am to noon and closed Saturday.

If you're interested in meeting the locals, the staff at the tourist office can arrange it. Local chapters of Rotary, Lions, Soroptimists, and Freemasons also extend a warm welcome to international members; contact the Tourist Information Office for meeting times and places.

CITY LAYOUT   It's pretty easy to find your way around this small city. The Central Bus Station and the railway station are just off the main highway on Ha-Ga'aton Boulevard, Nahariya's main road. Head down Ha-Ga'aton and you'll be going due west, to the sea. Don't worry about the weight of your bags, as you only have to walk about 5 blocks to get to a hotel.

BEACHES & OUTDOOR PURSUITS

The beaches of Nahariya, the town's raison d'être from a visitor's point of view, suffer, like other places on the northern Israeli coast, from the region's lack of a sewage treatment plant and the proximity of Lebanon, where decades of chaos have led to garbage dumping into the sea. The junk often swirls into Nahariya's waters, and at times in recent years, coliform bacteria counts per 100 milliliters of seawater at Nahariya were four times the Israeli Health Ministry's acceptable level (although within the more lenient standards of other Mediterranean countries).

The main beach, **Galei-Galil,** just to the north of Ha-Ga'aton Boulevard, has won prizes in the past for cleanliness and safety. Today, it also offers an Olympic-size outdoor pool, a heated, glass-enclosed indoor pool open year-round, a children's pool, dressing rooms, playgrounds for children, and restaurants. It is open June through September, daily from 8am to 6pm and October through May, daily until 5pm. Admission is NIS 12 ($3.40); discounts for children.

At the marina breakwater you'll see people **fishing** off the rocks, and you can rent a sailboat, or go snorkeling. **Tennis, basketball,** and **volleyball** courts are other attractions, as is the big water slide just on the north side of the beach.

If you just want to take a dip in the Mediterranean, the free **Municipal Beach** is 2 blocks south. The view from both beaches is lovely. On a clear day—and most of them are—you can see all the way from Rosh Ha-Niqra at the Lebanese border to the north to Haifa in the south.

For a hike with the **Friends of Nature (Hovevei Hateva),** check with the Municipal Tourist Office (☎ **04/987-9800**). Hikes are often scheduled for Saturdays.

MUSEUMS & ANCIENT SITES

Nahariya's **Municipal Museum** is in the seven-story Municipal Building, on Ha-Iriya Square. The fifth floor houses an art exhibit. The sixth floor, in addition to an interesting malacology (shell) collection, displays many artifacts from the area around Nahariya, with its fascinating history dating all the way back to the Stone Age. On the seventh floor is a department showing the history of the town. The museum is open Sunday to Friday from 10am to noon, plus Sunday and Wednesday afternoons from 4 to 6pm. Admission is free.

Nahariya's ruins of a **Canaanite temple** were accidentally discovered on Ha-Ma'apilim Street, a few yards up from the Municipal Beach, in 1947. Experts believe it to be a temple dedicated to the Canaanite goddess of the sea, Asherath (or Astarte), dating from about 1500 B.C.

The **beautiful mosaic floor of a 4th- to 7th-century Byzantine Church** can be seen on Bielefeld Street, near the Katznelson School. The mosaic depicts the hunting and working scenes as well as flora and fauna designs typical of mosaic floors found in Byzantine churches, but is one of finest yet discovered. Check with Tourist Information (☎ **04/987-9800**) to arrange a visit. There may be an admission fee of under $1.

WHERE TO STAY

Most of Nahariya's hotels are located, quite logically, at the western end of Ha-Ga'aton Boulevard near Galei-Galil Beach. You can also check with the Municipal Tourist Office (☎ **04/987-9800**) for lists of rooms to rent in private houses. Prices are around $30 to $35 per person, including breakfast, depending on season and facilities.

Carlton Hotel. 23 Ha-Ga'aton St., Nahariya. ☎ **04/992-2211.** Fax 04/982-3771. 200 units (all with bathtub). A/C TV TEL. $150–$200 double. Rates include breakfast. Add 15% service charge. AE, MC, V.

Located on the main street in the center of town, this six-story hotel is the best and most expensive in Nahariya. Rooms are comfortable, but not really up to this price category. There isn't a real beach atmosphere at this location, but the hotel's heated outdoor pool, which is covered in winter, provides the chance for off-season swimming. In summer and on weekends, the hotel is filled with activities that, together with late-night main street action, can be a bit too noisy for some. There is a sauna and Jacuzzi. Rooms are available for travelers with disabilities. There is a $100 surcharge per room during Passover and the Jewish New Year.

Days Inn Frank Hotel. 4 Ha-Aliyah St. (P.O. Box 58), Nahariya 22381. ☎ **04/992-0278.** Fax 04/992-5535. 50 units (all with bathtub or shower). A/C TV TEL. $110–$125 double. Passover and Sukkot, add 15% to high-season rates. MC, V.

Founded more than 50 years ago by a Nahariya family originally from Germany, the Hotel Frank is efficiently run with a careful, personal touch; it has recently become affiliated with Days Inn, but the same management continues and part of its business is with long established clientele. Located just back from Ha-Ma'apilim 2 blocks north of Ha-Ga'aton, this 1970s contemporary hotel is in a quieter neighborhood, relatively close to the beach. It offers a small outdoor swimming pool (the pool may soon be redone), rooms with good, moderately firm beds, heating, and at times, German-language TV channels. There are rooms for travelers with disabilities.

Erna House. 29 Jabotinsky St., Nahariya. ☎ **04/992-0170.** Fax 04/992-8917. 26 units (all with bathtub or shower). A/C TV TEL. $75–$86 double. Rates include breakfast. MC, V.

This neat, well-kept, two-star establishment is a converted house with the look of a solid, comfortable little hotel. It's a small family-run enterprise; the rooms come with heat, carpeting, and a TV if you request one, at no extra charge. Among other amenities is a video TV room.

WHERE TO DINE

Nahariya is not exactly what you'd call a gourmet's mecca. It's small and many vacation visitors take meals in their hotels. If you decide to go out, the first place to try is Ha-Ga'aton Boulevard, with its bistros, sidewalk cafes, and two commercial plazas, Ha-Banim Square (Kikar Ha-Banim), and Ha-Iriya Square (Kikar Ha-Iriya). The plazas are across Ha-Ga'aton from one another, at its intersection with Herzl Street, half a block west of the bus station. Each square has a cinema, lots of shops and other services, and some indoor-outdoor snack bar eateries.

El Gaucho. Ha-Ga'aton Boulevard. ☎ **04/992-8635.** Main courses NIS 45–100 ($10–$22). MC, V. Daily noon–midnight. ARGENTINEAN.

This restaurant specializes in Argentinean-style grilled meat, and lots of it, cooked over the coals behind the many cuts of fresh meat on display for all to see. The decor here is ranch—cowhide chairs, a South American pan flute, and wall-mounted cow horns. You can dine inside, or on the palapa-covered patio. The chefs are from South America; much of the meat served here is veal. Menu items range from an inexpensive half-chicken dinner to the house specialty, a 750-gram (about 1^{1}/2-lb.) mixed grill, a giant repast for two (or even more) people. All meat dinners are served with bread and butter, baked potato with butter and sour cream, vegetables, salad, dessert, and the special chimichurra meat sauce that's so scrumptious you'll be sopping it up with the bread.

Penguin Cafe. 33 Ha Ga'aton Blvd. ☎ **04/992-4241.** NIS 9–50 ($2–$11). Daily from 8am to midnight. ICE CREAM/SNACKS.

Located outside the big Penguin Restaurant complex (see below), the menu includes such hot-weather favorites as banana splits, milkshakes, and fruit cocktail, as well as blintzes, pancakes, pastries, and beverages. You can even order pizza with kosher "shrimp," for a change of pace. There are also low-calorie frozen yogurts mixed on the spot with fresh fruits of your choice.

Penguin Restaurant. 21 Ha-Ga'aton Blvd. ☎ **04/992-8855.** Main courses NIS 33–80 ($7.20–$17.60). V. Daily 8am–11pm.

The newly renovated Penguin is the nearest thing Nahariya has to a mall, with a bookstore and many trendy shops surrounding the dining space. The menu runs from pasta to schnitzel to Chinese food, fish, salads, and hamburgers. Photos on the walls remind you of the original tin-roofed Penguin and the bleak, empty landscape that was Nahariya in the 1940s.

Singapore Chinese Restaurant. Ha-Meyasdim and Jabotinsky. ☎ **04/992-4952.** Reservations recommended summer weekends. Main courses NIS 30–70 ($6.60–$15.40); set combination dinner NIS 60 ($13.20). DC, MC, V. Lunch daily noon–3pm; dinner daily 7pm–midnight. Closed Chinese New Year and major Jewish holidays. CHINESE.

Two blocks north of Ha-Ga'aton and across from the Yarden and Eden Hotels, you'll find this roomy place done up pleasantly in Chinese decor. The menu contains 110 items; as you'd expect, there are a number of Singapore specialties, including lemon chicken, a Singapore Sling cocktail, or Singapore ice cream with Chinese fruits for dessert.

SIDE TRIPS NORTH OF NAHARIYA
AKHZIV

Heading north along the main road, after 4 kilometers (2¹/₂ mi.) you'll see the road to **Akhziv Beach,** on the left (west). It's another kilometer (¹/₂ mi.) to the beach proper, where you'll find a parking lot, changing rooms, shelters, and snack stands, as well as freshwater showers. It's open daily from 8am to 7pm in summer. There's a charge of NIS 18 ($4) per person for admission during the summer swimming season.

Heading north again, a kilometer (¹/₂ mi.) past the Akhziv Beach road, you'll pass the parking lot and entrance to **Akhziv National Park** (☎ **04/982-3263**) with its sheltered beach, restaurant, picnic area, and changing facilities amid the ruins of a seaside Arab village.

Akhziv existed when Joshua assigned the tribes of Israel to their various territories, and is mentioned in the Bible as a Canaanite town that the tribe of Asher, to whom it was allotted, was never able to conquer. At the Nahariya Municipal Museum, you can learn about the varied history of the town through the wealth of archaeological artifacts on view.

In more recent times, Akhziv was an Arab village, but the inhabitants fled in 1948 and the village remained deserted for a number of years. In 1952, Eli Avivi, one of Israel's legendary eccentrics, received government permission to settle in Akhziv, and promptly declared the "independence" of **Akhzivland,** which is just north of the park boundary. The ramshackle building that is Akhzivland's main structure houses Mr. Avivi's living quarters and his personal museum of artifacts found on and near Akhzivland. You can visit the museum for a small admission charge.

There is a NIS 18 ($4) summer admission to Akhziv National Park, but off-season, you can sometimes just wander through the gates and up the hill through the lovely gardens. It's a beautiful spot for a picnic; there is a guarded but somewhat rocky beach for swimming. The park is open daily from 8am to 7pm. At the south end of the parking lot is the entrance to Club Méditerranée's vacation resort.

GESHER HAZIV & THE AKHZIV BRIDGE

While the town of Akhziv has a history dating from biblical times, the name is most often remembered in connection with a tragic, heroic event that took place here on the night of June 17, 1946. Attempting to cut British rail communications with neighboring Arab states, a Hagana demolition team was destroying railroad bridges along this line. At the Akhziv bridge, however, they were spotted by a British sentry, who fired a flare in order to get a better look. The flare ignited the team's explosives. The bridge was blown, but no one survived. The 14 who perished are commemorated by a large black metal monument across the road from the youth hostel.

Where to Stay

Kibbutz Gesher Haziv Country Lodging. ☎ **04/995-8568.** Fax 04/982-5971. 26 units (all with shower). A/C TEL. $75–$90 double. Rates include breakfast and service. AE, DC, MC, V.

Guests have access to the kibbutz's seaside diving center and horseback riding stables at discount prices. There are simple but comfortable rooms with refrigerators and coffeemakers, an outdoor swimming pool, and kosher dining facilities. For an extra charge, you can use the health club, Jacuzzi, and sauna, as well as two night-lit tennis courts. The location is excellent, just 5 minutes from the beach, and close to Akko and many sites in the western Galilee.

ROSH HA-NIQRA

This dramatic site borders Lebanon, astride a tall cliff overlooking the sea. On a clear day, standing atop the cliff, you can see the coastline as far as Haifa. Beneath the cliffs are **grottoes** carved out by the sea, reachable via cable car. Operating from 8:30am to 5pm (until 9 or 10pm in summer), on Friday until 3pm, the cable-car ride and admission to the grottoes costs NIS 35 ($7.70) for adults, with a discount for children and students. You can walk into the caves and passages and see the pools of water lapping the rocks. To see the artifacts that have been recovered from these caves, visit the **Municipal Museum** in Nahariya.

To reach Rosh Ha-Niqra, take the bus from Nahariya, which runs several times a day; sherut service is also available, in front of the Nahariya Central Bus Station, on Ha-Ga'aton Boulevard. You can dine at a reasonably priced self-service restaurant on top of the cliff called Mitzpe Rosh Ha-Niqra. The view is breathtaking. Open the same hours as the cable car.

Haifa 8

Some compare Haifa, beautifully situated on a hill overlooking a broad bay, to San Francisco or Naples. Israel's third-largest metropolitan area (population 300,000) and the capital of the north, Haifa is like a triple-decker sandwich—the industrial area that comprises Israel's most important port is the lowest tier; the business district (Hadar), higher up, is the second; and the Carmel district, with its panoramic vistas, nestled even higher on the upper pine slopes, constitutes the third. Just to the south of Haifa are magnificent beaches that locals flock to, but few tourists know about. Plans are now in progress to convert these unspoiled beach areas into Haifa's' own "Riviera"; you'll see a great deal of hotel, apartment, and marina construction underway along the shoreline during the next few years. Like much of the intensive development going on along Israel's Mediterranean coast, this project is controversial, with environmentalists and beach lovers who had wanted to turn the area into a national park opposing the loss of Israel's most accessible stretch of natural shoreline.

HAIFA TODAY Very different from either Jerusalem or Tel Aviv, the city is a pleasure to visit just to get a sense of its beauty and lifestyle. In a society unlike any other in the Middle East, Jews and Arabs live and work side by side; 25% of Haifa's population is either Muslim or Christian. In 1898, Theodore Herzl, the father of modern Zionism wrote his prophecy of the Jewish homeland that would one day be reborn: "Next to our temples, you find Christian, Mohammedan, Buddhist, and Brahmin houses of divine worship . . . my comrades and I make no distinction between people. We ask for no one's religion or race but let him be a Man, that is enough." With its Baha'i Center, churches, synagogues, and mosques, as well as its politically progressive, hard working Jewish and Arabic population, Haifa, more than any other city in Israel, has come to fit that vision.

Like the rest of the country, Haifa is booming. Construction of new hotels (including a totally new hotel district down near the shore) is already under way. Planned development of the truly beautiful beaches just to the south of Haifa will change the nature of the city as a travel destination over the next few years.

Haifa is a good base for exploring the northwestern part of Israel. You won't need to rent a car if you base yourself here; many organized day tours originate in Haifa, or, since Haifa is a major transportation hub, you can just use public transportation to explore cities like Akko or even Safed on your own. In the evening, after a day of touring the area, Haifa offers a good choice of restaurants, films, concerts, and urban strolling to keep you busy.

A LOOK AT HAIFA'S PAST Almost every square foot of Israel has been populated since earliest ages, and Haifa is no exception. The prophet Elijah knew this territory well—from the top of Mount Carmel he won a major victory over 450 priests of Baal during the reign of King Ahab and his notorious Phoenician wife, Jezebel. In late biblical times, the Phoenician port of Zalemona thrived here, with predominantly Greek settlers, and the Jewish agricultural village of Sycaminos (sometimes called Shikmona) clung to the northwestern peak of Mount Carmel (3rd-century Talmudic literature mentions both towns).

The crusaders called the area Caife, Cayphe, and sometimes Caiphas. Once a center of glass and cochineal-purple industries, Haifa was destroyed when the Arabs reconquered the area, and it virtually slept until the late 19th century when Jewish immigration helped bring about a revival.

Haifa got its first shot in the arm in 1905, when the Haifa-Damascus Railway was built. The Balfour Declaration and British occupation boosted it some more, as did a 1919 railway link to Egypt. But the real kickoff came when the British built its modern harbor—an arduous enterprise begun in 1929 and completed in 1934. Thereupon Haifa began its transformation into the vital trading and communications center it is today, taking on major importance as a shipping base, naval center, and terminal point for oil pipelines.

In 1898, when he visited Palestine and sailed past the spot that was to become modern Haifa, Theodor Herzl had a prophetic vision about the place: "Huge liners rode at anchor . . . at the top of the mountain there were thousands of white homes and the mountain itself was crowned with imposing villas. . . . A beautiful city had been built close to the deep blue sea." Herzl recorded this experience in his book *Altneuland* (Old New Land), and miraculously, Haifa developed precisely along the lines he predicted. Herzl's dream came alive for hundreds of thousands of homeless, scarred refugees who arrived here after the Nazi Holocaust. As they crowded the decks for their first glimpse of the Promised Land, the hills of Haifa must have seemed like a vision of heaven.

On April 21, 1948, Haifa became the first major city controlled by Jews after the end of the British Mandate and the U.N. Partition decision in 1947. Although Haifa's previous growth had already spurred development of residential areas such as Bat Galim, Hadar Ha-Carmel, and Neve-Shaanan, the new wave of immigration (more than 100,000) gave rise to others: Ramat Ramez, Kiryat Elizer, Neveh Yosef, and Kiryat Shprinzak. Haifa Bay, east of the port, became the backbone of the country's heavy industries, with oil refineries and associated industries, foundries, glass factories, fertilizer and chemical industries, cement works, textile manufacturing, and yards for shipbuilding and repair. Israelis are fond of saying that "Tel Aviv plays while Jerusalem prays. But Haifa works!" A visit here is filled with pleasures and new insights into what Israel is all about.

1 Orientation

ARRIVING

Haifa's inter city bus and train transportation center is at its northernmost tip, in the district called Bat Galim, about 2 kilometers (1¹/₂ mi.) northwest of the downtown port area.

BY PLANE At Ben-Gurion Airport contact tourist information *inside* the baggage claim area about taxi, sherut, and bus service to Haifa, approximately a 1¹/₂-hour trip.

The sherut (shared taxi) should be about NIS 67 ($15) per person. Service to Haifa and the north is not as well organized as service to Tel Aviv and Jerusalem.

For the return to Ben Gurion, **El Al Airlines** has an early baggage check-in service in Haifa, located at 6 Ha-Namel St. (☎ **04/867-7036**), open Sunday through Thursday from 5 to 9:30pm for flights departing the next day. El Al also offers a daily early morning bus transportation to Ben-Gurion Airport (available to anyone, not only to El Al's customers). The bus leaves the Egged central bus station daily at 3:30am, stopping at many hotels along the way, with its final departure from the Dan Carmel Hotel at 4:15am. It will pick you up anywhere along its route if you call in advance to request it. You can purchase tickets in advance from the El Al office, travel agents, or hotels (but not directly from the bus driver). For further information or to reserve a ticket, phone **El Al's office** (☎ **04/867-0170**). Shared taxi (sherut) service from Haifa to Ben Gurion Airport can be arranged through Amal Taxi (☎ **04/866-2324**). Fare is approximately NIS 65 ($14) one way per person. Another service to Ben-Gurion is **Kavei Ha-Galil,** 11 Berwarld St. (☎ **04/866-4444,** 866-4445, or 866-4446).

BY TRAIN   The New Central Railway Station is in Bat Galim, near the Central Bus Station. In the station you'll find a cheerful air-conditioned restaurant with set-price breakfasts or lunches if you're in transit, open Sunday through Thursday from 5am to 7pm, closing early on Friday and all day Saturday.

From Tel Aviv, trains along the coast to Netanya and Haifa leave approximately every hour from 5:45am to 7pm, Sunday through Thursday; the last Friday train leaves at 2pm; there's no Saturday service. The trip on the express train to Haifa takes one hour; the local train takes 90 minutes. Less frequent service from Haifa to Akko and Nahariya is available. Train information can be obtained by calling ☎ **04/856-4564.**

BY BUS   The Egged Bus Terminal, with intercity buses to and from all points in Israel, is next to the Central Railway Station in Bat Galim. From here, you'll have to take a city bus to either of my recommended hotel districts, in Hadar or Central Carmel. For Hadar, catch no. 10 or 12; for Central Carmel and the top of the mountain, you want no. 3, 22, or 24. Interurban bus information can be obtained by calling ☎ **04/854-9555.** For buses within Haifa, call ☎ **04/854-9131.**

Right in the Egged Bus Station in Bat Galim is the Egged Restaurant, not the most romantic place to dine, but just right for a meal before or after a long bus journey. There's a full set-price menu for lunch, and it's open Sunday through Friday from 7am to 4pm; closed Saturday.

BY CAR   Major highway networks connect Haifa with Tel Aviv, Jerusalem, and the Galilee.

BY FERRY   Your ship will dock right in the port at the Maritime Passenger Terminal. It's only a short walk to the Paris Square (Kikar Paris) station of the Carmelit subway that climbs the mountain to Hadar and Central Carmel.

VISITOR INFORMATION   The **Haifa Tourist Office,** is at 48 Ben Gurion Blvd. (☎ **04/853-5606**) in the German Colony, far from most hotels. From the hotel district in the Central Carmel, you can take the Carmelit down to Kikar Paris and then walk over to the German Colony, or check with the desk at your hotel about the best bus route to the office. There is also a small **Tourist Information Office in the Central Bus Station** (☎ **04/851-2208**). Both are open Sunday through Thursday from 8:30am to 5pm (till 9:30pm at the Bus Station), on Friday until 1pm; and closed Saturday. Here you can obtain the monthly calendar "Events in Haifa and the Northern

Region," plus detailed free maps, directions, and any other information you might need. You can telephone **Haifa's Tourist Information Hotline** at ☎ **04/837-4253.**

The **Israel Students Tourist Association (ISSTA)** has an office in Hadar at 2 Balfour St. (☎ **04/867-0222**). With a student card, you can get discounts on plane and ferry tickets; open Sunday through Thursday from 8:30am to 1pm, and 4 to 7pm; on Friday from 8:30am to 1pm.

CITY LAYOUT

Of all its graces, Haifa is richest in panoramic views. For purposes of orientation, you might think of Haifa as a city built on three levels. Whether you come by ship, bus, or train, you will arrive on the first, or **port,** level of the city. The second level, **Hadar Ha-Carmel,** meaning "Glory of the Carmel," is referred to simply as Hadar. This is the business section as well as the home of the Contemporary Art section of the Haifa Museum, and some very pleasant restaurants and budget hotels. At the top of the hills is the **Carmel** District, a patchwork of verdant residential neighborhoods with its own small but busy commercial center called **Central Carmel,** numerous hotels and pensions, restaurants, small museums, and two of Haifa's brightest cultural beacons: Haifa Auditorium and Bet Rothschild (the James de Rothschild Cultural Center).

Because Haifa is built all the way up the side of a mountain, many of its main streets are sinuous switchbacks, curving and recurving to accommodate the steep slopes of Mount Carmel. The streets are always and forever bewildering, and you will find it hard to orient yourself. If Haifa weren't so pleasant and beautiful, this would be a chore. About the only straight road in Haifa is the one that climbs the slopes of Carmel underground: the Carmelit.

2 Getting Around

BY SUBWAY The **Carmelit** is a fast and efficient and amazing means of getting up and down Haifa's various levels. Its lower terminal station is located on Jaffa Road, a few blocks north of the port entrance and not far from the old (Merkaz) railway station. The Carmelit's upper terminal is at the Carmel Center.

Pulled on a long cable up and down the steep hill, the Carmelit resembles a sort of scale-model Métro. From bottom to the top, the stops are: (1) Paris Square (Kikar Paris, lower terminus, port area); (2) Solel Boneh (Hassan Shukri Street); (3) Ha-Nevi'im (Hadar business district, tourist office); (4) Masada (Masada Street); (5) Eliezer Golomb (Eliezer Golomb Street); (6) Gan Ha-Em (Central Carmel business district, upper terminus).

Trains run every 10 minutes. The Carmelit operates Sunday through Thursday from 6:30am to midnight, Friday from 6:30am to 3pm, and resumes service on Saturday from one-half hour after the end of Shabbat until midnight; it is closed during Sabbath. Ticket machines have English as well as Hebrew instructions. The fare is NIS 5 ($1.10).

BY BUS Bus fares are charged according to destination, so you must tell the driver where you're going. Most fares to places inside Haifa itself are NIS 5 ($1.10). Haifa's municipal buses operate from 5am to 11:30pm Sunday through Thursday; on Friday, bus service halts around 4:30pm; there is limited Saturday service from 9am to midnight. For information on buses inside Haifa, call ☎ **04/854-9131.** For Inter-urban lines, call ☎ **04/854-9555.**

Fast Facts: Haifa

Bookstores   There are Steimatzky branches at 82 Ha-Atzma'ut St., 16 Herzl St. in Bet Ha-Kranot, 130 Ha-Nassi Blvd., and in the Central Bus Station. For a selection of used English books, try Beverly's Books, 18 Herzl St., second floor (usually closed Wednesdays).

Crime   See "Safety," below.

Currency Exchange   Banking hours are Sunday through Friday from 8:30am to 2:30pm. Afternoon hours are Sunday, Tuesday, and Thursday from 4 to 6pm.

Doctors   Call the Rambam Hospital in Bat Galim (☎ 04/854-3111).

Drugstores   Standard hours are Sunday through Thursday from 8am to 1pm and 4 to 7pm; Friday from 8am to 2pm. According to a rotating schedule, one or two pharmacies remain on duty nights and on Shabbat; their names will be posted in any pharmacy window.

Embassies/Consulates   The U.S. consulate is at 26 Ben Gurion Blvd., ☎ 04/853-1446; fax 04/853-1476. Consular services by appointment only; for emergencies, call the U.S. Embassy in Tel Aviv (☎ 03/519-7372).

Emergencies   Dial ☎ 101 for Magen David Adom first aid services; ☎ 04/851-2233 for an ambulance.

Hospitals   The Rambam Hospital in Bat Galim (☎ 04/854-3111), and Carmel Hospital, 7 Michal St. (☎ 04/825-0211), will accommodate tourists.

Hot Lines   Emotional First Aid (☎ 04/867-2222) is open 24 hours daily; English is spoken.

Laundry/Dry Cleaning   Laundromats in Haifa are not easily accessible from tourist areas; ask at your hotel.

Libraries   The main library is at 50 Pevsner St. (☎ 04/866-7766). Hours are Sunday through Thursday from 9am to 8pm, Friday 9am to 1pm.

Newspapers/Magazines   The *Jerusalem Post, International Herald Tribune* (including the English edition of the top Israeli newspaper, *Ha'aretz). Jerusalem Report Magazine* and *Eretz* (a magazine of history, nature, and travel) are readily available.

Police   See "Emergencies," above.

Post Office   Haifa's most accessible post office with the longest hours is in Hadar, at the corner of Shabtai Levi and Ha-Nevi'im streets (☎ 04/864-0917). It is open Sunday through Thursday from 8am to 7pm; Friday 8am to 1:30pm; closed Saturday.

Radio   English broadcasts are on Israeli radio 576 kHz and 1458 kHz at 7am, 1, 5, and 8pm.

Religious Services   "Events in Haifa," available at Municipal Tourist Information Offices, lists all major church, mosque, and synagogue services.

Safety   Haifa is generally a low-crime city. Extra care should be exercised near the port after dark.

Taxis   For special taxis to destinations outside Haifa, call Kavei Ha-Galil, ☎ 04/ 866-4444 or 04/866-4445. The fare for a taxi to Ben Gurion Airport is NIS 210 ($59); higher rates at night and on Shabbat. Amahl's Sheruts ☎ 04/

866-2324 offers shared taxi service to Ben Gurion for about NIS 44 ($12.40) per person.

Telegrams/Telex/Fax   Dial ☎ 171 for telegrams. You can send telegrams at the post office (see "Post Office," above). Ask at your hotel for fax services.

Television   Two Israeli channels carry many English-language programs. Channel 2 is the more highbrow; Middle East television from Lebanon specializes in American reruns.

Useful Telephone Numbers   The Israel Student Travel Association (ISSTA), 2 Balfour St., Hadar, can be reached at ☎ 04/867-0222 or 04/866-9139: discounts on plane and ferry tickets. Association of Americans and Canadians in Israel (AACI), 8 Wedgewood Drive, Haifa, can be reached at ☎ 04/838-7140 or 04/838-4319: help for absorption of North American immigrants, social and cultural programs, tours, lectures, and activities.

USO   Serving the needs of U.S. military in Israel; extremely busy when the fleet is in: ☎ 04/838-2057.

3 Where to Stay

With one exception, Haifa's recommended hotels are all up in the Central Carmel area, with its fabulous vistas. Despite the fact that you're way up on the top tier of Haifa, with the Carmelit, you're only minutes away from the other parts of the city.

HADAR
MODERATE

Haifa Tower Hotel. 63 Herzl St., Haifa. ☎ **04/867-7111.** Fax 04/862-1863. 49 units (all with bathtub or shower). A/C TV TEL. $105–$150 double. Rates include breakfast. AE, DC, MC, V. Carmelit: Ha-Nevi'im.

Located in a new 17-story office building in the downtown Hadar section of Haifa, this middle-ranking choice opened in the early 1990s and is the only decent hotel in this part of town. It doesn't have personality but it offers comfortable rooms (all with views of the harbor or the city, though not as spectacular as those from the higher Carmel neighborhood) and pleasant public areas. Business class guest rooms, with better furnishings and equipment, are $15 extra.

CENTRAL CARMEL
EXPENSIVE

✪ **Dan Carmel Hotel.** 85–87 Ha-Nassi Blvd., Haifa 34642. ☎ **04/830-3010.** Fax 04/83.0-3030. E-mail: dancarmel@danhotels.com. 219 units (all with bathtub). A/C MINIBAR TV TEL. $267–$380 double. Rates include breakfast. 15% service charge. AE, DC, MC, V. Carmelit: Gan Ha-Em.

For 40 years, the Dan Carmel has reigned as Haifa's most luxurious hotel. The building itself is a perfectly maintained example of 1950s modernistic architecture and decor—a style just now reaching the age to be appreciated for nostalgic as well as interesting esthetic value. There are spacious public areas, overlooking beautiful gardens, a large country club outdoor swimming pool, and a top-flight staff, all of which add up to a relaxing, pleasant experience. Deluxe rooms and suites, recently renovated, are beautifully furnished and decorated, with wall panels of Chinese or classic French textile designs that add a rich, intelligent touch. Superior (standard) rooms have not yet been updated, and show their age. Deluxe and Superior rooms are divided in price between rooms with interesting views and rooms with spectacular views.

Dining/Diversions: Two restaurants, lobby lounge, pub, poolside snack bar. The in-house **Rondo Restaurant,** perhaps the most elegant kosher choice in Haifa, is open Saturday through Thursday evenings; a fixed-price meal here is a worthwhile (kosher) splurge for a special occasion at $40 (Dan Carmel guests are exempt from the value-added tax (VAT) if the tab is charged to their room).

Amenities: Executive business center, 24-hour room service, hairdresser, swimming pool, sauna, health club, parking (fee).

✪ **Dan Panorama.** 107 Ha-Nassi Blvd., Haifa 34632. ☎ **04/835-2222.** Fax 04/835-2235. 267 units (all with bathtub). A/C TV TEL. $223–$270 double. Rates include breakfast. 15% service charge. AE, DC, MC, V. Carmelite: Gan Ha-Em.

This hotel, set in a high-rise built in 1986, is less expensive and usually has a busier pace than its sister hotel, the Dan Carmel, down the street. It's just steps away from the Carmelit Station and part of the upmarket Panorama shopping mall complex, which houses a choice of clothing shops, small eateries, and snack bars just off the hotel's polished stone lobby. The pool has been fitted onto the roof of one of the building's lower wings, and catches breezes on hot days. Rooms are compact, of efficient, modern design (even lower-category rooms have hair dryers), and classified in price according to their views (windows in many rooms are not really big enough to make the most of their vistas). The location, a short block from the Carmelit stop and the Carmel shopping district, is excellent. There are lots of pleasant Dan Hotel Chain touches, like the wonderful breads at the breakfast buffet.

Dining/Diversions: Three restaurants, piano bar lounge, Viennese cafe.

Amenities: Business service bureau, 24-hour room service, outdoor pool, children's pool, fitness club, parking (fee).

MODERATE

Holiday Inn Bay View. 111 Yefe Nof St. ☎ **04/835-0835.** Fax 04/835-0836. 100 units (all with bathtubs). A/C MINIBAR TV TEL. $144–$168 double. Rates include breakfast. AE, DC, MC, V. Carmelit: Gan Ha-Em.

Opened in 1999, this is Haifa's first international chain hotel and it provides excellent value in every way. The location, one street downhill from the Dan Hotels on Ha-Nassi Street, offers great vistas and is close to the Carmelit station. Rooms are up to the minute and have safes, satellite TV, and coffeemakers; hotel amenities include an indoor pool, fitness room, sauna, steam room, and fee parking. *Note:* The above rates are those offered when you call Holiday Inn's international reservation line; if you walk in, rates could range from $260 to $320.

Hotel Dvir. 124 Yefe Nof St., Haifa 34454. ☎ **04/838-9131.** Fax 04/838-1068. 30 units (all with bathroom or shower). A/C TV TEL. $110 double. Rates include breakfast. AE, DC, MC, V. Bus: 21, 28, or 37. Carmelit: Gan Ha-Em.

The 10 front rooms have an incredibly beautiful view of the city, the harbor, and across Haifa Bay to Acre and the mountains beyond. Each of these rooms has an entire wall made of glass as well as a balcony; get one of these if you can; back rooms (including singles) are cramped and confining. The service, however, is as significant as the view. The Dvir is run as a hotel training school for the Dan Hotel Chain, and the young people who serve you here are out to get good marks both from you and from their supervisors. Amenities include clock radios, heat, and wall-to-wall carpeting and use of the nearby Dan Panorama Hotel swimming pool. The long flight of stairs from the street to the Dvir's front door is a drawback for many visitors (call ahead if you need assistance carrying bags).

Haifa

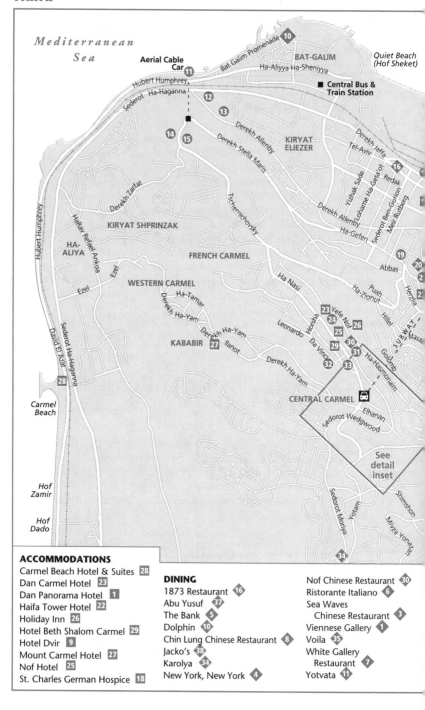

ACCOMMODATIONS

Carmel Beach Hotel & Suites 28
Dan Carmel Hotel 23
Dan Panorama Hotel 1
Haifa Tower Hotel 22
Holiday Inn 26
Hotel Beth Shalom Carmel 29
Hotel Dvir 9
Mount Carmel Hotel 27
Nof Hotel 25
St. Charles German Hospice 18

DINING

1873 Restaurant 16
Abu Yusuf 37
The Bank 5
Dolphin 10
Chin Lung Chinese Restaurant 8
Jacko's 38
Karolya 34
New York, New York 4

Nof Chinese Restaurant 30
Ristorante Italiano 6
Sea Waves
 Chinese Restaurant 3
Viennese Gallery 1
Voila 35
White Gallery
 Restaurant 7
Yotvata 11

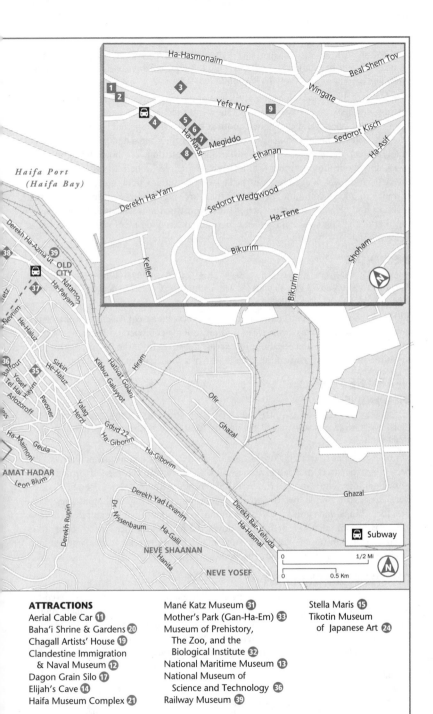

ATTRACTIONS

Aerial Cable Car **11**
Baha'i Shrine & Gardens **20**
Chagall Artists' House **19**
Clandestine Immigration
  & Naval Museum **12**
Dagon Grain Silo **17**
Elijah's Cave **14**
Haifa Museum Complex **21**

Mané Katz Museum **31**
Mother's Park (Gan-Ha-Em) **33**
Museum of Prehistory,
  The Zoo, and the
  Biological Institute **32**
National Maritime Museum **13**
National Museum of
  Science and Technology **36**
Railway Museum **39**

Stella Maris **15**
Tikotin Museum
  of Japanese Art **24**

Nof Hotel. 101 Ha-Nassi Blvd., Haifa 31063. ☎ **04/835-4311.** Fax 04/838-8810. 93 units (all with bathtub). A/C TV TEL. $176–$228 double. Lower prices Dec–Feb; higher prices July 15–Aug 31 and Jewish holidays. MC, V.

The Nof Hotel has a great location at the top of the Carmel Center, near the Carmelit Station and between the two Dan Hotels, yet it's less expensive than its neighbors. "Nof" means "view," and every guest room at the Nof has especially large windows to take in absolutely breathtaking vistas. Room refurbishing and a new wing are planned, but at present, decor in some rooms is starting to wear thin. The hotel dining room is good, and the in-house kosher Chinese restaurant (see "Where to Dine," below) is excellent. A drawback in summer is the lack of a swimming pool, but guests have free entrance to a local community pool and there are special hotel shuttles down to the beach in summer. Check about when planned construction is scheduled before reserving. Berta, the Nof's assistant general manager, offers Frommer's readers who book independently a 15% reduction if they stay 3 nights or more.

INEXPENSIVE

Hotel Beth Shalom Carmel. 110 Ha-Nassi Blvd. (P.O. Box 6208), Haifa 31060. ☎ **04/837-7481.** Fax 04/837-2443. 30 units (all with bathtub). A/C TEL. $70 double. Rates include breakfast. AE, DC, MC, V. Carmelit: Gan Ha-Em.

This is a modern, efficient German Protestant guest house equivalent to a three-star hotel, open to all comers, with clean and airy rooms equipped with heating. Minimum stay is 3 nights. The location, just across the street from the Carmel's three luxury hotels is great; extra amenities include use of a small garden and a library.

NEAR THE PORT
INEXPENSIVE

St. Charles German Hospice. 105 Jaffa Rd., Haifa. ☎ **04/855-3705.** Fax 04/851-4919. Units availabe vary (all with shared bathrooms). $55 double. Rates include breakfast. No credit cards.

On one of the port area's major thoroughfares, this hospice is surprisingly quiet, set back from the street in a large, stone-walled 120-year-old complex of gardens and stone buildings. The hospice is run by the Sisters of the Rosary, but it's open to all travelers. Rooms are simple, two or three beds to a room, with high ceilings, spare, practical furnishings, and running water in a sink in each room. There are ample, well-kept toilet, bathroom, and shower facilities down the hall, and a nice sitting room, too. You're welcome to use the kitchen to prepare meals, and to relax in the large garden. There is a 10pm curfew and 9am checkout.

ON THE CARMEL BEACH

This beautiful beachfront area just being developed at the edge of the city is served by buses during the day, but can seem somewhat isolated from the rest of Haifa at night. The area offers a beach resort atmosphere, but is also close to the **high tech Matam Industrial Park,** at the heart of Israel's own version of California's Silicon Valley. It is also convenient to Haifa's new **International Convention Center.** Parking is free.

EXPENSIVE

✪ **Carmel Beach Hotel and Suites.** 10 David Elazar St., Carmel Beach, Haifa. ☎ **04/850-8888.** Fax 04/850-0222. E-mail: carmel.beach@heihotels.com. 80 units (all with bathtub). A/C TV TEL. $260–$305 double; breakfast $20. AE, DC, MC, V. Free parking.

Eighty of the 300 rooms and suites in this lavish, new (1997) high-rise are set aside for hotel purposes; the rest of the units are residential and long-term rentals. Set on one of Haifa's best bathing beaches, the hotel offers superior (standard) guest rooms as well as one-bedroom, one-bathroom suites and a variety of two-bedroom, two-bathroom suites, all with kitchenette facilities, private safes, and voice mail. Guest rooms are new, sleekly furnished, and laptop friendly. The variety of suites makes this a good choice for vacationing families as well as long-term business travelers working at the nearby Matam Industrial Park. Kitchenettes compensate for the fact that the site is not near shops and restaurants. There are long-term discount plans available; ask about manager Neil Kaye's special: stay 5 nights, pay for only 4.

Dining/Diversions: Three restaurants, piano bar, beach snack bar.

Amenities: Business and secretarial center, synagogue, 24-hour room service, swimming pool, children's pool, beach, tennis court, shops, soccer on the beach. Health club for extra fee.

IN THE HILLS SOUTH OF HAIFA
EXPENSIVE

✪ Isrotel Carmel Forest Spa Resort. Carmel Forest, P.O. Box 90000 Haifa 31900. ☎ **04/832-3111;** 888/ISROTEL or 201/816-0830 in the U.S. and Canada; or 0181/997-6423 in the U.K. Fax 04/832-3988. E-mail: carmel-spa@isrotel.co.il. 126 units (all with bathtubs). A/C TV TEL. $375–$638 double. Rates include full board. Treatment programs extra. AE, DC, MC, V.

Opened in 1997, this luxury spa offers a green, tranquil alternative to the many massive spa hotels in the desert environment near the Dead Sea. The setting is beautiful. Rooms are freshly decorated, overlooking the distant Mediterranean or the acres of woods surrounding the hotel; there are electric kettles and personal safes for extra convenience. The spa includes indoor and outdoor pools, a gym, Jacuzzi, dry and steam saunas, and a real Turkish steam bath as well as a full array of weight-loss, cosmetic, exercise, massage, meditation, and outdoor nature programs. You can arrange for everything from aromatherapy, seaweed wraps, water aerobics, horseback riding, tai chi, and mountain biking to Shiatsu, Reiki, reflexology, Thai, or Swedish massage. Meals are well prepared, vegetarian, and filled with natural, wholesome ingredients.

BED & BREAKFAST ACCOMMODATIONS

The Haifa Tourist Board, 106 Ha-Nassi Blvd. (☎ **04/853-5606**), can arrange for a variety of accommodations. A double room in an apartment is $50. A double room in an apartment with a private bathroom is $65. A double room with a private bathroom and separate entrance is $70. The reservations service is open Sunday to Thursday from 9am to 3pm. Expect to pay host families in cash; breakfast is usually $5 extra per person.

4 Where to Dine

Haifa caters to every culinary taste and pocketbook. The city's **Falafel Row,** at the corner of Haneviim and Hechalutz streets, is one of the best spots in Israel for falafel; even an average Haifa falafel stand usually can hold its own with the best places in other towns. Haifa is also home to very authentic, popular Arabic restaurants, as well as excellent, personal French and Swiss dining spots.

HADAR/NORDAU STREET MALL

After observing the success of Jerusalem's lively Ben-Yehuda Street Pedestrian Mall, Haifa decided to take the plunge and turn Nordau Street, 1 block above Herzl Street, into a tree-lined pedestrian area. The result has brightened the whole Hadar District, and has brought some really wonderful restaurant choices to the center of town.

EXPENSIVE

Voila. 21A Nordau St. ☎ **04/866-4529.** Reservations recommended. Main courses NIS 45–100 ($10–$22); complete fixed-price lunches NIS 70 and NIS 90 ($l5.40 and $19.80). AE, DC, MC. Daily noon–midnight. SWISS/FRENCH.

A charming hideaway in the Nordau Street Mall, Voila is a labor of love on the part of its owners, who have provided a secluded, intimate atmosphere with specially designed rustic French Alpine touches, both indoors and in the garden. The style of the kitchen is rich, but this is a worthwhile place to set aside a diet, starting with the earthy pâté de foie gras. Other first courses include stuffed shrimp; mussels in a butter, garlic, parsley, and white wine sauce; and mushrooms in herb butter stuffed with either pâté de foie gras or white cheese. Fondue is a specialty: You can order a seafood fondue served with four cheeses and a basket of sliced baguette plus a salad (150 grams of shrimp, mussels, and other seafood; a considerably larger portion, which two can share, is only about NIS 27 [$6] more); a dazzling house-specialty meat fondue for two NIS 135 ($30) served with five sauces on a sizzling stone; or roasted mullard (hybrid of duck and goose) breast in apple cider and date sauce. Less expensive are dishes served with spaetzle, (Swiss flour and egg dumplings). A pan of Swiss rosti (a potato dish that's a Voila specialty), or a salad, is served with each main course. Ice cream crepes with lavish fruit sauces are sharable, if you're counting calories.

INEXPENSIVE

Kapulsky's. 6 Nordau St. ☎ **04/864-5633.** Desserts NIS 18–32 ($4–$7); light meals NIS 24–50 ($5.30–$11). MC, V. Sun–Fri 9am–11pm, Sat 1pm–midnight. CAFE.

Long a Haifa landmark for lavish pastries and beautiful light meals, Kapulsky's has a busy indoor cafe and outdoor tables that are great for leisurely people-watching. In addition to its famous European-style pies and tortes, Kapulsky's serves salads, soufflés, and lasagna and other light to major meals. Another branch of Kapulsky's is at the Panorama Center in Central Carmel.

CENTRAL CARMEL
MODERATE

○ **Karyola.** 117 Sderot Moriah. ☎ **04/826-5827.** Main courses NIS 48–88 ($10.70–$19.40). Reservations recommended. AE, DC. Mon–Sat noon–4pm and 7pm–midnight; Sun 7pm–midnight. MEDITERRANEAN BISTRO/FUSION.

This is a new place, worth the taxi, bus, or half-hour walk from the hotel district at the Central Carmel. You can have a feast here, or just gazpacho and salad. The menu spans the Mediterranean with dishes like seafood fettuccine; eggplant rolls stuffed with herbed cheese; moules marinières, succulent in a white wine and scallion sauce; seafood paella; chicken breast stuffed with nuts, leeks, mushrooms, and dried fruits. Karyola skirts fusion cuisine with dishes like crabs sautéed in soy, white wine, and ginger, however it never gets manically overinventive. Understated, easy decor, a cheerful staff, and a good wine list add to the ambience. Fixed-price luncheons run from NIS 54 ($12) to NIS 63 ($14).

New York, New York. 122 Ha-Nassi Blvd. ☎ **04/836-1501.** Hamburgers and light meals NIS 38–50 ($7.90–$11); main courses NIS 50–80 ($11–$17.60). AE, DC, MC, V. Daily noon–midnight. AMERICAN.

Step inside this convenient place located just beside the Carmel Carmelit stop, and you'll think you're in a suburban diner in the United States. Steaks and burgers, all weighing in at 300 grams (about ²/₃ lb.) are the big draws here, but you'll also find chicken and fish dishes served with your choice of potato and salad. More expensive than its American counterparts, this is a place to visit if you've got a yen for home. There's a fresh but unimaginative one-time salad bar costing NIS 36 ($8), but less if you order it with a main course.

Nof Chinese Restaurant. 101 Ha-Nassi Blvd. ☎ **04/835-4311.** Reservations recommended. Main courses NIS 55–80 ($12.10–$17.60). AE, DC, MC, V. Sun–Thurs noon–3pm and 7pm–midnight; Sat after Shabbat. Closed Fri–Sat until after Shabbat. CHINESE.

A comfortable and well-known kosher Chinese restaurant, the Nof Chinese specializes in hot-pot creations and a variety of regional styles of preparation. The view in the daytime is dramatic; there are fixed-price luncheon specials.

✪ **Sea Waves Chinese Restaurant.** 99 Yefe Nof St. ☎ **04/837-5602.** Reservations recommended evenings and weekends. Main courses NIS 55–100 ($12–$22); complete dinner special NIS 55–95 ($12–$21). AE, DC, MC, V. Daily noon–3:30pm and 7–11:30pm. CHINESE.

With its fabulous views, Sea Waves offers a sophisticated well-prepared menu with specialties that include skewered meats served on sizzling iron plates and hot-pot dishes. It also serves a large menu of more standard Chinese dishes at quite reasonable prices. Reserve a window table right up against the view; especially during daylight hours, it makes dining here memorable. Peking Duck (order in advance) is NIS 115 ($25) per person; there are good spare ribs and a very nice crispy duck with honey that you can order on the spot. Fried ice cream is a good dessert choice. There's a no-smoking area.

White Gallery. 125 Ha Nassi Blvd. ☎ **04/837-5574.** Appetizers, main courses NIS 40–80 ($8.80–$17.60). AE, DC, MC, V. Sun–Thurs 9:30am–1am; Fri 8am–3am; Sat 10:30am–3am. CONTINENTAL.

This stylish restaurant, both in terms of cuisine and design, with its sleek minimalist decor and a sidewalk terrace for people-watching, is both popular and affordable. Haifans come by for breakfast, which can be a simple coffee, a full Israeli-style meal, or a soft sesame roll (known locally as a bagel) with cream cheese and lox. For lunch and dinner, choose from inventive salads (that are meals in themselves) such as goose breast with fresh vegetables and mozzarella; the Far East salad, with chopped lettuce, chicken breast, rice noodles, and fresh vegetables in a sweet-and-sour coriander sauce; or the Hot Gallery Salad of lightly sautéed vegetables in a tasty vinaigrette. Pasta dishes are also a good choice, and include a rich lasagna filled with mushrooms, spinach, garlic, and onions. Fajitas, a variety of excellent chicken dishes, quality steaks, and a good wine list and cheese platters round out the upmarket end of the menu.

INEXPENSIVE

The Bank. 119 Ha-Nassi Blvd. ☎ **04/838-9623.** Light meals NIS 25–50 ($5.50–$11). MC, V. Daily 10am–11pm or midnight. Carmelit: Gan Ha-Em. CAFE.

This is a bright, stylish place, with summery furnishings, where you can enjoy sitting at the sidewalk tables and watching the activity around Central Carmel. The Bank is good for light meals—pancakes, blintzes, sandwiches, salads, crepes, cakes, and cappuccino, or many kinds of ice-cream confections. The hefty Bank salad is especially recommended.

Chin Lung Chinese Restaurant. 126 Ha-Nassi Blvd. ☎ **04/838-1308.** Main courses NIS 40–85 ($8.80–$18.70); Business lunch NIS 50 ($11). MC, V. Daily noon–3pm and 6:30pm–midnight Carmelit: Gan Ha-Em. CHINESE.

At first there seems to be no restaurant at all behind the sign and posted menu near the corner of Sea Road (Derekh Ha-Yam). But go down the adjoining steps and you'll discover a nice cellar dining room with a small-town American-style folksy Chinese decor, done in gold and crimson, with gold tablecloths and fresh flowers. The food is mostly Szechuan style, which can be spicy but needn't be if you don't like hot food. There are 50 items to choose from here; shrimp and calamari dishes are at the high end of the price range. Beer, wine, and cocktails are served.

✪ **Ristorante Italiano.** 119 Ha-Nassi Blvd. ☎ **04/838-1336.** Main courses NIS 35–65 ($7.70–$14.30). AE, MC, V. Sat–Thurs 5:30–11pm; closed Fri. EUROPEAN/ITALIAN.

A real favorite with Americans, this is a small, family run restaurant where you can have a filling meal of spaghetti, cannelloni, or a truly hefty pizza with fresh toppings for less than NIS 41 ($9). Breads and focaccia are served straight out the oven with heaping salads and wonderful main courses like goulash, just like my grandmother made; steaks; American home-style hamburgers; trout; and Saint Peter's fish. A rich bowl of vegetable soup and garlic bread makes a fine inexpensive lunch. The management here is very friendly and takes good care of returning customers.

NEAR THE PORT
MODERATE

Jacko's. 12 HaDekekim St. ☎ **04/866-8813.** Reservations not accepted. Main courses: NIS 65–85 ($14.30–$18.70). No credit cards. Sun–Thurs noon–11pm; Fri noon–5pm; Sat noon–6pm. FISH.

This little no-frills place in the market was once run by Jacko, a retired fisherman, and his entire family. Now, outsiders will wait on you, and the decor has improved, but the fish is still good, prepared without pretense, and the prices reasonable. As Jacko originally came from Izmir, on the coast of Turkey, you'll also find a Sephardic-Aegean touch in first courses like the Turkish-style "paella" or in the mezze of little salads that comes with your main course. The sesame shrimp and the shrimp sautéed in wine and garlic are fresh and tasty. Always ask the waiter what's special and what the catch of the day is. From the Carmelit stop at Kikar Paris, walk 2 blocks down S. Nathanson Street and turn right into the market. From there, anyone will point out the place for you—it's a Haifa institution!

INEXPENSIVE

✪ **Abu Yusuf.** 1 Ha-Meginim St. ☎ **04/866-3723.** Middle Eastern salad bar NIS 14 ($3) for one plate; main courses NIS 32–60 ($7–$13.20). MC, V. Sat–Thurs 9am–midnight; Fri 7am–4pm. Carmelit: Paris Square. ARABIC.

The sign is in Hebrew, English, and Arabic, and this restaurant has been loved by speakers of all three languages for decades. Newly redecorated but still basically no-frills, Abu Yusuf's food tends toward the Lebanese, with kubbeh, hummus with meat, grilled heart (delicious!), and roast chicken. One trip to the wonderful salad bar of 20 Middle Eastern dishes comes with a main course, or you can order the salad bar alone and have a fine meal with fresh pita bread and a shot ("jot") of anise-flavored arak brandy; two people will pay about NIS 32 ($7) each. A meal with a large main course would be NIS 45 ($10) to NIS 67 ($15). Abu Yusuf offers fresh fish and grilled lamb dishes and has won awards several years in a row. Very good value.

GERMAN COLONY

This neighborhood, filled with stone cottages built by German Christians in the late 19th century has great potential for charm and gentrification. The Haifa Municipality is helping things along with the construction of a new pedestrian promenade on the neighborhood's main street, Ben Gurion Boulevard, which is perfectly aligned with the dramatic Baha'i Shrine further up the slopes of Mount Carmel. During the time span of this edition, it should develop into much more of a tourist site.

EXPENSIVE

✪ **1873 Restaurant.** 102 Jaffa St. ☎ **04/853-2211.** Reservations necessary. Main courses: NIS 60–110 ($13.20–$24.20). AE, MC, V. Sun–Thurs noon–3pm; and 7:30–11pm; Fri 7:30–11pm; Sat 1–4pm and 7:30–11pm. FRENCH.

Occupying a restored German Colony cottage built in 1873, this restaurant offers the most superb new kitchen to debut in Israel in several years. Each dish is gracefully inventive and presented with visual elegance; sauces are fabulous. Among appetizers, look for giant mushrooms stuffed with a forcemeat of goose breast in a smooth cream sauce; giant New Zealand mussels in wine sauce accented by chopped chives, or exquisite foie gras wrapped in thin slices of smoked goose breast in a sauce of prune, apple, and wine or with a slightly tart reduction of blueberries in plum sauce (available also as a main course). Main courses, which constantly change, may include grilled trout in a Grand-Marnier–based orange sauce; scaloppini of ostrich under fruit glaze; or large, meaty quail stuffed with liver served on a bed of lightly sautéed vegetables in red wine sauce. Vegetables are fascinating here, desserts perfect. Decor is charming without being glitzy or pretentious. Ask about special fixed-price luncheons and dinners (true bargains) when you phone for your reservation. An upstairs wine bar is an added attraction.

BAT GALIM

Bat Galim means "Daughter of the Waves" in Hebrew, and you'll know how it got its name when you stroll along its beachfront promenade. If you take a ride on the aerial cable car between the beach and Mount Carmel, at the lower terminal you'll be right at the end of Bat Galim. The restaurants I'll mention are all within about a 5-minute walk from there.

If you're not coming from the cable-car terminal, you can easily walk over from the main bus or train stations—Bat Galim is located behind the stations. If you're at the Central Station, go through the underground tunnel that connects it to the train station; when you come out of the train station, you'll be in Bat Galim. You can also take bus no. 40, 41, 42, or 44, which go from the bus station to the cable-car terminal; or if you're driving, come across at Hel Ha-Yam, the main boulevard running just east of the bus station.

MODERATE

Dolphin. 13 Bat Galim Ave. ☎ **04/852-3837.** Reservations recommended evenings. Main courses NIS 55–100 ($12–$22). AE, DC, MC, V. Daily noon–4pm and 7pm–midnight. Bus: No. 40, 41, or 42. SEAFOOD.

À la carte prices are higher than in other neighborhood choices, but the reputation of the restaurant is very good. A typical dinner might include the excellent house fish soup, tomato-based and richly herbed; shrimp cocktail or fried calamari; followed by a main course of fresh fish. It's 1 block inland from Bat Galim Promenade.

INEXPENSIVE

✪ **Yotvata.** End of Bat Galim Promenade. ☎ **04/852-6835.** Light meals NIS 25–35 ($5.50–$7.70); main courses NIS 33–77 ($7–$16.10). AE, DC, MC, V. Daily 7am–4am. DAIRY/VEGETARIAN.

Right on the beach, at the lower terminus of Haifa's famous aerial cable car, this is an extremely popular emporium for dairy and vegetarian food. Everything is made from the best-quality produce bought directly from kibbutzim and from the famous dairy kibbutz at Yotvata. For under NIS 50 ($11) there are salads, cheese platters served with fresh herbs and vegetables, blintzes, pancakes, vegetable pies, pastas, and pizzas. At the upper end of the price range, you'll find a selection of fish, chicken, pasta and hamburgers as well as bagels and lox. The mixtures of natural fruit juices are famous, as are Yotvata's many ice-cream parlor desserts.

CAFES
CENTRAL CARMEL

On the loft balcony above the dairy self-service Cafe Carmel in the vast Panorama Center is the **Viennese Gallery** (☎ **04/835-2222**). The view is incredible from up here, and the distinctive architecture does everything to maximize the view, with a curved, two-story wall. The Viennese Gallery serves mostly desserts and coffees; but there is also a selection of quiches, salads, omelettes, soups, and cold platters. Although the surroundings are fancy, prices are really quite reasonable. You can get a gorgeous Viennese pastry with a whole pot of freshly brewed tea or coffee for NIS 32 ($7), or for NIS 27 ($6), the "Viennese Fantasy," a combination of as many flavors of ice cream and as many toppings as you like—you select the combinations. You'll find it open from 10am to 11pm daily (until midnight Friday and Saturday nights). If you're not a guest at the Panorama Hotel and therefore unable to put the tab on your VAT-free bill, you will pay an extra 17% above the dollar prices.

5 Attractions

Before setting out, check with the Haifa Tourist Information Office's "What's on in Haifa" and the Tourist Information Telephone Hot Line (☎ **04/837-4253**), which tell you what's doing while you're in town.

Suggested Itinerary

Day 1   Visit the Baha'i Gardens, enjoy the panorama, and take in a wing or two at the Haifa Museum while checking out central Haifa.

Day 2   Spend at least half the day at one of Haifa's fine municipal beaches if the weather's good. Hof Dado, south of the city, is accessible by bus. Choose from among Haifa's other fine museums, such as Clandestine Immigration, Mané Katz, or the Japanese Tikotin Museum for the rest of your day.

Day 3   Excursions! Take one to Mount Carmel, the Carmelite monastery at Mukraqa (with its sweeping view of northern Israel, the site of Elijah's contest with the prophets of Baal), and the Druze villages (see section 10); or to the artists' village at Ein Hod (see chapter 7, section 5); or to Old Akko (see chapter 7, section 6).

THE TOP ATTRACTIONS
IN HADAR

✪ **Baha'i Shrine & Gardens.** Free admission. Modest dress required. Shrine daily 9am–noon; gardens daily 9am–5pm. Bus: 22 from the port, 23, 25, and 26 from Hadar.

Haifa's most impressive sightseeing attraction is the splendid Baha'i Shrine and Gardens, reached from Zionism (Ha-Zionut) Avenue. The immaculate, majestic Baha'i gardens—with their stone peacocks and eagles, and delicately manicured cypress trees—are a restful, esthetic memorial to the founders of the Baha'i faith. Haifa is the international headquarters for the gentle Baha'i faith, which began in Persia in the mid–19th century in a bloodbath of persecution.

Baha'is believe in the unity of all religions and see all religious leaders—Christ, Buddha, Muhammad, Moses—as messengers of God, sent at different times in history with doctrines varying to fit changing social needs, but bringing substantially the same message. The most recent of these heavenly teachers, according to Baha'is, was Baha' Allah. He was exiled by the Turkish authorities to Acre, wrote his doctrines there, and died a peaceful death in Bahji House just north of Acre. (See "Acre [Akko]" in chapter 7 for more information.)

In the Haifa gardens, the huge domed **shrine** entombs the remains of the Bab, the Baha' Allah's herald. The tomb is a sight to see, with ornamental gold work and flowers in almost every nook and cranny. The Bab's remains, incidentally, were hidden for years after he died a martyr's death in front of a firing squad. Eventually, however, his followers secretly carried his remains to the Holy Land.

On a higher hilltop stands the Corinthian-style **Baha'i International Archives** building, modeled after the Parthenon, and the **Universal House of Justice,** with 58 marble columns and hanging gardens behind. These are business buildings, not open to tourists. They, and the shrine of the tomb of the Bab, all face toward Acre, the burial place of Baha' Allah.

The beautiful grounds were originally planned by Shoghi Effendi, the late Guardian of the Faith. The Baha'i gardens have recently undergone a massive redesign aimed at putting them on the world's horticultural map. They are now a geometric cascade of hanging gardens and terraces down to Ben Gurion Boulevard—a gift of visual pleasure to the city that gave the Baha'i religion its home and headquarters. In addition to tourists, you'll see pilgrims who have come from all parts of the world to pay homage to the first leaders of this universal faith. At the entrance to the shrine, where you must remove your shoes, you will be given a pamphlet providing further details on Baha'i history and doctrine.

✪ **Haifa Museums.** Admission good for all 3 branches of Haifa Museums Network NIS 22 ($4.80), NIS 16 ($3.50) students. Sun–Mon, Wed 11am–5pm; also Tues, Thurs 4–8pm; Fri 10am–1pm; Sat 10am–4pm. Hadar.

The Haifa Museum is composed of three branches scattered in different parts of the city: the Tikotin Museum of Japanese Art, the National Maritime Museum, and the Haifa Museum of Art. Each branch can be counted on to host beautifully planned and mounted visiting and special exhibits throughout the year.

The Haifa Museum of Art. 26 Shabtai Levi St. ☎ **04/852-3255.** Bus: 12, 22, or 41. Carmelit: Ha-Nevi'im station.

This branch contains a strong collection of contemporary painting, sculpture, and prints by Israeli and foreign artists, with emphasis on Israeli art. The library and slide collection is open to the public; lectures, art films, and slide presentations are held in the evenings.

Tikotin Museum of Japanese Art. 89 Ha-Nassi Blvd. ☎ **04/838-3554.** Admission good for all 3 Haifa Museums NIS 22 ($4.80). Bus: 22 or 23. Carmelit: Gan Ha-Em station.

The exceptional Tikotin has examples of almost all kinds of Japanese art and crafts, along with a library of approximately 3,000 books. The beautiful building hosts 10 to 12 special exhibits of Japanese arts and crafts, arranged to reflect the changing seasons. It's located near the Dan Carmel Hotel in Central Carmel.

National Maritime Museum. 198 Allenby Rd. ☎ **04/536-622.** Admission good for all 3 Haifa Museums NIS 22 ($4.80). Bus: 3, 5, or 43.

This third section of the Haifa Museum just up the street from the *Af-Al-Pi,* near Bat Galim, encompasses 5,000 years of seafaring in the Mediterranean and the Red Sea.

The **Museum of Ancient Art,** recently relocated here from the central Haifa Museum Complex, displays archaeological collections of Mediterranean cultures from the beginning of history until the Islamic conquest in the 7th century. There are outstanding collections of Greco-Roman culture, Coptic art, painted portraits from Fayyum, coins of Caesarea and Acre, terra-cottas of all periods, and finds from the Haifa area. The artifacts obtained through underwater archaeology are particularly impressive. The marvelous Ethnology Section of the Haifa Museum is also located here, but due to limited space, little of it is on display.

Mané Katz Museum. 89 Yefe Nof (Panorama Rd.). ☎ **04/838-3482.** Admission for visiting exhibits NIS 12 ($2.65); when Mané Katz collection is on display, free admission. Sun–Mon and Wed–Thurs 10am–4pm; Tues 2–6pm; Fri 10am–1pm; Sat 10am–2pm. Bus: 22, 23, or 31. Carmelit: Central Carmel.

This building, near the Dan Panorama Hotel in Central Carmel, was once a rustic mountaintop villa in which the French artist Mané Katz lived (the neighborhood has certainly changed). The museum now houses Mané Katz's own work and personal collection—drawings, aquarelles, gouaches, oil paintings, sculpture, and Judaica—as well as interesting, well-planned visiting exhibits of contemporary art.

Mitzpoor Ha-Shalom (Peace View Park). Zionism Ave.

The grounds of the Baha'i gardens are split by Zionism Avenue. Farther up the hill is the lovely Mitzpoor Ha-Shalom (Peace View Park), also called the Ursula Malbin Sculpture Garden, at the corner of Shnayim Be-November Street. Amid trees, flowers, and sloping lawns are 18 bronze sculptures by Ursula Malbin, of men, women, children, and animals at play. The view from here is magnificent—you can see all of Haifa's port area, Haifa Bay, Acre, Nahariya, and up to Rosh Ha-Niqra at the Lebanese border, plus the mountains all around.

IN CARMEL

Mount Carmel National Park. Bus: 37.

Israel's largest national park has 25,000 acres of pine, eucalyptus, and cypress forest. It encompasses a large area of the Carmel mountain range and contains many points of interest that are well marked and easily reachable. And, of course, it also has picnic areas, playgrounds, a restaurant, and rest rooms.

Technion City. Free admission. Visitor center Sun–Thurs 8am–2pm. Cafeteria Sun–Thurs 8am–2pm; Fri 8am–noon. Closed Sat. Bus: 17 from Central Bus Station, 31 from Central Carmel, 19 from Hadar at Daniel St., next to the Armon Cinema on Ha-Nevi'im St., just down from Masaryk Square.

Technion, the Israel Institute of Technology, is Israel's version of MIT. Founded in 1912, its 300-acre campus is a most impressive university complex with its view of the city, the bay, the coastline clear to Lebanon, and the snow-topped Syrian mountains.

Because so many people come to see the Technion, the **Coler-California Visitor Center** (☎ 04/832-0664) has been established to introduce the campus to visitors. You'll be greeted by a real working robot when you come in. There's also a free 20-minute video about the school, and there are high-tech multimedia touch-screen videos, Internet, and laser disc productions that offer additional information. You'll also receive a pamphlet and map of the campus, which you can use to take your own **self-guided tour.** The student-priced **cafeteria** downstairs is recommended for a good budget lunch.

Many **entertainment activities** are held every evening (except Monday) at Bet Student, the Technion's Student House (☎ 04/832-0664). Call during the daytime for info on folk, disco, and '60s dancing, films, and other activities. You can also stop in at Bet Student's pub, cafeteria, or restaurant for a meal at student prices.

Haifa University. ☎ **04/824-0093,** 04/824-0007, or 04/824-0097 for tour reservations. Campus tours Sun–Thurs 10am–3:30pm. Bus: 24, 36, 37, or 37A.

On the Mount Carmel road from Haifa to the nearby Druze village of Daliat-el-Carmel you'll see the buildings and tower of Haifa University. The campus was originally designed by the architect of Brasilia, Oscar Niemeyer; later new sections planned by other architects were added. The university began operation in 1963, under the joint auspices of the City of Haifa and the Hebrew University. At that time, the students numbered 650; now 13,000 full-time degree students attend the university.

The campus offers a magnificent view. From the 30th (top) observatory floor of the **Eshkol Tower,** which you can visit on your own, Sunday through Thursday from 8am to 3:30pm (admission free), you get an incredible view of practically the entire north of Israel. Throughout the university's public spaces you'll find a surprising amount of paintings and sculpture. The large murals located in the university lobby are especially notable.

The campus has several impressive art galleries. The **Oscar Ghez Gallery,** on the Eshkol Tower's 30th floor, houses a moving memorial collection of works by artists who perished in the Holocaust, compiled by Mr. Ghez over a 30-year period. The **University Art Gallery** in the Main Building displays important works by Israeli and foreign artists. The **Reuben and Edith Hecht Museum** contains a compact but impressive Israeli archeology collection, with rotating exhibitions; there is also a wing devoted to art—paintings by Impressionists and the Jewish School of Paris. Adjoining the Hecht Museum is the Maagan Michael Ship Museum, slated to hold the world's oldest vessel, a 2,400-year-old Phoenician-era merchant ship salvaged by University archaeologists off the coast just south of Haifa. The art galleries and the museum are open Sunday through Thursday from 10am to 4pm, Friday from 10am to 1pm, and Saturday from 10am to 2pm. Admission is free. To take a free **guided tour** of the campus, you must call in advance to reserve a spot (see above).

The Haifa University Students Association sponsors many activities throughout the academic year. Call the **Students Association** (☎ **04/824-0544**) for information. There is also a Hillel House (☎ **04/824-0762**) with a full schedule of activities.

Stella Maris Lighthouse and Carmelite Monastery. Stella Maris Rd. ☎ **04/833-7758.** English masses Mon–Sat 6:30am; Sun 7 and 9am. Modest dress required. Church open daily 6:30am–1:30pm and 3–6pm. Bus: 25, 26, or 31.

From Ha-Nassi Boulevard and Tchernichovsky Street go northwest to the Stella Maris French Carmelite church, monastery, and hospice (P.O. Box 9047). In the 12th century, during the crusader occupation of the region, groups of religious hermits began to inhabit the caves of the Carmeld district, in emulation of Elijah the Prophet, whose life was strongly identified with this mountain. Within a century, these monastic hermits were organized into the Carmelite order; although the Carmelite order spread throughout Europe, its founders on the Carmel range were exiled at the time of the Mamluk conquest in 1291 and did not return until the 18th century. Construction of the present monastery and basilica was begun in 1836. Situated across the street from the Old Lighthouse, with a magnificent view of the sea, the entire ensemble of buildings, including the Lighthouse, is known as "Stella Maris." An earlier monastery complex on this site served as a hospital for Napoleon's soldiers during his unsuccessful siege of Acre in 1799. The pyramid in front of the church entryway stands as a memorial to the many abandoned French soldiers who were slaughtered by the Turks after Napoleon had retreated from his toehold on the coast near Akko. It bears the inscription "How are the mighty fallen in battle," from King David's lamentation over Saul and Jonathan.

The **church** is a beautiful structure, with Italian marble so brightly and vividly patterned that visitors sometimes mistakenly think the walls have been painted. Colorful paintings on the dome, done by Brother Luigi Poggi (1924–28), depict episodes from the Old Testament, the most dramatic being the scene of Elijah swept up in a chariot of fire; but the statue of the Virgin Mary, carved from cedar of Lebanon, is also notable. The **cave** situated below the altar, which you can walk down into, is believed to have been inhabited by Elijah.

Be sure to visit the rooms to the right of the entryway, where you'll find a charming nativity scene, a **museum** with artifacts from the Byzantine church occupying this same spot before the Carmelites built here, and a small **souvenir shop.** One of the monks will gladly give you a free pamphlet with information about the history of this site, and the Carmelite order, dating back to the arrival of the crusaders on this mountain in the late 12th century. They will answer any questions you may have, and guide you to the various interesting details of the church, such as the many little votive candles burning on the altar above the cave, each representing a Carmelite community in another country (the United States has its candle up on the left).

IN THE PORT

Clandestine Immigration and Naval Museum. 204 Allenby Rd. ☎ **04/853-6249.** Admission NIS 8 ($1.80) adults, NIS 4 (90¢) students. Sun–Thurs 9am–4pm; Fri and holiday eves 9am–1pm. Closed Sat. Bus: 3, 5, 43, or 44.

The clandestine immigration movement of Jews into Palestine during and after World War II—called "Aliya Beth"—is one of the most harrowing phases of Israeli history. Throughout the time of the Holocaust, when Jews so desperately needed a haven, admission to British Mandate Palestine was largely denied to them by the British government. Nevertheless, Jews fleeing from the Nazis during World War II; and after the war, Jewish escapees from displaced persons camps constantly attempted to enter Palestine on rusty, unsafe illegal vessels. Some succeeded in making it undetected past British ships guarding Palestine's Mediterranean coastline; others were not so fortunate. The *Struma,* in 1941–42, waited for months at sea for some country to accept the 765 refugees aboard until at last it sank off Turkey. All but one on board perished. Others, like the *Patria,* went down in Haifa harbor, with hundreds killed in sight of safety; still others, like the *Exodus* (just after the war), ran the British blockade only to have its passengers shipped to a Cyprus detention camp, or, pathetically enough, returned to a detention camp in Germany. The blockade-running vessel *Af-Al-Pi Chen (Nevertheless)* is now a part of the Clandestine Immigration and Naval Museum, a memorial commemorating all the ships that defied the British blockade to smuggle immigrants into Palestine.

MORE ATTRACTIONS

The **Rothschild Community House** (Bet Rothschild) in Central Carmel near Haifa Auditorium at 142 Ha-Nassi Blvd. (☎ **04/838-2749)** often has something of interest for tourists. Call to see what's up. Interesting, too, are the changing art exhibits and folklore programs at **Bet Ha-Gefen** (☎ **04/852-5251)**, the Arab-Jewish Community Center, on Ha-Gefen Street opposite the Chagall Artists' House.

Aerial Cable Car. ☎ **04/833-5970.** Round-trip NIS 22 ($5), one way NIS 15 ($3.30) adults. Sat–Thurs 10am–5:30pm; Fri 10am–1:45pm. Bus: 26, 28, or 31 to the top terminal, or bus 40, 41, or 42 to the bottom terminal.

✪ Frommer's Favorite Haifa Experiences

Promenading. The view of Haifa from the promenade in Central Carmel makes you keep coming back for more. By day or night, it's always lovely. Combine it with a meal that gives you a table right by the edge, or coffee and an elysian vista with dessert (see "Cafes," above).

Beachcombing. Haifa's great beaches are to the south of the city, reachable by municipal bus or, in summer, special shuttle from the big Central Carmel hotels, as well as sheruts. At Hof Ha-Carmel (Carmel Beach) or the quieter Hof Dado just to the south, you can combine a dip in the warm gentle waves with shish kebab or falafel from one of the many beachside stands. Stay late and you'll see the sunset over the Mediterranean. For Haifans, such paradisiacal luxuries are routine!

A Day Trip to Old Akko. It's amazing to think that two such different cities could be located on opposite ends of Haifa's sweeping bay: modern Haifa with its panoramas, and medieval Akko, with its labyrinth of bazaars, caravansaries, and mosques. A short bus ride gets you the 14 miles up the coast where you can explore this largely unrestored architectural treasure, have lunch or dinner in true Mediterranean style at an outdoor harborside cafe, and even take a boat ride around the Old City walls.

Directly across the road from the *Af-Al-Pi* is the lower terminal of the Haifa Aerial Cable Car. The ride is not as dramatic as it looks from a distance, but it is a fast way to get up or down the side of the mountain. The popular Yotvata Dairy Restaurant, famous for its salads and ice creams is at the lower terminal. The cable car rides through the air from the beach at the western end of Bat Galim up to the tip of Mount Carmel, the site of the Old Lighthouse and Stella Maris. The top terminal also has a place for refreshments; the bottom terminal's downstairs hall contains an exhibit of a different featured artist's work each week.

Chagall Artists' House. 24 Ha-Zionut Ave. ☎ **04/852-2355.** Free admission. Sun–Thurs 9am–1pm and 4–7pm; Sat 10am–1pm. Bus: 10, 12, 22, 23, 25, 26, 32, or 41.

This gallery exhibits the works of contemporary Israeli artists. In 1998, there was a grand exhibition for the 50th anniversary of the State of Israel.

Dagon Grain Museum. Kikar Plumer. ☎ **04/866-4221.** Free admission. Tours Sun–Fri 10:30am; call for reservations. The museum is only open to the public for the guided tours. Bus: 10, 12, or 22. Carmelit: Plummer Square.

On display are earthen storage jars, striking mosaic murals, and various exhibits showing the development of one of humankind's oldest industries—the cultivation, handling, storage, and distribution of grain from ancient to modern times. There are even some grains of wheat here that are more than 4,000 years old—as well as fertility statues and flint grain sickles.

Elijah's Cave. 230 Allenby Rd. ☎ **04/852-7430.** Free admission, but donations are accepted. Summer: Sun–Thurs 8am–6pm; Fri 8am–1pm. Winter: Sun–Thurs 8am–5pm; Fri 8am–1pm. Closed Sat and holidays. Bus: 3, 5, 44, or 45 will let you off at the highway nearby.

From the *Af-Al-Pi*, it's just a short walk up to Elijah's Cave, nestled at the base of steep Cape Carmel, below the Stella Maris lighthouse and the Carmelite Monastery.

Tradition has it that Elijah hid here when fleeing the wrath of King Ahab and his wife, Jezebel. It's also the site where Elijah established his school upon his return from exile, thus earning the name "School of the Prophets," where Elijah, among others, studied. The cave is also said to be a place where the Holy Family found shelter for a night on their return from Egypt.

The cave is sacred to Jews, Christians, Muslims, and Druze, all of whom venerate the prophet Elijah. Pilgrimages and huge dramatic ceremonies are held at this cave many times each year. Head coverings are available at the entrance to the cave.

Israel Edible Oil Museum. In the Sherman Oil Factory. ☎ **04/865-4237.** Admission NIS 10 ($2.20). Sun–Thurs 9am–2pm. Bus: 2.

Many interesting items connected with the cooking oil industry in Israel, from more than 2,000 years ago up to the present, are housed in the original old stone factory building.

National Museum of Science and Technology. Old Technion Campus, Balfour St. ☎ **04/862-8111.** Admission NIS 25 ($5.50) adults; discounts for students. AE, DC, MC, V. Sun–Mon and Wed–Thurs 9am–6pm; Tues 9am–7:30pm; Fri 10am–3pm; Sat 10am–5pm. Bus: 18, 19, 21, 28, 37, 42, and 50 come nearby. Carmelite: Haneviim.

This museum showcase the latest discoveries in Israeli science and offers hands-on interactive science displays. Walk up the hill from Herzl St.; the museum is in the Old Technion campus, on the right.

Railway Museum. 2 Hativat Golani Rd. ☎ **04/856-4293.** Admission NIS 8 ($1.80). Sun, Tues, and Thurs 9am–noon. Bus: 41 or 42.

Two 1950s-vintage diesel locomotives, several cabooses, a club car built in 1922, and a passenger coach dating from 1893 are the major exhibits, but there are also displays of photographs, timetables, tickets, and other memorabilia going all the way back to the railroad's construction in Ottoman times (1882). This museum is in the old Haifa East railway station near Feisal Square, but it will be enlarged and move into the restored old Hedjaz Railway locomotive depot at the Haifa East Station during the year 2000.

6 Organized Tours

The Haifa Tourist Board, 84 Ben Gurion Blvd. (☎ 04/853-5606), offers a free 2¹⁄₂-hour **guided walking tour** of Central Carmel (atop the mountain), be at 10am every Saturday morning. The meeting point, marked by a sign, is on Panorama Road (Yefe Nof) at the intersection with Shar Ha-Levanon, right behind the Gan Ha-Em Carmelit station. To reach the meeting point, take bus no. 23 from Ha-Nevi'im Street, or bus no. 21 from Herzl Street, both in Hadar; they run on Saturday (note that the Carmelit does not). Modest dress is required. The Haifa Tourist Board also offers maps for a variety of self-guided tours throughout the city. For nature hike routes and walks through the vast, wild Park Ha-Carmel, contact the Haifa Hiking Club (☎ 04/ 838-4867) or the Carmel Field School (☎ 04/866-4159).

The following companies have all sorts of tour plans of the Haifa region: **Egged Tours,** 4 Nordau St. (☎ 04/862-3131) and **Mitzpa Tours,** 1 Nordau St. (☎ 04/ 867-4341).

The **Society for Protection of Nature in Israel (SPNI),** 18 Hillel St. (☎ 04/ 866-4135;** fax 04/866-5825), does excellent urban and nature trail tours of the Carmel Mountains.

7 Outdoor Activities, Sports & Other Pursuits

Ha-Peol and **Maccabi** are two sports leagues in Israel. By contacting either of the leagues—or the Haifa Tourist Board—you can get the latest data on where to go to play tennis, to exercise or work out in a gym, or take in sports events as a spectator.

BEACHES   Starting with **Bat Galim,** and moving south to **Camel, Dado,** and **Zamir beaches,** the miles of golden sands dotted with changing facilities and simple beach cafes are Haifa's great secret. Admission is free; bus 41, 42, 43, 45, 3a, or 99. In winter, at least one restaurant pavilion remains open until 7pm; in summer until 8:30pm. Never more than NIS 45 ($10), and usually less, dinner at a simple stand at the beach in summer, with the sunset over the Mediterranean at the end of an afternoon of swimming in the warm turquoise sea, is an experience Haifans love.

BICYCLING   Telephone Gideon at ☎ **04/822-1288** or 050/413-239 for information about his tours and group rides in the Carmel. The Haifa Tourist Board Office will have current biking information.

FOLK DANCING   Israeli **folk dancing sessions** meet Monday at 8:30pm at Haifa University and Tuesday and Thursday at 9pm at Bet Ha-Student at the Technion. **International Folk Dancers** meet Thursday at 8:30pm at Bet Rothschild, to the side of the Haifa Auditorium on Ha-Nassi Boulevard.

SWIMMING   In the Central Carmel section, you'll find the **Maccabi swimming pool** on Bikkurim Street (☎ **04/838-8341**), heated in winter, and serviced by bus no. 21, 22, or 23 and by the Carmelit. Admission is NIS 20 ($4.40), but the fee doubles in winter. Don't forget the pleasant gardened **pool at the Dan Carmel Hotel,** for a whole day's worth of pool privileges.

TENNIS & SQUASH   A 15-minute ride south of downtown Haifa, in the Kefar Zamir suburb, are the **Haifa Tennis Center** (☎ **04/852-2721** or 04/853-2014) and the **Haifa Squash Center** (☎ **04/853-9160**). Both have regular hours, and you're welcome to come and play—but you must call in advance to reserve a court. Take bus no. 43, 45, or 3A.

8 Shopping

Haifa has a number of modern indoor shopping malls, including the **Panorama Center** in Central Carmel, **Migdal Haneve'im** in the Hadar District, and the **Chorev Center** on Chorev Street at the intersection of Pica Street. **The Panorama Center** is most easily accessible to visitors staying in the Carmel Center, and offers branches of a number of the country's best women's clothing stores, including Dorin Frankfort and Oui Set. **Herzl and Nordau streets** make for an interesting window-shopping stroll, but the downtown center of Haifa is not what it once was for quality stores.

Massada Street, with its own Carmelit stop halfway up the mountain between Hadar and the Carmel Center has become home to a number of small, offbeat antique and curiosity shops. My favorite stop here is **Yad B'homer Contemporary Crafts Gallery** at 9A Massada St. (☎ **04/862-9239**). Here you can see the work of eight artisans, as well as special exhibits of guest craftspeople. There is also a shelf of very reasonably priced Ethiopian figurines and Judaica. Open Sunday and Monday, and Wednesday and Thursday from 10am to 1pm and 4 to 7pm; open Tuesdays and Fridays from 10am to 2pm. Most shops on the street keep similar hours. A walk down Massada Street gives you a feel for the architectural structure of Haifa's residential neighborhoods, with 1930s and '40s apartment buildings virtually climbing up and down the mountain on either side of the street.

If you take an excursion to the artists' village of **Ein Hod,** south of Haifa, you can shop for silver, enamel, and gold jewelry, hand-blown glass, pottery, and other contemporary crafts at the village's official gallery. See chapter 7, section 5.

9 Haifa After Dark

Haifa does not have as much nightlife as Tel Aviv, or even Jerusalem, but there are some nighttime activities. Check in the *Jerusalem Post,* which despite its name is a national paper covering events, cultural offerings, and movies throughout Israel. The Friday-morning edition includes the indispensable weekly calendar of happenings, some of which are in Haifa. Better yet, call the 24-hour telephone hot line for **"What's On in Haifa"** (☎ **04/837-4253**), and check with any of the tourist information offices, to find out about special events happening around town.

The student associations at the Technion and at the University of Haifa have entertainment of one kind or another going on almost every night. Check the universities for details.

THE PERFORMING ARTS

Haifa Auditorium. 138 Ha-Nassi Blvd. ☎ **04/838-0013.**

This is Haifa's largest concert hall, where you can find symphony, opera, the Israel Philharmonic, dance concerts, and many other cultural events and big happenings; there's also usually an interesting art display in the lobby, which you can see anytime for free, from 4 to 7pm (except Friday). Haifa Auditorium is just a short distance south of the Central Carmel commercial district, where Ha-Nassi Boulevard becomes Moriah Avenue. Ticket prices vary with performance.

Haifa Municipal Theater. 50 Yefe Nof St. ☎ **04/862-0670** box office.

Lots of shows are offered at this theater where the play performances are sometimes in Hebrew, sometimes in English, and sometimes both, in simultaneous translation. Ticket prices vary with performance; seats for many productions are in the NIS 115 ($25) to NIS 135 ($30) range.

James de Rothschild Cultural and Community Center. Bet Rothschild, 142 Ha-Nassi Blvd. ☎ **04/838-2749.**

Next to Haifa Auditorium, this community center always has something going on: a dance, exhibit, or concert. Also inside the community center is the Haifa Cinémathèque (see below).

THE CLUB & MUSIC SCENE

Looking for a club, a place to hang out, listen to music, have a drink, and dance? The **Haifa Tourist Board,** 84 Ben Gurion Blvd., in the German Colony, has compiled a list of recommendable spots; stop by for information.

Fever. Gan Ha-Em Promenade; open after 11pm. Thurs is over-25 night. No phone.

This disco is a favorite with teenagers. Summer weekend evenings are busiest.

Martef Esser (Cellar Ten). 140 Ha-Nassi Blvd. on far side of Rothschild Center. ☎ **04/824-0762.**

Once a Rothschild wine cellar, this is now a nightspot run by and for students, with live music of many kinds (jazz, classical, and more), and a nice wicker coffeehouse/bar atmosphere. There is a cover charge Thursday to Saturday evenings.

THE BAR SCENE

Many of Haifa's restaurants have bars with entertainment. Both the upper and lower terminals of the Aerial Cable Car, too, are enjoyable places to stop on an evening out, with restaurants, bars, and dancing; you can ride the cable car until 11pm; most of the year, until midnight. Haifa is a port of call for the United States Mediterranean Fleet. The **USO** is at 114 Yefe Nof St., around the corner from the Dan Panorama Hotel. When the fleet's in, pubs and bars all over the city become busy, especially near the USO.

Bear Pub. 135 Ha-Nassi Blvd. ☎ **04/838-6563.** Sun–Fri 11am–4am; Sat 6pm–4am.

Bear Pub offers indoor and outdoor spaces, and hefty sandwiches, pub food, and a nice atmosphere.

Little Haifa. 4 Shaar Ha-Levanon St. ☎ **04/838-1658.**

The oldest pub in town, conveniently located right next to the USO; open from 8:30pm until shore leave is cancelled; beer is the drink of choice.

Wine Bar at Restaurant 1873. 102 Jaffa St. ☎ **04/853-2211.** Thurs–Sat eves; reservations recommended.

Located in the newly gentrified German Colony, upstairs at the charming 1873 French Restaurant, this hideaway is an elegant spot for sampling wine, cheese, and gourmet snacks.

FILMS

Haifa Cinémathèque. 142 Ha-Nassi Blvd. ☎ **04/838-3424.** Tickets NIS 28 ($6.20).

Housed in the James de Rothschild Cultural and Community Center, this film repertory theater shows a wide variety of international films (up to three different movies every day, many in English, most with English subtitles), including special-interest art film screenings. The Cinémathèque hosts the **Haifa Film Festival** each fall at the time of Sukkot. Call for information about what's going on.

10 Day Trips from Haifa

DALIAT-EL-CARMEL & ISFIYA

These Druze villages are located 15 minutes from the Ahuza section of Carmel. If you're driving, just ask for the road to Daliat-el-Carmel. Isfiya is the first village you'll reach from Haifa; Daliat-el-Carmel is a very short ride farther. The trip takes about half an hour, and it's a splendid drive along the uppermost rim of Carmel. The Mediterranean is way down below you, and so is the entire city, the port, and the industrial area. Bring your camera.

Architecturally, the villages are no longer the quaint enclaves of 30 or 40 years ago; instead, they've become part of the urban sprawl at the outer edge of the city. Haifans visit the villages for the many home-style Middle Eastern restaurants that have sprung up, and for bargain basement shopping (see below).

The Druze are Arabic-speaking people who are, however, not Muslims. Theirs is a rather secretive religion; they draw heavily on the Bible and venerate such personages as Jethro (a Midianite priest and the non-Israelite father-in-law of Moses). The Druze were loyal to Israel during the 1948 war, and several of their brigades are highly respected detachments in the Israeli army.

They are an industrious people; you'll see their terraced hillsides, meticulously cared for and, as a result, very fertile. Many houses are new, and also square and boxlike in the Arabic style. Outside their own villages, Druze find employment on kibbutzim as electricians, builders, carpenters, and mechanics. Their hospitality is legendary.

In both villages, you can buy quite unusual souvenirs and handcrafted items, such as new or antique baskets and trays in the Druze style at moderate prices, but bargaining is necessary. (Markets will be closed on Friday, the Druze Sabbath day.) There are several pleasant cafes in both villages. You'll see older men in flowing gowns and headdresses, often wearing big mustaches, while the younger men wear Western-style clothes.

You can reach the villages on **bus no. 192,** which leaves infrequently from the Central Bus Station; but bus service back to Haifa seems to vanish by 3pm. Various tours also go to these villages (check with the Tourist Information Office for details). There's a sherut service that leaves Haifa during the evening from 6pm to 6am, departing from Hadar at the corner of Shemaryahu Levin and Herzl streets. Between 6am and 6pm, the sherut service from the port area is at the corner of Ha-Atzma'ut Road and Eliyahu Ha-Navi Street, near Kikar Paris. The sherut takes 25 minutes to reach Dali-at-el-Carmel and the fare is the same as by bus.

WHERE TO DINE

The Druze villages are lined with eating establishments geared to the weekend crowd.

Ganei Daliyah. Isfiya–Daliat-el-Carmel Rd. ☎ **04/839-5367.** Reservations recommended on weekends. Main courses NIS 33–70 ($7.20–$15.40). AE, V. Daily 10am–11pm or midnight. MIDDLE EASTERN.

This place has a pleasant garden filled with the sound of its fountain, a covered dining terrace, and a colorful proprietor, Mr. Toufik Halaby. Standard Middle Eastern dishes are a cut above normal, and there are a few well-prepared unusual offerings. The pigeon stuffed with onion, pine nuts, and sumac, grilled on an open fire, is earthy and excellent, as is the homemade Druze bread, and the oven-baked sweetbreads. This is a good choice for a leisurely roadside repast. If you come late at night and have had too much arak, Mr. Halaby rents rooms in a simple hotel above the restaurant. Arabic and Hebrew are spoken. Coming from Haifa, look for the restaurant with its front garden and sign on the right as you leave Isfiya, and before you enter Daliat-el-Carmel.

MUHRAKA

Half a mile south of Daliat-el-Carmel, the road to Muhraka forks off to the left side of the main road. Its destination is not posted, but it meanders and climbs through scrub oak and pine woods to the monastery at Muhraka, the place where Elijah defeated the prophets of Baal. You'll see a dramatic stone **statue of Elijah,** sword raised to heaven, and a lovely **Carmelite monastery,** open Monday through Saturday from 8am to 1pm and again from 2:30 to 5pm (on Friday until noon only). The view from the roof of the monastery (NIS 2 [44¢] admission) is unsurpassed; you can see halfway across Israel to Migdal Ha-Emek and the mountains near Nazareth. There are tables for picnics on the grounds outside the monastery. The name "Muhraka," or "place of burning," refers to a time when this extraordinary vista point was a sacred high place for burned offerings and sacrifices in Canaanite and early Israelite times. Interurban bus 192 or sheruts from downtown Haifa will take you to the fork in the road that leads to Muhraka for NIS 25 or 30 ($5.50 or $6.60). From there it's a half-hour uphill walk; returning buses are few, and seem to stop by 3pm. The Druze-Muhraka area is most easily visited by car, or as a daylong bicycle excursion from Haifa.

ORGANIZED TOURS

A 3-hour tour to **Ein Hod** leaves Haifa most weekdays at 9:30am. It includes a drive through the Carmel mountain range, visits to University of Haifa and the Druze market of Daliat-el-Carmel, and stops at art galleries, artists' studios, and other points of interest. (See chapter 7, section 5 for more about this fascinating artists colony.) Check with the tourist office for current schedules. The **Society for Protection of Nature (SPNI)** at 18 Hillel St. (☎ **04/866-4135**) sells excellent hiking and walking maps of the Carmel range.

9

Galilee

Roughly speaking, everything to the north and east of Haifa is known as "the Galilee" (Ha-Galil)—Israel's lushest region. In February and March, the residents of Israel pour into the Galilee to enjoy the ocean of wildflowers and blossoming trees that cover the valleys and slopes, and to marvel at the perseverance of the original late 19th- and early 20th-century settlers of the Galilee's Jewish agricultural communities who lived in tents, risked malaria, and performed back-breaking labor to cultivate land that had been neglected for centuries.

Beginning in March a vast blanket of green covers Galilee and its watchtowers, settlements, and stone Arab villages. The land is a carefully designed texture of olive groves, rich vegetation, vineyards, and fruit orchards.

In Herodian times, according to Josephus, 204 towns in these hills supported about 15,000 residents each, giving Galilee a population of three million. This estimate is regarded by most historians as high, but there is no doubt that the ancient Galilee supported a population unsurpassed until modern times. Today, this fertile countryside is the site of most of Israel's collective farms (kibbutzim), and it is also home to most of Israel's one million Arab citizens, who maintain a traditional way of life and close ties to the land.

It was only natural that this once fertile region should have been the first area to be redeveloped early in this century. Initially it was to the shores of the Sea of Galilee, in the Jordan Valley and around the Emek Yizreel (Valley of Jezreel, usually just called the Emek) that the early Zionist pioneers came with their dreams of a socialistic utopia, founded on principles of agricultural toil. Then, in the 1920s and '30s, they brought their communal settlements to the western plains and to the mountains of the north of Galilee. They established Israel's front line of defense, sweating out malaria attacks and returning the fire of Arab snipers. Babies born in these settlements grew into hardy young farmers, their playgrounds not the ghettos of Russia and Poland that their parents had known, but rather the meadows and fruit fields of their settlements. During the War of Independence in 1948, several Galilee settlements fought and farmed at the same time. War memorials throughout the region are a testament to these times.

TOURING THE REGION   You can approach the Galilee from the southeast on the road that runs northward up the Jordan Valley, or there are two good central routes for entering Galilee from the west:

One is from Haifa to Akko and east to Safed, then down to the Sea of Galilee. The other is due east from Haifa to Nazareth and straight across to Tiberias. An offshoot of the Haifa-Nazareth road is a route that detours down through the Jordan Valley, south of the Sea of Galilee; at the Jordan Valley, turn north. In summer, the Jordan Valley, which is far below sea level, can be oppressively hot. Give yourself time to enjoy the beaches of the Sea of Galilee, which can be paradisiacal.

The Galilee is filled with so many places of natural and historical beauty that it's worth it to rent a car, at least for a few days of travel.

1 Nazareth & the Yizreel Valley

Nazareth: 40 kilometers (26 mi.) SE of Haifa.

The largest and most fertile valley in Israel, the Yizreel Valley, often called simply Ha-Emek ("the valley"), lies between the Galilee mountains to the north and the Samaria range to the south. Nazareth, the town where Jesus grew up, was only a tiny hamlet in biblical times, scarcely recorded on maps or mentioned in historical works. Today, Nazareth is a bustling city, filled with industry and new construction. It is the major center for Israel's Arab community, and the first language of most inhabitants of Nazareth is Arabic.

ESSENTIALS

GETTING THERE   By Bus   Bus service is available to Nazareth from all major cities.

By Car   Nazareth is on the main road from Haifa to Tiberias and Tel Aviv to Tiberias, less than an hour from Haifa. Leave the port city via Ha-Atzma'ut Road and head inland over the four-lane highway that runs along the foot of the Carmel range. Nazareth is also connected by main roads to the Jordan Valley.

VISITOR INFORMATION   The **Tourist Information Office** (☎ 06/657-3003) is on Casa Nova Street near the intersection with Pope Paul VI Street, open Monday through Friday from 8:30am to 5pm, Saturday from 8:30am to 2pm.

Currency Exchange   use the centrally located **Bank Ha-Poalim** on Pope Paul VI Street beside the Hamashbir Department Store, open Monday and Tuesday and Thursday from 8:30am to 12:30pm and 4 to 6pm; Wednesday and Friday 8:30am to noon. **Change Spot Nazareth,** a money changer, is located in a jewelry store on Pope Paul VI Street near Casa Nova Street, open Monday to Saturday from 8:30am to 8pm. It's usually faster than the bank and charges no commission.

Bus Station   There is no actual bus station: intercity buses stop on busy Pope Paul VI Street near Bank HaPoalim. **Egged Information** is just across from the bank (☎ 04/854-9555), open daily 6am to 6pm. Buses to Haifa or to Tiberias leave approximately every 30 minutes. It is best to ask at the information counter for the number of the most convenient bus next departing for your destination.

Police   For **Police,** phone ☎ **100;** for first aid ☎ **101;** for fire ☎ **102.**

Pharmacy   Farah Pharmacy (☎ 06/655-4018), Pope Paul VI Street, beside Egged Information, open Monday and Tuesday and Thursday and Friday 9am to 1pm and 4 to 6:30pm; Wednesday and Saturday 8am to 2pm.

NAZARETH

This ancient part of town clings to the inside of a vast bowl, its stone houses tiered like the seats of an amphitheater. Today, the city houses Israel's largest Arab community outside Jerusalem—more than 80,000—approximately 35% to 40% Christian, and 60% to 65% Muslim. With Jerusalem, it is also the headquarters of the Christian mission movement in Israel, with more than 40 churches, convents, monasteries, orphanages, and private parochial schools. Nazareth's very name is used by Arabs and Israelis to designate Christians, just as Jesus was also known as the Nazarene. In Arabic, Christians are called Nasara, and in Hebrew Notzrim.

To see what the increasingly modern Nazareth would have been like 40 years ago, turn into the narrow alleys that wind up and back into the terraced limestone ridges, and wander through the narrow cobbled streets of the Arab Market. Keep in mind that Nazareth is completely closed on Sunday and in full swing on Saturday.

ORIENTATION

ARRIVING   Nazareth has a "bypass," a road that circles the town, which explains the confusing signs that point in opposite directions for the same destination. One of these destinations is **Nazareth Elit** (or Nazorat Ilit), the new, modern, mostly Jewish suburb to the north, built on land commandeered from the city of Nazareth, which is actually a separate municipality. You'll pass by it on your way to Tiberias.

CITY LAYOUT   Down Paul VI Street and into the center of Nazareth, you follow the signs to the Basilica of the Annunciation, Nazareth's principal religious monument off Paul VI Street on Casa Nova Street. Use the basilica's huge cupola, topped by a beacon, as your landmark—everything you'll need is within sight of the basilica. There are very few street signs and building numbers are often in Arabic. Remember that it's downhill to the basilica and the center of town from most points in the city.
Casa Nova Street is the approach to the basilica, and on it you'll find restaurants, cafes, hotels, and hospices and the Tourist Information Office.

The "Central Bus Station" in Nazareth is a stretch of Paul VI Street just east of Casa Nova Street, a few steps from the Basilica of the Annunciation.

WHAT TO SEE & DO

There are three things for tourists to do in Nazareth: shopping in the market, visiting the holy Christian shrines, and taking a glance at the new Jewish quarter.

CHRISTIAN SHRINES   The **Basilica of the Annunciation** is located on Casa Nova Street, on the spot where, according to Christian tradition, the angel Gabriel appeared before Mary, saying: "Behold, thou shalt conceive in thy womb, and bring forth a son, and shall call his name Jesus." The present Basilica of the Annunciation, a beautiful monument completed in 1966, was built over earlier structures dating from 1730 to 1877.

The earliest church was built over the grotto in which Mary sat when Gabriel spoke to her. As you enter the basilica, you'll be on the ground (or grotto) level, which is in fact the church's crypt. After you've toured the crypt, walk back to the entrance and you'll see steps up to the nave.

Unlike most Christian shrines in Israel, this basilica has a bold, modern design. Around the nave, on the walls, are murals that were created by artists from around the world. Note the Japanese mural of the Madonna and Child on the left (north) wall—Mary's robe is made entirely of Japanese seed pearls. The mural from the United States, on the right (south) wall, at first seems discordant and excessive, but it works when viewed from the basilica's north-side door.

Summer hours are daily from 8 to 11:45am and from 2 to 5:45pm; in winter, it's open daily from 9 to 11:45am and from 2 to 4:45pm. (Many of the churches in Nazareth observe these same hours, closing for the "noontime siesta" during the middle of the day.) Walk out the north side door to reach the other religious sites.

The **Church of Saint Joseph** is 100 yards away, constructed on the site thought to have been occupied by Joseph's carpentry workshop. From the sanctuary, stairways on either side go down to another floor below, where you can see old stone construction, an ancient water cistern, and a mosaic floor dating from the Byzantine period. Hours are the same as at the Basilica of the Annunciation, above.

On the main street in the bazaar is the **Greek Catholic "Synagogue" Church,** believed to be the site of the ancient Nazareth synagogue that Jesus frequented: "And He came to Nazareth, where He had been brought up; and, as His custom was, He went into the synagogue on the Sabbath day, and stood up to read" (Luke 4:16). Farther along the road is the **Franciscan Mensa Christi Church,** believed to occupy the spot where Jesus ate with his disciples after the resurrection.

Mary's Well, with its source inside the **Greek Orthodox Church of the Annunciation,** is another Christian holy site. The church was built at the end of the 17th century over the remains of three former churches. At the church entrance, on the archway above the stone staircase leading down to the well, there is a colorful mural showing the angel Gabriel coming to Mary and announcing in six languages, "Hail, thou that are highly favored, the Lord is with thee: blessed art thou among women." The ceiling is covered with brightly colored murals depicting scenes from the Bible. Proceed through the archway before you and you'll come to the well—a small spring and a round stone well.

The **Basilica of Jesus the Adolescent,** maintained by the French Salesian order, is one of the most beautiful churches in Nazareth. Built in 1918, the Gothic church contains pillars composed of clusters of slender columns that support the vaulted roof. There's a lovely marble statue of Jesus the Adolescent by the sculptor Bognio. It is a climb to get to the top of the hill north of the center of town, but it is worth the effort. Go down Casa Nova Street to Paul VI Street, turn left, go up two blocks, and go down the street to the left of the public fountain; the church is one short block up this street, straight ahead. It's open year-round daily from 8am to 5pm.

Our Lady of Fright Chapel, sometimes called the Tremore, is built on a wooded hill south of the center opposite the Galilee Hotel. It is on the spot where Mary watched while the people of Nazareth attempted to throw Jesus over a cliff—the Precipice, or Lord's Leap rock, a quarter of a mile away.

Although the majority of Nazareth's population was Christian before the 1950s, the city now has a Muslim majority, and is home to some lovely Islamic structures. Built between 1960 and 1965, the beautiful and modern **Al-Salam Mosque** is in the eastern quarter of town, a block away from Paul VI Street. In the southern part of the city is the new **Al-Huda Mosque.**

SHOPPING IN THE MARKET   The market streets, entered via Casa Nova, are narrow, crowded, and highly exotic. Remember that the deeper you get into the market, the smaller the shops become and the lower the prices. One of the first things to note is the trench running dead center of the street, and one of the first precautions is to stay out of it as much as possible—it's the donkey trail. Snaking upward, the narrow roadway is lined with tin-roofed shops in which you'll see everything from plows and ram's horns to cakes, leather goods, chandeliers, plastic buckets, and fine jewelry. Daily necessities are displayed side by side with antiques from Turkish times that sell for thousands of shekels. You can buy a *finjan* coffee set here or a *kefiya*, which is the Arab headdress. One shop, deep in the market, carries *narghilis* (bubble pipes). If you're a coin collector, try the tiny shops where you'll find a variety of coins and prices. Whatever you buy, be sure to shop around, and whatever you do, bargain over everything.

WHERE TO STAY

Nazareth has always been home to atmospheric, well-run Christian guest houses; in preparation for the year 2000, a number of international hotel chains have been building new hotels that will open during the time span of this edition. They will all be four-star properties with up-to-date rooms, swimming pools, and other amenities that will make Nazareth more of a base for exploring the area. If you're planning to stay in Nazareth, look for a new **Howard Johnson's Hotel** right in the center of town, within walking distance to the Church of the Annunciation and the heart of the old town; a new **Renaissance** (Ramada) hotel at the southern edge of Nazareth, near the Nazareth Gardens Hotel; and a new **Marriott,** in addition to the **Marriott** in **Nazareth Ilit,** the new Jewish town built on a hilltop next to Nazareth.

Hotel Galilee. Paul VI St., Nazareth. ☎ **06/657-1311.** Fax 06/655-6627. 93 units (29 with bathroom, 64 with shower). A/C TEL. $75–$105 double. Rates include continental breakfast. No credit cards.

This modern, pleasant three-star establishment is a 5-minute walk south of the basilica. The entire hotel has recently been renovated. The hotel has a bar and coffee shop, as well as heated rooms.

✪ **Nazareth Gardens Hotel.** Afula Rd., Nazareth. ☎ **06/656-6007.** Fax 06/656-6008. 120 units. A/C TV. $90–$150 double. Rates include breakfast. Add 15% service. AE, DC, MC, V.

Located in a small forest at the southern edge of Nazareth, the Nazareth Gardens Hotel is the most beautiful and restful place to stay in this bustling, busy city. This is another of the sprawling modern complexes with country club grounds originally built as a government retreat, with a vast swimming pool, sweeping lawns and landscaping, fish ponds, a basketball/handball court, fitness equipment, and a children's play area. Rooms are quite simple, but well serviced and comfortable enough; some are set around special courtyard gardens of cacti or roses, lovingly tended by a very dedicated staff. A fine base for exploring not only Nazareth, but the whole of the southern Galilee. The Merry Land Restaurant is a pleasant walk to the main road.

Nazareth Marriott. 2 Hermon St., Nazareth Ilit 17000. ☎ **06/602-8200.** Fax 06/602-8222. E-mail: nazareth.marriott@heihotels.com. 272 units. A/C TV TEL. $246–$296 double. Rates include breakfast. AE, DC, MC, V. Free parking.

Located in a rather isolated neighborhood of apartment blocks overlooking Nazareth, this new Marriott, opened in 1999, is the last word in comfort for those visiting the city. There are three executive club floors, which receive special service and attention from the staff. There is also a business center; heated outdoor swimming pool; fitness center (fee); and in-house restaurants, all of which make this a good stop for business travelers as well as for tourists and visitors on pilgrimage. Rooms are equipped with refrigerators; there are rooms for travelers with disabilities.

St. Gabriel Hotel. Salesian St. (P.O. Box 2318), Nazareth. ☎ **06/657-2133.** Fax 06/655-4071. 65 units (15 with bathroom, 50 with shower). TV TEL. $90–$125 double. Rates include breakfast. MC, V.

Built in the 1950s to serve as a monastery, this beautiful gardened, atmospheric building was recently converted into a hotel. The lobby is decorated with traditional crafts; guest rooms have exposed stone walls and offer fine vistas of the city. Bathrooms and furnishings are new, but this *was* a monastery and you must expect simple, rather small accommodations in exchange for the ambience. The location, in an upper neighborhood of central Nazareth, means a certain amount of climbing; a car can be very useful if you stay here. The hotel offers Saturday walking tours of Nazareth, including the

Basilica, some of the mansions of the Old Town and a bus ride back up the steep hill to the hotel, where you have lunch. Readers report breakfasts are bland here compared to the buffets found in most Israeli hotels.

Near Nazareth: Zippori

Two thousand years ago, Zippori (Sepphoris) was a thriving city and Nazareth a humble village less than 6 kilometers (10 mi.) away. Now those roles are reversed; Nazareth is the bustling city, and Zippori a cooperative agricultural village as well as the site of a vast and fascinating archaeological park. If you have a car, this is a placid and convenient place from which to explore the area.

Zippori Village Guesthouses. Moshav Zippori. ☎ **06/646-2647.** Fax 06/646-4749. 4 guest cottages (all with bathroom). A/C TV. $70 per couple per night. Weekends $80 per couple. $14 per child. Rates include breakfast. Discounts for large families or long-term stays. AE, DC, MC, V.

These cottages, built by hosts Mitch (a former New Yorker) and Suzy Pilcer (formerly from Colorado) in 1997, are fresh and pleasantly decorated. They sport front porches, a bedroom, a small living room with sofa bed, a kitchenette, and a Jacuzzi. A ladder leads to a loft area with a foldout bed. With extra floor mattresses supplied by Mitch, a large family can be accommodated. The management is personal and very well informed (Mitch is a tour guide), offering lots of brochures and advice about the area. A country breakfast (kosher) with organic bread, vegetables, eggs, jam, cheese, and goat's milk (all local products) is left each morning at 7:30am in a cooler beside your door. As public transportation is poor, you need a rental car in order to consider a stay here.

WHERE TO DINE

There are lots of places on Paul VI Street and Casa Nova Street near the Basilica where you can grab a falafel, a shwarma, or a mezze of Arabic salads and pita bread. There are also many spots for tea, coffee, and a piece of baklava. All have been around forever, and all serve good food, though few have much style. The best restaurant for a really good meal, Fahoum's, is also centrally located near the Basilica.

✪ **Fahoum Restaurant.** 303 Casa Nova St. ☎ **06/655-3332.** Reservations recommended Sat. Main courses NIS 36–56 ($7.70–$12.10). AE, DC, MC, V. Daily 8:30am–9pm. MIDDLE EASTERN.

Located at the intersection with Paul VI Street, 1 block from Basilica of the Annunciation, this bright, spotlessly clean restaurant serves delicious food and outshines its neighboring competitors. You can have a fine light meal by selecting some of the traditional Arabic salads (the tasty *hatselem,* or eggplant puree salad, is laced with lemon and garlic). But the restaurant is best known for meats cooked over wood fire, and for its authentic lamb ribs. Try the fine lamb or beef shashlik (cubes of meat on the skewer); the boneless fried chicken in lemon garlic; or the nicely seasoned kabobs (skewered ground meat). The oldest restaurant in town, Fahoum is spacious but no frills in style and presided over by the gracious, English-speaking owner, Mr. Naief Fahoum.

Merry Land Restaurant. Afula Rd. ☎ **06/656-0265.** Main courses NIS 25–90 ($5.50–$19.80). AE, DC, MC, V. Daily 9am–11pm. MIDDLE EASTERN.

At this modern roadside restaurant just at the southern edge of town, you can park right in front (avoiding the parking nightmare of busy central Nazareth). The menu includes the standard array of Middle Eastern salads followed by grilled meats and chips (french fries), but the interesting house specialty is a small whole pressed chicken seasoned with sumac and cooked on an open fire. This is an informal and pleasant option close to the Nazareth Gardens Hotel and the soon-to-open Renaissance Hotel.

Middle Eastern Desserts

On the left-hand side of Casa Nova Street, just before it meets the basilica, is **Abu-Diab Mahroum's Sweets** (☎ 06/657-1802). There are several stores named Mahroum's Sweets—make sure you go to the original near the Basilica of the Annunciation. The shop windows are filled with baklava, Turkish delight (maajoun) with nuts, Esh el-Bulbul ("Hummingbird's Nest," a shredded-wheat bird's nest filled with nuts and laced with honey), or burma (a roll of shredded wheat stuffed with pistachios and soaked in honey or syrup). Dessert and Turkish coffee costs about NIS 16 ($3.50) or less. Mahroum's is open daily from 7am to 9pm.

AN ATTRACTION NEAR NAZARETH **Mount Tabor** (or Tavor),at 1,800 feet above sea level, is the tallest of the Lower Galilee Mountains. It stands a little more than 6 miles southeast of Nazareth and must have been a dominant feature of the landscape Jesus knew in his childhood. At the summit stands the **Basilica of the Transfiguration,** which marks where Jesus was transfigured as he spoke to Moses and Elijah in the presence of three of his disciples (Luke 9:28–36). It was built in the 1920s over the ruins of long destroyed crusader and Byzantine churches. Also on the mount is the **Church of Elias** (Elijah), built in 1911 by the Greek Orthodox community. From here on a clear day, you can see the Sea of Galilee, Mount Hermon, the Mediterranean Sea, and the Emek. At this dramatic mountain, in the period of the Judges (c. B.C. 1150), the Prophet Deborah and her general, Barak, led the Israelite tribes to victory over the Canaanite General Sisera of Hazor (Judges 4:12–16). Like the summit of Mount Carmel, near Haifa, where the Prophet Elijah challenged the Canaanite prophets of Baal, the summit of Mount Tabor is believed to have been a Canaanite "high place" or altar from at least the 2nd millennium B.C. The defeat of the Canaanites at such a prominent sanctuary may have had a stunning psychological effect on the populace of that time.

Mount Tabor is accessible from Nazareth by Egged bus or taxi. Although it looks close, the way is circuitous. If you're driving from the northern part of Nazareth, take Route 754 to Route 77; from Route 77 at the Golani Junction, turn south onto Route 65 to Mount Tabor. From southern Nazareth, take Route 60 to Afula; at Afula take Route 65 to Mount Tabor. At the base of the mountain, in the Arabic village of Shibli, you'll find a very modest but charming **Center of Bedouin Heritage** (☎ 06/676-7875). It's open Saturday to Thursday from 9am to 5pm; admission is NIS 12 ($2.65). If you are driving or walking, the road becomes increasingly steep the higher you ascend, with absolutely hair-raising hairpin turns. Beware of vehicles in front of you conking out and rolling downhill. The descent can seem even more horrific, but the view from the summit is magnificent!

Where to Dine

Tzela HaTavor. Kfar Tavor (Village of Tavor). ☎ **06/769-9966.** Reservations useful; necessary on weekends. Light meals NIS 25–45 ($5.50–$10); main courses NIS 52–75 ($11.40–$16.50). AE, V. Daily 11am–10 or 11pm. COUNTRY FRENCH.

With stunning views of Mount Tabor from its windows, this rustic restaurant offers the chance to dine in relaxing style after an excursion up the mountain. If you're staying in Nazareth and have the freedom of a rental car, this is the finest restaurant in the area. The food is beautifully prepared, and you might almost imagine yourself in the south of France, prodded by the many different herbed cream sauces and classic appetizers. If you want something light, try a fine salad topped with slices of moulard (duck-goose hybrid), or giant mushroom caps stuffed with pecans, parsley, and garlic. Main courses, served with salad and potato baked in cream, range from veal medallions in a green peppercorn and cream sauce, or breast of moulard in a piquant orange glaze, to a simple Dan River trout baked in cumin and rosemary. The ostrich fillet stroganoff (delicious and low fat) is highly recommended. Excellent French desserts and an Israeli wine list round out the charms of this personal, delightful place.

THE YIZREEL VALLEY

The Yizreel Valley houses some of Israel's oldest and best-known settlements—**Mishmar Ha-Emek, Hazorea, Givat Oz, Ginegar,** and the giant moshav, **Nahalal.** The rich, dark soil is crisscrossed in checkerboard patterns of fruit trees, vineyards, and green vegetable fields. It is a breathtaking quilt of colors, some blocks golden with wheat, some black with heavy cultivation, others orange with brilliant flowers.

About 70 years ago, however, this lush area was a breeding swamp of malaria. In the early 1920s, the Keren Kayemet (Jewish National Fund) launched its biggest land reclamation project; over a period of time, the swampland was drained and every mosquito was killed. Russian, German, and Polish settlers filled the new settlements. The cultivation of the Emek became legendary, rhapsodized in dozens of romantic songs in which the tilling of soil and the smell of roses are common lyrics.

But as you look at this splendid fertility, remember also that this was one of the bloodiest battlefields in history. Here the Egyptians shed blood 4,000 years ago, as did the Canaanites, the Mongols, the Greeks, the Romans, and the crusaders in later centuries. From Mount Tabor, overlooking the Emek's northeast corner, the Prophet Deborah launched her famous attack against the Canaanite armies. And several years later, Gideon's forces came from Mount Gilboa on the Midianites and slaughtered the plundering Bedouin tribe.

But it was also on this fertile plain that the ancient Israelite nation suffered one of its most calamitous national defeats—when King Saul (the first king of Israel) and his sons, including Jonathan (the closest friend of David, second of Israel's kings), died during a clash with the Philistines. It is with regard to this battle that the book of Samuel records David's immortal lament.

> How the mighty are fallen!
> Tell it not in Gath,
> Publish it not in the streets of Ashkelon
> Lest the daughters of the Philistines rejoice . . .
> Saul and Jonathan were lovely and pleasant in their lives,
> And in their deaths they were not divided . . .
> Lo, how the mighty are fallen,
> And the weapons of war perished.

Later, the Turks fought here, as did Napoléon. In 1918, General Allenby defeated the Turkish forces on the Emek, and Israel's armies in 1948 overwhelmed the Arabs. It is ironic that the Emek region, which has been so ravaged, today flourishes in such splendor.

WHAT TO SEE & DO

As you travel from Haifa to Nazareth, you pass farm settlements, the most important of which are **Yagur** and **Allonim.** Yagur is one of the country's oldest kibbutzim, founded in 1922. About 30 or 40 minutes out of Haifa be sure to stop at the observation signpost on your right, after climbing into the foothills of Lower Galilee—the view of the Yizreel Valley spread out below is one of the loveliest in Israel.

Zippori (Sepphoris) National Park. 6.5km (4 mi.) northwest of Nazareth. ☎ **06/656-8272.** Admission NIS 22 ($5). Sat–Thurs 8am–5pm, in winter to 4pm; Fri 8am–3pm. No public transportation.

Now a small agricultural community, the ancient city of Sepphoris dates from the era of the Maccabees in the 2nd century B.C. An enormous period of expansion and building, starting in the 1st century A.D., turned the city into "the ornament of the Galilee," according to Flavius Josephus. With its worldly, mixed population of Hellenistic pagans and Jews, it is interesting to speculate about the influence of Zippori on Jesus, who grew up in what was then the small village of Nazareth, a mere 4 miles away. As **the traditional birthplace of Mary,** and as a city requiring the services of many skilled carpenters and builders, cosmopolitan Zippori may have been a place often visited by Jesus; the landscapes and vistas around Zippori, unlike those of modern, urbanized Nazareth, may still resemble the countryside Jesus knew.

The Jewish community in Zippori grew rapidly after the Bar Kochba revolt of A.D. 135, when thousands of refugees from Judea migrated into the Galilee. By the late 2nd century, Zippori was the seat of the Sanhedrin and the home of many great rabbinical sages, including Yehuda Ha-Nassi, who codified the Mishnah. During the Talmudic era, the city contained numerous synagogues; in 1993, archaeologists uncovered a **mosaic synagogue floor** from the 5th century A.D., decorated with an elaborate zodiac design and inscriptions in Hebrew, Aramaic, and Greek. Most impressive are the ruins of a 4,000-seat Roman amphitheater, and a late Roman-era Dionysian mosaic floor of a villa that includes the **"Mona Lisa of the Galilee,"** a hauntingly beautiful young woman that is one of the greatest examples of ancient mosaic portraiture ever discovered. There is also an intricate mosaic depiction of Nile landscapes, including the famous Nilometer. In other parts of the site, you'll find a crusader fortress and church.

Bet Shearim Burial Caves National Park. 20km (12 mi.) from Haifa. ☎ **06/983-1643.** Admission NIS 18 ($3.90). Apr–Sept, Sat–Thurs 8am–5pm, Fri until 3pm; Oct–Mar, Sat–Thurs 8am–4pm, Fri until 3pm. Bus: 301 from Haifa.

Somewhat reminiscent of the Sanhedrin Tombs in Jerusalem, the burial caves are located on the main road from Haifa that heads toward Afula (which is the principal town of the Jordan Valley).

In the 2nd century, Bet Shearim was the home of the Supreme Religious Council, the Sanhedrin, as well as headquarters of the famous Rabbi Yehuda Ha-Nassi, the compiler of the Mishnah. Many learned and famous Jews were laid to rest in the town's cemetery, a tranquil grove of cypress and olive trees. Over the centuries, however, the tombs were destroyed and the caves looted. Earth and rock covered the catacombs as if they had never existed. But finally they were unearthed, first in 1936, and then fully explored after the War of Independence.

Enter the burial chambers through an opening in the rock or a stone door. Inside are sarcophagi carved with rams' horns and lions' heads, and menorahs. So far, catacomb 20 is the most interesting, with its legible inscriptions, carvings, and interesting relics. Archaeologists claim that only a fraction of the original effects remain, that robbers have looted the almost 200 sarcophagi.

The entire site here is particularly well tended, with a parking lot, visitors' facilities, and outdoor cafe. The bus from Haifa runs every half hour. Ask the driver to let you off at the archaeological site.

Megiddo (Armageddon) National Park (☎ **06/652-2105**) is about 35 kilometers (22 mi.) southeast of Haifa. On the road, you pass Hazorea and Mishmar Ha-Emek, two old and large kibbutzim, before you come to ✪ **Megiddo** (Armageddon). This has always been the primary fortress overlooking the Emek, which due to its strategic position on the major route leading from Egypt to Syria and Mesopotamia, has always been coveted and attacked. Archaeologists have uncovered the remains of cities of more than 20 distinct historical periods here on this tel (Hebrew for an archaeological mound or hill), dating from 4000 to 400 B.C. It is mentioned frequently in biblical and other ancient texts.

In the Old Testament, the name Megiddo appears in a number of places, mostly in relation to war. In the New Testament, the book of Revelation names Armageddon (a corruption of the Hebrew *Har Megiddo*—Mount Megiddo) as the place where the last great battle will be fought when the forces of good triumph over the forces of evil.

Megiddo has been a place of battle continuing right down into our own century. General Allenby launched his attack against the Turks from the Megiddo Pass in 1917, and in 1948 the Israeli forces used the fortress site as a base of operations against the entrenched Arab armies. As you enter Megiddo today, now a national park, there is a **museum** with detailed information about the excavation, the artifacts found there, the biblical and historical references relating to its past, and a model of the site as it now exists. Many more artifacts discovered here have been removed, and may now be found in the Jerusalem Antiquities Museum and the Rockefeller Museum.

You can walk among the ruins, including a **palace** from the time of King Solomon, and **King Ahab's "Chariot City"** and what some archaeologists call **stables** with a capacity of almost 500 horses (other archaeologists claim that the structures are not stables, though exactly what they *are* is a matter of controversy). There is also a large **grain silo** from the reign of Jeroboam Ben Joash, king of Israel in the 8th century B.C., and a building from the time of King David (1006–970 B.C.). On strata way down below the later buildings, you can see excavated ruins of temples 5,000 and 6,000 years old, constructed during the Chalcolithic period.

Perhaps most amazing of all is the **water tunnel** dating from the reign of King Ahab in the 9th century B.C. You enter it by walking 183 steps (120 ft.) down into a large pit in the earth (the collection pool inside the city walls), whereupon you can walk along the tunnel extending 215 feet to a spring located outside the city, which was camouflaged by a wall covered with earth, designed to assure a constant supply of fresh water to the city even when it was under siege. (Read "The Psalm of the Hoopoe," in James Michener's *The Source,* to learn how tunnelers digging from both ends of a tunnel such as Megiddo's managed to meet underground using simple engineering techniques).

You can see remnants from Megiddo's imposing city walls, gates, and entryways, some of which were built during the time of King Solomon. The observation points offer a spectacular view of the huge valley below.

To get to Megiddo by bus, take bus no. 302 from Haifa, which leaves Haifa's Central Bus Station several times in the morning and returns from Megiddo several times in the afternoon. The **Visitors Center** at Megiddo and the **archaeological park** are open daily from 8am to 4pm, except for the water tunnel, which closes at 3:30pm. Admission is NIS 22 ($5) for adults and NIS 11 ($2.50) for children.

MA'ALOT TARSHISHA & NORTHWESTERN GALILEE

Nineteen kilometers (13 mi.) east of Nahariya, Ma'alot Tarshisha, with a population of 8,000, is at the center of the Northwestern Galilee (Crusader Castle Country), and sits astride the main road from the coast to the Upper Galilee. Its location makes it an ideal base for those who want to rent a car, and freewheel for a few days around the region. The 1997 opening of the Hacienda Mountain Resort, formerly a private retreat on the outskirts of the city, has made it possible to stay here in comfort.

Ma'alot is a development town founded in 1957; the municipality is united with the contiguous Arab-Israeli town of Tarshisha, whose history dates from Talmudic times and before. It's a pleasant, busy community, the center of the region's carefully planned checkerboard of agricultural, industrial and natural districts. The town made history in 1974 when terrorists who had infiltrated into Israel from Lebanon took a school filled with Israeli children hostage; 14 children were killed in the attack. To this day security around every town and city in the northern Galilee is very tight.

WHERE TO STAY

☉ **Hacienda Mountain Resort.** Yefe Nof, Ma'alot. ☎ **04/957-9000.** Fax 04/997-4404. 115 units. A/C TV TEL. $126–$221 double. Rates include breakfast. Jewish holidays 15% extra. AE, DC, MC, V.

Another of the network of country club–style retreats originally built in the 1970s for the federation of unions and now turned into a hotel, the Hacienda is surrounded by 17 acres of beautifully tended woods and gardens. With its heated indoor/outdoor swimming pool, and crisp, clear mountain it's a tranquil, well-run base for exploring the whole of the northern Galilee, from Bar'am Synagogue in the east to the Crusader castles at Yechiam and Montfort in the west. It's also so convenient to the coast that it provides a good alternative to the rather undistinguished hotel choices in Akko and Nahariya. Rooms with bathrooms have been freshly renovated and cost 10% more. Meals here are healthful, but rather institutional.

TOURING THE AREA

Yechiam (Judin) Castle. Kibbutz Yechiam. ☎ **050/813-227** (mobile phone). 12km (7.5 mi.) east of Narariya. Off Rte. 8833, which runs south of and parallel to Rte. 89.

The most easily accessible of all the country's crusader ruins, Yechiam is an atmospheric, romantic place, with windows and doorways framing vistas of the coastal plain it was designed to dominate. Probably built by the Templars in the late 12th century, Yechiam was destroyed by the Mamluk Sultan Baybars in the late 1200s. It's massive, strategic ruins were rebuilt in the 18th century by the local Bedouin warlord, Sheik Dahr El-Omar. Kibbutz Yechiam has renovated part of the castle and installed a series of restaurants, all quite pleasant, that have come and gone: At press time there is no restaurant at the castle. Check out whether the restaurant has reopened: Yechiam Castle is one of the most romantic places to dine in Israel, and restaurant guests can wander through the ruins of the castle until 11pm. Crusader castles were made for twilight; watching nightfall framed by the stones of Yechiam is a memorable experience. Yechiam is open daily 8am to 5pm. Admission is NIS 10 ($2.20); free if you come for the restaurant.

Montfort Castle. South of Route 899, accessible by trail from Goren Park.

Perched on a mountaintop in the wild, densely forested northern tier of the Western Galilee, Montfort was originally built by French crusaders; it was conquered by Saladin's armies in 1187, but recaptured by crusaders in 1192. In the 13th century it was bought by the German Knights of the Teutonic Order who renamed it Starkenberg Castle, and greatly added to its defenses. Despite its impregnable defenses, it was finally overrun by Sultan Baybars in 1271, who allowed its defenders safe passage to Akko. Goren Park offers a wonderful observation point, with a great sunset view of the castle; there is an uphill trail from the parking lot to the castle that could take from 30 minutes to an hour to hike, depending on your pace and fitness. SPNI can supply you with maps that will detail 4- and 5-hour hikes through the majestic countryside that lead to the castle.

Tefen Industrial Park Open Museum. ☎ **04/978-2977.** Off Rte. 89 1km east of Ma'alot Tarshisha.

A castle of modern industry and technology, Tefen's attraction's are its art gallery, the wonderful permanent collection of art that adorns the interiors of its building, and the beautiful contemporary sculptures that are part of the landscape of the complex. Among the very accessible Israeli sculptures in Tefen's permanent collection are Nubian sandstone pieces by Itzak Danziger, an op art portrait of Theodore Herzl by Uri Lipshitz, and a large ensemble called "The Walkers," in which Ofra Zimbalista created lifelike statues by casting plaster of Paris directly on human models. The casts obtained by this process were then removed, reassembled, and covered with a mixture of cement and sand. The Israeli sculptor Achiam's granite head of King David is especially fine. The pleasures offered by Tefen continue with a **Gallery of Modern Art,** offering well-mounted temporary exhibits, the **Museum of German Jewry,** documenting the history of that community, with special emphasis on German Jewry's contributions to the State of Israel, and a **Museum of Vintage and Classic Cars** displaying a collection of 40 vehicles, ranging from turn-of-the-century motor cars to a reproduction of a Bugatti and an actual 1946 Chevrolet. Open Sunday to Thursday from 9am to 5pm and Saturday 10am to 5pm. Admission NIS 15 ($3.30). After visiting Tefen, you might drive though the planned residential community of Kefar Vradim, the dream suburb for local professionals, and from there to the Israeli Arab town of Me'ona, and on to Yechiam Castle via the scenic Route 8833.

2 Tiberias

330 kilometers (198 mi.) N of Jerusalem; 116 kilometers (70 mi.) E of Haifa.

From Haifa the favorite road to Tiberias is the one from Nazareth, if only for that dip in the road and that sudden unfolding of the mountains when the Kinneret, the Sea of Galilee, is suddenly spread down below you. It happens best on a clear day, about 5 miles from Tiberias. Arab villages are sprawled on the hillsides, and sabra cacti, with their dangerous spiked arms and little orange fruits, line the road's edge. Then you round a bend and there it is—an incredibly beautiful azure lake set like a jewel in a pastoral valley.

Tiberias is the year-round tourist center for the Galilee and Golan regions, making an excellent base for explorations of these nearby areas as well as Lake Kinneret. Although the waterfront at Tiberias has large, modern hotels and the area is filled with beaches, Tiberias also offers a scattering of old, charming houses and the arabesque domes of Ottoman Turkish mineral water bathhouses as well as a scattering of archaeological digs, and the tombs of the great rabbinical sages. Two blocks inland from the lakefront, Ha Galil Street, with its black native basalt buildings filled with shops, brings to mind an old-fashioned, small-town American main street. The pubs and restaurants along the Waterfront Promenade pound with disco and heavy metal on summer evenings. Little of the town's splendid history is immediately visible. The climate is mild in the fall, winter, and spring, but brutally hot when Tiberias is busiest in July and August. In the winter, visitors are able to snow ski on Mount Hermon (1^1/$_2$ hr. drive, 9,000 ft. above sea level) in the morning, and (on warm days) water-ski on Lake Kinneret (700 ft. below sea level) in the afternoon. In the evening, you can eat a NIS 14 ($3) falafel packed with every salad or condiment imaginable at the pedestrian mall or a NIS 160 ($35) supper at one of Israel's most acclaimed restaurants, and go dancing or sailing afterward. In less than an hour you can drive from Tiberias to the Golan Heights, the Lebanese border, Safed, Nazareth, the Yizreel Valley, or down through the Jordan Valley to the south, as well as to any place on the Sea of Galilee.

The ancient town of Tiberias, built in A.D. 18 by Herod Antipas (son of Herod the Great), was named in honor of the Roman emperor Tiberias. With its hot springs and mild climate, it became one of the most elegant winter resorts in this part of the ancient world.

A century and a half after the Temple of Jerusalem was destroyed, Tiberias became the great Jewish center. It was here that the Mishnah was completed in A.D. 200 at the direction of Rabbi Yehuda Ha-Nassi, "Judah the Prince." Here the Jerusalem Talmud was compiled in A.D. 400, and the vowel and punctuation grammar was introduced into the Hebrew language by the learned men of Tiberias. Mystics, academicians, and men believed to have magic powers have been drawn to Tiberias throughout its history.

Both the town and the towering scholarship declined after the 5th century A.D., due to the many wars fought here by the Persians, Arabs, crusaders, and Turks. A medieval Arab historian named Al MuQadassi recorded that the residents of the town led a life of decadence—dancing, feasting, playing the flute, running around naked, and swatting flies.

Tiberias lies on one of the earth's major geological fault lines, the Syrian/African Rift, and in 1837 the city was virtually destroyed by an earthquake. A few portions of the city's black basalt medieval walls survived that catastrophe, but almost nothing else of medieval or ancient Tiberias can be seen today outside of the archaeological sites open to the public.

The entire area, geologically speaking, is known as the "Valley of the Rift." The fault line begins in southern Turkey and northern Syria, extends southward through Israel (from north to south, through the Hula Valley, the Sea of Galilee, the Jordan Valley, the Dead Sea, down to Eilat), and all the way to Lake Victoria in Malawi, Africa. Relative to one another, the east side is moving north, and the west side (where you are if you're standing by the lake) is moving south.

It is this rift that has given shape to the mountains and valleys, and it is the reason why you can stand at the Sea of Galilee, 700 feet below sea level, and look up toward the north and see Mount Hermon towering 9,000 feet above sea level. It's also the reason for the earthquakes and volcanic eruptions over the eons, as well as the mineral hot springs around the shores of Lake Kinneret and the Dead Sea. You can see evidence of it in the older buildings and in Tiberias's Old City Wall, which is composed of volcanic rock, called black basalt.

Another interesting feature of the Syrian/African Rift is that it forms an incredible highway for bird migration between Europe and Africa. Two of Israel's major wildlife reserves—Hula Valley in the north, Hai Bar in the south—serve as stopping-off points for the birds on their long journey, and are popular with bird watchers and nature lovers.

ESSENTIALS

GETTING THERE   By Bus   There is direct service from all major cities.

By Car   From Jerusalem via the Jordan Valley, it's a $2^{1}/_{2}$-hour drive; from Haifa, 1 hour and 20 minutes. Four main roads lead to Tiberias and the Sea of Galilee: from Safed, from the Jordan Valley, via Mount Tabor, and from Nazareth.

VISITOR INFORMATION   The area code is 06. The **Tiberias Tourist Information Office** is in the archaeological park in front of the Sheraton Moriah Plaza Hotel(☎ **06/672-5666** or 06/679-1981), open Sunday through Thursday from 8:30am to 3:30pm, on Friday from 8:30am to noon. There are often extended hours in July and August. The office gives out free maps and information and can direct you to lists of bed-and-breakfast accommodations.

The **Tzemach Junction Tourist Information Office** (☎ **06/675-2056**), is a good alternative for travelers coming up Route 90 from the Jordan Valley. The Tzemach Junction is formed just where Route 90 hits the southern tip of the Sea of Galilee.

Turn right at the junction: About 500 feet on the right is a small shopping center where you'll find the Tourist Information Office. Open Sunday to Thursday from 8:30am to 3:30pm, with hours on Friday and Saturday in season (call ahead), the office can help direct you to bed-and-breakfast accommodations and offers both free pamphlets and maps and books for sale. If you plan to stay on the eastern shore of the lake, the Tzemach Junction shopping center, with its supermarket open daily 7am to 8pm (and a Dr. Lek's Ice Cream store and plain, inexpensive restaurant), is a good place to keep in mind. You can stop for supplies without having to fight the tourist crush in Tiberias, which can be a madhouse in summer and Jewish holidays.

SPECIAL EVENTS   The **Ein Gev Music Festival** takes place at Kibbutz Ein Gev in spring during Passover week. Israeli folk dance and song festivals are organized along the waterfront in summer; ask the Tourist Information Office for details. The **Sukkot Swimathon** is across the Kinneret (3 mi.). Everyone is welcome to join, but bring a medical certificate stating that you are in good health. For information, contact the Tiberias Tourism Information Office, Ha-Banim Street, Tiberias (☎ **06/ 672-5666**).

ORIENTATION   Tiberias (or Teverya; pop. 45,000) spreads out along the Kinneret shore and climbs the hillside to the west. The very center of Tiberias is **Kikar Ha-Atzma'ut,** or Independence Square, in the Old City. Surrounding Ha-Atzma'ut Square is what little is left of historic Tiberias.

The **Central Bus Station** (☎ **06/679-1080** or 06/679-1081), on Ha-Yarden Street, is 2 blocks inland from Ha-Atzma'ut Square. Tiberias's main street changes names as it winds through the city. As it descends from the mountains to the lake it's called Ha-Nitzahon Road; in the residential district of Kiryat Shmuel up on the hillside it becomes Yehuda Ha-Nassi Street, and as it descends to approach the Old City its name changes to Elhadeff (or El-Hadeff or Alhadif) Street. After passing Ha-Atzma'ut Square, it becomes Ha-Banim Street, and this name serves it all the way to the southern limits of the city.

Northwest of the Old City, up on the hill that overlooks downtown, is the large residential district of **Kiryat Shmuel,** which has many moderately priced hotels. South of the Old City about 1¹/₂ kilometers (1 mi.) is the section called **Hammat,** or **Tiberias Hot Springs.** Ruins of an ancient synagogue and town, a national park, a museum, and the Tomb of Rabbi Meir Baal Haness are located near the springs.

North of the Old City, Gdud Barak Road skirts the water's edge and several beaches on its way to Magdala (where Mary Magdalene came from), Tabgha (where the miracle of the loaves and fishes took place), Mount of Beatitudes (where Jesus preached the Sermon on the Mount), and Capernaum (Kefar Nahum).

Fast Facts: Tiberias

Banks   Bank Mizrachi at the corner of the Pedestrian Mall and Ha Banim Street has an outdoor ATM that is connected to Visa, MasterCard, and CIRRUS and NYCE systems.

Bookstores   Steimatzky's is located at 3 Ha Galil St. (**06/679-1288**), open Sunday through Thursday from 8am to 1pm and 4:30 to 7pm; Friday 8am to 2pm; closed Tuesday afternoon and Saturday.

Emergencies   Magen David Adom (☎ **100** or 06/679-0111), at the corner of Ha-Banim and Ha-Kishon streets across from the Jordan River Hotel, is open 24 hours.

Maps Steimatzky's Bookstore and the Tourist Information Office sell a selection of regional road maps. In addition to standard road maps, look for Corazin Publishing's fold out *Go Galilee,* and *Map of the Galilee, Golan and the Northern Valleys.* It costs about NIS 22 ($5); Corazin also does a map on *The Northern Coast and Western Galilee.*

Police Telephone ☎ **100** or 06/679-2444.

GETTING AROUND

You can rent a **bicycle** at Hotel Aviv (☎ **06/671-2275**), at the southern end of Ha-Galil Street, starting at NIS 40 ($8.80) for standard bikes, NIS 50 ($1) for mountain bikes for a full day, with hourly and half-day rates available. It is open daily. For an additional fee, you can have pick-up service, if you don't feel up to biking back to Tiberias. You can also rent bicycles at comparable rates at the Lake Castle Hostel and Nahum Hostel (see "Where to Stay," below). You can rent a car at any of five different major rent-a-car companies with offices in Tiberias, many of them found in the block of Elhadeff Street north of Ha-Yarden Street, where the tourist information office is located. In alphabetical order, here's a listing of their telephone numbers: **Avis** (☎ **06/672-2766**), **Budget** (☎ **06/672-0864**), **Eldan** (☎ **06/672-2831**), **Hertz** (☎ **06/672-3939** or 06/672-1804), and **Reliable/Sixt** (☎ **06/672-4112**).

WHAT TO SEE & DO

Tiberias is the main city in the Eastern Galilee, and a centrally located base for exploring the area. The town has an interesting split personality. Ha-Galil Street (which is one way going south) is reminiscent of a tree-shaded main street in any small American town—it's lined with small shops serving the population from the surrounding countryside. If the old basalt rock buildings with their second-story balconies were renovated, the street could be charming. A block to the east is the other main street of Tiberias, Ha-Banim Street (running one way going north), passing high-rises, mega-hotels, and the *Midrehov,* or Pedestrian Mall, leading to the Waterfront Promenade, packed with Israeli and foreign tourists during the summer and Jewish holidays, throbbing at night with wall-to-wall discos, pubs, cafes, and restaurants. Ancient and Byzantine/Talmudic-era Tiberias was larger and more spread out than the modern town; many archaeological sites are outside the present town.

Ha Galil Street, the main shopping street, runs just outside the most recent of the town's old wall, destroyed over the past few centuries by a number of earthquakes that have struck the region. Here you can see the ruins of the **rampart** that enclosed the city; you can also see the **remains of mosques** and old buildings from the densely packed Arab town that once existed here. Floods during the British Mandate period, and the 1948 War of Independence, caused most of Tiberias's Arab population to flee.

The **Waterfront Promenade** has a magnificent view across the lake. One hundred yards to the left are the remains of a **crusader fort** (now the Castle Inn), jutting up in black basalt stone from the water. Directly across the lake is Kibbutz Ein Gev and other settlements. To the left is Mount Hermon. It is from these foothills that the sources of the Jordan River are formed. The mountains in the distance, opposite you, are part of the Golan Heights (see section 5 at the end of this chapter for a description of a Golan trip).

The **Galilee Experience** (☎ **06/672-3620**) is a multimedia exhibition depicting the history and heritage of the region. The entrance fee is NIS 27 ($6), and what you get is a 30-minute state-of-the-art multislide show that highlights Jesus and the rise of Christianity, and 20th-century Zionism. (Some visitors to the Galilee Experience are not prepared for the exhibit's attention to the area's most famous inhabitant, Jesus.) Strangely, little mention is made of Israel's large Arabic community, which makes up half the population of the Galilee. Located on the Waterfront Promenade, the Galilee Experience is open Saturday through Thursday, from 8am to 10pm, and Friday from 8am to 4pm.

Located off Yohanen Ben-Zakkai Street is **Rambam's (Maimonides's) Tomb.** Rabbi Moses Ben-Maimon, known as Maimonides, or Rambam, was the greatest Jewish theologian of the Middle Ages. A Sephardic Jew, born in Cordova, Spain, but who lived most of his life in Morocco and Egypt, he was an Aristotelian philosopher, a humanistic physician, and a leading scientist and astronomer. His principal work was *The Guide for the Perplexed.* The famous philosopher, who died in 1204, is now honored by a newly restored and beautified mausoleum and gardens. Nearby is the **tomb of Rabbi Yochanon Ben-Zakkai,** founder of the Yavne Academy in the years following the destruction of Jerusalem in A.D. 70, and on a hillside just west of town is the **memorial to Rabbi Akiva.** This great sage compiled the commentaries of the Mishnah before the Romans tortured him to death at Caesarea in A.D. 135 for his role in aiding the Bar Kokhba revolt.

The tomb of the 2nd-century A.D. **Rabbi Meir Baal Haness,** located on the hill above the hot springs, is considered one of Israel's holiest sites; pilgrims visit in search of medical cures and help with personal problems. Rabbi Meir, called the "Miracle-Worker" and the "Light-Giver," is remembered in a white building that has two tombs. The Sephardic tomb, with the shallow dome, was built around 1873 and contains the actual grave, close to the interior western wall of the synagogue; the building with the steeper dome is the Ashkenazi synagogue, erected about 1900. Huge bonfires are lit at his tomb by the Orthodox 4 days before the Lag b'Omer holiday in the spring. All the tombs are open daily between 8am and 4pm (possibly later in summer); there is a 2pm closing on Fridays.

Down on Tiberias's lakeside promenade, squeezed in among the fish restaurants and inconspicuously set back from the shore, stands **Terra Sancta.** The church and monastery are run by the Franciscans. Another name for the church is Saint Peter's Parish Church. The first church was constructed here by the crusaders around A.D. 1100. After the Muslims conquered Tiberias in 1187, the church was converted to a mosque; around the middle of the 17th century, the Franciscans began coming each year from Nazareth to celebrate the Feast of Saint Peter, paying the Muslims for the use of the site. Later on in the same century the Franciscans obtained the site for themselves.

The present church still contains part of the original crusader church, but only a part of the apse (altar), which, on the outside, is shaped like the bow of a boat. The rest was built by the Franciscans in 1848, except for the facade, which dates from 1870. The church's facade is identical to that of the Franciscan church in Assisi where the order began, with red stone imported from Assisi. In the courtyard facing the church is a white stone monument built by the Polish in 1945, dedicated to Our Lady of Czestochowa, and a bronze statue of Saint Peter, a copy of the statue in Saint Peter's Basilica in Rome. You can visit the church daily from 8 to 11:45am and from 3 to 5:30pm. Masses are weekdays at 7am, and on Sunday and holidays at 8:30 and 11am.

While you're here, you can also visit the historic **Greek Orthodox Church** located along the waterfront, a block or two south from Terra Sancta, or the **Church of Scotland,** which is a block or two to the north.

The **art gallery district** is located between Elhadeff and Dona Gracia streets, extending northward from Ha-Yarden Street. You'll find one gallery in the medieval castle on Dona Gracia Street, and many others nearby.

ORGANIZED TOURS

Every Sunday and Monday morning at 9am, and Thursday evening at 6pm, a free 2-hour walking tour of Old Tiberias leaves from the **Tourist Information Center** (☎ 06/672-5666), across from the Radisson Moriah Plaza Hotel; Saturday mornings at 10pm, a free walking tour leaves from the lobby of the **Sheraton Moriah Plaza Hotel,** under the hotel's sponsorship. These walks are a real pleasure, led by interesting guides; reconfirm all times with the Tourist Information Office. With Tiberias as a starting point, you can take guided tours of both the Golan Heights and the Sea of Galilee. Check the sections on those areas, below, for details.

In addition to the large tour companies, you may want to hire **private tour guides** to take you by sherut or taxi. Inquire at your hotel or youth hostel, at the major hotels, or at the Tourist Information Office. These tours can be reasonably priced and a welcome change of pace from the bus tours. The Society for Protection of Nature (SPNI) includes walks and hikes in the tours it offers in the Galilee Region. Check with the society's offices in Tel Aviv (☎ 03/638-8677) or Jerusalem (☎ 02/624-4605). SPNI's Alon-Tavor Field Study Center, M.P. Lower Galilee 14101 (☎ 06/676-7798), organizes hikes in the Jordan and Jezreel Valleys as well as elsewhere in the region; they offer information on trails and hotel accommodations in local field schools.

CRUISES & FERRIES

The **Kinneret Sailing Company,** on the Waterfront Promenade (☎ 06/665-8007), runs ferry service between Tiberias on the west side of the Kinneret and Kibbutz Ein Gev on the east side, departing daily from the Tiberias Waterfront Promenade and arriving at Ein Gev 45 minutes later. After spending an hour at Ein Gev, it departs for Tiberias. Schedules vary according to season, with three or four lake crossings in summer. The round-trip costs NIS 40 ($9). **Lido Cruises Sailing Company** (☎ 06/672-1538) does ferry runs between Lido Beach in the northern part of town, and Kibbutz Ginnosar, toward the northeastern corner of the lake, for NIS 28 ($6.20); bicycles are free and there is no discount if you only travel one way. Departures often depend on a minimum number of passengers.

Many people take this opportunity of crossing the lake by ferry to try out the excellent restaurant at Kibbutz Ein Gev, or just to stroll around the kibbutz. You can also plan to take the ferry one way, and take bus no. 18 or 21 back to Tiberias. Buses go between Tiberias and Ein Gev about every 2 hours.

The Lido Cruises Sailing Company also operates a daily ferry between Tiberias and Capernaum; call for details on this, as well as on water ski and sailboard rental.

Both of the above sailing companies offer evening cruises, some of which have dancing and meals on board; call for information or ask at the Tourist Information Office.

SPORTS & OUTDOOR ACTIVITIES

Water sports are offered on and around the lake, including waterskiing, water parachuting, sailboarding, giant water slides, kayak trips, and more. Call the Tourist Information Office for information.

BEACHES   The **Blue Beach** charges $5 for the use of its lake facilities and a beach-chair rental.

Tiberias

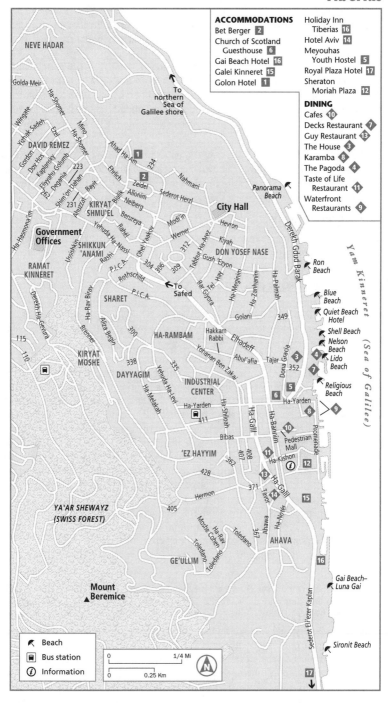

ACCOMMODATIONS
Bet Berger **2**
Church of Scotland
  Guesthouse **6**
Gai Beach Hotel **16**
Galei Kinneret **15**
Golon Hotel **1**
Holiday Inn
  Tiberias **16**
Hotel Aviv **14**
Meyouhas
  Youth Hostel **5**
Royal Plaza Hotel **17**
Sheraton
  Moriah Plaza **12**

DINING
Cafes **10**
Decks Restaurant **7**
Guy Restaurant **13**
The House **3**
Karamba **8**
The Pagoda **4**
Taste of Life
  Restaurant **11**
Waterfront
  Restaurants **9**

NEVE HADAR

Golda Meir

DAVID REMEZ

KIRYAT
SHMU'EL

**Government
Offices**

SHIKKUN
'ANAMI

RAMAT
KINNERET

KIRYAT
MOSHE

DAYYAGIM

SHARET

HA-RAMBAM

INDUSTRIAL
CENTER

'EZ HAYYIM

YA'AR SHEWAYZ
(SWISS FOREST)

GE'ULLIM

▲ **Mount
Beremice**

City Hall

DON YOSEF NASE

Panorama
Beach

To
northern
Sea of
Galilee shore

To Safed

Yam Kinneret
(Sea of Galilee)

Ron
Beach
Blue
Beach
Quiet Beach
Hotel
Shell Beach
Nelson
Beach
Lido
Beach
Religious
Beach

Pedestrian
Mall

Promenade

AHAVA

Gai Beach–
Luna Gai

Sironit Beach

≮ Beach
🚌 Bus station
ⓘ Information

0   1/4 Mi
0   0.25 Km

The **Quiet Beach**'s $4.20 fee includes all the swimming facilities, and is open from 8am to 6 or 7pm. The **Ganei Hammat Swimming Beach,** opposite the Ganei Hammat Hotel, near the Tiberias Hot Springs, is open daily from 9am to 5pm. It offers deck chairs, showers, and a snack kiosk. Admission is $3.50. The **Gai Beach**, a kilometer south of town, beyond the Galei Kinneret Hotel has a water park with incredible slides and a fine beach with all the requisite facilities; it is a $10 to $12 admission fee. **Sironit Beach** also south of town, is open from 8am to 5pm, April through October. There's also a **municipal beach** ($3 fee) south of Sironit Beach, open from 9am to 5pm.

HORSEBACK RIDING   In the countryside around the lake, you can join groups for trail riding in the Galilee; call **Vered Ha-Galil Restaurant(and Guest Farm)** (☎ **06/693-5785;** see Guest Farm, Restaurant, and Horseback Riding Facility under "Where to Stay Around the Sea of Galilee").

WHERE TO STAY

Tiberias has everything from youth hostels to five-star hotels, with a few religious guest houses as well. You should note that most hotels here have kosher kitchens and several are Orthodox.

DOWNTOWN TIBERIAS

Expensive

Howard Johnson Plaza Galei Kinneret. 1 Kaplan St., Tiberias. ☎ **06/672-8888.** Fax 06/679-0260. E-mail: hhemda@irh.co.il. 120 units. A/C MINIBAR TV TEL. $271–$313 double. Rates include breakfast. Add 15% service charge. AE, V.

Located a long block south of the landmark Sheraton Moriah Plaza (but not on the Waterfront Promenade), the Galei Kinneret, hidden from the main road by gardens, is the oldest of the quality hotels in town (it was a favorite of Ben-Gurion). In 1997, it joined a small group of unusual Israeli hotels that affiliated with Howard Johnson, but the old standards and personality of the hotel will continue. The original building from the early 1940s is a rather severe white International Style design to which a number of newer wings have been added. The general atmosphere is relaxing; unlike other downtown hotels, the Galei Kinneret has shaded lawns and its own beach directly on the lake. Public areas and guest rooms are comfortable but not all spectacular; however for Israelis, the hotel is a place to be seen in. The pool is heated and covered in winter. The hotel's prestigious in-house restaurant, Au Bord du Lac (open Saturday through Thursday, dinner only), is the only French restaurant in Tiberias. On Jewish holidays, rates go up $200 per room.

Dining/Diversions: Three restaurants, lounge/bar, live entertainment.

Amenities: Heated swimming pool, fitness center, floodlit tennis court, sauna, hot tub, water-sports rentals.

✪ **Sheraton Moriah Plaza Tiberias.** Ha-Banim St., Tiberias. ☎ **06/679-2233;** reservations through Sheraton Hotels. Fax 06/792-320. 272 units. A/C TV TEL. $200–$280 double. Rates include breakfast. Add 15% service charge. AE, DC, MC, V.

A modern 14-story high-rise with a pretty and convenient location at the southern end of the Waterfront Promenade, the Sheraton Moriah Plaza's public areas and light, elegant guest rooms are the most stylish in town. There is ongoing room redecoration; ask for an upgraded room, and one with a view toward the lake. The pool area is pleasantly sheltered from the Promenade; dining facilities are above average, with theme buffets at the main in-house restaurant; service is attentive; and in season and on weekends there is live entertainment.

Dining/Diversions: Three restaurants, lobby bar, cafes.

Amenities: Outdoor swimming pool, health club, sauna, Jacuzzi, massage, hairdresser, video games, shops.

Inexpensive

✪ **Church of Scotland Center Guest House.** P.O. Box 104, Tiberias 14100. ☎ **06/ 672-3769.** Fax 06/679-0145. E-mail: scottie@rannet.com. A/C. $80–$90 double; $10 extra for rooms with views. Rates include breakfast. AE, DC, MC, V.

A hidden enclave centrally located behind the Meyouhas Youth Hostel, this well-run guest house is surrounded by beautiful walled gardens and has stone terraces and balconies with sweeping vistas of the lake. Built 100 years ago as a Scottish missionary hospital, the ensemble of buildings is constructed of the black basalt stone native to the Galilee. All rooms have recently been renovated; they are simple but comfortable, and double-glazed windows help keep out the noise from Tiberias's summer disco scene; a gate through the garden wall leads to the Guest House's private beach. There's also a well-run hostel on the grounds, with double rooms (no air-conditioning and shared bathrooms) at $40.

✪ **Hotel Aviv.** Achva St. P.O. Box 1751 Tiberias. ☎ **06/671-2272.** 30 units. A/C TV TEL. $50–$80 double, winter and summer; add $5 per person Jewish holidays. Rates include breakfast. AE, DC, MC, V.

A perfect budget choice, built in 1998, and located on a quiet street in downtown Tiberias, the Aviv offers fresh, large, no-frills rooms with kitchenettes. The layouts of the rooms vary, so check a few if possible. Some contain completely separate kitchenettes; others are more like suites, with a living area, separate bedroom and kitchen—especially good for families. All have balconies, 36-channel cable TV, and some have whirlpool bathtubs. There are pleasant public areas, and street parking is permitted here. Do not confuse this with the nearby Hostel Aviv.

SOUTH OF DOWNTOWN TIBERIAS

Expensive

Gai Beach Hotel. Hamerchatzaot St. ☎ **06/670-0700.** Fax 06/679-2776. www. gaibeachhotel.com. E-mail: Gai_beach@netvision.net.il. 198 units. A/C TV TEL. $220, $257, $324 double low, regular, and high seasons respectively. Rates include breakfast. AE, DC, MC, V. Free parking. Located on the main road leading into downtown Tiberias from the south; a 5-min. walk into downtown.

Great for families with children, the Gai Beach is a sprawling low-rise right on the beach with an adjacent water park filled with slides, a vast wading pool, and a pool with artificial waves. The hotel is a bright, sparkling place with large windows in guest rooms and public areas that bring in the dazzling sunshine and vistas of the lake. The water park is open from Passover to October. The hotel contains rooms for travelers with disabilities, a fitness room for fee, business facilities, heated indoor and outdoor pools, and a private beach. High season includes July and August, Christmas, and Jewish holidays.

Royal Plaza Tiberias. Ganei Menorah Blvd., Tiberias. ☎ **06/670-0000,** or 800/670-0000 in Israel. Fax 06/670-0001. E-mail: roylplza@netvision.net.il. 160 units. A/C TEL. $202 double ($243 high season). AE, DC, MC, V.

Composed of two renovated hotels that have been joined together, the Royal Plaza doesn't offer architectural pizzazz, but it does have comfortable, roomy, rather formally decorated rooms, and prices that don't skyrocket as much as those at other Tiberias hotels during the summer. It is located 2 miles south of Tiberias center, on the main lakefront road not far past the hot springs. Amenities include swimming pool, free parking, pleasant Victorian pub/bar, Internet access, business facilities, and rooms for travelers with disabilities.

KIRYAT SHMUEL

Kiryat Shmuel is a residential and hotel district on the hill overlooking Tiberias and the Sea of Galilee. Unless otherwise mentioned, all of the following hotels have the equivalent of three-star facilities, private bathroom, air-conditioning, and heat. All these hotels have kosher dining rooms. Most have good views. But this is not an exciting neighborhood to be in—you don't get a feel for Tiberias or the Galilee staying in this urban residential area. Most tourists who choose this part of town are older Israeli or European tourists.

You'll want to take a taxi to get up to Kiryat Shmuel if you're arriving in Tiberias by bus—it begins a half kilometer (1/4 mi.) away from downtown, and that half kilometer is all uphill. Many of the hotels here are even farther uphill.

Moderate

Golan Hotel. 14 Ahad Ha-Am St. (P.O. Box 555), Tiberias 14222. ☎ **06/679-1901.** Fax 06/672-1905. 99 units. A/C TV TEL. 100–$125 double. AE, DC, MC, V.

This good-value establishment offers magnificent views and a swimming pool. It's quite a nice place, with an outdoor cafeteria and garden, and an intimate bar with dancing. In winter or at slow times, the lower rates can be obtained.

Inexpensive

Bet Berger. 25 Neiberg St., Tiberias. ☎ **06/671-5151.** Fax 06/679-1514. 45 units (15 with bathroom, 30 with shower). A/C TEL. $46–$75 double. MC, V.

This constantly expanding, well-run place has an excellent reputation in the budget category. Rooms are simple but clean, and have refrigerators, which helps cut down on your restaurant expenses. Some of the rooms have terraces. There is a video television room on the premises.

WHERE TO DINE

In addition to the choices in Tiberias, many travelers who have use of a car will enjoy dining at some of the delightful restaurants in the countryside and on the shore around Kinneret; see "Country Dining Around the Sea of Galilee," below.

ON THE WATERFRONT

The specialty in Tiberias is Saint Peter's fish, so-called because it is the very fish that swam in the Sea of Galilee when Jesus called Peter away from his nets to become a "fisher of men." It's a white fish that is indigenous to the Sea of Galilee and its taste resembles that of bass.

The best place to search out a good portion of Saint Peter's fish, or even shish kebab for that matter, is along the **Waterfront Promenade** in the Old City. You can get there by walking down Ha-Yarden Street until you reach the lake. Or just look for the minaret of the Great Mosque and pass by the mosque, heading for the shore. This is Old Tiberias, a municipal redevelopment project in which ancient crumbling buildings have been restored and new amenities, such as the popular waterfront promenade, have been added.

Three of the attractive waterfront restaurants have the same management, the same menu, the same prices, and the same delicious food. These are the **Nof Kinneret** (☎ **06/672-0310**), the **Galei Gil** (☎ **06/672-0699**), and the **Roast on Fire** (☎ **06/672-0310**). The indoor decor is different in each restaurant, although outdoor dining on the boardwalk is virtually the same, so stroll along and see which you like the best; but if the weather is good, you'll likely want to eat by the water. Plan to spend about NIS 45 to 60 ($12.60 to $16.80) for a large (more than a pound) serving of Saint Peter's fish, french fries, salad, and pita bread; if you add wine, coffee, and dessert besides, it could come to about NIS 70 ($20). All three restaurants offer the fish fried, charcoal grilled, or in a special sauce. Hours are daily from 8:30am to midnight; in summer, they may be open 24 hours.

Moderate

✪ **Karamba Restaurant/Bar.** Waterfront Promenade. ☎ **06/679-1546.** Reservations necessary on weekends and in summer. Main courses NIS 33–85 ($7.20–$18.50). AE, MC, V. Daily 11am–after midnight. SEAFOOD/VEGETARIAN.

This more unusual, attractive place along the waterfront has tropical decor and a tree-shaded patio. It offers hearty dishes such as vegetable pie topped with cheese, inventive hot and cold soups, light meals, fruit dishes, and salads that are meals in themselves—the Karamba special house salad has assorted vegetables, cheese, nuts, raisins, and yogurt dressing. Karamba's fish, served with a choice of sauces, is probably the best and most inventive on the waterfront. Most of Karamba's tables are on its patio, but you can reserve one of the restaurant's few tables right on the water's edge if you call ahead. There is also a tropical bar and after-hours spot, with nice music, open in summer from 11am to 2am, in winter from 5pm to 2am.

NEAR THE MOSQUE

This historic edifice is now incongruously surrounded by a supermarket and fast-food eateries. The *Midrehov,* or pedestrian street, a block from the mosque, leads down to the Waterfront Promenade. Both places are lined with restaurants, cafes, and pubs, almost all with outdoor tables.

For espresso, cappuccino, and excellent baked goods and pastries, try the **Contidoria Yatsek and Kapulsky,** which are right next to each other. At either place, a pastry and cappuccino at a sidewalk table will cost about NIS 27 to 32 ($6 to $7). Both also sell baked goods to go. They're open daily from 8am to 10 or 11pm.

DOWNTOWN

A bit away from the crush of the Waterfront Promenade, around Ha-Galil and Ha-Banim streets, you'll find less tourist-oriented restaurants, although you must remember that tourism is Tiberias's major industry. The north end of Ha-Galil Street, and Ha-Yarden Street next to Shimon Park is "**Falafel Row.**" The lineup starts right outside Ha-Atzma'ut Square and stretches up toward the bus station. Quality and fixings can vary, but the cost should be about NIS 10 to 15 ($2.20 to $3.30). The best falafel and shwarma stands offer a big selection of salads to tuck inside your pita with falafel. Many say the falafel here is the best in Israel.

Moderate

Little Tiberias Pub Restaurant. Ha-Kishon St. ☎ **06/679-2806.** Reservations useful. Main courses NIS 28–90 ($6.20–$19.80). AE, DC, MC, V. Daily noon–1am. CONTINENTAL.

To my experience, this is the best of the downtown restaurants: relaxed (perhaps too relaxed, as service can be *very* slow), and unpretentious. Everything comes out of the kitchen a bit more special than at other restaurants—even that Israeli standby, chicken schnitzel, is a pleasant surprise here. There are hefty salads that are meals in themselves, and good spaghetti and lasagna at the lower end of the main-course menu. In the upper price range, I strongly recommend the steaks and fresh fish; shrimp and calamari are also available. You can have a very good meal here, away from the hustle of the Waterfront Promenade; most main dishes are in the NIS 50 to 67 ($11 to $15) range.

Inexpensive

Guy Restaurant. Ha-Galil. ☎ **06/672-3036.** Main courses NIS 30–55 ($6.60–$12.10). No credit cards. Sun–Thurs noon–midnight; Fri noon–1 hour before Shabbat; Sat after Shabbat. SEPHARDIC HOME STYLE.

This friendly kosher, family style restaurant specializes in home-style Sephardic and Middle Eastern Jewish cooking. It is 1 block south of Ha-Yarden at the southern end of Ha-Galil Street, in a small white building. Delicious house specialties include eggplant, artichokes, tomatoes, or other vegetables stuffed with rice or rice with meat, as well as plums, dates, figs, and apricots stuffed with meat, rice, and nuts. Main meat courses are served with french fries and salad, pita bread, and pickles. Prices are very reasonable.

✪ **Taste of Life.** Ha-Kishon St. ☎ **06/671-2133.** Main courses NIS 25–40 ($5.50–$8.80) AE, DC, MC, V. Sun–Thurs 9am–11pm; Fri 9am–1pm; Sat after Shabbat. VEGAN.

You'll be amazed by this air-conditioned, no-frills restaurant's tasty natural vegetable meals: soy sausages, vegetarian shwarmas, wheat burgers, tofu falafels, veggie-steak sandwiches, and soy ice creams. My favorite is the barbecued twist on whole wheat pita served with medium spicy sauce and homemade mustard. Founded by the Hebrew Israelites, an African American religious group whose dietary laws prohibit milk or meat products, Taste of Life uses no milk or meat, nothing is fried, there is no cholesterol, and almost no salt, yet everything tastes great. Other delicious choices here are steamed vegetables and veggie stir-fries, tofu cheeses in assorted flavors, and okira sticks that seem a bit like fish sticks! Drinks include juices, veggie coffee, and carob milk; desserts include carob cakes and candies, and soybean ice creams in unusual flavors. There's fabulous live jazz Thursday and Saturday nights in the summer.

NORTH OF DOWNTOWN

Tiberias has three great restaurants that are about a 7-minute walk from downtown. They have great atmosphere, nice decor, and delicious food.

Moderate

✪ **Decks.** Gdud Barak St. ☎ **06/672-1538.** Reservations necessary. Main courses NIS 50–130 ($11–$26.40). AE, DC, MC, V. Sun–Thurs 7pm–after midnight; Sat after Shabbat. Call for possible lunch hours. BARBECUE.

This is the best new restaurant I've encountered in Israel, set on a large deck jutting over the Sea of Galilee, and serving wonderful meats, poultry, and fish barbecued over fires of citrus wood, olive wood, and American hickory imported from Georgia. Although it's kosher, Decks' meats are among the very best in the country. Pass the outdoor cooking fires, and continue through the sweeping open-air bar before reaching the dining area, on a wooden deck stretching over the lake, with its sweeping vistas and refreshing breezes; it is tented in winter. Waiters are well informed and helpful; most main courses are served at your table on specially designed plates over tiny glowing embers that keep your meal warm but not dried our during a leisurely dinner. Absolutely heavenly is the very reasonably priced breast of mullard, a local duck-goose hybrid as rich as steak, and cooked to perfection, filled with its own flavorful natural juices. The lamb is remarkable; all cuts are from delicate local female baby lamb. A specialty, not usually written on the menu is boneless shoulder of lamb, priced according to weight and of gourmet quality—it's worth requesting. Regular menu choices include herbed breast of chicken, prime rib steak, filet mignon, goose liver, and fish (the fish is good, but not as exceptional as the meats). All main courses are served with bountiful portions of grilled vegetables and fire-baked potatoes. There are nice salads and focaccias for first courses, and flambée crepes and nondairy ice cream touched with homemade berry sauces for dessert. The house drink of lemon and mint on crushed ice is a nice touch. Decks is often heavily booked by groups, creating something of a party atmosphere. Decks can easily run into the expensive price category, but is very worthwhile.

The Pagoda. Gdud Barak St. ☎ **06/672-5513.** Reservations recommended. Sushi fixed menu for two NIS 85–95 ($18.70–$21); main courses NIS 32–80 ($7–$17.60). AE, DC, V. MC, V. Sun–Thurs 12:30–3pm and 6pm–midnight. KOSHER CHINESE/THAI.

The Pagoda, with a kosher menu, gives you the chance to dine right on the water, with spectacular views of the lake. The building itself is an airy pavilion extending over the water, designed by Chinese architects to take advantage of the site. The pagoda-style roof, with its genuine Chinese beaming and joinery, is indicative of the management's attention to detail. The noodle soup overflows with chunks of tender stir-fried chicken, doughy homemade noodles, and crisp slices of fresh cucumber—but make sure to ask specifically for the homemade noodle version; the spicy Thai chicken coconut soup is an exotic light meal in itself. For light, healthful food, the Thai-style steamed dishes, including fresh fish, are good choices. There are Chinese choices, but the Thai side of the menu is the most interesting. Avoid the goose leg faux "spare ribs," that have been imposed upon the restaurant in the name of kashruth, replacing Pagoda's once famous lamb-spare ribs. During the Sabbath, the Pagoda opens its non-kosher affiliate, the **House Restaurant,** just across the road on Gdud Barak Street; it is open Friday 1pm to midnight and Saturday 1pm to 4:30pm. The menu, prices and phone number are the same as the Pagoda's.

COUNTRY DINING AROUND THE SEA OF GALILEE

Tiberias can become very hectic in the evening, especially during the summer. If you have a car, a drive out into the countryside for dinner can be very pleasant.

✪ **A Good Spot in the Middle.** Tiberias-Degania Rd. ☎ **06/675-2074.** Main courses NIS 35–75 ($7.70–$16.50); beer NIS 12–16 ($2.65–$3.50). AE, DC, MC, V. Summer daily 11am–4am; winter daily 11am–1am. GRILL/PUB.

Away from the rush of downtown Tiberias restaurants, this is a roadhouse restaurant/bar with a broad picnic table–covered porch overlooking the road and the lake across the street. Its always friendly spirit shifts in style according to the hour—it's a good choice for a hefty or light meal as you drive around the lake, but after dinner, A Good Spot in the Middle spends its summer evenings slowly building into a nightlong party as regulars and visitors filter in from the countryside. The restaurant is proud of its fried cheese, salads, and oven-smoked grilled pork steaks, pork fillet, and filet mignon. The traditional stuffed vegetables, especially the eggplant, were the best I've had in this part of the country. The home-style couscous dish is great—grab it on the days it's available. The restaurant is located 4 miles south of Tiberias on the right side of the road.

✪ **Kibbutz Ein Gev Fish Restaurant.** Kibbutz Ein Gev. ☎ **06/665-8035.** Reservations recommended. Main courses NIS 55–68 ($12.10–$15). 10% service charge added. AE, DC, MC, V. Daily 10am–10pm. SAINT PETER'S FISH.

For great freshly caught St. Peter's fish served indoors, or on covered and open terraces overlooking the lake, this is the place to come, either by excursion boat from Tiberias, or as you meander around the Sea of Galilee by car, bus, or bicycle. The fame of the fish here has spread; the restaurant is enormous, and constantly expanding. It is often filled with tour groups; nevertheless, this is a pleasant place for a meal. You can order your fish in two sizes: medium and slightly larger—it will come with chips (french fries) or oven-baked potatoes and salad on the side as well as a choice of good side sauces. The best time to come is in the evening; reserve a table on the terrace by the waterfront in good weather and watch the sunset over the Sea of Galilee and the soft twilight as you dine. Stick to the local St. Peter's fish—the other choices are not what the restaurant is famous for.

✪ **Vered Ha-Galil Restaurant.** Vered Ha-Galil Guest Farm, Korazim Rd. ☎ **06/ 693-5785.** Reservations recommended Fri–Sat. Main courses NIS 45–85 ($10–$18.70); light meals NIS 20–45 ($4.40–$10); desserts NIS 18 ($4). AE, MC, V. Daily 8am–9:30pm for meals; 8am–11pm for dessert. Follow Korazim Rd. a few miles north of the Sea of Galilee. AMERICAN.

This famous country lodge offers hearty American-style food in a lovely garden setting in the hills above the Sea of Galilee. You can choose hamburgers, grilled steaks, fish and ostrich, chicken in a basket with all the fixings, smoked trout fresh from the Dan River, as well as original house specialties, like trout in an orange and Cointreau sauce. There's a selection of less-expensive light meals; many just stop by for coffee and homemade pie (apple, pecan, or Golan boysenberry), or to talk over a bottle of wine. The scene is mellow and the clientele is largely into nature.

TIBERIAS AFTER DARK

There are summer shows and performances by local and foreign entertainers at the **Bet Gavriel Amphitheater** on the southern tip of the Sea of Galilee (across from the Tsemach Junction). With parklike grounds, snack bar/restaurant, and vistas of the lake, it's a memorable venue for concerts. Check with Tourist Information for a schedule of performances.

Folklore events are often scheduled at the hotels, where everyone is welcome to attend. For full details, contact the tourist information office at the end of the Ha-Banim Street Pedestrian Mall.

There are also many late-night pubs, cafes, bars, and restaurants. Good places for a quiet drink, with live music, include the **Sheraton Moriah Plaza** and the **Jordan River** hotels, at the southern end of the Old City.

There are plenty of opportunities to go dancing, as well. The most unusual, I'm sure, is the summer **disco dancing** on the boat operated by the Kinneret Sailing Company on the Sea of Galilee; call ☎ **06/665-8007,** or stop by its office at the Waterfront Promenade, for information. An evening **disco cruise** also leaves from the Lido Kinneret Beach (Lido Kinneret Cruises, ☎ **06/672-0330**) at varying times, depending on demand. Be there before 8pm.

For a lively pub and frenetic dancing crowd, there's **La Pirate**, just where the waterfront Promenade and the Pedestrian mall meet; its open nightly 5pm to 4am. **Big Ben,** on the Pedestrian Mall, has a more traditional indoor pub as well as a terrace; the crowd at times is a bit older and less rowdy.

Many, in fact most, of the hotels (and even the youth hostels) around town have nice bars and pubs where you can relax in the evening and enjoy a drink and conversation with fellow travelers.

EASY EXCURSIONS

Hot Springs of Tiberias. ☎ **06/672-8500.** Admission to the mineral pools NIS 64 ($14) midweek; NIS 74 ($16.20) for adults; discounts for children. Sun–Mon, and Wed 8am–8pm; Tues and Thurs 8am–10:30pm, Fri 8am–4pm; Sat 8:30am–8pm. Free shuttle bus to hotels in downtown Tiberias Sun–Fri 8am–2pm.

Located a mile south of Tiberias, the thermal baths have been famous for their curative powers for more than 3,000 years, and have continued to have a following to this day. Pharmacies in Israel keep well-stocked supplies of mineral salts from these Tiberias springs.

The hot waters contain high amounts of sulfuric, muriatic, and calcium salts, and over the centuries they've reportedly cured such ailments as rheumatism, arthritis, and gynecological disorders. They are probably the earliest-known thermal baths in the world, noted by Josephus, Pliny, church historians, and many Arabic writers. Some biblical commentators have surmised that Jesus cured the sick here. There's a local legend that Solomon entered into a conspiracy with demons to heal his kingdom's ailing people at this site, tricking them into perpetually stoking the fires in the earth below to heat up the water.

Several treatments are available, including the mineral bubble bath, physiotherapy, therapeutic massage, inhalation, mud baths, and so on. *Note:* Bring your own bathing suit and towel! There's an inexpensive restaurant on the premises.

To gain a better understanding of the waters, check out the **Lehman Museum** next to the springs. While visiting the springs, you can plan to spend some time exploring the ancient ruins of Hammat. See also "Hammat Gader" in the next section.

Hammat Tiberias National Park. ☎ 06/672-5287. Admission NIS 8 ($2.20). Daily 8am–4pm; Apr–Sept 8am–5pm. Egged bus: 2 or 5.

Hammat Tiberias (or Hammat), a spa and city 2 miles south of Tiberias, existed well before the founding of Tiberias in the 1st century A.D. Hammat and Tiberias existed side by side for hundreds of years as "twin cities." In Roman and Byzantine times, Hammat developed into a spa resort visited by travelers from all over the known world. The ruins of Hammat are now a national park.

Hammat contains the ruins of one of Israel's most magnificent ancient synagogues, as befits a town that would have hosted wealthy visitors from distant Jewish communities. Most spectacular is the synagogue's well-preserved **mosaic calendar floor** (4th century A.D.) that depicts the zodiac cycle and, in its outer corners, four women representing the seasons of the year. At the center of the zodiac, the sun god Helios rides on a chariot through the heavens; beyond the zodiac, a separate mosaic panel depicts traditional Jewish symbols, including the Ark of the Covenant flanked by two ceremonial menorahs. The famous naive zodiac floor of the Bet Alpha synagogue (which served a Byzantine-era farming village in the Jordan Valley) may have drawn on this very sophisticated mosaic for inspiration.

Entrance to the ruins is through the **Ernest Lehman Museum,** which inventories information on regional history and the curative powers of the hot springs. Beware that the open water flowing through the ruins comes directly from the hot springs and will scald you should you decide to do something foolish, like test it with your toe! Up the hill from the baths is the **Tomb of Rabbi Meir Baal Haness,** a disciple of Rabbi Akiva, and one of the great sages who helped to compile the Mishnah in the 2nd century A.D.

3 The Sea of Galilee

The Arabic and Aramaic poets called it the Bride, the Handmaiden of the Hills, and the Silver Woman. The ancient Hebrews called it the Harp in honor of the soothing harplike sounds of its waves, and because it roughly resembles the shape of an ancient harp. Today, Israelis still call the Sea of Galilee "harp"—in Hebrew *Kinnor,* or *Kinneret,* as it is popularly known. According to one lexicographer, an ancient sage has written: "God created the seven seas, but the Kinneret is His pride and joy."

Some 700 feet below sea level, the Sea of Galilee is 13 miles long, from the place where the Jordan flows in at the north to where it empties out in the south.

It was here that Jesus preached to the crowds and fed them by multiplying the bread and fishes; it is also where he restored the sick and maimed. Today, parts of the sea are filled with speedboats and water-skiers; other parts are as tranquil and mysterious as in ancient times.

Kinneret's waters are a vast reservoir of sardine, mullet, catfish, and the unusual combfish. They are the same fish once caught by the disciples, and they are caught in the same manner today, though some of the kibbutzim have developed careful methods of farming fish.

ESSENTIALS

GETTING THERE   A number of bus routes circumnavigate the late—check with the Tourist Information Office for current route and schedules. In summer, there is boat service from Lido Beach to Capernaum.

If you'd like to cruise up to the Christian sites on the northwest shore of the lake, **Lido Sailing Company** (☎ 06/672-1538) often operates an 11:45am cruise along the lake; you can also sometimes join one of their charter groups for a ride to Capernaum. Bicycles are free. The **Kinneret Sailing Company** (☎ 06/665-8007) leaves Tiberias for Ein Gev on the eastern shore of the lake at 10:30am, with returns at 12:15 and 1:15pm. Fare is NIS 22 ($5) one way; NIS 36 ($8) round-trip and bikes are free.

TOURING THE AREA

To tour the Sea of Galilee, we'll head north, starting a circle that will bring us back to Tiberias before heading into the Upper Galilee region. As of this writing there is no regular bus route that completely circles the lake, so you'll have to depend on a tour bus, rental car, bicycle, or boat.

MAGDALA & MIGDAL

Two miles north of Tiberias along the lakeside road, you'll come to the old village of Magdala, the birthplace of Mary Magdalene. There's not much to see, except for lovely scenery. The town was right down by the water's edge. On the hill just to the south of old Magdala, along the far (west) side of the highway, you can still see the sarcophagi (stone coffins) carved out of the rocks, in the place that was Magdala's cemetery. The modern town of Migdal, founded in this century, is about 1 mile to the north of the site of ancient Magdala.

THE GINOSSAR VALLEY

A little farther on, about 10 kilometers (6 mi.) north of Tiberias, you'll find yourself in a lush valley with many banana trees. These are part of the agriculture of **Kibbutz Nof Ginossar,** and the valley is the Ginossar Valley. In the kibbutz, you'll find the multimedia **Yigal Alon Museum of the Galilee** (☎ 06/672-2905), more a learning experience than a museum, offers only one genuine antiquity, a Galilee fishing boat, from approximately the 1st century A.D., preserved in the muddy sediment of the lake floor and revealed in the 1980s when, because of drought, the lake receded to record low levels. The boat is touted by some guides as "the Jesus boat." Although it may be typical of fishing boats on the lake from approximately the time of Jesus, there is, of course, no evidence that ties it to any specific persons. The wooden frame of the boat is preserved in a climate-controlled boathouse structure. The museum is open Sunday to Thursday 8am to 5pm and Friday from 8am to 1pm, and on Saturday from 9am to 5pm; admission to the museum and boat is NIS 20 ($4.40); to the boat only (of special interest to pilgrimage groups) NIS 12 ($2.65).

TABGHA
14 kilometers (8 mi.) north of Tiberias.

To reach Tabgha, where Jesus miraculously multiplied the loaves and fishes, proceed northward along the shoreline from Migdal, passing Minya, a 7th-century Arabian palace that is one of the most ancient and holy Muslim prayer sites. It's open daily from 8am to 4pm.

At Tabgha, you'll find the beautifully restored **Benedictine monastery** and the **Church of the Multiplication of the Loaves and Fishes** (☎ 06/672-1061). When the ancient church ruins, hidden for 1,300 years, were excavated, the mosaic basilica floor of a Byzantine-era church that once stood on this site was discovered. The floor is one of the most lyrical and skillfully made ever discovered in Israel. The section of the floor in front of the ancient altar is starkly unadorned and interesting mainly for what it depicts: two fish and a humble basket filled with loaves of bread. The main section of mosaic is a colorful tapestry of all the birds that once thrived in this area: swans, cranes, ducks, wild geese, and storks. The mosaic artist has captured the liveliness, humor, and grace of these creatures with a style rarely seen in this art form. The Nilometer, used to measure the flood levels of the Nile and famous throughout the ancient world, is also represented, leading some to speculate that the talented mosaic designer might have been Egyptian.

Be sure to read the history of this church posted just inside the entrance, in the church's courtyard. The early Judeo-Christians of nearby Capernaum (Kefar Nahum) venerated a large rock, upon which Jesus is said to have placed the bread and fish when he fed the 5,000. The rock, a natural **dolmen,** is believed by historians to have been a sacred place since prehistoric times, and was used as the altar in a Byzantine church erected over the spot in about A.D. 350.

The church is open Monday to Saturday from 8:30am to 5pm and Sun 10am to 5pm; modest dress is required. Admission is free, but donations are accepted. There's also a good bookstore and souvenir shop on the premises.

Just east of the Multiplication Church is the **Heptapegon** ("Seven Springs" in Greek), also called the Church of the Primacy of Saint Peter, or Mensa Christi. To reach it, you must leave the Multiplication Church, return to the highway, turn right, and climb the hill to a separate entrance. This Greek Orthodox church is open daily from 8:30am to 1pm and 2 to 5pm; modest dress is required, and admission is free.

It was here on the shores of Galilee that Jesus is believed to have appeared to his disciples after his crucifixion and resurrection. Peter and the others were in a boat on the lake, fishing, but with no luck. When Jesus appeared, he told them to cast their nets again. They did, and couldn't haul in the nets because they were so full of fish. As the disciples sat with their master having dinner, Jesus is said to have conferred the leadership of the movement on Peter, as first among the disciples. The theory of Peter's primacy, and the tradition of that primacy's being passed from one generation of disciples to the next, is the basis for the legitimacy of the Roman pontiff as leader of Christendom.

The black basalt church rests on the foundations of earlier churches. Within is a flat rock called **Mensa Christi,** or "Christ's Table," where Jesus dined that evening with his disciples. Outside the church, you can still see the stone steps said to be the place where Jesus stood when he appeared, calling out to the disciples; on the beach are seven large stones, which may once have supported a little fishing wharf. If it's not too hot, you can easily walk to nearby Capernaum (3km/2 mi.) and even to the Mount of Beatitudes.

MOUNT OF THE BEATITUDES

8 kilometers (5 mi.) north of Ginossar; 3 kilometers (2 mi.) north of Capernaum.

Just beyond Tabgha, on a high hill, is the famous Mount of the Beatitudes, now the site of an Italian convent. Here Jesus preached the Sermon on the Mount. There are many good views of the Sea of Galilee and its surroundings, but the vista from here is among the most magnificent. One odd fact about this church is the inscription on the sanctuary, which informs you that the entire project was built by Mussolini in 1937. The church is open daily from 8:30am to noon and 2:30 to 5pm. Admission is free. Take bus no. 459, 541, or 963 from Tiberias. Ask the driver to let you off at the closest stop, which is 1 kilometer (½ mi.) from the church.

CAPERNAUM (KEFAR NAHUM)

This site marks the prosperous lakeside town where Jesus preached, and his disciples, Peter and Andrew, made their homes. Today, you'll find a modern Franciscan monastery, which was built on the abandoned site in 1894, as well as ancient excavations spanning 6 centuries. Among the most impressive are the ruins of a 3rd- or 4th-century synagogue built on the site of an even earlier synagogue. Nearby are several houses of the period and a 5th-century octagonal church built over the ruins of the traditional site of Saint Peter's house. Byzantine architects frequently built domed octagonal structures over places of special veneration (the octagonal Dome of the Rock in Jerusalem, built by early Muslim rulers in A.D. 691, but designed by Byzantine architects, is an example of this type of structure). Other finds include an ancient olive press, and a 2nd-century marble milestone on the Via Maris (Coastal Road), the Roman route that stretched from Egypt to Lebanon (an inland extension to the Via Maris passed through this district).

Capernaum was the home of perhaps four of Jesus' other original followers; it was the place where Jesus began to gather his disciples around him, saying, "Follow me, and I will make you fishers of men."

Capernaum's splendid synagogue was built of imported white limestone rather than native black basalt. The ruins include tall columns, marble steps, shattered statuary, a doorway facing south to Jerusalem, and many ancient symbols: carved seven-branched menorahs, stars of David, palm branches, and rams' horns. It's not the actual synagogue in which Jesus taught, since it dates from around the 3rd or 4th century A.D., but it may stand on the same site. It is interesting to speculate on what the proximity of Saint Peter's house to the synagogue might tell us about the position of his family in the community. The excavations of basalt stone in the garden lead toward the sea, where you can still glimpse the remains of a small-boat basin with steps leading to the water. Admission is NIS 4 (90¢); the site is open daily from 8:30am to 4:15pm.

Where to Dine

Caper Naum Restaurant. Near Kfar Nahum. ☎ **06/672-4805.** Reservations recommended. Complete meals NIS 64–73 ($14–$16); Add 15% service. AE, DC, MC, V. Daily 9am–8pm. MIDDLE EASTERN.

Virtually the only place to eat on the northern shore of the Sea of Galilee, this restaurant caters to pilgrim bus groups that visit the nearby Christian sites at Tabgha and at Capernaum. If you're an independent traveler exploring this corner of the shoreline, the restaurant can provide a convenient breaking point between the area's churches and ruins, especially if you arrive during a lull in the bus arrivals. You can stop by just for a light meal of hummus and salads, or a soup, or you can have the house special meal of Saint Peter's fish, salad bar, and dessert. Though a mass production place, the fish is tasty and the location is superb.

KORAZIM

Four kilometers (6 mi.) north of the lake, on a rise of land, are the ruins of ✪ Korazim (Chorazin), a flourishing Jewish town in Roman times. According to the New Testament, Korazim was one of the towns chastised by Jesus. A large 2nd- or 3rd-century synagogue of black basalt has been excavated, as well as streets, houses, and ritual baths attached to the synagogue, which was apparently destroyed either by earthquake or during civil unrest in the 4th century. This is a hauntingly evocative site, with finely carved stonework ornamenting the ruins of the synagogue, and sweeping views of the lake. The national park office here (☎ 06/993-4982) is open from 5am to 4pm; in summer to 5pm. Admission to the site is NIS 16 ($3.50).

At the Korazim-Almagor crossroad between Tiberias and Rosh Pinna is the beautiful guest farm and dude ranch, Vered Ha-Galil Guest Farm, Restaurant, and Horseback Riding Facility (see "Where to Stay Around the Sea of Galilee," below).

LUNA GAL WATER AMUSEMENT PARK

Coming around the northern end of the lake, you reach a junction from which Highway 87 heads into the Golan Heights to its new capital, the town of Qasrin (see "The Golan Heights"). Where the Jordan River enters the lake, we come to Luna Gal (☎ 06/673-1750), on the eastern shore, one of the largest water parks in Israel. It offers a variety of activities including waterskiing, pedal boats, kayak tours of the Jordan River, sailboarding, water parachuting, and more. There is a substantial entrance fee of NIS 45 ($10), but it's worth it, especially for kids. Luna Gal is open Saturday through Thursday from 9:30am to midnight, Friday 9:30am to 5pm, April to October. From Tiberias, you can take bus no. 22.

KURSI

17 kilometers (10.5 mi.) from Tiberias; 7 kilometers (4.5 mi.) north of Ein Gev.

Kursi is on the eastern shore; according to the Gospels, it is the "country of the Gergesenes" (or Gadarenes), where Jesus cast the demons out of a man who was possessed and into a herd of swine, which then plunged into the lake and drowned.

For many years, speculation existed about the location of Kursi (also called Gergasa) and its church, but after the Six-Day War, a bulldozer clearing the way for a new road happened to uncover the ruins of a Byzantine church complex, complete with a monastery (perhaps the largest ever built in the Holy Land), dating from the 5th to 7th centuries. The monastery probably contained hostel facilities for the thousands of pilgrims who came to the Galilee during Byzantine times. Most remarkable among the discoveries was the underground crypt where more than 30 skeletons were found, all of middle-aged men, except for one child. The national park at Kursi (☎ 06/673-1983) is open daily from 8am to 4pm (till 5pm in summer); admission is NIS 12 ($2.60).

EIN GEV

12 kilometers (7.5 mi.) north of Tzemach Junction; 7 kilometers (4.5 mi.) south of Kursi.

About two-thirds of the way south along the lake's eastern shore brings you to **Kibbutz Ein Gev,** one of the loveliest places in Israel. You can stop by and take a free minitrain tour of the kibbutz (ask at the office next to the Ein Gev restaurant). Nestled between the hills of Golan and the lakefront, Ein Gev was founded in 1937 by German, Austrian, and Czechoslovakian refugees. (It was Jerusalem mayor Teddy Kollek's kibbutz.) These days Ein Gev has a 5,000-seat auditorium, which has presented some of the world's greatest musicians at its annual music festival. On the hillsides are tiers of vineyards, and elsewhere on the grounds are a banana plantation and date groves. Fishing is another big industry here; Ein Gev contains the country's largest restaurant, serving Saint Peter's fish straight from the Sea of Galilee. The

Central & Southern Galilee

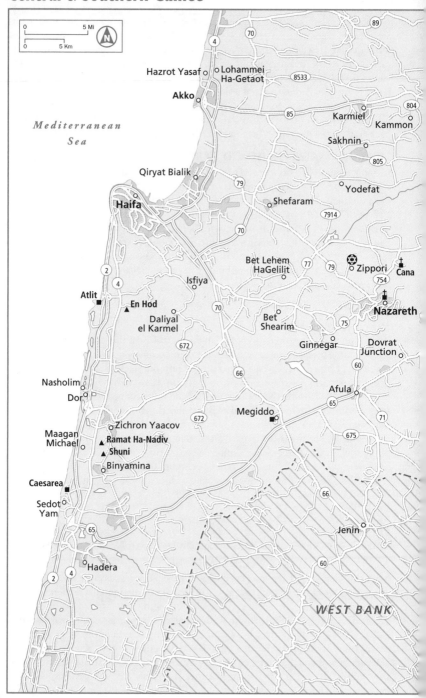

0   5 Mi
0   5 Km

N

Mediterranean Sea

Hazrot Yasaf
Lohammei Ha-Getaot
Akko
89
70
4
8533

Karmiel
804
Kammon
85
Sakhnin
805

Haifa
Qiryat Bialik
79
Shefaram
Yodefat
7914
70

Bet Lehem HaGelilit
77
79
Zippori
Cana
754

Isfiya
En Hod
Atlit
2
4
70
Daliyal el Karmel
Bet Shearim
Nazareth
75
672

Ginnegar
Dovrat Junction
60

Nasholim
Dor
66

Caesarea
Zichron Yaacov
Ramat Ha-Nadiv
Shuni
Binyamina
672
Megiddo
Afula
65
71
675

Sedot Yam
65
66

Jenin
60

Hadera
2
4

WEST BANK

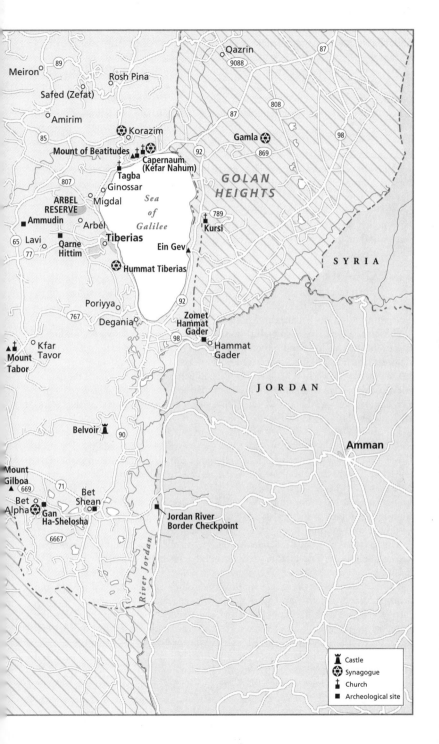

kibbutz also offers accommodations at Ein Gev Resort Village (see "Where to Stay Around the Sea of Galilee," below).

Not far from the auditorium, in a garden, is a bronze statue by the Israeli sculptress, Hanna Orloff, depicting a woman holding a child aloft, in memory of a young mother-to-be from the kibbutz who was killed in the 1948 battle for Ein Gev. This settlement bore the brunt of heavy attacks in the 1948 war, and its position at the foot of the Golan Heights, below heavy Syrian military emplacements, made it a perennial target. From 1949 to 1967, Ein Gev kibbutz members depended on an endless maze of slit trenches throughout the grounds, as well as concrete underground shelters.

It's easy to get to Ein Gev from Tiberias, by bus no. 22, or ferry. Farther south along the lake is a campsite, at **Kibbutz Ha-On** with its ostrich farm and moderately priced Holiday Village and Bed & Breakfast accommodations; continue south along the shoreline and you'll come to **Ma'agan,** with its **Holiday Village.** Ma'agan is very near the junction for the road to the hot-spring resort of Hammat Gader. (Ask at the tourism information office in Tiberias or at the Tzemach Junction for information on other campsites around the lake and in the vicinity.)

HAMMAT GADER

The **hot springs of Hammat Gader** (☎ 06/675-1039), east of the southern tip of the Sea of Galilee, are a favorite Israeli spa and vacation spot. Nestled in the valley of the Yarmuk River, this dramatic site has been occupied for almost 4,500 years.

The springs can be reached by bus from Tiberias. Bus schedules vary according to season, so check with the bus station for a morning departure and afternoon returns. Hammat Gader is 22 kilometers (14 mi.) southeast of Tiberias. If you're driving, it's 8¹/₂ kilometers (about 5 mi.) east of the junction with Route 92 that skirts the eastern side of the lake. As you wind down the steep road into the Yarmuk Valley, you'll pass several sentry and guard posts. The steep hillside on the other side of the valley is Jordan; you are also close to the Syrian border.

The Roman city here was first constructed in the 3rd century A.D., restored and beautified in the 7th century, and destroyed by an earthquake around 900. The ruins of the Roman spa city are extensive and significant, and several important parts (the baths, the theater) have been excavated and beautifully restored. The still-apparent elegance of the Oval Hall, the Hall of Fountains, and the Hall of Pillars in the Spring Area point to the magnificence of this rustic resort in ancient times. Don't miss the wonderful lions of the mosaic synagogue floor (5th century A.D.). The ruins are set up as a **self-guiding tour** (ask the park office about guided tours of the park).

The spa was known as El-Hamma to the Arabs and Turks, and the site is dominated by the minaret of a mosque that has fallen into disuse and been disfigured by graffiti.

There are swimming pools, hot sulfur springs, and baths for medical therapy and beauty treatments; there is an alligator farm in a jungle setting with elevated walkways. For the kids, the park has trampolines and water slides. You will also find showers, changing rooms, a bar, and a restaurant. Admission Sunday to Friday costs NIS 50 ($11); on Saturday and holidays, it is NIS 60 ($13); NIS 45 ($7) after 6pm. Bring your own towel and bathing suit. Sit in the far end of the warm-water pool and feel the mineral water crash down onto your back from the waterfall. Residents of the area as well as visitors come in droves, often bringing picnics; hence the evening (after work) hours. The many clay oil lamps found here may indicate the ancient inhabitants of the area also enjoyed night bathing. You'll find Hammat Gader's pools open Monday to Saturday 8am to 10:30pm; Sunday 8am to 4:30pm. Antiquities and children's activities close at 5pm. As if the ruins and hot springs were not

The Grand Old Man of the Lake

Ein Gev's patriarch fisherman, **Mendl Nun,** an expert on Lake Kinneret's nature, archaeology, and fishing traditions, has recently founded the **Anchor Museum,** a museum of the lake's nautical history, at Ein Gev. Those interested in the ethereal Sea of Galilee, both in modern and ancient times, should pick up his book, *The Sea of Galilee and Its Fisherman in New Testament Times.* Mr. Nun's writing is filled with real feeling for the place he has made his home for more than half a century. This and his other books about the Sea of Galilee are available at Kibbutz Ein Gev's gift shop beside the Ein Gev Restaurant in Kibbutz Ein Gev.

enough, an alligator farm and a Thai restaurant housed in a Thai-style building have been set up on the premises (if you dine at the restaurant, your admission to Hammat Gader is free). In 1993, there were rumors that alligators, either accidentally or through a deliberate act of sabotage, had escaped into the Sea of Galilee; no sightings or hunting parties led to anything more concrete than the Loch Ness monster.

KIBBUTZ DEGANIA

Located at the very southern tip of the Sea of Galilee, Degania is the country's very first kibbutz, founded in 1909 by Russian pioneers. Without any real experience in farming, this handful of self-made peasants left city jobs to fight malarial swamps and Arab bands. Much of the philosophical basis of kibbutz life was first formulated in this Jordan Valley settlement by its leader, A. D. Gordon. Gordon believed that a return to the soil and the honesty of manual work were the necessary ingredients for creating a new spirit in people. Although never a member of the kibbutz, he farmed until his death at age 74. On Degania's grounds a natural history museum, **Bet Gordon** (☎ 06/675-0040), contains a library and exhibition of the area's archaeology, flora, and fauna.

Degania grew so quickly that its citizens soon branched out to other settlements. The father of Moshe Dayan, the famous commander with the eye patch of the Sinai Campaign, left Degania to help establish Nahalal, Israel's largest *moshav* (cooperative settlement). Eventually, some of the Degania members split with the original Degania over political and philosophical issues and established their own kibbutz right next door, and called it simply Degania B. The older Degania is now called Degania A.

Outside the entrance to Degania, there's a small tank—a reminder of the battle the inhabitants of Degania waged against Syrian tanks in 1948 (the members fought them off with Molotov cocktails). Today, both Degania A and B are thriving.

HOF ZEMACH WATER AMUSEMENT PARK

Near Kibbutz Degania, there's another water amusement park called Hof Zemach (☎ 06/675-2440). The carnival atmosphere includes a beach, sunbathing areas, grassy picnic grounds, a buffet, and water-sports equipment rentals. Like Luna Gal, Hof Zemach is open only in season; check with the tourism office in Tiberias for current information.

RIVER JORDAN BAPTISMAL SPOT

Kibbutz Kinneret, just west of Degania, has established a spot where Christian pilgrims can immerse themselves in the waters of Jordan in safety and tranquillity. The

Baptismal Spot, called **Yardenit** (☎ **06/675-9111**), is 200 yards west of the lakeshore highway (follow the signs). The river seems to flow peacefully, but its currents can be dangerous, so no swimming is allowed. The area set aside for baptisms is sheltered and there are guide railings leading into the water. Snack and souvenir stands provide refreshment and sustenance (no charge for the baptismal dip). A special lift has been installed to enable visitors with disabilities to enter the water with a minimum amount of difficulty. It's open Saturday to Thursday 8am to 6pm; Friday 8am to 5pm; the last baptismal is one hour before closing.

WHERE TO STAY AROUND THE SEA OF GALILEE

✪ **Ein Gev Resort Village.** Kibbutz En Gev, Galilee. ☎ **06/665-9800.** Fax 06/665-9818. 184 units. A/C. $100–$120 double. 50% higher on weekends (Fri and Sat), Jewish holidays and July 15–Aug 31. Rates include breakfast. Discounts available on Kibbutz 7-Day Package. MC, V. The Village is 1 mi. south of Ein Gev Kibbutz.

Staying at this beautiful, historic kibbutz, founded in the 1930s (former Jerusalem Mayor Teddy Kollek and his wife were among Kibbutz Ein Gev's first members) is a special pleasure. Both the kibbutz itself and the guest facilities are so paradisical that it's hard to believe this was a barren, stony stretch of shoreline only 60 years ago.

Partly set in a date palm grove and a eucalyptus grove beside the lake, the Holiday Village offers basic, modern family or group accommodations in five-person bunga-lows that include a bedroom-kitchenette with dining nook and a small bunk-bed room off the main room. There are also standard double rooms in motel-style build-ings overlooking the lake but a bit away from the beach; these are also equipped with small kitchenettes. During 1997–98, a less-expensive part of the holiday village was demolished, and more double units were planned for construction during 2000. There is a minimarket for groceries; Kibbutz Ein Gev, down the road, has an excellent lake-side fish restaurant (see section 2 under "Country Dining Around the Sea of Galilee," above) with free transportation and discounts for Holiday Village guests. The Ein Gev Resort Village beach is the loveliest setting on the lake, but there are few special activ-ities for children. Off-season or midweek, see if it's possible to get a four-person bun-galow for the price of a double: the bungalows are in the area right beside the beach, under the date palms.

Kibbutz Lavi Hotel. Kibbutz Lavi, Lower Galilee Post 15267. ☎ **06/679-9450.** Fax 06/679-9399. 124 units. A/C TV TEL. $90–$140 double. Add 70% Jewish holidays and 50% July 15–Aug 31. Rates include breakfast. MC, V.

This beautifully gardened religious kibbutz offers a heated indoor swimming pool and comfortable accommodations plus lectures on kibbutz life. There is a synagogue on the kibbutz. Buses travel to Lavi direct from Tiberias, and the ride takes only 15 min-utes. There is a minimum weekend rate of one full board plus one half board, and holy-day prices are considerably higher. Meal facilities are glatt kosher. Discounts under Kibbutz Hotel Chain 7-Day Plan.

Kibbutz Ma'agan Holiday Village. Kibbutz Ma'agan, Sea of Galilee. ☎ **06/665-4400.** Fax 06/665-4455. E-mail: maaganhv@netvision.net.il. 148 units. A/C TV TEL. $100–$150 dou-ble; $160–$220 suite. Add 30% weekends, July 15–Sept 1, and Jewish holidays add $30 for double; $50 for suite. Rates include breakfast. Discounts available on Kibbutz 7-Day Package. AE, V.

Located on the southeastern shore of the Sea of Galilee, with a guarded beach and vis-tas, across the lake, Ma'agan sports 36 double rooms completed in 1999 (ask for these) as well as recently built minisuite units, arranged in subtle tiers so that each suite has a water view. The suites contain a living room/kitchenette with a couch that converts into a bed, and a separate bedroom in most units; many guests here do their own cooking. This holiday village is geared toward families, with a new outdoor swimming pool, children's pool, and a children's playground. There is a minimarket on the property; all rooms have refrigerators. Discounts available on Kibbutz 7-Day Package.

Kibbutz Nof Ginossar Hotel. Kibbutz Ginossar 14980. ☎ **06/670-0300**. Fax 06/679-2170. E-mail: ginosar@netvision.net.co. 170 units. A/C TV TEL. $130–$160 double. 15% above high rate for Jewish holidays. Rates include breakfast. MC, V.

This beautiful but rather expensive kibbutz hotel is on the kibbutz nearest to Tiberias—only a 10-minute ride from downtown. There is regular bus service, but it's a better choice for someone with a rented car. The kibbutz is next to the lake and offers very comfortable rooms; it has its own museum, outdoor swimming pool, beach, tennis court, gardens, and beach, with kayaks, sailboards, sailboats, and fishing poles for rent. The second-floor dining room (kosher) has a view of the Sea of Galilee. The guesthouse conducts a regular series of kibbutz tours and lectures with slides of kibbutz life. The **Yigal Alon Museum of the Galilee,** a media and educational exhibit, is on the grounds of the kibbutz, as is the 2,000-year-old Galilee fishing boat uncovered during a drought in the 1980s. Discounts are available on the Kibbutz Hotel Chain 7-Day Plan.

Poria Taiber Youth Hostel. P.O. Box 232, Tiberias. ☎ **06/675-0050.** Fax 06/675-1621. 140 beds. A/C. $17 IYHA member; $18.50 nonmember; $23 per person double. Rates include breakfast. No credit cards.

Located at Poria, in the hills overlooking the Sea of Galilee 4 kilometers (2.5 mi.) to the south of Tiberias, this rustic, small hostel in a beautiful setting can arrange for family rooms, kitchen facilities, clean sheets, and hot water, and is open all day long. Because it is so high above the lake, it's a bit cooler on summer nights than Tiberias itself, which is below sea level. This is a delightful inexpensive base for travelers with cars; there is no public bus, and it's often reserved for large groups who come with their own bus. Call for current information.

✪ Vered Ha-Galil Guest Farm, Restaurant, and Horseback Riding Facility. ☎ **06/693-5785.** Fax 06/693-4964. www.veredhagalil.co.il. E-mail: vered@veredhagalil.co.il. 18 units (all with bathrooms); 2 bunkhouse units with shared bathrooms. A/C TEL. Sun–Wed $110–$140 double; Thurs–Sat $130–$170; bunkhouse units $65–$75. Rates include breakfast and service charge. Jewish holidays supplement. AE, MC, V. Directions: 3$\frac{1}{2}$ km (2$\frac{1}{4}$ mi.) past the turnoff to the Mount of Beatitudes; the ranch is at the Korazim-Almagor crossroad.

This very personal place is the creation of Yehuda Avni, originally from Chicago (who immigrated to Israel in the late 1940s) and his Israeli-born wife, Yonah, who created a paradisiacal enclave with gardens, a pool, buildings that fit in with nature where there had once only been acres of impassable thistles. Now their children and grandchildren, as well as a carefully chosen young staff, contribute to the attentive but informal spirit of Vered Ha-Galil. The Guest Farm and its facilities are ideal for those who want to ride and to intimately explore the Galilee countryside. It is also a beautiful retreat and a fine base for travelers who want to explore the region by car. A well-informed tour desk will advise you about all kinds of special places in the area.

There are four kinds of accommodations: two simple bunkhouse rooms, each sharing bathroom facilities and available for from two to six people; rustic, 1960s northern California–style one-room cabins, each with private bathroom, double beds, and shaded porches overlooking the countryside; studio suites, with roomy living areas, kitchenettes, private bathrooms, and terraces; and a country apartment with cathedral ceilings, 1$\frac{1}{2}$ bathrooms, a spacious living room, separate bedroom, and private garden. A family or group of four or five can easily share these accommodations.

Backpackers are welcome to sleep on the lawn or in the barn for free, so long as they pick up their litter. Vered Ha-Galil will make special efforts to adapt to the needs of visitors with disabilities, in both accommodations and riding.

Yehuda Avni has designed trail rides by the hour, day, or week, into the hills or down toward the Sea of Galilee. Other planned tours last several days, exploring places such as Nazareth, and combining Arab meals with camping or hotel overnights to Gilboa, Mount Tabor, around the Sea of Galilee, and into the Golan Heights.

Riding lessons begin at $20 for a half hour. Horseback rides cost $25 for an hour, $42 for 2 hours, $80 for half a day on the trail, $150 for an entire day with lunch, and $190 for an overnight "Bonanza." There are also 2- to 5-day all-inclusive trips. All rides are accompanied by guides. There is a 10% discount for overnight guests at Vered Ha-Galil and if guests pay for riding in foreign currency as part of their hotel bill, the 17% VAT is also deducted.

In addition to the stables, Vered Ha-Galil has an outdoor swimming pool, rooms for changing and showers, an outdoor grill, picnic tables, a restaurant (see below), and a bar and grill, ping pong tables and a regulation horseshoe playing yard. There is a 10% discount for stays of 2 or more nights.

ROSH PINA

This small town, 26 kilometers (42 mi.) from Tiberias up the winding road to Safed, was founded by Jewish pioneers in 1882 as a cooperative farming settlement. The name "Rosh Pina" means "cornerstone," and indeed this settlement, the first new Jewish community to be founded in the Galilee in modern times became the cornerstone for Jewish resettlement of the region. A smattering of original 19th century cottages give this sleepy community a bit of architectural charm. A number of spots in the upper town, such as Auberge Shulamit, offer fine vistas, and the town itself is a crossroad on the routes between Safad, Tiberias, the Hula Valley and the extreme upper Galilee. It offers some of the best dining spots in the area.

WHERE TO STAY
Expensive
Auberge Shulamit. David Shuv Rd., Rosh Pina. ☎ **06/693-1485** or 06/693-1494. Fax 06/693-1495. 4 units. TV TEL. $140–$170 double. Rates include breakfast. AE, DC, MC, V.

In the style of a French country restaurant with a few rooms for overnight guests, the Auberge Shulamit offers a romantic overnight hideaway for travelers, be they from Tel Aviv or Toronto. You can have a long evening of wine and fine food without worry about driving home on the dark, hairpin-turn roads of the area. Guest rooms are country cottage in style, with four-poster beds, satin sheets, and down comforters; one room priced at $170 has an indoor Jacuzzi.

Mitzpe Hayamim Health Farm. Rosh Pina-Safed Rd., between Rosh Pina and Safed. ☎ **06/699-9666**. Fax 06/699-9555. E-mail: Sea_View@actom.co.il 82 units. A/C TV TEL. $200–$220 double; add $60 Thurs–Fri. Rates include breakfast. Add $48 per person for full board. Jewish holidays add $30 per room. MC, V.

The name of this health resort means "view of the seas," and from here you can see the Kinneret, and, on a clear day, the Mediterranean. This is not a place to lay your head after a hard day of touring the Galilee. Instead, it is a peaceful environment in which you pamper yourself with programs of Chinese, Thai, Indian, and Shiatsu message, aromatherapy, herbal baths, health and weight-loss programs, manicures, and pedicures. Vegetarian buffet meals are delicious, featuring with organically grown vegetables from Mitspe Yamim's own gardens; fish and local cheeses and yogurt are also served. Rooms are simple but comfortable and there is a heated indoor swimming pool as well as a small Jacuzzi open until the wee hours. Treatment programs vary in price; the clientele comes in all shapes and ages.

WHERE TO DINE
Expensive
✪ **Auberge Shulamit.** David Shuv Rd. ☎ **06/693-1485.** Reservations necessary. Main courses NIS 22-50 ($11–$22). AE, DC, MC, V. Daily 12:30pm–midnight. FRENCH.

With wonderful views, this restaurant occupies the upper floor of a building that had been a country inn during the 1930s and '40s. The view eastward toward the Sea of Galilee and the Golan Heights is so good that the inn was used as the monitoring center for the Israeli-Syrian Cease Fire Commission from 1948 to 1967 (since 1967, the Israelis have occupied the Golan Heights). The menu here is excellent, with chef Gadi Berkuz's famous smoked goose breast and spare ribs at the top of a list of smoked meats that includes trout, fillet of salmon, and Cornish game hen; beyond the smoked meat list, you might try filet mignon flambée served with a generous slice of foie gras. In autumn and winter, look for an incredible Turkish chestnut soup or hot Russian borscht. Other first courses include grilled portobello mushrooms with a special barbecue sauce; and a very rich Hungarian goose liver or confit of goose liver on a bed of fried apples and onions. There is a full wine list and house wine is served by the glass or half-carafe. If you care to stay the night, there are adjacent rooms that by Israeli standards are quite romantic (see listing under "Where to Stay," above).

Inexpensive
Indigo. 30 Hachalutzim St. ☎ **06/693-5333** or 06/693-0598. Main courses NIS 38–65 ($8.40–$14.30); light meals NIS 22–35 ($5–$7.70); breakfast NIS 35 ($7.70). AE, DC, MC, V. Daily 9:30am–11pm. ECLECTIC.

A charming rustic place decorated with interesting crafts, the menu here features delicious homemade goat cheeses and breads, which are served with fresh vegetables in NIS 54 or 70 ($7 or $12) portions. You'll find other choices on the menu, like cheese fondues, and wine by the glass at NIS 18 ($4) or a selection of Yarden, Gamla, and Rothschild wines ranging from NIS 45 to 180 ($10 to $40) per bottle. Good hefty salads (the management is thinking of using organic vegetables), quiches, and fish dishes round out the menu. Breakfast on the front porch has a 1960s California hippie ambience.

BED & BREAKFAST CHOICES IN THE GALILEE
There is a good range of bed-and-breakfast establishments in the region, including accommodations in private homes and in moshav and kibbutz facilities that are somewhat less expensive than those in the official Kibbutz Hotel and Guest House Chain. Most tourist information offices in major cities (including those in Tiberias, Haifa, and Safed) now are equipped with computers that let you access the current lists of bed-and-breakfast facilities available throughout the Galilee. You can telephone for reservations ahead of time, or play things by ear when you arrive.

The **Kibbutz Country Lodging Bed and Breakfast** network rents simple but pleasant rooms in various kibbutzim throughout the Galilee. Rooms are a bit less fancy than in the Kibbutz Hotel Chain, but they're adequate, often in beautiful locations, and give you a closer look at kibbutz life than the more insulated Kibbutz Hotels. At some kibbutzim, the rooms are in special guest buildings; in others, you get an empty kibbutz member's room or apartment that has been especially set up for visitors. Rates are $60 to $70 for a double most of the year. In North America, you can book a 1-week or more itinerary of Kibbutz bed-and-breakfasts as well as a package with a rental car through the **Israel Tourism Center** (☎ **888/669-5700** in the U.S. and Canada, or 201/556-9669; e-mail: Israelhotels@worldnet.att.net). There is a NIS 160 ($35) booking fee. Ask for a brochure of the bed-and-breakfasts so that you can plan which kibbutzim you'd prefer. Once you get to Israel, you can book kibbutz bed-and-breakfast accommodations through the **Kibbutz Hotels Chain Office,** 90 Ben Yehuda St., Tel Aviv (☎ **03/524-6161;** fax 03/527-8088); however the American office is better equipped to deal with your questions about accommodations and itineraries.

Among some of the recommended private families offering guest facilities are: **Mary and Sasson Soffer,** Mitzpe Tal El, M.P. Osrat 25167, Israel (☎ **04/996-6060**; fax 04/996-2336), offering charming rooms and fabulous breakfasts in a contemporary Israeli dream house with wonderful vistas. The house has four guest rooms, two with private showers. It is located at Tal El, north of Highway 85 between Akko and Karmiel. Prices range from NIS 180 to 203 ($40 to $45) per person with facilities and discount for children; credit cards: American Express, Diner's Club, MasterCard, and Visa. **Buki and Rochelle Cohen,** M. P. Bikat Beit Ha Kerem 25129, Israel (☎ **04/980-2471;** fax 04/980-3690), have four pleasant rooms in Har Chalutz, a community founded by Americans from the Reform Jewish Movement. Located in the Tefen Mountain Range of north-central Galilee, with lavish breakfasts, a Jacuzzi, and balconies and pergolas overlooking gardens the rates are about NIS 180 to 225 ($40 to $50) per person; no children and no in-house smoking. Free travel advice and homemade cakes and cookies are also part of the experience here.

At the completely vegetarian **Moshav Amirim,** Amirim, M. P. Karmiel, 20115, Israel (☎ **06/698-9571** office), you can arrange for bed-and-breakfast with a number of moshav families. You might request lodging with **Bella Shuldebrand** or **Yael Goldman;** both offer rooms in their beautiful chalet-style homes with lovely vistas. All families in Amirim's B&B program can prepare superb meals for you with advance notice; there is also a wonderful vegetarian restaurant (**Dahlia's**) on the moshav. Bed-and-breakfast arrangements in private homes are not generally recommended for families traveling with children.

Another interesting choice is the **Bed-and-Breakfast in a Galilee Arab Village Program,** which you can arrange by calling **Ruthi Avidor** (☎ **04/980-0708**). Rates per person are in the NIS 135 to 180 ($30 to $40) range. This program offers a unique opportunity to meet members of the Galilee's large Arabic community, and to experience the traditional hospitality of an Israeli Arab home. Accommodations are either in a family house or in a nearby apartment, to which the hosts will bring breakfast. You can specify whether you would like accommodations in which you have more personal contact with your host family. Many families in this program do not speak English fluently, but things work out. Rooms are comfortable, clean, and usually filled with little personal touches that the women of the house have planned for their guests' comfort. Most guests in this program so far have been Jewish Israelis, but the host families look forward to having foreign guests, and hope that the visits will help create greater understanding. Roads in Israeli Arab towns are hard to follow; be certain your hosts make a map, and note the way back to the main road from your lodgings.

If you are interested in encountering the Israeli Arab community of the lower Galilee, for a meal or a guided tour, contact the **Ali Baba Cave** (☎ **06/674-3156** or 050/327-229), which offers homemade traditional meals, rural accommodation, and hospitality in Israeli Arab homes, and does tours and excursions around the beautiful Saknine countryside (Saknine is one of the largest Israeli Arab towns in the Galilee). **Shadi Country Style Accommodations** (☎ **06/674-3222** or 052/ 485-973; fax 06/674-1616) is run by the Chaliala family of Saknine, and comes with good recommendations from readers; rooms have air-conditioning and TV. Breakfasts are delicious, and guided tours, lectures, and workshops can be arranged.

Among Kibbutz Bed and Breakfasts (Country Lodgings) in the NIS 135 to 160 ($30 to $35) per person range, try **Kibbutz Amiad** (☎ **06/693-3829;** fax 06/693-5337) and **Kibbutz Kedarim** (☎ **06/698-6300**), both in the vicinity of Korazim, just northwest of the Sea of Galilee; **Kibbutz Snir** (☎ **06/695-2508** and **Kfar Szold** (☎ **06/690-7176**), both in the extreme Upper Galilee; and **Kibbutz Sasa** (☎ **06/698-8699**) and **Kibbutz Yiron** (☎ **06/698-8394;** fax 06/698-0888), both in the beautiful, wild northern countryside near the ancient Baram Synagogue.

Readers' comments on especially good or bad experiences at bed-and-breakfast establishments are welcome.

4 Safed (Zefat)

36 kilometers (24 mi.) NW of Tiberias; 74 kilometers (46 mi.) E of Haifa.

From Tiberias and the Sea of Galilee, our next destination is the ancient and mystical city of Safed (Zefat, Zfat, Tsfat, Tzfat), an hour due north of Tiberias and less than 2 hours due east of Nahariya. Once Israel's major mountain resort, Safed is now more religiously oriented.

Skirting the Yermak mountain range (3,000 ft.), you finally climb up into Safed (pronounced with one syllable, *Tsfaht,* in Hebrew), which, at 2,790 feet, is Israel's highest town. This quiet city is built on three slopes and looks down onto a beautiful panorama of villages and tiered hillsides. Safed's name comes from a Hebrew root word, *tsafeh,* meaning to scan, or look—in other words, a lookout.

Safed's history began in A.D. 66, during the time of the Second Temple, when Flavius Josephus started building atop the Citadel mountaintop. In 1140, the crusaders built a fortress on this peak, the ruins of which can be seen today.

During the 16th century the Ottoman Turks chose Safed for the provincial capital, and it became the primary government, economic, and spiritual center for the entire Galilee region. It was during this period that the Sephardic Jews from Spain came here. Having escaped the horrors of Spain under the Inquisition, these Jewish intellectuals launched into a complex and mystical interpretation of the Hebrew scriptures called Cabala (Cabbalah, Kabala, Kabbalah). The town became a great center of learning, with a score of synagogues and religious schools. The first printing press in the East was introduced during this period of intellectual mysticism, and in 1578 the first Hebrew book—a commentary on the scroll of Esther—was printed. During this Golden Age of Safed, Ashkenazi Jews were also attracted to Safed, and the entire community and its rabbinical scholars became renowned and revered throughout the Jewish world. The Jewish community numbered about 10,000, but by the 18th century, Safed was in serious decline.

In 1837, the entire town was leveled by a powerful earthquake after which both the Jewish and Muslim communities of Safed struggled on in increasing poverty. The wave of anti-Jewish rioting that swept British Mandate Palestine in 1929 was particularly severe in Safed, where the Jewish population was mainly elderly and religious. During the 1948 war, control of the strategic heights of Safed was crucial to control of the Galilee. Although outnumbered, Israeli forces held the town, and the large Arab population of Safed fled. Since then, the center of Safed (pop. 24,000) has had three parts to its personality—a resort town, an artists' colony in the abandoned Arab neighborhoods of the city, and the long-established religious community. As Israelis have become more international in their vacation habits, Safed's tourism industry has withered; and the once vibrant Artists' Quarter is now relatively quiet. All the better for those who decide to explore the town. Although large apartment complexes have been built on the periphery, and Jerusalem Street is an architectural hodge-podge, the back streets of Safed, winding, cobbled, and resounding with the chant of prayers, are still medieval. July and August are the most popular months because of Safed's cool climate. In the winter, it can be windy and as much as 20° cooler than Tiberias. Year-round, especially at night, Safed is usually the coldest town in the country.

ESSENTIALS
GETTING THERE   By Bus   Buses run between Safed and Tiberias, Tel Aviv, and Jerusalem.

By Car   Follow the main but winding roads from Tiberias, Haifa, and Akko.

GETTING AROUND   Most city buses, such as no. 1, 1/3, 1/4, or 3, go from the center to the hotels on Mount Canaan.

VISITOR INFORMATION   The **Safed Tourist Information Office** is in the Municipality Building, 50 Jerusalem St. (☎ **06/692-0961** or 06/692-7485), open Sunday through Thursday from 8am to 1pm and 4 to 6pm, and until noon on Friday.

CITY LAYOUT   Safed is built on hilltops. The main part of town is compactly clustered atop one hill, while South Safed occupies another hilltop to the south, and Canaan perches on a hillside across the valley to the east. Although you may find occasion to go to Mount Canaan (a few hotels are there), you'll spend most of your time in the center of Safed. Jerusalem Street (Rehov Yerushalayim) is a circular street that girdles the hill, passing through the commercial street, the Artists' Quarter, and residential sections, before beginning its circle again. Walking the circle should take only 15 minutes, and it is a good way to see most of Safed.

The **Egged Bus Station** (☎ **06/692-1122**) is at the lowest point on Jerusalem Street's circle through town, where it intersects with Derekh Jabotinsky. Walk up to Jerusalem Street from the bus station and go right, and after 400 yards you will come to the Tourist Information Office. But if you come up from the bus station and go left, you'll be headed toward the commercial district. In any case, once you find Jerusalem Street you can't get lost in Safed.

WHAT TO SEE & DO
While there is much to see in Safed, a traveler unfamiliar with the city's crooked streets and unimpressive doorways may pass some of the city's best sites. I'll do my best to help you uncover the secrets of Safed, starting with its fascinating synagogues. But first, consider getting some local help by taking a **guided tour.** For $10 you can arrange for an informative walking tour of Old Safed with **Aviva Minoff,** an excellent licensed tour guide. The two-and-a-half hour tours generally leave from the Rimon Inn, Monday through Thursday at 10am and Friday at 10:30am. For information, call ☎ **06/692-0901,** preferably before your arrival. Note that modest dress is required when touring the religious quarter of Safed. Alternatively, look for the locally published book, *Six Self Guided Tours To Tzfat,* by Yisrael Shalem (approximately $4.75); it's sold at Greenbaum's bookstore on the Pedestrian Mall in the center of Safed.

THE SYNAGOGUES
During Safed's Golden Age in the 16th century, some of the synagogues here were devoted to the study of the Cabala, a mystical interpretation of the Bible and other sacred writings in which every single symbol in holy writ has deep, hidden significance: Each letter, number, and even accent in the holy books has meaning beyond its

face value. In Cabala, an offshoot of mainstream Judaism, Hebrew words, numbers, and the names of God have mystical powers in themselves, and can be used to ward off evil and to perform miracles.

Cabalists believed that the system originated with Abraham and was handed down by word of mouth from ancient times. Historians of religion dispute this, however, saying that Cabalism arose only in the 600s; it continued to be a thriving belief until the 1700s. Cabalism was, in a way, a reaction to the heavy formalism of rabbinical Judaism. It allowed for more latitude in the interpretation of holy writ and gained great popularity in the 1100s. The most significant Cabalist text is the *Zohar,* a mystical commentary on the Pentateuch (the first five books of the Hebrew scriptures). For an interesting fictionalized interpretation of what Safed was like at the height of its glory as a Jewish religious center, I recommend the chapter, "The Saintly Men of Safed," in James Michener's novel *The Source.*

It's not easy to describe exactly where the various synagogues are—the religious quarter has few street names, and is really a collection of alleyways and courtyards. Ask for "kiryat batei knesset," the synagogue section.

Among the most famous old synagogues here is the one named for the scholarly 16th-century **Rabbi Joseph Caro,** author of the *Shulchan Aruckh (The Set Table),* which is the standard guide for Jewish prayer and daily life today. Nearby is another named in honor of **Rabbi Moses Alsheikh.** Just a few steps away is the synagogue of **Rabbi Isaac Abuhav,** a sage of the 1400s; it contains an ancient Torah scroll said to have been written by the rabbi himself. Nearby is another, dedicated to **Rabbi Yosef Bena'a,** also called Ha-Lavan (The White).

The synagogue quarter has two houses of worship dedicated to the greatest of the Cabalist scholars, **Rabbi Isaac Luria** (known as Ha'Ari, or "the Lion," an acronym for Adoneinu Rabbeinu Itzak, "Our Master Teacher Isaac"). Although Luria lived, studied, and taught in Safed for only 2½ years at the end of his life (he died here at the age of 38), his work changed the face of Judaism forever. The fortresslike Sephardic synagogue, graced by fine carved-wood doors, is built where the rabbi studied and prayed, at the edge of the cemetery. The **Ashkenazi Ha'Ari Synagogue** is closer to Jerusalem Street, at a spot where the rabbi is said to have come to welcome the Sabbath with his followers. Rabbi Luria was the author of the *Kabbalat Shabbat (Receiving the Sabbath),* the liturgical arrangement of prayers recited at the start of the Sabbath in normative Judaism.

The original building, constructed after Rabbi Luria's death, was destroyed by an earthquake in 1852 and later restored. Its ark, done in the 1800s, is especially notable. If you come with an official guide, you will get a better sense of how every nook and cranny has a story and sometimes a supernatural occurrence connected with it.

At the end of the synagogue area is a **cemetery** containing the sky-blue tombs of many famous religious leaders; they're the ones with rocks placed upon them as symbols of love, respect, and remembrance. There is also a military cemetery containing the resting places of soldiers who fell in all the wars, and nearby is a third cemetery containing the graves of Israelis who served with the underground Stern Gang and Irgun groups at the time of the British mandate. Buried here are those executed by the British in Acre prison, including Dov Gruner, who is one of the best known of the outlawed fighters.

Another holy site is the **Cave of Shem and Eber** (or Ever), the son and grandson of Noah. This cave, located just off Ha-Palmach Street near where the Ha-Palmach stone overpass crosses Jerusalem Street, is said to be the place where Shem and Eber lived, studied, and were buried. Legend also has it that Jacob spent 14 years here studying before he went to the house of Laban, and that here he immersed himself in a ritual purifying bath before he wrestled with the angel. Today, there is a synagogue opposite the cave; if the cave is locked, you can ask the caretaker of the synagogue to open it for you.

20TH-CENTURY MEMORIALS

Going down the hill from Jerusalem Street, in the area between the synagogues and the Artists' Quarter, is a straight stairway: **Oleh Ha-Gardom.** Stand at the top of this stairway, where it intersects with Jerusalem Street, and you're within sight of a lot of Safed's 20th-century historical landmarks.

Oleh Ha-Gardom was the dividing line between Safed's Jewish and Arab quarters until 1948; that's why all the synagogues are clustered on the right-hand side, as you're facing down the stairway. The present Artists' Quarter is in what used to be the Arab section. Look up toward the Citadel and you'll see a small opening in the fortress from which a direct line of machine-gun fire could be sent straight down the stairway, a British attempt to keep an uneasy peace between the two communities. The same day the British withdrew, the Arab and Jewish factions went to war. Look at the walls of the old police station and you'll see it's pocked with bullet holes from the fighting.

Down Jerusalem Street from this intersection you can also see a war memorial, with a tablet describing how the fighting favored first the Arabs, then the Jews. Poised on a stone mount is a Davidka (little David), one of those homemade Jewish mortars that, though not too accurate or damaging, made a terrific noise and gave the impression of being much more dangerous than it actually was.

At the top of the hill, in the beautiful hilltop park, are the ruins of a Crusader fortress (unfortunately not well maintained at present) from which you can enjoy a fine view of Mount Meiron, Mount Tabor, the Sea of Galilee, and a smattering of tiny hill villages and settlements. This site, the highest in Safed, was once the scene of a 1st-century Galilean stronghold and later a 12th-century crusaders' lookout post. A war memorial commemorates the Israelis who were killed pushing the Arabs back from the heights.

MUSEUMS & EXHIBITIONS

The **Artists' Quarter** is the area down the hill from Jerusalem Street between the Oleh Ha-Gardom stairway facing the police station and the stone overpass that crosses Jerusalem Street. Here you will find picturesque houses, tiny streets, manicured gardens, and outdoor art displays. Many artists have galleries in their homes, and the homes themselves are often so charming and atmospheric that some owners charge a small admission. This is a good place to think about acquiring good, inexpensive gifts and souvenirs. Many of the exhibitions sell reproductions of the artists' work. Prices vary, but many are fairly inexpensive.

General Exhibition. Old Mosque, Artists' Quarter. ☎ **06/692-0087.** Sun–Thurs 9am–6pm; Fri 9am–2pm; Sat 10am–2pm. Directions: Downhill from the intersection of Jerusalem and Arlosoroff streets.

While many of the houses in the artists' colony may be closed in winter, the General Exhibition is open year-round. The galleries display everything from paintings to ceramics to silk. You can purchase objects here, or get in touch with artists whose work you find interesting. Next door is the New Immigrant Artists Exhibition.

Habad (or Chabad) House. ☎ **06/992-1414.** Free admission. Sun–Thurs 9am–4pm.

Located between Ha-Maginim Street between Maginim Square (Kikar Maginim) and the Oleh Ha-Gardom steps, this is a Jewish history museum, with special exhibitions for children. The museum is part of an outreach program of the Lubavicher Hassidic movement.

Hameiri House. Old City. ☎ **06/697-1307.** Admission NIS 8 ($1.75). Sun–Thurs 9am–2pm; Fri 9am–1pm.

Located down the hill, in south Safed, Hameiri House is the **Museum and Institute for the Heritage of Safed.** It's housed in a historic 16th-century edifice, the restoration of which was done over a 27-year period, completed in 1985. Artifacts and documents portray the history of Safed's Jewish community; photographs and videos of elderly residents are especially interesting if a translator is available.

Israel Bible Museum. ☎ **06/699-9972.** Free admission. Oct–May, Sun–Thurs 10am–2pm; Fri 10am–1pm; June–Sept, Sun–Thurs 10am–4pm; Fri 10am–1pm.

Dedicated in 1985, this museum (previously the home of the Turkish governor in Safed) is full of inspirational, dramatic art pieces by contemporary artist Phillip Ratner. The building is lovely, with dramatic vistas, and well worth the climb up the staircase at the north end of the Town Park. Or you can enter from the other side, walking down from Derekh Hativat Yiftah, which is the road that circles the Citadel.

Museum of Printing Art. Corner of Arieh Merzer and Arieh Alwail sts. ☎ **06/692-0947.** Free admission. Sun–Thurs 10am–noon and 4–6pm; Fri–Sat 10am–noon.

Safed was the site of the first Hebrew press in Israel, which was set up in 1576 and published Israel's first Hebrew book a year later. Here you can see a copy of the first newspaper printed in Israel (1863); a copy of the *Palestine Post* of May 16, 1948, announcing the birth of the State of Israel; a centuries-old Cabalistic text printed in Safed; examples of modern Israeli graphics; and many other things.

PLANT A TREE

Just outside the highway entrance to Safed is a **Keren Kayemet Le-Israel (Jewish National Fund) Tree Planting Center.** At this site, Joseph Caro wrote in the 16th century, and here during the British Mandate, Palmach soldiers built a fortress, which the British destroyed, only to have it built again. The **restored fortress** was opened to the public in 1971, with an exhibition of documents, press cuttings, and photographs relating to the site.

Here the Jewish National Fund has established the **Biriya Forest,** where you are welcome to plant a tree with your own hands. It costs about $10. Hours are Sunday through Thursday from 8am to 2pm, on Friday until 12:30pm. For further information, you can ask at the tourist information office.

SPORTS & OUTDOOR ACTIVITIES

SWIMMING   As you turn into town, in a hollow to the right of the road, near the Central Bus Station, is **Emek Hatchelet Swimming Pool** (☎ **06/692-0217**), which has been around since 1959. The area is beautifully landscaped, and has lounge chairs, tables, and big umbrellas. Admission is NIS 25 ($5.50), half price for children. There are two pools (one for children), game tables, a playground, plus a minigolf course. Aside from showers and dressing rooms, facilities include a restaurant serving everything from ice cream to a full steak-and-fries meal. It's open daily from June through part of September, from 9am to 5pm. Several days a week the afternoon hours are reserved for men-only or women-only swims.

TENNIS   Ask at the tourist information office for details about the new **Sports Center,** with tennis and basketball courts and more, and a capacity of 600 people. It's covered, and heated in winter. For more information about tennis courts, call ☎ **06/697-1222.**

WHERE TO STAY

Berinson House-Tel Aviv Hotel. Ridbaz St., Old City. ☎ **06/697-2555.** Fax 06/697-2535. 38 units. A/C TV TEL. $104–$138 double. Rates include breakfast. No credit cards.

If you want to stay in Safed, the acceptable choices beyond the Ruth Rimmon Inn (see below) are very limited. This is a clean place with simple but comfortable rooms that are heated in winter (all with private bathrooms). It's downhill, located at the bottom of Ridbaz Street.

✪ **Howard Johnson Ruth Rimon Inn.** Artists' Quarter (P.O. Box 1011), Safed 13110. ☎ **06/699-4666;** reservations through Howard Johnson Hotels. Fax 06/962-0456. 82 units. A/C MINIBAR TV TEL. $150–$200 double. July–Aug and Jewish holidays add $65 per room. AE, V.

This charming place in the Artists' Quarter, just a 5-minute walk from the center of town, is my favorite hotel in Safed, a lovely place. Part of the main building derives from the 17th-century Turkish period, when it served as a khan (inn) and a post office. The dining room was originally the stable, and you still can see where the horses were tied. In addition to the usual luxuries, you'll find acres of gardens, a swimming pool, more than half the rooms with large balconies, beautiful views, extra touches like a guitarist in the bar on weekends, and some interesting history as well. A recent addition has more than doubled the size of the Rimon Inn; the new rooms are comfortable and freshly furnished, but not as atmospheric as the rooms in the older section. In 1997, this hotel became affiliated with Howard Johnson, but will retain its own personal character and standards. A variety of deluxe rooms are $50 extra per room.

OUTSIDE OF SAFED

Motke and Mazel's B&B. Moshav Kerem Ben Zimra. ☎ **06/698-0603.** Units available varies (all with bathrooms). $85–$95 double. Rates include breakfast. No credit cards.

Located 6 kilometers (4 mi.) northwest of Safed, this is a pretty, rustic location facing the mountains. Decent accommodations in Safed are so scarce that this B&B might be a pleasant alternative for visitors with cars. There are nicely decorated rooms with bedrooms, and living room and kitchen areas. Delicious breakfasts include great omelettes and homemade jams.

WHERE TO DINE

The first thing you'll notice about Safed is its multitude of sandwich, snack, and falafel shops along Jerusalem Street, open day and night, except for the Sabbath, when the whole town is closed up tight.

Safed is not a great place for fine dining, but there are good choices in nearby Rosh Pina and in the surrounding countryside.

Golden Mountain Cheese Cafe. Kikar Meginim, Old City. ☎ **051/567-504.** Sandwiches and salads NIS 12–25 ($2.65–$5.50). No credit cards. Sun–Thurs 11am–midnight; Fri 11am–4pm. CHEESE.

Run by Fruma Goldberg, originally from Netherlands, this little place with lace cloths covering its plastic tables, is lined with shelves of homemade Dutch-style cheeses. Ms Goldberg makes fresh batches each week laced with cumin, herbs and onions, garlic, and other spices—no two batches are quite alike. You can order cheese platters by weight, sandwiches, salads, herbal teas, and for dessert, fruit and yogurt or (fat-free) whey shakes.

Ha-Mifgash. 75 Jerusalem St. ☎ **06/693-0510.** Main courses NIS 35–78 ($7.70–$16.80). AE, DC, MC, V. Thurs–Sun 9am–11pm (until midnight in summer); Fri 9am–4pm, Sat 10am–3pm and after Shabbat. ISRAELI.

Located on the main street in the center of town, this restaurant, which means "meeting place" in Hebrew, has four different parts. The first thing you'll see is the self-service falafel counter in front. Inside, there's the main dining room, and downstairs to the left side is a room with table service, which was once a large water cistern. Service is not great, but you can sit down to either a really full meat meal or a snack. There is a reasonable wine list.

Restaurant Pinati. 81 Jerusalem St. ☎ **06/692-0855.** Main courses NIS 35–80 ($7.70–$17.60). AE, DC, V. Sun–Thurs 9am–11pm; Fri 9am–2pm; Sat after Shabbat. ISRAELI.

Just a few steps down the hill from Ha-Mifgash, this plain but clean and friendly family run restaurant offers excellent filling meals of fish, grilled or baked chicken or meats, and goulashes, all with salad, potatoes, rice, and cooked vegetables. If you're feeling adventurous, you might try the unusual lung goulash. As amazing as the variety of dishes served is the decor, which is a monument to Elvis Presley! Breakfast and light meals such as salads, soups or hummus are also served.

COUNTRY DINING IN THE GALILEE MOUNTAINS

These choices are possible lunch or dinner excursions from Safed, but can also be reached from places like Rosh Pina, Vered Ha Galil, or even Akko, Nahariya, Maalot, Tiberias, or Haifa. Besides the opportunity to enjoy unusual meals, these restaurants offer a chance to explore remote parts of the countryside.

Bat Ya'ar Ranch Steak House. Birya Forest 5km (3 mi.) northwest of Safed. ☎ **06/692-1788.** Reservations necessary. Main courses NIS 46–100 ($10–$22). MC, V. Daily 11am–10:30pm. STEAKS.

You'll need a good map or careful instructions from the Tourist Information Office to get here, but once you've arrived, you could swear you're in Wyoming. A series of rough wooden buildings house a horseback riding farm; up the path, past a beautiful vista point, is the restaurant. It's grilled hamburgers, steaks, and chicken here, with fries or baked potato and salad served in a rugged, ranch-style room; the quality is good, and the fresh air and views demand a pre- or postdinner stroll, if not a full-scale hike. Out of character for Safed, but Israel is filled with such unexpected contrasts.

Ein Camonim. Route 85, 5km (3 mi.) west of the Kadarim Junction; 20 km (12.5 mi.) from Safed. ☎ **06/698-9894.** Fixed-price meal NIS 90 ($19.80). AE, DC, MC, V. Sun–Fri 11am–8pm. CHEESE & WINE.

At this dairy specializing in goat cheeses, they've set up an informal, restaurant with picnic tables and benches for enjoying their products. You get a platter of assorted cheeses, fresh baked bread, a carafe of wine, a basket of raw vegetables and dessert (go for the cheesecakes); everything is delicious, fresh, and leisurely. One order can be shared; children are half price.

✪ Kurdish Restaurant and Guesthouse at Shtula. Moshav Shtula, Western Galilee. ☎ **04/980-6068,** or 0050/269-406 mobile phone. Main courses NIS 25–40 ($7–$11.20); fixed-price dinner NIS 70 ($19.60). AE, DC, MC, V. Sun–Thurs noon–8:30pm; Fri noon–3pm. Call to check hours and discuss the kind of meal you want. HOME-STYLE KURDISH.

Mrs. Sara Hatan came to Israel from Kurdistan as a young wife and mother in 1951 and raised a large family in the Moshav of Shtula in the rugged Galilee mountains near the Lebanese border. Over the years, she became known as a fabulous cook, turning out Kurdish specialties according to the recipes she had learned from her mother, grandmothers, and aunts. In the mid-1990s, with the help of her Haifa University–educated daughter, Ora, she went public: the front of her house has been turned into a small restaurant where you'll find dynamite kubbe (cracked wheat meat or vegetable dumplings) soups, shuftas (Kurdish meat patties), stuffed vegetables, Kurdish breads, salads, pickles and festive dishes like special chicken and rice. A tasting menu of everything in Mrs. Hatan's repertoire (call ahead) is NIS 150 ($33); a less extravagant complete dinner goes for $20. To talk to Mrs. Hatan through an interpreter as she calmly makes her famous kubbe on a summer afternoon in the shade of her backyard fig tree is a truly special experience. Mrs. Hatan never abandoned her house in times of shelling from Lebanon ("Who would tend my goats and sheep?" she asks). In 1996, trusting in God and the goodness of strangers, she made a dangerous (and illegal) trip to her childhood town amid the warring factions of Kurdistan (northern Iraq) to see the friends and neighbors she left behind as a young woman ("It was my dream to go back. If not then, when?") Meals like hers are made not only with skill and traditional recipes, but with strength of character. Pleasant guestrooms for overnight stays with country breakfasts are $70–$80 for a double. Get to Route 899, the road that parallels the northern border, and take the turn-off to Even Menachem. In Even Menachem, you'll have to ask for the way through this moshav and on to Shtula. The Kurdish Restaurant is on the main road of Shtula, on the left, not far from the entrance to the town. Look for a Coca-Cola sign.

✪ **Tova Admoni.** Mitspe Kamon. ☎ and fax **04/998-8647.** Reservations more than a day in advance required. Fixed-price meal NIS 140 ($31). No credit cards. Fri dinner and Sat lunch only; midweek by reservation only for parties of 6 or more. RUSTIC FRENCH/ MEDITERRANEAN.

More and more marvelous cooks in the Galilee are opening their country homes for dining. Tova Admoni is one of the best in the hills, with a great reputation and a beautiful location. You are served a five-course meal at tables in her own picturesque living room. There are country breads and a choice of soups, followed by many interesting salads, stuffed pastries, and then a choice of meats (as much as you want). Tova's main course specialties are usually smoked chicken or wild boar served in a wine, sour cream, and mustard sauce. Then comes dessert! You must call ahead to reserve places and discuss the menu choices for the week. Everything is heavenly. Standard opening hours are Friday evenings and Saturday afternoons, but if you have a party of 6 or more, Tova may be able to schedule a midweek meal for your group. You must have a good map to get here. Mitspe Kamon (Kamun) is down a road off Route 85 1½ kilometers (2 mi.) east of Karmiel. From Safed, take Route 89 to Route 866. Turn left (south) onto 866; where 866 meets Route 85 at the Hananya Junction, take Route 85 towards Karmiel and Akko. About 3 kilometers (5 mi.) after Route 85 passes Route 804, is the left turn to Kamun. You must call Tova for directions to her house. Plan for a 50-minute drive; daylight is always easier.

SAFED AFTER DARK

Summer is the time for most of Safed's musical events. About eight chamber music concerts are held throughout the year, mostly in the summer, as well as a summer musical workshop. The **Klezmer Festival of East European Jewish Music** is the highlight of the summer programs. Check with the tourist office for the weekly scene. For piano concerts, check out **Hemdat Yamim** (☎ **06/698-9085**) on the Acre-Safed highway, which usually has concerts every Monday and Saturday evening during the summer.

The new **Yigal Alon Cultural Center and Theatre** on Jerusalem Street (☎ **06/697-1990**) has everything from Shakespeare to ballet and popular folk dancing. It's named for the man who led the forces that liberated Safed in the 1948 war.

EASY EXCURSIONS
MEIRON

Five miles west of Safed is the town of Meiron, a holy place for religious Jews for 1,700 years. Meiron has had a continuously Jewish population for nearly 18 centuries. When Judea fell to the Romans in after the Second Revolt against Rome in A.D. 135, the mountainous northern Galilee took on many refugees. One early Meiron inhabitant, a 2nd-century Talmudist named Shimon Bar Yochai, was ultimately forced to hide in a cave in Peqiin, outside Meiron. There, according to legend, he wrote the *Zohar*, or *Book of Splendor,* which is central to the Cabalist belief.

Meiron is the scene of considerable pageantry during the holiday of **Lag b'Omer,** which occurs in the spring just 3^1/$_2$ weeks after Passover. Thousands of Orthodox Jews pour into Safed and there follows a torchlight parade to Meiron, with singing and dancing. Here they burn candles on top of Rabbi Shimon's tomb and light a great bonfire into which some, overcome by emotion, throw their clothes. In the morning, after the all-night festivities, 3-year-old boys are given their first haircuts, and the cut hair is thrown into the fire.

There still exists a **ruined ancient synagogue** from the 3rd century A.D., as well as **Rabbi Shimon's tomb,** and a rock called the **Messiah's Chair.** Reputedly, on the day the Messiah arrives, he will sit right here while Elijah blows the trumpet to announce his coming. **Mt. Meiron,** the highest peak in the Galilee at 2,926 feet, dominates the rugged countryside, with vistas that sweep virtually across northern Israel. The local **SPNI Field School** (☎ **06/698-0023**) offers trail maps and information about a number of hikes through the beautiful, wooded Meiron Nature Reserve.

SASA & THE BAR'AM SYNAGOGUE

Kibbutz Sasa is on the northern foothills of Mount Meiron 16 kilometers (26 mi.) northwest of Safed. In 1949, American and Canadian settlers built atop a 3,000-foot-high hill and persevered despite many problems, including a polio epidemic. The thriving kibbutz is now the center of an area of forest reservations.

Just 5 kilometers (8 mi.) to the north, the 3rd- to 4th-century A.D. ✪ **Bar'am Synagogue** is probably the best preserved and most beautiful of all the ancient synagogues in Israel. Its location, in the wild mountains near the Lebanese border, is breathtaking. According to some scholars, the synagogue may have been in use through early medieval times. In the style of early Galilee synagogues, the building faces south, toward Jerusalem. Beautifully carved clusters of grapes ornamenting the main entrance testify to the town's abundant vineyards and orchards. At some point the design of the synagogue was changed and the main entrance walled over with large ashlars that can be seen in a 19th-century engraving of the ruined site, made from an early photograph. Archaeologists theorize that over the centuries, it became customary for worshippers to face both the Ark of the Torah and Jerusalem while praying, and the central doorway, on the southern wall of the synagogue, was walled over in order to build a Torah shrine. By the late 19th century, the ashlars walling the entrance, as well as other chunks of the synagogue, had been carried off by locals for reuse in other buildings.

Medieval through 19th-century travelers record the existence of a second, smaller ruined synagogue at Bar'am, now totally obliterated. According to one visitor, an inscription on the lintel of one of its doorways read: *"Do not be surprised by snow in*

Nisan [April]. We have seen it in Sivan [June]." Although this lintel stone has vanished, the inscription over the main doorway was preserved and carted off to the Louvre in 1861. Its message: *"May there be peace in this place and in all the places of Israel...."* The **National Park at Bar'am** (☎ **06/698-9301**) is open daily from 8am to 4pm (till 5pm in summer); admission is NIS 12 ($2.60).

The ruins of the Christian Arab village of **Birim** surround the cleared areas around the synagogue. As noncombatants during the 1948 War of Independence, the residents of Birim had quartered Israeli troops in their homes. Late in the war, the people of Birim were told by the Israeli army to evacuate their town for what was promised would be a short time during a possible enemy offensive. They were never allowed to return, despite a ruling by the Israeli Supreme Court in the early 1950s upholding the villagers' rights to their homes. Since then, the former inhabitants of Birim, who all possess Israeli citizenship and are now scattered throughout the Galilee, have maintained an unending legal struggle to reclaim their village.

Past the synagogue, you can follow a path to the left and uphill to the **Church of Birim,** still maintained by the people of the village for weddings and funerals. If you climb the rather difficult stairs onto the roof of the church, you will be rewarded with a dramatic panorama of countryside so intensely loved by two peoples. Arabic graffiti on the Church walls promise that the members of the congregation will return.

5 Upper Galilee & the Golan Heights

TOURING THE REGION

From Tiberias or Rosh Pina, Highway 90 heads north toward Kiryat Shmona and Metulla. North of Kiryat Shmona, roads head west and south along the Lebanese border back toward Safed, and east to Hurshat Tal National Park, Baniyas Waterfall, and the Mount Hermon Ski Center in the Golan Heights.

GUIDED TOURS I highly recommend a 1-day guided tour. Several are available from Tiberias. A 1-day tour of the Golan Heights will cost you NIS 135 to 180 ($30 to $40), depending on which tour you choose. **Egged Tours** (☎ **06/672-9220**) does full-day tours from Tiberias to the Galilee and the Golan for the same prices, going to about the same places. The Egged tours go at 8:30am on Tuesday, Thursday, and Saturday, leaving from the Tiberias Central Bus Station; you can also arrange to be picked up at your hotel for no extra charge. The **Society for Protection of Nature in Israel** also offers quality tours and hikes of the region.

A third option, especially popular with younger travelers, is to see the Golan with various **local taxi drivers,** who pick up tourists from all the Tiberias youth hostels every morning during the summer season (call in advance to reserve your space through any hostel). The price, NIS 115 ($25) per person, is a bit less than many official bus-company tours, and it must be noted that these are not official government-licensed tour guides. However, the tours are lively and personal. Many readers have been disappointed with standard tours, and this is a colorful alternative.

Yet another option is to check with Tiberias's major hotels, many of which will have information about private guided tours. If you want to start out from somewhere other than Tiberias, Egged and Galilee offer tours leaving from Haifa, Tel Aviv, and Jerusalem; check their information booklets, or call, for details.

UPPER GALILEE

North of the Sea of Galilee are Israel's northern panhandle and the area leading up to it—a small area dense with natural beauty and tranquillity—at least off-season when it is not flooded with Israelis on vacation. The region connects naturally into the Golan. If you're overnighting, try to make arrangements in advance. If you don't phone ahead, travel early from Tiberias or Safed and pin down a place to stay as soon as possible. Highway 90 will take you right into the heart of this area, passing by the outskirts of Rosh Pina (see above).

FROM MISHMAR HA-YARDEN TO AYELET HA-SHAHAR

Along the main road is the turnoff to Mishmar Ha-Yarden, Galilee's oldest moshav, established around the turn of the century, and one of the few Jewish communities overrun and destroyed during the 1948 war. Beyond the moshav, crossing the Jordan into Golan, is the bridge called **Benot Yaakov (Daughters of Jacob),** believed to be the place where Jacob crossed the river on his return from Mesopotamia. The bridge is also on the ancient caravan route from Damascus to Egypt, which is part of the Via Maris.

On the left (west) side of the road is **Tel Hazor,** a prehistoric mound that serves as yet another reminder of this land's history. Canaanite Hazor was one of the region's most important cities; but after the Israelite conquest (around B.C. 1200) the city's power declined. After Hazor was destroyed by the Assyrians in B.C. 732, it never became a sizable community again, and fell into oblivion. Artifacts from the area are exhibited at the **Hazor Museum** (☎ 06/6934-855), near the entrance to Kibbutz Ayelet Ha-Shahar. Displays are from 21 different archaeological strata spanning 2,500 years, from the early Bronze Age to the Hellenistic period in the 2nd century B.C. The excavation of Hazor is recorded in the extensively photographed book, *Hazor,* by Yigael Yadin, whose writing makes archaeology truly accessible and exciting for all readers. Admission to the National Park at Hazor (☎ 06/693-4855) including the Hazor Museum is NIS 16 ($3.50). It is open daily from 8am to 4pm; until 5pm in summer.

Where to Stay

Kibbutz Ayelet Ha-Shahar. Upper Galilee 12200. ☎ **06/693-2611.** Fax 06/693-4777. E-mail: atlashot@netvision.net.il. 136 units. A/C TEL. $115–$130 double. Rates include breakfast. 5% off-season discounts available; add 15% in high season. AE, DC, MC, V.

A short distance past Tel Hazor, on the east side of the road, this kibbutz hotel is a romantic, slightly historical accommodation choice, set close to the ruins and next to the Hazor Museum. There are beautiful gardens; rooms have radios, central heat, and glorious views. Facilities include an outdoor pool, tennis courts, a playground for children, and a TV/video room.

THE HULA VALLEY

The best view of this beautiful reclaimed swampland is from the **Nebi Yusha fortress** just off the main road, on the Hill of the 28. A memorial in front of the British Taggart Fort recalls the time when these Hagana soldiers climbed the hill from Hula in the dead of night and fought to gain this strategic point. The odds were against them as they weathered a rain of machine-gun fire and grenades from the windows of the fort. When efforts to dynamite the building failed, the group's commander strapped the dynamite to his back, ignited it, and threw himself at a weak point in the wall. In all, 28 fighters died in taking this hilltop strongpoint, and today, birds make nests in the many shell holes on the walls of the fort.

Beyond the memorial plaques is an observation point with a magnificent view of the valley below. This breathtaking area, which stretches in both directions as far as the eye can see, was once a vast marshland teeming with wildlife. It was the smallest of the

Upper Galilee & the Golan

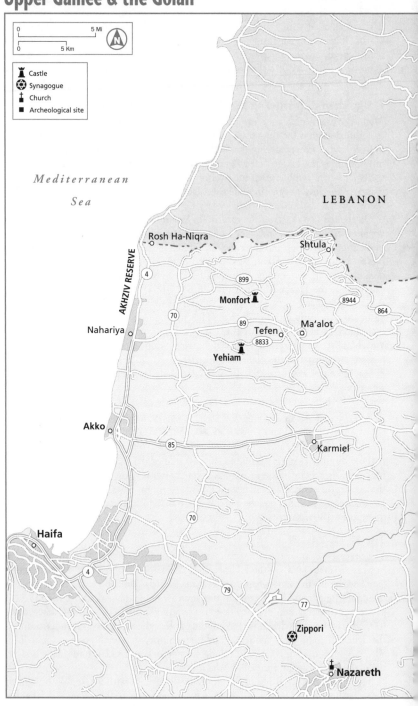

Castle
Synagogue
Church
Archeological site

Mediterranean
Sea

LEBANON

Rosh Ha-Niqra
Shtula

AKHZIV RESERVE

899
Monfort

70
89
Ma'alot
Tefen
Nahariya
8833
Yehiam

8944
864

Akko

85
Karmiel

70

Haifa

4

79

77

Zippori

Nazareth

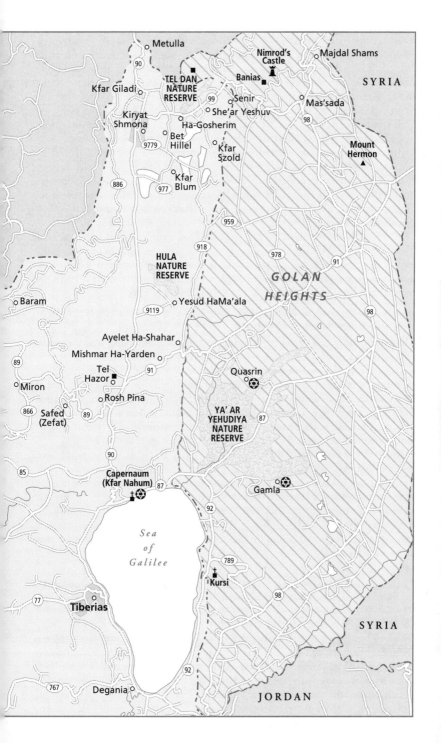

three lakes fed by the Jordan—the Sea of Galilee and the Dead Sea are the other two. To Israelis who remember the marshland, the Hula was a lovely place—a home for water buffalo, wild boar, exotic birds, and wildflowers. Species of cranes and storks would migrate here, coming and going from as far away as Russia, Scandinavia, and India. To those who knew its thickets of papyrus, its dragonflies and kingfishers, and its tropical water lilies (some claim it looked a little like the shores of the Nile), the Hula was a bit of paradise. The Arabs had legends about the Hula's charms, where spirits walked in the evening mist luring young people into the mysterious marsh.

After years of wrangling with neighboring governments—as well as with the French and British—the Israelis finally drained the marshes after they achieved independence. Because the country needed every drop of water and every square foot of fertile land, only one small section of the valley was left as a wildlife preserve. Control over the Hula's waters was also a necessary phase of the Lowdermilk and other Jordan River diversion plans, which bring water to the barren southern reaches of Israel.

However, the project upset the ecosystem and harmed the region's natural aquifer. The draining of Hula Lake and the marshes also deprived millions of migrating birds of a strategic watering hole on the migration route from Europe and Western Asia down the Jordan Valley to Africa. In 1970, a reconstruction project to re-create the marshes was launched, and the Hula Nature Reserve was created.

Hula Nature Reserve. ☎ 06/693-7069. Admission NIS 20 ($4.40) adults, NIS 10 ($2.20) children. Sat–Thurs 8am–4pm; Fri 8am–3pm.

The reserve today is once again alive with gray herons, cormorants, ducks, pelicans, wild boar, water buffalo, and other former species of the area that had died off or gone elsewhere when the swamps were drained. The best hours for a visit are early in the morning, especially in summer, when the birds and animals of the Hula are active. A new path has been constructed, suitable for wheelchairs. At the visitors' center, free films about the reserve are shown. The reserve is located 15 kilometers (9 mi.) south of Kiryat Shmona and 3 kilometers (1¹/₂ mi.) east of the highway. A combined ticket with the nature reserves at Baniyas, Dan, Gamla, and Ayun costs NIS 40 ($9).

Right in the center of the Hula Valley, at Yesud Hama'ala, is the picturesque, restored **Dubrovin Farm,** housing an agricultural museum and a fine rustic French restaurant (see below). The Dubrovin Farm, a series of stone houses built at the turn of the century, was the homestead of a family of Russian Christians who converted to Judaism and turned this section of the Hula swamp into a model farm. In 1986, the farm was donated to the Jewish National Fund, and opened to the public. Save your entrance ticket of NIS 10 ($2) to the museum, and it will be deducted from the price of your main course.

Where to Stay

✪ Kibbutz Kfar Blum Hotel. Kibbutz Kfar Blum, Upper Galilee 12150. ☎ **06/683-6611.** Fax 06/683-6600. E-mail: hotelf_p@kfarblum-hotel.org.il. 105 units. A/C TEL TV. $120–$165 double. Rates include breakfast. 15% increase for Jewish holidays. Discounts are available on the Kibbutz Hotel Chain 7-Day Plan. AE, MC, V.

Set amid flowering gardens this country hotel offers modern rooms, some with terraces and balconies, and many with views of the Hula Valley and Mount Hermon in the distance; all are comfortably heated against the winter Galilee chill. During 2000, a new wing of deluxe suites will be completed, but the older rooms with their gardens already capture the spirit of the area. There's an Olympic swimming pool as well as a children's pool, two night-lit tennis courts and a sauna; the office will give advice on fishing, bird watching, and jogging, which are prime kibbutz activities. The lobby is comfortable after a day of touring, and good cappuccino is served at the lobby bar until late in the evening. In summer, there is a short Chamber Music Festival. There's also a kosher dining room (praised in readers' letters) and a synagogue. There are rooms for disabled guests. You can arrange Jordan River kayaking through the Hotel, as well as local tours and hikes. As you head north from the Hula Nature Reserve, you'll pass the turnoff to the hotel (to the right, east) toward Kefar Blum.

Where to Dine

Dubrovin Farm. Yesud Hama'ala. ☎ **06/693-4464.** Main courses NIS 50–110 ($11–$24); complete fixed-price gourmet meal NIS 130 ($28.60); complete business lunch NIS 80 ($17.60). DC, MC, V. Mon–Sat noon–11pm; Sun noon–6pm. FRENCH/CONTINENTAL.

The restored, century-old Dubrovin Farm is a delightful setting for a leisurely meal as you explore the area. This restaurant is known for its rich cream sauces—you'll find shrimp in a lively lemon cream sauce, or fabulous foie gras touched with red currant jam and served in a rich totally different cream preparation. If you're looking for something lighter, try the smoked trout, or a salad or pasta dish. The nut pie heads the list of fine desserts; there is also an excellent wine list. The choices on the business lunch are rather limited, but the quality of everything here is tops.

Outdoor Activities

Kayaking in one- and two-person kayaks can be arranged at Kibbutz Kfar Blum ☎ **06/683-6611.** The cost for 1 hour is NIS 115 ($25) per couple and includes transportation back to Kibbutz Kfar Blum at the end of the run. March to October is kayaking season, but even then, a wetsuit could come in handy. Abu Kayak, at Ha-Yarden Park (☎ **06/692-0622**), where the Jordan River runs into the northern end of the Sea of Galilee, rents kayaks and tubes at similar prices. Look for its ad with a 10% discount in area tourist magazines.

KIRYAT SHMONA

This is the "big town" in Upper Galilee (pop. 18,000), with a wide main boulevard: you'll find lots of fast, inexpensive falafel and shwarma places here if you're looking for a quick meal. At the junction of Highway 90 and Route 99 (to Banias and Nimrod's Castle) you'll find a small shopping center with a Burger Ranch.

Kiryat Shmona is an especially attractive Israeli town, with carefully laid-out residential districts, a busy bus station, and a fascinating monument to the turbulent past: three old army tanks, painted in bright basic colors, next to a gas station on the left side of the road as you enter from the south.

Where to Stay

Kibbutz Kfar Giladi. Upper Galilee 12210. ☎ **06/690-0000.** Fax 06/690-0069. E-mail: kfar_giladi@kibbutz.co.il. 175 units. A/C TV TEL. $110–$140 double. Rates include breakfast. 15% increase for Jewish holidays. Discounts are available through the Kibbutz Hotel Chain 7-Day Plan. AE, MC, V.

Halfway between Kiryat Shmona and Medulla, this kibbutz hotel is set on a wooded hilltop offering pleasant walks and great views. The kibbutz offers tidy rooms, a heated pool, indoor and outdoor swimming facilities, health club, night-lit tennis courts, a playground, synagogue, and kosher dining facilities. There are rooms for the disabled.

EN ROUTE TO METULLA

From Kiryat Shmona, you can head north past Kefar Giladi and Tel Hai to Metulla, then backtrack to Kiryat Shmona before heading east, to Golan.

Situated along the Lebanese border, Metulla is as far north as you can go in Israel proper. Founded in 1896 by a Rothschild grant, Metulla is a pretty, pine-scented

Joseph Trumpeldor & the Founding of Kiryat Shmona

Kiryat Shmona was founded in memory of a legendary episode in the Jewish movement to resettle the Galilee during the early years of the 20th century. The name Kiryat Shmona, which means "Town of the Eight," refers to Joseph Trumpeldor, leader of a group of six men and two women who died at nearby Tel Hai defending their settlement from Arab attackers in 1920. Trumpeldor is the Israeli model of courage and heroism; he was born in Russia in 1880, served in the czar's army, lost an arm, and was decorated for gallantry by the czarina of Russia. The Zionist leader came to Palestine in 1912, and with his self-styled Zion Mule Corps, fought on the side of the British in Gallipoli during World War I. After the war he became a leader of Palestine's pioneer agricultural youth movement and settled at the Tel Hai kibbutz. Trumpeldor defended the settlement against marauding Arabs, until one day, when a particularly heavy attack came, and he refused to leave the kibbutz grounds. In a last-ditch stand, he and seven comrades were killed. His memorial, a few miles north at Tel Hai, is a statue of a lion at the edge of a cliff, head thrown back and mouth open, bellowing at the skies.

Today, Kiryat Shmona is a development town, largely populated by Israelis of Middle Eastern descent, with a smattering of new immigrants from the former Soviet Union. In the tradition of the early settlements of the region, Kiryat Shmona at times comes under attack by katushya rockets fired from Lebanon.

orderly little community where residents farm and cultivate bees. During the rainy season you can see a waterfall cascading from the Tanur Pass into the Iyon River. Because of its proximity to the border, the town has many soldiers and has experienced a considerable amount of military action.

Metulla became a bustling place during the Israeli invasion of Lebanon, but now that the troops are withdrawn it has settled back into its picturesque serenity. With its limestone buildings accented by dark wood, cypress, and evergreen trees, Metulla is reminiscent of a Swiss mountain village, tidy and tranquil.

Metulla has a tiny museum, and the Nahal Ayoun Picnic Ground is by the Lebanese border, shaded by tall eucalyptus trees and furnished with picnic tables and campgrounds. Past the picnic ground, a rough road skirts the Lebanese border, heading east and south to the **Nahal Ayoun (or Ha-Tanur) Nature Reserve (☎ 06/695-1519)** that runs along the entire east side of Metulla, along the Ayoun Stream, between Metulla and the Lebanese border. You can drive or walk into the reserve from here; admission is NIS 16 ($3.50) for adults, half price for children. It's open daily from 8am to 4pm (till 5pm in summer) and until 3pm on Friday.

Ha-Tanur, the Tanur Waterfall, is in the Ayoun Nature Reserve, 2 kilometers (1¹⁄₂ mi.) south of Metulla. To get to the waterfall, you can come down through the nature reserve, or you can take any bus, or walk downhill out of town toward Kiryat Shmona, and after 2 kilometers (1 mi.) turn left (east) and walk down into the valley another 400 yards. After the 20-minute walk, you'll find the waterfalls, one of Israel's loveliest spots. In all but the driest months, the falls tumble into tempting, shaded pools.

About a kilometer (¹⁄₂ mi.) west of Metulla you can visit the **Good Fence,** the border crossing between Israel and Lebanon. The fence got its name in 1976 when a Lebanese child was brought across into Israel to receive medical care, and the name stuck. Today, Lebanese cross the border daily to work in Israel.

If you have a car, or if you don't mind a bit of a hike, go to **Lookout Mountain,** the peak about 1 kilometer ($^1/_2$ mi.) west of Metulla, for a bird's-eye view of the area.

Where to Stay
Guests at Metulla hotels receive discount admission to the Canada Sports Center.

Alaska Inn. P.O. Box 13, Metulla. ☎ **06/699-7111.** Fax 06/699-7118. 49 units. A/C TV TEL. $110–$140 double. Rates include breakfast. AE, DC, MC, V.

Comfortable guest rooms, all equipped with Jacuzzis, plus an outdoor swimming pool, sauna, and health club make this a pleasant place in which to pamper yourself a bit. The desk will arrange tours in the area; the hotel has a communications center for journalists. Again, the vistas here are splendid.

Hotel-Pension Arazim. Metulla 10292. ☎ **06/699-7143** or 06/699-7144. Fax 06/699-7666. 34 units. A/C TV TEL. $110–$130 double. Rates include breakfast. AE, MC, V.

This comfortable hotel in the center of town pays old-world attention to service and quality. It has a bar, gift shop, outdoor swimming pool, and tennis courts. The food is kosher and there is central heating. The hotel serves as a communications center for journalists when things get hot on this portion of the Lebanese border.

EN ROUTE TO MOUNT HERMON & THE GOLAN HEIGHTS
East from Kiryat Shmona, along Route 99 to Mount Hermon—that snowcapped peak you've probably already noticed—is a beautiful national park, hot springs, a crusader fortress, and a ski center.

Hurshat Tal National Park. ☎ **06/694-2360** or 06/694-2440. Admission NIS 14 ($3). Daily 8am–4pm; until 5pm in summer. Bus: 26, 27, or 36 from Kiryat Shmona stop close to the park entrance.

You can swim, picnic, and camp (in season) just 5 kilometers (3 mi.) from Kiryat Shmona. The national park is famous for its ancient oak trees, set among lawns filled with picnicking families on Saturdays and in summer. Some of the trees may date from the time of Jesus and the Second Temple. According to Muslim legend, ten soldiers of the Prophet Muhammad camped here at the time of the Muslim conquest in A.D. 638. Finding no place to tie their horses, they thrust their staffs into the ground and used them as hitching posts. When they awoke the next morning, the staffs had become enormous trees shading a paradise of wildflowers. The Dan River, a tributary of the Jordan, passes down this valley, collecting in a series of artificial lakes and ponds. The freezing (or refreshing) swimming pool in the park is also fed by these streams. In the springtime, this is a lush green place, good for picnics.

Where to Stay
Kibbutz Ha-Goshrim Hotel. Kibbutz Ha-Goshrim. ☎ **06/681-6000.** Fax 06/681-6002. E-mail: hg2@hagoshrim.org.il. 180 units. A/C TV TEL. $110–$160 double. Rates include breakfast. 15% increase for Jewish holidays. Discounts are available through the Kibbutz Hotel Chain 7-Day Plan. AE, MC, V.

Located next door to the beautiful Hurshat Tal National Park, this very popular kibbutz guesthouse is another good base for exploring Upper Galilee and the Golan. Founded by Turkish Jews in 1948, it has a kosher dining room, a large new swimming pool a fitness room (fee), a sauna, Jacuzzi, children's playground, tennis courts, and a video/TV room. The kibbutz offers a water sports program that includes kayak rentals and trips. 20 guestrooms have been recently renovated and 60 new rooms will have been added by late 2000. Try for the new or renovated rooms, which are a bit higher in price. There are rooms for travelers with disabilities.

Where to Dine

Pub Gosh. Kibbutz Hagoshrim, Upper Galilee. ☎ **06/695-6753.** Main courses NIS 45–70 ($10–$15.40); light meals also available. AE, MC, V. Daily noon–10pm or later; open May–Oct only; call to verify schedule. KOSHER VEGETARIAN/FISH.

For those seeking a good kosher restaurant in this part of the countryside, Pub Gosh, run by Kibbutz Hagoshrim, is kosher, despite the fact that it's open 7 days a week (food is brought from the kibbutz hotel, which has a kashruth certificate and operates on Shabbat). The pub is a rustic wooden building set in a forest beside a stream. The menu includes hefty portions of soups, salads, pasta dishes, pizzas, and the restaurant's star attraction, excellent local trout prepared in a number of ways. Soups, meals in themselves, are served inside a small loaf of country bread (quite a stylish presentation for a kibbutz-run place), but as at many restaurants, the stock seems powder-based. In good weather, there are outdoor tables along the side of the stream; the building is blessedly heated and air-conditioned. A good choice for nonkosher as well as kosher visitors.

TEL DAN

The prehistoric settlement at Tel Dan, 9 kilometers (5^1/$_2$ mi.) east of Kiryat Shmona and then 3 kilometers (1^1/$_2$ mi.) north, was a thriving Canaanite community when Joshua led the conquering Israelites here more than 3,000 years ago. In fact, Dan was the northern limit of the Promised Land (the southern limit was Beersheva).

Tel Dan Nature Reserve. ☎ **06/695-1579.** Admission NIS 20 ($4.40) adults, half-price children. Sat–Thurs 8am–4pm; Fri 8am–3pm.

Cold-water springs gush right up from the ground here, forming the Dan River, which is one of the three principal sources of the Jordan River. The dense vegetation around the site is lovely, but swimming is not permitted. Excavations in the reserve, which include a pre-Israelite cult center, are ongoing. In 1993, an inscription bearing what may be a reference to the "House of David" was found here, an exciting discovery, as it would be the first extrabiblical mention of King David's royal family to be discovered.

There is also a 700-year-old Arabic stone flour mill. Reconstructed by the National Parks Authority, it is run by water power, and is near a 2,000-year-old pistachio tree, walking trails, and picnic areas.

If you come by bus, it's a 30-minute walk from Kibbutz Dan. Buses run between Kibbutz Dan and Kiryat Shmona about every 2 hours. You can buy a combination ticket for all nature reserves in the area for NIS 40 ($9).

In nearby Kibbutz Dan is a nature museum, Bet Ussishkin (☎ **06/694-1704**), with exhibits covering the flora, fauna, geology, topography, and history of the region. Bet Ussishkin also contains a Society for the Protection of Nature in Israel (SPNI) station where you can get excellent maps and information about hiking safely in the Golan. *Important:* You must check in at an SPNI station before hiking independently through the Golan Heights. You can also pick up information about seasonal bird watching in the area here. Hours are Sunday through Thursday from 8:30am to 4:30pm, Friday until 3pm, and Saturday 9:30am to 4:30pm. Admission is NIS 16 ($3.50). Keep your receipt: The admission fee here gets you a discount at the National Park.

Where to Dine

Dag Al HaDan Trout Restaurant. Off Kiryat Shemona-Banias Rd. ☎ **06/695-0225.** Reservations necessary weekends. Main courses NIS 65–75 ($14.30–$16.50). AE, DC, MC, V. Daily noon–11pm. FISH.

Set amid the streams of the Dan River's headwaters, this is a delightful spot for a meal, except on weekends, when it often gets frantically busy. You can eat outside, on tables beside willow trees and brooks, or on picnic tables inside the rough stone and wood pavilion. A quick walk around the trout pools and tanks will assure you that the trout is spectacularly fresh—you can have yours grilled with garlic butter sauce, smoked with mustard sauce, baked with herbs and a lemon or mushroom sauce or fried with almond sauce; you can also order salmon fillet or steak, but fresh trout is the raison d'être for this place. You can start your meal with an assortment of small Middle Eastern salads (included with homemade bread in the dinner price) or you can just stop for something lighter, like a salad and delicious fish soup. There is a grilled shish kebab children's plate for NIS 45 ($10), and a good assortment of beers, nonalcoholic drinks, and desserts.

THE GOLAN HEIGHTS

The wild plateau, with its vistas of the Galilee below, is especially worthy of a visit. Occupied since 1967 by Israel, which annexed the Golan for security reasons in 1981, the heights are lightly populated with Druze villages and Jewish towns constructed by the Israeli government specifically for security purposes. Unlike the occupation of Gaza and the West Bank, the period of Israeli control in the Golan has been marked by economic development, prosperity, and tranquil relations between the Druze and the Israeli settlers, who do not share the sometimes fanatic ideologies of settlers in the West Bank. The future of the Golan is not clear. Prime Minister Rabin was quoted as stating that in exchange for a genuine peace with Syria, most of the Heights may be returned to that country. Meanwhile, the Golan affords visitors the pleasure of flowing winter springs and waterfalls, and a variety of ancient sites ranging from **prehistoric dolmens** to the ruins of 1,900-year-old synagogues, as well as Israel's only ski resort and one of its best **wineries**. The region's most spectacular site is the **ruin of Gamla**, a Jewish town destroyed in A.D. 67 during the First Revolt against Rome, located on an especially beautiful and dramatic mountain ridge. The Golan is one of the areas where a rental car is most useful. In summer, the plateau is blazing hot; in winter it can be bitterly cold and windy.

Warning: When touring the Golan area, do not go exploring for shell fragments or souvenirs in the hills near the bunkers. As many as 100,000 to a million Syrian mines were planted in this area, and it may be 10 or 20 years before the Israeli army finishes minesweeping. It must be done inch by inch, and since many of the mines are plastic—not detectable by metal-seeking devices—laboriously slow probes and earth-turning machines must be used. En route you will see a couple of places where the tour buses stop to give visitors a look at the bunkers. Two million visitors (mostly Israeli) have been there before you—so you can be sure it's safe. The barbed-wire fences that line much of the road, and the triangular yellow-and-red Hebrew signs on them, all mean the same thing: minefield.

Hiking in the Golan Heights must be arranged in advance through an SPNI field school or information station. The SPNI Field School in Qasrin (☎ **06/696-1234**) is on Zavitan Street, off Daliyot Street; in the Upper Galilee SPNI is at Beit Ussishkin at Kibbutz Dan (☎ **06/694-1704**).

Banias (Hermon River) Nature Reserve. Off Route 99. ☎ **06/695-0272.** Admission NIS 20 ($4.40). Sat–Thurs 8am–4pm; in summer to 5pm; Fri 8am–4pm.

For thousands of years, Banias has been a holy place to a dozen peoples and half a dozen religions. Banias figures in the New Testament as the place where Jesus designated Peter as "the rock" on which the church would be built. In ancient times the

Canaanites, and later the Greeks, built shrines and temples here. The Greek name Paneas (after Pan, the god of pastures, flocks, and shepherds) was modified in Arabic to Banias as Arabic has no "p" sound. Though an earthquake collapsed the impressive grotto of the Greeks, you can still see little shrines, most of which date from the Hellenistic period. Under the Romans, the settlement was named Caesarea Philippi after Philip, son of Herod, who followed in the ancients' ways and also built a temple.

The crusaders fortified the nearby hilltop with what is now called **Nimrod's Castle.** Christians built a chapel to Saint George on the hillside, which Muslims later converted into a shrine dedicated to El-Khader (the prophet Elijah). A steep path still leads up to the shrine. While the shrine is usually closed, you should still go up for the view.

WHAT TO SEE & DO
Banias Waterfall
The beautiful and legendary Banias Waterfall is less than a mile inside the Golan, some 15 kilometers (9¹/₂ mi.) from Kiryat Shmona, and less than 1 kilometer (¹/₂ mi.) off the main road. Banias is one of the principal sources of the Jordan River. Head down to the stream for a look at the waters, which begin several hundred feet higher on the Hermon slopes. From here the destination, after dropping into the Jordan River, is the Sea of Galilee. Jordan (Yared-Dan) means "descending from Dan," and the river, whose origins are right here, picks up again south of the Sea of Galilee for a twisting, turning run of 70 miles before emptying into the Dead Sea and becoming a stagnant, oily mixture.

This ancient site has been landscaped by the Nature Reserves Authority. You can go swimming, if you can stand the icy waters.

You can buy a combination ticket to the Banias, Hula Tel Dan, Nahal Ayoun, and Gamla nature reserves for NIS 40 ($9).

Nimrod Castle (Kalat Nimrod). ☎ **06/698-4316** (mobile phone). Admission NIS 18 ($4.). Sat–Thurs 8am–4pm; Fri 8am–2pm; closing 1 hour later in summer.

Nimrod's Castle, now a national park, is one of the biggest and best-preserved Crusader ruins in the area, and has a spectacular view. You can visit by car, but in cooler weather, the 1¹/₂- to 2-hour hike from Banias is well worth the effort.

As you come under the wall of the castle you'll see the narrow vertical slits where archers were once stationed. Inside, see many deep water-filled cisterns, some 30 feet deep.

As you can see from up here, whoever controlled Nimrod in bygone days controlled the traffic from Lebanon to Tiberias and the Jordan Valley. To the left is the zigzagging cleft of Banias rift. In a lush, green pocket farther on, you see Tel Dan kibbutz, then a series of carp ponds, Kiryat Shmona on the hills beyond, and the rectangles of brown and green of the Hula Valley extending southward for miles and miles. Behind the castle to the north sits Mount Hermon, rising to 6,500 feet.

To get to Nimrod Castle, follow the signs to Kalaat Namrud. It is approximately 1¹/₂ kilometers (1 mi.) northeast and uphill from Banias.

The Druze Villages
The Druze villages on the slopes of Mount Hermon are inhabited by the fiercely independent people whose religion is something of a mystery to outsiders. They are farmers for the most part, and don't mind tilling the steep, rocky ground so long as they are left in peace. For the past 1,000 years, the Druze have had considerable autonomy. It just wasn't worth the time and expense to conquer them.

The Druze religion is an offshoot of Islam, but very different from either of the major branches, Sunni and Shiite. It all starts with the Fatimids, an Islamic dynasty that grew powerful in the 900s. The Fatimids conquered most of North Africa and parts of the Mediterranean, even taking Genoa for a time. Among their caliphs (leaders with both religious and secular powers) was Al Hakim (996–1021), the sixth of the Fatimid line, who in the year 1020 proclaimed himself to be the reincarnation of God. Many people disagreed with his assertions, and he was assassinated within a year. But he was believed by some followers in Syria and Lebanon, especially among the people who would come to be called Druze. Thus, the foundation of the Druze faith is that Hakim was and is an incarnation of God, that he did not die (because God can't die), but rather is in hiding and will reappear to rule the world when the time is ripe. The Druze also revere Jethro, the Midianite father-in-law of Moses.

The Druze believe in loyalty to the countries in which they reside, and Israeli Druze have served with distinction in the Israeli army. The Druze of the Golan, however, though they admit they have had a tranquil and prosperous existence since the Israeli occupation began in 1967, also feel they must uphold their commitment to Syria, and publicly, most support a return of the Golan Heights to Syrian control.

Between the Druze villages of Majdal Shams and Mas'ada is the small lake of **Birkhet Ram,** now used as a reservoir. Although its round shape hints at a volcanic origin, Birkhet Ram was actually formed by the action of underground springs. Visit the **Birkhet Ram Restaurant** if you're hungry, because you won't find many restaurants in Golan, and it offers the best view of the lake from its balcony. It's open from 8am to 6pm. There's a falafel stand and snack shop here as well.

En Route to Qasrin

After the slow, bouncing ride back from Hermon to the main road, the road becomes well paved. Fifteen kilometers (24 mi.) south of Mas'ada is an observation point from which you can see across the Israeli-Syrian border, which is patrolled by a UN peace-keeping force. In the distance is the abandoned Syrian border city of Kuneitra; beyond is the wide, barren plain that leads to Damascus.

Kuneitra (or Quneitra, now in Syria) was the chief Syrian city in Golan before the war. It was occupied by Israel from 1967 to 1974. Under terms of a disengagement withdrawal brokered by the United States, Kuneitra was returned to Syria. Israel had hoped that a repopulated Kuneitra would be incentive for Syria to defuse tension on the border, but the city has remained largely deserted, one of many ghost towns created by politics and war.

Nearby, on the Israeli side of the border is **Kibbutz Merom Ha-Golan,** a commune of settlers from all over the world initially set up by the Israeli government to help secure the Golan border.

QASRIN

Qasrin is 20 kilometers (12.5 mi.) from Merom Ha-Golan; 38 kilometers (23.5 mi.) from Tiberias. Situated in the center of Golan, the new (1977) Israeli "capital" of Golan, Qasrin (Kazrin, Katzirin), with a present population of about 3,000, was founded on the site of a 2nd- to 3rd-century Jewish town of the same name. Qasrin is the region's administrative hub, with new apartments, offices, schools, factories, and a few shops. It is a good place to stop for groceries or snacks and emergency services. And there are many interesting sights nearby. Bus service is from Kiryat Shmona (take bus no. 55).

A few unlikely contrasts serve as strong reminders of the town's strategic locale: a pleasant suburban town surrounded by barbed wire, bomb shelters encircled by rose gardens, and bomb shelters that house recreation centers, clubhouses, and music halls. Qasrin is known for its sweet, **natural mineral water,** which is bottled and exported to the rest of the country.

What to See & Do

Golan Archeological Museum and Ancient Qasrin Park. P.O. Box 30, Qasrin, Golan Heights 12900. ☎ **06/696-9636.** Admission to each section NIS 18 ($4); discounts for combined visits. AE, DC, MC, V. Sun–Thurs 8am–5pm; Fri 8am–5pm; Sat 10am–4pm. Call ahead to confirm opening hours.

A small **museum of regional history** that is modern, light, and well planned is the heart of the complex. Here you can also see an exhibit and short film about the Golan stronghold of Gamla, destroyed by the Romans in A.D. 67, during the First Revolt against Rome. The museum is open Sunday through Thursday from 8am to 5pm, Friday until 3pm, and Saturday from 10am to 4pm.

The **Ancient Qasrin Archeological Park** (☎ **06/696-2412**), is just outside Qasrin to the southeast along the main road. Here you'll find the partially restored ancient synagogue of Qasrin, dating from the Byzantine and Early Arab periods. You'll also find two reconstructed houses from the Talmudic era, complete with reproductions of furnishings and implements from those times. This reconstruction helps give a revealing picture of what daily life in the early Jewish communities of the Golan and Galilee would have been like.

The Jewish Heritage Doll Museum. Main Plaza. ☎ **06/696-2982.** Opposite the Golan Archeological Museum.

Despite its recent opening in 1994, this has quickly become one of the country's special, although little-known, attractions. The creation of Leonardo Nisemblatt and Shalom Kahila, who worked on this project for many years, 80 often poetic, wonderfully detailed, and charmingly human dioramas depict the entire history of the Jewish people, starting with the Garden of Eden, and continuing through Abraham's abandonment of Hagar and Ishmael, the parting of the Red Sea, the revolts against Rome, the Diaspora, the Inquisition, the Dreyfus Affair, and the resettlement of Israel. As if this were not tour de force enough, additional dioramas portray the Jewish holidays and storybook fantasies. A newly created diorama, filled with hope for the future, portrays "The Peace Between Israel and Jordan," with dolls representing Clinton, Rabin, Peres, King Hussein, and Crown Prince Hassan. Truly wonderful for everyone from children to history buffs and even those who normally hate dolls and dioramas, the museum is open Sunday through Thursday from 9am to 4pm, Friday from 9am to 1pm, and Saturday from 10am to 4pm. Admission is NIS 18 ($4) for adults; NIS 9 ($2) for children.

Golan Heights Winery. ☎ **06/696-8409.** www.golanwines.co.il. Route 87, 2km (3 mi.) east of central Qasrin.

Producing wines in the Golan, Yarden, and Gamla series, this winery is one of the great business success stories in Israel. A skilled staff, state-of-the-art equipment, the Golan's cold winters and cool summer nights have all combined with the unusual volcanic soil of the winery's vineyards to produce red and white wines that have changed the international reputation of Israel's wine industry. The Yarden series is the most prestigious, but in each series, you'll find notable Cabernet Sauvignon and Merlot wines, as well as Chardonnay and Sauvignon Blanc. Look for Blanc de Blanc, a sparkling wine, as well as a variety of dessert wines. Tours and tasting visits can be made Sunday to Thursday 8am to 4pm and Friday 8am to 1pm. Admission is NIS 18 ($4); credit cards accepted include American Express, Diner's Club, and Visa.

Where to Snack

Qasrin Bakery. Downtown Shopping Center, Qasrin. Sun–Thurs 7am–11pm; Fri 7am–3pm.

The Golan is not thick with restaurants, but the town bakery has baguettes, burekas, and also sells sandwiches on freshly baked breads. It's a great spot to pick up the makings of a picnic; there are also a few tables in case you care to eat in.

Ya'ar Yehudiya Nature Reserve

The reserve stretches from Qasrin to the shores of the Sea of Galilee, and is famous for its ancient oaks, forested valleys, and **waterfalls.** Within the reserve are several waterfalls (especially at Mapal Gamla) and rivers.

Berekhat Ha-Meshushim, a pool amid natural hexagonally shaped columns, is also worth seeing. The columns were formed when mineral-rich molten rock cooled slowly, taking on the crystalline structure. Also in Ya'ar Yehudiya are several **ancient dolmens,** the use and provenance of which is still something of a mystery. The dolmens are not far from Gamla (see below).

Gamla

Gamla National Park. Off Route 808. ☎ **06/696-3721.** Admission NIS 18 ($4). Sat–Thurs 8am–4pm, till 5pm in summer; Fri 8am–3pm.

Gamla, where Jewish residents battled Roman legionnaires in A.D. 67, is a dramatic historical as well as nature site, 12 kilometers (7 mi.) southeast, near Zomet Daliyot. Gamla was one of the early Jewish strongholds recaptured by Rome during the First Revolt against Rome (A.D. 66–70). At the end of this war, Jerusalem and the Second Temple were destroyed (A.D. 70), and the Zealots of Masada committed mass suicide rather than fall into Roman hands (A.D. 73). The story of the battle at Gamla is chillingly similar to that of Masada, but the number of dead was many times higher.

The well-fortified town of Gamla was first conquered by Jewish forces under Alexander Yannai in 90 B.C. Its name came from the site: a hill that looks like the hump of a camel (gamal). Shortly after the Revolt against Rome broke out in A.D. 66, Gamla filled with Jewish refugees fleeing Roman control. The inhabitants at first held out against a Roman siege army, but in the end (according to the Roman Jewish historian, Josephus), when the Romans breached Gamla's defenses, 9,000 people flung themselves from the cliff—choosing death before subjugation. If this indeed happened, the resistance to the death at Gamla in A.D. 67, was different in strategy and spirit from the mass suicide at Masada 6 years later, when all hope of Jewish victory had long been lost. In Gamla, at the start of the Revolt against Rome, the Jews wanted to demonstrate that they would pay any price to stop Rome from regaining control of the Galilee and Judea. There was hope that their sacrifice would result in victory, or at least a compromise with Rome.

There is a shorter trail to the ruins as well as a longer nature hike. Both routes are marked; the longer hike from the road to the site of Gamla, though an arduous 1 to 1¹/₂ hours, is especially beautiful amid the waterfalls and wildflowers of late winter and the spring. The dramatically located synagogue, one of the very few that can be dated from the time of the Second Temple, is memorable. Bring drinking water in warm weather.

Mount Hermon Ski Center

The moshav of Neve Ativ has developed the Mount Hermon Ski Center (☎ **06/698-1337**), high on the slopes of Mount Hermon. The ski center caters to skiers and nonskiers alike. There's even a lift that is exclusively for nonskiers that goes 1 mile to the 6,630-foot summit, where there's an observation point and cafeteria. The snow season usually begins in December or January and lasts until about mid-April. There are times when there's real snow cover, but often, there's just about nothing. Despite Israeli enthusiasm for a ski resort of their own, this is not a must stop for serious skiers.

Roads up to the site are subject to blockage by heavy snow, so check on conditions in advance by telephone, radio report, or newspaper. On Saturday in ski season, the hotels in this region, the roads, and the parking lot fill up early. Also, on Saturday and holidays a special traffic pattern is in effect for the narrow roads in this region: You must approach the resort via Masada and Majdal Shams only; you exit via Neve Ativ. Those driving should just follow the flow of Saturday traffic. Or take the bus from Kiryat Shmona.

The parking lot is below the ski center. You'll be stopped on the road to pay an entrance fee of NIS 36 ($8) to the site. From the parking lot, shuttle buses run you up to the base station.

As for the slopes, there are four runs from the upper station, the longest of which is about 1¹/₂ miles, for average to good skiers. Beginners can use the short chairlift, which is a 1,300-foot trip to a height of 885 feet above the base station. Gentle slopes at the bottom of the hill are good for first runs and for children.

Other facilities include picnic tables and a snack bar at the base, a ski school, and an equipment rental shop. Most Israelis rent equipment, which is yet another reason why you should arrive early if you plan to ski on Saturday. Plan on spending about NIS 405 ($90) per person for a day on the slopes: admission and lift fees, equipment rental, and a snack for lunch.

The ski center is open daily from 8:30am to 3:30pm, weather and security conditions permitting.

6 South of Galilee: The Jordan Valley

Although the River Jordan is at times little more than a desert stream, its waters, which come from the Sea of Galilee, are crucial to the agriculture of the area. It has brought fertile silt down from the Sea of Galilee for so many centuries that its valley is one of the most bounteous farming regions in the country.

ALONG THE JORDAN RIVER

From the Tzemach Junction at the southern tip of the Sea of Galilee, you approach the Jordan Valley **from the north** on Highway 90, following the route of the Jordan River, beginning at its source at the southern shore of the lake.

A CRUSADER CASTLE

Belvoir (Kochav Ha-Yarden) National Park. ☎ **06/658-1766.** Admission NIS 18 ($4). Daily 8am–4pm (to 5pm in summer).

This park, in the Jordan Valley 19 kilometers (31 mi.) south of the Zemach Junction, contains the most spectacular crusader castle ruins in the region. Constructed by the Knights Hospitalers in 1140, this fortress, with dramatic views of the Jordan Valley, was conquered by Saladin in 1189, and dismantled in 1218 to prevent a crusader reoccupation. Especially interesting are carved basalt stones that can be seen in secondary use at various places in the crusader ruins. Some of this stonework, bearing the menorah and other Jewish motifs, has been identified as having originally been part of a synagogue, and testifies to the ravaging of the land by the crusaders. A car is necessary if you wish to visit the site on your own.

BET SHEAN

As you approach the pass at Bet Shean, the temperature increases as the altitude plummets to 300 feet below sea level. Despite the burnt-orange rocky hillsides and the low rainfall of 12 inches annually, this is a highly fertile area. Springs and streams from Mount Gilboa have been directed toward the Jordan Valley's fields, and the fertile soil here supports thousands of acres of wheat, vegetables, banana groves, and cotton fields.

Bet Shean, now an agricultural center and a quiet development town, is another ancient city that, due to its position on the great caravan route from Damascus to Egypt, has had a long succession of foreign rulers.

At ✪ **Tel Bet Shean,** archaeologists have cut into layer upon layer of civilization. They uncovered five separate strata of Canaanite and Egyptian civilizations, with altars and ruins of the Ramses II period, and early Israelite ceramics dating from the time King Saul's body was hung by the Philistines on the Bet Shean wall. Later strata revealed a Scythian period (the Greeks named the town Scythopolis), and in a higher stratum the layers of dirt and rock revealed fragments from Roman times. Some 70 feet into the "tel" (Hebrew for an archaeological mound or hill), the dig uncovered a 6th-century Byzantine town with mosaic floors and delicate columns. Closer to the top they uncovered the remains of crusader castles from the Middle Ages, and still higher up, the jugs and farm tools of the Arab and Turkish settlers of the last 5 centuries.

Elsewhere at Bet Shean you'll see the best-preserved **Roman theater** in Israel. This 8,000-person playhouse has 15 tiers of white limestone in nearly perfect condition, and several more tiers of crumbling black basalt. Broken columns and statue fragments are scattered on the floor. Outside the archaeological park to the north, at the edge of modern-day Bet Shean, is the late-Byzantine **Monastery of the Noble Lady Mary,** with an extremely beautiful and complicated series of mosaic floors. Information about the many sites in the vast archaeological area, which is in the process of being developed for the public, is best obtained at **Bet Shean National Park Visitors Center** (☎ **06/658-7189**). Admission is NIS 22 ($5). The park is open daily from 8am to 4pm, and to 5pm in summer.

THE JORDAN VALLEY

Once you head south from Bet Shean, you are in the abundantly fertile Jordan Valley. You'll see emerald-green splashes of farm settlements in the distance, and soon you'll come to the straight rows of beautiful fruit trees. The vegetation is particularly apparent in the Bet Shean Valley, at the entrance to the Jordan Valley. One ancient sage has written: "If Paradise is in the land of Israel, its gate is Bet Shean."

You are now in subtropical country—notice the profusion of date palm trees, banana groves, pomegranate and grapefruit orchards, and mango trees as well as the neat blue rectangles of carp-breeding ponds. It's hard to imagine the heavy toll this land took on the lives of early settlers.

The river Jordan often dwindles to a mere trickling stream, and rarely looks like it's supposed to—lush and green, with myrtle and reeds.

THE WESTERN APPROACH TO THE JORDAN VALLEY: FROM AFULA TO BET ALPHA

The road from Afula follows a historic route, although road signs announce only communal settlements. Throughout history, pilgrims have traveled along this path to reach the waters of the River Jordan.

Southeast of Afula, you'll pass **Kibbutz Yizreel.** The road then skirts the slopes of **Mount Gilboa,** where the tragedy of Saul occurred. There is a farm collective and a road running right to the top of the mountain, where there is a view of everything—the Galilee mountains, the Emek, the Mediterranean, and Jordan.

On the left is a string of communal settlements—**Ein Harod, Tel Yosef, Bet Ha-Shita.** A large, well-developed settlement, founded in 1921, Ein Harod has a population of nearly 2,000 settlers. It has a hostel, an amphitheater, a culture hall, an archaeological and natural history museum, and an art gallery that has exhibited works by Chagall, Hanna Orloff, Milich, and the American artist Selma Gubin.

Just after Ein Harod, the road sign points to Kibbutz Heftziba and Kibbutz Bet Alpha, both communal settlements. **Kibbutz Bet Alpha** was one of the early Jordan Valley settlements, founded in 1922 by pioneers from Poland and Galicia who cleared the swamps. In 1928, during regional swamp-draining operations, a remnant of a 6th-century rural synagogue, called the Bet Alpha Synagogue, was uncovered in what is now Kibbutz Heftziba. An excavation financed by Temple Emmanu-El of New York City revealed what has become one of the most beloved examples of ancient Jewish art in Israel.

✪ **Bet Alpha Synagogue.** Kibbutz Heftziba, Route 669. ☎ **06/653-2004.** Admission NIS 12 ($2.60). Daily 8am–4p, to 5pm in summer.

The ruins of the Bet Alpha Synagogue contain a highly ornamental and charmingly naive 5th-century A.D. mosaic floor (probably the most famous in Israel) that is divided into three panels: a depiction of Abraham's near sacrifice of Isaac, a depiction of the sun pulled by a star chariot surrounded by the signs of the zodiac, and a tableau representing the Temple of Jerusalem and religious objects associated with the Jewish religion. Many mosaic synagogue floors have been uncovered throughout the Holy Land in the past 75 years; numerous floors, despite the traditional Jewish avoidance of "graven images," depict biblical figures, sacred objects, and a variety of local flora and fauna. The Beit Alpha mosaic has been the subject of many scholarly theories about the meaning of its zodiac, and about the nature of the Jewish communities in Byzantine Palestine that created such representational art.

Interestingly, the signs of the zodiac in the Bet Alpha floor move counterclockwise and do not correspond to the surrounding representations of the four seasons. According to one theory, this indicates that the mosaicists and the Bet Alpha community did not understand the astronomical and astrological relationships of the zodiac, and merely used the design for decorative purposes. Another theory holds that the artisans deliberately rearranged the zodiac to negate its pagan implications. Other archaeologists theorize that Cancer, the sign of Judaism, was deliberately placed at the top of the wheel, ascendant to Leo, the sign of Rome in order to depict an astrological belief in the eventual victory of Judaism over its oppressor. A number of scholars believe that the zodiac motif discovered here (as well as at synagogues uncovered at Na'aran, near Jericho, Hammat Tiberias, and Zippori), was used to symbolize the orderly rhythms of God's universe, or perhaps even the concept of God. It has also been suggested that the geometric mosaic designs to the side of the main floor were boards for games similar to backgammon and chess, and that this may indicate the synagogue was a Jewish community center in every sense of the word! A Greek inscription commemorates Marianos and his son Hanina, two Jewish artisans who created the floor; it is interesting to note that an inscription on the mosaic floor of the Samaritan synagogue found in Bet Shean attributes part of that floor, so similar in style, to the same father-and-son team.

Gan Ha-Shlosha National Park. ☎ **06/658-6219.** Admission NIS 32 ($7); NIS 18 ($4) for children. Daily 8am–4pm; in summer Sat–Thurs until 6pm, with a 4pm closing on Fri. 3 km (5 mi.) southeast of the Bet Alpha Synagogue.

Fed by aquifers, **Sachne,** Israel's large and unique natural swimming pool, is remarkably clear of solvents and silt, and miraculously warm year-round. With its waterfall, tall trees, and distant mountains, Gan Ha-Shlosha/Sachne is a favorite Israeli picnic and swimming site.

Nearby in Gan Ha-Shlosha Park is the **Museum of Regional and Mediterranean Archeology,** an interesting exhibition that attempts to place ancient Palestine within the framework of Mediterranean civilization. There are displays of locally collected statuary, pottery, metalwork, jewelry, and coins dating from the Neolithic to the Mameluke eras, as well as objects from more distant places. Open Sunday through Friday from 8am to 2pm, and admission is NIS 10 ($2.20).

10 The Dead Sea & the Negev

If you have the usual preconception of what a desert is like—nothing but sand—you're in for a surprise. The Negev is not a desert in that sense at all. In fact, the Hebrew word for this southern region is *midbar,* meaning wilderness. There are stretches of sand in the Arava region just north of Eilat, but for the most part, the Negev is a great triangular swath of boulders, pebbles, wind-sculpted mountains, eroded landscape, Bedouin encampments, and brave, lonely settlements. The people of the region are different—they have to be. The Negev could easily be regarded as a sort of Israeli Siberia; instead, the taming of the desert is the prime challenge of the idealistic, and perhaps the greatest single achievement of the people of Israel.

Just a few decades ago the Negev reached north and lapped at the settlements of Rishon-le-Zion and Gedera. But today, the desert has been pushed back beyond Beersheva. Where vultures and scorpions once reigned, winter crops and early vegetables are grown. Inch by inch, a dead land is being reclaimed, and if there is ever peace in the region, the most arid of lands will be taught to bloom again.

It is a pity that so many tourists overlook the Negev in favor of the more conventional sites. The historical artifacts of the wilderness are as intrinsic to Jewish history as the more settled regions in the far north. Flying over the area on the way to Eilat will give you a general appreciation of the region, but to really understand what Israel is about you have to smell the desert, wipe the sand out of your eyes, and tread the paths of the Hebrew nomads.

TOURING THE REGION   Because of the sometimes extraordinary desert heat, it's best to see it by rented car, if at all possible. If you are traveling by bus, choose one or two places to see intensively, rather than scurrying from site to site in the heat. Dehydration occurs very quickly. Keep emergency water with you at all times. It's a good idea to bring along salt pills and insect repellent.

1 South to Beersheva

83 kilometers (52 mi.) S of Jerusalem; 113 kilometers (70 mi.) SE of Tel Aviv.

A few years ago, this town of 170,000 was the "Dodge City" of Israel—only the adventurous came here to work and live. Today, Beersheva is the capital of the Negev, and that old spirit is dwindling, as housing developments and municipal buildings go up in the new part of town.

Still, as you travel from Tel Aviv to Beersheva, the face of the countryside changes; hills disappear and green fields turn dustier; housing projects give way to occasional black tents; the metal of the car burns you as you rest your arm on the window.

Beersheva is another of the ancient cities of Judah. The book of Genesis contains two versions of the story of the town's origin. The first tells of a covenant made between Abraham and Abimelech over a well that Abraham had dug in the desert here. The second story also involves a well (in Hebrew, *be'er*), dug by the servants of Isaac, who gave the well and the town its name: "And he called it Shebah: therefore the name of the city is Beer-sheba unto this day." The phrase "from Dan to Beersheva" appears repeatedly throughout the Bible. Dan is at the northern boundary of the Israelites' territory; Beersheva at the southern end.

Beersheva has been a watering place and trading post for thousands of years, due to its locale on the northern fringe of the Negev. But its modern history dates only from its founding as an outpost of the Ottoman Turkish Empire in 1907.

Increasingly, tourists use this ancient biblical town as their base of operations for excursions into the desert. From here, it's only an hour to Sodom and the Dead Sea and $3^1/2$ hours by bus to Eilat.

ESSENTIALS

GETTING THERE   By Bus   From Jerusalem or Tel Aviv, several buses make the $1^1/2$-hour ride every hour. There is no bus service in Shabbat.

By Car   From Jerusalem I strongly advise the long route via Kiryat Gat, which circumvents the West Bank; from Tel Aviv, via Kiryat Gat.

VISITOR INFORMATION   The **Municipal Tourist Information Office** (☎ 07/ 623-6001) is at 6A Ben-Zvi St., located directly across the street from the Central Bus Station, in the Ein Gedi Building. It's open Sunday through Thursday from 8am to 4pm.

All the shops and businesses in Beersheva close between 1 and 4pm, reopening from 4 to 7pm.

ORIENTATION   Beersheba's **Central Bus Station** is located on Eilat Street, across from the modern Canion Ha-Negev Shopping Center. To the left of the entrance to the bus station are stops for local buses to the Old City, where most of the hotels and restaurants listed below are located. A new railway station has been constructed nearby, but at present there is limited rail service to Beersheva. Other trains may be added, however, if a planned railway heading south to Eilat is put into operation.

West of the bus station, you'll find a Muslim cemetery, and beyond that, a small, densely packed business section of Beersheva. The **Old Town,** or the original Turkish and British Mandate–era town, is laid out as a grid. It is the commercial "downtown" of Beersheva, where you will find the shops and budget and moderately priced hotels and restaurants.

Herzl Street is the major downtown north-south thoroughfare. Main streets east and west are **Ha-Atzma'ut (Independence) Street** and **Keren Kayemet Le-Israel,** which has been made into a pedestrian mall. Right where Herzl and Ha-Atzma'ut intersect is the old Turkish city hall, the Allenby Garden; and behind the Turkish city hall is the Great Mosque, now the Negev Museum, which at press time, after years of closure, was under renovation.

The rest of modern, apartment-complex Beersheva sprawls northward from the old downtown section.

WHAT TO SEE & DO
THE BEDOUIN MARKET

The famous Bedouin market is next to the municipal market, on the southeastern edge of downtown. Although the Thursday morning market, when the Bedouin tribes come in from the desert to buy and sell in the colorful marketplace, is no longer the exotic event it once was, you can still see Bedouins in long gowns, bartering over sacks of flour and coffee, and holding conferences on the dollar rate of exchange for hand-woven rugs and baskets. Most of the marketeering goes on between 5 and 7:30am.

While you watch the Bedouins, you can also pick up some (sometimes question-able) bargains yourself. Although most of the beautiful tribal crafts have vanished, you can find spices, sheared wool in sacks, copper and brass coffee sets with decorated trays, long knives, wood carvings, fancy Arabian saddles, nargeilas, and rugs and bas-kets. You can also climb aboard a camel and be photographed (don't be perturbed by his protesting spits and snorts).

Plans are now in the works for the construction of several permanent shops at the market site, so that the arts and crafts can be displayed all the time. A motel is in the planning stages here as well; you can ask at the Municipal Tourist Information Office for current details.

MUSEUMS

Negev Museum Complex. 60 Ha-Atzma'ut St. ☎ **07/623-4338.** Partly closed for renovation; call for details on admission fee and hours.

The museum's small collection combines antiquities, historical artifacts, and contemporary art, all presently housed in the turn-of-the-century Turkish governor's house on the corner of Ha-Atzma'ut and Herzl streets, adjacent to Beersheva's Turkish mosque, in a pleasant little park in the center of the Old City. Until recently, the collection was also housed in a graceful, neighboring mosque that had not been in use since the 1948 War of Independence, when the Muslim inhabitants of Beersheva fled the city. During the 1990s, Israeli Arabs living in the region began to demand the museum exhibits be displayed elsewhere and the mosque be returned to its original state as a house of worship; at press time, the mosque is closed for repairs, and the museum has retreated into the Governor's House. Old photographs of pashas, provincial governors, staff officers in ancient motorcars, and early settlers provide a glimpse into Beersheva's early days as a municipality. You may also see displays about the Chalcolithic (3500 B.C.) civilization of the Negev, characterized by underground cities and houses, as well as 6th-century mosaics depicting desertscapes from the church of Kissufim in the Western Negev. As you approach the mosque, the most beautiful and interesting building in Beersheva, note the graceful *tughra* (the Ottoman sultan's monogram) in a medallion over the main door.

Joe Alon Museum of Bedouin Culture. Kibbutz Lahav. ☎ **07/991-3322.** www. lahavnet.co.il. Admission NIS 16 ($3.50). Sun–Thurs 9am–4pm; Fri 9am–2pm.

This museum, located 24 kilometers (14 mi.) north of Beersheva, is well worth a visit. Displays illustrate the way of life for Bedouin tribes in the Negev and the Sinai, and also the Jbaliyya (Jebaliya) tribe that has been associated for centuries with the Santa Katerina Monastery on Mount Sinai. There are folklore guides, lectures, and there is a traditional Bedouin tent where you can stop for spiced dessert tea or coffee. Displays of Bedouin rugs, textiles, embroidery, jewelry, and tools will make you aware of the strikingly beautiful objects that were (and still are) part of the everyday life of these nomadic people. Today, of the 100,000 Bedouin living in the Negev, 60,000 have been settled into permanent housing and the ancient Bedouin culture, so closely attuned to the nature of the Negev, is threatened with assimilation into the 21st century.

To get there, drive north from Beersheva on the road to Tel Aviv; after 24 kilometers (14^1/$_2$ mi.), you'll see a sign for Lahav, or Kibbutz Lahav, and the Joe Alon Center. Turn right here; go another 7 kilometers (4 mi.) until you see the sign directing you uphill to the **Joe Alon Regional and Folklore Center;** the Bedouin Museum is part of this center. As you go uphill, you'll go through part of the Jewish National Fund forest, a shady place to stop for a picnic. There is no bus service.

MORE ATTRACTIONS

Abraham's Well is located at the southern end of Keren Kayemet Le-Israel Street, at the intersection of Derekh Hevron, down by the riverbed. Two large round stone walls, one open, the other covered by an arched stone roof, are surrounded by a stone courtyard, some desert date palm trees, and a wooden water wheel for drawing up the water. The wells are no longer in use, but you can still see the water far down below.

It may have been here that Abraham watered his large flocks almost 4,000 years ago, and settled a dispute with Abimelech over rights to the water. Scholars still cannot decide whether "Beer-Sheva" means "Well of the Covenant" or "Well of the Seven" for the seven ewe lambs that Abraham gave Abimelech as a peace offering. Behind Abraham's Well, look for signs to the **Ethiopian Jewish Handicrafts Exhibit,** which opened here in 1994. Its future at this location is not certain.

The pride of Beersheva is the **Ben-Gurion University of the Negev,** whose faculties include the humanities, the sciences, and a medical school. Many of the more than two dozen departments emphasize the development of the Negev. The imaginative architecture combines awareness of climatic conditions with practical needs of the students and teachers.

The **old railway station** on Tuviyahu Street is worth a look. It was along the Beersheva line that ran to Egypt that Lawrence of Arabia played his train-blowing tricks.

ATTRACTIONS IN TEL BEER SHEVA

Of all Israel's war memorials, the **Monument to the Negev Fighters Brigade,** completed in 1969, is possibly the most original, certainly the most evocative. It is the work of Dani Caravan, one of Israel's most famous artists. It's on the northeastern edge of the city, just off the road that leads to Hebron, and commemorates the Palmach brigade that captured the Negev during the 1948 War of Independence.

The memorial, consisting of 18 symbolic sections, flows like a fantastic cement garden over the summit of raw windy hill. Here the entire Negev campaign has been reduced to its essentials: a concrete tent wall, a bunker, a hill crisscrossed by communications trenches, a pipeline, nine war maps engraved in the floor of the square. You can climb all over these structures and to the top of the tall cement tower (representing the watch and water towers that were shelled on the Negev settlements); you can file singly through the inclined walls of the pass that lead into the Memorial Dome, and enter the symbolic Bunker. Sadly, this memorial to those who fell in the battle for the Negev is not always well maintained and has been vandalized with graffiti.

3 kilometers (1^1/$_2$ mi.) northeast of Beersheva on Route 60, at **Tel Beer Sheva National Park** (☎ 07/646-7286), the digs of many seasons have unearthed an ancient Israelite city dating from the 12th to the 8th centuries B.C., built over the ruins of earlier levels of habitation. A dominant feature of the Iron Age Israelite city is a circular street with rows of buildings on both sides. A massive, 90-foot-deep well of

great antiquity was found right outside the 3,000-year-old city gates—some speculate that this may actually have been the well of Abraham. A huge, four-horned ashlar altar was also found at the site—the original is now in the collection of the Israel Museum, and a reproduction is displayed near the entrance to the tel. Though a dramatic object, and central to the ancient religions of the area, this altar is made of carved stone, in violation of biblical law; it therefore was probably not an altar used by early Israelite worshippers. The tel is open Sunday to Thursday from 8am to 5pm; Friday 8am to 3pm; and Saturday 8am to 4pm. Admission is NIS 12 ($2.60).

The **Israel Air Force Museum,** on Route 233, 7 kilometers (4 mi.) west of Beersheva (☎ **07/990-6890**), contains at least 100 planes that have played a role in Israel's history, ranging from one of the four Czech Messerschmitts that helped stop the Egyptian advance into Israel in 1948 to a Boeing 707 that was used in the famous 1976 rescue of Jewish passengers aboard an Air France plane that had been hijacked and taken to Entebbe, Uganda. Open Sunday to Thursday noon to 5pm and Friday 8am to noon. Admission is NIS 28 ($6.20).

OUTDOOR ACTIVITIES

SWIMMING   The brand-new **Negev Paradise Hotel** (☎ **07/640-5444**) has a heated pool, a children's pool, and a health club with dry and wet saunas and a Jacuzzi; you will have to pay a nonguest fee. In the Old City, the **Bet Yatziv Youth Hostel** and **Bet Sadot Valev Guesthouse** (☎ **07/627-7444**) share a large swimming pool behind the hostel. You'll find it at 79 Ha-Atzma'ut St., about 3 blocks northwest of Herzl Street, past the Turkish mosque. Admission is NIS 22 ($5) with a discount for guests of the hostel. It's open Sunday through Friday from 8:30am to 5pm, Saturday from 8:30am to 4pm.

ORGANIZED TOURS

It is possible, while in Beersheva, to join a group tour for a visit to a **Bedouin encampment and a Bedouin-style dinner.** Ask at the Tourist Office across from the Central Bus Station. The cost will be anywhere from NIS 54 ($12) for the "short visit," which consists of a chat with the sheik over coffee or tea, camel ride, and Bedouin music, to about NIS 115 to 135 ($25 or $30) for the full "sunset visit" with Bedouin dinner, which includes the above as well as a typical rice, mutton, and fruit meal, eaten with the fingers or in pita. Prices include transportation, and can be higher if there are fewer than 25 people in the group. It is a good idea to phone ahead before reaching Beersheva to find out when the next group is going out.

WHERE TO STAY

Desert Inn (Neot Midbar). Shderot Tuviahu, Beersheva. ☎ **07/642-4922.** Fax 07/641-2772. 164 units. A/C TV TEL. $98–$133 double. Rates include breakfast. Add 15% service charge. AE, DC, MC, V.

Built in the 1960s and located away from the center of town, this was (until 1996) the only hotel in Beersheva above the rock-bottom level. It's utilitarian, rather than stylish, but comfortable, with a friendly staff, heated outdoor swimming pool, a children's pool, three tennis courts, basketball courts, a sauna and hot tub. There are also three in-house restaurants.

Negev Paradise Hotel. Henrietta Szold St., Beersheva. ☎ **07/640-5444.** Fax 07/640-5445. 262 units. A/C TV TEL. $178–$200 double. AE, DC, MC, V. Fee for parking.

Completed in 1996, this 15-story hotel is by far the best in Beersheva, within walking distance of the City Hall, the municipal theater, and downtown restaurants.

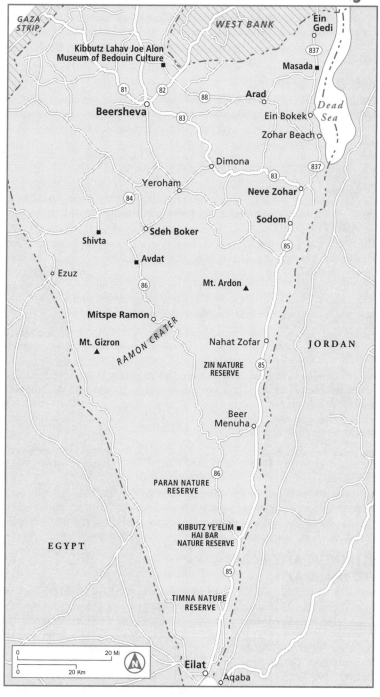

The Negev

GAZA STRIP

WEST BANK

Ein Gedi

837

Kibbutz Lahav Joe Alon
Museum of Bedouin Culture

Masada

81   82

88   Arad

Beersheva

83   Ein Bokek

Zohar Beach

Dead Sea

Dimona

83   837

Yeroham

Neve Zohar

84

Sdeh Boker   Sodom

Shivta

85

Avdat

86   Mt. Ardon

Mitspe Ramon

RAMON CRATER

Nahat Zofar   JORDAN

Mt. Gizron

ZIN NATURE
RESERVE   85

Beer
Menuha

PARAN NATURE
RESERVE

86

EGYPT   KIBBUTZ YE'ELIM
HAI BAR
NATURE RESERVE

85

TIMNA NATURE
RESERVE

0   20 Mi
N
0   20 Km

Eilat

Aqaba

Ezuz

It contains a heated swimming pool, a children's pool, a full health club, a Jacuzzi and wet and dry saunas, as well as a business center, and no-smoking and handicapped-accessible guest rooms. The relatively new rooms are still freshly decorated and very comfortable; some have minibars or kitchen facilities.

WHERE TO DINE

Beersheva has never had a stunning culinary reputation, but the dining situation is starting to improve. For an inexpensive meal, there are many quick-service counter restaurants in the pedestrian mall on Keren Kayemet Le-Israel Street. The air-conditioned Kanion Shopping Mall across from the Central Bus Station has Pizza Hut, Burger Ranch, China Town, and a number of other places to grab a bite for NIS 18 to 27 ($4 to $6). Also, the omnipresent shashlik and french fries aren't bad.

✪ **Apropo.** 140 Keren Kayemet St. at Herzl St. ☎ **07/623-6711.** Reservations recommended. Appetizers and main courses NIS 34–85 ($7.50–$18.70). 12% service charge. AE, DC. Sun–Thurs 9am–midnight; Fri 9am–2pm; Sat after Shabbat to midnight. EUROPEAN/INTERNATIONAL.

The most stylish restaurant in town, in terms of both food and decor, Apropo offers a large variety of menu items, ranging from salads and omelettes to genuine Thai dishes, and inventive dishes with an Asian touch. You can even order kosher faux "shrimp" in a number of styles, or fish steamed in the Thai manner but seasoned with Mediterranean-style herbs. With its kosher dessert list, this is also a good choice for a leisurely coffee and cake. Service is usually excellent; the service charge is obligatory.

Bet Ha-Fuul. In Gan Ha-Nassi Park. No phone. Light meals NIS 15–30 ($3.30–$6.60). No credit cards. Sun–Thurs 10am–midnight; Fri 10am–3pm; Sat after Shabbat. HUMMUS/FELAFEL.

Located near Ilie Restaurant, between Herzl, Ha-Histadrut, Ha-Avot, and Smilansky streets, this place is not much in terms of decor, but it's popular with the locals for its good food. A hearty lunch might include hummus or Egyptian fool beans with sauce and a boiled egg, assorted salads, and fresh, thick pita bread. The outside falafel counter is open daily until 8 or 10pm, and serves a fine falafel.

Ilie Steak Restaurant. 21 Herzl St. ☎ **07/627-8685.** Reservations not accepted. Main courses NIS 50–80 ($11–$17.60). AE, DC, MC, V. Sun–Thurs noon–midnight; Fri noon–3pm. STEAK.

What this place lacks in decor it makes up for in good, fresh food. This restaurant is not fancy; decor is a wall-size photograph of camels, and a meat-and-fish display. House specialties include Romanian kebab, sirloin fillet steak, and fresh fish grilled over charcoal. Regular customers even do the grilling themselves!

BEERSHEVA AFTER DARK
PERFORMING ARTS

Beersheva is justifiably proud of its **Israel Sinfonietta** (☎ **07/623-1616**), which performs throughout the country. Tickets are by subscription, but you may be able to buy a ticket before the performance at the box office. The concerts start promptly at 8:30pm. Concerts are also given by the Beersheva Music Conservatory's Chamber Orchestra (☎ **07/627-6019**). Many superb musicians perform with these groups. The **Beersheva Theater** performs at Bet Ha-Am, in the Hever Community Center, the large white building in Gan Moshe Park. Performances are usually in Hebrew only. Check with the Tourism Information Office (6A Ben-Zvi St., ☎ **07/623-6001**) for current programs. Tickets are approximately NIS 115 ($25).

PUBS & CAFES

Beersheva has a number of cozy, constantly changing pubs that spring up and close down, especially on the southern side of Old Town. Stroll around Trumpeldor, Smilansky Streets and the little lanes of the neighborhood, listen to the music, and see the lights flood the streets from the open doors. **Hatzer Ha-Yayin Wine Bar** (☎ 07/623-8135), in the Artists Quarter, is the classiest place around, serving wine and tapas at a pace that works well with quiet conversation.

EN ROUTE FROM BEERSHEVA TO ARAD

As soon as you leave Beersheva, you'll see clusters of Bedouin tents and flocks—and also houses, for today the Bedouin are being strongly encouraged by the government of Israel to settle down.

At the first major intersection not far from Beersheva take the right turn for Arad and the Dead Sea. A bit farther on you'll begin to see Bedouin villages—the Abu-Rabiya tribe has four such settlements between Beersheva and Arad, all fairly close together. The villages consist largely of huts and some planned housing projects. At times it may be possible to see a few traditional black goat-hair tents, which are amazingly cool in summer and warm in winter. Some villages may be quite large; others may be nothing more than three houses and five tents. Another thing to note is that the Bedouin here do a lot of farming, growing mostly wheat, but also other grains, and fruits and vegetables, most of which they sell in the Beersheva markets. A great deal of experimental agricultural work is being done along this road: sisal is grown without irrigation; tamarisk, eucalyptus, and other trees are planted in small areas, where their growth is watched carefully by scientists who are planning to cultivate even more of Israel's desert.

When the road starts snaking around tight curves, you'll know you're approaching Arad.

2 Arad, Neve Zohar/Ein Bokek & Sodom

Arad: 46 kilometers (28 mi.) E of Beersheva.

ARAD

The modern desert city of Arad, with a population of 22,000, is not a mirage, but rather a well-planned town located on the site of an ancient Israelite settlement—a concrete testimonial to the continuity of Jewish history. There is bus service to the city from Jerusalem, Tel Aviv, and Beersheva and sheruts and taxis travel the road to the Dead Sea spas at Ein Bokek and Ein Gedi. Arad is a logical place to stay if you're exploring the desert region. At 2,000 feet above sea level, the town's ultradry, mold-free climate is especially good for people who suffer from allergies or asthma, and hotels in Arad cater to such visitors.

It is interesting to note that Arad is a planned Western-style city, begun in 1961, and mapped out to efficiently meet the rigid desert conditions in the most comfortable manner. Today, however, many believe a city plan more rooted in desert tradition, with narrow, shaded, labyrinthine streets, might have been more successful. The cityscape is bleak here, and even more so in some of the other planned settlement communities in the Negev, such as Yeroham and Dimona. However, people are working to make these places succeed—a good part of Israel's territory (and future) is here.

ESSENTIALS

GETTING THERE **By Bus** There is regular bus service from Jerusalem, Tel Aviv, and Beersheva.

By Car Main highways run east from Beersheva and west from the Jordan Valley at the southern end of the Dead Sea.

VISITOR INFORMATION You will probably come into town from the main highway **via Hebron Street.** The third cross street is **El'azar Ben-Yair** (named for the leader of the stronghold at Masada in A.D. 73). The corner of Hebron and Ben-Yair is the town's principal commercial center. The post office is at the corner of Hebron and Ben-Yair. The **Tourist Information Office** is in the **Arad Visitors Center** at 28 Ben-Yair St. (☎ **07/995-4409**). Follow the signs to find the office in the commercial center of town, opposite the Community Center. It's open Saturday through Thursday from 9am to 5pm and on Friday from 9am to 2pm. There are publications of the Society for Protection of Nature in Israel (SPNI) here (some free, some for sale), including information about the area (including a video presentation), books, maps, and desert hiking gear. The Visitors Center can also give you advice about hotels and rooms in the area, and book you onto tours, treks, and other desert activities. Admission to the very worthwhile multimedia desert exhibit at the Visitor's Center is NIS 20 ($4.30).

WHAT TO SEE & DO

Most people come to Arad's high, dry location for relief of asthma rather than for sightseeing. However, you should make the effort to see the spare landscape from the far eastern end of Ben-Yair/Moav Street near the Hotel Masada. At the road's end, a path begins, heading out to a modern sculpture on the promontory.

Most everything can be found at the commercial center, including food, clothing, cosmetics, stationery, banks, a hairdresser, pharmacy, and a photography store.

Many activities take place at the **Matnas Cultural Center** opposite the Tourist Information Office. Youngsters meet on Friday night, and local activities like the **Chess Club** and **Melave Malka,** the **Bridge Club,** and the **folk dancing group** meet once a week. You can obtain a schedule of events from the Tourist Information Office.

For the past decade, in mid-July, a **Hebrew Song Festival** (mostly rock music) has turned Arad into a desert mecca for teenagers and students, but in the summer of 1995, a stampede at the festival resulted in a number of deaths and injuries and left the country in a state of shock; the future of this event is now in doubt.

Arad is such a friendly place that it's a good spot to meet area residents willing to participate in activities with tourists. Ask at the tourist office.

Four miles west of Arad is Tel Arad, a partially reconstructed 5,000-year-old Canaanite town with a 3,000-year-old Israelite fort. It's open October through March, Sunday to Thursday, from 8am to 4pm; until 5pm the rest of the year, closing an hour earlier, respectively, on Friday and holiday eves. The entrance fee is NIS 12 ($2.60).

WHERE TO STAY & DINE

Arad offers a selection of simple but adequate hotels. The town has few restaurants, but snack places can be found in the commercial center.

Margoa Arad Hotel. Moav St., Arad 80750. ☎ **07/995-1222.** Fax 07/995-7778. 146 units. A/C TV TEL. $143–$160 double. Rates include breakfast. Add 15% VAT. AE, DC, MC, V.

This choice, as luxurious as you'll get in Arad, offers hotel rooms and cottages as well as a pleasant restaurant/dining room. The large heated swimming pool is open from the spring (Passover) to the late fall (Sukkot). There is a fitness room (fee) and the Margoa also offers a clinic for asthma sufferers.

Nof Arad Hotel. Moav St., Arad 80750. ☎ **07/995-7056.** Fax 07/995-4053. 117 units. A/C TV TEL. $94–$114 double. Rates include breakfast. Add 15% VAT. MC, V.

Across the street from the Margoa, this establishment has cabins and hotel rooms. Rooms in the hotel's newer (1984) wing are more luxuriously furnished and cost about $7 per person more. The hotel features a swimming pool and offers self-service breakfasts.

EN ROUTE TO NEVE ZOHAR & SODOM

If you're traveling during Israel's 7 dry months, be sure to get an early start; by noon an eerily languid, breathless heat settles over the entire area.

The ride from Arad to the Dead Sea (just 45 min.) is almost all downhill—the word *steep* is hardly adequate. From Arad's heights, where the land is a chalky sandy color, the wilderness to the west turns increasingly darker, changing to tans and then deeper shades of brown. During the 28½-kilometer (17-mi.) trip, the scenery will doubtlessly hold your attention. You'll pass through the **Rosh Zohar** fields of large underground reservoirs of natural gas. Don't miss an observation point to the left, called **Mezad Zohar.** For the best view, be sure to lean against the rail of the sun-shelter and look out and down. Here are remains of a **Roman fortress,** in the valley that once served as the major roadway from the Dead Sea. (These desert valleys, or *wadis,* were carved out over the centuries by fierce and sudden rains.) A second observation point is a bit farther down; there is a huge map to help you identify what you're looking at. Then the road swings down to reveal a vista of the Dead Sea and part of the Judean wilderness beyond it.

If you come directly from Beersheva (by bus, sherut, or private car), you'll drive just over an hour, and you can take the road through another of those desert development towns, **Dimona.** The most famous of Israel's hastily constructed boomtowns, Dimona was the subject of considerable controversy, because at one time many thought it was inhuman and impossible to expect people to live and work in such a climate. However, the handful of tents that started the town in 1955 soon became a community of 22,500 people living in cement housing complexes—a town complete with movie theaters, cultural centers, textile and phosphate plants, and even an atomic reactor. Its population consists of desert visionaries and members of many immigrant groups that were settled there by the Ministry of Absorption. Most famous of these groups are the Hebrew Israelites (or Black Hebrews), an African American group that originally came to Israel as tourists in the 1970s, and never left. Most Hebrew Israelites have been settled in Dimona. Their vegan restaurants in Tel Aviv and Tiberias, and their jazz and blues musicians, are famous throughout Israel.

Three miles farther, on the right, is a deserted stone blockhouse—a former police station on a high hill that stands on the site of **Mamshit** (see below; access via Dimona), an ancient Nabatean-Byzantine town. Nearby, in a deep gorge, are the ruins of three **ancient dams,** behind which 6th-century A.D. engineers were able to store enough water to sustain Mamshit's residents. Mamshit is one of the many old desert cities under close scrutiny by Israel's modern scientists, who are convinced that many of the inventive methods of water collection and desert living devised by these ancient cities are still applicable in the Negev.

THE DEAD SEA

Beyond the ruins of a Roman fort called **Tamar** (20km/12 mi. farther on), the road descends rapidly. Abruptly, around a turn, you are confronted with one of Israel's most amazing sights—and certainly the most bizarre. Surrounded by the Moab and Edom mountains, the Dead Sea is 3,000 feet below, in a heavy haze.

Soon you pass the sea-level sign, as you descend through the Arava plain, passing potash and bromide factories along the way. Signs commemorate the workers who were ambushed constructing this road in 1951, and the actual opening of the road to Sodom in 1953. Suddenly, you are at the edge of the **Dead Sea,** the lowest point on earth, 1,300 feet below sea level. (Death Valley in California, America's lowest point, is only 282 feet below sea level.)

Half of the 48-mile Dead Sea is in Israel's territory (about 100 square miles of it), but even working with that little area, technicians find that they can scarcely deal fast enough with the vast reservoir of chemicals being constantly removed from the sea. This water is 25% solids, of which 7% is salt—six times as salty as the ocean. Each day, tons of chlorides, bromides, and sulfides are removed for processing and export. No fish can live in these miles of mineral-rich liquid.

NEVE ZOHAR/EIN BOKEK & THE DEAD SEA
ZOHAR SPRINGS

Unlike the waters of the Dead Sea further north, near Ein Gedi, those in the area of the big spa hotels at Neve Zohar and Ein Bokek are believed to be very helpful for skin diseases like psoriasis. These were Cleopatra's favorite waters for her beauty needs, and today the waters are said to be cleansing for skin and scalp, improving skin texture, and even smoothing wrinkles.

Experts came out here in the 1960s, had the waters analyzed by Hadassah technicians, and found that they contained the highest mineral content of any waters in the world: 300 grams per liter. In the baths here, they explain, you take 10% to 14% more oxygen than in any other water in the world, which is helpful for people with respiratory problems and heart disease. In addition, when tired and nervous people come here for a week, the atmosphere seems to change their lives. At the area's hotels and spas, experts will tailor the treatment baths to your specific ailment. If you want the whole spa treatment, though, you'll have to have a medical okay. You can be examined by a resident physician, but a doctor's note certifying that your blood pressure can stand the stimulation of the waters will suffice. In order to really get any benefit from the Dead Sea spas, you must stay here for at least 1 or 2 weeks. The four- and five-star hotels at Ein Bokek, though expensive, are the only way to really do an intensive program of spa treatments.

The Hammei Zohar spa is quite a luxurious place. It is equipped with a central air-conditioning system, excellent facilities in the sulfur baths and pools, mud baths, vibration and electrogalvanic baths, underwater massages, and cosmetic treatments. The baths are open Sunday to Thursday from 7am to 3pm and Saturday 7am to 1:30pm. The sulfur pool costs NIS 40 ($11.20); the sulfur bath NIS 66 ($18.50); and the mud treatment NIS 100 ($56). It's advisable to check your valuables.

WHERE TO STAY

All hotels in this community offer health and beauty programs, but these should not be your only reason for staying at a hotel in Neve Zohar or Ein Bokek; they also provide a very comfortable base for exploring the desert and enjoying the Dead Sea.

Expensive

Crowne Plaza. Ein Bokek. ☎ **07/659-1919.** Fax 07/659-1911. 320 units. A/C MINIBAR TV TEL. $258–$290 double. Rates include breakfast. Add 15% VAT. AE, DC, MC, V.

Opened in 1997, the Holiday Inn is half the size and not quite as dazzling as its rival, the new Hyatt Regency, but it is a tasteful, state-of-the art hotel and spa, with every possible therapeutic, health and resort program you could want. There are indoor and outdoor pools, and a wide range of sulfur, mineral, and mud baths. The breakfast, lunch and dinner buffets are sumptuous, perhaps outdoing those at the Hyatt; there is also a kosher branch of Tel Aviv's stylish Giraffe Noodle Bar, serving inventive Asian fare. The Holiday Inn has the added advantage of actual Dead Sea beachfront. As at all first class Dead Sea hotels, a tour desk will arrange outings throughout the area.

✪ **Hyatt Regency Dead Sea Resort and Spa, Ein Bokek.** ☎ **07/659-1234.** Fax 07/659-1235. 600 units. A/C MINIBAR TV TEL. $250–$314 standard double; $289–$352 deluxe double. Rates include breakfast. AE, DC, MC, V.

This gleaming new (1996) 17-story blockbuster, the largest spa hotel in the Middle East, is a climate-controlled world unto itself, with most comforts and facilities imaginable. There are heated indoor and outdoor swimming pools, including a lengthy serpentine swimming pool (bathtub-warm in summer) that sprawls across the hotel's property; sulfur pools and Dead Sea mineral baths. There's also a Jacuzzi, sauna, massage, and Dead Sea mud treatments, a medical center offering a wide variety of services including postsurgery, and 14 separate facilities for beauty and fitness programs. Guest rooms are spacious and have polished stone bathrooms; many contain both tubs and glass stall showers. Food services are under the direction of a talented chef brought in from Austria. Restaurants, set around the gardened atrium, range from Caribbean, Italian, and Middle Eastern to Far Eastern. The lavish breakfast buffet should get you through most of the day; lunch and dinner buffets are generous and top quality. Though polished marble and glass abound, the hotel's design also includes classical columns and other touches that bring to mind a theme of lavish Roman baths. There is a beach on the Dead Sea for Hyatt guests, but the hotel itself is not directly on the Dead Sea.

Lot Hotel. Ein Bokek. ☎ **07/658-4321.** Fax 07/658-4623. 199 units. A/C TV TEL. $160–$210 double. Rates include breakfast. MC, V.

This is one of the few (somewhat) less-expensive hotels in the bustling resort center. It's been around for more than 20 years and if you had come to take the waters before the great hotel boom of the '90s here, this is the kind of place you would have stayed. It's functional and comfortable, but lacking the glamour of its neighbors, and has two in-house restaurants and an outdoor pool, plus a full range of health and beauty treatments. Rooms are equipped with minibars or refrigerators. The clientele is largely Israelis and older Europeans.

✪ **Nirvana Resort and Spa Hotel.** Ein Bokek. ☎ **800/221-0203** or 212/541-0203 in the U.S. and Canada; 07/668-9444 in Israel. Fax 07/668-9400. E-mail: info@nirvana.co.il. 388 units. A/C MINIBAR TV TEL. $290–$320 standard double; $374–$444 deluxe double. Rates include breakfast. 15% service charge. Seven-night packages including breakfast, dinner, and treatments begin at $290 double for 2 persons. AE, DC, MC, V.

This place is different from the maze of megahotels lumped together at Ein Bokek. It's by itself a few kilometers to the south of the other hotels, with its own private beach and lagoon and gives you a real feeling for the Dead Sea's serene mystery. With a large new wing completed in 1999, and the rest of the hotel renovated at the same time, the Nirvana is more stylish and livelier than many of the places nearby, where many guests are staying for long-term treatment programs, There's a large freshwater pool, and there are also saltwater, and mineral pools, complete health and beauty packages at Nirvana's spa, three restaurants, bar and disco, fitness center with sauna and hot tub, and an in-house synagogue. Readers report the dining facilities as superior: Lunch and dinner are each NIS 162 ($36). Public areas and new guest rooms are also among the best in the area.

WHERE TO DINE

The in-house hotel restaurants offer the best possibilities for a major meal. Many visitors staying here hotel-hop to try out the different lunch or dinner buffets. They're all vast, and you're sure to find something interesting; the price range is from NIS 100 to 200 ($22 to $44). A kosher branch of Tel Aviv's always interesting and inventive Asian restaurant, Giraffe, is at the Crowne Plaza Hotel.

Kapulsky. Ein Bokek, Dead Sea. ☎ **07/658-4382.** Main courses NIS 22–50 ($6.20–$14.); cakes and desserts NIS 12–20 ($3.40–$5.60). MC, V. Daily 8am–midnight. CAFE/LIGHT MEALS.

For passers-through as well as guests at local hotels, this is one of the better choices, with a glassed-in terrace overlooking the Dead Sea. Kapulsky's is a national chain, famous for rich desserts and pleasant, light meals. At this branch, the selection is often limited (depending on demand and what's been shipped into this remote location), and prices are somewhat higher than elsewhere in the country. When supplies are in you can order fish, pasta dishes, salads, and sandwiches.

SODOM

Retrace your drive along the shore, back to whichever highway (Arad or Beersheva) brought you to the sea-hugging road. Don't turn there; just keep going and you'll reach Sodom in 10 kilometers (6 mi.). The wicked city of Sodom, the lowest inhabited place on earth, is no more (Gen. 19:12–29). The famous community of degeneracy is now a potash concession, not a real town as such. Here the road that runs along the Dead Sea shore is bordered on the left by a wall of solid salt. Reportedly, one of the pillars along the bordering wall is Lot's wife. According to the biblical story of the destruction of Sodom and Gomorrah, angels intended to save Lot, nephew of Abraham, and his family; in telling them to run for it, they also admonished them not to look back. Lot's wife, however, turned back in curiosity and was mummified in perpetuity as the pillar of salt. The legendary pillar—which does suggest such a shape—stands above the entrance to the Sodom cave (now closed).

The fire and brimstone that hit Sodom and Gomorrah was probably a Tertiary-era volcano that shattered this area, according to scientific evidence. A proposal to construct a gambling casino here drew a wrathful protest from religious leaders. Their objection? The city was destroyed once for its wickedness; don't tempt history to repeat itself.

The calm, oily sea is on one side; bizarre, agonizing mountain slopes on the other. Clumps of white foam, a solid brine, cling to the dried shrubs and clumps of whitened stone. There is a noxious smell of sulfur in the air, and some of the trees next to the sea are petrified and laced with gypsum and bitumen crystals. Nearby, however, is Moshav Neot Ha-Kikar—proof that even the most arid and desolate desert land can be reclaimed.

3 Ein Gedi & Masada

Ein Gedi: 50 kilometers (30 mi.) S of Jericho; 15 kilometers (10 mi.) S of Ein Gedi.

Your adventure into the Negev can start from Jerusalem eastward through the Judean desert to the outskirts of Jericho, and then south along the dramatic Dead Sea road via Ein Gedi and Masada. The route from Jerusalem south through the West Bank cities of Bethlehem and Hebron to Beersheva is not recommended at this time. Don't fail to see Masada, and to take a dip in the Dead Sea at Ein Gedi. The road from Jerusalem along the Dead Sea coast passes the ruins of **Qumran,** near the caves where the first Dead Sea Scrolls were found in 1947. In addition to the Scrolls, hidden at the time of the First Jewish Revolt against Rome in A.D. 70, archaeological excavations of caves in this region during the early 1960s uncovered mysterious and beautiful copper ritual objects, used 5,000 to 6,000 years ago by members of a prehistoric civilization, as well as artifacts and personal documents and letters hidden by refugees from the Second Jewish Revolt against Rome in A.D. 135. Other caves in the area, their openings or interior reaches sealed by rockfalls over the centuries, may conceal still more treasures.

ESSENTIALS

GETTING THERE   By Bus   There is service from Tel Aviv via Jerusalem and from Eilat four times daily.

By Car   There are main roads to Eilat and Beersheva via Arad, and from Jerusalem via the Jordan Valley and the Dead Sea.

EIN GEDI

Ein Gedi has been an Eden-like canyon oasis for thousands of years, attracting human beings for thousands of years before recorded time. More than 5,000 years ago, Chalcolithic people built a sanctuary amid the waterfalls and springs here—in the 1960s, Israeli archaeologists searching for Jewish scrolls (from the period 150 B.C. –A.D. 135) amid the crevasses and depths of inaccessible caves nearby, came upon a cache of elegant, mysteriously designed copper wands, crowns, and scepters from 3,000 B.C. that scholars believe were the sacred vessels of a long-forgotten prehistoric culture centered at Ein Gedi (the copper objects are now displayed at the Israel Museum). It was to Ein Gedi that the young David fled as a fugitive from the paranoid King Saul; here David had the chance to kill his pursuer, but he would not lay a hand on his king, the anointed of God. The Song of Solomon rhapsodized thus: "My beloved is unto me as a cluster of camphire from the vineyards of Ein Gedi." Rare herbs and spices grown at Ein Gedi from approximately the 6th century B.C. until the late 8th century A.D. were famous throughout the ancient world and used to produce the most exotic incense, lotions and perfumes. The secret of these plantations was carefully guarded by the Ein Gedi community until its demise in early Islamic times. Indeed, an inscription in the mosaic floor of a Byzantine-era synagogue discovered at Ein Gedi warns members of the community not to divulge the "secret of the town" to outsiders; many scholars believe this refers to the secret formulas for balm, incense, and perfumes. After more than 1,000 years of complete desolation, the region was resettled in 1949 by a group of pioneers who planted it with cotton, grapes, vegetables, and flowers. Beginning with nothing but fertile land, the settlers created a beautiful kibbutz with stunning views of the wild, unearthly area, including the desert cascade of **Ein David Gorge,** where the water drops from a height of nearly 300 feet.

WHAT TO SEE & DO

There is no modern town at Ein Gedi. The area now called Ein Gedi is spread out along 3 miles of the shore of the Dead Sea, and divided into four basic sections, each with its own bus stop. If you're coming from Jerusalem by bus, the first (northernmost) stop at Ein Gedi is where you'll find the entrance to the **Nature Reserves,** the **youth hostel,** and the **SPNI study center/field school.** The second stop is the **bathing beach,** with its self-service restaurant and gas station. The third stop is for **Kibbutz Ein Gedi** and its kibbutz hotel. The fourth, and southernmost stop is for the **Ein Gedi Spa.**

The spectacular waterfalls and hiking trails are within the **Ein Gedi Reserve's Nahal David and Nahal Arugot** canyons (☎ **07/658-4285**). Maps and suggested trail routes are available at the entrance; more detailed maps and trail advice for hikes of several hours through these two neighboring canyon systems are available at the SPNI Center, near the hostel and the Nahal David entry gate. Follow the trail and the signposts, winding through tall pines and palm trees up and into the desert hills. You proceed between slits in the rock formations, under canopies of papyrus reeds, and, after about 10 minutes of steady climbing, you'll hear the wonderful sound of rushing water. In another 5 minutes, your appetite whetted, you arrive at what is surely one of the wonders of the Judean desert—the **Nahal David–Ein Gedi waterfalls,** hidden in an oasis of vegetation that hangs in a canyon wall. A second trail involving a 30-minute climb takes you to the **Shulamit Spring** and then to the **Dodim Cave** at the top of the falls. A 20- to 30-minute walk to the left brings you to the fenced-in ruins of a **Chalcolithic sanctuary** dating from about 3000 B.C. Mysterious copper wands and crowns, probably belonging to this sanctuary, and hidden in nearby caves for more than 5,000 years, are displayed in the antiquities section of the Israel Museum. Another walk leads to the ruins of Byzantine-era Ein Gedi's synagogue, with its marvelously intact mosaic floor. The reserve is open from 8am to 4pm; in summer until 5pm. You must make arrangements with the Nature Reserves Authority if you plan to do any of the 5- to 6-hour hikes into the depths of the Nahal (canyon) systems, especially if you plan to go beyond the **Hidden Falls.** Always carry with you at least 5 liters of water if you're planning a major hike in summer. From autumn to spring, it is important to be aware of the possibility of flash floods caused by rain in distant places. No food or cigarettes are allowed on the grounds. Admission is NIS 20 ($4.40). There is a snack kiosk at the entrance.

At the Ein Gedi National Antiquities Park, the ruins of **Ancient Ein Gedi,** one of Israel's most important archaeological sites may be visited. Admission is NIS 10 ($2.20). From First and Second Temple times until the end of the Byzantine era, Ein Gedi was a largely Jewish outpost famous throughout the ancient world for its production of rare spices, fragrant, intoxicating balsam oil, and priceless myrrh. Perhaps Ein Gedi was permitted to survive the tumultuous decades of wars and rebellions against Rome because its secret formulas for spice and incense production were not only beyond value, but also irreplaceable. At Ein Gedi, the **mosaic floor** of a 6th-century A.D. synagogue has been uncovered. If you visit other mosaic synagogue floors discovered in the Jordan Valley and the Galilee, you'll find that a number of Byzantine era synagogues (at Bet Alpha, Hammat Tiberias, and Zippori) contained a circle with a depiction of the zodiac as the centerpiece of their mosaic floors. Some scholars believe the zodiac was meant to represent the orderly patterns of God's universe. At Ein Gedi, in place of a zodiac circle, the mosaic floor is dominated by a central circle design of peacock chicks and adult birds, perhaps illustrating continuing patterns of birth and growth through which divine presence is revealed. It may be that the Jewish community at Ein Gedi, less influenced by outside cultures than the Jewish communities further north, was reluctant to employ pagan motifs in the ornamentation of its synagogue.

The extraordinary personal papers, letters, and possessions found in the Dead Sea caves and dating from the Second Jewish Revolt against Rome (A.D. 135) belonged to Jewish inhabitants of Ein Gedi who attempted to escape the Roman armies by hiding in the region's almost inaccessible caves. Yigal Yadin's book, *Bar Kokhba,* details these dramatic finds.

Across the Dead Sea to the far left are the **Moab Mountains,** where Moses was buried, and where Gad, Reuben, and half the Manasseh tribe settled after helping

Joshua claim the rest of the Promised Land. To the right it seems the sea ends, but it's actually the **Ha-Loshon** (The Tongue)—a strip of peninsula from the Jordanian side that reaches across the middle of the Dead Sea.

The ✪ **Ein Gedi Beach** is often mobbed with tour buses and weekending Israelis, but it's a fun place to try the experience of floating on the Dead Sea. There are showers on the beach, and changing rooms available for NIS 5 ($1). This section of the Dead Sea does not purport to have the same healing properties as the more mineral-heavy waters further south. The **Pundak Ein Gedi Cafeteria** (☎ 07/659/4761), just beside the beach, is the only restaurant in the region, and serves basic (kosher) chicken, meat, and vegetarian meals for under NIS 45 ($10). It is open daily 10am to 6pm; an adjacent minimart is open daily 7:30am to 8pm.

About 3 kilometers (2 mi.) south of Ein Gedi Beach is the well-run, often very busy **Ein Gedi Sulfur Springs and Spa** (☎ 07/659-4934), housed in a modern building. Here you can take the mineral-rich spring waters on the shores of the Dead Sea. Admission to the spa costs NIS 55 ($12.10) for adults; NIS 65 ($14.30) Saturdays and holidays. Facilities include a total of six single-sex and coed indoor warm and hot mineral pools. There's a bland fish and dairy restaurant downstairs that serves lunch for NIS 45 to NIS 54 ($10 to $12) (you get a discount by presenting your receipt from the spa). The spa has its own Dead Sea swimming beach and plenty of the famous Dead Sea black mud to smear on your skin. Open daily from 7am to 6pm in summer; until 5pm in winter. Any bus to Ein Gedi will drop you here.

WHERE TO STAY

Ein Gedi is not a full-fledged resort with hotels, but Kibbutz Ein Gedi has a popular and dramatically sited guesthouse as well as an excellent youth hostel. Make sure to reserve in advance. Beds are scarce and in great demand.

Moderate

✪ **Kibbutz Ein Gedi Resort Hotel.** Kibbutz Ein Gedi, Mobile Post, Dead Sea 86980. ☎ **07/659-4222.** Fax 07/658-4328. 120 units. A/C TV TEL. $146–$178 double. Discount available on Kibbutz Chain 7-Night Package. AE, DC, MC, V.

Dramatically located on a hill overlooking the Dead Sea, this kibbutz and its low-rise hotel units are set amid the exotic plantings of the only internationally registered botanical garden in which people live. Containing hundreds of species (including baobab trees and 900 types of cacti), the garden is the creation of the kibbutz, but it draws upon the ancient tradition of Ein Gedi's priceless trees and shrubs. For visitors, it's hard to believe that before 1949, there was nothing but barren rock here.

Rooms are simple but comfortable. What makes this place special are the remarkable surroundings, and an enthusiastic management that offers a program of desert excursions as well as great Bedouin evening barbecues. There's a large outdoor swimming pool, an indoor pool, and tennis courts. The rates for most guests include use of the Ein Gedi Spa, daily transportation to and from the sulfur springs and the beach, movies, slides, and lectures. The office is open from 8am to 8pm, and the kiosk for supplies opens twice daily. Lowest rates here are for January, February, and July. Reserve well in advance. It is possible to arrive here by bus, but a car is virtually essential in order to stay and explore the area.

Inexpensive

Bet Sara Youth Hostel. Mobile Post, Dead Sea 86980. ☎ **07/658-4165.** Fax 07/658-4445. 200 beds. A/C. $26 per person double; $18.50 dorm bed. Take the bus from Beersheva via Arad, or from Jerusalem; ask the driver to stop near Bet Sara.

I highly recommend Bet Sara. Located off the main road, about 1¹/₂ kilometers (1 mi.) north of the kibbutz, this very clean, homey, and efficient hostel offers a fantastic view of the sea and mountains. There are eight beds per room, and each room has its own bathroom; if you reserve ahead, and the hostel is not at capacity, you may be able to rent a room as a double. The hostel has an outdoor cafe/bar and serves dinners for NIS 40 ($9). The hostel has its own swimming place in the Dead Sea. The snack bar, open from 5 to 8pm, sells simple supplies at higher than in-town prices, but you're far from civilization. There's no curfew or lockout.

WHERE TO EAT

There's a nearby self-service restaurant at the Ein Gedi beach called **Pundak Ein Gedi.** Guests staying at the hotel get a 15% discount. The air-conditioned restaurant serves breakfast, lunch, and "tea" until 6pm. Main courses are NIS 27 to 45 ($5.40 to $10). Guests also get discounts for the Ein Gedi Spa restaurant and for the Ein Gedi Nature Reserve.

MASADA

It is a national tradition to have made the ascent at least once, for Masada is the scene of what many believe is one of the most heroic and tragic incidents in Jewish history. Few non-Jews outside Israel had heard of Masada until the events were dramatized in a book and a subsequent television miniseries in 1981. The story of a small garrison that defied the Roman army, as the historian Flavius Josephus recorded and perhaps embellished it, is worth retelling.

King Herod had built a magnificent palace complex and fortress atop this nearly inaccessible desert plateau mountain around 30 B.C. Underground cisterns assured the fortress of a lavish water supply for the palace's baths and gardens, as well as for Herod's court. Most impressive was Herod's personal winter villa, the extraordinary hanging palace on the northern tip of Masada, calculated to catch the breathtaking vistas of the lake as well as the refreshing breezes from the north. He furnished the luxurious place with every comfort as well as storehouses of food and arms, protecting the entire establishment with impregnable fortifications. The audaciousness of such an undertaking tells much about Herod's personality. After Herod's death, a small Roman garrison occupied the mount. However, during the Jewish revolt against the Romans in A.D. 66, a small band of beyond-the-mainstream Jewish zealots attacked and overtook the almost unattended fortress. They lived off the vast storehouses of food and had more than enough arms with which to defend themselves. The weapons were even put to use in raids on the surrounding countryside.

Finally, in A.D. 73, three years after the fall of Jerusalem and the end of the First Jewish Revolt, the Romans became so incensed with the Masada situation that they decided to put an end to this last pocket of Jewish resistance. After a lengthy attack using siege engines, flaming torches, rock bombardments, and battering rams, the Masada fortress was still in Jewish hands. But with 10,000 Roman troops camped on the hillside and daily bombardments smashing at the walls, it became only a question of time until the 900 defenders would succumb.

One brutal night attack spelled the end: Flaming torches thrown at the fort's wall were whipped by a wind into the midst of the defenders, and the garrison's gates caught fire. The Romans, seeing that Masada was practically defenseless now, decided to wait until dawn and take it over in their own good time.

During that final night, the 900 men, women, and children who inhabited Masada held a strange meeting. Their leader, Eliezer Ben-Yair, in a lengthy and dramatic speech, as reported by Flavius Josephus (who, of course, was not actually present),

Masada

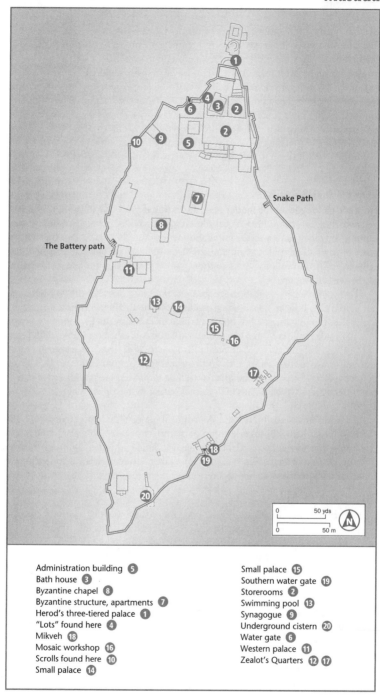

Snake Path

The Battery path

0 ____ 50 yds
0 ____ 50 m

Administration building ⑤
Bath house ③
Byzantine chapel ⑧
Byzantine structure, apartments ⑦
Herod's three-tiered palace ①
"Lots" found here ④
Mikveh ⑱
Mosaic workshop ⑯
Scrolls found here ⑩
Small palace ⑭

Small palace ⑮
Southern water gate ⑲
Storerooms ②
Swimming pool ⑬
Synagogue ⑨
Underground cistern ⑳
Water gate ⑥
Western palace ⑪
Zealot's Quarters ⑫ ⑰

persuaded his followers to accept death bravely, on their own terms. In the darkness at Masada nearly 2,000 years ago, one of history's greatest mass suicides occurred. Ten men were chosen by lot as executioners. Members of families lay side by side and bared their throats. After the rest had been killed, one man killed the other nine and ran himself through on his own sword. Two women and five children survived, hiding in one of the caves on the plateau. The Romans, who had expected to fight their way in, were doubly astonished at the lack of resistance and at the "calm courage of their resolution . . . and utter contempt of death." So, Flavius Josephus wrote, ended the Jewish resistance against Rome. Like almost everything in Israel, the meaning of Masada has become a matter of controversy, with many contending that the current glorification of a political stand that resulted in mass suicide is not good for the national psyche.

CLIMBING THE ASCENT

From the parking lot at the foot of **Masada National Park** (☎ 07/658-4207), you've got two choices—climb on foot or ride the cable car that carries you almost to the summit. If you climb, especially in the summer months, be sure to start literally at the crack of dawn. The heat is murderous by the middle of the day. Climbers are frantically urged by the National Parks Authority to wear hats and drink as much as possible before starting up.

Climbers have two choices: the route from the Dead Sea side, or the Roman siege ramp originally built in A.D. 73 on the side of the mountain facing in the direction of Arad (this Roman ramp path is only accessible by car from Arad). The route from the Dead Sea side requires from a half hour to an hour; it is called the **Snake Path** because of the steep, hairpin curves. The Snake Path opens at 4:30am and closes at 3:30pm, and you must start down by then just to get to the bottom before dark. The same hours apply to the path up the other side. The mountainside path is called the **Battery**, after a battery the Romans built there. Getting to the top via that route takes only 15 to 30 minutes.

Admission to Masada is NIS 22 ($5); admission plus round-trip cable car is NIS 40 ($8.80); NIS 35 ($7.70) for admission plus a one-way cable car ticket. Students and children get a third discount. Cable cars operate Sunday through Thursday from 8am to 4pm, on Friday and eves of holidays (including Saturday) from 8am to 2pm. The cable car will deposit you about 45 very steep steps from the fortress top.

THE RUINS OF MASADA

Masada excavations have unearthed perhaps the most exciting ruins in the entire country in terms of physical drama and historical mystique. Masada remains a symbol of courage, and has long moved scholars, laypeople, and soldiers to make the ascent. Yigael Yadin's beautifully photographed book, *Masada,* carefully recounts the archaeological expedition that uncovered the original palace, walls, houses, straw bags, plaits of hair, pottery shards, stone vessels, cosmetic items, cooking utensils, synagogue, and important scroll fragments. Among the most intriguing finds are the ways the palace was adapted for use as a stronghold for guerrilla fighters and their families. Evidence from this period includes ritual baths *(mikvehs)* built by the observant defenders, and the ostraca marked with Hebrew names that might have been the very lots cast by the defenders in their final moments as they decided who among them would be chosen to kill the others rather than die at the hands of the Romans. You can also see the ruins of the Roman siege encampments, which provide an amazingly preserved visual lesson in Roman military field strategy. A later Byzantine chapel with a mosaic floor was built on Masada, and there are signs of Byzantine-era habitation in the ruined buildings of the palace.

WHERE TO STAY

✪ **Isaac H. Taylor Youth Hostel.** Mobile Post, Dead Sea 86935. ☎ **07/658-4349.** Fax 07/658-4650. 140 beds. A/C. $17 with IYHA card; $18.50 nonmembers; $26 per person double room. Rates include breakfast. Check in 4–7pm.

The youth hostel at Masada is the place to sleep if you want to roll out of bed and make the predawn climb up the Snake Path, experiencing dawn at Masada without the hassle of driving or taking a taxi in the night from Jerusalem or Tel Aviv. This state-of-the-art hostel offers dormitory-style beds and kitchen privileges. Each six- to eight-bed room has its own shower and can be easily converted into a family or private accommodation if you reserve ahead and there is room. Meals are available for $10. Reserve in advance—the other options are 42 kilometers (25 mi.) away in Arad—the Ein Gedi Resort Hotel, or the big spa hotels at Ein Bokek.

4 Into the Negev

The Talmudic scholars say that Negev means "dry," and Old Testament experts claim it means "south." Both are correct—in literal terms. A vast wasteland of almost 4,000 square miles, this desert is Israel's future—for population expansion, for chemical industries, and for farming. In fact, studies show that one-fifth of the desert can be used for some form of agriculture.

This region is a constantly varying landscape of red, black, and yellow, accented by valleys, deep craters, and burnt-brown mountains. Craggy limestone walls, mounds of sandstone, red and green dunes of sand are everywhere strewn with great blocks of black volcanic silex. Saw-toothed mountain ridges, abruptly hollowed out by the wild gorges left from the Great Middle Eastern Earthquake, starkly point back to the day when these mountains just fell down and this desert opened its granite jaws to everything living on top of it. In this petrified desert world, temperatures can range from 125°F during the day to 40°F in a winter dawn.

There are two possible routes into the Negev. The faster route is to head toward the Jordanian border and take the highway from Sodom to Eilat, but the scenery is stark. Or you can go to Beersheva and take the older and slower but more interesting route through the heart of the Negev to the port of Eilat on the Red Sea. If you choose the latter, there are several major points of interest along this bleak but fascinating road. If you're going by sherut or driving yourself, stop the car at some uninhabited spot and listen to the almost frightening stillness. Equally mysterious are the secondary roads—cryptic paths winding their way into the flatlands and beyond the dunes, toward agricultural collectives. The port of Eilat on the Red Sea is at the end of the road. Be sure to bring extra water when you drive this road, both for yourself and your car.

You will see black-tented Bedouin camps, though these will grow sparser as you proceed farther south—all natural growth is in the northern part of the Negev, so even the perennial wanderers do most of their wandering in the northern desert regions.

Roughly 32,000 Bedouin roam Israel's deserts and hills—an estimated 27,000 in the Negev, 5,000 in the Galilee mountains. Until recently they haven't respected border lines very much, but Israel has been campaigning to entice them with benefits: Clinics and hospitals give their babies free service, the government has provided them with land, and some have settled down to become nonmigratory workers.

SHIVTA

Shivta is an impressive site, but it's in the middle of nowhere and has no facilities. If you have a car or plan to go on a tour, this can be a very worthwhile, atmospheric excursion; otherwise spend your time at Avdat.

Shivta is about 50 kilometers (30 mi.) southwest of Beersheva, in the military zone about 5 miles off the Nizzana road. It's important not to get lost in the military zone, so here are explicit directions: From the highway, the Shivta road is two lanes and paved for the first 2¹/₂ kilometers (1¹/₂–2 mi.). It then narrows, and after another kilometer you pass a road, on the left, to the military installation. After passing this road, it's another 5 kilometers (3 mi.) over a rough, curvy one-lane road to Shivta. There are few signs. Officially Shivta is a national park, but there is no office or telephone at this deserted location. Admission, if anyone is around to collect it, is NIS 12 ($2.60); half price for children under 18.

The Nabateans, a desert merchant people whose capital was the legendary city of Petra, in Jordan, established Shivta in the 1st century B.C., but Shivta (or Subeita) reached its high point during the time of Justinian the Great (500s), when Byzantine wealth and power were at their height. Caravans laden with pilgrims and merchandise made their way between Egypt and Anatolia, the Red Sea and the Mediterranean, and many stopped at Shivta. Besides this commercial wealth, Shivta's ingenious citizens built an elaborate irrigation system that allowed them to farm the barren soil. Israelis are studying Nabatean irrigation techniques to this day.

But Shivta's location on major trade routes proved its undoing; the easily accessible city was overrun by Arab armies. Trade routes slowly changed, and, though Shivta survived as an Arab outpost for many centuries, by the 1100s it was a ghost town.

The ruins of Shivta remained in fairly good condition throughout the centuries because they were too far away from newer building sites to make pillage economical. As a result, the city, which dates from the 500s, is still somewhat intact. Restoration work began in 1958. Buildings restored include three churches, a mosque, a caravansary, and houses. Signs identify and discuss the principal buildings.

SDE BOKER & AVDAT

About 50 kilometers (30 mi.) due south of Beersheva, surrounded by sand and parched mountains, you suddenly come to a farm settlement—the famous Ben-Gurion kibbutz, Sde Boker. The settlement was begun in May 1952, at the prime minister's instigation, when the country was first encouraging settlers to populate the Negev. Ben-Gurion became a member of this kibbutz in 1953; he lived and worked here until his death in 1973, at the age of 87. He and his wife, Paula, are buried here, and many of his papers and eclectic collection of books on history, philosophy, and religions may be seen in the **Paula and David Ben-Gurion Hut** (☎ 07/656-0320). The hut remains as it was when Ben Gurion lived in it. Visiting hours are Sunday through Thursday from 8:30am to 3:30pm, on Friday, Saturday, holidays, and holiday eves from 8:30am to 2pm. Groups are asked to phone in advance. Bus no. 60 from Beersheva runs to the kibbutz every hour from 8:30am to 2:30pm. The stop for the Ben-Gurion house is the first after the kibbutz.

Over the years Sde Boker began to thrive, as did several other young settlements in the Negev. A campus of the Ben-Gurion University of the Negev has been established at Sde Boker. A modern library, housing the **Ben-Gurion Institute and Archives** (☎ 07/655-5057), and containing 750,000 documents associated with Israel's first chief of state, is located here. The institute also contains a **Research Center for Solar Energy** and a **Museum of Desert Sculpture,** a collection of art created from natural objects and materials found in the desert. The Institute also serves as a center for the study of desert areas. It's open daily from 9am-5pm; you must phone ahead for tours, which are given by appointment for $2.

Ten kilometers (6 mi.) south of the Paula and David Ben-Gurion Hut is the national parks archaeological site of **Avdat** (☎ 07/655-0954). This was another city built by the Nabateans in the 2nd century B.C. as a caravan city on a route that ran from the Red Sea to the Nabatean trading capital at Petra, then to Avdat, Beersheva and onward to Gaza on the Mediterranean coast. The city reached its peak of importance during Roman and Byzantine times, and went into decline after the Roman conquest in the 7th century A.D.

Situated on a cliff 2,000 feet above sea level, Avdat offers dramatic vistas across the desert; along with the ruined Nabatean city of Mamshit, it was used for location shots in the film *Jesus Christ Superstar.* The western half of Avdat's acropolis contains the ruins of two Byzantine churches; the eastern section is dominated by the city's fortress. Beyond the acropolis are a large Byzantine-era winepress and olive press, evidence of the Nabateans' amazing ability to irrigate and farm the desolate Negev 1,500 years ago. Restored with the aid of U.S. government funds, Avdat is administered by the national parks department. Admission is NIS 14 ($3.08); half price for those under 18. It is open from 8am to 5pm, but if no one is on duty during these hours, just enter. Beside the ruins of Avdat, the Hebrew University has operated an experimental farm for the past forty years, in which Nabatean agricultural techniques, as uncovered by archaeologists, are being explored and redeveloped. To visit the farm, call ☎ 08/948-1211 for an appointment.

MAMSHIT NATIONAL PARK

This third ruined Nabatean city 6 kilometers (4 mi.) Southeast of Dimona, is probably a few centuries older than Avdat, and was built on a slightly more important trade route. It was a town of large caravansaries, warehouses, and accounting offices; by Roman times, the town sported large public bathhouses, villas, with wall murals, and houses of pleasure. The two large Byzantine-era churches may have been converted to mosques after the Muslim conquest in A.D. 635, judging from Koranic verses inscribed on the walls of their ruins; however the city seems to have been permanently abandoned not long after that time, and the inscriptions may have been made after the city was no longer inhabited. The ruins are set above Makhtesh Ha-Gadol, one of the Negev's dramatic erosion craters. The site is open daily 8am to 5pm; admission is NIS 14 ($3.10).

WHERE TO DINE

✪ **Dushara Nabatean Restaurant.** Mamshit National Park. ☎ 07/655-5596. Reservations advisable. Complete set-price meal NIS 105 ($23). AE, DC, MC, V. Sat–Thurs 12:30–10:30pm; Fri noon until start of Shabbat. ANCIENT-STYLE CUISINE (KOSHER).

A number of restaurants in Israel have begun to do "Biblical" menus and decor for tourists and Israelis alike. This restaurant is by far the best of the group, offering truly delicious food, and an absolutely awesome setting. Unlike the others, it is not in the least bit hokey. The thoughtful menu, carefully grounded in authentic ingredients, begins with hot wine flavored with honey served in rough ceramic cups, and a basket of hot carob bread made with tamarind flour served with olive oil and strong desert spices. There will also be a number of first courses and ancient-style salads such as a delightful concoction of barley, green onions, and fresh herbs. Main courses include quail baked in a date-honey garlic sauce with dried fruits and a dash of vinegar; lamb baked with lentils; and a meat couscous, all baked and served in individual desert-style clay casserole dishes. Biblical desserts and a date drink round out a fascinating dining experience that should be on every visitor's itinerary.

MITZPE RAMON

Mitzpe Ramon (pop. 7,000), lies 139 kilometers (84 mi.) south of Beersheva and appears to be a typical Negev development community if you approach it from the north. What you don't immediately see is the town's location right at the edge of the spectacular **Ramon Crater,** a vast, breathtakingly beautiful geologic depression formed by erosion that has exposed a virtual encyclopedia of fossils and geologic structures. Founded in 1954 as a clay-mining town and way station on the long road then being built through the desert to the isolated outpost of Eilat, Mitzpe Ramon was bypassed by the new, more direct road to Eilat built through the Arava Valley after the 1967 war.

Mitzpe Ramon struggled to survive as a viable economic community during the 1970s and '80s. The Ramon Crater (which had not been picked up by aerial surveys during British Mandate times, and which was only discovered after the 1948 War of Independence) had not yet captured the imagination of travelers. It has only been since 1990, with the establishment of the Ramon Inn to accommodate middle- and upper-range visitors, that a tourism industry has begun to develop here. The community has a great public spirit, and gives you an opportunity to get a feel for day-to-day life in the kind of Negev community that Ben-Gurion envisioned as an important part of Israel's future. You can also feel the isolation and mystery of the Negev plateau. Sunsets and twilights at the edge of the crater usually bring out an extraordinary vista of changing colors, as the landscape slowly sinks into darkness.

WHAT TO SEE & DO

The **Mitzpe Ramon Visitors Center** (☎ 07/658-8620) at the edge of the crater, housed in a large modern structure designed to resemble the spiral-shaped sea fossils embedded in the local rocks, is staffed by people trained by the Israel Nature Reserves Authority; the bookstore/gift shop is a good place to pick up background and hiking information as well as topographical maps. There are slide and film shows, and a museum exhibit of the area's geology, flora, and fauna. Admission is NIS 40 ($4.40). It is open Saturday through Thursday from 9am to 4:30pm and Friday 9am to 4pm.

The Ramon Crater is perhaps at its most accessible in the spring or fall, when it's not too hot or too bitterly cold. Whenever you happen to visit, it is worthwhile to invest in a professional tour or guide. **Desert Shade** (☎ 07/658-6229; fax 07/658-6208), a tour company based in Mitzpe Ramon, offers a range of activities including 2-hour Jeep tours that leave Mitzpe Ramon several times a day and cost NIS 124 ($27) for adults, NIS 90 ($20) for children. Camel tours fit in better with the intense quiet, and run NIS 45 ($10) per hour; a full-day tour including a visit to the Alpaca Farm (easy to do on your own) is NIS 396 ($88). Desert Shade also arranges 2- and 3-day desert expeditions, including accommodations in Bedouin-style tents, camel tours, mountain-bike rentals, rappelling, escorted hikes, and Bedouin evenings, complete with dinner. **SPNI** offers excellent nature hikes, but you must book in advance. SPNI's office in Jerusalem is at 13 Helena Ha-Malka St. (☎ 02/624-4605); in Tel Aviv, 3 Hashfela St. (☎ 03/ 638-8674); in Haifa, 18 Hillel St. (☎ 04/866-4135). Guided bus tours to the crater (minimum of 20 people generally required) run about NIS 22 ($5) per person.

For an overview of the Ramon Crater, turn left as you exit the Visitors Center, and follow the 1-kilometer (¹/₂- mi.) promenade alongside the crater's rim. Sunset is a good time for walking; with luck, you'll spot an ibex in the distance, or an eagle aloft on the evening wind. In the opposite direction, you'll find the wonderful **Desert Sculpture Park,** with the sky and the crater as backdrop for works by a number of international and Israeli artists. To get there, drive out of the Visitors Center, make a left onto the main road, and past the gas station on the right, make a right turn at the sign for Ma'ale Noah.

The **Alpaca Farm** (☎ 07/658-8047) is 3 kilometers (1.8 mi.) outside of town. Founded in 1987, this establishment raises both alpacas and llamas, and produces fine alpaca and llama wool. The alpacas have a charm of their own, and after the Ramon Crater, they have become the town's most memorable tourist attraction. Adorable, gentle, and fluffy, they quickly bond with anyone carrying a small paper bag of feed sold on the premises for NIS 5 ($1.10). At times, they may spit (they are distantly related to camels), but they mean nothing personal. You can also visit the llama herd, but the llamas are not as whimsical. Guided **llama treks** through the Ramon Crater can be arranged through the Alpaca Farm, with gentle, intelligent llamas carrying your packs and serving as mounts for small children. The Alpaca Farm has an open-air snack bar with light meals costing NIS 14 to 22 ($3 to $5). Admission is NIS 12 ($2.65); children pay NIS 8 ($1.75). The farm is open daily 9am to 6pm.

WHERE TO STAY

✪ **Isrotel Ramon Inn.** 1 Aqev St., Mitzpe Ramon. ☎ **07/658-8822,** 800/552-0140 in the U.S., or 800/526-5343 in Canada. Fax 07/658-8151. E-mail: ramon-inn@isrotel.co.il. 96 units. A/C TV TEL. $118, $139, $174 double in high, regular, and low seasons; units are for 2 to 6 persons. Rates include breakfast. Half-board $20; full board $45. Substantial discounts on Isrotel and Kibbutz Hotel Chain plans. AE, DC, MC, V.

With its comfortable accommodations, the Ramon Inn has made the beautiful countryside around the Ramon Crater accessible to the kind of traveler who was unwilling to stay in the youth hostel or the field school. The inn has also brought hope of a genuine tourist industry to the economically depressed community, and the entire town is helping to make the project a success. An apartment block was totally renovated to create the inn: The very comfortable, tastefully decorated living room/bedroom suites with kitchenettes were once small apartments. Public areas are sleek but friendly, and the lobby sports a freestanding fireplace for chilly desert nights. The spirit of the staff is wonderful, but perhaps best of all are the inn's fabulous buffet meals (see below). There is no swimming pool yet, but the community pool is just across the road. Although this is not a kibbutz, you can include the Ramon Inn on the Kibbutz Hotels Chain Guest House Plan and get a considerable discount.

✪ **Succah in the Desert.** P.O. Box 272, Mitzpe Ramon 80600. ☎ **07/658-6280** or 07/658-8267. Fax 07/658-6464. www.succah.co.il. E-mail: succah@netvision.net.il. 8 succot (desert shelters made of natural materials) (all with shared bathrooms). $100 double weekdays; $130 Shabbat. Rates include breakfast and evening meal. AE, MC, V.

Succah in the Desert, 7$^1/_2$ kilometers (4$^1/_2$ mi.) outside of Mitzpe Ramon, on the road to the Alpaca Farm, is a place to live on the earth as a guest and not as a settler. The special creation of Rachel Bat Adam, a German immigrant to Israel, here you can experience the desert's immense silence, the wind and stars. Eight *succot* (simple shelters), dot the landscape around the central succah, which serves as the place for meals and as a central place for guests to meet. Each succah is different, but all are made with walls of sheltering rocks, roofs of natural materials, and have areas open to the air. There are carpets covering earthen floors, comfortable mattresses, blankets and bed linens, an enormous clay jar in which water is kept miraculously cool, copper vessels for washing, and ecologically correct solar-powered lamps. In winter, there are solar heaters. For those who do not wish to blend totally into nature, there is a nonpolluting toilet and a solar shower near the main succah. The staff of this encampment has an agenda of meditation and spiritual renewal, but you are free to come and go as you like as long as you do not intrude on the quiet of others. Only vegetarian meals are served. The evening meal is NIS 30 ($6.60) for outsiders on weekdays; NIS 60 ($13.20) on weekends. If you have no car, call from Mitzpe Ramon for transportation or hiking instructions. For students, prices may be a bit negotiable.

Staying in a Bedouin-Style Tent

For a less-expensive desert experience, **Desert Shade Tours** (☎ **07/658-6229; 03/575-6885** reservations made from Tel Aviv; fax 03/613-0160) rents space in simple cabin cubicles with meals in an Bedouin-style tourist tents in the crater. Bed-and-breakfast is NIS 126 ($28); other meals are NIS 67 ($15). Call ahead for reservations. In-season only.

WHERE TO DINE

✪ **Ramon Inn Restaurant.** In the Ramon Inn. ☎ **07/658-8822.** Reservations necessary. Set price full meal NIS 115 ($25). AE, DC, MC, V. Dinner 7–9pm. INTERNATIONAL.

Like the Ramon Inn hotel, the restaurant is an effort that involves many residents from the town of Mitzpe Ramon. The menu here is composed of family recipes prepared by the best local cooks and served in an all-you-can-eat buffet that varies from night to night; when it's good it is one of the best meals you'll find in Israel. The choices change each night, but represent traditions that range from Morocco and Yemen to Russia and Hungary, and I strongly urge you to sample everything! Then zero in on a dish with herbs, seasonings, or sauce that catches your fancy. Dessert, sometimes exotic, sometimes average, is included, as are coffee, tea, and other beverages. The restaurant also serves a buffet breakfast and lunch, with many special homemade jams, salads, and other unusual items. If you are a guest at the Ramon Inn and charge your meal to your room, the 17% VAT should be deducted from the price if you pay your bill in foreign currency.

KADESH-BARNEA

Scholars have three different versions of the route they believe Moses took as he led the Jewish people out of Egypt and into the Promised Land. But all three versions converge at Kadesh-Barnea, located about 40 kilometers (24 mi.) to the east of Mitspe Ramon.

Kadesh-Barnea served as a center for the confederation of tribes that wandered in the Negev and the Sinai during the time of Abraham; it was also called Enmishpat at that time. But most of the biblical references to it are connected with the time of the Israelites' sojourn in the desert under Moses. It was from Kadesh that Moses sent 12 men to spy out the land of Canaan, at Kadesh that he smote the rock and got water, and here that his sister, Miriam, died and was buried.

There has been a longstanding controversy over the location of the biblical Kadesh; early in this century, a general consensus emerged, identifying the site with **Tel el-Qudeirat,** located in the fertile valley watered by the spring of Ain el-Qudeirat. Excavation has unearthed three fortresses built one atop the other, the earliest dating from the early 10th century B.C., the latest existing up until the time of the destruction of the First Temple (A.D. 586). Numerous examples of pottery and *ostraca* (tablet writings) have also been found here, but no traces of the followers of Moses, a fact not inconsistent with the nomadic character of that society. But although we see no evidence of their passing, it is very moving to stand here and look around at the scenes where the great biblical stories took place. Kadesh-Barnea is well represented at the Negev Museum in Beersheva, and also in the Rockefeller Museum in Jerusalem.

5 Eilat

243 kilometers (151 mi.) S of Beersheva; 356 kilometers (221 mi.) SE of Tel Aviv.

This city of 36,000 at the southern tip of the Negev is the country's leading winter tourist resort. Eilat's chief claims to fame for the tourist are fine beaches, coral reefs filled with exotic fish, and year-round sunshine. At the moment, the once easygoing, relaxed desert and Red Sea resort town is undergoing a construction boom, with gargantuan four- and five-star hotels being erected wherever possible. The architectural style of Eilat's hotels and shopping malls has been agreed upon—new buildings are all of white concrete with straight, crisp geometric lines; older hotels are being redesigned to conform to the light, airy look. There is a unity to the new Eilat, but from the outside, most hotels seem to vary only in size and shape. Planners have not emphasized the desert and Bedouin traditions of the region—instead they've aimed for the generic look of a gleaming white international resort, like Cancún, Mexico. If you're hoping for a touch of regional color in your hotel, you'll have to try the Sinai or the new five-star establishments in Petra (Jordan).

Eilat is also a combination military outpost and shipping port—you'll see ample evidence of this all along the shoreline. The city's first-class hotel area is less than a mile from the Jordanian border and you can see the Jordanian port city of Aqaba, with a population of 20,000 across the bay, dazzling in a haze of desert sand, ringed by date palms. For almost 50 years, until Israel and Jordan signed a peace treaty in 1994, Aqaba seemed as unattainable as a mirage. There is now a border crossing for tourists just north of Eilat, and you can also book excursions to Jordan's fabulous Petra from Eilat. At present you cannot go across merely to check out Aqaba for a few hours; to enter Jordan you have to have a valid visa and stay at least overnight. For some time, Egypt, Israel, and Jordan have quietly been planning a regional coordinating committee and international park that will protect the ecosystem of this end of the Red Sea, in anticipation of the regional peace agreement. Meanwhile the area remains the most peaceful of Israel's borders. A few years ago, before the peace agreement, when one of King Hussein's prize racehorses bolted and swam from Aqaba to Eilat, he was returned as if such incidents were an everyday occurrence. Saudi Arabia is 20 kilometers (12 mi.) south of Aqaba; to the west are the mountains of Sinai.

It was from the port of Eilat that King Solomon sent and received his ships from the land of Ophir, laden with gold, wood, and ivory, dominating this exotic trade route with Hiram of Tyre, Solomon's famous naval ally (Hiram was king of the Phoenician trading city of Tyre on the Mediterranean coast north of Israel). It is even thought by some that the Queen of Sheba landed at Eilat when she came to Jerusalem to see Solomon and "commune with him all that was in her heart." From 1000 to 600 B.C., Phoenician shipping from Eilat plied the shores of East Africa and at times developed trade with the coasts of India and even Southeast Asia. There is evidence that on occasion, Phoenician vessels circumnavigated the African continent. Today, the port is again bustling.

Eilat has a youthful, adventurous spirit that seems to move the entire population. Israelis who had begun to find the north too confining and cramped have moved down here for the challenge; so, too, have a few who practice yoga, pluck guitar strings, and who, in general, were displeased with "the people up north." This is an individualist's town, and it's also an entrepreneur's dream.

During summer, the outdoor afternoon heat in Eilat can exceed 110°F; it's best to stay in the shade between noon and 3pm, to avoid sun poisoning. In winter, the thick dusty heat is gone, the air is cool and dry, yet the water is warm enough for swimming.

ESSENTIALS

GETTING THERE   By Plane   Several daily Arkia flights (☎ **800/444-888** toll-free inside Israel) arrive from points north. The downtown airport can receive only small aircraft; larger planes land at **Ouvda airport,** 60 kilometers (37 mi.) north of Eilat. Aqaba's International Airport, just on the border near Eilat, will be rebuilt in the next 2 years so that arriving planes will be able to taxi to either Israeli or Jordanian gates at the new Shalom-Salaam International Terminal. One-way flights from Tel Aviv or Jerusalem are approximately $100; if you fly both ways, you'll miss the Negev Desert close up, but there are good flight/hotel packages offered by Arkia. El Al passengers can also purchase an add-on to Eilat with their flight ticket to Israel. The bus ride from Ouvda to town can take an hour.

From Eilat to Jordan   Bus service is now available from Eilat to Aqaba, Jordan, at the United Tours Terminal in Eilat. Fares are NIS 8 ($1.75) each way. Buses stop at the hotel district, the airport, and the New Commercial Center in Eilat before continuing on to Aqaba via the Arava Crossing north of Eilat. Passengers must have a Jordanian entry visa and must pay a crossing fee of NIS 75 ($16.50) from Israel into Jordan. For those coming from Aqaba to Eilat, the crossing fee is $6. As regulations are constantly being revised, check with the Eilat Tourist Information Center for the latest information.

If you arrive at Eilat's little **downtown airport,** you will be right at the bottom of the hill, where Hatmarim Boulevard meets Ha-Arava Road (the road north to Beersheva). It will be a 10-minute walk to almost any of our Hatmarim Boulevard hotels and hostels, or to the hotels on the North Beach. All the local city buses (no. 1, 2, or 15) run every 20 to 30 minutes or so, from early morning until about 7 or 8pm. They run daily except Saturday, stopping early on Friday (about 3 or 4pm) in observation of the Sabbath.

By Bus   There are a number of daily buses (except on Shabbat) from Jerusalem and Tel Aviv to Eilat. The trip takes about 4¹/₂ hours. If you arrive by bus, you will be planted in the center of town on the main street—Hatmarim (or Ha-Temarim) Boulevard. From there, hostel row, just around the corner on Ha-Negev Street, is within walking distance; local city buses no. 1 and 2 go from the Central Bus Station to the North Beach area, around the lagoon, and down as far as the Jordanian border. You must take a taxi, or city bus no. 15, if you're heading out to Coral Beach. You can also leave your luggage at the bus station. It is best not to even think about carrying luggage even short distances in Eilat's hot weather. For your return bus ride out of Eilat, the Egged information phone number is ☎ **07/637-5161.** Reserve your bus seat leaving Eilat at least 2 days ahead; weekends, holidays, and summer vacations, 4-day advance reservations are necessary.

For hotel reservations at the Central Bus Station   At the **Egged Tours Office** (☎ **07/637-5625**) (on the right as you leave the bus arrival area), you can nail down a hotel room in town on your arrival. I wouldn't count on arriving without reservations in summer, on weekends or on Jewish holidays and Christmas, but at other times, especially midweek or off-season, this office works as a clearinghouse for hotels that are not fully booked, and can often get you rooms at considerable discounts. The office seems to have close contact with the brand new, comfortable, though not very

Eilat

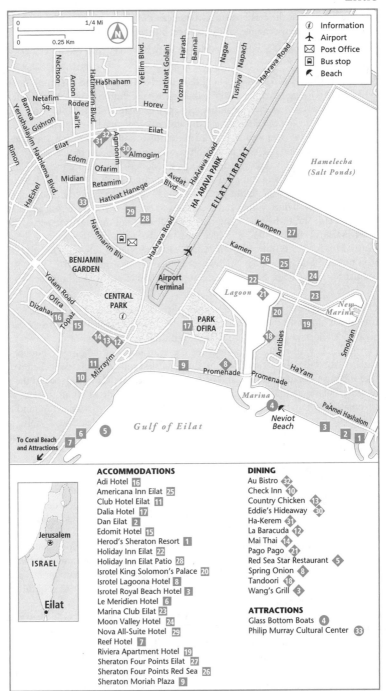

ACCOMMODATIONS
Adi Hotel 16
Americana Inn Eilat 25
Club Hotel Eilat 11
Dalia Hotel 17
Dan Eilat 2
Edomit Hotel 15
Herod's Sheraton Resort 1
Holiday Inn Eilat 22
Holiday Inn Eilat Patio 28
Isrotel King Solomon's Palace 20
Isrotel Lagoona Hotel 8
Isrotel Royal Beach Hotel 3
Le Meridien Hotel 6
Marina Club Eilat 23
Moon Valley Hotel 24
Nova All-Suite Hotel 29
Reef Hotel 7
Riviera Apartment Hotel 19
Sheraton Four Points Eilat 27
Sheraton Four Points Red Sea 26
Sheraton Moriah Plaza 9

DINING
Au Bistro 32
Check Inn 10
Country Chicken 13
Eddie's Hideaway 30
Ha-Kerem 31
La Baracuda 12
Mai Thai 14
Pago Pago 21
Red Sea Star Restaurant 5
Spring Onion 8
Tandoori 18
Wang's Grill 3

ATTRACTIONS
Glass Bottom Boats 4
Philip Murray Cultural Center 33

exciting hotels near the Bus Station, but you can ask about more interesting choices. At press time there was no fee for this service, but check to be sure.

By Car The trip takes approximately 4 hours by direct road from Tel Aviv and Jerusalem.

VISITOR INFORMATION The **Eilat Tourist Information Center** (☎ **07/ 637-2111**) is located in a new white building set back from the road at the corner of Arava and Yotam roads. Pick up an English-language map for NIS 4 (80¢) and a copy of *Events in Eilat.* You can also get help and advice on booking hotel and hostel accommodations and tours as well as bus schedules, discount coupons, and schedules of events in the region. The staff here is often well attuned to the problems of budget travelers. The center accepts American Express, MasterCard, and Visa when booking rooms, travel tickets, and tours. In the same building, you'll find the **E.T.I. Attractions Office** (☎ **07/637-0380;** fax 07/637-0434). At E.T.I., you can book tours of the Eilat region, diving cruises, and excursions to Sinai (see below) as well as package tours to Petra and to Egypt. At the center, you'll also find the highly respected **Neot Ha-Kikar** (☎ **07/633-0425**), which does similar tours and bookings at quality places. Hours for the Tourist Information Center are Sunday through Thursday from 9am to 9pm; Friday, Saturday, and eves of holidays from 8am to 3pm.

Eilat has no VAT tax, but since many supplies have to be shipped in, prices tend to be higher.

ORIENTATION There are three easily distinguishable areas in Eilat: the town itself, built atop hills that roll toward the sea; Coral Beach, with its great snorkeling, about 6 kilometers (3¹/₂ mi.) south of town on the western shore of the harbor; and North Beach, a 10-minute walk from the center of town on the eastern shore of the harbor. North Beach is the most central and busiest public beach, and where you'll find the most restaurants, bars, and better-quality accommodations. It is also the site of an elaborate marina system that started with the building of an artificial lagoon, cutting several hundred yards inland in back of the "hotel row" section. Around this lagoon are hotels, restaurants, and a promenade filled with pubs, discos, shops, and street vendors. Here tourists can enjoy the sun, the red-tinted green waters, the calm, the dusty hills, and the cool desert breezes of night.

SPORTS & OUTDOOR ACTIVITIES

BEACHES Although the waters around Eilat are safe, always take the elementary precaution of not going out too far alone, keeping in mind that depth is deceptive and that the numerous sharks are not particularly hungry for you; spiny sea urchins are the major danger.

North Beach is a sandy beach in front of the Radisson Moriah Hotel that extends as far eastward as the Dan Hotel; because it's free of coral and sea urchins, this is a good beach for ordinary swimming. Water skis and boats can be rented, but make sure you know where you're going, because you don't have to ski very far to get into both Jordanian and hot water.

Coral Beach, which is a short drive or bus ride around the curve of the bay, is the better beach for **snorkeling** and **diving.** It's inundated with coral and fish, and snorkeling equipment can be rented. Much of Coral Beach is now a nature preserve, perfect for both first-time and intermediate snorkeling and scuba diving. *Warning:* Spiny sea urchins and sharp, burning corals are always to be avoided here; footwear or flippers are advisable when swimming at this beach. Never put your feet down on the floor of the sea unless you can see that you will be standing on a clear, urchin-free space.

The ✪ **Dolphin Reef** is a new attraction and certainly the prettiest beach in Eilat, dotted with palm trees and thatched-roof palapa structures for shade. Once in the water, you'll find the area designated for humans, with its sandy floor, is also the best in Eilat for swimming. The dolphins are an added attraction. As you swim and sun, you can watch them frolicking and being fed just beyond the roped-off human zone; you can also walk out to a wooden observation pier in the dolphins' free-swimming area for a closer look. Or, for about NIS 200 ($44) per person, you can join a guided group of snorkelers for a 20-minute **swim among the dolphins.** (Advance reservations are recommended.) Sometimes, especially when the dolphins are ready for a meal, this can be an expedition of wonderful close encounters; at other times, the free-swimming dolphins (which are under no obligation to perform) keep their distance. You must be a good swimmer. There are no guarantees, refunds, or rain checks. For NIS 95 ($21), you can sit right on the float while the dolphins come up to the trainers for snack and trick sessions. The Dolphin Reef also hosts a program of scientific studies, as well as a program in which people with medical or emotional problems may visit and interact with the dolphins as part of their therapy. From time to time you may notice participants in these programs on a raft in the dolphins' free-swim zone. The reef's institute believes in informal, personal relationships between humans and dolphins, and has even had plans for the dolphins to witness a human underwater birth.

There is a reasonably priced cafeteria serving hot and cold drinks, snacks, and full meals on the premises, as well as a pub and a program of films on dolphins. The whole feel of the beach is friendly, easygoing, and interesting. Many evenings and nights, when admission to the beach is free, there is live or disco music and dancing. All in all, this is one of the best places in Eilat to spend a day or an evening.

Dolphin Reef is on Southern Beach (P.O. Box 104, Eilat; ☎ **07/637-5935**) and is open daily from 9am to 5pm. Admission is NIS 32 ($7), NIS 22 ($4.80) for children, from 9am to 5pm, with no admission fee after 5pm, when the restaurant and beach continue to be open, but when the dolphin sessions finish for the day.

BOATING   You can hire boats 24 hours a day at the North Beach marina and lagoon—boats for waterskiing and water parachuting, sailboats, fishing boats, paddle-boats, motor sea-cycles, sailboards, and kayaks are all available.

GLASS-BOTTOM BOATS   Boats leave from the jetty just north of Coral Beach, or from North Beach near the Neptune Hotel. These boats offer a wonderful view of a fairy-tale marine world, with mounds of coral and clusters of rainbow-colored fish. **Israel Yam** (☎ **07/637-5528**) operates daily 1^1/2-hour glass-bottom boat trips, leaving North Beach several times during the day for about $12 per person. For a trip down by the Coral Beach Nature Reserve and the underwater observatory/aquarium, a newer state-of-the-art vessel that offers underwater vistas is the ***Jules Verne Explorer*** (☎ **07/637-7702**). The price is $18 per person for a 2-hour tour. Mornings, when the sea is calm, usually provide the clearest water for viewing. A 50-minute dive in the ***Yellow Submarine*** (☎ **07/637-6666** or 07/636-2000) runs about $65 for adults, $36 for children, including entrance to the Coral World Observatory. Off season and midweek, there are sometimes deals like a child in the company of two adults goes for free.

SAILBOAT CRUISES   Several yacht and sailboat cruises will take you on a full-day (10am to 5pm) excursion to **Taba,** on the Egyptian border, or to **Coral Island and the Fjord**—two points of interest along the Egyptian Sinai coast south of Eilat. If you go to the Egyptian coast, you can't land (you won't have a visa, and there's no Customs post on the beach!), but you can swim from the boat, snorkel, scuba dive, relax in the sun on board, and have a lunch that is included in the cost of the cruise. For a bit more money, you can also water-ski or go sailboarding for a full or half day. Cost for all day is about NIS 160 to 203 ($35 to $45), lunch included (several of the boats have kosher kitchens); prices start at around $10 for a simple sail. Special diving cruises can, of course, go above the NIS 225 ($50) range. Walk along the marina in front of the North Beach lagoon and see which boat or itinerary appeals to you; you can reserve in advance at most travel agencies, at the marina, or at large hotel desks.

SNORKELING & SCUBA DIVING　　The best-equipped firm for snorkeling and scuba diving is **Aqua Sport,** also called the International Red Sea Diving Center (P.O. Box 300, Eilat; ☎ 07/633-4404). Right across the highway from the Red Sea Sports Club Hotel on Coral Beach, the Aqua Sport center can fulfill your needs for mask, fins, and snorkel ($8 per day for the complete ensemble), as well as wet suits, weight belts, depth gauges, buoyancy compensators, cylinders, and other gear. One-day dive cruises are ($39), including lunch, introductory dives are $42; diving lessons (in English), diving tours (half or full day), and even 3-day camping/diving or snorkeling safaris are also available. A 5-day diving course ($275) leads to internationally recognized two-star diver certification; with 6 days' bed-and-breakfast at the divers' hostel, the cost comes to $370. Many other programs are offered as well, including rental and lessons in sailboarding. Bed-and-breakfast at the Aqua Sport hostel is $22 per day in double or quadruple rooms. Aqua Sport also has a program of weeklong summer camps for kids ages 10 to 15 during July and August; parents can leave the kids and go off for a week, and the kids are exposed to a world of underwater and maritime activities and fun. Also operating through Aqua Sport is the **School of Underwater Photography,** with half-day to 14-day programs on underwater video and still photography. In the evening, there's a pub, underwater video films, and occasional live entertainment, and dancing. Aqua Sport is open every day from 8:30am to 12:30am. Write directly to Aqua Sport for information on prices, programs, and to arrange for courses and trips. Aqua Sport accepts Diner's Club, MasterCard, and Visa.

　　Red Sea Sport Club's Manta Dive Center, located at the Red Sea Sport and Ambassador Hotel (☎ 07/637-6569), is another highly recommended diving center at the Coral Beach. It offers facilities similar to those at Aqua Sport, plus other activities including sailing, windsurfing, and boating, deep-sea fishing, night cruises, organized diving trips to Sinai, desert safaris, horseback riding, camel treks, canoes and paddleboats, waterskiing, and bicycle rental, in addition to its diving and sailboarding programs. There is even a special sauna facility for divers. It's open daily from 8:30am to 4:30pm in winter, until 6pm in summer.

　　Both of the above places offer introductory dives for people who have never experienced diving before and want to try it out. It costs about $44 for an hour-long, one-to-one session with a diving instructor, who spends about half an hour giving you the instruction you need to go down and another half hour with you 18 to 20 feet below the water, out in the Red Sea coral reefs. This is a great way to get a short introduction to diving before committing yourself to a full 6-day program.

OTHER OUTDOOR ACTIVITIES
Bird Watching

Eilat is one of the best places on earth for bird watching, due to its prime location on the Jordan Valley–Red Sea–Great African Rift Valley migration path between Europe and Africa. Migration times are twice a year: from **September through November** the birds head south to Africa, and from **March through May** they head back north to Europe.

Eilat's **International Birding and Research Center,** P.O. Box 774, Eilat 88106, on Hatmarim Boulevard (☎ **07/633-5339;** fax 07/633-5319; e-mail: IBRCE@ EILATCITY.CO.IL), in the small City Centre Shopping Mall, is a storehouse for information and activities relating to bird watching around Eilat. It conducts guided bird-watching tours daily between February 15 and May 30, from 8 to 10am, for a fee of $5; for a minimal fee, you can rent a pair of binoculars to use on the hike. Between February 15 and May 15 a general spring census of birds is conducted, in which you may participate. The center will also offer advice on birding throughout the country. The International Birdwatching Center is open Sunday through Thursday from 9am to 1pm and 5 to 7pm, on Friday from 9am to 1pm. Also visit the bird-banding station during the morning hours on most days of the week. Similar activities take place again in the fall. Lectures, nature films, literature, and background material are also offered.

If you would like to be in Eilat at the best time for bird watching, you should know that each year in March, the center hosts an **International Birdwatchers' Festival** of growing renown. Write to the International Birdwatching Center, P.O. Box 774, Eilat 88106, for information about the many special programs and discounts on accommodations and car rentals at the time of the festival. Throughout the year, the center currently can help arrange discount car rental programs.

✪ **Coral Beach Nature Reserve.** ☎ **07/637-6829.** NIS 22 ($4.80) adults, NIS 11 ($2.40) for children ages 5–18. Daily 9am–5pm. Closed Yom Kippur. Bus: 15.

This is where you can explore Israel's small, but fascinating chunk of the Red Sea's reef system, teeming with colorful, exotic fishes and sea creatures of every description. Located south of the city, between downtown Eilat and the border with Egypt, the reserve consists of a pleasant, unfrenzied beach dotted with shade structures. The sand here is the original course beige sand of the shoreline—the imported, powdery white sand of North Beach tends to blow into the water and suffocate the coral. There are comfortable changing rooms with showers, and there's an open-air snack bar. Illustrated books about the reserve are for sale at the snack bar/gift shop.

The Reserve will give you a flyer pointing out a number of underwater trails. For NIS 23 ($5), you can rent a snorkel, mask, and fins, or you can bring your own gear. There is a refundable deposit of NIS 100 ($22) for each snorkel set. A walkway takes you into the water beyond the reef (which parallels the shore) so that coral is not broken underfoot by visitors. You enter at the northern end of the reef. Since the wind and current usually move southward, all you have to do is drift and paddle a bit to observe the reef through your mask.

The nature reserve also operates a scuba program for novices called "Snuba," in which you can dive tethered to an oxygen tank on a floating dingy—the safest, easiest way to dive! It costs NIS 180 ($40) for 1¹/₂ hours, including instruction. There are showers and changing areas. *An important warning:* Be very sure to wear some sort of foot covering every time you enter the water here: Spiny sea urchins are almost everywhere you might want to try to stand.

City bus no. 15 from downtown Eilat runs half-hourly, and takes you to Coral Beach in about 15 or 20 minutes.

✪ **Coral World Underwater Observatory and Aquarium.** ☎ **07/376-666.** Admission NIS 60 ($13.20) adult, NIS 40 ($8.80) children ages 5–16. Sat–Thurs 8:30am–4:30pm; Fri 8:30am–3pm. Bus: 15.

Located just south of Coral Beach is this fascinating complex. The complex consists of three one-story buildings on the beach with distinctive rounded roofs, and two

Wings over Israel

After the Second Revolt against Rome in A.D. 135, Judea was left so desolate that olives, the ancient staple of the region, were not harvested again for more than a century, and according to tradition, even birds avoided the once verdant hills. The loss of the birds must have been especially noticeable. Today in Israel are found 91 resident species, 121 regularly migrating species, and more than 200 winter or summer residents—an amazing number and variety for so small an area. In ancient times, the variety and number of birds must have been even larger. Israel is located on the main migration route of the birds of Europe and Western Asia to and from Africa. For millions of years migrating birds have followed the line of the below-sea Jordan Valley to the Great Rift Valley because they need warm air thermals to help them cover the distance between Europe and Africa. At times in the migration season—an amazing spectacle that includes overflights of 500 million birds—Israel hosts an estimated 85% of the world's stork population! Birds stop for several days' rest in the Galilee among the thriving kibbutz fishponds and farms along the Jordan River before continuing south across the Negev to Eilat.

The flight over the desert can be so difficult that exhausted birds commonly drop dead out of the sky, in the Western Negev and Sinai, sometimes only a short distance from a watering hole on the fringe of Israeli agricultural land. Some migrants, including a dozen families of storks, have become so habituated to the lush agricultural scene developed in Israel over the past decades that they have begun to breed in Israel rather than their traditional European nesting areas. During migration season the skies can be so thick with birds that they are a major hazard to military and commercial flights in the area. With the new peace agreements between Israel, Egypt, and Jordan, the governments of those countries have begun plans to build a network of migrating bird radar-tracking stations throughout the area in an effort to save the lives of both human passengers and the birds themselves. Over the next several years, this network will also be put to use for the benefit of worldwide bird enthusiasts who visit the region. Meanwhile, the first station of the network, the **Inter-University Institute for Research of Bird Migration,** is under construction at Latrun, in the foothills of the Judean Mountains not far from Jerusalem. It is scheduled to open in 1997, in cooperation with the Hebrew University of Jerusalem, Tel Aviv University, and Haifa's Technion, and will include a research center, a museum, and an auditorium for screening films. The institute will join Eilat's International Birdwatching Center, the Society for Protection of Nature in Israel, the Zipori Bird Park in Tel Aviv, and the Nature Reserve Center at northern Israel's Beit Ussishkin in Kibbutz Dan as a major resource for bird-watching enthusiasts traveling in Israel.

underwater observatories, which are 100 yards out to sea in what is called the Japanese Gardens. A pier binds the observatories to the coast. In addition to the underwater observatories, you'll also find the **Maritime Museum and the Aquarium.** The aquarium is built so that you stand in the middle and the fish swim around you in a huge circular tank. The third building is a pleasant snack bar/cafe. There are also large outdoor observation pools—one for big sharks, and another for sea turtles and rays. The tower of the observatory rises out of the sea to a height of 20 feet; inside, a spiral staircase of 42 steps leads down to the observatory itself. Since the water in the gulf is generally crystal clear, observation of the magnificent fish and coral life is unparalleled.

The best time to visit the observatory is between 10am and noon, when the light is good and the water is usually calm and clear. The Eilat local city bus no. 15 comes this way every half hour.

WHERE TO STAY

If there is a low season here, it is from May to June. Europeans tend to come from October to April; Israelis come July to August and during the September-October high holidays. Jewish and Christian holidays are also times when prices skyrocket even above high-season levels. In the past, winter was Eilat's high season, but with the prevalence of air-conditioning, and the development of the town for tourism, it's become a popular year-round spot. Many hotels have developed their own systems for determining when to charge high- and low-season rates. Nobody in his right mind actually pays full price here. A good travel agent or packager in Israel or your own country can get you fabulous deals. The **Egged Tours Office,** right at the Central Bus Station, can often come up with discounted hotel rooms, if you want to play things by ear, and make your arrangements as you stop off the bus in Eilat. They specialize in walk-ins.

We'll start with hotels on the main centers of downtown Eilat (such downtown as exists), Hatmarim Boulevard and the New Tourist Center. Then we'll look at hotels in the bustling North Beach area, with many restaurants, nightclubs, and discos, both attached to and separate from hotels. This area is within walkable distance of downtown Eilat, especially in the relative cool of the evenings. A third hotel area is the Coral Beach, several miles south of town. For those into exploring the reefs, this is a good choice, since North Beach is basically coral-free. In the streets west of the Bus Station are numerous private hostels; the Tourist Information Center is the place to check on which are currently up to standard. You can also gather information there about rooms in private homes and rental apartments.

HATMARIN BOULEVARD & NEAR THE BUS STATION
Moderate
Holiday Inn Eilat Patio. 3 Shifton Alley, Eilat. ☎ **07/636-4364.** Fax 07/634-0118. 115 units. A/C MINIBAR TV TEL. $135–$170 double. Rates include breakfast. No charge for up to 2 children under 19 years of age sharing parents' room. AE, DC, MC, V. Free parking.

Less fancy and in a less-prestigious area than the Crown Plaza Eilat (see North Beach below), the Patio is one of a number of bright new hotels in the moderate range that have popped up in the center of town around the Central Bus Station. The "kids are free" policy makes this a good base for families and offers a generic, comfortable room and heated outdoor swimming pool and Jacuzzi, but no beach or desert ambience. A health club (extra charge), baby-sitting, room safes, and pleasant outdoor dining terrace are the pluses.

Nova All Suite Hotel. 6 Hativat Hanegev St., Eilat. ☎ **07/638-2444.** Fax 07/638-2455. E-mail: atlashot@netvision.net.il. 193 suites. A/C TV TEL. $127–$177 suite. Rates include breakfast. AE, DC, MC, V.

Built in the mid-1990s, the one- and two-room suites of this six-story hotel overlook a swimming pool courtyard. Rooms are functional and simple, with rattan furniture and kitchenettes that help make a stay in Eilat a bit more economical. There's room service, a children's club, minimarket, restaurant, and poolside snack bar and a cool underground parking lot that keeps your car from becoming an oven. Larger suites run $50 extra.

NEAR THE NEW TOURIST CENTER

The New Tourist Center, right across (west of) the main highway from North Beach at the corner of Derekh Ha-Arava and Derekh Yotam, is a useful landmark and a prime nightlife area for Eilat's younger crowd.

Expensive

Club Hotel Eilat. Ha-Arava St., Eilat. ☎ **07/636-1666.** Fax 07/632-2613. 135 units. A/C MINIBAR TV TEL. $363–$402 for up to 4 adults or 2 adults and 3 children in 1-bedroom suites; add $80 for 2-bedroom suite. July–Aug, Jewish and Christian holidays, add $150 per suite. Breakfast $12 per person extra. AE, DC, MC, V.

This vast new (1997) all-suite hotel located 2 blocks from North Beach is family oriented and superfriendly for kids. It offers tons of activities, seven swimming pools surrounding a garden with more than 90,000 plants, and an intensely nautical decor that makes you feel like you're on a self-contained cruise ship. There's an entertainment center with video games, an Internet cafe, lots of shops, two discos, and a "submarine" from which kids can view the adult swimming pool from underwater. There are also five restaurants and a bar. These are the most state-of-the-art suites in town, all bright and comfortable; most overlook the gardens and pools, but a few face a bleak parking lot. Avoid them. Since many of the suites have been purchased as timeshares, the hotel is filled with Israeli families. It's lively, but *not* a romantic hideaway.

Moderate

Edomit Hotel. New Tourist Center, Eilat. ☎ **07/637-9511.** Fax 07/637-9738. 85 units. A/C TV TEL. $127–$160 double. Rates include breakfast. DC, MC, V.

This three-star-equivalent, eight-story hotel, located to the rear of the New Tourist Center, has a swimming pool and offers rooms with heat, radio, and a sea view in the distance from its higher floors. The Edomit also can arrange triple or quadruple rooms, and family plans. Many rooms have been recently renovated; try to get them.

NORTH BEACH

This is the high-powered, high-priced hotel district, covering the area from the northern shore of the Red Sea inland to the local Eilat Airport. Most of the hotels here are mammoth blockbusters, although here and there a smaller holdover from pre-1993 Eilat has survived. An artificial lagoon has been created in the heart of this neighborhood, but it's not for swimming. A few hotels are right on the beach, but most hotels (including some of the most expensive) are anywhere from one to four blocks inland.

Very Expensive

Dan Eilat Hotel. North Beach, Eilat. ☎ **07/636-2222;** 800/223-7773 for reservations in the U.S., or 0171/439-9893 in the U.K. Fax 07/636/2333. 378 units. A/C MINIBAR TV TEL. $276, $345, $525 standard, deluxe, and family double. Rates include breakfast. Add 15% service charge. AE, DC, MC, V.

Opened at the end of 1995, this five-star blockbuster is the newest of the well-managed Dan Hotels. Its location, right on a palm-dotted piece of North Beach just next door to Isrotel's Royal Beach Hotel, is excellent and especially good for swimming. The hotel itself is new and impressive. Rooms come in three categories: superior (standard), deluxe, and family (with additional sleeping alcove). Designer Adam Tihany, who has done the interiors of trend-setting hotels and restaurants on three continents, decorated the Dan Eilat with bold colors and shapes unlike anything else in Israel; the look is lively and inventive—I like it, but there are partisans on both sides. The gardened pool areas are most attractive.

Dining/Diversions: 10 restaurants (including Polynesian and Mexican), bars and cafes, nightclub, jazz cellar, virtual reality laser arena.

Amenities: Two pools, fitness center, concierge, secretarial services, 24-hour room service, children's programs, Turkish bath, sauna, massage, Jacuzzi, squash courts.

✪ **Herod's Sheraton Resort, Spa and Convention Center.** North Beach, Eilat. ☎ **07/638-0000;** reservations through Sheraton Hotels. Fax 07/638-0100. 468 units. A/C MINIBAR TV TEL. $320–$400 double; $600 Easter/Passover; $670 Christmas. Rates include breakfast. AE, DC, NC, V. Free parking

Completed in early 2000, the Herod's Sheraton complex, with its own piece of Eilat beachfront, is the most expensive and lavish hotel in Israel. Visually, the towering ensemble of buildings, pools, and enormous, enclosed, light-filled space touched with Arabesque and Roman architectural elements looks like the stuff dreams are made of. There are domes, networks of bridges, waterfalls, a Roman Cardo (colonnaded street) and elegant optical illusions and tricks of perspective (like the Roman style pool, placed at the end of an avenue of date palms, and seeming to flow into the Red Sea). Some compare this Middle East Deco extravaganza to a set for the most fabulous Fred Astaire–Ginger Rodgers film ever conceived. Staff members are garbed in Arabian Nights costumes. The fantasy, however, does not extend into the guest rooms, which are tasteful, equipped with every comfort a top hotel should offer, but perfectly normal (try for a room with a Red Sea view; some simply face other towers in the complex). The hotel is divided into three parts: Herod's Palace, which is the main section, encompassing 268 rooms and suites; Herod's Vitalis Health and Lifestyle Resort, a spa par excellence (and largely a no-children zone) containing 64 balconied no-smoking rooms, all with Jacuzzis; and Herod's Forum Convention Center, a venue for special events and business meetings, with 104 rooms, suites, and cottages, a wing of exhibition booths, meeting halls, a business center, simultaneous translation and complete audiovisual services.

Dining/Diversions: The Tamarind, a "fusion" Moroccan restaurant; Birdwatchers, a breakfast and dinner buffet restaurant with a more lavish spread than any other hotel in Israel; the Terrace, for light meals and an evening al fresco fish grill; and the Officers' Club, a British Empire–style bar with pool table and darts.

Amenities: Rooms for travelers with disabilities, outdoor pools, beachfront, water sports, complete fitness center, sauna, steam bath; children's sports, handicrafts and antiquities activities; health, beauty, massage and business facilities.

✪ **Isrotel Royal Beach Hotel.** North Beach, Eilat. ☎ **07/636-8888;** 888/669-5700 or 201/556-9669 in the U.S. and Canada. Fax 07/636-8811. 363 units. A/C MINIBAR TV TEL. $253–$630 double. Rates include breakfast and service charge. AE, DC, MC, V. Free parking.

Opened in 1994, this is the newest star of the Isrotel Chain, with a palm-shaded beach, airy, sparkling, beautifully furnished public areas, and a swimming pool landscaped around natural rocks and artificial waterfalls. Architecturally, this is one of the best hotel buildings in the country, filled with light and soaring space and with glass upper-story corridors that look out onto wonderful vistas of Eilat and the desert mountains. Rooms are graceful, decorated with well-chosen artwork and noninstitutional touches like wooden moldings around the ceilings; every room faces directly onto the Red Sea. There are standard, deluxe, and family rooms (which include a sleeping alcove for two children) as well as a variety of suites. Electric kettles with a supply of teas and coffees in each room are a convenient extra touch. Ask about package deals.

Dining/Diversions: Ten restaurants, including a wide variety of ethnic and theme restaurants; most popular is the American-style Ranch House serving prime rib, barbecue beef spare ribs, and charcoal-grilled steaks. Cocktail lounge, English pub, disco, entertainment lounge, piano and terrace lounge.

Amenities: Swimming pool, 24-hour room service, paddling pool, sauna, steam bath, fitness room, gym, shops.

Le Meridien All Suite Hotel. North Beach, Eilat. ☎ **07/638-3333.** Fax 07/638-3300. 138 suites. A/C MINIBAR TV TEL. $330–$390 smaller suites regular season; add $150 per suite Christmas, Easter, and July–Aug. Rates include breakfast. AE, DC, MC, V. Free parking.

Another of the 1999 crop of new Eilat hotels, Le Meridien brings suite hotels to new levels of luxury and service. There are a number of kinds of one and two bedroom suites, all strikingly decorated (and some no-smoking). Among the services and amenities offered are a large outdoor heated pool overlooking the Red Sea; health club for additional fee; playground; and hairdresser. The beachfront location, at the southern edge of North Beach, is central. Rates for the larger class of suites begin at $50 above the rates for smaller suites.

Expensive

Crowne Plaza Eilat. North Beach, Eilat. ☎ **07/636-7777;** reservations through Holiday Inns. Fax 07/633-0821. 266 units. A/C TV TEL. $258 double; $368 Passover, Christmas. Rates include breakfast. Add 15% service charge. AE, DC, MC, V.

On the Lagoon Waterfront Promenade, but a few blocks inland from the beach, the new (1994) nine-story Holiday Inn is a beautiful structure, but can seem a bit jumbled at busy times, with activities in its Carnival Lobby and Pub. Guest rooms are attractively decorated; an entire floor is reserved for nonsmokers. Facilities include a pool, heated in season, a health club, and a sauna.

✪ **Isrotel King Solomon's Palace.** North Beach, Eilat. ☎ **07/636-3444;** 888/669-5700 or 201/556-9669 in the U.S. and Canada. Fax 07/633-4189. 415 units. A/C MINIBAR TV TEL. $181–365 double; less on packages. Rates include breakfast and service charge. AE, DC, MC, V.

If you decide to experience Eilat in its new incarnation as a luxury resort, this hotel, built in the early 1980s and the first of the city's five-star blockbusters, is a worthy choice. Located right in the center of things on the Lagoon Promenade (but, like many downtown hotels, a walk to the beach), the King Solomon is luxurious, with freshly redecorated rooms, and has perfected an amazing program of daytime and evening activities for kids, teens, and under and over 25ers. The pool is gracefully shaped around an island and is heated in winter; you can join the daily poolside aerobics there, or enjoy the open-air tropical snack bar. There's tennis, a health club, sauna, and Jacuzzi. For kids, in addition to daytime activities, there's a well-organized Snoopy Disco from 5 to 9:45pm. Adult entertainment is from 10:30pm on, and the downstairs Sheba Disco, with its laser sound-and-light system, is the acknowledged high-powered nightspot in town. The hotel's many restaurants are among the best in Eilat for quality kosher dining. Five-person suites with large terraces and private Jacuzzis can be a viable choice if you're with a family or group.

Isrotel Lagoona Hotel. North Beach, Eilat. ☎ **07/636-6666;** 800/552-0140, 888/669-5700, or 201/566-9669 in the U.S. and Canada. Fax 07/636-6699. 256 units. A/C MINIBAR TV TEL. $197–$320 double. Rates include breakfast and service charge. AE, DC, MC, V.

Located on the lagoon, just beside the Isrotel King Solomon's Palace, the Lagoona is smaller and quieter than its more lavish neighbor, but certainly comfortable. There are many returnees among its clientele, and this branch of the Isrotel Chain often may have fewer children than the other branches. An atmospheric Bedouin Tent restaurant, with excellent food, a heated pool, and direct access to the Lagoon Promenade, are the strong features of this comfortable hotel. The highly recommended Tandoori restaurant is in the Lagoona's waterfront promenade.

Sheraton Four Points Red Sea Paradise Hotel. North Beach, Eilat. ☎ **07/636-3636.** Fax 07/636-3630. 282 units. A/C MINIBAR TV TEL. $195–$270 double. Rates include breakfast. Add 15% service charge. AE, DC, MC, V.

This sprawling three-story complex is a choice in the lower part of the expensive price range. It's newer and prettier than its fellow Four Points Sheraton Eilat (see below) but a bit further from the beach. The hotel consists of a series of large atriums and courtyards connected by lattice-shaded outdoor passageways. Guest rooms resemble those in a standard American motel; most look out on a vast central swimming pool. The hotel's design is among the best in Eilat, but the location, in the part of North Beach most distant from the actual beach, can be difficult for those without rental cars. There are adult and children's pools, as well as a fitness center (fee), Jacuzzi, sauna, tennis court, entertainment lounge, and dance floor. There are rooms for travelers with disabilities.

✪ **Sheraton Moriah Plaza Eilat.** North Beach, Eilat. ☎ **07/636-1111;** 800/221-0203 or 212/541-5009 in the U.S. Fax 07/633-4158. 296 units. A/C MINIBAR TV TEL. $280–$350 double. 15% service charge. Rates include breakfast. AE, DC, MC, V.

The glistening, elegantly designed Radisson Moriah Plaza ranks just below the Royal Beach and the Dan as one of the three most luxurious hotels on North Beach. The entire hotel was rebuilt in 1992. Polished-stone public areas lead out to meandering, natural-form swimming pools laid out amid rocks and small cascades. Staff and dining facilities are excellent. A light, attractive touch marks the guest rooms, most of which have balconies and water views. As the jewel in the Radisson Moriah Hotels Chain, this hotel is not always available in the Radisson Moriah Package plans, but it is excellent value when it is included. The location, on the beach and in walking distance to town, is a plus.

Dining/Diversions: There is a pub and two restaurants, including Trattoria Italian restaurant (a favorite among locals), which features a special low-budget pasta menu in summer.

Amenities: Three swimming pools, including a water jet and a children's pool, health club, shopping arcade, 24-hour room service, concierge, business center, hairdresser.

Moderate

Marina Club Eilat. North Beach, Eilat 88141. ☎ **07/633-4191.** Fax 07/633-4206. E-mail: marinac@netvision.net.il. 132 suites. A/C TV TEL. $151–$259 two people in suite for up to six people; $202–$363 six-person suite. AE, DC, MC, V.

Pushing 12 years old, but bright and well maintained, this apartment hotel has two- and three-room suites that are ideal for families or small groups. Suites vary according to number of rooms and type of view, which determine the rate (pool view is $20 to $30 extra per suite), but each suite has its own kitchenette equipped with basics for producing anything from coffee to a full meal. The hotel surrounds a magnificent gardened pool (heated in winter) and all services are provided. The high end of the price range is during July, August, and Jewish holidays and Israeli school vacations, but at other times the hotel is an excellent deal for three- to six-person groups. Sunday to Thursday is the best time for bargaining a bit or finding a "special" rate. On weekends, prices go up $50 per suite. Bargain in off-seasons or if you are only two people. There are handicapped-accessible rooms and children's programs during school holidays.

Moon Valley Hotel. North Beach, Eilat. ☎ **07/636-6888.** Fax 07/633-4110. 182 units (all with bathroom). A/C TV TEL. $115–$160 double. Rates include breakfast. AE, DC, MC, V.

Another low-rise hotel, about 2 decades old, with units opening to outdoor walkways or overlooking the large pool, the Moon Valley has recently been completely renovated. Its lobby and guest rooms now sport light, pleasantly tropical furnishings and decor. Rooms are small but efficient. Much of the clientele is 20- to 30-something. Despite the careful update of the hotel, service is average. Low season is May, June, September, and October except for Jewish holidays. High season includes Christmas.

Reef Hotel. North Beach, Eilat. ☎ **07/636-4444.** Fax 07/636-4488. 79 units. A/C TV TEL. $152, $161, $200 double, low, regular, high seasons. Rates include breakfast. AE, DC, MC, V.

One of the few human-sized hotels left in Eilat, the Reef has a great waterfront location just south of busy North Beach, walkable to shops, diving centers, and the North Beach Promenade. All rooms have balconies with sea views, and have refrigerators; they're comfortable but not exceptional. There's a medium-size pool surrounded by a deck, and direct access to the hotel's slice of beach.

Riviera Apartment Hotel. North Beach, Eilat. ☎ **07/633-3944**; 888/669-5700 or 201/556-9669 in the U.S. and Canada. Fax 07/633-3939. 172 units. A/C TV TEL. Suite for two to four persons $100–$160 low season; $121–$190 regular season; $230–$345 Jewish holidays and Christmas and July 15–Sept. 15. Substantial discounts on Isrotel or Kibbutz Hotel Chain plans. AE, DC, MC, V.

Especially good for families or people traveling in small groups, this busy, brand-new establishment, just across the street from the luxury King Solomon's Palace Hotel, offers a number of pleasantly furnished and decorated suites (many with their own garden terraces or balconies), a vast swimming pool, and state-of-the-art kitchenettes set up with the basic equipment (including, in some suites, a microwave oven) and cleaning supplies you'll need to prepare your own meals during your stay. The hotel's buildings are low-rise, set around the pool, and the feel is less formal than the big high-rise places in the area. Readers report a number of nice touches on the part of the management, such as packages of herbal teas. Although not located on a kibbutz, this hotel is one of the choices available at a discount rate on the Kibbutz Fly and Drive Plan when you book through the Israel Tourism Center. Check with the center about any specials available through the Riviera's parent company, Isrotel, or in conjunction with Arkia Airlines.

Sheraton Four Points Eilat. North Beach, Eilat. ☎ **07/630-4444.** Fax 07/633-2348. 247 units. A/C MINIBAR TV TEL. $160–235 double. Rates include breakfast. Add 15% service charge. AE, DC, MC, V. Free parking.

Built in 1991, this is one of two low-rise Sheraton Four Point hotels in North Beach. The guest rooms surround a pleasant central pool area, which is the heart of the hotel; there's a large reception area (good for receiving groups) but a rather jumbled lounge/lobby. Guest rooms are adequate, but motel-like. The location is a few blocks inland from the actual beach. Rooms are often available at a discount in packages. There is a fitness club (fee) and rooms for travelers with disabilities.

Inexpensive

Americana Inn Eilat. North Beach (P.O. Box 27), Eilat. ☎ **07/633-3777.** Fax 07/633-4174. E-mail: americana@eilatcity.il. 140 units. A/C TV TEL. $114–$149 double. $9 supplement for units with kitchenettes. Add $10 per person for Jewish holidays; $10 for pool view. AE, DC, MC, V.

This busy low-rise hotel, built in the 1970s, has a young, festive atmosphere, and is one of the best deals in Eilat. The rooms are situated around a large swimming pool/terrace with one huge, heated pool and another children's pool; 36 rooms have private balconies, 50 have private kitchenettes; all are recently refurbished and contain safes, refrigerators, and hair dryers. Films are shown daily in the TV room; watersports bookings, billiards, and table tennis are all available and a new fitness room with a sauna and Jacuzzi are free to guests. If you book 7 nights or more, the management will offer a 10% reduction. From this hotel, and from its neighbor, the Moon Valley Hotel (see above), it's a hike of a few blocks to the beach, which can be a problem on a 100° day. There is a minimarket on the premises.

Dalia Hotel. North Beach. ☎ **07/633-4004.** Fax 07/633-4072. 63 units. A/C TV TEL. $82–$122 double. Rates include breakfast. AE, MC, V.

At the beginning of North Beach, just in from the intersection of Durban and Arava roads, this well-located hotel, built in the early 1970s, has no view and offers utilitarian rooms, but 1997 redecorations make it one of the better affordable choices in the lower-moderate price range. Pluses are a small but pleasant swimming pool and the Check Inn Chicken restaurant on the premises, where you can dine well on the $9 all-you-can-eat buffet.

Coral Beach & South to The Border
Very Expensive

✪ **Eilat Princess Hotel.** Eilat. ☎ **07/636-5555.** Fax 07/637-3590. 418 units. A/C MINI-BAR TV TEL. $270–$460 double. Rates include breakfast. Add 15% service charge. AE, DC, MC, V. Free parking. Bus: 15.

Built in 1992, the Eilat Princess has set a new standard for hotel design and room decor in Israel. More expensive deluxe rooms offer a variety of design themes, ranging from European to Chinese and Philippine (there are no genuine Negev and Bedouin motifs). As the southernmost of Eilat's hotels, 2 miles south of the Coral Beach, the Princess is somewhat isolated unless you have a car, but it's a self-contained resort, with soaring, light-filled public areas, swimming pools designed around artificial cascades, continental, Cajun (kosher and terrific), and Asian restaurants, as well as the standard range of hotel cafes and lounge/piano bars. There is also a fitness club (fee) and spa with therapeutic and beauty programs. The beach, along a strip of water containing some reefs, is just across the highway; at present it's narrow and bare, but there are plans for upgrading.

   Dining/Diversions: Six very good restaurants and cafes, disco, piano bar, live entertainment.

   Amenities: Two swimming pools, heated in season, two tennis courts sports facilities, fitness room, health and beauty spa. 24-hour room service, desert and diving bookings, shuttle into Eilat.

Expensive

Ambassador Hotel. Coral Beach, Eilat. ☎ **07/638-2222.** Fax 07/638-2200. 160 units. A/C MINIBAR TV TEL. $250–$350 double. AE, DC, MC, V.

If you want to be close to snorkeling at the Coral Beach Nature Reserve, this new (1997) hotel offers the perfect location, less than a 5-minute walk across the road. On the hotel's property, you'll also find the excellent Red Sea Sport Club Diving Center, with a wide selection of scuba classes and excursions. Guest rooms are comfortable though a bit small for the price, and surround a vast swimming pool.

Orchid Hotel and Resort. Coral Beach, Eilat. ☎ **07/636-0360.** Fax 07/637-5323. E-mail: orchird@netvision.net.il. 136 bungalows. A/C TV TEL. $280–$380 double; $500–$2,500 suite. Rates include breakfast. Add 15% service charge. AE, DC, MC, V. Bus: 15.

Designed to suggest a Thai village, with a beautifully authentic wooden Thai pavilion serving as both a centerpiece and Thai/Asian restaurant, the Orchid is one of Eilat's most architecturally interesting hotels, especially if you can conceive of a Thai community transported to the barren, rocky desertscape of the Negev (a fire destroyed the hotel's tropical landscaping, but new plantings are slowly being installed). Located half a mile south of the Coral Beach, on the inland side of the road leading along the coast to Taba, the Orchid has graceful public areas surrounding a large, often busy pool, and further uphill, wooden A-frame guest units with a double room and bathroom on the ground floor, and a sleeping loft reached by ladder/steps. A golf cart shuttle carries guests up to their accommodations, which are decorated with non-Thai print curtains and bedspreads. There is an in-house restaurant serving a daily buffet, piano bar, disco in high season, and entertainment for children and adults, usually in Hebrew. Off-season, the Orchid can have a tranquil charm; during school vacations it's packed with Israeli families, which means lots of children.

Moderate

Club Inn Villa Resort. Coral Beach, Eilat. ☎ **07/638-5555.** Fax 07/638-5533. 168 villas for up to 6 people. A/C TV TEL. $250–$420 per villa 6-person occupancy. Add 15% service charge. Breakfast $10 per person extra. AE, DC, MC, V. Bus: 15.

Set around a very pleasant, gardened swimming pool, the Club Inn is a low-rise complex of units built in the late 1970s and completely renovated in 1994. Each unit, with simple, clean, practical decor, contains two bedrooms and a kitchenette; two units are designed for travelers with disabilities. There are minimarkets on the premises, and just outside the property. You can easily walk to the Coral Beach Nature Preserve from here, but it can be a hot 10-minute walk in the summer sun. Quieter rooms face away from the pool. The swimming pool is heated in winter; other facilities include a fitness room, two floodlit tennis courts, children's programs, bar, disco, and restaurant. Rates are lower for two or four people.

JUST ACROSS THE BORDER: TABA

Just across the Israeli-Egyptian frontier at the southern edge of Eilat, Taba came under Israeli occupation, along with the rest of Sinai, at the end of the 1967 Six-Day War. When Israel returned the Sinai Peninsula to Egypt as part of the Camp David peace accord in the early 1980s, Taba remained in dispute. International arbitration in the late 1980s decided in favor of Egypt, but by then it had become a very valuable few acres, encompassing the site of the Taba Hilton, which visitors and residents alike had come to think of as a southern precinct of Eilat. Today, travelers from Eilat can pass across the border to the Taba Hilton for a few hours without problem, but to venture into Sinai beyond Taba requires a special visa. Guests at the Taba Hilton may and frequently do walk the few hundred feet across the border and taxi or bus into Eilat; however, Egyptian rental cars may not currently be taken across the border, nor can Israeli rental cars be taken out of Israel.

✪ **Taba Hilton Resort Hotel and Casino.** Taba Beach, Sinai, Egypt. ☎ **62/530-140** in Egypt; 07/632-6222 in Israel; reservations through Hilton Hotels International. Fax 62/578-7044 in Egypt; 07/632-6660 in Israel. 326 units. A/C MINIBAR TV TEL. $140–$175 double. Nelson's Village and suites $270–$438. Breakfast $10 per person; tax and service extra. AE, DC, MC, V.

One of the most comfortable hotels in the Eilat area, built before Israel returned Taba to Egypt, the Hilton is a comparatively good bargain because it is priced according to Egyptian standards. During Israeli school holidays, the Taba Hilton can be as busy as any downtown Eilat hotel, but at other times the atmosphere can be refreshingly tranquil. Everything here is equal to the best hotels in Eilat. The Egyptian staff is very professional and attentive, the snorkeling and diving center facilities are exceptionally good, with a reef right off the private beach, and the hotel's gardens and palm trees have had time to gracefully mature. Among unique attractions are the casino (easily visited by travelers from Eilat) and a large saltwater swimming pool. Other special attractions here are a bazaar filled with interesting Egyptian crafts and souvenirs, and the new (1997), low-rise Nelson's Village section of the hotel, providing a more intimate atmosphere. Among standard rooms, prices differ according to sea or inland views.

Eilat's bus no. 15 takes you to the Taba Border crossing; you must show your passport at the Israeli and Egyptian sides of the border. Make it clear to passport control officials that you are only going to the Hilton, and you avoid border crossing fees, though you may need to show a receipt from the hotel or casino as you return into Israel. If you have suitcases and a reservation at the Taba Hilton, a free hotel van will be arranged to take you from the border to the hotel. In any case, a Hilton courtesy van will usually be waiting at the border to take hotel guests, and visitors to the casino or bazaar to the hotel. The walk is less than 5 minutes from the Egyptian side of the border.

Dining/Diversions: Four restaurants, four bars, casino.

Amenities: Travel and cruise bookings, 24-hour room service, outdoor pool, five floodlit tennis courts, diving and water-sports center, windsurfing, jet-ski, waterskiing, children's club.

PRIVATE ROOMS & APARTMENTS

Ask at the **Tourist Information Center** (☎ 07/673-2111) at the corner of Yotam and Arava roads. It's best to use the Tourist Office for referral, since there have been complaints from people using other sources. Prices for a two-bedroom apartment (for four people or more) are about NIS 270 ($60) per day during most of the year, and NIS 360 to 450 ($80 to $100) or more per day during high season (July, August, and holidays). Especially for a group, this is one of the best ways to economize in Eilat.

WHERE TO DINE
NEAR HATMARIN BOULEVARD
Expensive

✪ **Au Bistro.** Eilot St. ☎ **07/637-4333.** Reservations required. Main courses NIS 55–110 ($12.10–$24.20); lobster and chateaubriand for two $47–$60; fixed-price special dinners $20–$25. AE, DC, MC, V. Daily 5:30–11:30pm. FRENCH.

At this small gem of a restaurant, chef Michel Tourjeman turns out a nightly menu of dishes in the Belgian/French tradition. Among first courses, a house specialty is a flawlessly presented goose liver in Cassis sauce, its richness enhanced by the subtle cakelike toast on which it is served, and the taste variations of almonds and peeled grapes in the sauce. Fish and seafood are exquisitely fresh, turned into small masterpieces like grouper fillet with shrimp in an exotic sauce served on a bed of seafood mousse, or the house seafood bisque, rich with shrimp, calamari, and fresh fish. Everything is perfectly executed, and although the understated decor and service are in the formal style, the staff is knowledgeable and helpful, and the atmosphere relaxed. Prices are very reasonable and very good value; the list of French and Israeli wines is superb, with the more exceptional choices at $150 a bottle. Nothing in Eilat's hotel restaurants comes close to a meal here.

Eilat's Street Food

A local favorite is the **Family Bakery,** 133 Hatmarim Blvd. (☎ 07/633-5846), a partly open-air stand where you can get all kinds of delicious breads, rolls, and minipizzas (sold by weight) for about NIS 3 to 6 (65¢ to $1.30) per piece. There are also lots of fresh-from-the-oven pastries. It's open Sunday through Thursday 24 hours, on Friday until 4pm, and Saturday after Shabbat.

Also, you should know about Eilat's small **Indian and Natural Foods** shop (☎ 07/637-5266) in a small shopping courtyard on Hatmarim Boulevard across the street from the bus station. Soy milk and natural fruit juices sold here are nourishing and a good defense against dehydration. It's open normal business hours; closed for Shabbat.

Just south of the New Tourist Center, facing the road to Coral Beach and Taba, you'll find **Acapulco Chicken** (☎ 07/637-6222) where you can get a fresh (not frozen) rotisserie-style chicken with a unique flavor. They'll deliver to your hotel. **Pizza Hut** (the American chain) (☎ 07/637-3166), is the best pizza choice in Eilat; there are branches at the Lagoon Promenade under the Lagoona Hotel and at Pnat Eilat, at the entrance to North Beach. There's delivery and take away and unlike American Pizza Huts, these often have coupons in tourist magazines for a free glass of wine with your order.

The intersection of Ha-Arava Road (the north-south highway) and Yotam Road, at the western limits of North Beach, is the place for beach snacks and light fare.

Moderate

✪ Eddie's Hideaway. 68 Almogim St. ☎ **07/637-1137.** Reservations required. Main courses NIS 32–95 ($7–$21). AE, DC, MC, V. Daily 6pm–midnight. CONTINENTAL.

One of Eilat's very best restaurants, this quality establishment serves an enormous menu in a variety of inventive styles, yet manages to keep its prices reasonable and its customers very happy. Main courses, designed by Eddie himself, include personal creations such as Nairobi shrimp cooked in butter and hot paprika with onion, fresh mushrooms, and a touch of pineapple; moist, delicate Shanghai fish, smothered in a spicy soybean paste; or goose liver in a Middle Eastern date sauce. I'm also a fan of the homemade lasagna, the steaks, and the honey barbecued ribs. In addition, the menu includes lean, light dishes like grilled sea bass or bream. Salad, vegetable, and potato are included with most main courses. A 10% service charge, which covers the tip, is added to the bill. Because Eddie's is out of the way, Eddie may deduct the price of your taxi (from any hotel in Eilat) from your bill—just give the waitress your receipt.

Eddie's is aptly named, as it's not directly on Almogim Street, and once you locate the building you must enter from around back. To find it, go up Hatmarim Street past the bus station, turn right on Almogim Street, and turn left at Peace Cafe.

Inexpensive

Ha-Kerem Restaurant. Eilat St., corner of Hatmarim. ☎ **07/637-4577.** Light meals NIS 15–22 ($3.30–$5); full meals NIS 32–60 ($7–$13.20). No credit cards. Sun–Fri noon–3pm; Sun–Thurs 6–9:30pm; Sat after Shabbat. YEMENITE.

At this kosher home-style Yemenite restaurant, service is friendly though often in limited English. The decor is basic, except for a few family photographs in traditional

Yemenite costumes, but the food is delicious and reasonably priced. Melawach, the traditional flaky Yemenite pancake, starts at NIS 14 ($3), depending on what you have on it. A full selection of Middle Eastern appetizers is available, and meat dishes are served with rice, salad, or fries. A glass of arak (anise brandy) costs NIS 9 ($2). A 10% service charge is added.

NEW TOURIST CENTER
Expensive
La Barracuda. In front of the Sonesta/Sun Suites Hotel. ☎ **07/632-5222.** Reservations recommended. Main courses NIS 95–120 ($21–$26.40); lobster $50. AE, DC, MC, V. Daily 1pm–midnight. FRENCH SEAFOOD.

Excellent fresh fish from the Red Sea, shrimp, crab, calamari, and lobster are the heart of the menu here, grilled, fried, or served in a variety of sauces, but you'll also find choices like veal or chicken cordon bleu, and steak if you're not up for fish. Among specialties of the house is the oven-baked fillet of baby shark prepared without skin in a garlic sauce with melted butter. There is an excellent house seafood soup; good wines and desserts round out this very comfortable, enjoyable place.

Moderate
✪ **Mai Thai.** New Tourist Center. ☎ **07/637-0104.** Reservations recommended. Main courses NIS 33–75 ($7.20–$16.50); business lunch NIS 42 ($9.20). AE, DC, MC, V. Daily 1–3:30pm and 6:30–11:30pm. THAI/CHINESE.

Housed in a glassed-in upper-story pavilion with a virtual garden of paper parasols and bamboo basket lampshades hanging from the ceiling, Mai Thai serves a menu that is 75% Thai, 25% Chinese, and entirely excellent. There are *patai* noodle dishes, both vegetarian and with meat; classic Thai dishes like *omm olai* (chicken in a coconut, chile, and mint sauce); or heavenly Beef Chang My Style, all of which the management will adeptly tone down in case you're not yet used to Thai seasonings. Excellent for Thai food fans, and a great place to learn a new cuisine. It's located at the edge of the New Tourist Center facing Yotam Road. There is a no-smoking section.

Inexpensive
✪ **Country Chicken.** 6 New Tourist Center. ☎ **07/637-1312.** Main courses NIS 40–70 ($8.80–$15.40). DC, MC, V. Sun–Thurs 9am–midnight; Fri 9am–3pm; Sat after Shabbat to midnight. ISRAELI/AMERICAN.

Tucked away in a corner of the New Tourist Center, you might not notice this restaurant, but it's where many Eilat residents go when they want good value and hefty portions without the touristy glitz. There are lots of surprises once you step inside. First, the place is quite large, though no-frills in decor. Second, chicken is not really the main thing here; the menu includes excellent goulash, kabobs, schnitzel, and liver (all less than NIS 40 ($9) and served with fries or rice and salad), as well as very upmarket lamb chops and even fresh Red Sea fish in wine and garlic sauce (priced according to weight) as good as you'd get in the fanciest restaurant, and much cheaper. Third, if you strike up a conversation with the very hospitable family running the place, you'll find they are Israelis from Karachi, Pakistan; and although the menu offers nothing Pakistani, you'll be delighted with the nice little Israeli extras that are served when you order a full meal. Finally, ask if they're at the end of a batch of their "Kentucky Fried Chicken" (which, despite its name, is not like the American franchise recipe); it's best when really fresh. Home-style soups and appetizers are a good choice for a light meal.

NEAR NORTH BEACH

Expensive

Pago Pago. Eilat Laguna. ☎ **07/637-6660.** Reservations recommended evenings. Main courses NIS 55–120 ($12.10–$26.40). AE, DC, MC, V. Daily 1pm–3am. SEAFOOD/FRENCH.

Moored in the North Beach Lagoon near the King Solomon Hotel, this floating restaurant, club, and bar offers a South Seas tropical ambience, and a menu of exotic seafood, fresh fish, and meats prepared and served with flair. You might try gratinée of shrimps and calamari in cream sauce or the royal platter catch-of-the-day for two (NIS 130 [$40]) served in a giant ruffled clam shell, as well as tropical drinks and mellow desserts served with chocolate liqueur coffee. A 10% service charge is added to the bill.

Wang's Grill. Royal Beach Hotel Beachfront Promenade. ☎ **07/368-8888,** ext. 8781. Reservations recommended. Main courses NIS 75–110 ($16.50–$24.20). AE, DC, MC, V. Sat–Thurs 7:30–11:30pm (Sat after Shabbat). PACIFIC RIM/CHINESE.

This elegant restaurant uses Asian cooking techniques to produce dishes that have a Chinese influence, but are often far from standard Chinese food. Appetizers, in the NIS 32 ($7 to $12) range, include interesting variations of traditional Lo Mein or wonton soup, but you will also find ginger lamb dumplings with wild mushrooms, ginger and garlic sauce, or tangerine duck with toasted almonds and crispy wontons on a bed of lettuce. Main courses include grilled sirloin steak with a spicy Szechuan sauce and vegetables; grilled beef fillet served with a crispy noodle pancake and spicy garlic sauce; grilled sea bass with sautéed Chinese cabbage and mustard vinaigrette; and a number of variations of Peking duck. Side dishes of vegetables are extra. Chocolate hazelnut terrine, poppy seed parfait, and a dynamite hot chocolate cake with a molten interior are among the dessert choices. Wang's has a kashruth certificate.

Moderate

The Golden Duck. In the Neptune Hotel. ☎ **07/633-4333.** Reservations recommended. Main courses NIS 30–70 ($6.60–$15.40). AE, DC, MC, V. Sun–Thurs 1–3pm and 7–11pm; Sat after Shabbat. KOSHER CHINESE/THAI.

This is a pleasant, affordable place that offers one of the few unusual kosher choices in town; it's also a good choice for anyone looking for good food in the center of town. There are well-prepared standard Chinese restaurant dishes, but also house specialties touched with Thai variations. I liked the sliced fillet of fish in a spicy Bangkok coconut sauce, the modestly priced the patai noodles, the spicy Thai soups, and the crispy duck served with Thai crispy noodles and Chinese salad. Thai dishes are served mild, but if you ask for authentic fiery seasonings, the Golden Duck will oblige.

✪ Red Sea Star Underwater Restaurant, Pub and Observatory. Next to the Le Meridien Hotel. ☎ **07/634-7777.** Reservations necessary. Main courses NIS 40–70 ($8.80–$15.40). AE, MC, V. Daily noon–midnight. CONTINENTAL.

This amazing restaurant is 5 meters (over 15 ft.) below the surface of the Red Sea, with thick Plexiglas windows that give you an octopus-eye view of the surrounding fish, corals, and other creatures. The decor is fantasy oceanesque, with sand floors covered by a layer of clear epoxy, velvet, sea urchin cushions on the chairs, starfish lighting fixtures and wavy blue underwater light filtering through the subsea pavilion from natural sources by day, and artificial sources by night. It may sound campy, but the details are so well done that the effect is enchanting—you find your attention torn between the underwater vistas outside the windows, and the interior decor, overflowing with marine shapes and textures (the work of a young Israeli, Ayala Serfaty, whose aquatic designs have received international attention and exhibition). Not resting on its one-of-a-kind location and design, the Red Sea Star serves meals that are quite good. Dennis, a fish from the Red Sea, leads the list of well-prepared fish (though you may not feel comfortable dining on a sea creature while its family and friends glide past the windows). Grilled ostrich fillet in a Dijon berry sauce with mushrooms; spare ribs in a melon and chile sauce; as well as pastas and salads round out the menu. If you dislike smoke, request the no-smoking area when you make your reservation.

✪ **Tandoori.** In the Laguna Hotel. ☎ **07/633-3879** or 07/633-3666. Reservations recommended. Main courses NIS 32–65 ($7–$14.30); 15% service charge. AE, DC, MC, V. Daily noon–3pm and 6:30pm–midnight. INDIAN.

Located in the Laguna Hotel on King's Wharf, this is one of Eilat's most special restaurants. Beautifully decorated with Indian artifacts, the restaurant serves a variety of Indian dishes, although specializing in tandoori cooking. Tandoori's kitchen does everything with a light, elegant touch. All traditional styles are spectacular, and house creations, such as giant prawns in ginger marinade, are very much worth trying. Look into the reasonably priced luncheon specials, which include soup, breads, four choices for your main meal plus vegetable curry, basmati rice, dessert, tea or coffee, wine, or soft drink. As if this weren't enough, Tandoori also provides live traditional instrumental music, with performances by a classical or regional Indian dancer every evening. If you are wondering why an Indian restaurant has become such a landmark in Eilat, remember that the Red Sea has been the West's gateway to India since ancient times. The homemade desserts are both exotic and delicious, and lassi, a yogurt-based tropical drink, is a cool antidote to Eilat's torrid temperatures.

Inexpensive

Check Inn. In the Dalia Hotel. ☎ **07/633-0389.** Self-service buffet NIS 40 ($9); main courses NIS 30–50 ($6.60–$11). AE, MC, V. Daily noon–11pm. EUROPEAN/MIDDLE EASTERN.

The self-service buffet is the great deal here, including a salad bar with lots of fresh ingredients and Middle Eastern appetizers. From there you go on to the hot counter, where there's a daily selection of fish, meat, chicken, vegetables, and rice and potatoes. The food is solid, but generally good, and you're sure to find things you especially like. Some of the dishes, like chicken or pot roast, will be safe, Western-style choices; others like spicy Moroccan fish will have a bit of local style to them. You can come back for more. The restaurant's food is kosher; because of its affiliation with the Dalia Hotel, Check Inn is open on the Sabbath.

Spring Onion Restaurant Cafe. North Beach Promenade near the bridge. ☎ **07/637-7434.** Light meals NIS 25–40 ($4.40–$8.80); main courses NIS 32–75 ($7–$16.50). AE, DC, MC, V. Daily 8am–after midnight. VEGETARIAN/FISH.

A favorite of Eilat vegetarians, with fresh, nicely prepared food, this small modern place expands to a large outdoor terrace after the sun goes down, and is a good spot for watching promenaders as you dine. Salads are excellent and enormous here, and can easily be shared by two people. Pastas and fresh fish fill out the main courses, and there's also an assortment of rich cakes for dessert in the NIS 18 to 32 ($4 to $7) range. The sign is in English, but if you're asking directions from locals, the Hebrew name actually translates as "Green Onion."

SOUTH OF TOWN & THE CORAL BEACH

Moderate

Last Refuge. Coral Beach. ☎ **07/6373-627.** Reservations recommended. Main courses NIS 60–100 ($13.20–$22). AE, DC, MC, V. Daily 1–4:30pm and 6–11:30pm. SEAFOOD.

Right across the street from the Fisherman's House, this rather expensive but good fish restaurant has weather-beaten nautical decor (not unlike something you'd find on

Cape Cod or Long Island), tables inside or out on the seaside terrace, and generous portions of seafood. Simple, very fresh grilled fish is an excellent choice here. A 10% service charge is added to each bill.

Inexpensive

Dolphin Reef Seafood Restaurant. Dolphin Reef. ☎ **07/637-1846.** Reservations useful. Light meals and snacks NIS 20–40 ($4.40–$8.80); main courses NIS 40–65 ($9–$14.30). MC, V. Daily 11am–after midnight. SEAFOOD/PUB.

This thatched-roof, tropical pavilion at the easygoing Dolphin Reef is a good place for lunch, should you have paid admission to the Dolphin Reef's private beach for the day; it's also a congenial place to hang out in the evening, when admission to the Dolphin Reef is free, and when the management often provides live entertainment and dancing on the sand. The floor is sand, the bar is lively in the evening, and the menu choices range from cold yogurt and Greek salad to grilled whole fish or hamburgers. There's also a cafeteria on the premises of the Dolphin Reef beach.

Fisherman's House. Coral Beach. ☎ **07/637-9830.** Reservations not accepted. All-you-can-eat buffet NIS 38 ($8.40). No credit cards. Daily noon–midnight. Bus: 15 to Coral Beach. SEAFOOD.

I enjoy this place immensely. It is a large, very informal self-service, all-you-can-eat restaurant with long indoor and outdoor tables—a great place for a casual meal. Choose from a selection of six kinds of fish cooked in different ways, savory rice, baked potatoes, cooked vegetables, and several kinds of spicy Middle Eastern salads. Children up to age 11 eat for half price. Or, for the same price, you can order meat or chicken from the grill (one big serving) and still get all you can eat of everything else. Some of the fish offered may be rather fatty or greasy, but don't be afraid to try all the offerings until you find something you like. Desserts and drinks cost extra.

EILAT AFTER DARK

In this sun-and-fun resort the crowds move from beach to bar, disco, or club after the sun goes down. The Government Tourist Information Office's weekly bulletin, "Events in Eilat," available for free at the tourist office, will let you know what's happening where.

Several of the major hotels have **nightclubs, piano bars,** and **discos.** These are some of the liveliest places in town, patronized by international tourists, Israelis, and native Eilatis alike. Of the discos, **Sheba,** in the **King Solomon's Palace Hotel,** is the most popular, with spectacular laser and sound effects; **Ha-Nesiha,** at the **Princess Hotel** just before the Taba border, runs a close second. Cover charges at these top hotel discos run NIS 45 to 63 ($10 to $14). Best of all for easygoing beach atmosphere and spirit is the **Dolphin Reef** (☎ 07/637-4292), with its thatched-roof restaurant/bar: There's dancing on the beach Monday and Thursday nights, and Friday afternoon/evening. Take bus 15; cover charge is NIS 25 ($5.50). The **New Tourist Center** and the **North Beach Waterfront Promenade** also have a lot going on in the evening, with numerous pubs and indoor/outdoor cafes humming with activity. **The Three Monkeys** on the Promenade near the Royal Beach Hotel is Eilat's biggest, busiest, and trendiest spot for drinking and dancing, with live music every night, a dual level indoor area, an outdoor section beside the water, and an international crowd, largely in the 25 to 30 age range. It opens every night at 9pm, gets busy toward midnight, and has a dress code: no shorts or flip-flops and neat (preferably informal but stylish) clothing. For dining and dancing cruises with live music and stars or moonlight, call Eilat Cruises (☎ 07/633-3351) at the Marina, or Red Sea Sports Club (☎ 07/637-9685) at King's Warf. Prices start at about NIS 100 ($22.).

Various Israeli **folklore evenings** are sponsored by the big hotels, usually beginning about 9:30pm several nights a week. Music for dancing, or a disco, often follows the performance. The fee (usually about NIS 23 to 32 [$5 to $7]) includes first drink, or perhaps wine and cheese. **Kibbutz Elot,** 5 kilometers (3 mi.) north of Eilat, offers Saturday evening performances of **Israeli Folk Dancing and Song.** The price, including transportation and a kibbutz-style buffet dinner is NIS 150 ($33). **Desert Shade Tours** (☎ 07/633-5377), offers a **Saturday night Bedouin Tent Dinner,** with traditional music, food, and hospitality. The price, including transportation, is NIS 145 ($32).

The **Cinémathèque Club** screens films in English at the **Philip Murray Cultural Center** (☎ 07/633-2257), at the corner of Hatmarim Boulevard and Hativat Ha-Negev. Regular starting time seems to be around 9pm; admission is charged. The major hotels show films and videos about excursions in the Eilat area as well. Check the tourist office's bulletin "Events in Eilat" for details.

SHOPPING

Eilat stones, a form of green and turquoise polished malachite, are sold throughout Israel in settings that range from contemporary to traditional Yemenite. They were popular in the 1960s and '70s; less so now. Most hotel gift shops offer a selection of Eilat stone jewelry. You can visit **Malkit** (☎ 07/637-3372), an Eilat stone jewelry workshop in the Ha-Dekel part of town. Open Sunday to Thursday 8am to 7pm and Friday 8am to 1pm. The **Egyptian Bazaar at the Taba Hilton Hotel** offers the chance to peruse Egyptian crafts and souvenirs you'd otherwise have to travel to Cairo to find. Some stock is tourist stuff; a few really beautiful crafts and objects will be found amid the stalls. It's easy to cross the border at the southern city limits of Eilat. See the listing on the Taba Hilton Hotel (above) for details.

EASY EXCURSIONS

Timna Valley National Park. 27km (17 mi.) north of Eilat. ☎ **07/635-6215** for information. Admission NIS 22 ($5) adults, half price for children. Daily 8am–4pm. Tour buses daily 8am. Leave from Eilat daily for Timna at 8am.

If you're driving, head north, pass the Timna Mines (on your left, to the west), and after a few kilometers you'll see a sign for Timna. Turn left onto the road indicated, and head west toward the striking, jagged black hills. Not far in from the highway is the main gate; follow the road 3¹/₂ kilometers (2 mi.) to a right turn for the **ancient Egyptian copper mines,** another kilometer along. The mines consist of sandstone arches, underground mining shafts, and galleries. About 3 kilometers (2 mi.) from the mines, along another side road, is a parking area from which you make the short walk to see a **wall face carved with figures in chariots.** All these twists and turns are marked clearly by signs.

Along the roads you will have noticed **"The Mushroom,"** a curious rock formation with a huge boulder resting on a column of sandstone, the result of erosion. But the most striking formation in the preserve is undoubtedly **Solomon's Pillars.** Go back to the main road of the preserve and head east for several kilometers. The pillars, a series of sandstone fins jutting out of a rock face, are at the end of the road. Climb into the fins along a path with steps to see some **Egyptian rock carvings,** and then down the steps on the other side to the remains of a **small temple** dedicated to the Egyptian goddess Hathor.

The spare, clean air of the desert, the hot sun, the quiet of the preserve are sure to make a lasting impression. You can get information on **hiking trails** from the staff at the main gate. The development of Timna Valley National Park has become a major project of the Jewish National Fund of America. An artificial recreational lake and architecturally stunning **Visitors Center** have been built in the **Nechushtan Recreation Area** not far from Solomon's Pillars and the Sphinx. The lake provides facilities for swimming, boating, and fishing. The Visitors Center pavilion includes a cafeteria and a shop for traveling supplies.

Hai Bar National Biblical Wildlife Reserve. 40km (24 mi.) north of Eilat. ☎ **07/637-3057.** Admission including guided tour NIS 34 ($7.50) for adults, NIS 20 ($4.40) for children; NIS 18 ($4) for Predator Center only. Sun–Thurs 8:30am–5pm; Fri–Sat 8:30am–3:30pm.

If you have no car, you can take a guided tour from town, which takes about 2 hours. The purpose of the 8,000-acre reserve is to save rare and endangered desert animals mentioned in the Bible, as well as other rare desert animals of western Asia and northern Africa, breeding them for eventual release into the wild. Among the 450 kinds of animals found here are the Nubian ibex, the Dorcas gazelle, the Persian onager, the scimitar-horned oryx, the addax antelope, and the Arabian gazelle, as well as wolves, hyenas, foxes, desert cats, leopards, cheetahs, wild donkeys, lots of ostriches, and many species of snakes, lizards, and even predatory birds. Many of these animals are nocturnal, due to the blistering desert heat, but a special dark room makes it possible to observe these creatures during your daylight visit. You can ride around the reserve in special coaches (closed vehicles only) and observe the animals at close range.

You'll notice that the Hai Bar Reserve has many trees, signifying that water is lying below the arid desert. This area is known as the **Yotvata Oasis,** and it is believed that it was one of the places where Moses stopped as he brought the Children of Israel up out of Egypt.

6 On to Sinai

The Sinai is a place of fateful, haunting crossings. If human beings originated in Africa, it was through this harsh, unrelenting land bridge connecting Africa to Asia that the ancestors of much of the human race had to pass as they migrated toward the far corners of the earth. The Sinai Peninsula, mountainous and awe-inspiring, is the unearthly triangle of wilderness in which the Israelites wandered after the Exodus from Egypt. It was here that the Torah was given to them; after their journey through this vast crucible of monotheistic faith, the Israelites were transformed, and human civilization was set onto new pathways. Even if you were unaware of its history, the primordial splendor of Sinai can be an overwhelming personal experience.

Mount Sinai and the ancient Byzantine **monastery of Santa Katerina** on its slope have been a destination for pilgrims for 16 centuries, almost miragelike in their sanctity. Over the past 30 years, the coast of the **Gulf of Aqaba** has become a second awe-inspiring Sinai attraction. It's a diver's and snorkeler's paradise, with some of the most beautiful and unusual coral reef systems in the world.

Since the Sinai was restored to Egypt in 1982, after a 15-year Israeli occupation, the area has been developed as never before in its isolated history. The few simple beach hut accommodations, with their accompanying restaurants and dive shops that were the sum total of Nuweiba, Dahab, and Sharm-el-Sheik in the late 1960s, are as forgotten now as a lost civilization, while Hilton, Hyatt, Movenpick, Novotel, and Sonesta Hotels, as well as other international chains dot the coastline, and new vacation complexes continue to rise. Here and there, you'll find a few pleasant, small hotels at isolated spots along the coast. There are also literally hundreds of beach hut hotels and encampments along the Gulf of Aqaba, with discos throbbing under the starry desert nights, surrounded by rudimentary accommodations for well under $10 per person (insect repellent is a must). The Sinai is now on the superhighway of touristic civilization, and gaining a worldwide reputation as a fun place, but the old austere majesty and mystique is still close by, accessible to those who seek it out.

PLANNING A TRIP
VISA REQUIREMENTS & TRAVEL PERMITS

Coming from Israel, there are two kinds of visas available, depending on what your travel plans may be. The first is a **Sinai Only visa,** obtainable at the Egyptian consulate in Eilat, which permits you to travel along the Gulf of Aqaba Coast to Nuweiba, Dahab, Na'ama Bay, and Sharm-el-Sheik as well as to Mount Sinai and the Monastery of Santa Katarina. If you want to hike in the mountains near Santa Katarina, or to visit the extraordinary reefs at Ras Mohammed National Park, just south of Sharm-el-Sheik, or travel on to Cairo, you'll need a **standard Egyptian visa,** which is more of a procedure and expense. It's best to obtain the standard visa ahead of time from the Egyptian Embassy in Tel Aviv or from the Egyptian Embassy in your own country. You cannot change or expand your Sinai Only visa once you are in the Sinai, and you cannot use it to go on to Cairo and the rest of Egypt.

Note that no tourists are allowed to hike or travel alone off the main roads and tourist centers in Sinai without a guide and special permit. Bedouin guides at the main tourist centers are always available, and can arrange the necessary permits for the itineraries you plan. Make sure your guide has the required permits. Escorted tours can be arranged from Eilat through most travel agencies there.

CROSSING THE BORDER   The regulations, crossing schedules, and fees on both the Israeli and Egyptian sides of the border are constantly being revised. The **Tourist Information Center in Eilat** will give you current information and practical advice about what to expect in terms of regulations, fees, and ongoing bus connections. Do not plan to cross the border without checking here first. Expect Israeli and Egyptian crossing fees to amount to $20.

MONEY   The Egyptian pound (abbreviated LE) is valued at press time at a bit less than 30¢ in U.S. currency, and 18 new pence in pounds sterling. Expect this rate to change during the time span of this edition. It's approximately LE 3.4 to one American dollar.

CURRENCY EXCHANGE   There are exchange desks at banks and hotels in the tourist centers of Nuweiba, Dahab, Sharm-el-Sheik, and at the village of Milga near Mount Sinai.

TOURS & PACKAGES   The **Society for Protection of Nature in Israel (SPNI),** with offices in Jerusalem, Tel Aviv, and New York, offers a range of hiking, camping, and nature exploration tours to the Sinai. The scale of SPNI's accommodations ranges from quality and modest hotels to Bedouin tent and sleeping bag.

The Eilat Tourist Information Center (see above) is especially in touch with the tourist market in Sinai, and can direct you to tours of the Sinai leaving from Eilat and book you into hotels (at times with considerable discounts) as well as onto excursions to Santa Katarina and diving packages on the Aqaba Coast.

GETTING THERE
BY PLANE   From Eilat, you can fly to Santa Katerina and Sharm-el-Sheik on Air Sinai, either as an independent passenger, or on package trips and guided tours.

BY BUS   Egyptian buses leave from the Egyptian side of the Israeli–Egyptian border at Taba, near Eilat, a number of times a day on routes southward to Nuweiba, Dahab, and Sharm-el-Sheik. Buses will either let you off at your hotel in any of these centers,

Sinai Hotel Tips

Sinai Hotels, whether small isolated motel-like establishments along the coast, moderate establishments in places like Nuweiba or Dahab, or luxury resorts in Sharm-el-Sheik, are far less expensive than their counterparts in Israel; in general, many have more interesting design and architectural character. Remember that all hotel bills are charged 17% tax and at least a 10% service charge. Breakfast is often not included in the room rate. When reserving a room as an individual or through a packager, always check to see whether tax, service, and breakfast charges are included or extra and get it in writing!

or you can take a shared taxi from the bus station to your hotel. There are also buses from Taba and Nuweiba to Santa Katarina and to Cairo. Schedules are unpredictable. It is always wise to reserve a seat if possible, and arrive at the bus station more than an hour ahead of time. The Tourist Information Center in Eilat can give you advice about current schedules and prices. The trip from Taaba to Sharm-el-Sheik should be no more than $10 to $12, on a scheduled bus. Private Bedouin taxis will also take you all the way to Sharm-el-Sheik. You have to bargain over the price; the best I've been able to do is $60 from Taba to Sharm-el-Sheik. On a hot day, when you are at a bargaining disadvantage, twice that amount could be the price. If you want a taxi that will stop at various sights along the way, you'll have to bargain, taking into consideration how many hours of the driver's time you plan to take. If you can get a group of four people together, an $80 to $100 taxi ride with a few stops along the coast is quite reasonable.

BY CAR   You cannot take an Israeli rental car across the border from Eilat into Sinai; if you want to rent a car, you must make arrangements at Taba, on the Egyptian side of the border, where most international car rental agencies have offices. The most convenient place is the car-rental desk at the Taba Hilton, just a few hundred feet across the border. If you decide to rent a car, you always get a better deal by making your reservations from overseas, or with a prepaid package. Driving can be unnerving, if not downright dangerous, in Sinai, with massive long-haul trucks charging around curves on the wrong side of narrow two-lane highways with small concern for a rented Fiat coming from the other direction.

MOUNT SINAI & SANTA KATERINA

Located in the rugged interior of the peninsula, this is not the isolated pilgrimage site it once was; nevertheless it is a charismatic and powerful place. Nestled on the lower slopes of Mount Sinai (Gabal Mussa, or the Mountain of Moses in Arabic), is the **Monastery of Santa Katerina,** with origins reaching back to the times of the cave-dwelling monks of the 2nd century A.D. Much of the monastery is more than 1,500 years old; its library includes what is probably among the most important collections of rare and ancient manuscripts outside of the Vatican. The unrestored Byzantine mosaics of the Chapel of the Burning Bush and a vast collection of ancient icons are among the dramatic monastery's other treasures.

The climb up steep pathways and staircases to the top of Mount Sinai is arduous. Most people do it in the cool (or cold) of night and enjoy the incredible sunrise. The hike can take from 2 to 4 hours, depending on your strength. It's by no means an easy ascent—you may want to consider taking a Bedouin guide and renting a camel at a cost of $12 for the climb. The view from the summit (if you can get away from tour groups) is transcendent.

Sinai

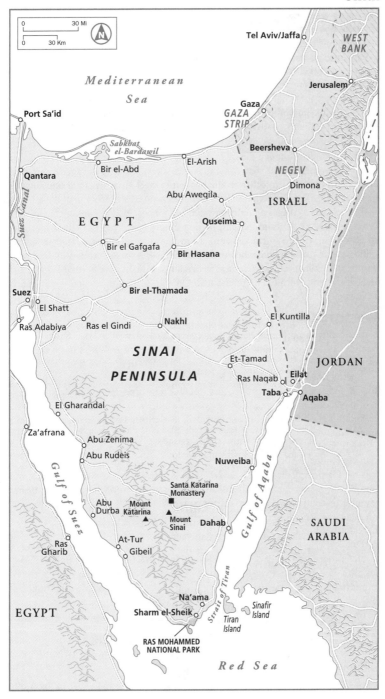

0   30 Mi
0   30 Km

Mediterranean Sea

WEST BANK

Tel Aviv/Jaffa

Jerusalem

Port Sa'id

Gaza
GAZA STRIP

Sabkhat el-Bardawil

El-Arish

Beersheva

Bir el-Abd

Qantara

NEGEV

Abu Aweqila

Dimona

E G Y P T

ISRAEL

Quseima

Bir el Gafgafa

Bir Hasana

Suez

Bir el-Thamada

El Shatt

Ras Adabiya

Ras el Gindi

Nakhl

El Kuntilla

SINAI

PENINSULA

Et-Tamad

JORDAN

Ras Naqab

Eilat

Taba

Aqaba

El Gharandal

Za'afrana

Abu Zenima

Abu Rudeis

Nuweiba

Gulf of Suez

Gulf of Aqaba

Abu Durba

Mount Katarina

Santa Katarina Monastery

SAUDI ARABIA

Mount Sinai

Dahab

At-Tur

Gibeil

Ras Gharib

Na'ama

Strait of Tiran

Sharm el-Sheik

Sinafir Island

Tiran Island

EGYPT

RAS MOHAMMED NATIONAL PARK

Red Sea

443

Sinai Telephone Tips

The country code for Egypt is 20. When calling the Sinai from outside Egypt, remember that the initial zero in the Sinai area code is dropped. A telephone number such as 062/600-000 becomes 20-62/600-000 when dialed from outside Egypt.

Six kilometers (9.6 mi.) to the south is **Gabal Katarina** (Mount Catherine), the highest in Egypt. The path to the summit of this mountain is more beautiful and less trafficked by hordes of tourists than Mount Sinai; from the village of Milga the climb can take 6 hours. Although the tradition of identifying Mount Sinai as the place where the Ten Commandments were given to Moses is very strong, there are other traditions and theories attached to other mountains, and Gabal Katarina could possibly be the genuine place. There is a chapel and a source of water at the very top of the mountain.

The village of **Milga,** a kilometer from the monastery, has banking facilities, groceries, a bread bakery, and inexpensive restaurants where you can take a meal for $3 to $8. Those with Egyptian visas can ask in Milga about hiring a Bedouin guide for hiking in the surrounding countryside. Guided hikes start at around $20 for a guide and permit. Whatever tour packages or guides you might have booked before coming to Milga, in the end, all hiking tours are led by guides from the Bedouin syndicate here in town.

WHERE TO STAY

One of the most atmospheric and economical choices is the **Santa Katarina Monastery Hostel** (☎ **062/470-343,** 62/470-345, or 62/470-346), on the left side of the monastery complex. Rooms are hot and airless in summer, and rather cramped with seven or eight beds to a chamber, but they are clean—the place seems like a locale for an Indiana Jones adventure, and you'll always find interesting fellow travelers. Dorm beds are $12 a night; beds in rooms with three to four beds and a private bathroom are $17; if the hostel is not crowded, it is at times possible to rent a room as a private double for $20 per person. A tasty, simple breakfast and dinner are included in the price. Check-in is from 8am to 1pm and from 4 to 9pm. You cannot enter the monastery after 9:30pm.

The **Daniela Village** (☎ **062/771-379;** fax reservation office in Cairo 02/360-7750). Situated at the edge of Milga, this is a plain but relatively comfortable, with 52 air-conditioned rooms in desert stone buildings all with private bathrooms. A double runs $65, breakfast included. It is located 2 miles from the monastery and includes a Middle Eastern restaurant and shopping facilities. No credit cards are accepted.

St. Catherine's Tourist Village/El Raha Hotel (☎ **062/770-221** or 062/770-456; fax 062/770-221), located 2 kilometers (1.2 mi.) from the monastery, is the most comfortable place to stay when visiting Mount Sinai. It has 124 air-conditioned doubles (with televisions) that run from $145 to $180, including breakfast. They accept MasterCard and Visa.

ALONG THE COAST BETWEEN TABA & NUWEIBA

This is some of the loveliest shoreline in the Gulf of Aqaba, dotted with isolated encampments and small hotels. They are inexpensive but tranquil places; most offer simple snorkeling and beaching, and can arrange hikes and Jeeps trips in the region as well as tours to Mount Sinai. The following are the best.

✪ **Basata.** 43km (26.6 mi.) on the Taba-Nuweiba Rd., South Sinai. ☎ and fax **062/500-481.** 18 bamboo huts; communal ecological bathrooms. $16 double plus 10% tax. No credit cards. 43km (26.6 mi.) south of Taba.

A unique place where you can experience the Sinai shore with nothing between yourself and the beach, *Basata* means "simplicity," and the beautiful bamboo huts and central pavilion of this small complex offer shelter and delight the eye, but do not separate you from nature. Created by manager Sharif El Ghamrawy, who has studied ecology and design in Europe, Basata's rules are as careful as its physical design. All materials at Basata are biodegradable; rooms are lit by candles (they can be quite chilly at night in winter). You are allowed to make simple meals for yourself in the kitchen, where every dish must be washed; guests must not litter, use drugs or alcohol (mainstays of many Sinai beach encampments), play loud music, or be naked in public. You must bring your own sheets/sleeping bags, and plan to do your laundry elsewhere. Wonderful communal meals are served each day for $6 to $8; the nightly dinner alternates between a fish meal and a vegetarian evening. Guests snorkel, stargaze, and read; green safaris and hikes can be arranged with Bedouin guides. Impossible to get into on Israeli holidays or during Ramadan, you must make reservations in advance throughout the year if you have any hope of getting in. The management tries to screen out guests who may not fit into Basata's quiet, econature way of life.

Sally Land Village. Taba-Nuweiba Rd., South Sinai. ☎ **062/530-380.** Fax 062/530-381. 65 units. A/C. $40 double. Rates include breakfast. Add 10% tax. V. 37km (23 mi.) south of Taba.

Located all by itself on a beautiful, quiet stretch of beach about 20 minutes by car south of Taba, Sally Land is a sprawling enclave of one-story whitewashed and natural stone units. Each guest room opens onto one of Sally Land's sandy, gardened courtyards. The complex was designed and is managed by an Egyptian-American from Chicago and his partner, an American Chicagoan. Many European groups come through, many of them into nature and meditation. The atmosphere is tranquil and quiet (especially when meditation groups check in). Rooms are simple but comfortable, and most guests come to beach out. The office will organize tours, hikes, and snorkeling for you, and simple in-house meals for about $10. Taxi fare from the Taba border should be LE 80 ($25) or less, but you must bargain. You can prearrange with the hotel for a vehicle to meet you at the Taba border for LE 65 ($20).

NUWEIBA

Nuweiba is a small port and industrial center with beautiful beaches at its outskirts, and along the coast to the north of town. Truckers from Cairo come to Nuweiba, from which they can catch daily ferries up to Aqaba, in Jordan. From there, the truck routes continue on to Amman, Damascus, Saudi Arabia, and the Gulf States. On busy days, the line of trucks waiting for the ferries can stretch for half a mile. Separate from the port is Nuweiba's other incarnation as a beach resort. Resort Nuweiba consists of a mixture of sprawling camps and beach-hut hotels, especially to the north at **Tarabin,** where you can easily find a place in the $4 to $10 per person a night range. Tarabin is filled with little restaurants, cafes, and outdoor discos and pubs. Elsewhere on the Nuweiba coast are moderately priced, more mainstream Holiday Villages and pleasant, low-rise hotels. From Nuweiba, there's a main road to Santa Katarina and Mt. Sinai.

The modest but solid **El Sayadin Village Hotel** (☎ **062/520-341**) offers air-conditioned rooms, restaurant facilities, and a private beach. Doubles are in the $44 to $62 range.

The Nuweiba coast's best hotel, located south of the port, is the ✪ **Nuweiba Hilton Coral Resort** (☎ 062/520-320; fax 062/520-327). This is a sprawling, low-rise 200-unit complex set around desert gardens and a pool. It has doubles for $88 to $108, and beautiful, isolated swimming and snorkeling beaches. At times, a good travel discounter in Eilat can book you in here for $55 for a double room, including breakfast. The more expensive bungalow rooms are located close to the beach; they're very spacious, with domed ceilings, a bit of atmosphere, and are worth the extra money. Rooms are air-conditioned, and have TVs, phones, and refrigerators. As at all Hilton Hotels in Sinai, there is a quality diving center, in this case PADI Resort certified. Facilities include a swimming pool, private beach, snorkeling and water-sports center, and a fine international buffet restaurant as well as à la carte seafood and Italian restaurants. A bank (open only mornings) and a small selection of Egyptian craft and carpet shops are on the premises. The hotel often provides free evening performances of Egyptian folk troupes brought in from Cairo. Tours and hikes of the area can be arranged from the tour desk. Credit cards accepted include American Express, Diner's Club, MasterCard, and Visa.

The **Helnan Nuweiba Hotel** (☎ 062/500-402; fax 062/500-407), is closer to the port and industrial center of Nuweiba, but it has its own beach and gardens. It has 117 air-conditioned, rather plain contemporary doubles in its main building for $70 to $80; there are suites in the $150 to $200 range, and also bungalow accommodations in the hotel's adjacent camping grounds, with doubles for $35 to $50 (or less if you bargain). There is a diving center, pleasant beach, tennis courts, and breakfast, lunch, and dinner buffets as well as à la carte Italian restaurant; credit cards include Master-Card and Visa.

DAHAB

Once the flower child of the Aqaba Coast during the years of Israeli occupation, Dahab has not grown old gracefully and is now distinctly seedy. Diving opportunities and dive schools, however, are superior to those at Nuweiba. Among the many dive centers in the Dahab area, I had a good experience with **Nesima Dive Center** (☎ 062/640-320; fax 062/640-321). Nesima offers daylight- and night-diving tours for $55 as well as packages for up to 10 days.

As at Nuweiba, hutlike accommodations abound. They have no phone numbers—just ask about rooms at places that strike your fancy. There are tons of beachfront Bedouin restaurants, cafes, and discos.

Most comfortable choice in town is the new ✪ **Hilton Dahab Resort** (☎ 062/640-310. fax 062/640-424;), a low-rise village of 163 air-conditioned units with its own nicely landscaped beach and grounds, top-flight diving center, two outdoor pools and a buffet restaurant. Rates are $74 to $135 for a double without breakfast, but there are packages and special Hilton weekend rates that can get you a double with breakfast for $66; credit cards accepted include American Express, Diner's Club, MasterCard, and Visa.

The **Novotel Dahab Coralia** (☎ 062/640-301; fax 062/640-305) is another comfortable choice. It is older than the Hilton, but well maintained, with 141 varied air-conditioned units in a low-rise complex, ranging from small, simple bungalows (without televisions) to spacious rooms and suites with full amenities. It has no Egyptian ambience, but offers a truly beautiful beach, an assortment of restaurants, a pool, tennis courts, and its own water-sports and diving center. Doubles range from $65 to $110; suites from $200 to $300, but are much less through a good travel agent or package plan; credit cards accepted include American Express, MasterCard, and Visa.

SHARM-EL-SHEIK

At the southernmost point of the Sinai Peninsula, Sharm-el-Sheik itself is a sprawling center for commercial and industrial action as well as a mecca for divers.

Na'ama Bay, a low-rise resort for beaching out, snorkeling, and diving, is a 5-minute drive from commercial Sharm-el-Sheik. When I first saw Na'ama Bay in 1970, there was absolutely nothing but sparkling sea, sky, and a pristine beach with a few reed shelters. It now contains over two dozen moderate and expensive hotel complexes catering largely to European visitors on package vacations (but there's lots of room for individual travelers). Most of the better hotels are located directly on Na'ama Bay, and most have a slice of beach reserved for its guests. A pedestrian promenade runs along the beach, connecting all the hotel properties; it then runs on to the Na'ama Bay Shopping Mall. Less-expensive hotels are located at the Mall area, 1 to 3 blocks inland from the beach. Shops here are filled with Egyptian souvenirs and crafts; interspersed among the stores are a growing number of inexpensive Chinese, Middle Eastern, or pizza restaurants offering meals in the $5 to $12 range.

Diving is good at Na'ama Bay, and the hotels and dive centers offer a large variety of snorkeling and diving options. The best diving and snorkeling, perhaps in the world, is just south of Sharm-el-Sheik, at the **National Park at Ras Mohammed.** You must have the standard Egyptian visa, rather than Sinai Only visa in order to enter this most elysian of the earth's coral reefs. Admission to the National Park is $5. Many divers arrange to get to Ras Mohammed by chartering a boat and diving or snorkeling from the boat; most hotels and diving centers offer tours to Ras Mohammed. Diving and snorkeling areas are carefully marked. It is forbidden to damage the reefs or to remove sea shells. The park is open daily from 8am to 5pm.

WHERE TO STAY

The area is filled with low-rise international hotel chain resorts. Most of the best hotels are located around Na'ama Bay area, 7 kilometers (4.5 mi.) north of Sharm-el-Sheik itself, and offer very good value when compared to such properties elsewhere in the world. At Na'ama Bay, you'll find a pleasant but often crowded swimming beach, diving and snorkeling reefs accessible by boat, a good selection of moderate and expensive accommodations, and more of a holiday atmosphere than at the rather bleak, downtown Sharm-el-Sheik. However, prices are on the rise, and demand is very great: More than 3,000 new hotel rooms are planned for Na'ama Bay in the next few years. If you plan to stay in one of the better complexes, book way in advance, as diving groups and tours fill the most desirable (as well as the less desirable) places as much as 6 months or more in advance. In addition to the choices listed below, be aware that along the coast between the sheltered Na'ama and Shark Bays, there is a **Hyatt Resort,** a **Marriott,** a **Holiday Inn,** and a **Novotel,** among the many new complexes opened in 1998–99.

Expensive

✪ **Fayrouz Hilton Resort, Na'ama Bay, Sharm-el-Sheik.** ☎ **062/600-136** or 062/600-140; reservations throught Hilton Hotels International. Fax 062/601-040. 150 units. A/C TV TEL. $145 standard double; $165 deluxe double. Service, tax, and buffet breakfast extra. AE, DC, MC, V.

The Fayrouz Hilton, built in the late 1980s, is the most experienced of the international complexes at Na'ama Bay. Located at the very center of the bay, with the choicest stretch of palm shaded beach, the Hilton is an informal, desert beige low-rise complex set amid gardens that have had time to develop. Rather than one central pool, you'll find smaller swimming pools hidden amid the gardens and terraces; restaurants are also spread throughout the grounds, rather than centralized. The dive and water sports center is tops in Sinai, state of the art, and knows its stuff completely. Many members of the staff have a long time commitment to the area, and the knowledgeable guest relations manager is one of the organizers of major ecology and preservation programs for South Sinai. All this shows in the hotel's savvy ambience. Guest rooms are four-star; comfortable but less luxurious than at other newer complexes such as Movenpick or Sofitel. The Wadi Restaurant features a sumptuous buffet with lots of Egyptian spe-cialties, and waiters in Pharonic costume; the Pirate Bar is a genuine Sharm-el Sheik meeting place, with dancing and karaoke. The hotel is so heavily booked that you must make reservations well in advance. When making phone reservations, don't confuse the Fayrouz resort at Na'ama Bay with the Hilton Residence Hotel in Sharm-el-Sheik.

✪ **Movenpick Sharm-el-Sheik Beach Resort.** Na'ama Bay, Sharm-el-Sheik. ☎ **062/ 600-100;** reservations through Movenpick Hotels International. Fax 062/600-111. 337 units. A/C TV TEL. $195–$215 double. Rates include breakfast, service, and tax. AE, MC, V.

This vast, low-rise outpost of the Swiss Movenpick Hotel Chain is a complete vaca-tion enclave in itself, catering only partly to travelers who come to Sharm for the div-ing. Lattice-covered outdoor passageways and open air pavilions provide an architectural theme and connect the white, contemporary structures of the complex. Deluxe rooms are in the front section, along the beach; less expensive rooms are fur-ther inland across the highway to downtown Sharm-el-Sheik, near the sports facilities. Electric golf carts convey you to these distant reaches of the complex. Special facilities include fresh- and saltwater swimming pools, a complete diving center, tennis courts, a casino, the best quality shopping arcade in town, and a bookstore stocked with mate-rial about the area. Movenpick is famous for its restaurants; the daily buffet restaurant, and the inventive à la carte Seagull's Restaurant are both a pleasure. President Clinton stayed here during the 1996 Sharm-el-Sheik Conference. January and February, June and July and other times of the year look for special Run of the House rates: $120 for a double including breakfast, service, and tax.

Dining/Diversions: Two restaurants, plus cafes, pubs, and casino.

Amenities: Two swimming pools, diving center, fitness room, health and mas-sage spa, shops and hairdresser, shuttle to Sharm-el-Sheik Airport, desert excursion bookings.

Sheraton Sharm Hotel Resort. Shark Bay, Pasha Coast, Sharm-el-Sheik. ☎ **062/ 602-070;** reservations through Sheraton Hotels. Fax 062/602/099. 300 units. A/C MINIBAR TV TEL. $120 double. Rates include breakfast. AE, DC, MC, V.

Opened in November 1999, and located at the up-and-coming, sheltered Shark Bay, 15 kilometers (10 mi.) north of Na'ama Bay, the Sheraton is a multitiered low-rise that sprawls down a rise to the beach. It offers sparkling new accommodations—the best at the wonderful Shark Bay diving and snorkeling site, an area less built up and with clearer water than at Na'ama Bay. Rooms have balconies and beach views, facing Tiran Island, and offer extra amenities such as voice mail and hair dryers. There are rooms for travelers with disabilities; and a variety of suites are available at higher rates.

Dining/Diversions: Four restaurants including one for dining and dancing; four bars and numerous snack bars.

Amenities: There is a diving center, swimming pool complex with cascade and two children's pools, fitness club, sauna, massage and steam bath, two tennis courts and snorkeling, parasailing, and windsurfing facilities.

Sofitel Coralia Sharm-el-Sheik. Na'ama Bay, Sharm-el-Sheik. ☎ **062/600-081;** reserva-tions through Sofitel Hotels. Fax 062/600/085. E-mail: h1970@accor-hotels.com. 304 units. A/C MINIBAR TV TEL. $193–$252 double plus service and tax. Breakfast $9. AE, DC, MC, V.

Completed in 1998 and a few years newer than the above hotels at the more central, sandy section of Na'ama Bay's beach, the Sofitel's five whitewashed, slightly arabesque levels step down the rocky side of the horseshoe-shaped bay. There are four restaurants, two bars, a diving and water-sports center, fitness center, sauna, Jacuzzi, steam bath and massage room, and beauty salon. The free shuttle to the airport, the Na'ama Mall, and to downtown Sharm-el-Sheik means you can avoid tangling with taxi drivers and compensates for the hotel's location at the far end of the bay.

Sonesta Beach Resort. Na'ama Bay, Sharm-el-Sheik. ☎ **062/600-725** or 800/766-3782 in the U.S. Fax 062/600-733. 228 units. A/C MINIBAR TV TEL. $150–$210 double; $400–$500 suite. Add 20% for service and tax. Rates include breakfast. Children under 12 in room free. MC, V.

Architecturally this is the most interesting and beautiful complex on Na'ama Bay, located at the center of the swimming beach area. From a distance it looks like a whitewashed desert village filled with dome-roofed houses and arabesque arches. Guest rooms are marked by Egyptian crafts and pleasant touches such as terraces, alcoves, and domed ceilings, as well as practical amenities like hair dryers in every room. There's a swim-up bar in one of the three pools, a rooftop cafe/bar for sunsets, a health club with sauna and Jacuzzi, and, of course, a complete diving and water-sports center. In addition to the main breakfast and evening buffet restaurant, there is an Italian restaurant on the premises. The Sonesta offers live entertainment nightly.

Dining/Diversions: Five restaurants, cafes, and bars, offering everything from falafel to continental cuisine.

Amenities: Desert and diving excursion bookings; complimentary shuttle to airport.

Moderate

✪ **Sanafir Tourist Village** (☎ **062/600-197;** fax 062/600-196) is located in the Shopping Mall area of Na'ama Bay. From the outside, all you see is a doorway. The entrance passageway leads to a delightfully designed complex that is half traditional Middle Eastern traveler's *khan,* with courtyards and sunken conversation areas around fire pits (great for evening gatherings and conversation), and half whitewashed desert village, with domed roofs and labyrinths of passageways and outdoor stairways leading to guest rooms. Designed by followers of Hassan Fathi, contemporary Egyptian architect who employed North African village design in his structures, the place has an exotic feel, and the management maintains a friendly, younger, more adventurous travelers' ambiance. There are simple buffet breakfasts and dinners and there's live entertainment a number of times a week. A swimming pool and new guest room section were completed in 1997; the new section is more comfortable, with airy, modern rooms, but not nearly as intriguing as the older section, and a bit more expensive. Double rooms are in the $90 to $170 range including breakfast and tax. Prices here have skyrocketed over the past 2 years and reflect the hotel's special style, but you get better value for your money, in terms of amenities, at the international complexes on Na'ama Bay's beach. Try to reserve far in advance for this popular, atmospheric choice. MasterCard and Visa are accepted.

The moderate **Helnan Marina Sharm Hotel** (☎ **062/600-170;** fax 062/768-385), also on Na'ama Bay's central beach, has 105 rooms with private bathrooms, air-conditioning, and televisions as well as a swimming pool; it is located close to good diving reefs. Rooms are comfortable, but without the glitz of neighboring complexes. Doubles are $95 to $110; suites run $250 to $350. American Express, MasterCard, and Visa are accepted.

Oona's Diver's Club Hotel (☎ **062/600-581;** fax 062/291-937) is the another moderate place on the beach at Na'ama Bay, with 20 simple motel-like doubles with air-conditioning, TV, and private bathrooms. Heavily booked with diving tour groups, Oona's offers diving excursions and lessons—the atmosphere is young, informal, and very friendly if you're a diver. Doubles are $70 to $90. MasterCard and Visa are accepted.

The **Pidgeon House Hotel** (☎ **062/600-996;** fax 062/600-995) is the best budget choice at Na'ama Bay, right across the road from the big, expensive hotels that line the beach. Doubles in huts are $20; in standard rooms with shared bathrooms and fans, but no air-conditioning are $30; and pleasant, new superior rooms with private bathrooms, air-conditioning, and refrigerator are $52. Breakfast is included in all categories. Prices vary according to season. This is a rambling, friendly place with interesting architectural style, including palm tree trunks that support the roofs, in traditional Sinai style. Chef Juergin's Restaurant (see below), serving tasty food, is just across the terrace. There are 90 units. Visa accepted.

WHERE TO DINE

Evening dinner options consist of the lavish buffets that most deluxe hotels offer, or $5 to $10 Italian or Chinese dinners at restaurants in the Shopping Mall. Hotel guests who are not on full board often buffet hop in the evening, trying a different buffet each night. The Hilton's vast buffet on its outdoor terrace is the most atmospheric, with waiters in Pharonic garb, a large fresh barbecue of meats, poultry, and fish, and a buffet containing many Egyptian specialties. The Movenpick buffet, indoors and equally lavish, emphasizes continental cuisine, with occasional Middle Eastern flourishes. At around $25 or less, these feasts are a wonderful deal.

Two nonhotel restaurants deserve special mention. **The Sinai Star,** in Sharm-el-Sheik, serves the best fresh grilled fish in the area, along with wonderful bread and salads and chips. It is a simple, no-frills place that many travelers in the know visit; a full meal should be under $10. It's worth the taxi fare from Na'ama Bay and every driver knows the place. **Chef Juergin's Restaurant** at the budget Pigeon House Hotel, across the road from the Sonesta is a friendly, informal place with long tables where long-term visitors come for a good meal. You can have just soup, or an entire feast. Chef Juergin, who ran the food services at one of Na'ama Bay's luxury hotel complexes for many years, decided to settle here; his lively European menu is always excellent. A meal could run in the $9 to $16 range.

Exploring Jordan 11

The Hashemite Kingdom of Jordan offers a new horizon for travelers to the Middle East. It contains dazzling, unspoiled desertscapes and countryside and legendary lost cities from ancient times, but it's also an orderly country with a modern infrastructure and a population that has a long tradition of natural hospitality and courtesy. Since 1994, when Jordan and Israel signed a peace agreement ending a 46-year-long state of war, the Kingdom of Jordan has been host to a wave of international and Israeli tourists. The word is out that sights are magnificent, roads are excellent, and prices for lodgings and restaurants are far, far lower than in Israel.

In terms of history, as well as logic, the lands east and west of the Jordan River have traditionally existed in a close relationship. Ruth, the Moabite ancestor of King David, came from what is now a central region of Jordan; Herod the Great, an Ideumean, came from what is now the southern part of the country; Jesus was baptized by John the Baptist in Jordan; and the crusaders, who swept in from Akko, Jerusalem, and the Galilee, built the most formidable of their mountaintop castles at Kerak. An excursion to the Nabatean canyon city of Petra, one of the wonders of the world, should be a highlight of any visit to the Middle East. For the first time, visitors to Israel can include in their itineraries the wonders of Wadi Rum (backdrop for the filming of *Lawrence of Arabia*); the sweeping views from Mount Nebo, reputed to be the place where Moses died; the vast Byzantine mosaics at Medaba; the Red Sea coral reefs at Aqaba; and the Hellenistic/Roman ruined city of Jerash (ancient Gerasa), which hosts a world-famous festival of Western and Middle Eastern performing arts each July.

Although the barriers to travel between Israel and Jordan have fallen, an excursion to Jordan still involves some amount of hassle. Border-crossing regulations and procedures (as well as fees) are still in the process of evolving: the rules constantly change. The country is at times overwhelmed by the numbers of international tourists and Israeli visitors. The touristic and ecological capacity of Petra, the most dazzling of Jordan's attractions, is being mightily taxed. Admission to Petra may have to be limited to 1,000 visitors a day or less.

Under these circumstances, many tourists find it best to book onto a tour of Petra that will guarantee admission, or book a guided tour of all the country's highlights. Although Jordanians are very helpful, many travelers will feel more comfortable on a tour, rather than having to contend with the megalopolis of Amman, and a transportation system in which even bus numbers may not be written in symbols an English-speaking person can recognize. For those booking tours from Israel, it is worthwhile to check out the better operators. We have reports that some bargain-tour operators, both in Israel and Jordan, are blatantly cutting corners on tours, guides, transportation expenses, accommodations, meals, and activities that were supposed to be included in packages.

Jordan, however, is a fresh, exhilarating destination, and the rewards and memories will far outweigh any obstacles.

A LOOK AT JORDAN'S PAST

The Hashemite Kingdom of Jordan encompasses boundaries defined by the Allied victors of World War I. Emir Abdullah, son of Sherif Hussein of Mecca, whose ancestry can be traced to the Prophet Muhammad, was awarded Trans-Jordan, the former Ottoman territories east of the Jordan River, in gratitude for Arab support during the war against the Ottoman Empire. Under British supervision, the Emirate of Trans-Jordan moved toward independence in 1946; with independence, Emir Abdullah became King Abdullah of Trans-Jordan. In 1949, with the annexation of the West Bank, the name of the country was changed to the Kingdom of Jordan.

In 1951, King Abdullah was assassinated in front of the El Aksa Mosque in Jerusalem by forces who felt the king was working for reconciliation with the new State of Israel. Abdullah's 14-year-old grandson, the future King Hussein, was at his side when he was struck down. Hussein ruled from 1953 until his death in 1999, bringing his country through more than 4 decades of wars and crises, walking a delicate tightrope between the larger powers in the Middle East. During this time, Jordan has absorbed and given citizenship to well over a million refugees from the 1948 and 1967 wars, as well as to more than 300,000 Palestinians expelled from Kuwait and other Gulf states in the wake of the 1991 Gulf War. In the last years of his life, King Hussein made the search for peace in the Middle East into a personal crusade. Few in the region will forget his committed words and presence at the funeral of Prime Minister Rabin or his personal condolence visits to the mourning Israeli families of Beit Shemesh, whose children had fallen victim to violence. Hussein's son, the Western-educated, innovative King Abdullah, has vowed to continue his father's work for peace.

In a land devoid of oil and with few natural resources, Jordan has created one of the most progressive and energetic societies in the Middle East, but the burden of absorbing so many refugees, largely without help from the outside world, has taken its toll on the nation's economy. The annual per capita income, approximately $2,000 in 1990, fell to less than $1,400 in subsequent years. The opportunities afforded by peace may turn this trend around. If it does, tourism will be an important element in Jordan's economic revival.

1 Planning a Trip to Jordan

VISITOR INFORMATION, ENTRY REQUIREMENTS & MONEY
VISITOR INFORMATION

There's not a great deal of advance information about travel to Jordan available outside Jordan itself. Royal Jordanian Airline offices are the main sources for travel material on the country. **Jordan Tourist Information Offices** in the United States are at the Jordanian Embassy, 3504 International Dr. NW, Washington, DC 20008

(☎ **202/966-2664,** ext. 116), or call Royal Jordanian Airlines at ☎ **800/RJ-JORDAN.** In the United Kingdom, Jordan Tourist Information Offices are at 32 Brook St., London W1Y 1AG (☎ **0171/878-6333**); in Canada, 45 St. Claire Ave., W., Toronto, ON, M4V1K9 (☎ **416/962-3999**). In Australia, 403 George St., Sydney, NSW 2000 (☎ **02/9321-9222**). In New Zealand, Manchester Courts, Room 6c, 160 Manchester St., Christchurch (☎ **03/365-3910**). In Ireland, 3 Clyde St., Baldbridge, Dublin 4 (☎ **01/842-3144**). In Israel, 5 Shalom Aleichem St., Tel Aviv (☎ **03/ 516-5566**). In the past, these offices were equipped mainly with nicely photographed brochures, but with the tourist boom, they may offer more detailed information and services.

On the **Internet** try Jordan On Line (http://jordan-online.com) for current information on news, upcoming cultural events and travel sites in Jordan.

Excursions Unlimited, 545 Madison Ave., Suite 800, New York, NY 10022 (☎ **800/726-8687** or 212/980/7032; e-mail: go2israel@usa.net), a wholesaler and tour operator that specializes in Israel and Jordan, is a good source of information about tours and travel between Israel and Jordan, and can book transportation, package tours and individual hotels in Jordan, usually at discounted rates.

ENTRY REQUIREMENTS

You must have a valid passport, preferably one that does not have an expiration date within 6 months of your planned visit. American, British, and Canadian citizens are issued visas upon arrival at Queen Alia Airport in Amman. Travelers from the United States, Canada, the United Kingdom, Ireland, Australia, and New Zealand planning to enter Jordan over land from Israel can get their visas after paying a fee at the **Beit Shean/Sheik Hussein Bridge Crossing** or **the Eilat/Aqaba Crossing.** Travelers wishing to cross into Jordan from Israel at the **Allenby Bridge/King Hussein Bridge** must already have a visa stamp, obtainable in person or by mail at Jordanian embassies and consulates upon completing the necessary forms; a recent photograph is required. The fee is $45 for U.S. citizens. Those applying for visas at the Jordanian Embassy in Tel Aviv should allow a minimum of 2 days for visa application processing. If you entered Israel from Jordan via the Allenby Bridge, you may reenter Jordan via the Allenby Bridge provided you have a valid multiple-entry visa.

Most visas are issued for 15 days, renewable at local police stations without an additional fee; the renewable visa is usually good for an additional 3 months. Good travel agents, abroad as well as in Israel, and reputable tour companies can generally handle the arrangements for their clients' visas. Visa fees are not included in most package tour prices, but there should be no charge for the service of obtaining the visa.

The Jordanian Embassy in the United States is at 3504 International Drive NW, Washington, DC 20008 (☎ **202/966-2664**); in Canada, 100 Bronson Ave., Number 701, Ottawa, Ont. KIR 6G8 (☎ **613/238-8091**); in the United Kingdom, 6 Upper Philimore Gardens, London W8 7HB (☎ **0171/937-36-85**); and in Australia, 20 Roebuck St., Red Hill ACT 2603, Canberra (☎ **02/6295-9951**). In Israel the Jordanian embassy is at 14 Aba Hillel St., in Ramat Gan, a suburb of Tel Aviv (☎ **03/751-7722**). If you book a tour to Jordan in Israel, the travel agency can usually arrange your visa paperwork for you.

MONEY

The Jordanian dinar is valued at approximately US$1.40, £0.86, or about NIS 6.4. US$1 = JD 0.71; £1 = JD 1.143.

The **Jordanian dinar** (JD) is divided into 1,000 **fils:** 10 fils are 1 piaster; 500 fils are generally referred to as 50 **piasters.** Paper currency comes in denominations of JD

1, 5, 10, 20, as well as 500 fils (half a JD); there are silver coins for 25 fils, 50 fils, 100 fils, and 250 fils; copper coins are 5 and 10 fils.

GETTING THERE

BY PLANE Royal Jordanian Airlines has service between Ben-Gurion Airport and Amman Tuesday through Friday and on Sunday in the evening. Call ☎ **800/ RJ-JORDAN** or 212/949-0050 in the U.S. for information. El Al also offers service between Amman and Ben Gurion.

BY LAND VIA ISRAEL *Note:* Conditions, regulations, and border fees are in a constant state of flux. Check with the East Jerusalem agencies or with Royal Jordanian Airlines in Tel Aviv for the most current information.

Most visitors from Israel who already have Jordanian visas enter Jordan from Jerusalem via the Allenby/King Hussein Bridge at the Jordan River near Jericho; visitors without visas can purchase them upon entrance at the Eilat/Aqaba Arava Crossing just north of Eilat (initially opened for non-Israeli visitors in 1994); or at the Sheik Hussein Bridge Crossing near Beit Shean, in the northern Jordan Valley. Crossing at the Allenby Bridge can be very slow, as this is the main crossing point into Jordan for Palestinians—lines are long and security checks can be laborious. Many tours originating in Jerusalem are routed into Jordan via the Sheik Hussein Bridge, a new and less busy Jordan River Crossing Point in the northern Jordan Valley, near the Israeli city of Beit Shean. From there, tours continue on to Jerash, north of Amman, and then proceed to Amman for the night. Independent tourists can also use this crossing. At press time, travelers with passports from English-speaking countries will be issued visas for Jordan on the Jordanian side of the Sheik Hussein Bridge. At press time, Israel departure fees at crossings into Jordan are NIS 57 ($12.60).

Independent travelers from Jerusalem are advised to make arrangements with an East Jerusalem travel agency for sherut service to the Allenby Bridge or to the Sheik Hussein Bridge. You must disembark, carry your baggage across the border checkpoints, and connect with ongoing Jordanian service sheruts or air-conditioned **Jordanian Express Tourist Transport (JETT)** buses from the Allenby Bridge to Amman; the cost is JD 7 ($10). At the Sheik Hussein Bridge, there are taxis (service) to Amman. You must check with your East Jerusalem travel agency for information about current flat-rate fares from the Sheik Hussein Bridge to Amman, and be prepared to bargain taxi drivers down to approximately that fare.

From Eilat, you can cross into Aqaba, where a number of JETT buses (equipped with air-conditioning, hostess service, sandwich service, and Arabic videos) as well as minibuses and private taxis leave for Amman each day.

ORGANIZED TOURS

Royal Jordanian Airlines (☎ **800/RJ-TOURS** in the U.S.) offers a range of well-tested land packages and tours for its passengers and has air service between Tel Aviv and Amman.

TOUR ORGANIZERS IN ISRAEL Travel agencies in Eilat can arrange package tours of Jordan that originate in Eilat. Traveli, in the New Tourist Center (☎ **07/ 637-1820**), and Johnny V.I.P. Tours, in the Shalom Center (☎ **07/634-0368**), are two experienced agencies. Tours can also be booked at the Eilat Tourist Information Center itself (☎ **07/637-2111**).

In Jerusalem, tours are offered by **Galilee Tours** (☎ **02/625-8866;** 800/874-4445 in the U.S.), 3 Hillel St.; **B.T.C. Tours,** 1 Ha-Soreg St. (☎ **02/623-3990**); and **Mazada Tours,** 9 Koresh St., corner of King Solomon Street (☎ **02/623-5777**).

Jordan

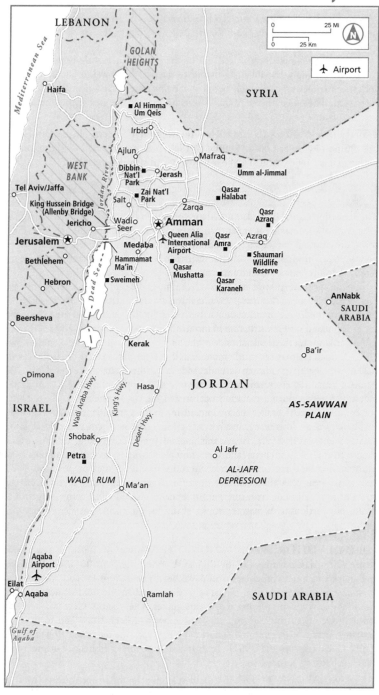

From the United States, you can book tours from Israel into Jordan with **Excursions Unlimited** (☎ **800/726-8687** or 212/980-7032). Readers' feedback on this company has been excellent.

There has been mixed reader feedback on the performance of almost all Israeli tour companies dealing with Jordan, partly due to the fact that travel to Jordan has undergone a sometimes unmanageable boom in the first year of the Israeli-Jordanian peace agreement. The budget-range Mazada Tours has evoked the greatest number of readers' complaints.

TOUR ORGANIZERS IN AMMAN **International Traders,** Shemaysani District (☎ **06/560-7014;** fax 06/566-9905), is the representative of American Express in Jordan. Their arrangements will be top quality and very dependable.

2 Amman

The sprawling capital of Jordan undulates over seven hills, and is home to more than a million people, making it larger than any of Israel's cities. There is an older "downtown" area around the ancient, beautifully restored Roman Amphitheater, but there is no one main business center or hotel district in Amman. Offices and hotels are scattered randomly across the entire sprawling city.

In biblical times, Amman was Rabbath-Ammon, the capital of the Ammonite people; in the Hellenistic/Roman period, this was the formidable city of Philadelphia, a member of the league of cities known as the Decapolis—impressive ruins from those times still blend into the structure of modern Amman. During the early 1920s, when Trans-Jordan was carved out of the wreckage of the Ottoman Empire, centrally located in Amman (at that time little more than a village), rather than the larger town of Salt to the north, was chosen as Emir Abdullah's administrative center. Until 1948, Amman remained essentially a small town with a population of less than 12,000. Palestinian refugees from the 1948 war swelled the city's population; like the rest of the country, more than half the inhabitants of Amman are of Palestinian origin.

The city is an interesting, lively base for exploring northern and central Jordan. Independent travelers will, of necessity, spend time here making touring arrangements. Amman has fabulous (and very affordable) Middle Eastern restaurants as well as interesting local craft cooperatives and shops to visit. A walk or drive through the residential areas of Abdoun, not far from the American Embassy, reveals street after street of new and under construction stone mansions and villas; some are garish and flashy, but you'll also see many examples of interesting, exciting modern design.

ESSENTIALS

JORDAN VISITOR INFORMATION The Ministry of Tourism's new **Downtown Visitors' Center** is near the Roman Amphitheater (☎ **06/464-6264**), offers free maps and tourist brochures, will make hotel reservations for you, arrange rental cars, give out information on the latest of the ever changing border and visa regulations, and advise you on tours and private guides. The Visitors' Center is open daily April to October from 9am to 7pm; November to March from 9am to 5pm. The Jordan Tourism Board, in the Kalbouni Building, opposite the Jordan Tower, near the Third Circle (☎ **06/464-7951**), offers similar brochures and maps, but provides no hotel or booking services.

GETTING AROUND Taxis are the best option for first-time tourists. Most taxi rides in the central city come to JD 2 ($2.80) or less. A taxi from Queen Alia International Airport to a hotel in the center of Amman should run JD 13 to 15 ($18.30

to $21). There is no additional charge for baggage, nor is a tip expected unless the driver carries heavy baggage a considerable distance for you. Airport Express buses to downtown Amman's Abdali Station depart from outside the Arrivals Hall every 30 minutes from 6am to 10pm; and every 2 hours from 11pm to 5am. The fare is JD 1 ($1.40) with a charge of 250 fils (35¢) for each suitcase or large bag. The 35-kilometer (56-mi.) trip from the airport to central Amman takes around 45 minutes.

Yellow shared taxis, called *service,* ply definite routes, much like buses. Service taxis bear the numbers of their routes. Check with your hotel about the nearest service routes, and always ask at the desk about the best service routes for your day's destinations. Drivers are usually very helpful to foreign visitors, as are fellow passengers. Standard fares in the center of Amman are generally 90 to 120 fils (about 20¢), but on a few routes the fare is 160 fils.

ORIENTATION

There are few addresses in Amman, and street signs in any language are rare. Neighborhoods are known in relationship to landmarks and to the eight traffic circles that are stretched across the hills and valleys of the city. For this reason, it is best to take taxis, which are inexpensive and generally fair to foreigners. Very seldom will a taxi fare across the city come to more than JD 2.50 ($3.50); most taxi rides will be in the $2 range. Because the city is built on hills and around ravines, it is difficult to judge walking distances or accessibility from maps. The good thing is that people are very friendly about giving directions (basic English is widely spoken) and the vistas from high points throughout Amman have become part of the city's charm. You orient yourself by the direction of the landmark hills of the city.

King Feisal Street running toward the Al Husseini Mosque, surrounded by the city's seven hills, is at the heart of **Al Balad,** the downtown center of Amman. The main market area lies several blocks southwest of the Al Husseini Mosque; the ancient **Roman Amphitheater,** another landmark, is to the northeast. The hill of **Jabal Amman** is the upper-class hotel and government district; the well-to-do foreign community makes its presence felt here. Beyond Jabal Amman is the district of **Shemaysani,** with more expensive hotels, cafes, and the Petra Center, which houses an American Pizza Hut and a Kentucky Fried Chicken. The American Express representative (see below) is located in this area, across the street from the Ambassador Hotel.

Fast Facts: Amman

American Express   The representative is **International Traders** (☎ 06/560-7014) in the Shemaysani district, on Abdul Hamid Sharif Street, opposite the Ambassador Hotel. You can book tours here, and American Express card holders can receive mail.

Area Code   The telephone Area Code for Amman is **06.** The country code for Jordan is **962.**

Embassies   The U.S. Embassy (☎ 06/592-0101; fax 06/592-0102) is in Abdoun near the Fifth Circle; the Canadian Embassy (☎ 06/566-6124; fax 06/568-9227) is in Shemaysani, in the Philadelphia Bank Building Complex; the U.K. Embassy (☎ 06/592-3100; fax 06/592-3293) is also in Abdoun, near the Fifth Circle and the Orthodox Club; the Australian Embassy (☎ 06/593-0246) is near the Fourth Circle (in Jabal Amman, opposite the Embassy of Kuwait). The Israeli Embassy (☎ 06/552-5407) is at Rabia, near the Embassy of China;

it is open Sunday to Thursday 8am to 4pm. Always call first to confirm the hours the desk for visas to Israel will be open.

Emergencies   Throughout Jordan, for Police dial ☎ **191** or 192; for an ambulance dial ☎ **193.**

Newspapers & Publications   Most helpful is *The Visitor's Guide,* followed by *Your Guide to Amman,* a free tourist publication put out each month and available at major hotels and many travel agencies. The weekly *Jerusalem Star* lists Amman performances and cultural events; the *Jordan Times* has interesting English-language reporting of Middle Eastern news as well as practical information such as current government price guidelines for fruits and vegetables. The *International Herald Tribune* generally arrives in Amman late in the second day after its publication. *Time* and *Newsweek* are also available.

Telephones   The country code for Jordan is **962.** The area code for Amman is **06.** If you are calling an Amman phone number from outside Jordan, you must omit the "0" preceding the 6: dial 962-6 and the local Amman number. When calling from within Jordan, you don't use the country code, but you do use the initial "0" in the area code for places beyond your area code. You can only make collect or calling card calls from private phones in Jordan. Directory assistance is in Arabic.

WHAT TO SEE & DO

The **Roman Theater,** on Jabal al-Qala'a, near the center of downtown Amman, built in the 2nd century A.D., is the most famous and easily accessible of the city's ancient sites. It was restored in the late 1950s and can accommodate 6,000 spectators. The theater is used for special events and performances. It is open from Wednesday to Monday from 9am to 5pm; there is no admission fee, but you may be thronged by potential "guides." Their going rate is JD 2. The **Museum of Folklore, Costume, and Jewelry,** filled with spectacular examples of Jordanian embroidery and regional costumes, is part of the restored theater complex. The museum is open the same hours as the theater; admission is JD 1.50 ($2.10).

A colonnaded Roman Square that was once part of the city's forum lies in front of the theater. To the east, at the far end of the ancient forum, is the **Odeon,** a smaller 2nd-century theater used for music performances. The ancient buildings have been woven into the main flow of city life with a busy, newly built piazza.

Jabal al-Qala'a (the Citadel Hill), is a steep walk up from the Roman Theater complex. This was the site of the acropolis and fortress of ancient Rabbath-Ammon. The views from the top of the hill are beautiful, encompassing all of the modern, hill-strewn city. The Citadel Hill includes Byzantine and early Islamic ruins, and the **Archeological Museum,** containing finds from all over Jordan.

Walk down the hill to the landmark **al-Husseini Mosque,** the bustling center of modern downtown Amman. In the triangle between the Citadel Hill, the al-Husseini Mosque, and the post office, you'll find the streets of the **Gold Market,** open Saturday through Thursday from 9am to 9pm, and on Friday until about 1pm. Very few shops in the maze sell old Bedouin and tribal silver.

WHERE TO STAY
EXPENSIVE
Amman Marriott Hotel. Shemaysani, Amman. ☎ **800/228-9290** reservations in North America and U.K. through Marriott Hotels International; or 06/560-7607. Fax 06/567-0100.

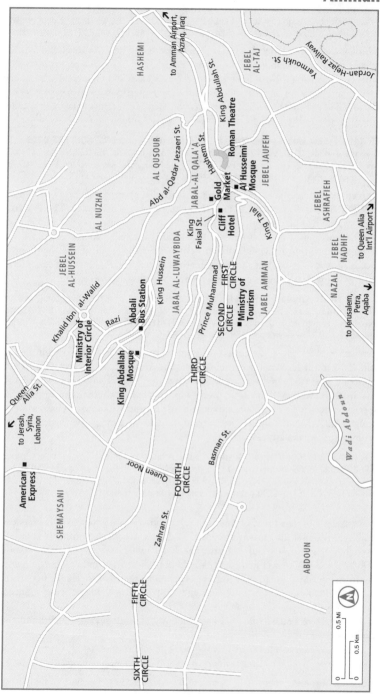

E-mail: marriott@cns.go.com.jo. 296 units. A/C MINIBAR TV TEL. $133–$175 double. Rates include breakfast. Add 10% service charge and 13% tax. AE, DC, MC, V. Free valet parking.

A bit less expensive and less luxurious than the other top hotels in town, the Marriott offers a good health club, indoor/outdoor pool facilities, and two tennis courts. More expensive rooms on the top floor are especially spacious and offer good vistas; many lower-floor rooms are small, but less expensive, and often available at special low rates. There is 24-hour room service, a good selection of in-house restaurants, live music and entertainment in the evenings, and a business service office.

✪ **Amra Forum Hotel.** Amra St., near the Sixth Circle, Amman. ☎ **800/327-0200** in the U.S. and Canada; 0181/847-2277 (London) or 0345/581-444 in the U.K.; or 06/551-0001. Fax 06/551-0003. 277 units. A/C TV TEL. $135–$145 double. Rates include breakfast. Add 10% service charge and 13% tax. AE, DC MC V.

This attractive four-star hotel with recently renovated rooms has an excellent staff and provides most of the services and facilities to be found in deluxe hotels. There's an out-door swimming pool, terrace cafe, comfortable hotel restaurant, fitness and massage room, tennis courts, and a business center as well as a travel booking desk and 24-hour room service. Minibars are available in some rooms and in all suites. The shopping arcade contains a good craft shop as well as a number of sleek, upmarket stores. Standard rooms with pool views are slightly more than those facing the street.

Grande Hyatt Amman. Hussein Bin Ali St., Jabal Amman, near the Third Circle, Amman. ☎ **06/465-1234;** reservations through Hyatt Hotels. Fax 06/465-1634. E-mail: info@ammgh.com.jo. 330 units. A/C MINIBAR TV TEL. $162–$197 double. Rates include breakfast. Add 10% service and 13% tax. AE, DC, MC, V.

Opened in 1999, this is the newest of Amman's quality hotels. The location is excellent, close to the Intercontinental Hotel, and the Amman Trade Center. Guestrooms, equipped with safes, are large and freshly decorated. Rooms with better views of the city are $176; regency club rooms, on the top floor, with the most dramatic vistas and special services, are $197. There are six in-house restaurants, cafes, and bars, as well as a nightclub. Amenities include indoor and outdoor swimming pool; state of the art business center; and a fitness center.

✪ **Hotel InterContinental Jordan.** Jabal Amman, near the Third Circle, Amman. ☎ **800/327-0200** in the U.S. and Canada; 0181/847-2277 (London) or 0345/581-444 in the U.K.; or 06/464-1361. Fax 06/461-9695. E-mail: ammha@go.com.jo. 400 units. A/C MINIBAR TV TEL. $215–$230 double. Rates include breakfast. Add 10% service and 13% tax. AE, MC, V. Parking $7.50 per day.

Perhaps the most fast-paced of Amman's deluxe hotels, with a Reuters News service at its business center, this massive, modern landmark is a very comfortable choice for both business travelers and tourists. The hotel underwent massive renovation in 1998–99 and visitors will find guest rooms and facilities fresh and bright. A center for Amman's social life, there are wedding parties and banquets here almost nightly; the goings and comings add extra interest and excitement to the hotel. Four rooms are designed for travelers with disabilities.

Dining/Diversions: Two restaurants, indoor and outdoor cafes, English pub, bar, nightclub.

Amenities: Large outdoor swimming pool, children's pool, tennis courts, 24-hour room service, executive business floor, travel agency, shops, hairdresser.

Meridien Amman. Shemaysani, Amman. ☎ **06/569-6511.** Fax 06/567-4261. E-mail: meridien@go.com.jo. 303 units. A/C TV TEL. $180–$210 double; higher rates for suites. Rates include breakfast. Add 10% service charge and 13% tax. AE, DC, MC, V.

This modern, comfortable high-rise hotel is next to the busy Housing Bank Complex, one of the city's landmarks in which more than 100 shops and businesses are located in a convenient but rather drab shopping center. Not quite as high-powered as the InterContinental (see above), the Meridien is known for its excellent staff. Diplomatic and economic missions (including the Israeli mission) have headquartered here. Rooms are very spacious, with large dressing and storage areas as well as pleasant touches of Arabic decor; doubles contain two double beds. The in-house restaurants are above average in quality and reasonably priced, with attendants in traditional dress bringing coffee and Jordanian desserts. Among the in-house shops, the prominent Al Dalal Craft Shop is run-of-the-mill, but tucked away on a lower level you'll find a store with excellent Bedouin embroideries and Palestinian crafts. The hotel has a swimming pool, fitness room, tennis courts, sauna, live evening entertainment, and 24-hour room service.

MODERATE

Commodore Hotel. Shemaysani, around the corner from Safeway. ☎ **06/607-185.** Fax 06/668-187. 96 units. A/C TV TEL. $80 double. AE, DC, MC, V.

The building is contemporary Middle Eastern, with recently redecorated guest rooms and public spaces; it's not atmospheric but the location in upmarket Shemaysani is good, close to the Safeway complex with a variety of moderate and fast-food eating choices. Most rooms have minibars or refrigerators and there is 24-hour room service. Extra perks include use of the nearby Middle East Hotel's outdoor in-season swimming pool. There are shops, a beauty salon, and a car-rental desk on the premises.

Shepherd Hotel. Zaid Ben Al Harith St. between 1st and 2nd Circles. ☎ **06/463-9197.** Fax 06/464-2401. 42 units. A/C TV TEL. $66 double. Rates include breakfast. AE, DC, MC, V.

A good hotel choice in the moderate price category, the Shepherd is well run, with a pretty cafe terrace out front, and a great location in one of the few areas of town that has some character. The building has a 1960s decor, but it's spotlessly clean, has some style, and comfortable if not memorable rooms, all with refrigerators and private bathrooms with tubs. There is a lot of variation in guest rooms—some are larger; some contain newer furniture, so ask to see a few possible choices. The staff is helpful; the fondue at the in-house restaurant is quite good.

INEXPENSIVE

There is no lack of inexpensive hotels in Amman. At discount rates, package trips can book you into moderate-range hotels that are well above the quality of the following suggestions, but for independent travelers, these are some of the best bets.

Canary Hotel. Jabal al-Luwaybida, across from Terra Sancta College. ☎ **06/463-8353.** Fax 06/465-4353. 21 units. TV TEL. $38–$44 double. Rates include breakfast. MC, V.

Comfortable rooms in a building overlooking one of Amman's pleasant, older neighborhoods, plus a pleasant garden and a very helpful management, make this an extremely popular choice for budget travelers. It makes up in friendliness for whatever it may lack in amenities.

Caravan Hotel. Sulaiman Al-Nabulsi St., Jabal al Weideli P. O. Box 9062, Amman. ☎ **06/566-1195.** Fax 06/566-1196. 25 units. $38–44 double; slight discount Nov–May. Rates include breakfast. MC, V.

Located on a quiet street near the Abdali Bus Terminal and the King Abdullah Mosque, the Caravan is under the same friendly management as the Canary Hotel (see above). In good weather, guests socialize in the hotel's front garden/terrace. Ask for rooms with renovated decor and bathrooms. Like the Canary, this is a modest place with personal service; the manager, Mr. Ihsan Twal, offers good advice, can arrange delicious Arabic-style meals cooked on the premises, and may offer off-season discounts. Sulaiman Al-Nabulsi Street is also known as Abdali Police College Street.

Dove Hotel. Qurturbah St., between 4th and 5th Circles. ☎ **06/569-7683.** Fax 06/567-4676. 25 units. TV. $40–$46 double. Rates include breakfast. MC, V.

Another hotel run by the very hospitable Twal family (see Canary and Caravan Hotels, above), this is a bit more out of the way, located on a quiet street in a neighborhood with a number of Middle Eastern embassies. The building is relatively new, and many rooms are quite spacious, but in summer, some can be unusually hot. There's a pleasant bar in the basement, and very delicious food available at the in-house restaurant.

WHERE TO DINE
EXPENSIVE

L'Olivier Restaurant. Abdoun, Amman. ☎ **06/592-9564.** Reservations required. Complete meals $25–$40. MC, V. Daily 12:30–3:30pm and 7:30pm–midnight. Best visited by taxi. FRENCH.

This is one of the most elegant and expensive restaurants in the city, offering a menu of classic French cuisine. You can be confident of a relaxed, gracious atmosphere here, and a good selection of standard dishes and desserts as well as one of the best wine lists in the country. In summer, there is garden dining. À la carte choices and fixed-price dinners make the cost of dining here somewhat lower.

MODERATE

Very reasonably priced restaurants with delicious food are one of the pleasures of the Amman scene. You'll find them everywhere; those in the Middle Eastern style are usually the best bets. The following are two especially pleasant suggestions that offer extra style and quality at modest prices.

✪ **Abu Ahmed's New Orient Restaurant.** 10 Orient St., near the Third Circle. ☎ **06/464-1879.** Reservations recommended. Main courses JD 4–10 ($5.60–$14). MC, V. Daily noon–midnight. MIDDLE EASTERN.

This centrally located place, an Amman institution, is one of the city's real gems, presided over by the courtly Abu Ahmed himself. Set in a rambling stone bungalow, it offers garden dining in good weather and a large Arabic menu in which every dish is exquisitely prepared from the best ingredients—many traditional dishes, especially among the first courses, are virtually works of art here. The venerable Abu Ahmed, a proud patriarch with grandchildren educated at universities throughout the world, personally supervises the buying of meats and vegetables for his restaurant each day. There are fresh breads, and the standard array of appetizers and grilled main courses, all served with style by a courteous staff. Another branch of Abu Ahmed's, with equally good food but less decor, is on Basman Street (☎ **06/463-6069**).

Al-Bustan. Jordan University Rd. near the Jerusalem Hotel. ☎ **06/566-1555.** Reservations recommended. Meals $8–$15. MC, V. Daily 12:30–11:30pm. MIDDLE EASTERN.

Al-Bustan (the Garden) is generally acknowledged to be one of the best Arabic-style restaurants in Amman, yet despite its reputation, prices are quite reasonable by most travelers' standards. The restaurant offers a wide choice of traditional appetizers, baked dishes, grilled meats, and desserts. Breads are freshly baked. In summer, there is terrace dining.

⭐ **Kan Zeman Restaurant.** Yadudda, 7 mi. south of Amman off the Desert Hwy. ☎ **06/412-8392.** Reservations recommended. Middle Eastern/International Buffet $16. AE, MC, V. Daily 9am–1am. *Note:* A $6–$10 taxi ride from the center of town. MIDDLE EASTERN.

The name of this restaurant means "once upon a time," and the old, atmospheric buildings have been renovated and turned into a complex of artisan's workshops and top-flight craft stores as well as an establishment serving traditional Middle Eastern food. Although this is an enjoyable spot on the tourist circuit, Jordanians love it as well, and there's an interesting mix of tour groups and locals. You can enjoy a very fine buffet for a relatively modest price, watch bread being made, and stroll around the charming shopping area. There is often live music, and you may catch folk or belly dancing. A must for every visitor to Amman.

Romero's. Jabal Amman, near the Third Circle and Intercontinental Hotel. ☎ **06/464-4227.** Reservations necessary. Main courses JD 4–10 ($5.60–$14). MC, V. Daily 1–3pm and 8–11pm. ITALIAN.

Famous throughout Jordan, with a branch at the Royal Yacht Club in Aqaba, this is a solid restaurant of high standards serving traditional Italian dishes, including pastas, meat, and chicken. The antipasti has a touch of the Middle East to it; portions are large and you can't fail to have a good meal here.

Tanoreen. Shatt-al-Arab St., near the Sixth Circle. ☎ **06/551-5987.** Reservations recommended. Main courses JD 4–10 ($5.60–$14). MC, V. Daily 1–4pm and 8–11pm. MIDDLE EASTERN.

Decorated with hand-painted Armenian tiles from the Palestinian Pottery Workshop in Jerusalem, and offering a garden dining terrace in good weather, this is a charming spot for a leisurely meal. There are fabulous *mezze* choices, and the list of grilled meats is headed by *shish tawook,* a delicious Lebanese-style marinated chicken breast. Prices here are a bit higher than at similar Arabic restaurants, but many dishes are presented with an imaginative extra twist that makes them special.

INEXPENSIVE

The overwhelming majority of restaurants in Amman, many of them quite good, are in the lower price range. Most budget Middle Eastern-style restaurants do not serve alcoholic drinks; unless they are listed in the menu, it is a good idea not to ask for them, especially during Ramadan. Upper-class neighborhoods like Shemaysani and Abdoun are dotted with Western (and Eastern) fast-food spots like Pizza Hut, Kentucky Fried Chicken, Chicken Tikka, and Arby's. But with some of the tastiest Middle Eastern foods you'll ever find, Amman is really a place to explore the local cuisine. You can't go wrong with any of the little places in downtown Amman serving *shwarma* (meat sliced from a spit), hummus, or falafel.

El Quds (Jerusalem) Restaurant. King Hussein St. near the First Circle. ☎ **06/463-0168.** Meals JD 3 ($4.20) and under. No credit cards. Daily 7am–11pm. MIDDLE EASTERN.

The window is filled with Arabic pastries, but inside this busy workers' establishment, you'll find all kinds of traditional Middle Eastern appetizers and dishes. *Mensaf,* a rice, meat, and yogurt dish served *on'aish tanoor* (with freshly baked, extra-thin pita-like bread) is one of the specialties here; you can also get *mahalabiya,* a traditional thin custard dessert with pistachios. Less daring are the very good grilled meats. There's no English menu, but the staff and fellow customers are usually very understanding, and the quality of everything served is tops. Acknowledged as the best place of its kind in Amman.

SHOPPING

Traditional Jordanian and Palestinian crafts are sold in many shops throughout Amman. The following offer some of the best quality and selections in the country.

Jordan River Designs, near First Circle, Abu Bakr al Siddiq (Rainbow) Street (☎ 06/461-3081), sponsored by Save the Children, sells a wide range of Palestinian and Jordanian embroidery, including pillowcases, quilts, wallets, and purses. Quality is very high, and proceeds go to the women who produce these beautiful items. Most of the hand-woven rugs are contemporary interpretations of traditional designs done in soft, attractive colors. Look for traditional kilim rugs, pillowcases, and wall hangings of the formerly nomadic Bani Hamida tribes, who have been settled in villages near the Dead Sea; the rich desert colors and textures produced by the special Bani Hamida dyes and wool are extraordinary.

Al Bawadi House is located between Mecca Street and Ash Shahid Wafsi al Tal Street. Sponsored by the Queen Alia Social Welfare Fund, this shop displays a careful selection of traditional crafts, including weavings, kilim rugs, and ceramics.

Al Aydi, located near the Intercontinental Hotel (☎ 06/464-4555), carries a selection of fine quality Palestinian embroideries, antique silver, jewelry, Bedouin woven carpets, and inlaid mother of pearl and olive-wood items.

Artisana Jordan Arts and Crafts Center is near Second Circle (☎ 06/464-7858). Filled with an especially attractive collection of traditional and contemporary crafts, this is always a worthwhile stop. Signs at the Second Circle direct you to the shop; closed Fridays.

3 Petra

Some 3¹/₂ to 5 hours by public transport, or a 2¹/₂-hour drive south of Amman, this is the jewel in the crown of Jordan's attractions, and the main objective of travelers to the country. The canyon city of Petra is vast, mysterious, and really demands a 1- or 2-night stay and 2 full days of exploring to get a feel for the atmosphere, to say nothing of the contents of the ruins. You could easily spend 3 or 4 very full days exploring Petra and the surrounding countryside. If you're staying at one of the luxury resort hotels near Petra, you can plan for a relaxing, exotic desert holiday amid marvelous surroundings, enjoying local foods, entertainment, and the opportunity to browse shops filled with tribal crafts. For those on a budget, the many less expensive hotels at Wadi Musa, 5 kilometers (3 mi.) from the entrance to Petra, are reasonably comfortable, and offer the chance to meet interesting fellow travelers on the treks and tours of Petra. A hard day of exploring Petra will work up your appetite. In the evenings, many budget hotels offer very reasonably priced buffet dinners where travelers can meet to try traditional Middle Eastern dishes, make plans, and recount experiences. Many travelers buffet hop, and look for the most interesting and freshest deals being offered each night.

ESSENTIALS

GETTING THERE   JETT offers day excursions from Amman, leaving at 6:30am; the price is JD 40 ($56), including lunch and a guide; $14 bus fare and the admission to Petra are extra. You must reserve well in advance, especially in the fall and spring. Petra needs lots of time, and you would do better to try to stay at least 1 or 2 nights. From Eilat, travel agencies offer all kinds of tours and excursions.

VISITOR INFORMATION   The **Visitors Center** at the entrance to Petra (☎ 03/215-6060) is open Saturday through Thursday from 6:30am to 5pm. You can stay inside Petra until you are shooed out at sunset. Admission to Petra is JD 20 ($28) for 1 day; JD 25 ($35) for 2 days; JD 30 ($42) for 3 days. Children are half price. If you have hired a Jordanian guide, you should know that the admission price for Jordanians is JD 1 ($1.40). At the Visitors Center, independent travelers can hire guides for $12 to $80 per trip, depending on how long and how extensive you want your tour to be. Many of the guides are colorful, and most know their stuff. It's a good idea to hire a guide, at least for your first foray into Petra, and especially if you plan to do a hike to some of the more remote parts of the city. At the Visitors Center, you'll also find a variety of books and maps of Petra for sale. A good guidebook and map are *very* useful investments, even if you hire a guide; most books make a basic self-guided tour of Petra quite easy, especially if you have a chance to read up before your visit. Officially, the park is open daily until 6pm, but in summer guards usually let visitors stay a bit later in order to take in the sunset and twilight. A flashlight is necessary if you plan to stay until dark. It's a good idea to bring your own bottle of water when you enter Petra; as the day progresses you'll need to buy more bottled water from the Bedouins, who until recently inhabited the site. A number of stands inside Petra sell refreshments and food. Prices will be high, but don't hesitate to shell out for water and keep drinking even if you're not especially thirsty to avoid the dangers of dehydration! In summer, you'll need four $1^1/_2$-liter bottles of water to get through the day.

Fast Facts: Petra

Banks The Arab Bank and the Housing Bank in the center of Wadi Musa, and the Cairo Amman Bank in the Movenpick Hotel just outside the entrance to Petra all change money with higher commissions than you'll encounter in Amman. They also give Visa cash advances. Banking hours are Saturday to Thursday 8:30am to 12:30pm. The Housing Bank has an ATM machine connected to Cirrus and Plus.

Hospitals The Petra Emergency Clinic (☎ 03/215-6694), across the parking lot from the Petra Forum Hotel, is not a hospital, but it has an X-ray machine, an operating room, and other modern equipment. It is open daily 8am to 8pm. In an emergency, your hotel or the police (☎ 191) can help get you there.

Pharmacies The Wadi Musa Pharmacy (☎ 03/215-6444) is also on the main traffic circle in Wadi Musa, and is open daily 24 hours. The Modern Petra Pharmacy, a block from the Wadi Musa Traffic Circle, has an English-speaking staff and carries tampons, condoms, and other items not normally stocked by local pharmacies.

Telephones The area code for Petra is **03.**

EXPLORING PETRA

You enter Petra through the *siq,* a narrow crevice-canyon lined with niches that once held statues of gods and spirits that protected the city. The incredible siq winds its way through the rocks for almost a mile before opening to Petra's wonders of rock and light. Traditionally, visitors entered on horseback, or in special carts. Most visitors now walk from the entrance (beside the Visitors' Center) through the siq. As you proceed through the siq, you feel as if you are in the prologue to a mysterious adventure. The siq's dreamlike, sculptural turnings are almost hallucinatory and separate Petra from the outside, real world. Indeed, Petra was chosen as the location for the climatic sequence of the film *Indiana Jones and the Last Crusade.* If you walk through the shadowed siq at twilight, listen for the sound of the evening owl, once the symbol of the city.

The Nabataeans, who carved the elaborate palaces, temples, tombs, storerooms, and stables of their city into the solid rock of the cliffs, dominated the Trans-Jordan area from the 3rd century B.C. through Byzantine times. Little is known of the individual personalities who created Nabatean society. The Nabataeans, a Semitic people from northern Arabia, moved into the Negev and the southern portions of what is now Jordan in the 6th century B.C. They commanded the trade route from Damascus to Arabia; through here the great caravans passed, carrying spices, silk, jewels, gold, and slaves from as far away as Yemen and East Africa. As a trading people, the Nabataeans developed cosmopolitan tastes, and easily incorporated Hellenistic and Roman design into their architecture, and into their style of life. The fabulous facades carved into the rose sandstone cliffs of Petra are exotically Hellenistic rather than classical Greek or even Roman, and reflect the mixture of Western and Eastern, Semitic and European influences in which Nabatean civilization developed.

Nabatean religion was centered around two deities: **Dushara,** the God of Strength and Masculine attributes, and **al-Uzza,** also known as Atargatis, the Goddess of Water and Fertility. Slowly, these deities took on the characteristics of Greek and Egyptian gods; al-Uzza, especially, became associated with elements of Aphrodite, the Greek goddess of love, Tyche, the goddess of fortune, and the Egyptian mother goddess, Isis.

In addition to their hidden capital at Petra, the Nabataeans developed lucrative trading and caravan cities at **Avdat, Shivta,** and **Mamshit,** in the Negev. Using careful methods of conserving dew and rainwater, and developing amazingly efficient methods of irrigation that are being studied by modern agronomists, the Nabataeans made the desert bloom and managed to sustain a population in the Negev and south Jordan far larger than the population of that region today.

Until the first century A.D., the mysterious Nabataeans skillfully maintained their independence from the Parthians, an Iranian people who ruled Mesopotamia to the east, as well as from the briefly successful Hasmonean Jewish Commonwealth (which lost its independence to Rome in 63 B.C.) and from the Hellenistic and Roman powers to the west. Nabatean neutrality and aloofness was legendary. In 40 B.C., the young Herod, who had recently been made governor of the Galilee and Judea by the Romans, was overthrown by Jewish insurgents. Desperate and pursued, Herod made his way with a small entourage across the desert to Petra to beg for sanctuary and reinforcements. Despite the fact that Herod's mother had been a Nabatean princess, the ever-cautious rulers of Petra denied him permission to enter the siq and the confines of the city (the indefatigable Herod eventually made his way to Rome, obtained reinforcements, put down the rebellion, and ruled as Rome's "King of the Jews" until his death in 4 B.C.). In A.D. 106, the Nabataeans were finally annexed into the Roman Empire. The emperor Hadrian (who put down the Jewish Bar Kochba Revolt of A.D. 132–35, and who built the defensive wall separating Britain from Scotland), visited Petra in A.D. 130. Thereafter the city was known as Petra Hadriane in his honor; it continued to be the center of a highly profitable trading route, with connections to all parts of the Roman Empire.

In the early fourth century, Christianity became the dominant religion of the Nabataeans. Important churches were built in every Nabatean community; the Bishops of Petra participated in ecumenical councils that helped shape the development of the early church. As the Roman Empire collapsed, and the amount of trade moving on the exotic desert routes through Petra shrank, the city's economy faltered. What trade there was tended to be shipped up the Red Sea to Egypt, bypassing the overland route through Nabatean territory. A series of earthquakes in late Byzantine times hastened the Nabataeans' decline. After Petra's conquest by the armies of the newly formed Muslim religion in A.D. 633, traditional trading routes changed, and the region became a forgotten backwater. Petra was briefly fortified by the crusaders, but after its surrender to Saladin in 1189, it sank into almost total oblivion. Not until 1812, when the Swiss explorer Johann Ludwig Burkhardt (who had carefully studied Islamic rituals in order to disguise himself as a Muslim) bribed Bedouin tribesmen to take him to Petra, was the ruined, uninhabited city restored to the knowledge of the world. Only since 1958 has a careful exploration of the site been undertaken.

A Walk into Petra

A guide (or a good guidebook) is necessary as you wander among the hidden city's monumental cliff edifices and sites ranging from prehistoric to Crusader times. It is important to remember that many of the sites and buildings at Petra were given fanciful names in modern times that have nothing to do with what we now know as their original functions. Also remember that once inside Petra, a fast, but reasonably inclusive tour, without hikes to the sacred high places that overlook the city, can take 5 to 6 hours. Petra deserves at least 2 full days. Give yourself time to respond to the romantic mystery and beauty of the place, and to explore at your leisure. Every walk and hike will be filled with objects of interest and vistas that are remarkable. Petra changes dramatically as the light of day changes: The colors and mood of the city in early morning are different from the colors of Petra at noon or at sunset.

1. **The siq.** Beginning just near the Visitor's Center, the winding 3/4-mile walk through the narrow fissure, or canyonlike siq that leads into Petra can take from 45 minutes to 11/2 hours, depending on your pace. The journey through this mysterious, highly sculptural passageway can be one of the most memorable parts of the Petra experience (especially in the soft twilight as visitors depart from Petra for the night). At the entrance to the siq and a various points throughout the passageway, you'll notice channels cut into the rock that once held pipes for the water system which carried the waters from the spring of Ain Musa into Petra. There is also a modern dam to prevent flash flooding during the winter rains; it is modeled after the ruins of an ancient Nabatean dam uncovered by archeologists at this site. According to Nabatean and local Bedouin legend, Petra's water source, Ain Musa ("the Spring of Moses"), was created when Moses, leading the Israelites through the desert after the exodus from Egypt, struck a rock with his staff in despair as he watched his people close to death from thirst. The rocks burst forth with cool water. (Petra's Ain Musa is one of many springs in this part of the world that claims to be the site of this miracle). Niches in the walls of the siq once held the images of gods that protected the city, and that served to intimidate foreign visitors as they made their way into Petra.

2. **The Khazneh** (Treasury). Suddenly a turn in the siq reveals the most famous structure in Petra, a royal tomb that has come to be known as the Treasury. Bedouin believed that the solid urn sculpted into the monument's facade was actually hollow and contained treasure; often they fired bullets at the urn in hopes of having the treasure spill out (you can detect their bullet marks across the magnificent facade). The Khazneh's stone facade changes color during the day: In the morning it's often a soft yellow-rose peach hue; by late afternoon it

becomes a pure, sometimes jewel-like rose; at sunset, it turns an amazing intense red before slipping into the dusty twilight. Beyond the Khazneh (continuing to the right as you face the Khazneh), the siq widens into what is called the:

3. The outer siq. Here you'll encounter the busy modern denizens of Petra, sand artists and water sellers. The outer siq is lined with countless carved tomb facades in styles ranging from classical Roman to designs that echo Assyrian and nomadic desert influences. Honoring the dead was an important part of Nabatean culture. The outer siq also contains caves until recently inhabited by Bedouins—the soft sandstone interiors are as wildly patterned as marbleized paper, and are atmospheric spots to rest and shelter from the hot midday summer sun. To the left, opposite the Uneishu Tomb (which an inscription identifies as the tomb of the brother of a queen), is a flight of rough ancient stairs that leads to an uphill trail to the:

4. High Place of Sacrifice and the **Tombs of Wadi Farasa.** This can be an arduous hike for those out of shape, but it is very worthwhile. A hike to the High Place of Sacrifice and back down to the colonnaded main street of ancient Petra by a different route can take $1^{1}/_{2}$ to 3 hours. This hike is an option to come back to at a later time; it's probably wise to invest in a guide if you decide to make the excursion. Continuing on down what is now the main street of Petra, you come to the:

5. Roman Theater. Originally built by the Nabataeans, who were always adapting elements of other cultures into their way of life, the theater, facing the cliff-side facades of tombs, may have been used for religious ceremonies. In the 2nd century A.D., the theater was enlarged by the Romans, who apparently cared little for Nabatean traditions, and cut into nearby Nabatean tombs to create a vast 7,000-seat venue. The theater has been restored and after a 1,500-year hiatus, will be used again for performances and other events. Further along, on the opposite side of the canyon from the theater, are the:

6. Royal Tombs, so named because of their elaborate facades, and not because of any certainty that they were indeed created for royal burials. The first of these is the:

7. Urn Tomb, named for the carefully sculpted urn above its pediment. In A.D. 446, the Byzantines converted the inner chamber of this tomb into a church. A few facades beyond is the:

8. Corinthian Tomb, with a facade that actually includes a small-scale reproduction of the **Khazneh.** After the Corinthian tomb is the:

9. Palace Tomb, built in two stories that jut out from the side of the canyon. Part of the Palace Tomb was constructed of stone, rather than carved into the canyon rock. Around to the right is the heavily eroded:

10. Tomb of Sextius Florentinus, built around A.D. 130 for a Roman governor of the Provence of Arabia who so admired Petra's network of tombs that he asked to be buried in a tomb of his own design in this far outpost of the Roman Empire. A faint Latin inscription and a Roman eagle mark the facade of this tomb. A route of processional staircases and corridors began here and wound uphill to sacred high places on the mountain beyond. Staying on the main path to the city center, you come to the:

11. Nymphaeum, a two-story fountain dedicated to the water nymphs, and a major landmark of Petra. How amazing to travelers from the desert this lavish structure of flowing water, piped in from Ain Musa, must have seemed. The Nymphaeum was a place of both refreshment and worship. The open water channel that fed the Nynphaeum continued on along the:

12. Colonnaded Street, built by the Romans after A.D. 106 over the route of an earlier Nabatean thoroughfare. The street was lined with shops, but also served as a civic and ceremonial route for processions. On a rise of land to the right (north) as you walk down the Colonnaded Street, is the:

13. Temple of the Winged Lions, named for the winged lions that serve as capitals for its columns, and probably a temple dedicated to the worship of the female deity, al-Uzza. Built in A.D. 27, this was one of Petra's major temples until it was heavily damaged, apparently by fire, in the second century. The structure was then used to house families until it was destroyed by an earthquake in A.D. 363. That the temple was not rebuilt as a religious structure after the fire in the second century may indicate the old region of Petra had gone into decline under the Roman occupation. The temple is under excavation by an American-sponsored archaeological team. Also several hundred meters to the right of the Colonnaded Street is the:

14. Byzantine Church, a large structure with triple apses, and extremely beautiful and well-preserved mosaic floors that have been uncovered by the joint Jordanian-American team excavating the site. On both sides of the Colonnaded Street are the outlines of ruined buildings. According to some theories, the Roman forum of Petra would have been among the structures to the left (south) of the Colonnaded Street. At the end of the Colonnaded Street is the:

15. Triple Arched Gate, adorned with carved panels containing bas relief busts, animals, and geometric and floral designs. These monumental gateways would have borne wooden doors that opened to the *temenos,* or sacred precinct of the:

16. Qasr al Bint (Palace of the Pharoah's Daughter) Temple, perhaps the most important temple in Petra (again, despite its romantic name, the temple has nothing to do with a Pharoah's daughter). This massive structure was built of stone, rather than carved from rock, and is the most impressive building in Petra. It faces north, toward the Sharra mountains, from which the name of the chief Nabatean god, Dushara ("he of Sharra") is derived, and may have been a sanctuary for the Dushara cult. This temple was built around the time of Jesus, and seems to have been destroyed late in the 3rd century. Just to the south of the Arched Gate, but not accessible at present to visitors, were the:

17. Baths of Petra, which had access to a corner of the temenos. Beyond the ruins of the Qasr al Bint Temple, you'll find the:

18. Petra Museum, which contains a small collection of sculptural artifacts, jewelry, and pottery found at Petra. The museum building also houses the Petra Forum restaurant, as well as restrooms. A second part of the museum is housed in a nearby tomb.

OTHER HIKES & EXCURSIONS AT PETRA

In addition to the hike up to the High Place of Sacrifice (see number 4, above), a number of longer walks away from the center of Petra are very worthwhile and give you important vistas of this extraordinary place. These walks involve some amount of climbing as well as scrambling over rocks and ruined pathways, therefore it's best to have some walking companions with you. Guides at Petra will escort you for about JD 35 to 50 ($50 to $70). *Note:* It is required to have a guide with you when you go to more remote areas.

Jabal Haroun (the Mountain of Aaron, brother of Moses) is a climbing trek that can take as much as 4 to 8 hours depending on your route. The way passes **Ad Deir** (the Monastery), Petra's largest carved tomb monument, built in the first century A.D., with an interior adorned by carved and painted crosses from the Byzantine period. Across the canyon from Ad Deir is Jabal Haroun, the highest peak in the area. A small white church containing the **tomb of Aaron** stands at the top of the mountain. In winter, you might ask your guide to descend on the route that passes **Wadi Siyah,** where winter rains create a waterfall. This difficult but beautiful winter hike will take at least three hours, and a few additional hours if you return via Wadi Siyah. The Jabal Haroun trek requires a guide.

Wadi Turkimaniya is a pleasant 45-minute or so round-trip walk down the wadi that starts behind and to the left of the Temple of the Winged Lions. The easy road through the wadi supports rich vegetation in winter and leads to a Petra's only tomb with a Nabatean inscription.

Qasr Habis (the Crusader's Castle) is a climb that takes you from near Petra's muse-um to the not very impressive ruins of Petra's crusader stronghold; however, the path-way leads to wonderful vistas that overlook beautiful canyons. The round trip can run from 1 to 1¹/₂ hours.

The High Place of Sacrifice is one of the most popular destinations for hikers, tak-ing you to the great altars carved from rock (with drainage channels for the blood of sacrificial animals) far above the city. The panorama of Petra is dazzling; the round-trip hike can take from 1¹/₂ to 2¹/₂ hours and is not for visitors who are out of shape.

Additional treks to the **Snake Monument** and to **Jebal Numair** entail a minimum of 5 or 6 hours and require guides. There are also car tours and hikes available to **Al Madras** and **Al Barid,** nearby satellite towns of Petra. Al Barid is a kind of mini-Petra, entered through a smaller version of Petra's siq, and is filled with carved canyon struc-tures. Unlike at Petra, some of Al Barid's structures carved into cliff sides seem to have served as houses. Archaeology buffs can also take a taxi excursion (or hike with a Bedouin guide, about 6 hours round-trip) to the site of **El Beidha,** a Neolithic village from the 8th millennium B.C. A full day or overnight camping tour from Petra to the beautiful desertscapes of **Wadi Rum** is also highly recommended.

WHERE TO STAY
EXPENSIVE

✪ **Petra Movenpick Hotel.** Petra. ☎ **800/344-6835** in the U.S. for reservations through Movenpick Hotels International; 03/215-7111. Fax 03/215-7112. E-mail: hotel.petra@ movenpick. 183 units. A/C TV TEL. $175–$210 double. Rates include breakfast, service charge, and tax. AE, MC, V.

Opened in 1996, this is the top hotel in town, and the best location as well—just steps from the entrance to the Petra National Park. In the tradition of Middle Eastern palaces tucked away amid the labyrinths of walled cities, the Movenpick's contempo-rary exterior is deceptively plain. Inside, however, there are towering atriums dotted with latticed windows; fountain terraces like Arabian nights fantasies, and public areas that seem to have been painted and furnished by medieval master craftsmen from Cairo, Fez, and Marrakech. Relatively spacious guest rooms come with polished stone bathrooms that are pleasant but not luxurious. Included in the complex are a medium-size outdoor swimming pool that is covered and heated in winter, a fitness center, sauna, and steam bath, and a wood-paneled library with reading material about Petra and Jordan. There are a number of restaurants and cafes; on the roof garden, guests can meet in the evenings and talk over their adventures amid strawberry-flavored

Petra

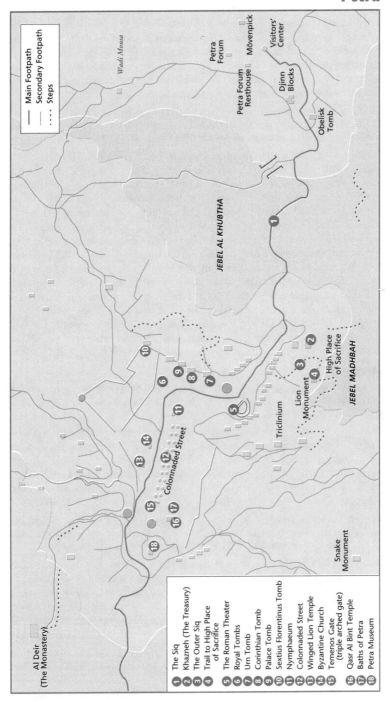

- 1 The Siq
- 2 Khazneh (The Treasury)
- 3 The Outer Siq
- 4 Trail to High Place of Sacrifice
- 5 The Roman Theater
- 6 Royal Tombs
- 7 Urn Tomb
- 8 Corinthian Tomb
- 9 Palace Tomb
- 10 Sextius Florentinus Tomb
- 11 Nymphaeum
- 12 Colonnaded Street
- 13 Winged Lion Temple
- 14 Byzantine Church
- 15 Temenos Gate (triple arched gate)
- 16 Qasr Al Bint Temple
- 17 Baths of Petra
- 18 Petra Museum

nargilehs and the kind of camaraderie you seldom find in hotels of this class. There are rooms for travelers with disabilities, three bars, a shopping arcade with arts and crafts galleries, a local pastry shop, and a Movenpick bakery. Check with Movenpick's central reservations for special discount periods. In summer, a standard double can be as low as $125, including breakfast, tax, and service. Dinner buffet, at $18, is the best in town, and visited by many from outside the hotel.

✪ **Taybet Zeman Hotel and Resort.** Petra. P.O. Box 2 Wadi Musa, Petra. ☎ **03/ 215-0111.** Fax 03/215-0101. A/C MINIBAR TV TEL. $170–$200 double; $700 royal suite. Rates include breakfast. Add 13% for tax and 10% service. AE, DC, MC, V.

Taybet Zeman is the most beautiful and unusual hostelry in Jordan. The rustic buildings of an abandoned 19th- to early 20th-century village, 5 miles from Petra, have been renovated and decorated in a Bedouin-style chic that could easily grace the pages of *Architectural Digest.* (Indeed, Taybet Zeman has been featured in a number of interior design and architecture publications.) Everything has been carefully done. The rooms have hidden heating and air-conditioning, and such modern amenities as minibars are blended into the hotel's design. The complex, with its quality tribal crafts for sale in rustic shops and galleries, reminds one of Santa Fe. There is a small swimming pool, Jacuzzi, sauna, a fitness center, an attentive staff, and spectacular vistas of the countryside. A traditional bakery and a variety of restaurants are offered. A full range of tourist and guide services for Petra and the vicinity are available. A sumptuous buffet dinner, often accompanied by traditional music is $18 per person. Totally delightful, Taybet Zeman is a memorable addition to the Petra experience. The Royal Suite contains two bedrooms and two bathrooms. The drawback is the taxi ride from the hills down to Petra each morning, and worse, each evening.

MODERATE

Kings' Way Inn. Main St. (P.O. Box 71) Wadi Musa. ☎ **03/215-6799.** Fax 03/215-6796. E-mail: nebo@nets.com.jo. 77 units. A/C TV TEL. $80–$110 double. Add 10% service charge and 13% tax. AE, DC, MC, V.

Built in 1994, this is a comfortable modern choice with spacious rooms, a touch of traditional style and an efficient staff. The pluses include a swimming pool, 24-hour room service, and pleasant extras like hair dryers in bathrooms. The hotel is located at Ain Musa, at the far end of sprawling Wadi Musa from the entrance to Petra, 4km (6.4 mi.) away. There are good, affordable but comparatively pricey breakfast and dinner buffets.

Petra Crowne Plaza. P.O. Box 30, Wadi Musa. ☎ **03/215-6266.** Fax 03/215-6977; reservations through Bass Hotels & Resorts. E-mail: petrafh@nets.com.jo. 146 units. A/C MINIBAR TV TEL. $130–$140 double. Add 10% service charge and 13% tax. AE, DC, MC.

Located on a slight hill above the entrance to Petra, until recently this modern, very professional hotel was the most expensive and luxurious lodging in the Petra area. The hotel has a swimming pool, a number of restaurants, comfortable rooms, and an experienced staff. You can obtain good touring information here and the hotel will even send you off on your explorations with a picnic box. There are suites, which are useful for families; slightly more expensive standard rooms offer more interesting views.

Petra Palace. P.O. Box 70, Wadi Musa. ☎ **03/215-6723.** Fax 03/215-6724. E-mail: ppwnwm@go.com.jo. 83 units. A/C MINIBAR TV TEL. $80 double. Add 10% service charge and 13% tax. AE, MC, V.

Located on the block of hotels and restaurants leading up to the entrance to Petra, this new, pleasantly decorated hotel is very comfortable and a comparative bargain. Guest rooms have pleasant extras such as hair dryers; amenities include a medium-size landscaped swimming pool, an in-house bar and restaurant, underground parking, a business center, and fitness room.

INEXPENSIVE

Al Anbat 1 Hotel. P.O. Box 43 Wadi Musa, Petra. ☎ **03/215/6265.** Fax 03/215-6888. 40 units. TV TEL. $21 double. Rates include breakfast, tax, and service. MC, V.

Located at the edge of Wadi Musa, with beautiful views and a location overlooking great sunsets, the modern Al Anbat 1 has spiffy though uneven decor and attracts the backpacking crowd. Private rooms are basic but comfortable, with fans; air-conditioning may be available. There is camping for $2, a dorm in the basement at $6 a bed, and endless screenings of *Indiana Jones,* as well as free transportation to Petra. The newer Al Anbat 2 (☎ **03/215-7200;** fax 03/215-6888), built in 1996, is a small six-story tower in the center of Wadi Musa with 20 slightly nicer rooms, but without the overview of the sunset. I'd go for the sunset, an occasion that adds to Anbat 1's congeniality. When making reservations, specify which hotel you prefer.

✪ **El Rashid Hotel.** Main Traffic Circle, P.O. Box 96, Wadi Musa, Petra. ☎ **03/215-6800.** Fax 03/215-6810. 40 units. A/C TV TEL. $20 per person in a double room (no single supplement). Rates include breakfast. Add $8 per person for half-board. DC, MC, V.

In the heart of bustling Wadi Musa, 5 kilometers (3 mi.) from the entrance to Petra, you'll find the friendly El Rashid with large, clean, carpeted rooms and free transport to Petra. Of the many hotels that have sprung up in Wadi Musa, this one is the best value in its price range and offers very good meals in its dining room.

Petra Guest House and Hotel. P.O. Box 30 Wadi Musa. ☎ **03/215-6246;** reservations through Petra Crowne Plaza. Fax 03/215-6977. E-mail: petrafh@nets.com.jo. 74 units. A/C MINIBAR TEL TV. $84.50 double. Add 10% service charge and 13% tax. Breakfast not included. AE, DC, MC, V.

The best choice in the inexpensive range is this well-located place, right at the entrance to the siq of Petra and under the management of the Petra Crowne Plaza. The rooms are clean and simple, though not air-conditioned, and all rooms have private bathrooms. The building is somewhat bland but the restaurant has been built into an ancient Nabatean tomb, and travelers you meet here tend to be interesting people. When making fax reservations, be sure to specify you want the Petra Guest House, as the number is also used for another hotel. All guest staying at the Guest House have access to the facilities of the Petra Crowne Plaza.

4 Side Trips in Jordan

NORTH OF AMMAN

Travel agencies in Amman can arrange private or group tours to important sites throughout the country.

JERASH & AJLOUN CASTLE

An interesting excursion from Amman is to the Hellenistic/Roman ruined city of **Jerash,** 50 kilometers (80 mi.) north of Amman. The impressive, beautifully preserved ruins of the city include buildings from Byzantine and early Muslim periods; the entire setting is quite lovely. Excavations began in the 1920s and are still going on today. Guided tours are very rewarding and can easily be arranged through agencies in Amman.

A 24-kilometer (15-mi.), 30-minute drive west of Jerash brings you to the Islamic castle of **Ajloun,** built in 1184 by a nephew of Saladin as a defense structure against

Getting Connected in Amman

Books@Cafe (☎ **06/465-0457;** www.books-cafe.com) is the most fun and atmospheric place to get connected in Amman. It's located near the First Circle on Omar bin Khattab Street, around the corner from Jordan River Crafts, in a neighborhood filled with old stone bungalows and villas. Computer access is $3.50 an hour, but the cafe is also a meeting place where travelers and Jordanians connect in person over a menu that ranges from Tex-Mex to iced mocha lattes. There is a film program here, with weekly showings; live music many nights a week (cover charge $1.50); cantaloupe, mint, mango and grape-flavored nargilehs; an excellent array of Green Mountain coffees; a tiny bookshop, art, and photo exhibits; and a small but good selection of Jordanian tribal crafts for sale.

marauding Crusaders. The well-preserved, atmospheric castle offers dramatic views of the Jordan Valley and a good part of the rich countryside of northern Jordan.

The dramatic structures of Jerash are the venue for the **Jerash Festival of the Performing Arts,** which features local and international folklore troops, theater, ballet and opera performances, concerts, and sales of Jordanian crafts. The Jerash Festival is held each year for 2 weeks in July (contact Jordanian Tourism Information offices for current information). The **Jerash Visitors' Center** (☎ **04/451-272**), near the South Gate of the city, is open daily from 7:30am to 7pm (until 8pm in summer) sells books and maps of Jerash and can arrange group or private tours. **The Jerash Archeological Museum** (☎ **04/452-267**) is open Saturday to Thursday from 8:30am to 5pm (to 6pm in summer); closed Fridays. **Ajloun Castle** is open daily 8am to 5pm; till 6 or 7pm in summer. Admission is JD 1 ($1.40).

Where to Dine

❂ **Um Khalil's Lebanese House Restaurant.** Ajloun Rd. 5 min. drive west of the ruins of Jerash. ☎ **04/451-301.** Reservations recommended on Fri. Appetizers $1–$3.75; main courses $3–$15; mezze for two $14. No credit cards. Daily 9am–midnight. ARABIC.

One of the best Arabic restaurants in the Middle East, and crowded with Jordanians from Amman on Fridays and holidays, the Lebanese House is famous for its *mezze,* a large selection of traditional appetizers and salads, seasoned with herbs and spices that are grown in the restaurant's own gardens. Um Khalil (mother of Khalil) is actually Mme Antoinette Rami, originally of Beirut, and her kitchen turns out unusual specialties, like quail in wine and mushrooms, and *shinklish,* a traditional dish of seasoned cheese fried in olive oil. In good weather, visitors can dine overlooking a large, delightful garden surrounded by pomegranate trees and views of the terraced hills and countryside.

SOUTH OF AMMAN HIGHLIGHTS BETWEEN AMMAN & PETRA
MEDABA & MOUNT NEBO

The city of **Medaba,** 33 kilometers (20 mi.) south of Amman, offers a rich collection of remarkable Byzantine-era mosaic floors, including one that contains the famous **Medaba Map,** a 25-by-5-meter representation of the entire eastern Mediterranean as it was 15 centuries ago, with a detailed depiction of Jerusalem at its center. Medaba was a center for mosaic artists in the Byzantine period, and the works of the town's mosaic craftsmen adorned 5th- and 6th-century Medaba as well as the surrounding region. On the main street of modern Medaba, the Church of St. George (Greek

Orthodox) was built in 1896 over the famous **Medaba Map,** once the mosaic floor of a 6th-century Byzantine church. The original floor was made up of 2.3 million pieces of mosaic stones. Of special interest is the mosaic's depiction of Jerusalem (the oldest known representation of that city), showing the classical column-lined main streets that archaeologists have discovered indeed existed in Byzantine-era Jerusalem. The Church of St. George is open Monday to Thursday and Saturday 8:30am to 6pm, Friday and Sunday 10:30am to 6pm; admission is JD 1. Nearby, the Medaba Museum, the Archaeological Park, and the Apostles Church display a large group of Byzantine-era mosaic floors as well as a folklore exhibit and other local antiquities. Open daily 8am to 4pm; combined admission JD 3. Across the street and slightly to the right of the Church of St. George, a number of shops sell locally made kilim (flat-weave) rugs; 300 yards up the street to the left, you'll find **Haret Jdoudna,** a charmingly restored, century-old courtyard complex for tourists containing craft shops, a pizzeria with wood-burning oven, and a restaurant good for light Middle Eastern meals. If you have a car and are hungry, a more serious dining option is the rustic Syaga Restaurant (see below) on the road between Medaba and Mt. Nebo.

From Medaba, you have two choices for traveling further south. The first is to travel on the old King's Highway, through some of the most dramatic mountain country in Jordan, and visit **Kerak,** the most massive and best preserved of the Crusader castles in the region. The castle is open daily 8am to 5pm; admission is JD 1 ($1.40). In the town of Kerak, below the castle, you'll find **Kan Zeman Kerak** (☎ **03/355-102**), a traditional Bedouin/Jordanian-style restaurant in a beautifully restored 19th-century fortified desert villa. It's run by the same management as the Taybet Zeman resort village overlooking Petra, and the Kan Zeman Restaurant complex outside Amman, and is a delightful place to stop for lunch buffet midway between Amman and Petra. The buffet is $16. Phone numbers in the area are being upgraded to seven digits during the time span of this edition; Jordan Tourism Investment Co. in Amman (☎ **06/ 553-7677**), or Taybet Zeman Resort Hotel near Petra (☎ **03/215-0111**), can give you the current phone number for reservations.

The second choice is to descend the steep winding road toward the Dead Sea, where you can visit the remarkable **Hammamat Ma'in,** a series of natural hot springs and waterfalls, some of which have been channeled into pools and baths. King Herod frequented the springs here, and built a villa for himself at nearby Mukawer. It was at this palace that in later years, Salome danced, and, according to tradition, John the Baptist was beheaded (Matt. 14: 1–12). Further south along the Jordanian shore of the Dead Sea are two excellent spa resorts.

Where to Dine

✪ **Syaga Restaurant.** 10-min. drive south of Medaba on road to Mt. Nebo. ☎ **08/ 540643;** 079-36391 (mobile phone). Reservations recommended. Lunch buffet noon–6pm JD 7 ($10); main courses JD 3–6 ($4.20–$7). No credit cards. Daily 8am–midnight.

This roadside restaurant serves a bountiful all-you-can-eat luncheon buffet that contains more than 25 hot and cold choices and also includes dessert. Try to visit in time for an early lunch, when all the courses are freshly cooked and set out on display—everything is good, but the oven-baked lamb is absolutely superb! A new rough stone wing with Bedouin rugs and vistas of the olive trees and countryside behind the restaurant is more atmospheric than the first dining area just inside the front door. Country-style breakfasts are served from 8am to 11am for JD 3 or 4 ($4.20 or $5.60).

The trip from Amman to Medaba can easily be combined with an excursion further south to the nearby cascading hot springs at **Zarqa Ma'in,** and to **Mount Nebo,** where according to tradition, Moses died and was buried. The views from Mount

Nebo are dramatic, and on clear days include the towers of Jerusalem, crowning the mountains far beyond the Dead Sea (prophetically, the one glimpse of the Promised Land Moses was granted, included the city that would one day become the Land's spiritual center). A modern church with a towering, sculptural cross has been built on the site of a 4th-century church that by the 7th century had been expanded into a large monastery complex and pilgrimage center. Elements of a triple-apse Byzantine basilica were uncovered by archaeologists in the 1930s, and have been incorporated into the structure of the modern church building, which displays archaeological finds and exceptional ancient mosaic floors. In summer the church is open daily from 9am to 5pm; in summer until 7pm. Admission is 500 fils (70¢).

Other Attractions

Zarqa Ma'in. 30km (48 mi.) southwest of Medaba. Admission JD 2 ($2.80); combined general, Roman Bath and pool admission JD 4 ($5.60). Open daily 24 hours.

This large area of the hot springs and cascades is entered through one access road, across which is an entrance gate where admission fees are paid. The main entrance gate is open 24 hours; a JD 2 admission fee lets you into the area, but a higher admission fee also includes entry to the Roman Bath and steam room, and the swimming pool at the Ashtar Hotel, which is inside the Wadi Zarqa Ma'in gorge. The torrential waterfalls, ranging from 105°F to a scalding 150°F, are what's really unusual here (there is a special fenced-in "family" waterfall, safer for women, to the side of the Ashtar Hotel). Many visitors enjoy just finding an isolated collection pool amid the rocks and relaxing in relative solitude. Daily Jett buses leave Amman each morning at 8am for Zarqa Ma'in. Round-trip ticket, including all admissions and a simple lunch, is JD 10 ($14). Return is at 5pm (4pm in winter). A round-trip taxi from Medaba, including a reasonable wait at the springs, should run around JD 8 to 10 ($11.20 to $14) depending on your bargaining skills. Ma'in is impossibly crowded on Fridays, and very busy in the spring and autumn.

JORDAN'S DEAD SEA SPAS

A 30-minute drive from Medaba to the eastern shore of the Dead Sea brings you to **Sweimeh,** the area of the Jordanian side of the Dead Sea where a resort center has begun to develop. This side of the Dead Sea is far more tranquil than the booming high-rise resort center across the lake in Israel. The atmosphere at these hotels on the Jordanian shore is very restful, and you'll feel more in touch with the desert and the quiet of the surrounding wilderness (in addition, Jordanian hotel rates are also much lower). Despite the isolation of the area, the spa hotels are beautiful, and professional in every way, offering a good selection of health, therapeutic, and beauty treatment packages. In addition to the Dead Sea Spa Hotel, and the new Movenpick Hotel, with its fascinating desert-style architecture, a Marriott resort is slated to open here during the time span of this edition. If you're coming from Amman to stay at one of these spa hotels, it is a 50-minute taxi ride that will cost approximately $30.

Dead Sea Spa Hotel. Sweimeh, Jordan. ☎ **06/560-1554.** Fax 06/568-8100. E-mail: dssh@nets.com.jo. 100 units. A/C MINIBAR TV TEL. $100–$120 double. Rates include breakfast. Add 10% service and 13% tax. AE, DC, MC.

Built in the mid-1990s, this airy white complex with gardened terraces and a large freshwater pool overlooking a sandy beach dotted with thatched shelters is a peaceful enclave right on the Dead Sea. Guest rooms are large and comfortable, both in the main four-story structure, or in bungalows around the gardens. There is a comfortable restaurant, with an $18 fixed-price lunch or dinner buffet; a beach cafe and indoor pool bar. Other facilities include outdoor, heated, and children's pools, as well as a Jacuzzi and two night-lit tennis courts. Doctors are in attendance at the in-house medical center, which offers dermatology and relaxation programs. Packages for mud pack, physiotherapy, and beauty treatments are also available. Tours and car rental can be arranged from the hotel.

✪ **Movenpick Dead Sea Resort and Spa.** Sweimeh, Jordan. ☎ **05/325-2030.** Fax 05/325-2020. E-mail: dseamp@globalone.com.jo. 230 units. A/C TV TEL. $190–$220 double. Rates include breakfast, tax, and service. AE, DC, MC, V.

Using elements of traditional desert rock and plaster architecture, Movenpick has created a new (1999), exotic Dead Sea retreat, that is a pleasure to the eye and fun to explore as well. The complex is a low-rise labyrinth of arches, covered passageways, and terraces that give the feeling of an old traveler's *khan*, or inn. Guest rooms are tastefully decorated; all have balconies with flowering vines. There are large swimming pools, mineral baths, beautiful stretches of Dead Sea Beach, and an exotically designed Wellness Spa and Fitness Center run by the Sanctuary of London. You can arrange 3- to 7-night packages with board, as well as a large variety of Dead Sea therapeutic, massage, and beauty treatments. The Asian, Italian, Grill, and Buffet restaurants are all up to Movenpick's strict Swiss standards. In winter (except Christmas) and much of the summer, rates go down to $140 to $153 for a standard double, including breakfast, service, and tax. There are full-board plans for an additional $36 per person— something to consider, since there are no restaurants in the region. Most visitors do very well, however, on the buffet breakfast and the $21 buffet dinner. There are special rooms for travelers with disabilities. A full range of five-star facilities and services are offered.

AQABA

For decades, travelers to Eilat were tantalized by the green, palm-dotted shoreline of Aqaba, just across the curve of beach shared by both cities on the northern curve of the narrow Red Sea. The 1994 peace treaty between Jordan and Israel has made it possible for tourists to cross into Jordan at an inland point just north of the two cities after going through border procedures and paying exit and visa fees, but you still cannot simply walk or taxi back and forth between Eilat and Aqaba. All this is due to change, perhaps during the time span of this edition, as plans to unify both cities into a single tourist zone develop, and a joint international airport opens exactly on the border between Israel and Jordan.

Aqaba, like Eilat, is a port city with a tourism industry based on the fragile, ecologically endangered **coral reefs** just below the surface of its sparkling, clear waters—Jordan, Israel, and Egypt are working jointly to preserve the incredible reef system of the Gulf of Aqaba. The Aqaba shoreline is longer than Eilat's and contains richer, more varied reefs. When the joint tourist zone develops, travelers to Eilat will be diving and snorkeling in Aqaba's waters and using Aqaba's dive centers.

Aqaba is quieter than Eilat, but at press time, it is going through the kind of frantic reconstruction of its tourism infrastructure that Eilat went through in the early 1990s. Small, pleasant but undistinguished hotels built in the 1960s, '70s, and '80s are being torn down to build up-to-the-minute megahotels that can compete with Eilat's choices, and a shoreline promenade that will connect the two towns is under development. For the moment, the beaches are less friendly to women alone, but that will change as Aqaba becomes more of an international tourism destination.

Where to Stay

The top-quality choice in Aqaba is the **Movenpick Aqaba Resort,** slated to open in the first half of 2000. Right on the beach, and part of a tourism promenade complex that will extend to downtown Eilat, the Movenpick will offer the highest standards for guest rooms, in-house restaurants, amenities, and services, all at rates that will be a bargain compared to those at similar hotels in Eilat. Movenpick International Reservations will have all information on this hotel.

The best moderate hotel choice is the modern, 192-room **Aqaba Gulf Hotel** (☎ **03/201-6636;** fax 03/201-8426), on the Beach Corniche just beyond the downtown center. A double room with air-conditioning, TV, telephone, and refrigerator—comfortable, but nothing special, is $124 plus 13% tax and 10% service. The pool is large and the location is close to downtown restaurants. A good travel agent can get you in here at discount rates.

A good inexpensive hotel choice is the centrally located, 32-room **Shweiki Hotel,** Hammamat Street, town center (☎ **03/202-2657;** fax 03/202-2659). A standard double room is $45 to $60, plus 13% tax and 10% service; all major credit cards are accepted. Guest rooms all have private bathroom, air-conditioning, minibar, TV, and telephone; guests receive a free voucher for the large pool at the nearby Aqaba Gulf Hotel.

Where to Dine

Ali Baba Restaurant. Town Center. ☎ **03/201-3901.** $5–$15 full meals. AE, DC, MC, V. Daily 8am–11pm.

With an outdoor dining terrace facing the central square, this is a meeting place both for Jordanians and the foreign community; it has a large menu of Middle Eastern dishes, good grilled meat, fresh grilled fish, pastas, and excellent curry. The grilled *shish taok* (garlic chicken) is a specialty; wine and beer are served as are breakfasts.

✪ Captain's Restaurant. Next to Aquamarina II Hotel. ☎ **03/201-6905.** Reservations necessary for dinner. Main courses $4.20–$11.20; set-menu dinners $12.60–$9.80. MC, V. Daily 9am–11pm.

Shaped like a ship, this tiny, busy place serves delicious fresh fish and seafood, as well as chicken and meat dishes, and good, small, Arabic seafood and mezze dishes. Soft drinks and nonalcoholic beer served. Reservations are essential at night.

Royal Yacht Club. Town Center, at the Main Corniche. ☎ **03/202-2404.** Reservations necessary. Meals $11–$20. MC, V. Daily 11:30am–3:30pm and 7:30–11:30pm.

The best, most elegant restaurant in town, run by Jordan's top-quality Romero's of Amman, this is a calm, dignified place to dine. There is a spacious dining room, a terrace overlooking the marina, and a menu that includes excellent pastas, fish, and seafood. There is an adjacent bar.

Diving Centers

The **✪ Royal Diving Center** is located 17 kilometers (27 mi.) south of Aqaba (☎ **03/201-7035;** fax 03/201-7097). With its own private beach beside a superb reef, this is the best run snorkeling and diving center in Aqaba, offering a complete array of equipment rentals, lessons, dives and diving tours. There are lockers, changing rooms, and a snack bar, making this a nice place to spend the day. A shuttle bus (JD 1/$1.40) picks guests up from the hotel district at 9am and returns to town at 5pm. Open daily 9am to 5pm in summer; 9am to 4pm in winter. Admission is JD 2 ($2.80); mask, fins, and snorkel rental is JD 3 ($4.20); taxi from town is JD 3 ($4.20).

Appendix A:
Israel in Depth

To millions of Jews, Christians, and Muslims, Israel is the Holy Land where Solomon reigned in all his glory, where Jesus died on the cross, and where Muhammad visited during a miraculous night journey.

Religion is the basis of Israel's political importance. Were it not for its sacred character, few people would choose to live on this narrow strip of land between the sea and desert. Jews have been living here since the time of Abraham, almost 4,000 years ago; Christianity began in the Galilee 2 millennia later. During the very early days of Islam in the 7th century A.D., before Mecca became a sacred city, the Prophet Muhammad advised Muslims to face in the direction of Jerusalem for prayers.

All three religions have battled to capture and hold the holy territory: Israelites fought Canaanites, Philistines, Assyrians, and Babylonians; Jews fought Hellenists and Romans; and Muslim armies fought Crusaders. In the 20th century, Muslim Turks were driven out by the British, and the British in turn were driven out by groups of Zionists and Palestinian Arabs.

Israel looms large in the great political happenings of our times. Realizing the ancient Jewish dream of a homeland has meant the displacement of many Palestinians, which, in turn, has meant alienating the surrounding Arab countries in the already unstable Middle East. The problem of finding a truly fair solution to the many valid and conflicting claims on the Holy Land is one of the great challenges facing the Christian, Jewish, and Muslim communities in Israel and throughout the world.

1 The Natural Environment

Israel is a surprisingly small country, but the land itself is remarkably varied and contains some of the earth's most unusual geological oddities. Depending on your itinerary, you are likely to find anything from beaches to lush valleys rugged, wooded mountains rambling foothills, flat plains, snowcapped peaks, the hot wilderness that surrounds the mineral-saturated waters of the Dead Sea, desert regions, and the multicolored crags and crevices of the Negev. There are coral reefs teeming with rare marine life off Eilat and the Sinai Peninsula, and vast erosion craters in the Negev near Mitspe Ramon, that are geological encyclopedias of the eons. The mineral-laden Dead Sea (in which it is impossible to sink) is by far the lowest point on the face of the earth—the dense atmosphere at this extremely low altitude is heavy with oxygen, and beneficial to those with heart and respiratory problems; it also blocks some of the sun's rays and permits psoriasis sufferers to expose their skin for longer periods of time without risk of sunburn. The dramatic geology of the country also brings a varied climate. It can be a raw, cold, sleety January day in Jerusalem, in the Judean Mountains, and an hour away, at the Jordan Valley oasis of Jericho or at Ein Gedi, a canyon near the Dead Sea, it can be sunny, dry, and 75°F!

Israel is part of a land bridge connecting Africa and Asia. The below sea-level Jordan Valley, running along the Israeli-Jordanian border, is a northern continuation of the Great Rift Valley of Eastern Africa, which runs through the Red Sea and surfaces at Eilat-Aqaba. Since prehistoric times, this has been a natural route of migration for birds, animals, and human beings. The enormously varied flora, fauna and peoples who have come to inhabit this small region are a reflection of Israel's unique location and geological structure.

2 History 101

Dateline

- **600,000 B.C.** Early human habitation of caves in Carmel Mountains near Haifa.
- **15,000 B.C.** Appearance of farming settlements in the Galilee and Jordan Valley.
- **7000 B.C.** Defensive wall built around Jericho in the Jordan Valley. Early domestication of animals. Evidence of early centers for cult and fertility worship.
- **4500–3100 B.C.** Towns develop at Bet Shean, Ein Gedi, Megiddo, and Beersheva.
- **3100 B.C.** Start of Early Canaanite era; development of cities.
- **1600 B.C.** Hebrews enslaved in Egypt.
- **1250 B.C.** Exodus of Hebrews under Moses. Early Canaanite-Hebrew alphabet begins to develop.
- **1100 B.C.** Israelite tribes settle in much of Canaanite highlands. Philistine people occupy Canaanite coast. Deborah judges loose confederation of Israelite tribes.
- **1025 B.C.** Saul anointed first Israelite king by the prophet Samuel.

continues

Recorded Jewish history dates from the time of Abraham, between 2000 and 1800 B.C. Many elements of the patriarchal chronicles have been confirmed as accurate by recent archaeological discoveries. Modern scientific methods reveal that human beings have lived in the Holy Land since the Old Stone Age, some 600,000 years ago. But a history so deep and full of universal significance is almost impossible to grasp in its entirety. I've provided an outline of the major periods before 1917.

A BRIEF LOOK AT THE PAST In Israel's museums, and at Israel's archaeological sites, you will encounter the terms used to define the many time periods in Israel's long history.

Old Stone Age (600,000–12,000 B.C.): Cave dwellers, hand axes, hunting, fire.

Middle Stone Age (12,000–7500 B.C.): Cultivation of grain, more sophisticated tools.

Late Stone Age (7500–4000 B.C.): First villages appear, including Jericho; animal husbandry, irrigation, and pottery begin.

Chalcolithic (Copper) Age (4000–3200 B.C.): Copper used in tools; towns grow; designs show on pottery; a culture develops at Beersheva.

Early Bronze (Canaanite) Age (3200–2200 B.C.): Towns are fortified, temples and palaces built.

Middle Bronze (Canaanite) Age (2200–1550 B.C.): The Age of the Patriarchs; Abraham's travels; trade develops; the Hyksos invade Canaan and Egypt.

Late Bronze (Canaanite) Age (1550–1200 B.C.): Israel captive in Egypt; the alphabet develops; the Exodus from Egypt; Ten Commandments delivered on Mount Sinai; Israel conquers the Promised Land.

Early Iron Age (1200–1020 B.C.): Period of the Judges; Philistine invasion.

Middle Iron Age (1020–842 B.C.): The united monarchy under King Saul and King David (1000 B.C.); Jerusalem is capital of kingdom; in 961 King Solomon builds First Temple; golden age of Israelite culture and power.

Late Iron Age (842–587 B.C.): Period of the later kings and prophets; in 587, destruction of First Temple.

Babylonian and Persian Periods (587–332 B.C.): Israel captive in Babylon, followed by Persian domination; the Second Temple is built; times of Ezra and Nehemiah.

Hellenistic and Maccabean Periods (332–37 B.C.): Domination by Alexander the Great, by the Ptolomies and Seleucids; the Maccabean struggle; Hasmonean Dynasty.

Roman Period (37 B.C.–A.D. 324): Herodian Dynasty; birth of Jesus, his ministry and crucifixion; wars against Rome; Second Temple and Jerusalem destroyed (A.D. 70); fall of Masada (73); Talmud and Mishnah compiled; Bar Kokhba's revolt against Rome (132–35).

Byzantine Period (324–640): Jewish revolt, Byzantine domination; Jerusalem Talmud completed; Persian invasion and sack of Jerusalem (614); birth and rise of Islam in the Middle East.

Arab Period (640–1096): Jerusalem conquered by Islamic armies (638); Arab Empire capital first at Damascus, later Baghdad; joint Christian-Muslim protectorate of holy places; Christian pilgrimage rights curtailed.

The Crusades (1096–1291): First Crusade (1096–99), sack of Jerusalem, Crusader Kingdom under Godfrey of Bouillon. Second Crusade (1147–49): Saladin captures Jerusalem for Islam (1187). Third Crusade (1189–92); Fourth Crusade (1202–04).

Mameluke and Ottoman Turkish Period (1291–1917): Mongols and Seljuks replace Arabs and Byzantines as overlords of the Holy Land; Ottomans conquer Palestine; Suleiman the Magnificent rebuilds Jerusalem; Jews,

- **1004–1000 B.C.** David, second king of Israelites, makes Jerusalem his capital; begins conquest of territories from southern Syria to Eilat.
- **950 B.C.** King Solomon builds First Temple of Jerusalem.
- **928 B.C.** After death of Solomon, David's kingdom divided into Israel in the north, and Judah, with its capital at Jerusalem.
- **870–722 B.C.** Pagan religions flourish. Assyria conquers Kingdom of Israel.
- **701 B.C.** Judah devastated by Assyrian invasion. Jerusalem, led by King Hezekiah and inspired by the prophet Isaiah, remains unconquered.
- **627–586 B.C.** Prophet Jeremiah in Jerusalem.
- **586 B.C.** Nebuchadnezzar destroys Jerusalem and Temple of Solomon. End of First Temple period. Jews exiled to Babylon.
- **540 B.C.** Babylon defeated by Persians. Jews allowed to return to Jerusalem.
- **515 B.C.** Second Temple built upon ruins of Solomon's Temple in Jerusalem.
- **445 B.C.** Ezra the Scribe begins public reading of Torah in Jerusalem.
- **332 B.C.** Alexander the Great conquers Judea. Hellenistic era begins.
- **167 B.C.** Antiochus IV desecrates Jerusalem temple; outlaws Jewish religion.
- **164 B.C.** Judah Maccabee captures Jerusalem; temple rededicated. Judea independent under Maccabee (Hasmonean) Dynasty; borders greatly expanded.
- **63 B.C.** Judea incorporated into Roman Empire.
- **37 B.C.** Romans proclaim Herod the Idumaean king of Judea.
- **18 B.C.** Herod begins vast renovation of Second Temple.

continues

- **8–4 B.C.** Jesus born in Bethlehem.
- **A.D. 62** Completion of Herodian renovation of Second Temple.
- **66–73** Jewish revolt against Rome. Jerusalem and Second Temple captured by Rome and razed; Masada falls.
- **132** Second Revolt against Rome led by Bar Kokhba; ruins of Jerusalem freed; temple service resumed.
- **135** Bar Kokhba defeated. Hadrian orders Jerusalem rebuilt as Aelia Capitolina, a Roman city forbidden to Jews.
- **160–300** Early Talmudic era. Classical synagogues built throughout Holy Land; Galilee center of Jewish population.
- **313–326** Emperor Constantine recognizes Christianity as new religion of Roman Empire. His mother, Queen Helena, visits Holy Land to identify sites of Jesus' life and ministry.
- **326–614** Hundreds of Byzantine churches and monastic communities built. Restrictions against Jews.
- **351** Jews of Galilee rebel against Byzantine/Christians.
- **400** Codification of Palestinian Talmud.
- **614–629** Jerusalem conquered by Persians, recaptured by Byzantines.
- **638** Islamic conquest of Palestine. Omar Ibn El Khattab conquers Jerusalem.
- **691** Dome of the Rock built on Temple Mount.
- **720** El Aksa Mosque built on Temple Mount.
- **1008** Caliph Al Hakim destroys churches and prevents Christian pilgrimage.
- **1099** Crusaders conquer Jerusalem. Muslims and Jews massacred.

continues

expelled from Spain and Italy, welcomed into the Ottoman Empire; Napoléon's campaign in Egypt and Palestine (1799); movement to re-create a Jewish homeland led by Theodor Herzl (1860–1904), published The Jewish State; the first Zionist Congress in Basel (1897).

THE BRITISH MANDATE The Balfour Declaration in 1917 announced British support for the creation of a national home for the Jewish people in Palestine. In 1920, after Great Britain had captured the region of Palestine from the Ottoman Empire at the end of World War I, the League of Nations granted the British a "mandate" to govern Palestine, and Sir Herbert Samuel, a Jew, was named first British high commissioner. In 1922, Great Britain separated Trans-Jordan (present-day Jordan) from British Mandate Palestine and established a separate Arab country in that area.

Within Palestine, enormous progress was made during the first 20 years of British administration. Hospitals and schools were established in both Jewish and Arab areas, and in Jewish areas of the country, dazzlingly modern, planned communities, both urban and agricultural, were built; much desolate land was reclaimed for agricultural use. The Arab population of Palestine resented British policy in the early 1920s, which encouraged Jewish immigration and the development of the Palestinian Jewish community, and almost immediately after the British Mandate took effect, political disorders developed. The era of the British Mandate was characterized by three-way disputes between British, Jewish, and Arab factions and by Arab attacks on Jewish communities, especially in 1921 and 1929. Jewish immigration increased during the early Hitler years. An Arab insurrection from 1936 to 1939 led the British, in 1939, to severely limit Jewish immigration before cutting it off entirely. Thus, during World War II, Jews seeking to escape the Nazi Holocaust in Europe were denied refuge in Palestine. After the outbreak of World War II, political tensions within Palestine diminished somewhat, and the area became an important Allied military base for the Middle East. However, the coming conflict was inevitable. In 1946, Arab and Jewish terrorism against the British increased, the King David Hotel was blown up by a Jewish underground group at odds with Ben-Gurion's more mainstream

Zionist organization, and the cycle of violence rose to new heights.

In November 1947, with Britain abstaining, the United Nations General Assembly voted to partition Palestine into two separate states, one Arab and one Jewish. On May 14, 1948, with the Jewish parts of Jerusalem under Arab siege, with fighting widespread across Palestine, and with 400,000 Arab Palestinian civilians fleeing their homes, the British Mandate ended in shambles, and the State of Israel was proclaimed. The Palestinian state proposed for those areas that remained under Arab control did not come into being. The West Bank and East Jerusalem including the Old City, were annexed to the Kingdom of Jordan. Although most of the international community did not recognize this act, Jordan granted citizenship to all Palestinians under its control, the only Arab nation to do so. Egypt occupied but did not annex the Gaza Strip. Its inhabitants were declared stateless.

THE MAKING OF AN INDEPENDENT STATE In the beginning of the State of Israel's history there was enormous exhilaration, but also a grim determination. The double weight of the horrors of World War II and the enormous casualties suffered in the 1948–49 War of Independence drove the country to hang on, to protect every sand dune, to force life out of the desert, and to create a haven for any Jews who might ever find themselves in danger. Life was austere in the newly won state. For years, food, clothing, razor blades, and paint were severely rationed as the country struggled to survive as well as to feed and shelter the thousands of new immigrants who arrived each month. In less than a decade, the nation's population quadrupled as hundreds of thousands of Holocaust survivors from Europe and Jewish refugees from the Middle East arrived and were absorbed. Hundreds of thousands more were added in the 1960s as the Jewish communities of North Africa fled to safer havens in France and Israel.

Slowly, with enormous effort, conditions grew more stable. Basic housing was built, uprooted people began to develop new identities, and although life was still spartan (Ben-Gurion and the founding fathers refused to allow television stations to be established in Israel, claiming that the nation had more

- **1187** Saladin recaptures Jerusalem from crusaders.
- **1189–91** Third Crusade. Crusader Kingdom along coast with Akko as capital.
- **1240** Turkish armies plunder Jerusalem.
- **1261** Mongols devastate countryside.
- **1267** Postcrusader Jewish community reestablished in Jerusalem.
- **1291** Mameluke conquest. Akko falls; end of Crusader Kingdom.
- **1517** Ottoman Turkish conquest of Jerusalem.
- **1538** Ottoman Sultan Suleiman the Magnificent orders walls of Jerusalem rebuilt.
- **1550** Safed becomes center of Jewish scholarship and mysticism.
- **1569** Recodification of normative Judaism (Shulkan Aruckh) in Safed.
- **1776** Jezzar Pasha rebuilds Akko.
- **1799** Napoléon attacks but fails to win Akko.
- **1841** First Protestant mission in Jerusalem.
- **1863** First Hebrew newspaper in Jerusalem.
- **1870** Mikvah Yisrael, first agricultural school, founded.
- **1878** Petah Tikva, near Jaffa and Rosh Pinna, in Galilee, first Jewish farming settlements, founded.
- **1882** First aliyah from Europe and Jewish immigration from Yemen.
- **1897** First Zionist Congress in Basel.
- **1898** Herzl meets German kaiser in Jerusalem.
- **1909** Tel Aviv founded.
- **1911** First kibbutz founded at Degania in the Galilee.
- **1914** Jews from Russia and Allied countries expelled by Ottoman Turks.
- **1917** Balfour Declaration supporting Jewish national

continues

home in Palestine. British free Jerusalem from Turks.

- **1920** Official start of British Mandate.
- **1922** British create Trans-Jordan (now Jordan) from Palestinian lands east of the Jordan River.
- **1925** Hebrew University founded in Jerusalem.
- **1929** Arab-Jewish riots. Jews massacred at Hebron.
- **1936–39** Arab strikes and uprisings.
- **1939** British White Paper curtails Jewish immigration on eve of World War II.
- **1939–45** Six million Jews killed by Nazis in Europe.
- **1947** United Nations votes partition of Palestine into Jewish and Arab states. First Dead Sea Scrolls found.
- **1948** State of Israel declared. Five Arab countries attack.
- **1949–56** Cease-fire. Terrorist attacks on Negev from Egypt.
- **1956** Israel joins Anglo-French attack on Egypt. Conquers Sinai Peninsula.
- **1957** Israel returns Sinai. United Nations peace-keeping force installed in Egypt.
- **1967** Egypt expels peace-keeping force. Israel wins Six-Day War, occupies Sinai, Golan, West Bank, and Gaza.
- **1972** Palestinian terrorists massacre Israeli athletes at Munich Olympics.
- **1973** Egypt and Syria attack. Yom Kippur War.
- **1976** Israelis rescue Jewish hostages at Entebbe Airport.
- **1977** Likud wins elections. Sadat of Egypt comes to Jerusalem.
- **1979** Camp David peace treaty with Egypt.
- **1981** Israel bombs atomic reactor in Iraq.
- **1982** Israel invades Lebanon.

continues

important things to attend to), the country began to flourish. Modern farming and irrigation, along with dedication, made the desert bloom, and the long season ensured by the Mediterranean sun made marginal land wonderfully fruitful. Jaffa oranges, Israeli tomatoes and avocados, and the wines of Mount Carmel became famous. But even more important than its agriculture were Israel's developing industries. Today, the country manufactures its own tools and machinery, arms and airplanes, and is becoming an extremely important center for high-tech electronics. It also supports a burgeoning diamond and fashion industry—Israeli designs are highly regarded throughout the world. The Dead Sea, heavily saturated with minerals, has only begun to be exploited. Oil, however, must be imported. Israel's brilliant medical community, scientific establishment, and computer industries may one day benefit the entire region.

WAR & THE SEARCH FOR PEACE

During the Suez War of November 1956, Great Britain and France invaded Egypt in order to secure the Suez Canal, which Egypt had nationalized, and Israel, in coordination with Great Britain and France, conquered Egypt's Sinai Peninsula and the Gaza Strip hoping to put an end to 9 years of Egyptian terrorist attacks on southern Israel. In exchange for the stationing of a United Nations peacekeeping force on the Egyptian side of the Israeli-Sinai border, and with promises of freedom to send its shipping through the Red Sea and the Suez Canal, Israel withdrew entirely from the Sinai Peninsula and Gaza in early 1957. Ten years of relative peace followed, punctuated by periodic Syrian sniping attacks on the Galilee from Syrian batteries on the Golan Heights.

Then, in May 1967, the United Nations peacekeeping force that had maintained security on the Israeli-Egyptian border for 10 years was unilaterally ordered out by Egypt's President Gamal Abdel Nasser, in violation of international guarantees. At the same time, Nasser blockaded the port of Eilat on the Red Sea, economically strangling Israel, while from the Golan Heights, Syria stood ready to attack the Galilee. For Israelis, only too aware that the nation was less than 10 miles wide at Tel Aviv, and that the Jordanian Army in East Jerusalem was aimed point blank at Jewish West Jerusalem, the agony of these weeks, while the

Israeli government tired to rally international diplomatic support, was unbearable. The pace of Arab propaganda against Israel reached new pitches of frenzy and Arab armies mobilized to deliver what was claimed would be a crushing blow.

On June 5, 1967, Israel made a preemptive strike against the air forces of Egypt and Syria; Jordan, despite diplomatic pleas that it stay out of the conflict, began to shell West Jerusalem. In the Six-Day War that followed, Israel swept to an unimaginable victory, occupying the Sinai Peninsula, the Gaza Strip, the Golan Heights, East Jerusalem, and the entire West Bank. The Egyptian blockade of Eilat was broken. The Arab world was left in a state of shock. Suddenly Israel was no longer a struggling state hanging on tenaciously to its hard-won independence. Land areas had more than trebled. Infusions of new immigrants swelled the country's Jewish population. The economy was burgeoning and tourism was increasing at a rate greater than ever before.

For travelers, Israel, with its artifacts, excavations, and kibbutzim, always had a lot to offer. After the 1967 war, it had more. Most important of all, there was united Jerusalem, the Western (Wailing) Wall, the Levantine veneer of the Old City. For Christians, Israel became a synonym for the entire Holy Land. Both sides of Jerusalem were joined together. Concrete walls and barbed-wire fences that had divided the Israeli and Jordanian sides of the city became things of the past. In the early days of what most hoped would be a short and benign occupation, Israelis and tourists alike enjoyed the exotic bazaars and holy sites of East Jerusalem and the West Bank. Bethlehem, once virtually inaccessible from Israel, was only minutes away from Jerusalem. Jericho, believed to be the oldest city in the world, and Hebron, where the ancient Hebrew patriarchs were buried, were open to visits. In the north, the Golan Heights provided a double meaning: tranquillity in Galilee and a new area for tourist inspection.

- **1984** Labor-Likud Coalition. Withdrawal from most of Lebanon. Aliyah of Ethiopian Jews.
- **1987** Intifada begins.
- **1989** Great Soviet aliyah begins.
- **1991** Iraq attacks with Scud missiles. First peace talks with Arab states in Madrid.
- **1992** Labor Coalition government, headed by Yitzhak Rabin, elected. Rabin pledges new peace effort.
- **1993** Rabin and Arafat sign Declaration of Principles for Peace at White House.
- **1994** Israel withdraws from Jericho and Gaza as first step toward peace with Palestinians. Peace treaty signed with Jordan.
- **1995** Further Israeli withdrawals from West Bank. Prime Minister Rabin assassinated; world leaders attend his funeral in Jerusalem.
- **1996** Likkud Party and Benjamin Netanyahu elected. Traditionally opposed to the Rabin-Arafat Declaration of Principles, Netanyahu pledges to continue peace process.
- **1997** Peace process deteriorates. Terrorist attacks resume; Israeli settlement expansion and land confiscation in West Bank continues.
- **1999** Death of King Hussein of Jordan. Election of more moderate government led by Ehud Barak in Israel.

In the south, there was a new accessibility to the great historic wilderness called Sinai. Eilat, once considered by Israelis as the end of the earth, awoke one morning with a deep and fascinating hinterland. The craggy isolation of the Santa Katerina Monastery, at the base of Mount Sinai where Moses was believed to have received the Ten Commandments, provided an unforgettable experience. Command cars, Jeeps, buses, and airplanes began penetrating the desert that had once sustained the ancient Israelites during their 40-year odyssey from Egypt to the Promised Land.

History of Israel

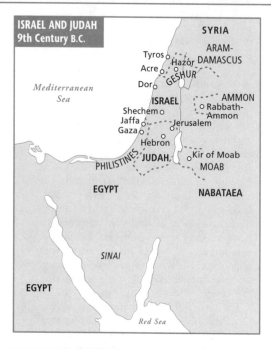

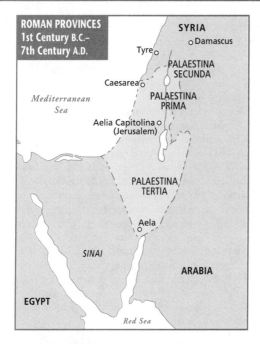

ROMAN PROVINCES
1st Century B.C.–
7th Century A.D.

SYRIA
Damascus
Tyre
PALAESTINA
SECUNDA
Caesarea
PALAESTINA
PRIMA
Mediterranean
Sea
Aelia Capitolina
(Jerusalem)
PALAESTINA
TERTIA
Aela
SINAI
ARABIA
EGYPT
Red Sea

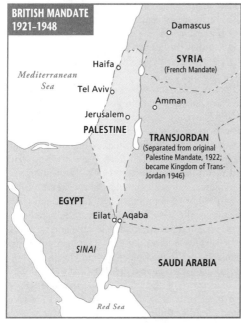

BRITISH MANDATE
1921–1948

Damascus
Haifa
SYRIA
(French Mandate)
Mediterranean
Sea
Tel Aviv
Amman
Jerusalem
PALESTINE
TRANSJORDAN
(Separated from original
Palestine Mandate, 1922;
became Kingdom of Trans-
Jordan 1946)
EGYPT
Eilat Aqaba
SINAI
SAUDI ARABIA
Red Sea

In those days the mood was optimistic. No one any longer questioned the premise that Israel was on the map for good. As the years passed, however, the Arab world continued to refuse to recognize Israel diplomatically, and the plight of the Palestinian refugees scattered throughout the Middle East continued to be ignored by the world at large. In the absence of a peace settlement that would trade most land captured in 1967 for peace, the occupation of the West Bank and the Gaza Strip began to seem less temporary. The small political movement for Jewish settlement of the Occupied Territories began to grow, although initially opposed by the Israeli government. Resentment among the Palestinians under occupation quietly rose.

The country experienced a sharp change in fortune in October 1973. The Yom Kippur War, a completely unexpected simultaneous attack against Israel launched by Egypt and Syria, had a sobering effect on the entire nation. In the first days of the attack, the Golan Heights were almost retaken by Syria, and Egyptian forces, crossing the Suez Canal, overwhelmed Israeli troops in Sinai. More than 2,500 young Israelis were killed in 1 month, losses proportionately higher than the casualties the United States sustained during the entire Vietnam War. Egyptian and Syrian casualties were enormous. While the war ended with Israeli forces closer to Cairo and Damascus than ever before, the initial setbacks and the high cost in lives shook the nation's confidence, and tarnished the images of its leaders. In a backlash, voters turned against the Labor Party, which had led the state since its founding, and elected a new government dominated by the right-of-center Likud led by Menachem Begin.

A few weeks after he assumed office in 1977, Prime Minister Menachem Begin quietly asked neutral intermediaries to arrange a meeting with Egypt's President Sadat anywhere in the world. This set in motion a series of events highlighted by President Sadat's dramatic visit to Jerusalem, the conclusion of a framework for the Middle East peace agreement in Camp David, and the treaty with Egypt in March 1979 terminating 30 years of war between the two countries. Accordingly, Israel withdrew from the Sinai, and Mount Sinai with the Santa Katerina Monastery reverted to Egypt. With the state of peace, it remains open to tourists from Israel.

The hopes for a regional peace agreement, which the Egyptian-Israeli settlement raised, were not quickly realized. No additional Arab countries came forward to negotiate. The 1982 invasion of southern Lebanon put further strains on Israel's relations with its neighbors, and provoked a great deal of debate in every sector of Israeli society. Triple-digit inflation and deteriorating relations with Palestinians in the Occupied Territories, as more land was appropriated for Jewish settlements, marked the early 1980s. The withdrawal from Lebanon and the economic stability achieved under Shimon Peres's brief tenure as prime minister from 1984 to 1986 promised better times, but in late 1987, the Palestinian population of the West Bank and Gaza, under military occupation since 1967, decided it could no longer allow its land and future to be endlessly controlled by Israel. The Intifada, a grassroots program of daily commercial strikes and demonstrations (both violent and nonviolent) against the military authorities, began. The Israeli people suddenly had to face long-postponed decisions about the nature of their democracy, and about how much of their tiny margin of security they dared to trade for uncertain promises of peace. The Intifada continued through the early 1990s.

The year 1990 brought unexpected challenges to Israel, initially with a massive wave of 350,000 immigrants from the dissolving Soviet system, and in the summer of 1990, with the Kuwait crisis. Israel was not a direct participant in the Allied coalition against Iraq; however, in an attempt to win support for his policies throughout the Arab World, Saddam Hussein threatened to "incinerate half of Israel" with missile-borne chemical attacks if the Allied coalition moved against him. The United States asked Israel to refrain from retaliating if it came under attack and pledged that any Iraqi missile threat to Israel would be destroyed by American bombing within the first hours of war. Nevertheless, Israelis found themselves sitting in sealed rooms, experiencing Scud missile attacks almost nightly for the entire 6 weeks of the Gulf War. Iraq's missiles turned out to be armed with high explosives instead of chemical weapons, but the ordeal of the Scuds and their threat of chemical annihilation left its mark on Israeli society. Faced with the prospect of terrible chemical, bacteriological, and nuclear weapons in the future, many Israelis have come to believe it is worth taking extraordinary risks to try to achieve peace and create stability in the Middle East now. Other Israelis are more determined than ever to avoid any further concessions.

THE PEACE PROCESS STALLS Negotiating directly with Palestinians and with moderate Arab governments, Israel began a planned withdrawal from the West Bank and Gaza in 1994. In the same year, a peace treaty was signed with the Kingdom of Jordan. The assassination of Prime Minister Rabin by a Jewish opponent of the peace process in November 1995 was a blow for those who hoped to create a new Middle East. The extraordinary gathering of world leaders for Rabin's funeral in Jerusalem showed the depth of concern throughout the world for the future of the peoples who live in the Holy Land. The hope engendered during Rabin's leadership has not so far been realized, but slowly, dialogue and progress toward peace between Israel, the Palestinians and the Arab World continue.

3 Israel's Famous People

Menachem Begin (1913–1992) Polish-born Zionist leader, arrived in Palestine during World War II, having lost much of his family in the Holocaust, and assumed command of an underground organization responsible for attacks against the British presence in Palestine. Condemned by Ben-Gurion and the Israeli provisional government for these tactics, Begin led the opposition to the Labor governments of 1948–77. He became prime minister in 1977, and presided over the Camp David negotiations and peace treaty with Egypt in 1979. Though he approved the invasion of Lebanon in 1982, he resigned as prime minister in 1983. With Anwar Sadat, he was the recipient of the Nobel Prize for Peace.

David Ben-Gurion (1886–1973) Polish-born Zionist leader, he immigrated to Ottoman-ruled Palestine in 1906. Exiled by Ottoman Turks during World War I, he fled to the United States, where he met his wife, Paula. Ceaseless architect of the emerging Jewish state in the 1920s and 1930s, he became Israel's first prime minister and led the country in the 1948 War of Independence. Deeply committed to the land, a visionary who believed Israel's future lay in the development of the desert, he retired to the Negev kibbutz of Sde Boker after his final term in office. In the euphoria after the 1967 war, Ben-Gurion urged magnanimous terms for a peace settlement, including the return of conquered lands. He lived just long enough to see his country survive the onslaught of the Yom Kippur War in 1973.

Abba Eban (b. 1915) A South African–born, Cambridge-educated author, diplomat, and former foreign minister, he is noted for an eloquence and wit unrivaled among Western leaders since Winston Churchill. An Arabic scholar and a supporter of more moderate policies regarding the West Bank and Gaza, he is known for his PBS television series, *Civilization and the Jews.*

Teddy Kollek (b. 1910)   Indefatigable mayor of Jerusalem for 28 years, Kollek arrived in Palestine from Vienna during the rise of the Nazis in the 1930s, and was originally a member of Kibbutz Ein Gev. Leader of the One Jerusalem Coalition, his commitment to maintaining peace among the many ethnic and religious groups in the city has been matched by his determination to adorn Jerusalem with every kind of artistic, cultural, and civic treasure possible. Amazingly accessible to the people of Jerusalem during his long tenure, Teddy often answered the municipal phones himself in the early morning hours before his staff arrived.

Golda Meir (1898–1978)   Born in Russia, she emigrated to the United States as a child. As a young Milwaukee schoolteacher and ardent Zionist, she decided to emigrate to British Mandate Palestine in 1921. Meir held many posts in the Labor Party and was famous for personal courage: In 1948, on the eve of Israeli independence, she traveled to Jordan at great risk, disguised as an Arab woman, to plead with King Abdullah not to make war on the new Jewish nation. Prime minister from 1969 to 1974, her government was criticized for failing to detect the Egyptian and Syrian Yom Kippur surprise attack in 1973, and bore responsibility for heavy casualties. Named by Ben-Gurion as "the only real man in the government," Meir projected a grandmotherly image, often doing business with Israeli and foreign leaders in her kitchen.

Yitzhak Rabin (1922–1995)   Rabin was the first Israeli prime minister to be born in the land that was to become Israel. Originally a student of agronomy, he joined Palmach, the elite Haganah strike force, and served with Allied forces fighting in the Middle East during World War II. A brilliant strategist, as commander in chief of Israel's armed forces during the Six-Day War in 1967, he led the country to its greatest military triumph. Rabin's first term as prime minister, from 1974 to 1977, was distinguished by the successful raid on Entebbe Airport in Uganda, which rescued almost 100 Jewish and Israeli hostages. As defense minister in a Likud-Labor Coalition government, in 1987 he supported a hard line against Palestinian demonstrators, but came to be increasingly committed to creating a world in which Israelis and Palestinians could live side by side, "In dignity. In empathy. As human beings." Rabin was a modest, noncharismatic leader, and public faith in his caution and judgment enabled him to make concessions and territorial withdrawals in the search for peace. He was the recipient of the Nobel Peace Prize. Rabin was assassinated by an Israeli opponent to his policies in November 1995.

Boris Schatz (1866–1932)   Lithuanian-born sculptor and ardent follower of Theodor Herzl, Schatz arrived in Jerusalem in 1906 and founded the Bezalel Academy of Arts and Crafts with the purpose of developing an indigenous artistic tradition for the nation he believed would one day be reborn. The Bezalel Academy planted the seeds for a modern cultural scene in Jerusalem, which had previously been a remote, religiously oriented community. Israel's extraordinary commitment to the arts is in no small part due to Schatz's vision of art as a necessary component of Zionism.

Abraham Ticho (1883–1960)   Born in Moravia, Dr. Ticho arrived in Jerusalem in 1912 determined to battle against trachoma and other endemic eye diseases that caused thousands of cases of blindness among the local population. As founder and head of Jerusalem's first ophthalmic hospital, he became a modern Jerusalem legend, working devotedly to save the eyesight of all who approached him (including Emir Abdullah, later king of Jordan). He was known for sometimes brusquely dragging off children he spotted on the streets for treatment at his clinic. When he was stabbed and left for dead during the political unrest of 1929, thousands in Jerusalem's Jewish, Christian, and Muslim communities prayed for Dr. Ticho to recover, which he did. As one whose life's work was bringing light to others, Dr. Ticho was fascinated by Hanukkah menorahs, sometimes accepting Hanukkah lamps in exchange for treatment. His remarkable collection of menorahs is now in the Israel Museum. The 19th-century mansion he shared with his wife, the artist Anna Ticho, is now a downtown branch of the Israel Museum.

Yigael Yadin (1917–1984)   A leading member of the Haganah during the 1940s and was responsible for drawing up and implementing Haganah's operations during the War of Independence. After serving as chief of staff of the Israel Defense Forces until 1952, Yadin devoted himself to archeology, leading and writing about excavations at Hazor, Masada, and in the caves of the Judean Desert, and publishing extensively on the Dead Sea Scrolls. A brilliant lecturer, Yadin made archaeology so exciting and accessible to the Israeli people that he virtually became a national hero. In the1970s, Yadin led an unsuccessful movement to reform the Israeli political system.

4 Architecture

Casting a shadow over all other structures in Israel are two that long ago vanished: the legendary First Temple, built by King Solomon in approximately 960 B.C. and destroyed by the Babylonians, and the Second Temple, originally put together on the ruins of the First Temple. In front of the First Temple, a Canaanite-style sanctuary building embellished with decorations of cedar, ivory, and gold, King Solomon is recorded in the Bible to have prayed: "The heavens, even the heaven of heavens, cannot contain Thee; how much less this house that I have built." The reconstruction of the Second Temple into a vast Hellenistic-style pilgrimage complex was begun by the Roman-installed King Herod in 18 B.C., not to be completed until A.D. 64, almost 70 years after Herod's death.

This ceremonial center did not endure for long. In A.D. 70, Jerusalem was destroyed by Roman armies. On the eve of this destruction, according to the Roman historian Tacitus, the Roman general, Titus, called a council to decide whether, in victory, Rome should destroy "the Temple, one of man's consummate building achievements." This hesitation on the part of the Romans to level the symbolic religious center of a stubbornly rebellious subject nation is an indication of the Herodian structure's grandeur and charisma. The Western Wall is part of the retaining-wall system that held up the vast artificially created ceremonial plaza that surrounded the Herodian temple. A few architectural details found in archaeological excavations since 1967 have been identified with the structures that formed part of the Second Temple complex, but no fragment of the actual Second Temple building has yet been found.

Of all the ancient buildings that still stand in Israel, nothing is more incredible than the Dome of the Rock, built on the site of the First and Second Temples by the early Islamic rulers of Jerusalem in A.D. 691. The Byzantine architects who were commissioned to design the Dome of the Rock may have been inspired by the legends of the two vanished structures. In the 16th century it was adorned with Persian tiles by Sultan Suleiman the Magnificent. One of the world's most beautiful buildings, this shrine acts as a crown to a site that is both physically and spiritually sublime. With its golden dome, like a gilded balloon against the skies, offering intimations of ascension to the heavens (as Koranic tradition records the Prophet Muhammad did from this very spot), it combines simplicity with intricacy in a way that does equal justice to the monotheistic concept and the complex traditions associated with the site.

From the crusader period, two remarkable Frankish Romanesque churches remain: the heavily restored Church of Saint Anne in Jerusalem, and the church in Abu Ghosh, near Jerusalem, which is more in its original state. Designed using Eastern and Western techniques to create marvelous acoustics, both are musical instruments to be played by the human voice: a single soprano in either will sound like a choir of angels.

The Street of the Chain and the Temple Mount in Jerusalem offer many dramatic examples of architecture from the Mameluke period (A.D. 1267–1517), characterized by intricately carved arabesque stonework, and Mameluk "stalactite"-adorned recesses over the doorways of its important buildings. The labyrinthine Old City of Akko, with its medieval khans and Ottoman Al-Jazzar mosque, deserves to be considered a national treasure. Unfortunately, the fascinating bazaars and residential quarters of Old Akko have been left in ill repair due to local political considerations.

The International Style of the 1930s and 1940s was brought to British Mandate Palestine by refugee architects who had studied at the Bauhaus and worked in the studios of Le Corbusier, Gropius, and Mies van der Rohe in Europe. Tel Aviv has one of the world's largest urban concentrations of such buildings, with their crisp white concrete curvilinear and blocklike shapes. These buildings were recorded in international architectural publications of their time as visionary gems, but a combination of civic unconcern and the fact that the sand-laden bricks used for construction did not weather well, has left many of these structures in a state of near ruin. Many are now being restricted.

The British Mandate period also left an architectural legacy in Jerusalem, where the high commissioner issued an ordinance that all construction must be faced with Jerusalem stone. Both the YMCA building on King David Street (designed by the same American firm that did New York City's Empire State Building) and the Rockefeller Museum, designed by the noted British architect Austin S. B. Harrison, exhibit an interesting mixture of art deco, Byzantine, and Islamic themes.

The vast uninspired neighborhoods constructed after 1948 in Israel's main cities and development towns, hastily built to fulfill a practical need, dominate the landscape. Most Israelis detest these postindependence apartment blocks, locally known as egg boxes. Today renovation and restoration are necessary to save what architectural heritage Israel still possesses. The reconstruction of the old quarter of Jaffa and the Jewish Quarter in Jerusalem's Old City, along with the gentrifying of 19th-century Jerusalem neighborhoods like Yemin Moshe, Ein Kerem, and the German Colony, have produced places with real charm and a sense of community. Other urban planning projects, like the expanded routing of a major road system alongside the walls of Jerusalem's Old City (complete with pedestrian under- and overpasses to the Jaffa Gate) and the piecemeal destruction of West Jerusalem's 19th-century Ha-Nevi'im Street neighborhood, may prove to repeat the kind of mistakes already made in many Western cities.

Israel had two official languages: Hebrew and Arabic. English is widely spoken or understood, Arabic is the daily language and language of instruction for Israel's Arabic citizens, but for Jewish Israelis, who comprise 83% of the country's population, the day-to-day language is Hebrew—the resurrected language of biblical times. Hebrew has only come to life again as a vehicle for everyday speech during the past 100 years. Although Hebrew ("the tongue of Canaan," according to the Prophet Isaiah) was the language of much of the time period of the Old Testament, it was gradually supplanted after the Babylonian Captivity (586 B.C.) by Aramaic, another Semitic language, which became the lingua franca of the region for the next 500 years. As Jewish history moved into the Diaspora, Jewish communities spoke Greek and Greek koine, Judeo-Persian, Latin and Arabic, Ladino—the late medieval Spanish of the Jewish community expelled from Spain in 1492 (spoken by many of their descendants to this day)—and expressive, irony-prone Yiddish, a medieval Rhine Valley German written with Hebrew letters, which the Jewish communities of northern Europe maintained and developed as they wandered deeper and deeper into eastern Europe over the centuries.

At the end of the 19th century, as Zionist leaders began to envision a return to Israel of Jews from all parts of the world, they wondered what language should be spoken the a Jewish homeland whose inhabitants' native tongues ranged from Yiddish, Russian, English, and Hungarian to Moroccan Arabic, Argentinean Spanish, Urdu, and Uzbekistani. Many important leaders believed the official language of the Jewish homeland should be what at that time was considered the preeminent language of science, culture, music, medicine, and philosophy: in short, German! A handful of Zionists had other ideas.

When Eliezer Ben-Yehuda (1858–1922), a Polish-born linguist, came to Jerusalem in 1881, he believed that ancient Hebrew, used mainly as a liturgical language since the 5th century B.C., should be the language of the reborn Zionist vision. He codified Hebrew grammar, wrote the first modern dictionary, and coined words necessary for a modern vocabulary. Ben-Yehuda and his wife, also a linguist, spoke only Hebrew to their son, Itamar, who became the first primarily Hebrew-speaking person in the modern world.

From the initial determination of the Ben-Yehuda family and their friends, the Hebrew language, with its uniqueness and vitality, was brought back to life, changing and growing each day—the Israeli people's great communal work of art. Modern Hebrew is being stretched by the hour by its Israeli speakers as they take the language and vocabulary of a laconic, pastoral Iron Age civilization and reshape it to the needs of an enormously cosmopolitan, gregarious, heterogeneous society of the 21st century.

Written in its own alphabet, Hebrew must be transliterated into the Latin alphabet for non-Hebrew speakers. The varying ways in which Hebrew names are transliterated is sure to confuse you—most places seem to have several different names and spellings. Is it Jaffa, Joppa, or Yafo? Safed, Safad, Zfat, or Zefat? Lake Tiberias, the Sea of Galilee, or Kinneret Lake?

The confusion stems partly from Israel's long history, partly from myriad cultures and languages, and partly from Hebrew itself. Vowels are not normally written in Hebrew (this is also true of Arabic), and so in transliteration you get such unpronounceable words as Sde (for Sede) and Sderot (Sederot). Further confusions are added by sounds like the guttural "kh" sound, a rasping in the back of the throat usually rendered as "ch," but pronounced very differently from the "ch" in "church." You might come across "Hen" and "Chen," which are the same Hebrew word, pronounced more like "khen." How does one cope? The only way is to pronounce the word you want and compare it to the one you've found. If it sounds the same, it probably is: Mikveh Israel, Miqwe Yisra'el, Elat-Eilat, Tiberias-Teverya, and so on.

Arabic is the second official language of Israel, and English is Israel's major international language, so you will find that street and road signs are in Hebrew, Arabic, and English. English will work in virtually every shop, restaurant, and hotel in the three major cities, as well as most other places. If, however, you chance to encounter a storekeeper who speaks only Russian, Hebrew, Arabic, or one of the 17 or so other relatively common languages, just look for his 12-year-old son, who's studying English in school.

If you find yourself groping for another language, try French, German, or Yiddish. Many Israelis of Romanian origin know French, and Israelis from Morocco, Algeria, and Tunisia, often speak fluent French.

You can use the Hebrew and Arabic glossaries at the back of this book as a crutch—you'll find that your stabs at speaking the native tongues will be warmly appreciated.

6 Religion

Israel is special, if not sacred, to more faiths than is any other country in the world. Today, for at least 15 different Jewish sects, several Christian sects, Muslims, Druze, Baha'is, Samaritans, Circassians, Karaites, Bedouins, and still others, Israel is holy, and although many of the groups claim the land as "their own," the differing faiths are practiced side by side. This calls for daily tolerance. For instance, many Jews from English-speaking countries find Israel isn't "Jewish" in the way they personally practice or understand Judaism. Christians traveling in Israel are often perplexed by certain Israeli Christian customs—entrance fees at holy shrines, or famous churches subdivided (with actual lines of demarcation on walls and floors) among different sects of Christianity. Protestants are often amazed to find most holy places tended by Catholics; Catholics are surprised to find their Israeli counterparts functioning as Catholics did hundreds of years ago rather than following the modern practices of most of the Catholic world.

To Islam, the patriarchs were holy men and Jesus was a prophet, though not the final one. Islam, in some ways, is closer to Judaism and the nomadic-type culture of the patriarchs than to the Greek-influenced culture of Christianity. Islam is dedicatedly monotheistic: The profession of faith declares, "There is but one God, Allah, and Mohammed is His prophet." Muslims pray five times a day, fast in daylight hours during the month of Ramadan, make a pilgrimage to Mecca, and give alms. The Muslim Sabbath is from Thursday's sunset to sunset on Friday. However, the prohibition against work is less severe than in Judaism. Like Jews, Muslims are enjoined from eating pork. Gambling and drinking alcohol are also prohibited to Muslims, and they may not make paintings or sculptures of human beings or animals. The men may marry up to four wives, although this tradition is practiced very rarely.

7 A Taste of Israel

DINING CUSTOMS
THE SABBATH (SHABBAT)   You will need to know a few things about Shabbat dining. On Friday afternoons and afternoons before holidays, shops,

offices, and kosher restaurants close around 2pm in preparation for Shabbat, which begins at sunset. Most restaurants don't reopen until Saturday evening after dark. In summer, the Saturday evening reopening can be quite late. Depending on the volume of business, some restaurants may stay open beyond normal closing hours on Saturday night. An increasing number of nonkosher restaurants remain open on Shabbat in most cities.

Saturday's breakfast is usually provided by your hotel, but you will need to deal with Friday's dinner and Saturday's lunch. By Saturday dinnertime, restaurants will be open again. If you're kosher, eat a hearty lunch on Friday, and buy snacks or picnic supplies for Friday evening and Saturday lunchtime.

KOSHER FOOD   To those unfamiliar with kosher food, the prohibitions against eating pork and serving meat and milk products at the same meal are the most noticeable laws of kashruth.

According to the rigorous regulations of kashruth, only peaceful animals that chew their cuds and have cleft hooves and birds that do not eat carrion may be used for food, but only if they have been killed instantly according to methods supervised by religious authorities. If there is reason to believe that an animal may have died in pain, or of disease, it cannot be considered kosher (which means no hunted animals). Only fish with fins and scales can be eaten, which means no shellfish or dolphins.

A restaurant may maintain a kosher menu, but if it prepares and cooks food or does business on Shabbat, it will generally not be able to receive a kashruth certificate. Many hotels prepare meals before Shabbat for their anticipated guests, and either serve cold Saturday meals, or meals that have been kept warm on fires that were started before Shabbat.

Kosher restaurants that serve milk will not serve any food containing meat or poultry, although they are permitted to serve fish. This means that cheese lasagna must be meatless. In restaurants serving meat, your coffee will be served with milk substitute.

In many cases, kosher restaurants may be 5% to 10% more expensive than comparable nonkosher restaurants. If kashruth is not a concern, you can save a bit by seeking out nonkosher places. Glatt kosher (strict adherence to the rules of kashruth) almost always means a higher price. Most kosher restaurants have adapted so skillfully to their constraints that you will notice nothing very unusual in your dining experience.

CUISINE

For the first half of Israel's existence, the restaurant scene was almost as spartan and no-nonsense as the State of Israel itself. Kibbutz cuisine was king, starting with hotel breakfasts, where you could have your fill of bland but healthy chopped tomato and cucumber salad, hard-boiled egg, heavy, government-subsidized white bread, soft cheese, olives, and orange juice or punch. A typical tourist lunch was falafel, hummus, or shwarma in pita bread with chopped salad, and for dinner, there was no lack of places with Formica tables where you could get turkey schnitzel or a chicken thigh with french fries and that ubiquitous, healthful chopped salad. Anyone looking for a bagel and lox with cream cheese or corned beef on rye would be directed to New York (*beigele* still means a pretzel in Israel) and the one consolation was that most visitors returned home able to fit comfortably into clothes that had previously been tight.

Gone are those days! After 1967, things began to change. Israeli restaurants began to offer a wide variety of main and side dishes done in real Middle

Israeli Street Food

Falafel and shwarma tucked into a pita bread with chopped salad and eaten on the run have become the national fast foods of Israel.

1. A quality falafel (spiced chickpea fritter) sandwich should contain at least four falafels and include your choice of a number of fresh salads.

2. Buy from places with a big turnover and fresh, hot falafels. You should be able to see falafels being fried; if the oil is dirty or idle and not constantly boiling, move on.

3. A good, fresh salad bar is an indication of fresh falafel and shwarma.

4. A sandwich made with giant napkin-size Iraqi pita bread (available at stands in Jerusalem's Mahane Yehuda and Tel Aviv's Hatikvah) costs half a shekel more and fills you up for most of the day.

5. Shwarma (spiced turkey or lamb on a spit) should be freshly sliced from the spit. If the proprietor must turn on the flame and heat the spit of shwarma for you, move on.

6. Many stands offer hummus (spiced chickpea paste) either as a separate sandwich choice or with falafel. Avoid it after 11am on a hot summer day.

7. Falafel sandwiches, especially with lots of essential techina sauce, tend to be messy. Grab tons of napkins. Pay extra for a place where you can sit.

Eastern tradition. Israeli fish farming began to thrive, and with it, choices such as Saint Peter's fish from the Galilee, trout from the Dan, and even home-grown salmon, which over the years has been refined to a high level of excellence. A new fast food, the *boureka,* a flaky, salty cheese pie of Greek origin, swept the nation. People began to envision possibilities beyond hummus and falafel. Pizza hit the streets of every downtown district. Israelis from Asian and North African countries—Yemenites with their melawach dishes, Iraqis with their spicy kubbehs, Moroccans with their exotic sauces—all began to challenge the notion that east European borscht, blintzes, and chicken soup were the only true Jewish cuisine. In the 1970s, Israel began to admit boat people as well as other Asians. Chinese and Thai restaurants cautiously opened and many Asians found jobs in traditional Israeli restaurants, where they began to make interesting suggestions. Israelis, hitherto hampered by a heavy travel tax, suddenly found themselves free to visit other lands when the tax was removed in 1977. Exotic tastes began to develop.

Israeli cuisine simmered for a decade and finally burst forth in the late 1980s with a new generation of restaurants offering inventive, intelligent menus that find their roots in the country's remarkably international character. Israeli restaurant owners are falling in love with elegant sauces and exotic seasonings, and customers are responding to quality meals. The country has become the vanguard of a new approach to cooking that mixes the informal rustic cuisines of countries around the Mediterranean Rim with an easy touch of Far Eastern restraint and elegance. Tel Aviv–Herzlia is the center for this movement, with glistening, inventive deluxe restaurants like **Roshfeld, Ocean, Capot Tmarim, Keren,** and the kosher **Twelve Tribes;** in Jerusalem, the stars of the field are **Ocean Bistro, Arcadia,** and the kosher **Michael Andrew;** in Haifa, it's the new **1873 Restaurant.** Strangely, trendy Tel Aviv is also the center for old-world east European Jewish dishes like potato latkes (pancakes), stuffed cabbages and derma (intestines), and matzo ball soup, which locals devour at places like **Batya** and **Bebele.**

You can find interesting food at all prices. Jerusalem has great ethnic choices like **Misadonet,** a Kurdish-Jewish home-style restaurant, in the moderate range, where you can have a rich dish of creamy lamb hearts stuffed with rice, pine nuts, walnuts, and raisins in a curried apricot sauce, or the budget range **Yemenite Step,** with its exotic spices and melawach (phyllo pancake) dishes. In the luxury range, food traditions of Moroccan Jewry can be sampled at the excellent and authentic **Darna Restaurant.**

A new phenomenon is the rise of restaurants serving "biblical" food in "ancient" settings. Among the best of these are the **Dushara Restaurant** in the dramatic Nabatean ruins of Mamshit in the Negev Desert and the vegetarian restaurant at the **Neot Kedumim Biblical Reserve,** which has been praised by American food critic Mimi Sheraton. Without going biblical, Moshe Basson, of Jerusalem's **Eucalyptus Restaurant,** has been called a "veggie archaeologist," rediscovering the herbs, spices, recipes, and traditional cooking techniques of the countryside and putting the Jewish people, so long away from Israel, back in touch with the culinary roots of their land. Mixing authenticity with his own skill and inventiveness, Moshe Basson makes works of art out of typical Israeli cuisine.

But what is typical Israeli cuisine? It draws on Arabic traditions like the mezze, or a vast array of spiced salads and spreads that opens a lavish Middle-Eastern–style feast. It includes the Arabic falafel, still the staff of fast-food life in Israel despite the recent arrival of McDonald's, Burger King, and Kentucky Fried Chicken. Like Arabic cuisine, Israeli cuisine loves lamb, grilled organ meats, and fresh grilled fish. But Israeli cuisine is stretching to encompass other traditions as well. The skewers of grilled hearts, chicken, and goose livers that workers love to eat in places like Jerusalem's Mahane Yehuda vegetable market, and at Tel Aviv's Etzel Street in the Hatikva district, have evolved into an extraordinarily fine foie gras, which Israel exports to France, and which dominates the first-course lists at quality restaurants all over Israel. Israeli cuisine means mussels jetted in from Brittany at Tel Aviv's **Mul Ha Yam Restaurant,** kosher sushi bars, and the **Pagoda Restaurant** in Tiberias, where you can dine on world-class Thai cuisine (kosher) while enjoying vistas of the Sea of Galilee. Israeli cuisine also means the baklavaries and hummus parlors of Jerusalem's Old City (**Abu Shukri,** long a master of hummus, has been immortalized in the pages of *Playboy*) and the inventiveness and gusto of places like **Margaret Tayar's Fish Restaurant** in Jaffa, or the unexpected exoticism of **Tandoori** in Eilat, where classical Indian musicians and dancers perform during your meal.

Israel in the 1990s is a genuine food festival that's nothing like what Grandma used to make. Enjoy! Eat and be well! *Betayavon!*

ISRAEL'S WINE

The wine scene is fairly new in Israel. At one time, only parochial kosher wines of little interest to the outside world were produced, but since the 1980s, the wine industry in Israel has undergone a major revolution. The **Golan Heights** (Ramat Ha Golan) **Winery,** which opened at Qatzrin in 1983 set new standards of quality and inventiveness. Its 1984 Cabernet Sauvignon won a gold medal at the International Wine and Spirit Competition, and the winery has three times received the Chairman's Award for Excellence at Vinexpo. A wave of other new, smaller wineries throughout the country followed this success.

Sampling the Grape

Israel's symbol has long been the familiar picture of the spies sent into Canaan by Moses returning with a bunch of grapes so huge they had to hang it from a pole to carry it. Now modern Israel is using grapes in a new way, to produce notable, prize-winning wines.

Among the best Cabernet Sauvignons to look for are Barkan Reserve, 1993; Yar-den Gamla 1994; Carmel Private Collection 1995; and Dalton 1995. Less expensive but recommended are Baron Tishbi 1995, and Carmel Selected 1995. Excellent Merlots include Yarden 1994; Barkan Reserve 1995, and Carmel Private Collection.

For Sauvignon Blanc, look for Yarden, Binyamina Special Reserve, Dalton, Carmel Private Collection, Barkan Reserve, and Gamla. Yarden and Dalton Chardonnays, 1995 and 1996 are highly recommended; the Barkan Reserve, and the Gamla Chardonnays are also quite good.

Among semidry wines, Yarden Johannesburg Riesling is outstanding; the less-expensive Golan, Carmel Mizrachi Selected, and Binyamina Reserve Emerald Rieslings are well regarded. Carmel's Carmel Nouveau Red and Golan Winery's Golan Blanc are at the top of the very long list of young red and white wines offered in many places.

Information about Israeli wines is available in Jerusalem at the remarkable **Avi Ben Wine Store,** 22 Rivlin St. (☎ **02/622-3018**), and also at **Fink's Bar,** 2 Ha-Histadrut St. (☎ **02/623-4523**), which *Newsweek* has declared "one of the 50 best bars in the world," and the **Gaffen** wine shop, 42 Emek Refaim St. (☎ **02/561-9617**), in the German Colony. In Jaffa, the gourmet and atmospheric **Yoe'ezer Wine Bar** (☎ **03/683-9115**), opposite the Clock Tower on Yefet Street, offers a wonderful chance to sample fine Israeli and imported wines, accompanied, if you like, by excellent food. The owner of Yoe'ezer Wine Bar, Shaul Evron, a noted Israeli journalist and food critic, is usually on hand to offer careful advice and suggestions. In Haifa, **Special Reserve** (☎ **04/837-9750**), the wine shop adjoining the Dan Carmel Hotel, run by Andre Suiden, is an especially good resource.

The Golan Heights Winery remains the leader in the climb toward new standards of excellence, concentrating on the production of Cabernet Sauvignon, Merlot, as well as crisp, dry Sauvignon Blanc and Chardonnay, and a good semidry Emerald Riesling. Golan Heights wines are produced in the "Yarden," "Gamla," and "Golan" series. "Yarden" is the most prestigious of the three, known especially for its deep red Yarden Cabernet Sauvignon, but all Golan Heights series are good.

Carmel Mizrachi, the largest winery in Israel, also underwent a quality revolution. Its "Rothschild" series is increasingly prestigious, and includes quality Cabernet Sauvignon and Merlot, as well as well as Chardonnay, Emerald Riesling, and Sauvignon Blanc.

The smaller **Baron Winery** and the **Barkan Winery** are also worthy of note, as are the interesting wines of the Latrun Monastery near Jerusalem, and the wines of the West Bank's **Bet Jalla Monastery,** which are sold inside Israel at the Monastery at Bet Jimal, south of Beit Shemesh. The **Binyamina Winery,** near Zichron Yaacov, has recently begun to produce quality wines.

Among the up-and-coming "boutique" wineries, look for the **Dalton Winery** north of Safed, the **Amiad Winery** near Korazim northeast of the Sea of Galilee, the **Tzora Winery** in the hills west of Jerusalem, and the legendary **Margolit** wines, produced by the owner of an Italian restaurant in Jerusalem, which are generally available only by advance reserved purchase.

8 Recommended Books

GENERAL BACKGROUND
Josephus's *The Jewish Wars* is on every English-speaking Israeli's bookshelf. A Jewish general in the Galilee during the revolt against Rome in A.D. 66—and an eventual traitor—Josephus was also a historian who provided volumes of historical commentaries and anecdotes about almost every area you'll see in Israel. *The Earthly Jerusalem,* by Norman Kotker (Scribner's, 1972), is a graceful, wryly intelligent history of Jerusalem from earliest to modern times; *Jerusalem: City of Mirrors*, by Amos Elon, is another highly readable history of that city. *Jerusalem on Earth,* by Abraham Rabinovich (Macmillan, New York and London, 1988), contains wonderful real-life stories about people in contemporary Jerusalem by one of the *Jerusalem Post's* finest human-interest writers.

ARCHAEOLOGY
Yigael Yadin, the Israeli archaeologist whose father, Professor E. L. Sukenik of Hebrew University, identified the first fragments of the Dead Sea Scrolls in 1947, has written a beautifully photographed, thrilling book about the final archaeological search of the Dead Sea Caves in the early 1960s. The book, *Bar-Kokhba* (Harper & Row, 1971), reads almost like a novel, is available in bookstores throughout Israel and in most American libraries. Perhaps no other book allows you to share the excitement of each amazing discovery and lets you understand what archaeology means to those who love Israel. Yigael Yadin is also the author of books on the Masada and Hazor archaeological projects.

Other recommended books about archaeology include *Judaism in Stone,* by Hershel Shanks (Harper & Row, New York and London, 1979), a heavily illustrated survey of ancient synagogues in Israel and the Middle East; and *In the Shadow of the Temple,* by Meir Ben-Dov (Harper & Row, New York, 1985), a lavishly illustrated and photographed volume that details recent archaeological discoveries in the Jewish Quarter of Jerusalem.

FICTION & POETRY
Israeli writers face the problem of creating a literature in a language that was mainly used for prayer and religious study for more than 2,000 years. Working in a tradition so long interrupted, writers face many problems.

Among the Israeli writers most accessible to English-speaking readers are Amos Oz, whose early novel, *My Michael,* with its delicate narrative voice, has been beautifully translated into English; Yehuda Amichai, whose poetry is personal, yet filled with evocative Israeli locales, imagery, and a graceful, visionary wit; and Aharon Appelfeld, who writes in the surreal, European tradition of Kafka. S. Y. Agnon, Israel's first Nobel Prize–winning writer, worked in a disciplined Hebrew that drew intensively on a knowledge of east European legends and Jewish intellectual and religious history; try his novel, *The Bridal Canopy.* Emile Habiby is an award-winning writer from Israel's Arabic community; his wry approach can be sampled in *The Secret Life of Saeed, The Ill-fated Pessoptimist: A Palestinian Who Became a Citizen of Israel.* Anton Shamas displays an interesting blend of both Hebrew and Arabic style and sensibility. His novel, *Arabesques,* points to rich, new directions in which Israeli writing may develop. Among other outstanding modern novels are *The Smile of the Lamb,* by David Grossman, and *A Late Divorce,* by A. B. Yehoshua.

For a sampling of Israeli poetry, read *The Modern Hebrew Poem Itself,* an anthology edited by Stanley Burnshaw (Holt Rinehart & Winston, 1965); and *Poems of Jerusalem* (Harper & Row, 1988) and *Even a Fist Was Once an Open Palm with Fingers* (Harper Books, 1991), both by Yehuda Amichai.

OTHER BOOKS

Footloose in Jerusalem, by Sarah Fox Kaminker (a former American who held a seat on the Jerusalem City Council and led a movement from neighborhood preservation), and *Jerusalemwalks,* by Nitza Rosovsky, are two books filled with detailed, interesting guided walking tours in Jerusalem.

9 Recordings

The Oranim Zabar Troup featuring Geula Gill orchestrated and performed many of the classic 1950s Israeli songs that are known to Israeli folk dancers around the world. Look for "Salom!," "Hora," and "On the Road to Eilat" (Electra Records).

The noted ethnomusicologist Deben Bhattacharya has compiled a wonderful four-record collection of traditional Israeli musicians from Morocco, Uzbekistan, Bukhara, Yemen, and other lands, called in Israel Today (Westminster Recordings).

Israeli popular music reflects a lively, unusual blend of Western and Middle Eastern styles and sensibilities. Among the current favorites to look for are Ethnix, a group that does orientalized versions of Western dance rock; Zehava Ben, a wildly popular songstress of Jewish-Moroccan ancestry (her song, "Ketourne Massala," in collaboration with Ethnix, was one of Israel's biggest hits in recent years); Ofra Haza, who died suddenly in 2000, was one of the few Israeli singers to break into the international market, with a repertoire that includes both traditional Yemenite songs and rearrangements of these pieces into disco (*Shadai* is her most popular album: *DesertWind* is geared to the dance market); and Yehuda Poliker, the son of Holocaust survivor from the Greek community of Salonika, whose 1985 best-selling album *Enayim Sheli* (My Eyes) opened the door to Hebrew interpretation and rendition of Greek music. Finally, of special interest to Westerners is Ahinoam Nini (outside of Israel, she's know as "Noa"), who grew up in the United States and has returned to dazzle her homeland with her extraordinarily pure voice (she was invited to the Vatican to perform "Ave Maria" before the Pope). Her original songs and renditions of classics range from witty to dramatic and reflect a lively New York, English-language, Yemenite-Israeli sensibilities that are absolutely dynamite! Bustan Avraham (The Garden of Abraham), a group that does lovely interpretation of traditional Middle Eastern music, is also very worth checking out.

Appendix B: Useful Terms & Expressions

1 Hebrew Terms & Expressions

The Hebrew alphabet is, of course, entirely unlike our Latin ABCs. Fortunately for us, however, Israelis use the same numerals that we use: 1, 2, 3, 4, and so on.

Hebrew has a number of sounds that we don't use in English. They're difficult to communicate in writing, and until you hear them spoken correctly, you may not get the flavor of them. The first is the "ch" or "kh" sound, which you'll find repeatedly in many words throughout the vocabulary. This is not the sound of "ch" in either "change" or "champagne." We don't use this sound in English, and the closest to it are the "ch" sounds in the German exclamation "ach," and in the Yiddish-Hebrew toast "le-chaim." It's a raspy, hacking sound that comes from the back of the mouth.

Another difficult sound, and also very common in Hebrew words, is the "o" sound. The best advice for practicing this sound is to say the word "oh" and halfway through saying the word suddenly cut your voice off. That's what many call a short "o." You get an approximation with the "o" sound in the word *on* and the German word *von*, although they're not exactly it either. You just have to cut the "o" short, so when you say the Hebrew word *boker*, meaning "morning," you don't say *bowker*.

USEFUL WORDS

hello **sha-*lom***
good-bye **sha-*lom***
good night ***lie*-la-tov**
I **ah-nee**
you **ah-tah**
he **hoo**
she **hee**
we **an-*nach*-noo**
where is? ***eye*-fo?**
there is **yesh**
there isn't **ain**
little **m'*aat***
much **har-*beh***
very **m'*od***
so-so ***kac*-ha-*ka*-cha**

good **tov**
hot **ch***aa***m**
bad **rah**
see you later **le-hit-rah-*ott***
friend **cha-*vare***
excuse me **slee-*cha***
yes **ken**
no **lo**
please **be-var-kah-*sha***
thank-you **to-*dah* rah-*bah***
you're welcome **al low da-*vaar***
good morning ***bo*-ku tov**
good evening **erev tov**
I speak English **ah-*nee* m'dah-*behr* ang-leet**
I don't speak Hebrew **ah-nee lo m'dah-*behr* ee-vreet**
today **hah-*yom***
tomorrow **ma-char**
yesterday **et-*mohl***
right (correct) **na-*chon***
too much **yo-*tair* mee-die**
patience ***sav*-la-*noot***
hands off *blee* **yah-*die*-im**
what? **mah?**
why? ***la*-ma?**
how? **aych?**
when? **mah-tiee?**
how long? **kama-zman?**
pleasant **nah-*im***
excellent **met-soo-*yan***
wow, far out **shiga-on**
crazy **me-shugg*a***
healthy **ba-*ree***
sick **cho-*leh***
doctor **row-*feh***
dentist **row-*feh* shin-eye-yim**

POST OFFICE

post office **dough-are**
letter **mich-tav**
stamp **bool (pl. bool-im)**
envelopes **ma-ata-*foth***

postcard **gloo-yah**
telegram **miv-rock**
airmail **dough-are ah-*veer***

SHOPPING & STORES

how much is it? ***ka*-mah zeh oh-*leh*?**
store **cha-*noot***
pharmacy **bait mer-kay-*chat***
barber, hairdresser **mahs-peh-*rah***
shampoo **ha-fee-*fah***

manicure ***mah*-nee-koor**
appointment **p'gee-*shah***
expensive **ya-*kar***
cheap **zol**

THE COUNTRYSIDE

sea ***yaam***
sand **chol**
desert **mid-*bar***

hill **giv-*ah***
house **bay-yit**
synagogue **bait k-*ness*-et**

forest **yah-**_are_
cold **car**
village **k'far**
road _der_-ech
mountain **har**

school **bait say-**_fer_
newspaper **ee-**_tahn_
spring, well **ayn, ma-ay-in, ay-in**
farm _mesh_-ekh
valley _eh_-mek

HOTEL TALK

hotel **meh-**_lon_
room _che_-der
water **my-im**
toilet **bait key-**_say_**, no-chi yoot
she-roo-**_teem_
where is? _ay_-fo?
key **maf-**_tay_-ach
manager **min-ah-**_hel_
accommodations **ma-**_kom_

dining room _che_-der _oh_-chel
bill _chesh_-bon
Mr. (sir) **ah-don-ee**
Mrs. (madam) _g'ver_-et
money _kes_-sef
bank **bank**
do you speak English? **ah-**_tah_ **m'dah-**
behr ang-_leet_?
balcony **meer-**_pes_-eth

LOCAL TRAVELING

station **ta-cha-nah**
railroad **rah-**_keh_-vet
airport **sde t'u-**_fah_
bus **auto-boos**
taxi **taxi**
taxi (sherut) **shay-**_root_
straight ahead **ya-**_shar_

street **re-**_chov_
stop here **ah-**_tsor_ **kahn**
to **le**
wait _reg_-gah
trip **tee-**_yule_

west **m'ar-**_av_
north **tsa-**_fon_
near **ka-**_rov_
far **rah-**_chok_
central **meer-ka-**_zith_
bus stop **ta-cha-**_naht_ **ha-auto-boos**
which bus goes to . . .? _eh_-zeh
auto-boos . . .?
no-_say_-ah le . . .?
to the right **yeh-**_mean_-ah
to the left **smol-**_ah_
south **da-**_rom_
east **miz-**_rach_

RESTAURANT & MENU TERMS

to eat **le-eh-**_chol_
to drink **lish-toth**
restaurant _miss_-ah-dah
food **o-chel**
cafe **ca-**_fe_
menu **taf-**_root_
breakfast **ah-roo-chat** _bo_-ker
lunch **ah-roo-**_chat_ **tsa-ha-rye-im**
dinner **ah-roo-**_chat_ **erev**

waiter **mel-**_tsar_
ice cream **glee-**_dah_
wine _yah_-yin
milk **cha-**_lav_
ice **ker-**_ach_
veal **e-**_gel_
chicken **tar-ne-**_gol_-et
fish **dag**
tea **tay**
coffee **cafe**

apple **ta-**_poo_-ach
orange **tapooz**
tomatoes _ag_-von-ee-_oat_
butter **chem-**_ah_
cheese **g'-vee-nah**
egg _bayt_-sa
hard-boiled egg **bay-**_tsa_ **rah-**_sha_
soft-boiled egg **bay-**_tsa_ **rah-**_kah_
scrambled eggs **bay-**_tsim_ **m-bull-**
bell-et
fried egg **bay-**_tsee_-ah
soup **ma-**_rock_
meat **bah-sahr**
cucumber **mah-la-fe-**_fon_
pepper **pil-**_pel_
salt **me-**_lach_
sugar **sue-**_car_
omelette **cha-vi-**_tah_
sour **cha-**_muts_
sweet **mah-**_tok_

vegetables *yeh*-rah-*koht*
salad **sal**-*at*
fruit **pay**-*rote*

bread *lech*-hem
satisfy *save*'a
hungry **ra**'*ev*

DAYS & TIME

Sunday *yom* ree-*shon*
Monday *yom* shay-*nee*
Tuesday *yom* shlee-*shee*
Wednesday *yom* reh-vee-*ee*
Thursday *yom* cha-mee *shee*
Friday *yom* shee-*shee*
Saturday *sha*-baht
what time? *ma* ha-sha-*ah?*

minute **da**-*kah*
hour **sha**-*ah*
seven o'clock ha-sha-*ah* *shay*-va
day **yom**
week **sha**-voo-*ah*
month *cho*-**desh**
year sha-*nah*

NUMBERS

1	eh-*had*
2	*sht*a-yim
3	sha-*losh*
4	*ar*-bah
5	cha-*maysh*
6	shaysh
7	*shev*-vah
8	sh-*mo*-neh
9	*tay*-shah
10	*ess*-er
11	eh-*had* ess-ray
12	*shtaym*-ess-ray
20	ess-*reem*
21	ess-*reem* v'eh-*had*
30	shlo-*sheem*
50	cha-mee-*sheem*
100	*may*-ah
200	mah-tah-*yeem*
300	shlosh may-*oat*
500	cha-*maysh* may-*oat*
1,000	elef
3,000	shlosh-*et* elef-*eem*
5,000	cha-maysh-*et* elef-*eem*

2 Arabic Terms & Expressions

USEFUL TERMS

please **min fadlak**

thank you **shoo-khraan**

hello **a-halan, mahr-haba**

good-bye **salaam aleikum,
ma-ah-salameh**

right **yemina**

left **she-mal**

straight **doo-ree**

today **il-yaum**

tomorrow **boo-kra**

what is your name? **shoo ismak?**

my name is . . . **ismay . . .**

how much is this? **ah-desh ha dah?**

yes **ay-wah**

no **la**

good, okay? **tay-eeb**

where is? **wain?**

how are you? **kee falak?**

in the hand of Allah (**reply to
"how are you?"**) **'hahm du'allah**

do you speak English? **te-kee
Ingleesi?**

pardon **sa-mekh-nee**

coffee **kah-wah**

market, bazaar **suk**

MEASURES & NUMBERS

one kilo **wahad kilo**

half kilo (500 grams) **noos kilo**

100 grams **mia gram**

1 **wa-had**

2 **ti-neen**

3 **talatay**

4 **ar-bah**

5 **ham-seh**

6	**sitteh**
7	**sabah**
8	**tamanyeh**
9	**tay-sa**
10	**a-sha-rah**
50	**ham-seen**
100	**mia**

Index

FROMMER'S® COMPLETE TRAVEL GUIDES

Alaska
Amsterdam
Arizona
Atlanta
Australia
Austria
Bahamas
Barcelona, Madrid &
  Seville
Beijing
Belgium, Holland &
  Luxembourg
Bermuda
Boston
British Columbia & the
  Canadian Rockies
Budapest & the Best of
  Hungary
California
Canada
Cancún, Cozumel &
  the Yucatán
Cape Cod, Nantucket &
  Martha's Vineyard
Caribbean
Caribbean Cruises & Ports
  of Call
Caribbean Ports of Call
Carolinas & Georgia
Chicago
China
Colorado
Costa Rica
Denmark
Denver, Boulder & Colorado
  Springs
England
Europe

European Cruises & Ports
  of Call
Florida
France
Germany
Greece
Greek Islands
Hawaii
Hong Kong
Honolulu, Waikiki &
  Oahu
Ireland
Israel
Italy
Jamaica
Japan
Las Vegas
London
Los Angeles
Maryland & Delaware
Maui
Mexico
Miami & the Keys
Montana & Wyoming
Montréal & Québec City
Munich & the Bavarian
  Alps
Nashville & Memphis
Nepal
New England
New Mexico
New Orleans
New York City
New Zealand
Nova Scotia, New Brunswick
  & Prince Edward Island
Oregon
Paris

Philadelphia & the
  Amish Country
Portugal
Prague & the Best of the
  Czech Republic
Provence & the Riviera
Puerto Rico
Rome
San Antonio & Austin
San Diego
San Francisco
Santa Fe, Taos & Albuquerque
Scandinavia
Scotland
Seattle & Portland
Singapore & Malaysia
South Africa
Southeast Asia
South Pacific
Spain
Sweden
Switzerland
Thailand
Tokyo
Toronto
Tuscany & Umbria
USA
Utah
Vancouver & Victoria
Vermont, New Hampshire
  & Maine
Vienna & the Danube Valley
Virgin Islands
Virginia
Walt Disney World &
  Orlando
Washington, D.C.
Washington State

FROMMER'S® DOLLAR-A-DAY GUIDES

Australia from $50 a Day
California from $60 a Day
Caribbean from $70 a Day
England from $70 a Day
Europe from $60 a Day

Florida from $60 a Day
Hawaii from $70 a Day
Ireland from $60 a Day
Italy from $70 a Day
London from $85 a Day

New York from $80 a Day
Paris from $85 a Day
San Francisco from $60 a Day
Washington, D.C.,
  from $60 a Day

FROMMER'S® PORTABLE GUIDES

Acapulco, Ixtapa &
  Zihuatanejo
Alaska Cruises & Ports of Call
Bahamas
Baja & Los Cabos
Berlin
California Wine Country
Charleston & Savannah
Chicago

Dublin
Hawaii: The Big Island
Las Vegas
London
Maine Coast
Maui
New Orleans
New York City
Paris

Puerto Vallarta, Manzanillo
  & Guadalajara
San Diego
San Francisco
Sydney
Tampa & St. Petersburg
Venice
Washington, D.C.

FROMMER'S® NATIONAL PARK GUIDES

Family Vacations in the
    National Parks
Grand Canyon

National Parks of the
    American West
Rocky Mountain

Yellowstone & Grand Teton
Yosemite & Sequoia/
    Kings Canyon
Zion & Bryce Canyon

FROMMER'S® MEMORABLE WALKS

Chicago
London

New York
Paris

San Francisco
Washington D.C.

FROMMER'S® GREAT OUTDOOR GUIDES

New England
Northern California

Southern California & Baja
Southern New England

Washington & Oregon

FROMMER'S® BORN TO SHOP GUIDES

Born to Shop: China
Born to Shop: France

Born to Shop: Italy
Born to Shop: London

Born to Shop: New York
Born to Shop: Paris

FROMMER'S® IRREVERENT GUIDES

Amsterdam
Boston
Chicago
Las Vegas

London
Los Angeles
Manhattan
New Orleans

Paris
San Francisco
Seattle & Portland
Vancouver

Walt Disney World
Washington, D.C.

FROMMER'S® BEST-LOVED DRIVING TOURS

America
Britain
California

Florida
France
Germany

Ireland
Italy
New England

Scotland
Spain
Western Europe

THE UNOFFICIAL GUIDES®

Bed & Breakfasts in
    California
Bed & Breakfasts in
    New England
Bed & Breakfasts in
    the Northwest
Beyond Disney
Branson, Missouri
California with Kids
Chicago

Cruises
Disneyland
Florida with Kids
Golf Vacations in the
    Eastern U.S.
The Great Smoky &
    Blue Ridge
    Mountains
Inside Disney

Hawaii
Las Vegas
London
Miami & the Keys
Mini Las Vegas
Mini-Mickey
New Orleans
New York City
Paris

Safaris
San Francisco
Skiing in the West
Walt Disney World
Walt Disney World
    for Grown-ups
Walt Disney World
    for Kids
Washington, D.C.

SPECIAL-INTEREST TITLES

Frommer's Britain's Best Bed & Breakfasts and
    Country Inns
Frommer's Britain's Best Bike Rides
The Civil War Trust's Official Guide
    to the Civil War Discovery Trail
Frommer's Caribbean Hideaways
Frommer's Food Lover's Companion to France
Frommer's Food Lover's Companion to Italy
Frommer's Gay & Lesbian Europe
Frommer's Exploring America by RV
Hanging Out in Europe
Israel Past & Present

Mad Monks' Guide to California
Mad Monks' Guide to New York City
Frommer's The Moon
Frommer's New York City with Kids
The New York Times' Unforgettable
    Weekends
Places Rated Almanac
Retirement Places Rated
Frommer's Road Atlas Britain
Frommer's Road Atlas Europe
Frommer's Washington, D.C., with Kids
Frommer's What the Airlines Never Tell You